THE AUSTRALIAN ADVENTURE *atlas*

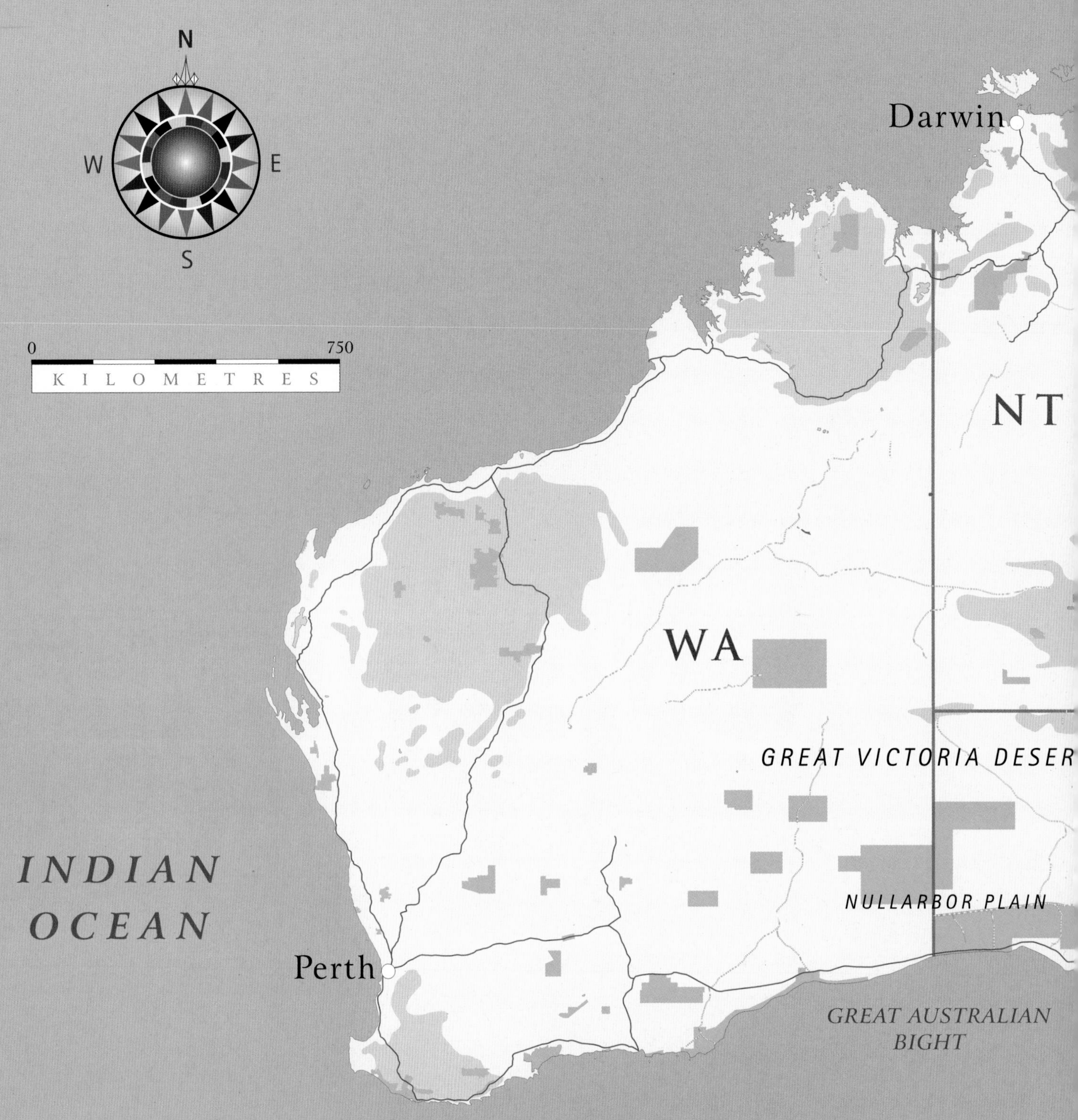
N
W
E
S
0
750
KILOMETRES
Darwin
NT
WA
GREAT VICTORIA DESER
NULLARBOR PLAIN
INDIAN OCEAN
Perth
GREAT AUSTRALIAN BIGHT
SOUTHERN OCEAN

PACIFIC
OCEAN
GREAT
BARRIER
REEF
GULF OF
CARPENTARIA
GREAT
DIVIDING
RANGE
QLD
SIMPSON DESERT
SA
Brisbane
NSW
Sydney
Adelaide
Canberra
VIC
Melbourne
TAS
Hobart

MAP KEY:

 Adventure Activity Icon

 Approximate Regional Boundary

 State Boundary

 National Park, Conservation Park, State Forest Area

 Key No.: National Park, Conservation Park, State Forest Area

 City, Town

Feature, Cave, Gorge, Waterfall

Roadhouse, Settlement

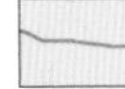 Highway, Road

 Walking Track, 4WD Track

ABNER RANGE — Mountain Range, Hills

+ Mountain

 River, Stream, Creek

 Lake, Pond

KEY TO ICONS:

 Abseiling, Rock Climbing, Canyoning

 Ballooning

 Bungy Jumping

 Bushwalking

 Caving

 Cycling & Mountain Biking

 Fishing

 Gliding

 Hang Gliding, Microlighting, Paragliding

 Helicoptors, Acrobatics, Jet Flights

 Horse Riding

 Hot Laps, Karts, Cars, Motorbikes

 Jet Boating, Water Skiing, Wakeboarding

 Kayaking & Canoeing

 Off-Road Driving

 Sailing

 Scuba Diving

 Skiing & Snow Boarding

 Skydiving

 Surfing

 Whale Watching, Marine Encounters

 White Water Rafting

 Windsurfing & Kitesurfing

ACKNOWLEDGEMENTS

The information in this Adventure Atlas was compiled with the assistance and information provided by state, regional and local tourism associations and National Parks and Wildlife Services.

The author would like to thank the following organisations:

Canberra Tourism
Environment ACT
Tourism NSW
Tourism Victoria
NSW National Parks and Wildlife Service (NPWS)
Parks Victoria
Queensland Parks and Wildlife Service
Brisbane Marketing
Tourism Queensland
South Australian Tourism Commission
South Australian Department for Environment and Heritage (DEH)
Northern Territory Tourism Commission
Tourism Western Australia
Western Australia Department of Conservation and Land Management (CALM)
Tourism Tasmania
Tasmanian Parks and Wildlife Service

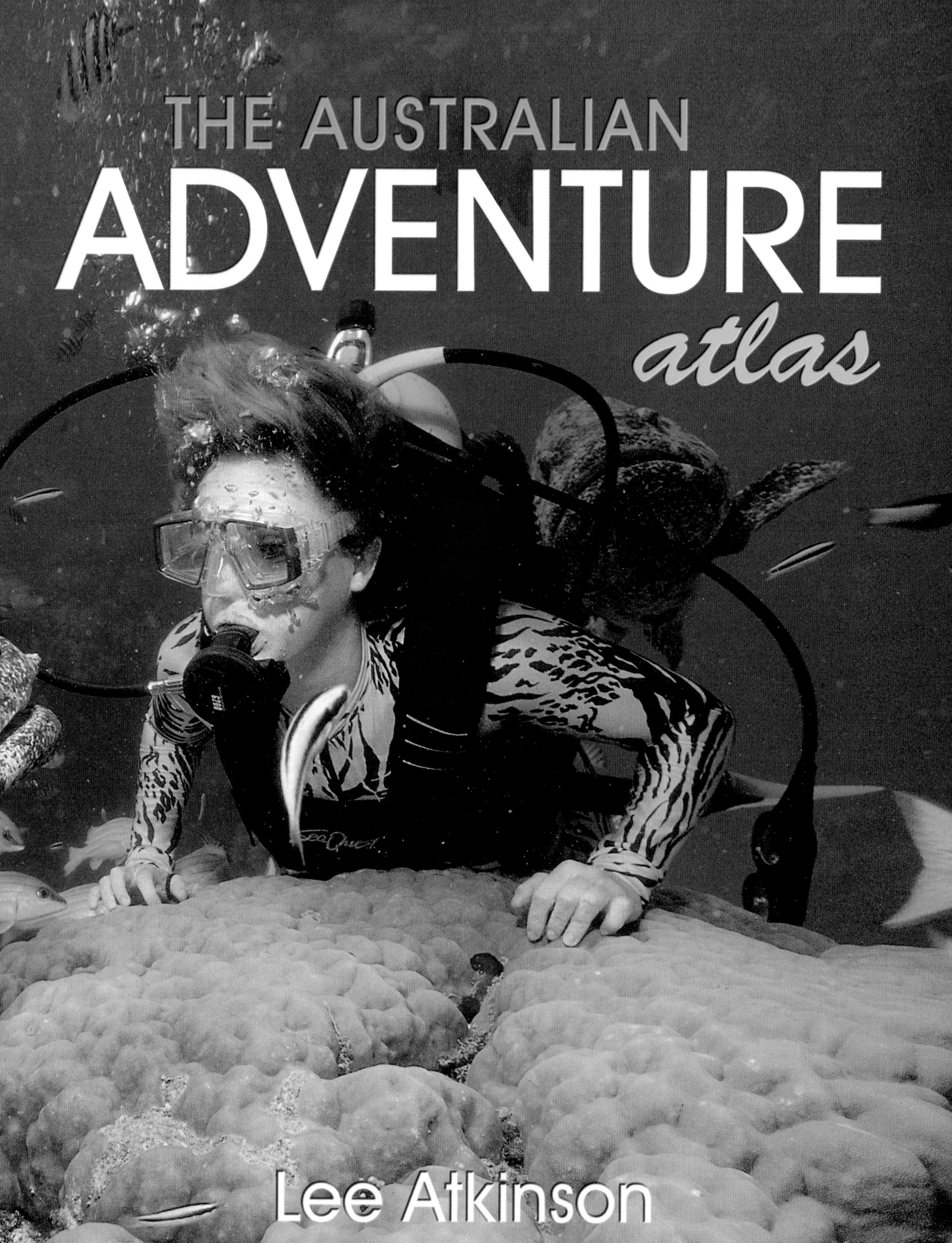
THE AUSTRALIAN
ADVENTURE
atlas
Lee Atkinson

First published in Australia in 2007 by
New Holland Publishers (Australia) Pty Ltd
Sydney • Auckland • London • Cape Town

www.newholland.com.au

14 Aquatic Drive Frenchs Forest NSW 2086 Australia
218 Lake Road Northcote Auckland New Zealand
86 Edgware Road London W2 2EA United Kingdom
80 McKenzie Street Cape Town 8001 South Africa

National Library of Australia Cataloguing-in-Publication Data:
Atkinson, Lee.
Adventure Atlas of Australia.

Includes index.
ISBN 978 174 110 4516 (hbk).
ISBN 1 74110 451 3 (hbk).

1. Australia - Guidebooks. I. Title.

919.40466

Publisher: Fiona Schultz
Managing Editor: Martin Ford
Production: Linda Bottari
Project Editor: Michael McGrath
Designer: Barbara Cowan
Picture Research: Lee Atkinson, Grace Gutwein, Barbara Cowan, Michael McGrath
Cover Design: Barbara Cowan
Cover Images: Sam Tinson, onsight.com.au, Tourism Queensland, Tourism Victoria, South Australian Tourism Commission
Printer: Toppan Printing Co. (China)

contents

introduction

AUSTRALIA IS AN ADVENTURE PLAYGROUND; a vast wild-at-heart island continent—the sixth largest country in the world and 50 per cent larger than Europe—with the lowest population density in the world at just two people per square kilometre. With 7000 beaches—more than any other nation in the world—14 World Heritage listed wilderness areas, the longest living coral reef in the world, rugged snow-capped peaks, raging rivers, ancient rainforests, fertile valleys and harsh deserts, there's something for everyone with a spirit of adventure.

This is a guide for those who like active and adventurous holidays, those who want to join in rather than sit and watch when they travel, those who like a pinch of adrenalin to spice up their day. It's a holiday guide for those who want to get out and get into it: snorkelling and diving, tackling outback tracks, rafting rapids, paddling or sailing waterways, climbing peaks, skiing slopes, surfing waves or trekking through rainforests. You'll find everything you need to help you plan an adventure holiday in Australia.

Forty comprehensive chapters, with detailed maps, cover every region across the country in depth. There's information on national parks, where to camp, the best bushwalks, scenic highlights, attractions and adventure tours. You'll find information on local weather and where to find more information.

There are chapters on responsible travel and safety, whale watching, fishing, bird watching and Australia's unique wildlife, including a useful list of dangerous creatures you should avoid. You'll find information on skiing, diving, snorkelling and more, all written by leading experts in their field. There's a guide to driving in Australia with handy tips and vehicle preparation know-how, gourmet getaways for food and wine lovers and an inspirational list of Australia's top 100 things to see and do.

Whether you're out and about or home thinking what you'd like to do next, *The Australian Adventure Atlas* brings you the best of Australian adventure holidays. Get out there!

Lee Atkinson, 2006

travelling responsibly in australia

Most travellers have heard the term 'ecotourism', which largely refers to 'treading lightly' on natural areas. 'Responsible tourism' takes this a step further: it's tourism that respects the natural environment as well as the country's people, their rights and their cultural heritage. It emphasises conserving the natural environment; learning and understanding; interacting meaningfully with the local people, and it strives to be sustainable.

By following responsible travel guidelines, you'll not only be a considerate global citizen, you're sure to have a far more rewarding, insightful and awe-inspiring adventure!

Treading lightly on the land

Australia has some of the most remote and unblemished wilderness areas on earth, but in many cases these ecosystems are in very delicate balance, easily disrupted by careless humans. Wherever you are in Australia, here are some tips for leaving only your footprints:

- Whether you're walking, riding or four-wheel-driving, stick to the trail if there is one, rather than cutting your own, which can cause damage to slow-growing plants; fragile soils and animal habitats.
- Australia is the second-driest continent on earth. Even our major cities have water consumption restrictions. Conserve water whenever possible (take short showers!), particularly on islands and in rural areas where often the only water comes from the skies.
- Avoid contaminating water sources, such as streams and dams. Wash away from the water if you're using soap and move at least 100m away if you need to go to the toilet.
- Fire is a serious hazard in this dry country–bushfires rage out of control every summer. Be aware of fire-lighting restrictions (listen to the weather forecast) if you're thinking of lighting a barbecue or campfire. And dispose of cigarette butts carefully!

Great Ocean Road.

- Throughout Australia, there are Aboriginal sacred sites–places of great spiritual significance that usually have a Dreaming story associated with them. If you visit a sacred site, be respectful of the traditional owners' wishes and traditions, particularly regarding photography and gender protocol (some sites may not be visited by women; others are off-limits to men). Leave any artefacts where you find them.
- The most famous site, of course, is Uluru, or Ayers Rock. The local Anangu people ask visitors not to climb the rock, yet thousands still do every year. Try listening to the Anangu story of Uluru first, and then decide if you still want to climb it. You can find more information on Aboriginal culture and tourism at **www.ataust.org.au**
- Don't feed animals or birds in the wild. Native animals can become ill and/or become scavenging pests, which can be dangerous for both man and beast.
- Please dispose of your litter properly (we have fines of up to $200 if you don't!).

Jim Jim Falls. *(Tourism NT)*

Getting along with the locals

Australians are renowned as a friendly, laid-back bunch–and they like to think of themselves that way, too. The population is culturally diverse, with citizens hailing from all corners of the planet, and proud of their cultural traditions. As with meeting people anywhere, if you abide by the 'do unto others as you would have them do unto you' credo, you're unlikely to cause serious offence.

Over the past 60,000 years Aboriginal and Torres Strait Islander people have developed a unique and extremely complex culture that is tied strongly to respect for their land and which delineates strict rules for social interaction. Each Aboriginal language group (there are more than 300) has its own set of rules, so it's impossible to generalise, however there are a few things to keep in mind when you meet indigenous people.

- Many Aboriginal people are naturally shy and English may be their second (or third, or fourth!) language. Speak clearly–but there's no need to raise your voice.
- Direct eye contact and the typical 'white fella' style of interrogative questioning can be confrontational to indigenous people: their way is more oblique and reserved and conversations are often as much about silence as words.
- Older people, particularly, command great respect within Aboriginal society.
- Referring to dead people or showing their photograph in many instances is taboo.

Although etiquette can be quite rigid, there's a healthy, leavening dose of humour peppering most conversations.

Choosing a responsible tourism operator

Just because a resort or a tour uses the 'eco' label, doesn't mean they abide by eco or responsible tourism principles. Most genuine operators will be keen to tell you about their environmental and cultural credentials: you'll find information on their websites, often including operating policies.

- Select tours that keep group sizes small–you'll make less impact on wilderness, animals and local people than a bigger group.
- Choose a tour operator that emphasises education and interpretation and exhibits a good understanding of environmental and cultural issues.
- There is a growing number of excellent indigenous tour operators across Australia. Aboriginal guides can give you an extraordinary insight–and a completely different appreciation–of their country.
- Consider the environmental credentials of the accommodation you choose. For example, a small-scale eco-lodge, hidden in the trees, utilising solar power and recycling its water is a far more sustainable option than a large-scale resort built around a resource-hungry golf course.

By staying at locally-owned accommodation and eating at locally-owned restaurants rather than international chains, and by using public transport when you can, you'll not only minimise your personal environmental 'footprint', you'll be contributing to the local community and you'll get to know the 'real' Australia!

Staying Safe in the Great Outdoors

Australia is famous for its dangerous fauna–deadly spiders and snakes; killer crocodiles–and the unforgiving vastness of the outback. The reality is, accidents are rare and you can travel safely in Australia if you abide by some common-sense guidelines:

- If you don't already know first aid, do a course–you never know when it will come in handy. Carry a small first aid manual and first aid kit with you when you're travelling.
- If you're heading off for an adventure–even if it's just a day-long bushwalk–tell someone where you're going and what time to expect you back.
- Whether you're in a national park, at the beach or on the road, heed the safety signs.
- Most popular surf beaches are patrolled by lifesavers–swim in the patrolled area between the red and yellow flags and if you get into trouble, raise your arm. If the beach isn't patrolled, try to identify any potential undercurrents, rips or sandbars and proceed with caution.
- Other beaches, rivers and billabongs sometimes have signs warning of dangerous wildlife. Crocodiles can be a danger in the Top End–you shouldn't swim in any watercourse unless you've been assured it's croc-free. Likewise in the Top End, at certain times of year there are stingers in the ocean–check with a local before you dive in!
- Don't assume that, because there isn't a sign, it's safe to take the plunge–use your common sense. In lakes and rivers, beware of submerged logs and rocks. If you can't see the bottom, ease your way in: don't dive.

- Australia has more than its fair share of poisonous snakes and spiders,but again, the chances of being bitten are remote. Summer is snake season: avoid walking through long grass and if you're in the bush, wear boots and socks and keep your eyes open. Never approach a snake or try to pick it up. For the most part, snakes are 'shy' and will get out of your way.
- There are several poisonous spiders in Australia including the red back, funnel web and white tail spiders. Be careful when turning over rocks or moving timber, or collecting firewood (wear gloves if you can).
- The chances of being bitten by a snake or spider are slight, but if you are bitten or stung, apply first aid and seek medical attention immediately.
- Tick bites can cause severe illness. If you're bushwalking in tick-infested areas, check your body all over for tell-tale lumps. Apply methylated spirits and use tweezers to remove the tick, being sure to keep it intact.
- If you're 'going bush' for more than a day–either on foot or by car–or heading out on the water, be prepared for contingencies. Take plenty of water and know where you'll be able to source more. Make sure you have any relevant maps or charts, spare food and fuel, warm clothing (don't forget the desert can be freezing at night). On a boat, make sure you have a functioning two-way radio, flares and appropriate safety equipment. And of course, check the weather forecast before you go.
- If you're taking a road trip away from the east coast, remember it can be hundreds of kilometres between towns, fuel and food stops. Plan your stops and ensure you're self-sufficient. Carry extra spares, particularly if you're travelling on dirt roads. Make sure you know the road rules.
- Outside cities, stock and wild animals such as kangaroos and wombats can pose traffic hazards, especially at night and in the half light of early morning and dusk. Maintain a sensible speed, look well ahead and avoid driving in the outback between dusk and dawn.
- Don't forget that in Australia, we drive on the left-hand side of the road. As you step off a pavement, make sure you look to your right for on-coming traffic.
- Theft is relatively rare in Australia, but nevertheless you should take care of your belongings–don't leave valuables lying around, or visible through a car window.
- For all of Australia's dangerous wildlife and unforgiving wilderness, undoubtedly the most common afflictions suffered by travellers are heat exhaustion and sunburn. Make sure you keep hydrated (don't wait until you feel thirsty to drink water), wear a wide-brimmed hat and long sleeves and avoid exertion during the hottest part of the day. Your skin can start to burn in just 10 minutes–most travellers (and locals) underestimate its intensity. Cover up, apply protective cream or stay out of the sun between 11am and 2pm when the sun's rays are most damaging.
- The number to dial in case of emergency is **000**. This will connect you to ambulance, police or the fire brigade.

Emergency services: ☎ 000

the big Trip

driving around australia

Lasseter Highway. *(Tourism NT)*

Australians have always loved a good road trip—whether it's a leisurely Sunday drive through the wineries or to the beaches near our capital cities; a quick weekend getaway into the mountains; a summer family holiday travelling our beautiful coastline; or roughing it on a remote outback track—hitting the road is a favourite way to spend our holiday time.

Most Australians dream of heading off on The Big Trip at some stage: taking a few months holiday and staying in hotels, motels and guesthouses; loading up the campervan or 4WD and hitting the campsites and national parks; or planning a retirement spent driving around the country with a caravan in tow. Not everyone can afford the six months or so that you really need to see and do all there is in this great continent, so we've broken the trip up into easy stages that cover some of the highlights. Do one close to home, or do the whole thing. Either way, it's time to hit the road ...

Across Tasmania: Hobart to Strahan

The beauty of Tasmania is that everywhere is only a few hours drive from anywhere with plenty to see in between.

Start in Hobart's Battery Point on a Saturday morning with the Salamanca Market. Here you'll find lots of bargain-priced hand-spun, hand-knitted jumpers, beautifully-turned native Tasmanian timberwork and freshly-picked garden produce.

Shopping done, head to New Norfolk and Lake St Clair on the Lyell Highway. It's a pretty drive that will take around four hours, through the Derwent Valley, past farmlands, hop fields, forests and remnants of rainforest.

Break your journey west at Lake St Clair. There are some lovely walks here, ranging from 45 minutes to a few hours. The really energetic can try the 65km Overland Track to Cradle Mountain. The more sedate can take the ferry to the northern end of the lake and take a five-minute walk to the rainforest from there.

The drive from Lake St Clair to Strahan is magnificent. The first 80km section winds through the Franklin-Gordon Wild Rivers National Park, where it seems as if a new jagged-edged mountain rises up around every curve of the road.

By bizarre contrast, at Queenstown the alpine wilderness is transformed to a moonscape of treeless, eroded hills where the vegetation has been killed by almost 100 years of tree felling, sulphurous pollution from smelters and bushfires.

It's 37km on to Strahan, home of the Gordon River Cruises. Thrill seekers can try the 50-minute jet boat ride to King River. Alternatively, if the weather is nasty, you can always while away the afternoon sitting by the fire with a bowl of soup watching the fishing boats dock at the wharf.

Length: 245km

Tourism Tasmania: ☎ 1800 623 191
www.discovertasmania.com.au

Great Alpine Road: Wangaratta to Bairnsdale

The Great Alpine Road is one of Australia's great mountain drives. It begins in pastoral northern Victoria and takes you high into the ski fields of the Australian Alps and finally brings you out, a stone's throw from the coast in east Gippsland.

Take the Ovens Highway out of Wangaratta towards Myrtleford and Mt Buffalo through hop fields and vineyards. This area was once an important tobacco growing area, but has been replanted in the last few years with more lucrative grape vines. Keep an eye out for the oddly-shaped tobacco curing sheds that still dot the countryside. Other crops you'll see (and taste at roadside stalls in season) around here are chestnuts, walnuts and blueberries.

If you are planning to drive further during winter, Myrtleford, or the smaller village of Porepunkah 24km further on, are the places to buy your wheel chains–it is compulsory to carry chains during the snow season, from June to October.

Take the turn-off to Mt Buffalo National Park at Porepunkah. The park is a massive granite mountain, and here you'll see fantastically-shaped granite boulders and cliffs, waterfalls, alpine lakes and snow gum woodlands.

Queenstown Hills, Tasmania. *(Joe Shemesh)*

From Bright, The Great Alpine Road snakes its way through the valley via little villages such as Smoko, once set amongst fields of tobacco. MT Feathertop dominates the scenery and soon after Harrietville the road begins to climb. This is a terrific piece of road: sharp bends wind through forests of mountain ash and stringy bark before traversing the ridgeline for 30km, giving superb views on both sides of the road.

The road passes through the ski villages of Mount Hotham and Dinner Plain before it begins to descend, winding its way through extensive forests, following various rivers and streams, almost all the way to Bairnsdale.

Length: 298km

www.lakesandwilderness.com.au

The Princes Highway: Melbourne to Sydney

Put the fun back into the Melbourne-Sydney commute by taking the coast road and turn the trip into a three-day holiday.

The first few hours are through lush farmlands–gourmet deli country. Try some famous Jindi or Tarrago cheese at Yarragon, then head inland to Sale and across to Bairnsdale to explore the Gippsland Lakes, Australia's largest waterway system. Spend the night at Paynesville, the boating capital of Australia and take the ferry out to Raymond Island, home to a large koala colony.

At Lakes Entrance cast a line from a jetty, riverbank or beach, and then head to the historic timber town of Orbost and on across the border into NSW.

Eden, on the shores of Twofold Bay, is one on the best places to watch whales and the Eden Killer Whale Museum is a must. Stop at the Bega Cheese Factory and wander through the twin villages of

Outback Highway. *(Sam Timson)*

Central Tilba and Tilba Tilba. Both are Heritage listed, and look much the same as they would have 100 years ago. Stay the night at beach-side Narooma.

The highway spears north to Sydney. Check out the surfing kangaroos at Pebbly Beach, stop at Ulladulla for some great fish and chips, browse the boutiques in Berry, catch a wave whooshing thorough the Blowhole at Kiama and visit Wollongong's Nan Tien Temple, the largest Buddhist temple in the Southern Hemisphere. And if you want one last look at the coast pull into Stanwell Tops for the big view south.

Length: approximately 1130km, depending on detours.

www.visitvictoria.com www.visitnsw.com.au

The Pacific Highway: Sydney to Brisbane

Relive the best summer holidays of your childhood on a holiday drive between Sydney and Brisbane.

Head out of Sydney on the F3 freeway, but take the Gosford exit and meander through the string of seaside villages and resorts. Give the kids a break at The Entrance and let them burn off some energy at Vera's Playground, a free-play pool with lots of colourful sculptures to climb on.

Continue north through Newcastle, where new foreshore developments like Honeysuckle are giving the former industrial city a makeover, and on to Port Macquarie. Stop here overnight and chill out on one the town's 13 beaches.

Back on the road, stop for a snack at Freddos Pies at Frederickton–home to the best pies in the country–and then on to beautiful Bellingen, with its galleries, restaurants and cafes.

You can't drive through Coffs Harbour without a visit to the infamous Big Banana. Check out the fun rides, including the toboggan, ice skating, a real snow slope, and the best chocolate-covered frozen bananas you've ever tasted. Another big thing is just three hours up the road–Ballina's big prawn.

Stretch the legs at Uki, a cute town overshadowed by the dominating peak of Mt Warning and then cross the border into Queensland. Have some quality quiet time with the glow worms of Springbrook National Park, before succumbing to the non-stop action of the Gold Coast theme parks.

On the way into Brisbane, stop and check out the views across the Brisbane River at Kangaroo Point.

Length: approximately 940km, depending on detours.

www.visitnsw.com.au www.queenslandholidays.com.au

The Tropical North: Rockhampton to Cairns

Escape to the tropics in Far North Queensland on a three-day, 1000km drive from the beef capital of Rockhampton to lush and steamy Cairns.

Make your first stop Cape Hillsborough, north of Mackay. Surrounded by national park, it's a nature lover's paradise–but be warned, you may have to fight the local wallabies for space on the beach. Continue north to Bowen, gateway to the Whitsunday Islands. It's an undiscovered paradise with dozens of unspoiled bays and beautiful beaches and a great place to explore the stunning coral of the Great Barrier Reef Marine Park.

But just because you have a car doesn't mean you can't get off shore. At Townsville, take the car ferry to Magnetic Island and spend a day or two relaxing–or for a change of pace head for Horseshoe Bay on the far side of the island for a little bit of jet ski action or some horse riding along the beach.

Leaving Townsville the countryside gets greener as you head into sugarcane country. Spend a night in the historic country town of Ingham and take a 40-minute detour to one of the north's little known wonders, Wallaman Falls.

If you have the time on the final 233km leg to Cairns, head out to Hinchinbrook Island, stop at Mission Beach and check out the Spanish castle ruins and rainforest gardens at Paronella Park.

Length: 1070km

www.queenslandholidays.com.au

The Savannah Way: Cairns to Broome

From sea to sea, the trip across the top of Australia along the Savannah Way is one of the greatest trans-continental road trips in the world. You'll need at least three weeks to drive the whole thing comfortably, although you can break it up into shorter sections, such as Katherine to Broome for a week, if you are short of time.

While there are unsealed 4WD alternative sections, the main route (apart from a 700km section between Normanton and Borroloola) is technically sealed, but often only for the width of one lane, so you need to move on to the dirt shoulder to pass oncoming traffic. There are plenty of road trains as well, so the best strategy is to take it slow and watch for flying stones hitting the windscreen. If you're hiring a car, take the extra insurance option that covers you for windscreen damage–on this road it's not a case of if, but when. Even though the road may be blacktop (ashphalt) almost all the way these days, it's still a long drive through a remote landscape. It's a dry season trip only with some of the sections impassable between November and April.

Highlights of the eastern section include Undara lava tubes 285km west of Cairns, Karumba's sunsets, Burketown, the Barramundi capital of Australia and a great place to hook a whopper or catch yourself a monster mud crab, the palm-filled oasis of Lawn Hill Gorge National Park, the fossils of Riversleigh World Heritage site, and Limmen National Park's Lost City bushwalks.

Soak away any road-weariness at Mataranka Hot Springs, before spending a night or two in Katherine, roughly the half-way point of the Savannah Way. A highlight here is the sunset cruise in Nitmiluk National Park, where the Katherine River carves a series of 13 deep gorges through towering red sandstone cliffs.

Continue on to Broome, travelling through more rough and rugged gorge country beyond Lake Argyle, one of the largest man-made bodies of water in the country, through remote national parks such as Keep River and Gregory national parks, through tall stands of boab trees and past the magnificent Purnululu National Park or the Bungle Bungles, though tiny blink-and-you'll-miss-it Aboriginal communities selling investment-quality art pieces and on to, finally, the white sands of Cable Beach at the pearling port of Broome.

Length: approximately 3500km.

www.savannahway.com.au

The Coast Road: Monkey Mia to Perth

Hit the road in the country's biggest state and drive the coast from dolphin central, Monkey Mia, to Perth. It's a 900km trip, but take a few detours to see the best mother nature has to offer.

There's no shortage of beaches and marine life, including the wild dolphins of Monkey Mia who have been visiting the beach since the 1960s, playing up to the rangers who look after them and the tourists who love them. The Shark Bay World Heritage area is also home to the oldest living organisms on earth, the stromatolites at Hamelin Pool and Ningaloo Reef where you can dive with the world's biggest fish, the whale shark.

Highlights of the next stretch include the colourful coastal cliffs and river gorges of Kalbarri, the mysterious Pink Lake and convict history at Lynton Historic site. Stop and check out the twisted trees on the way to Geraldton and the WA Museum with the shipwrecked Batavia and HMAS *Sydney* memorial, the then head for the historic pioneer settlement of Greenough before dipping your toes in the Indian Ocean at Jurien Bay.

Don't miss the Pinnacles, some of the most photographed rocks in WA. Around 30,000 years old, they are the result of centuries of weathering by water and wind. Stretch the legs in Gingin and check out the old waterwheel in the centre of town, then head into the city of Perth via the Swan Valley wine region with lots of vineyards and gourmet food producers.

Length: approximately 900km.

www.westernaustralia.com

Across the Nullarbor: Perth to Port Lincoln

Australia's other great trans-continental road trip is the journey across the Nullarbor Plain, one of the longest, straightest, flattest roads in Australia. From Perth follow the Goldfields Pipeline through the wheat belt and goldfields of the south-west to the historic gold-mining towns of Southern Cross, Coolgardie and Kalgoorlie-Boulder–full of grand gold rush era buildings that testify to the riches that were found here. Once on the Nullarbor Plain the road runs due east with hardly a turn or hill. A 100 or so kilometres past the WA/SA border the highway hits the coast and side tracks spear off to the right, each leading to a lookout over the spectacular Bunda cliffs where the immense, treeless plain falls into the Southern Ocean over the Great Australian Bight. Explore the Eucla Telegraph station ruins; take a scenic flight over the Head of Bight whale breeding grounds and climb the sand-dunes just east of Border Village.

The outback meets the sea on the Eyre Peninsula. The cold southern waters that wash this rugged coastline produce some of the freshest and tastiest seafood in the country and the best way to taste it is to follow the seafood and aquaculture trail, visiting abalone and crayfish farms, oyster sheds and fish hatcheries, that open their doors

Boab Tree. *(WATC)*

for tours, and even a seahorse farm. Cast a fishing line off a jetty in a seaside town along the way; visit celebrated surf spot Cactus Beach; or go four-wheel-driving in Coffin Bay and Lincoln national parks.

Length: around 2300km

www.nullarbornet.com.au www.epta.com.au

The Red Centre: Adelaide to Alice Springs and beyond

Take a detour into the red centre and head up the Stuart Highway from Adelaide to the Alice.

Before you head out into the wild yonder visit the Wadlata Outback Centre in Port Augusta, then spend some time in the beautiful Flinders Ranges. Star attractions are the bushwalking and scenic flights over the massive bowl-like shape of Wilpena Pound and Parachilna Pub, a little slice of luxury in the middle of nowhere. Be sure to try the feral mixed grill, it's their signature dish.

From here on in the countryside gets drier and hotter as you pass through the ghost town of Farina and on to Marree, home of the mysterious Marree Man, a 4km long image carved into the earth. Stop at Mutonia, a sculpture park 30km out of Marree, take a look at the vast white salt lake at Lake Eyre South and the mini oasis of Coward Springs before stopping for a cold drink at William Creek the smallest town in South Australia.

Next stop, Coober Pedy, opal capital of the world, where most of the locals not only work underground, they live there too. Check out the underground Serbian Church and the golf course where the greens are black, the fairways are rough and the only piece of grass you'll see is the tiny plastic square that you carry around with you.

From here it's a straight seven-hour, all-sealed run to Alice Springs where you can hook up with the Mereenie Loop Road (also often called the Pioneers Path) a 1050km loop that leads you through the beautiful West MacDonnell Ranges, past several spectacular gorges and swimming holes and on to Kings Canyon, Uluru and Kata Tjuta.

Length: 2500km

www.ntexplore.com.au

(Sam Timson)

Great Ocean Road: Warrnambool to Torquay

Finish your round-Australia trip with one of the country's best known, and best loved, scenic routes–the Great Ocean Road. Built between 1919 and 1932, the cliff-hugging road was hewn from the rock by returned World War I soldiers using picks, crowbars and shovels.

Great Ocean Road begins (or ends) on the coast at Warrnambool meandering through pastoral farmlands to Peterborough and then on through Port Campbell National Park past all the dramatic rock formations and rugged cliffs that make this drive one of the most famous in the world. There's London Bridge, which dramatically lost one of its arches in 1990, stranding two startled sightseers on the newly formed tower, and Loch Ard Gorge, site of a tragic shipwreck in 1878 that left just two survivors.

DRIVING IN THE OUTBACK

- The most important thing to remember when driving on remote tracks in the outback is to ensure you are carrying enough water, basic spare parts, food and fuel. Remember, fuel and supply outlets in remote areas are not often open after hours or at weekends.
- If you do get into trouble in the outback, never, ever leave your vehicle. Most people who have perished in the outback have died while trying to walk to help. Wait until help comes to you.
- Station properties are often unfenced in the outback—keep an eye out for wandering cattle and wildlife on roads and avoid driving at night.
- Watch out for road trains. Slow down and if there is an escort vehicle watch for signals. If you move off the road, reduce speed and watch for guide posts and soft edges.
- Bulldust patches can appear without warning. Shift down a gear quickly if you're bogging down and steer carefully. Watch carefully for the end of the dust patch which can often have a hard edge that can damage your tyres or even the wheel rims.
- When driving over sandhills or through drifts of sand lower your tyre pressure to around 15 psi to help avoid getting bogged. If you need to stop, either face down a dune or find a section of hard-packed sand. Generally, you don't need to brake on sand—sudden braking can bury the nose of the vehicle. Be aware that some dunes have double—even triple—crests, and that you may need to power through even though you think you're at the top.
- Slow down at dips. Brake on entry and accelerate again as you exit to give maximum clearance.
- Check tracks across creeks for clear passage and water depth.
- Do not camp in dry creek beds in case of flash flooding, which may arise without warning from rainfall hundreds of kilometres away and many days earlier.

Along this stretch the road climbs the high plain which falls into the sea in sheer cliffs, sometimes just metres from the edge of the road. Highlights include the Twelve Apostles rock formations, the result of wind and wave erosion that carved the towers out of the surrounding cliffs. The cliffs rise to nearly 70m in some places and the highest Apostle is around 50m from base to tip.

The road then leaves the coast and cuts through dense rainforest of Otway National Park, before emerging on the eastern side of the coast near Apollo Bay, and continues to hug the coastline, with plenty of jaw-dropping views, to Anglesea. In between are the stylish resort towns of Lorne and Aireys Inlet, great for a stroll and cup of coffee or lunch at one of the many restaurants that line the main streets.

Final stop is Torquay, surfing mecca. Visit surfworld, an interactive museum dedicated to the art and culture of wave riding. Shop for surf wear or check out the waves at Front Beach. Famous Bells Beach is a short detour away and it's a quick run into Geelong and Melbourne.

Length: around 250km

www.greatoceanrd.org.au

Driving on unsealed roads

Many of the roads in country areas are unsealed. After heavy rains, they may take up to 24 hours to dry out. Travelling on roads that have a 'closed road' sign, even if you are in a 4WD vehicle, may incur a fine of up to $1000.

Driving in the snow

Snow chains must be carried on certain roads between June 1 and October 10 in alpine areas of NSW and Victoria. Unless you intend to do a lot of driving in snow and ice affected regions, the best decision is to hire your chains. There are many places you can hire the correct chains to fit your vehicle in the towns near both areas. Make sure you ask for a demonstration on how to correctly fit your chains before you leave.

Coffin Bay, SA (LA)

ROAD READY

Before you leave home, give your car the ten step once over.

1 **Ask the expert:** play it safe and get your vehicle serviced by a licensed mechanic before you leave home.

2 **The good oil:** engines like fresh oil, so treat your engine to a lube. And check it regularly while on your trip to make sure it doesn't get low.

3 **Power rangers:** you'd be amazed how many people get stranded with a flat battery, especially if they are running portable fridges, chargers or night lights. Carry a spare and make sure that you turn appliances off overnight.

4 **Keep your cool:** check your radiator coolant level and top it up if necessary. If you're heading a long way from help, carry some spare hoses and a bottle of coolant with you.

5 **Keep the pressure on:** carry, and use, a tyre gauge. Before you leave, check the tread and make sure you have a spare in good condition.

6 **The right tools:** a basic tool kit should include a jack, jacking plate and wheel replacement tools, spare tyre, fire extinguisher, emergency fuel supplies if heading off the beaten track, engine oil, coolant, jumper leads, spare radiator hoses, fan belts and the tools you'll need to replace them.

7 **First aid:** never travel without a first aid kit and always carry extra drinking water.

8 **Pack it in:** don't overload your car or carry unrestrained items in the back seat–even a flying book can cause serious injury in crash. If it won't fit in the boot, don't take it. If you're traveling in a wagon or 4WD, install a cargo barrier.

9 **Take the right maps:** sounds simple, but most people don't. Fighting over which is the right way to go is a major cause of holiday (and marital) breakdown.

10 **Play it safe:** make sure your vehicle and home insurance is up to date. Cancel any home deliveries, get the neighbours to collect your mail and install a light timer so the bad guys don't know you've left home. Join your state auto club, such as the RAA or NRMA, to help you out in the event of a breakdown.

australia's top 100

Australia is a vast continent, a place of geographical and climatic extremes with enough unique things to see and do that you could spend a lifetime exploring and still not see it all. Knowing where to begin your adventure can be daunting, so to help you decide where to go and what to see we've compiled a list of 100 things worth seeing and doing. From the best outback tracks and most popular walking trails, to our favourite forests, caves, waterfalls, rivers and gorges, from amazing animal encounters to adrenalin-pumping aerial adventures, indulgent luxury camping safaris and awesome natural attractions, we've put together a list of some of Australia's best.

Of course, no list like this can ever hope to be complete. There are hundreds of very special spots and remarkable experiences that we have left out. Rather, this Top 100 is a starting point, just a handful of Australia's unique places and adventures that are out there waiting for you.

Devils Marbles *(Tourism NT)*.

Birdsville Hotel *(Queensland Tourism)*.

outback tracks

1 Birdsville Track, Qld

First established in the 1880s as a stock route between Marree in South Australia and Birdsville in Queensland, the Birdsville Track is one of Australia's most legendary outback tracks. Back then, it took about a month to complete; the route was long and extremely harsh and cattle often didn't survive the trip. Now the track is passable to conventional vehicles, most of the year. Highlights include salt lakes, homestead ruins, crossing the dog fence and visiting the gushing hot water bores beside the track, the Natterannie sand hills where the Tirari and Strzelecki deserts meet, and of course, the famous Birdsville Hotel.

Length: around 520km.

Wirrarri Information Centre: ☎ (07) 4656 3300
email: wirrarri@hotmail.com

2 Gibb River Road, WA

The Gibb River Road is a trip for those who want a true outback adventure. It's 4WD only; remote, rugged, hard on your vehicle and seriously out there. You'll need to be pretty much self-sufficient, carry spares, tools and extra fuel and be willing to camp most nights, but it is one of the most beautiful outback drives in the country. The track starts in Kununurra, and cuts through the heart of the Kimberley to meet the sea at Derby. Highlights are forests of boab trees, spectacular gorges, crocodiles, cool billabongs and waterfalls. Most people continue on to Broome and then circle back to Kununurra via the bitumen Great Northern Highway and explore the Bungle Bungles on the way home. Roads are impassable November to April.

Length: around 700km.

www.derbytourism.com.au www.westernaustralia.com

3 Corner Country, NSW

This drive takes you up the Silver City Highway to Tibooburra and Cameron Corner, where three states meet: New South Wales, Queensland and South Australia. The mostly unsealed road spears north from Broken Hill, through endless red dust plains studded with salt bush and mulga, mobs of kangaroos, emus and cackling galahs. Highlights include the ghost town of Milparinka; Depot Glen where explorer Charles Sturt was forced to wait out the summer heat in 1845; Sturt National Park, with its startling jump ups, flat mesa-like mountains rising dramatically from the surrounding plains; Cameron Corner, where the states meet beside the Dingo Fence, the red dunes of the Strezlecki Desert and vast gibber plains.

Length: around 480km.

www.outbacknsw.com.au www.nationalparks.nsw.gov.au

4 Oodnadatta Track, SA

Linking Marree in the south to Marla in the north, the Oodnadatta Track traverses some of South Australia's most remote outback, following in the footsteps of explorer John McDouall Stuart, who crossed the continent from Adelaide to Darwin in 1862. The Overland Telegraph Line was built along his route just 10 years later, which was followed by the now abandoned original Ghan railway line, opened in 1929. It can be a bumpy, dusty trip, but nothing like the horror stretch it once was. Today, with care, even a conventional two-wheel-drive sedan can travel the main track. Explore old train carriages in Marree, have a beer at William Creek (population seven), visit the white salt vastness of Lake Eyre, bubbling mound springs, old Telegraph Station and homestead ruins and the outback outpost of Oodnadatta. You need a Desert Parks Pass for access and camping in the national parks along this track. These cost $95 including an information pack and detailed maps. Call 1800 816 078.

Length: around 620km.

www.environment.sa.gov.au/parks/lakeeyre/visit.html
www.southaustralia.com

5 Eyre Peninsula, SA

One of the best kept beach secrets in the country is the Eyre Peninsula, a triangle of land jutting into the sea between Adelaide and the Great Australian Bight. If you like empty beaches, this is the place. On this three- to four-day drive from Whyalla to Ceduna via Port Lincoln you'll find beach after beach, visited only by the occasional fisherman and screeching seagulls. Campsites are on the edge of the sand and you're often the only ones there. Highlights are oysters and fresh seafood, stunning five-kilometre cliff drive at Elliston, fishing from town jetties, four-wheel driving in Lincoln and Coffin Bay national parks and swimming with sea lions at Baird Bay.

Length: 580km.

www.epta.com.au

6 Flinders Ranges, SA

The weathered crags of the Flinders Ranges in central South Australia is an ancient landscape, full of almost primeval colours: rich purples and deep blues, cut through with red rock gorges and acres of white, yellow and purple wildflowers in spring. Main roads are accessible to conventional sedans, but most side tracks are 4WD only. Highlights include the Wadlata Outback Centre in Port Augusta, Pichi Richi steam railway at Quorn, Brachina and Mount Chambers gorges with their galleries of Aboriginal rock art, Wilpena Pound (best seen on a scenic flight) and Arkaroola's stunning ridge-top tour.

Length: around 650km loop.

www.flinders.outback.on.net

7 Pioneers' Path, NT

This drive will take you to all the icons of the Australian outback in one three-day trip: Alice Springs, Kings Canyon and Uluru. From the Alice, head west through the ancient purple West MacDonnell Ranges to Hermannsburg, home of Albert Namatjira, then on to The Mereenie Loop Road. This dirt road will take you to Kings Canyon, where you can hook up with the bitumen road to Uluru. Highlights along the way include Glen Helen Gorge, the Gardner Range, Finke Gorge, Mount Connor and Palm Valley. Four-wheel drive is recommended on the Meerenie, although conventional cars have been known to survive the trip. *(ed's note: due to be sealed in 2007)*

Length: 630km.

www.travelnt.com

Aerial view of Uluru. *(New Holland Image Library)*

Menindee Lakes, NSW. *(TNSW)*

Simson Desert dune. *(SATC)*

8 The Simpson Crossing, Qld/NT

The Simpson Desert crossing is one of the last frontiers of the outback. It was the last of the Australian deserts to be explored by Europeans–the first to cross its expanse of red dunes was Ted Colson, on camel, in 1936; the first vehicle in 1962. Now, it's top of the list for serious four-wheel drivers, and while thousands of people cross the Simpson each year, it is still not a trip to be taken lightly. You'll need to be self sufficient, carry good maps, make sure your vehicle is in tip-top condition, carry enough water for several days and basic spares. Crossing east to west is the easiest way, from Birdsville to Dalhousie hot springs, and allow three days.

Length: 645km.

www.environment.sa.gov.au/parks/simpson_cp

9 Across the Nullarbor, WA/SA

The trip across the Nullarbor is an iconic journey through the Australian outback. The longest, straightest, flattest piece of road in Australia stretches from just east of the historic gold mining town of Kalgoorlie in Western Australia to the fishing port of Ceduna on the Eyre Peninsula in South Australia. Highlights include semi-arid desertscape, the flat Nullarbor Plain so devoid of features you feel as if you can see forever, towering cliffs along the Great Australian Bight, Eucla Telegraph Station ruins, whale watching at Head of Bight and fresh seafood in Ceduna.

Length: around 2500km.

www.nullarbornet.com.au

10 Kidman Way, NSW

The fully-sealed Kidman Way runs almost 800km through outback New South Wales, and is a great introduction to the wide open expanse of the western plains, particularly for those who prefer to stay on the bitumen. Along the way you can visit the scene of some of bushranger Ned Kelly's more notorious raids at Jerilderie, enjoy the wineries and restaurants of cosmopolitan Griffith and the surrounding Riverina region, learn about the true story behind the legend of the 'black stump', discover a rich local history at the copper mining town of Cobar and explore the town that has become synonymous with the bush and the outback–Bourke.

Length: around 800km.

www.kidmanway.org.au

Yarra Ranges, Victoria. *(Tourism Victoria)*

forests

11 The Otway Fly, Vic

Perched high in the rainforest tree tops of Victoria's Otway Ranges midway along the Great Ocean Road, the Otway Fly provides a unique walk within the canopy of beautiful beech myrtle forest. Get close-up views of the rainforest on the elevated boardwalk 25m above the ground. If you have a head for heights, climb the 47-metre lookout tower for stunning views. The walk is suitable for all ages, but does have some steep sections. The visitor centre has lots of information on this amazing rainforest, plus a licensed restaurant.

12 Yarra Ranges, Vic

The Yarra Ranges, just a couple of hours drive from Melbourne, is home to two of the most beautiful forest drives in Victoria. The Black Spur between Healesville and Narbethong is a narrow 10km section of the Maroondah Highway that winds its way up into the Great Dividing Range through towering mountain ash and lush green fern forests. Continue on to Marysville and visit Steavenson Falls, which, at 82m high, are Victoria's highest cascades. If you are staying overnight, come back after dark when the falls are floodlit. From Marysville, take Lady Talbot Forest Drive, a round trip of 46km into the Yarra Ranges National Park. There are several walking trails that will lead you through old-growth myrtle beech forest to waterfalls tumbling over huge granite boulders and through dense rainforest. Unless you've got a 4WD, it's a dry weather road only.

13 Snowgums, Vic/NSW/ACT

Nothing characterises the Australian 'High Country' more than the wind-twisted, multi-trunked forms of snowgums, especially after rain when the bark comes alive in varying shades of pink, grey, brown and white. The best place to see them is above the snowline in Alpine National Park, Victoria's largest national park. With adjoining national parks in NSW and the ACT, it forms a protected area that covers almost all of Australia's high country. Downhill and cross-country skiing are the main winter attractions; spring and summer bring stunning wildflower displays and are the best time for bush-walks, four-wheel driving and horse riding.

14 South East Forests, NSW

About 50 to 60km inland from the far south coast township of Eden, the South East Forests National Park protects some of the most important areas of eucalypt forest in Australia. Many of the old growth trees in these areas are almost three metres across in diameter and are many hundreds of years old. There are several walking tracks and lookouts and two very good scenic drives–a 100km loop from Bombala takes you to the Myanba Gorge, Pheasants Peak (steep 1km rough walking track) and White Rock River via the towering canopies of old growth forest trees; the 140km drive from Bega to Six Mile Creek, Postman's Camping Area, and Myrtle Mountain Lookout takes you through hinterland wet fern forest.

15 Dorrigo Skywalk, NSW

Dorrigo National Park is about 60km from the popular beach-side town of Coffs Harbour on the NSW north coast via the very scenic Waterfall Way. It's a great place for either a quick one-hour visit or you can spend all day on one of the longer, five-hour walks. Don't miss the Rainforest Centre, which has an excellent interpretive display and Skywalk, a dramatic board-walk above the rainforest canopy that leads out over the edge of the escarpment for spectacular views across the rainforest and down to the coast. The Canopy Café does good coffee and cake.

16 Cape Tribulation, Qld

The rainforest meets the sea in the coastal section of Daintree National Park, home to a variety of habitats including rain-forests, mangroves, swamps and heathlands. There are two popular boardwalks: Maardja boardwalk at Oliver Creek and the Dubuji boardwalk at Cape Tribulation. Explore the rain-forest along short tracks at Jindalba or walk along Kulki or Myall Beaches. Fit walkers can climb to a lookout over the Daintree coast along the Mt Sorrow ridge trail. Swimming is not recommended as estuarine crocodiles live in the park's creeks and nearby coastal waters. Beware of marine stingers from October to May. Access roads are narrow and winding and not recommended for caravans. Roads may be closed after heavy rain. Check current road conditions with RACQ.

☎ (07) 4033 6433 ☎ 1300 130 595

Enjoying the rainforest

17 Treetops Walk, Qld

If you'd like to really give your hiking boots a work out next time you're on the Gold Coast head to the World Heritage-listed Lamington National Park. Protecting one of the largest remaining tracts of subtropical rainforest in Australia, Lamington is also part of the Scenic Rim. Highlights include waterfalls, stands of 15,000-year-old Antarctic beech trees and more than 160km of walking tracks and the treetops canopy walk, a 20m-high suspended walk amongst the rainforest canopy and across nine swinging suspended bridges. O'Reilly's Guesthouse inside the park has restaurant and bar facilities.

18 Boondal Wetlands Reserve, Qld

Mangrove forests form some of Australia's most important and widespread coastal ecosystems, covering some 750,000 hectares around the coastline. One of the best places to walk amongst them is at Boondall in Brisbane. Boondall Wetlands lies on the edge of Moreton Bay and includes more than 1000 hectares of tidal flats, mangroves, saltmarshes, melaleuca wetlands, grasslands, open forests and woodlands. Keep an eye out for flying foxes, bats, possums and squirrel gliders. There are also a variety of frogs, reptiles and butterflies and an amazing array of birdlife including mistletoe birds, tawny frogmouths, eastern curlews, kingfishers, rainbow bee-eaters, grass owls and wrens. At low tide, shorebirds feed on the mudflats.

19 Tahune AirWalk, Tas

An easy day drive from Hobart, the southern forests near Geeveston are home to Tahune Forest Reserve, where you can wander above the treetops on the Tahune Forest AirWalk, a 600m-long elevated treetop walk that leads out over the canopy of the wet eucalypt forest to a cantilever 50m above the ground for stunning views of the Huon and Picton rivers. Apart from the elevated walkway there are several lookouts and short walks leading off the Arve Forest Drive including the 10-minute riverside loop at the Arve River Streamside Reserve and the 20-minute Huon Pine boardwalk underneath the AirWalk.

20 Valley of the Giants, WA

About 420km from Perth near the south coast town of Walpole is Walpole Nornalup National Park, 20,000 hectares of towering karri and tingle forests. The Tree Top Walk leads you along a 420m-long steel-truss walkway which takes you up and over a deep, red tingle gully. Because it is built on the side of a natural valley, the walkway rises up above the forest floor on a gentle grade suitable for kids, people in wheelchairs and the elderly. The highest point in the 600m loop is about 40m. Below, a boardwalk winds though a grove of veteran tingle trees known as the Ancient Empire.

Fraser Island, Qld (TQ)

best walks

21 Yankee Hat, ACT

Just 45 minutes drive from the manicured lawns and gardens of Canberra's suburban sprawl is Namadgi National Park an untamed wilderness and the most northern of all the Australian Alps parks. At almost 106,000 hectares, this one park makes up more than half of the Australian Capital Territory.

During winter, snowfalls are common, and the highest peaks, such as Bimberi Peak, which at 1911m is just 318m lower then Mt Kosciuskzo, and the Brindabella Ranges are permanently capped with snow.

The central Namadgi Ranges, with their bold outcrops of granite, are of great importance to Aboriginal people, who have lived and roamed this country for more than 21,000 years. There are 170km of marked walking trails throughout the park, but one of the best is the 6km short trail to Yankee Hat, great for family trips with kids or grandparents in tow. The trail meanders through open grasslands past mobs of eastern grey kangaroos and along boardwalks skirting the edge of the Bogong Swamp to end at the lower slopes of Yankee Hat Aboriginal Rock Art Site where you'll find an excellent rock art gallery of ancient art depicting human figures, kangaroos, wombats, koalas, dingos and birds.

Length: 6km, two to three hours.

Level: easy.

www.environment.act.gov.au/bushparksandreserves/namadgi.html

22 The Six Foot Track, NSW

Following the 44km route of the original 1884 bridle track from Katoomba to Jenolan Caves, the Six Foot Track (named for its width, not its length) is a strenuous but beautiful walk through the heart of the World Heritage-listed Blue Mountains National Park west of Sydney.

The track begins at the Explorer's Tree, just off the Great Western Highway, 6km west of Katoomba. The track winds down the through the rainforest and waterfalls of Nellies Glen and across the Megalong Valley through open pastures and along the banks of the wild and stony Cox's River.

Day two and it's a steep climb up and over the Mini Mini saddle (not so mini) and the Black Range, while day three is a descent through thickly forested slopes to Jenolan Caves.

The walk is not for the unfit: you need to carry your own water and arrange transport from Jenolan Caves back to Katoomba at the end. Spare a thought for those who enter the annual Six Foot Marathon and run the entire course in less than four hours!

Length: 44km, three days.

Level: moderate to difficult.

www.bluemts.com.au

23 Coogee to Bondi Cliff Walk, NSW

One of the best urban walks you'll find anywhere, the 6km Coogee to Bondi walk is a spectacular cliff-top walk that links several of Sydney's most iconic beaches and offers stunning views. It's an easy walk, with paved pathways, about 100 steps, railings along the steeper, more vertiginous parts, and few steep slopes or hazards (apart from dogs and joggers, and traffic on the strip linking Tamarama with Bronte). Allow about an hour to complete the one-way stretch. Many walkers make a day of it, stopping at intervening beaches for a dip, or taking a bus to the Coogee end and walking back to Bondi. Beachside parks offer picnic shelters, coin-operated barbecues, play areas, kiosks, toilets and change-rooms. Sculpture by the Sea is an annual international sculpture competition that sees the pathway lined with sculptures each November.

Length: 6km, two hours return.

Level: easy.

www.waverley.nsw.gov.au

24 Fraser Island Great Walk, Qld

The Queensland Government is creating a series of 'Great Queensland Walks' through some of the state's most beautiful natural areas, including three World Heritage Areas. The first to open was the Fraser Island Great Walk, a 90km track that winds between Dilli Village and Happy Valley.

Following the pathways of the island's original inhabitants, the Butchulla people, old logging roads and tramlines, the track passes iconic sites such as Lake McKenzie, Wanggoolba Creek, Lake Wabby and Central Station, as well as some of the island's most popular spots like the Valley of the Giants.

There are also short walks from Central Station, Kingfisher Bay Resort, Lake McKenzie, Lake Wabby, Lake Boomanjin and Eurong. Additional tracks link the Great Walk to the island's main barge landings, accommodation and supply centres.

Length: 90km, six to eight days or can be broken into a series of half- and full-day walks.

Level: some moderate sections.

www.epa.qld.gov.au/parks_and_forests/great_walks/

25 The Riesling Trail, SA

The Riesling Trail is a 27km walking and cycling track that follows a disused railway line between Clare and Auburn. It's sealed and suitable for bicycles as well as wheelchairs and strollers. What's more, you don't have to compete with road traffic, so it's great for families and small children.

Named after the grape and wine variety that the Clare Valley is famous for, the Riesling Trail travels past many cellar doors and other visitor attractions, making it ideal for those wanting a leisurely walk with a few distractions along the way. It begins at Auburn, birthplace of CJ Dennis, of *Sentimental Bloke* fame, before heading through paddocks and vineyards and up through the Skilly Hills. Stop for some refreshment at Sevenhill Winery, founded in the mid-19th century by early Jesuit settlers, and offering tastings and sales in the old monastery cellars, as well as tours of the underground cellar, museum, St Aloysius Church, historic cemetery, crypt and shrines. Clare is just 6km up the road at the end of the Trail.

Length: 27km, three leisurely days, or broken into shorter sections.

Level: easy.

www.clarevalley.com.au or
www.southaustraliantrails.com/top_trails.asp?riesling

26 Kings Canyon, NT

The western end of the George Gill Ranges rises sharply from the surrounding flat desert plains, producing a rugged landscape of ranges, rockholes and gorges, the best known of all being Kings Canyon in Watarrka National Park. Sculptured by the elements and rising up 100m to a plateau of rocky domes, Kings Canyon is home to one of the most dramatic short walks in the outback–the Rim Walk.

The best time to tackle the 6km Rim Walk is either early in the morning, before the heat and flies begin to fray tempers, or late in the afternoon, when the setting sun lights up the sheer sandstone walls of the canyon to their best advantage.

The first half-hour or so is a lung-busting, muscle-destroying climb up the side of the canyon, but if you can make it that far, the remainder of the two-hour to three-hour walk is an easy stroll around the rim of the canyon where breathtaking 300m sheer cliffs cut deep into the rock. Highlights include the weathered, buttressed domes of the 'Lost City', and the 'Garden of Eden', a sheltered valley with permanent waterholes and lush vegetation.

Length: 6km, three hours.

Level: easy with a challenging start.

www.nt.gov.au/ipe/pwcnt

27 Cape to Cape, WA

Think Margaret River and most people automatically think 'great wine'. And rightly so. The Margaret River region, a wild knob of land jutting into the sea off the bottom corner of WA, crowned in the north by Cape Naturaliste and Cape Leeuwin in the south, is home to some of the finest white wines (and plenty

Kings Canyon, NT. *(Sam Tinson)*

Cradle Mountain, Tas. *(Garry Moore)*

of terrific reds) produced in Australia. But it is also home to one of the country's greatest walking tracks, the Cape to Cape that stretches 140km along the coastline between the two headlands. There's lots of sandy ups and downs, but you'll walk across cliff tops with breathtaking views, sandy beaches with spectacular surf and through magnificent karri forests. The two historic lighthouses at either cape are both worth a visit.

Time your trip for September and you'll be treated to one of the world's best wildflower shows as the dunes and countryside are carpeted in kangaroo paw, deep blue karri hovea, old man's beard, yellow cone bushes and yellow Patersonia. From April to June and October to December you can see humpback and southern right whales from various vantage points along the coast.

Length: 140km, around seven days.
Level: some challenging sections.

www.calm.wa.gov.au/national_parks

28 Great Ocean Walk, Vic

First there was the Great Ocean Road, and now there is the Great Ocean Walk. The 91km coastal walk links Apollo Bay to the Glenample Homestead, near Port Campbell. The walk includes many of the prime attractions of the Great Ocean Road and passes through the dense mountain forests and spectacular coastal margin of the Otway Ranges and Otway Plain through the Otway and Port Campbell national parks, coastal reserves and road reserves. It's knock-your-socks-off gorgeous, with highlights including the Bay of Martyrs, Loch Ard Gorge, Twelve Apostles and London Bridge, Maits Rest rainforest boardwalk, giant mountain ash gums, fern gullies and rugged, inaccessible beaches and the historic 150-year-old Cape Otway Lighthouse. Many of the beaches along the walk are exposed to tides, rips and reefs and are not patrolled and the safest time to walk along them is during low tide. Check tide times before setting off.

Length: 91km, around eight days.
Level: some challenging sections.

www.parkweb.vic.gov.au

29 The Overland Track, Tas

The Overland Track between Cradle Mountain and Lake St Clair is a true wilderness walk through some of Tasmania's best alpine scenery. Taking the best part of six days, the track travels through spectacular dolerite mountains, beside beautiful waterfalls, through a variety of landscapes including alpine pastures, swamps and beech forests, includes a side trip to climb Tasmania's tallest mountain, Mt Ossa, and finishes at Australia's deepest lake, Lake St Clair.

The best time to tackle the track is in summer, but even then temperatures can drop suddenly so be prepared with some winter woollies. To help manage numbers, a booking system is in place for the peak walking season, November to April. An Overland Track fee of $100 per person is charged to cover the costs associated with maintaining the track, and as part of this system, walkers are required to walk the track from north to south during the peak walking season.

Length: 65km, five to seven days.
Level: some challenging sections.

www.overlandtrack.com.au www.parks.tas.gov.au

30 Wineglass Bay, Tas

One of the most photographed curves of sand in Australia, Wineglass Bay in Freycinet National Park on the east coast of Tasmania is a perfect crescent of fine white sand, lapped by crystal clear, azure waters. Drop in a backdrop of wild bushland and remove all traces of human habitation–beaches just don't come much better than this one!

Jutting out from the sea the craggy but beautiful Freycinet Peninsula is largely national park and consists of bare granite mountains (known as the Hazards) surrounded by sheltered bays and white sand beaches. The one-hour climb up to the lookout over Wineglass Bay with its breathtaking view is worth the steep slog. What's more, while you'll see a few people on the trek, if you continue down to the beach you're just as likely to have it to yourself, as the walk unjustly deters most day trippers, who seem happy enough to snap a picture and continue on their way.

Length: 6km, two and a half hours return.
Level: some steep sections.

Longitude 131, NT. *(Voyages)*

luxury camps

31 Slumber safari, Vic

If you can't get to Africa this is the next best thing. Werribee Open Range Zoo's Slumber Safaris include up-close animal encounters, a delicious African BBQ feast, an African drumming lesson and an evening of fun around the campfire. Get close to the action of Africa sleeping in four-star canvas safari tents and wake to watch the savannah come to life while enjoying a delicious cooked breakfast. All Slumber Safari guests receive special discounts on all special tours of the zoo, including the canoe safari along the Werribee River and the open vehicle adventure where you can come face-to-face with the animals.

www.zoo.org.au ☎ (03) 9731 9600

32 Emma Gorge, WA

With an address like Number 1, Gibb River Road, you know you're in for an adventure. Emma Gorge is part of the million-acre Wilderness Park, El Questro, set in some of the most dramatic country of the Kimberley in the remote north-west of Western Australia. Accommodation is in luxury timber-floored tents with ensuite and just a short walk from the base of the gorge and waterhole, perfect for swimming. Chefs serve locally grown tropical fruits for breakfast–barbecues of fresh fish and Kimberley beef are specialities for lunches and dinners, served in the open air of the Headquarter's verandahs.

www.elquestro.com.au ☎ (08) 9169 1777

33 Kooljaman, WA

Kooljaman at Cape Leveque is a multi award-winning Aboriginal-owned wilderness camp, 220km north of Broome on the Dampier Peninsula, which can be reached either by air from Broome or by 4WD on a fairly rugged road. Activities include whale watching in season, cultural tours led by local Aboriginal guides, fishing, snorkelling and scenic boat tours. The tents are built on raised timber decking, high on the hillside below the lighthouse, to take advantage of the panoramic ocean views. Each has its own large balcony with barbecue, private bathroom, full-size fridge/freezer and all cooking equipment. Alternatively you can always eat at Dinkas Restaurant on the beach.

www.kooljaman.com.au ☎ (08) 9192 4970

34 Longitude 131, NT

They may call it a 'tent' but the suites at Longitude 131 is about as luxurious as outback 'camping' can ever hope to be. Elevated high above the sand and spinifex a stone's throw from Uluru, tents are lavishly appointed with all mod cons–marble bathrooms, television, stereo, king-size bed, objets d'art on the walls. That's right, these tents have walls, the front one made entirely of glass so as not to miss the view. There's even a neat remote control so you can open the blinds in the morning to watch sunrise over Uluru from your bed!

www.longitude131.com.au ☎ 1300 134 044

35 Minjungari Safari Camp, NT

Tucked in a remote corner of Litchfield National Park a couple of hours south of Darwin, this campsite overlooks beautiful Minjungari billabong, home to two saltwater crocs. Most people stay as part of an Odyssey Tour, which includes trips to swimming holes and waterfalls that most day visitors to the park don't get to, as well as savannah sunset tours, although you can arrange to drive in if you have a four-wheel drive. Facilities include insect-proof dining shelter where a three-course dinner is served, permanently erected tents with single beds, solar hot water for showers and composting toilets.

www.odysaf.com.au ☎ 1800 891 190

36 Arnhemland Safari, NT

Davidson's Arnhemland Safaris take you to Mount Borradaile, in the north-west corner of Arnhem Land next to Kakadu National Park and Cobourg Peninsula, a vast sub-tropical savannah rich with Aboriginal rock art and culture. Comfortable, airy twin-share tents surround the main complex, a fully screened social hub incorporating a kitchen, dining area and library. Permanent toilet and shower blocks with hot and cold water are situated at the outer fringe of the camp, as is a laundry facility. If you can't catch a barramundi here, it's time to give away the rod and reel and take up lawn bowling.

www.arnhemland-safaris.com ☎ (08) 8927 5240

37 Gunya Titjikala, NT

Gunya Titjikala offers an authentic indigenous experience as a guest in a remote desert Aboriginal community, 120km south of Alice Springs. Exclusive itineraries can vary from aboriginal art, culture, landscapes, dreamtime, bush tucker or just sit down in the dirt with the locals and share cultures. Accommodation is one of three luxury safari tents overlooking the Simpson Desert with the most spectacular views, dawns and sunsets. Each tent features private ensuite with flush toilet and deep bath, expansive decking, extensive Aboriginal library and exclusive Gunya skin and body products. Enjoy a fusion of western and 'bush tucker' dishes prepared by the resident chef.

www.gunya.com.au

38 Paperbark Camp, NSW

One of Australia's first eco-friendly luxury camps, Paperbark Camp on Jervis Bay south of Sydney, is The Spot for a beach holiday. The unique tents have private ensuite facilities, comfortable queen or twin beds, pure wool doonas, insect screens and solar powered lighting. They're also stylishly furnished with locally handcrafted bush furniture. Activities include whale watching, bushwalking, canoeing and swimming. Dining is in the Gunyah, a chic space built high off the ground to enjoy the sea breeze and a wonderful position amongst the tree tops. The menu focuses on local produce and seafood and Australian native ingredients.

www.paperbarkcamp.com.au ☎ 1300 668 167

39 Jabiru Camp, Qld

Wake up to a dawn chorus alive with the sounds of the kookaburra and brolga and listen to the distinctive call of the Southern Boobook while stargazing under the southern sky. Set in the heart of a 5000-acre wetlands conservation reserve near Mareeba in the Cairns highlands, Jabiru Camp overlooks beautiful lily-covered lagoons alive with birds and other wildlife. The safari-style tents have private ensuite facilities, queen or twin beds and insect screens. Each one has a private timber verandah with comfortable chairs and a table, perfect for birdwatching, reading or a glass of champagne as the sun sets over Clancy's Lagoon.

www.mareebawetlands.com ☎ (07) 4093 2514

Wilson Island, Qld. *(Voyages)*

40 Wilson Island, Qld

A tiny coral cay on the Great Barrier Reef, Wilson Island is your own island paradise. With a maximum of just 12 people on the island at any one time, accommodation is in one of just six comfortable tents, set on raised timber decks–each with views of the reef and ocean and designed for your comfort. Each tent has its own designated private shower and dressing area though this is not ensuite. Toilets and vanities are also located in this separate building. Visit rare turtle and bird breeding grounds, snorkel the reef, do some bird watching or just kick back and enjoy the stunning views from your private retreat.

www.wilsonisland.com ☎ 1300 134 044

Queensland's tropical fish. *(TQ)*

marine life encounters

41 Swimming with sea lions, SA

Ocean Eco Tours run half-day trip swimming trip with wild sea lions in the waters off Baird Bay on the Eyre Peninsula, South Australia. These cold southern waters are home to a large breeding colony of 70 or more Australian Sea Lions, one of the rarest of seal species. The entire population of these friendly creatures is only around 12,000 and about two thirds of the population live in South Australian waters. This is no theme-park splash-about with highly-trained, tamed and well-fed captive animals. These are wild creatures in their natural environment, but they do appear to enjoy the interaction–the more you splash about in the water and duck-dive, mimicking their frolicking, the more they respond. The sea lions are never fed and all interaction is initiated by the animals. They come to you.

Masks and snorkels are provided and wet suits are available for hire. You must be able to swim and parents or guardians must accompany children under 12. The best season is from September through to May.

www.bairdbay.com ☎ (08) 8626 5017

42 Seal Bay, SA

If you prefer walking among the mammals then head for Seal Bay on Kangaroo Island's southern coast and join a tour, wandering on the beach through a colony of dozens of huge, sleepy sea lions, resting after spending three days at sea hunting for food. Seal Bay is the only place in Australia where you can approach this close to the sea lions since all the other colonies are located on craggy and inaccessible rocky headlands. If you don't want to join a tour, there is a self-guided boardwalk you can stroll along, but it does not allow you to get onto the sand or as close to the sea lions. From Seal Bay, drive a couple of hours west to Cape du Couedic. The rocks below the lighthouse are home to a colony of New Zealand fur seals, wallowing in the sun or frolicking in the surf under the dramatic rock arc of Admirals Arch. Be warned–they smell worse than they look.

www.tourkangarooisland.com.au

Baird Bay, SA. (SATC)

43 Penguin parade, Vic

One of Australia's most popular wildlife events takes place each day at dusk when a parade of little penguins emerge from the sea and make their way to their burrows in the sand dunes of Phillip Island, 90-minutes drive from Melbourne. You can watch the parade from the viewing stands and observation board-walks at Phillip Island Nature Park. Built to protect the penguin's habitat, these viewing areas also ensure that the 500,000 visitors that attend the event each year all get a good look at the penguins.

The island is also home to a large number of koalas, and a colony of up to 16,000 fur seals that take up residence at Seal Rocks at the western tip of the island from October to December. There is also abundant bird life, including shearwaters, which can be seen flying to and from their nests on Cape Woolamai, and many different species of waterbirds at Rhyll Inlet.

www.visitvictoria.com

44 Polperro Dolphin Swims, Vic

Swim with seals and dolphins in Port Phillip Bay on Victoria's Mornington Peninsula near Melbourne. Despite the high amount of commercial traffic (freighters, ferries and leisure craft) the bay is home to a resident population of more than 100 bottlenose dolphins and a number of Australian Fur Seals. Polperro Dolphin Swims, led by passionate marine conservationist Judith Muir, runs regular dolphin swims in the bay teaching people about local marine life while giving them the opportunity to be in the water with dolphins and seals.

➲ Trips depart Sorrento Pier, daily in summer (8am and 1pm) and by arrangement in winter.

www.polperro.com.au ☎ (03) 5988 8437

45 Diving with sharks, NSW

If you really want to commune with sea creatures try dating a grey nurse on the Central Coast of New South Wales. Les and Fran Graham of Terrigal Dive Centre are the experts when it comes to diving with grey nurse sharks. If you are an experienced diver they run boat trips to an underwater cave, called Foggy Cave, about three miles out from Terrigal Beach. From March to the end of May, these endangered sharks come to here to breed. Les says you can see up to eight sharks on any one dive. "The sharks will come quite close to you," says Les. "They just slowly cruise past you, very close and very slow, in a trance like state, and look at you. It is such a beautiful thing." If you want to swim with the sharks you will need to be an experienced diver as the dive is 40m deep.

www.terrigaldive.com.au

46 Finding Nemo, Qld

Although the Great Barrier Reef spans more than 2000km of Queensland's coastline, Cairns is one of the closest gateways to the spectacular coral beds of the outer reef and there are literally dozens of snorkelling, diving and glass-bottomed, observation boat cruises available. Most trips take a full day and head out to coral cays and islands around 90 minutes to two hours from shore and cater for all levels of swimming abilities. Nearby, Green and Fitzroy islands give you the chance to dive, snorkel or reef walk. If you've always wanted to try scuba diving this is a good place for it, as there are lots of places that offer introductory dive course for underwater first timers–and all that competition means you're sure to find a trip to suit your budget.

www.queenslandholidays.com.au

47 Whale watching, Qld

Australia is directly in the path of the southern whale migration route, so between May and November there are hundreds of great vantage points to see whales along much of the Australian coastline. The most common are humpbacks and southern right whales, although Bryde's and sperm whales, and a variety of others may be seen as well. One of the most popular places to take a whale watching cruise is Hervey Bay off the southern coast of Queensland. The Hervey Bay Marine Park is protected from prevailing winds by nearby Fraser Island, providing a sheltered area for humpback whales on their annual migration from Antarctica. Humpbacks mate and calve along this part of the Australian coast and you can often see mothers and young calves together which is a delight. Humpbacks are also the most acrobatic of the whales (breaching, tail slaps, deep dives, etc) so they are one of the best for whale watching. More than 12 operators offer whale watching tours with vessels departing the Hervey Bay Boat Harbour daily between late July and early November.

www.frasercoastholidays.info

48 Whale sharks, WA

From mid-March to mid-May at Ningaloo Reef on the northern coast of Western Australia you can dive with the awesome whale shark, the world's biggest fish–often reaching more than 12m long and weighing more than 11 tonnes. Ningaloo Reef is Australia's second largest marine park, covering 5000km^2 of ocean around the North West Cape from Exmouth to Red Bluff. It is the largest fringing coral reef in Australia, and is the only large reef in the world found so close to a continental land mass; about 100m offshore at its nearest point and less than 7km at the furthest. Ningaloo Reef is the only easily accessible place in the world where these giants appear in large numbers at predictable times of the year. You don't even have to be a scuba diver to swim with them, as they swim close to the surface.

www.westernaustralia.com

49 Dolphin feeding, WA

Monkey Mia, on the north-west coast at Shark Bay, Western Australia's first World Heritage-listed area, is one of the few places on earth where wild dolphins interact with humans. The bottlenose dolphins have visited the beach for about 30 years, and are famous for their almost daily ritual of swimming to shore. Seven of them make regular beach visits, with up to 20 others occasionally stopping by to greet a captivated audience. You can feed the dolphins under the supervision of a national park ranger. The shallow waters of the lagoon are also home to more than 180 species of coral, including cabbage corals, brain corals, lavender corals, and delicate branching corals and you can often spot whales, dolphins, dugongs, manta rays, huge cod or sharks on nearby Ningaloo Reef.

www.westernaustralia.com

50 Crocodile cruise, NT

The place to look a saltwater crocodile in the eye is in the Northern Territory's Top End. At Adelaide River Bridge, about halfway between Darwin and Jabiru, you can join a 90-minute Jumping Crocodile Cruise. The double-decker boat takes you on a leisurely trip up the river, enticing the crocodiles sunbathing on the muddy banks into the water to jump up and snatch a pork chop dangling from a big stick. Although the crocs are wild, the slightly vaudevillian tour smacks a little of trained animals, but it is a good chance to get a close-up look at some huge crocodiles–especially if you sit downstairs, where you will be eye to eye with the giant reptiles through the large glass windows. Inside Kakadu National Park, head for Cooinda, where you can do the much better Yellow Water billabong cruise, a two-hour cruise on a breathtakingly beautiful landlocked billabong fringed by pandanus, paperbark swamps and monsoon rainforest. Take the sunset or sunrise cruise and you'll see thousands of birds and more than likely a few big crocodiles as well.

www.travelnt.com

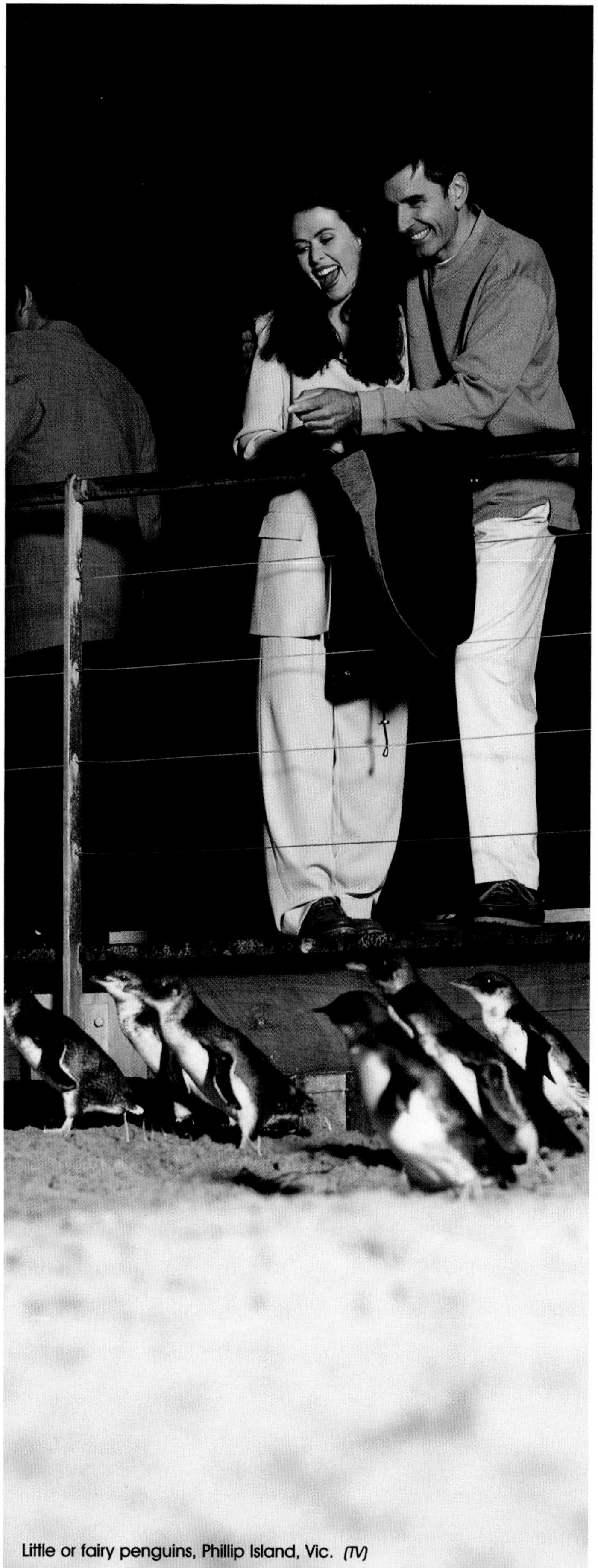

Little or fairy penguins, Phillip Island, Vic. *(TV)*

Bright, Victoria.

flying high

51 Microlights, Vic

Soar like an eagle in a tandem microlight with the Eagle School of Microlighting and Hang Gliding. Based at Porepunkah at the base of Mt Buffalo the flying school offers tandem instructional flights for absolute beginners. The adventure begins as you suit up and climb into the flimsy aircraft–basically a hang glider with a small engine and propeller attached to the back. Whilst in the air, the pilot demonstrates how the glider is controlled, and if you like, you can even take over the controls yourself–all this in less than 10 minutes! At the highest point of your flight the pilot switches off the engine and you glide silently back to the airstrip. Twin flights are available so you and a friend can fly together–wingtip to wingtip.

www.eagleschool.com.au ☎ (03) 5750 1174

52 Hang gliding, NSW

There's no greater way to fly like a bird than hang gliding and the beachside cliffs of Bald Hill at Stanwell Park an hour's drive south of Sydney is the best place to try it. The undisputed hang gliding capital of Australia, you can undertake full instruction courses that will have you flying solo with your pilot's license as soon as you're ready. If you prefer to try before you buy, there are tandem 30-minute sightseeing flights available, providing spectacular ocean views and flying over the Royal National Park to the north and the escarpment and to the south. No prior experience is necessary but you will need to book ahead and all flights are weather dependent.

www.hangglideoz.com.au

53 Paragliding, NSW/ACT

Fly from the top of Australia's highest mountain and other sites in and around Thredbo in a paraglider–similar to a hang glider but using a parachute rather than a rigid wing frame. The Australian Paragliding Centre specialises in paragliding courses for complete beginners–from tandem flights and two-day introductory courses to full license courses run over a week. It's a full-time professional school based in Canberra and teaches year round, with additional teaching facilities in Sydney, Tumut and Corryong in Victoria.

www.paraglide.com.au

54 Jet fighter flights, NSW/Vic

If you've secretly harboured dreams of being a fighter pilot just like Tom Cruise in Top Gun you can live the dream on a Strikemaster jet fighter flight as you bomb a secret base hidden in the mountains, take evasive action from enemy fire and return home unscathed. Each half-day adventure includes a full safety and mission brief covering the area of operations, weapons delivery and G-force preparation. You will be outfitted in a full military pilot flying suit, helmet, oxygen mask and gloves. After final briefing and flight clearance, be prepared for the exhilarating acceleration from 0 to 600kph in less than 20 seconds!

Jet Fighter Flights operate from Bathurst NSW (2.5 hrs from Sydney), Newcastle NSW (1.5 hrs from Sydney), Mangalore Vic (1.5 hrs from Melbourne), and soon from Hobart, Tasmania.

www.jetfighterflights.com

55 Bridge climbs, NSW/Qld

It's a long way down from the top of Sydney Harbour Bridge, but the view is unbeatable. The climb, which takes three hours, begins with a briefing in BridgeClimb's training centre, where you are provided with a grey climbing suit and a harness that is linked to a static line once you reach the catwalk. Once ready, you walk out onto the catwalk to the pylon and climb up the ladder onto the arch, or main span, itself. Out on the arch, any fear or anxiety disappears as you take in the views. It is an easy walk, just lots of steps. At all times you are attached to the static line and there is always a handrail for extra support. You will need to wear rubber-soled shoes. Day and night climbs are available, but the climbs are popular so bookings are essential.

You can also climb Brisbane's Story Bridge, not quite as high as Sydney's but designed by the same man, Dr J Bradfield, and a great way to get some high-altitude thrills and spectacular, uninterrupted 360° views of the river city. Morning, day and night climbs are available.

Sydney: www.bridgeclimb.com

Brisbane: www.storybridgeadventureclimb.com.au

56 Bungy Jumping, Qld

The uninitiated might think it's a crazy thing to do, but once you plucked up the courage and taken your first bungy jump you'll be back for more. Inspired by the manhood ritual on Vanuatu's Pentecost Island, where the young men jump from 35m towers with vines tied around their feet, the modern bungy jump using latex rubber cords is the ultimate swan dive. The 50m-high Cairns Bungy Tower is 15km north of Cairns and is surrounded by lush tropical rainforest with panoramic views out to the Great Barrier Reef. Night Bungy is available once a month during the famous Full Moon Party.

www.ajhackett.com.au

57 Scenic flights, WA

Scenic flights are a great way to see what's happening on the ground below from a completely different perspective, particularly if you are flying over a remote or inaccessible area. If you only take one scenic flight in Australia, do it over the Kimberley in north-western Australia. One of the most impressive sights in outback Australia, Purnululu National Park or the Bungle Bungles, was only discovered by Europeans in the 1980s and is best seen from the air, where you can look over the huge expanse of distinctive beehive-shaped towers made up of sandstones and conglomerates, their alternating orange and black or grey banding caused a skin of silica and algae. Most flights also fly over Lake Argyle, the body of water created by the Ord River Scheme, one of the world's largest man-made bodies of water and the huge open cut Argyle Diamond mine.

www.alligatorairways.com.au

Cape Crawford, NT. *(Tourism NT)*

58 Helicopter tours, NT

Cape Crawford on the Gulf of Carpentaria in northern Australia, is home to the Heartbreak Hotel and little else, but worth a mention as the place to take a helicopter sightseeing tour over the Lost City, a large expanse of tall sandstone columns only accessible by air. The flight takes you over the Abner Escarpment onto a plateau on McArthur River Station. The area was once an inland sea, the water seeped into the rock and eroded it, breaking it into columns up to 25m tall, and from the air you get a good idea of how these natural sky scrapers were formed. You can also do a two-hour ground tour that includes a 1.5km walk around the base of a small section after being dropped off by the chopper, which returns to pick you up and fly you back later.

www.capecrawfordtourism.com.au

59 Hot air ballooning

Ascend into the heavens on a sunrise hot air balloon flight. It'll mean an early start–most flights begin set up well before dawn in order to catch the stable, gentle early morning breezes, but at least you won't have to cook breakfast later as most flights include a champagne breakfast as part of the deal. Suitable for all ages, the most difficult thing about hot air ballooning is getting out of bed so early and climbing in and out of the high wicker basket. Once up in the air, the flight is very still and surprisingly tranquil as the balloon becomes one with the breeze. Mornings are a magic time to be aloft. Often a misty layer of soft fog reflects the first rays of the sun. On other days the light quickly changes the colours as it spreads across the plains below. This is as close to walking in the sky as it is possible to get. There are plenty of great places suitable for hot-air ballooning around Australia, with the best being the Yarra Valley in Victoria, Hunter Valley in NSW, Alice Springs in the Red Centre and Canberra. Broome in north-west WA is the latest addition.

www.hotairballooning.com.au, www.balloonaloft.com
www.outbackballooning.com.au

60 Skydiving

If you're after the ultimate adrenaline rush, then skydiving wins. For pure fear, it's hard to beat sitting in the open doorway of a very small plane, very high up in the air, knowing you're about to jump out into absolutely nothing. And for sheer exhilaration, it's hard to beat the incredible sense of freedom and speed as you plummet very quickly towards the ground. Best way to get your first taste is on a tandem skydive.

Skydiving suits are supplied, but you'll need a sturdy pair of shoes. The instructor runs you through a practise drill from a parked plane on the strip, before you pile into the plane for take-off. At 12,000 feet, you clumsily make your way to the open door (it is hard to manoeuvre around a moving plane with a fully-grown instructor strapped to your back!) count down from three and before you know it, you're out the door.

Flight time is around 15 minutes or so, free fall around 45 seconds, the entire jump lasts around four to five minutes. The adrenaline rush lasts much longer.

Tandem skydives are available in regional centres across Australia.

www.australia.com

Floating over Alice Springs. (Sam Tinson)

Lake Cave, WA. *(WATC)*

going underground

61 Mole Creek, Tas

The Mole Creek Karst National Park in the central north of Tasmania, about 40 minutes drive west of Deloraine, contains more than 200 caves, which began to form about 30 million years ago and include gorges, large underground streams and springs. You can take a guided tour of Marakoopa and King Solomons Caves. Both are home to a range of fascinating animals which have evolved features which allow them to adapt to their lightless environments. The glow-worm display in Marakoopa Cave is the largest you'll see in any public access cave in Australia. When you've toured the caves take some time to walk through the beautiful forests in the national park.

www.parks.tas.gov.au/natparks/molecreek

62 Princess Margaret Rose Cave, Vic

Semi-translucent and backlit stalactites, stalagmites, helictites and flow stone form sculptures, rarely seen cave coral and miniature landscapes that could be from another planet are among the beautiful limestone decorations you'll find at Princess Margaret Rose Caves, in Lower Glenelg National Park, near Nelson, 2km east of the South Australian border in western Victoria. Most limestone caves are formed by water seeping down through cracks and faultlines in the limestone, dissolving the rock and creating fissures and tunnels. The formation of Princess Margaret Rose Caves, however, was assisted by water from the Glenelg River which worked its way along a faultline for 300m. The water scalloped the walls of the cave and wore a reasonably level floor. Guided tours lasting about half an hour are conducted on most days.

www.parkweb.vic.gov.au

63 Buchan Caves Reserve, Vic

Buchan Caves Reserve is north of Lakes Entrance in Victoria's Gippsland region. These ancient caves have spectacular limestone formations created by underground rivers cutting through limestone rock almost 400 million years ago. Guided tours are conducted daily in Royal Cave and Fairy Cave. Both caves are lit and have walk-ways. Royal Cave has beautiful calcite-rimmed pools; Fairy Cave has elaborate stalactites and stalagmites. Tours to 'wild' unlit caves can be arranged for small groups. Other caves have been opened and you can book tours of the less accessible Murrindal Caves, just north of Buchan.

www.parkweb.vic.gov.au

64 Naracoorte Caves National Park, SA

A series of marine transgressions and regressions–the sea moving in and out–near Naracoorte in the south-east of South Australia helped form the World Heritage-listed Naracoorte Caves National Park. Giant prehistoric marsupial remains were discovered in what's now known as the Victoria Fossil Cave in 1969, and the Wonambi Fossil Centre brings these giant marsupials back to life as fantastic robotic re-creations. You can view bats from the Bat Observation Centre (via infrared technology), try your hand at adventure caving or take a guided tour of the many beautiful caves dotted throughout the park. Wet Cave can be explored without a guide, while regular guided tours of Alexandra Cave and Victoria Fossil Cave showcase beautiful limestone formations and the fossil site.

www.environment.sa.gov.au/parks/naracoorte

65 Undara Lava Tubes, Qld

The Undara Lava Tubes in the heart of the Savannah Gulf Country in outback Queensland are part of the longest lava flow from a single volcanic crater on the planet. These lava tubes, which extend more than 160km, were formed around 190,000 years ago, when a large volcano in the McBride volcanic province erupted violently, spewing molten lava over the surrounding landscape. The molten rock, which has been estimated at 233 cubic kilometres or enough to fill Sydney Harbour in just six days, flowed rapidly down a dry riverbed. The top outer layer cooled and formed a crust while the molten lava below drained outwards leaving behind a series of hollow tubes. There are 68 separate sections of lava tube that have been identified from more than 300 lava tube roof collapses and more than 164 volcanoes in the area. You can explore some of the longer lava tubes on one of the daytime tours run by Undara Experience.

www.undara.com.au

Undara lava tube, Qld.

66 Margaret River, WA

Twenty minutes drive south from the wine producing region of Margaret River in the south-west corner of Western Australia, the limestone that forms the rugged coastline also has numerous caves, with two open for self-guided tours. Spectacular Calgardup Cave has water covering the floor of two caverns, resulting in beautiful reflections and features elevated platforms throughout the cave. Adventure sections of Calgardup Cave are available with a guide and can be arranged by talking to staff at the entrance. Giants Cave is about 800m long and is a through cave, meaning you can enter a spectacular doline and reappear out of another via elevated platforms and marked paths. The Cape Naturaliste Tourism Association runs Ngilgi Cave, while Augusta-Margaret River Tourist Association has regular tours of Mammoth, Lake, Moondyne and Jewel Caves.

www.calm.wa.gov.au

67 Jenolan Caves, NSW

There are 280 known caves in the Jenolan Reserve in the Blue Mountains west of Sydney, many richly decorated with stunning limestone formations–stalactites and stalagmites, columns, shawls and canopies. Nine of the caves are open to the public and tours leave regularly, ranging from one to two hours. There are also candlelight ghost tours at night, 'off the track' tours where guides take you to their favourite places in the caves the tourists don't normally get to visit and extended adventure caving tours for groups. If you prefer to stay above the ground there are many bushwalking tracks. Climb up to Carlotta's Arch, the Devil's Coachhouse lookout or stroll more sedately beside the river to the cyan-coloured Blue Lake. Jenolan Caves is also a good starting point for the stunning cliff-top walks at Kanangra Walls, a 30-minute drive away in Kanangra-Boyd National Park.

www.jenolancaves.org.au

Blue Lake, Jenolan Caves. (TNSW)

68 Yarrangobilly Caves, NSW

Just a few kilometres off the Snowy Mountains Highway in Kosciuszko National Park, the limestone caves at Yarrangobilly are among the most richly-decorated in Australia and are open for self-guided tours. South Glory Cave, first explored in 1834, contains massive decorations and vast rockpiles. Jersey Cave, featuring a rare display of black and grey flowstones, is home to some of the most stunning and diverse cave decorations found at Yarrangobilly. Don't miss Cleopatra's Needle, a remarkable four-metre stalagmite that almost touches the cave's ceiling.

Relax in the surrounding reserve with a dip in a warm thermal pool where the water remains at a constant and comfortable temperature of 27°C. There are also a range of excellent bushwalking and picnic facilities.

www.nationalparks.nsw.gov.au

69 Wellington Caves, NSW

The turn-off to Wellington Caves on the Mitchell Highway in central western NSW is hard to miss, marked by the Wellington Gateway–a huge, fantastic and grotesque wind chime made from the girders of the old Wellington Bridge. The caves reserve includes two show caves–Cathedral and Gaden caves–and a series of smaller caves. These are limestone caves, with wonderful displays of stalagmites and stalactites, including what is reputed to be the world's largest stalagmite, 'the alter'. Also in the reserve is a restored phosphate mine, which apart from a few palaeontologists looking for fossils, has remained virtually untouched for the past 80 years. The walls of the Bone Cave in the eastern loop of the mine are embedded with thousands of fragments and fossils. Lit by ultra-violet light, the ancient bones glow eerily in the darkness. The 350m-long mine cave has been developed with easy access in mind so it is accessible for wheelchairs and strollers. Most tours take around an hour and a half.

www.wellington.nsw.gov.au

70 Abercrombie Caves, NSW

Just as spectacular as Jenolan Caves, but without the crowds and long queues and busloads of visitors, these caves are only 11km south of Trunkey in the state's central west. The largest feature is 'the Archway' which is 221m long and 60m wide at both ends. On a self-guided tour you'll find a wooden dance floor that was built by gold miners more than 100 years ago. Guided tours of the four caves run everyday. Some tours involve steps and climbing up ladders and squeezing past formations, but they are a lot of fun for those tired of larger, more sedate, cave tours. Children love the Bushranger's Cave with its many tunnels that was once used as a hideout for the Ribbon Gang in 1830, long before the reign of more well-known bushrangers like Ben Hall or Ned Kelly and before the caves were 'officially' discovered in 1842.

www.jenolancaves.org.au

Millaa Millaa Falls, Qld. *(TQ)*

best waterfalls

71 Ellenborough Falls, NSW

Reputed to be the largest single drop of water in the southern hemisphere, Ellenborough Falls is one of the hidden secrets of the NSW mid-north coast, tucked away in the hinterland west of Port Macquarie. There are picnic and barbecue tables here and a lookout at the top where locals abseil down the side of the falls. You can take the 642 steps to the bottom (we counted!) or follow the much easier walk through the rainforest to view the falls from the other side of the gorge.

72 Oxley Wild Rivers National Park, NSW

Situated east of Armidale and Walcha, the World Heritage Oxley Wild Rivers National Park encompasses more than 500km of rivers, which fall from the New England Escarpment in spectacular waterfalls then flow through dramatic gorges and valleys to join the mighty Macleay River. Attractions include Wollomombi Falls, often quoted as Australia's tallest waterfall, but this is only so if measured from its highest point, where the land has a much gentler gradient and the water does not truly 'fall'. Other falls in the park include Apsley Falls, Dangarsleigh Falls, Gara Falls, Bakers Creek Falls and Chandler Falls.

73 Atherton Tablelands, Qld

Forget the highest, Millstream Falls, 3km from the small town of Ravenshoe in the Atherton Tablelands west of Cairns, are the widest falls in Australia. The falls, which spill over an old basalt lava flow, are best seen during the wet season when they are at their most spectacular. The Atherton Tablelands are also home to several other dramatic falls: follow the scenic Tully Falls Road from Ravenshoe to the spectacular Tully Gorge Lookout. The falls only run in a big wet season, but the walls of raw rock and rainforest which plunge 300m (984 feet) down to the Tully River are still an awe-inspiring sight. An 800m walking track leads to the Tully River above the falls. Do not venture onto the rocks at the top of the falls–they are slippery and dangerous.

Further south, nearer to Innisfail, Millaa Millaa is the centre of the Waterfall Circuit, which includes Mungalli Falls, Millaa Millaa Falls, Zillie Falls and Ellinjaa Falls.

74 Barron Falls, Qld

Also in the Atherton Tablelands just out of Cairns, Barron Falls are amongst the most accessible of all Australian waterfalls–you can view them from the Kuranda Scenic Railway as well as the skyrail cable car that runs above the falls. Due to its hydro-electric potential, waterflow of the Barron River above Barron Falls is controlled by releases. Releases are timed to allow water to go over the falls when the Kuranda train passes filled with passengers. Like many other falls in northern Australia, in order to see them in their full glory (which is a very impressive sight), you need to see them during the wet season.

75 Mackenzie Falls, Vic

Renowned for rugged mountain ranges and stunning wildflower displays, Grampians National Park (Gariweed) is a vast patch of wilderness in the western heart of Victoria. There are more than 50 marked trails in the park, but if you only have time for a short one, choose the half-hour descent to Mackenzie Falls. 265 steps later you'll emerge at a beautiful waterhole at the foot of the falls. Despite the huffing and puffing the walk is sensational.

76 Waterfall Gully, SA

Cleland Conservation Park in the Adelaide Hills, just 12km from Adelaide city centre, conserves a vital area of natural bushland on the Adelaide Hills face and includes the Cleland Wildlife Park, the viewing platform of Mt Lofty Summit and scenic Waterfall Gully, one of the more popular waterfalls in the Adelaide foothills. Water flows year round but the cascade is at its most spectacular in the wetter winter months. Walk the many trails in the area. There is also a chalet kiosk and café as well as a picnic area with free gas barbecues.

77 Russell Falls, Tas

Mount Field National Park, in central Tasmania, is the state's oldest national park–the 120ha around Russell Falls were first proclaimed a reserve in 1885. The park features a variety of scenery including rainforest and alpine moorlands, but the most popular attraction of the park is the famous Russell Falls, a three-tier waterfall dropping 45m into rainforest. This area has many stunning walks through enormous fern forests and some of the tallest trees in the world. One of these walks, the Tall Trees Walk, is a 900m wheelchair accessible boardwalk with signs detailing the history of these 45m giant swamp gums. Other waterfalls in the area are Horseshoe Falls and Lady Barron Falls.

78 Mitchell Falls, WA

These falls are about as remote as you can get, deep in the heart of the Kimberley at the end of a rough 240km track that spears off the Gibb River Road, through thick red bulldust with several creek crossing and corrugations. But the trip through the changing landscape of Livistonia Palms up to the Mitchell Plateau is well worth doing. The track ends at Mertens Creek, from here a walk of about one hour (round trip) takes you to Little Merten Falls, great for swimming. It's another couple of hours walk to the triple-cascades of Mitchell Falls, over rough country. The track is marked with stone cairns and is reasonably well-worn, but if in doubt walk in close vicinity to the creek. Take care near the many cliffs.

79 Jim Jim Falls, NT

One of the iconic images of the Top End, Jim Jim and Twin Falls in southern Kakadu are two of the most widely photographed falls in the country. The falls run in the wet season only, so unfortunately most people who visit the national park in the dry season are disappointed, despite having negotiated the rough track to get there. Even in the dry access to the Jim Jim Falls area is by 4WD only and your vehicle will require a snorkel to cross the Jim Jim Creek. In the wet when the falls are at their most spectacular it is impossible to drive any vehicle into the area. Those photographs of the falls at their most dramatic were all taken by people who entered the area by light plane or helicopter.

80 Litchfield National Park, NT

The Top End is spoilt for choice as far as waterfalls go, but unfortunately, the large crocodile population means swimming is often out of the question. Not so in Litchfield National Park a couple of hours south of Darwin, which has numerous falls and waterholes safe for swimming. Wangi Falls is the most popular: here, two waterfalls cascade into a very large plunge pool set amidst rainforest. It is the most accessible of the swimming holes, and includes wheelchair access into the water, although the swimming is sometimes closed during and after heavy rain due to powerful currents in the plunge pool. Other good spots for swimming include Buley Rockholes and Florence Falls, and the 4WD-only Sandy Creek Falls and Surprise Creek Falls.

Jim Jim Falls, Kakadu. *(Tourism NT)*

Wall of China, Mungo National Park, NSW. *(New Holland Image Library)*

natural wonders

81 Uluru and Kata Tjuta, NT

It doesn't matter how many photos you've seen of Uluṟu (Ayers Rock) and Kata Tjuṯa (The Olgas) nothing can prepare you for the stark beauty of the desert and the overwhelming sense of spirit of place that the rock radiates. Hyperbole aside, it really is that special: nobody is ever disappointed with their first glimpse of Uluṟu. Join the throng of awestruck tourists who gather like religious pilgrims to watch the rock turn red, then purple, then blue and finally black in the setting sun on any given evening, and it's highly unlikely you'll hear a disappointed complaint among them. There are a number of walks and tours available. Kata Tjuṯa, 53km from the resort, with its huge, weathered domes, is just as impressive as Uluṟu. The 8km 'Valley of the Winds' walk winds along a rocky trail past sheer rock faces and unusual rock formations to a magnificent lookout. Ayes Rock Resort is 445km by sealed road from Alice Springs. Flying time is approximately 45 minutes. The resort is 18km from Uluṟu and shuttle buses are available.

www.travelnt.com

82 Kings Canyon, NT

From monolith to chasm, the contrast between Uluru and Kings Canyon (Watarrka National Park) is startling. Here, rising from the surrounding stark desert plains, the canyon is actually part of the rugged George Gill Range. Atop the plateau, 300m cliffs cut deep into the ground, the sheer-sided red sandstone walls of the canyon looking as if they've been sliced with a giant hot knife. There are a number of walking trails, with the most popular the 6km Rim Walk that takes you to the top of the plateau and around the edge of the canyon, although there are other walks including the shorter, shady Kings Creek walk along the valley floor and the Giles Track, a 22km walk between Kings Canyon and Kathleen Springs. There are also scenic helicopter flights available from the Kings Canyon Resort.

www.travelnt.com

83 Walls of China, NSW

15,000 years ago the vast, sparse mulga-studded plain that makes up most of Mungo National Park in far-south-western NSW near Wentworth, was a huge lake. Along the eastern shore of the ancient lakebed is a 22km crescent-shaped wall of sand and clay, eroded into fantastic formations. Called the Walls of China by Chinese station workers in the 19th century, the lunette has preserved countless Aboriginal campfires, cooking hearths and burials. It was here that the oldest recorded cremation in the world was found–an Aboriginal woman more than 40,000 years old. Skeletons of ancient megafauna and Tasmanian tigers have also been found. There is a short walk from the car park to a viewing platform at the Great Walls, or you can take a 60km sign-posted drive tour around the park through Mallee country and the north-eastern shore of the lake.

www.nationalparks.nsw.gov.au

84 Bald Rock, NSW

The biggest granite monolith in Australia is the water-streaked dome of Bald Rock at 750m long, 500m wide and 200m high. Almost straddling the NSW/Qld border (the view from the top is mainly Qld), Bald Rock is part of Bald Rock National Park, near Tenterfield. A number of walks make the most of the park's granite landscape, including the track to the summit, which includes canyons, stone arches and panoramic views. The summit walk takes approximately three hours to complete.

www.nationalparks.nsw.gov.au

85 Remarkable Rocks, SA

On the far-western reaches of Kangaroo Island, in Flinders Chase National Park, Remarkable Rocks are a cluster of huge, weather-sculptured granite boulders perched precariously on a granite dome that swoops 75m to the sea. Wander freely among the fantastically shaped rocks and natural archways, but be wary if conditions are slippery–the sea below the rocks is treacherous and rescues are rarely successful.

www.southaustralia.com

86 Lake Eyre, SA

The bright, white salt vastness of Lake Eyre is one of the largest internal drainage systems in the world and overlies the Great Artesian Basin. Normally dry, Lake Eyre is an extensive 'salt sink' deriving its mineralisation from countless years of floodwater evaporation. Lake Eyre has had water in it a number of times in the last century but has filled to capacity only three times in the past 150 years, but when it does the dry salt pans are transformed into wetlands supporting large flocks of pelicans, gulls and terns. The park is largely inaccessible and travellers must be well prepared. Tracks are suitable for 4WD vehicles only–although the lakebed looks firm and safe to drive on, it is only a thin crust and many vehicles have come to grief sinking in the dark sticky ooze that lies just beneath the surface. Don't even think of visiting between November and March as the weather is to extreme and make sure you carry spare fuel, water and food. Scenic flights are available.

www.environment.sa.gov.au/parks/lakeeyre

87 Wave Rock, WA

Wave Rock, as the name suggests, looks like giant 15m-high, 100m-long wave, frozen solid just as it is about to break. Located near the small town of Hyden, about 350km east of Perth, it is officially a granite inselberg, created by the erosion action of water and wind over eons of time. Inselbergs are usually composed of rock that is more erosion resistant than the surrounding rock. There are other rock formations within the Wave Rock Reserve including Breakers, Hippo's Yawn, and the Humps. There are also some fantastic Aboriginal rock paintings within the nearby Mulka's Cave.

www.westernaustralia.com

Wave Rock. *(WATC)*

88 Purnululu, WA

The 45,000 hectare Bungle Bungle Range, with its huge expanse of striking, banded beehive structures, sandstone cliffs and towers is one of Australia's most recent discoveries, found by Europeans less than 30 years ago. Twenty million years of weathering has produced the eroded sandstone towers, the dark bands formed by cyanobacteria, (single cell photosynthetic organisms), winding horizontally around the domes, contrasting with the lighter sandstone. Ground access to the domes is still difficult: although it is only 55km from the main road into the park, it is negotiable by 4WDs only and takes a couple of hours. The most visited site is the serene Cathedral Gorge, a fairly easy walk, although the best way to see the domes is on a scenic flight from Kununurra.

www.calm.wa.gov.au

89 The Twelve Apostles, Vic

One of the most photographed sections of Australian coastline, Port Campbell National Park on the Great Ocean Road in Southern Victoria is home to the Twelve Apostles, stacks of rock formed up to 20 million years ago. The wild and powerful Southern Ocean that sculpts the area's limestone landscape also hides a remarkable seascape beneath the waves–a submarine labyrinth of towering canyons, caves, arches and walls. Breeding colonies of seabirds regularly inhabit the rock stacks and islands. The cliffs rise to nearly 70m in some places and the highest Apostle is around 50m from base to tip. The coast is continuously changing and there are frequent small rock falls. There are also less frequent major events, such as the collapse of a large stack in July 2005, and the loss of London Bridge, which dramatically lost one of its arches in 1990, stranding two startled sightseers on the newly formed tower. Along this stretch of coastline you'll also find the Bay of Martyrs, the Bay of Islands, Loch Ard Gorge, site of a tragic shipwreck in 1878 that left just two survivors

90 The Great Barrier Reef, Qld

No list of Australia's greatest natural wonders is complete without mentioning the Great Barrier Reef. It is the largest natural feature on earth stretching more than 2300km along the north-east coast of Australia, from the northern tip of Queensland down to just north of Bundaberg, including the fabulous Whitsunday Islands. Said to be the only living structure visible from outer space, the World Heritage-listed Great Barrier Reef is often referred to as the eighth wonder of the world and is home to one fifth of all the coral reef on earth. It is actually made up of more than 2800 coral reefs and is home to tens of thousands of species of brilliantly coloured fish, coral and other marine life including whales, dolphins and turtles.

www.gbrmpa.gov.au www.barrierreefaustralia.com

Gordon River, Tasmania. *(Geoff Murray)*

rivers & gorges

91 Nymboida River, NSW

Sixty kilometres as the sea eagle flies from Coffs Harbour is the beautiful Nymboida River, one of Australia's best white-water rivers. Between banks clothed in rainforest and untouched bushland there are world-class grade-three and grade-four rapids, and some grade fives (rapids are graded from an easy grade one up to grade six, the most difficult and treacherous). The 50km length of river lures white-water enthusiasts from around the world and there are plenty of rafting companies that are keen to take you on the ride of your life.

www.coffscoast.com.au

92 Hawkesbury River, NSW

Join the last riverboat postman in Australia on a three-and-a half-hour cruise up the Hawkesbury River on the northern outskirts of Sydney as he (or she) delivers the mail and essentials like bread and milk to isolated residents. Posties always have the best gossip and anything the postie does not know about the area is not worth knowing–which makes the commentary about the area and its history even more fascinating. Cruises include lunch.

☎ (02) 9985 7566

93 Mutawintji National Park, NSW

In contrast to the surrounding plains and lakes, Mutawintji, in western NSW, near Broken Hill, is spectacular gorge country. The Mutawintji Local Land Council tour guides will show you Aboriginal rock art that dates back more than 8000 years, explain the significance of the area and the many uses of the flora and fauna of the park. Take a self-guided tour of the Homestead Creek Gorge to Wright's Cave to see more engravings and stencils, or the longer walk to Old Mootwingee Gorge, a delightful swimming hole surrounded by towering red cliffs.

www.nationalparks.nsw.gov.au

94 Murray River, Vic

The Murray is Australia's longest river, stretching 2520km from the Snowy Mountains of NSW to the ocean near Goolwa in SA, and forms the border between NSW and Victoria. The river is navigable for 1986km from Goolwa to Yarrawonga Weir with 13 weirs incorporating locks. Vegetation along the river ranges from extensive displays of wildflowers in summer in the high country and Upper Murray, to irrigated pastures, riverine forests and woodlands. River Red Gum and Black Box woodland dominate the banks. There are a wide variety of river cruises, paddleboats, steamers and houseboats available for hire and tours.

www.murrayriver.com.au

Olives. *(LA)*

nsw/act

Hunter Valley

The Hunter Valley, two hours north-west of Sydney, is one of Australia's premier gourmet regions and a favourite weekend getaway for Sydneysiders. Centred around the Pokolbin, Broke and Lovedale areas in the Lower Hunter Valley, and the Muswellbrook area in the Upper Hunter, there are more than 120 wineries and cellar doors open to the public. Many have restaurants and galleries as well as tastings room and picnic areas. Home to more than just winemakers, you can also try some of the local gourmet fare at Hunter Valley Chocolates and the Hunter Valley Cheese Factory or follow the olive trail and try some of the extra virgin olive oils produced by nine local growers and producers.

www.winecountry.com.au

Mudgee

For serious foodies, Mudgee, around four hour's drive west of Sydney, has all the attractions of the Hunter Valley but none of the crowds. There are around 30 wineries in and around the town, most open to the public for tastings and cellar door sales. Many are small, boutique operations, so you'll find labels you haven't seen before in retail bottle shops. The region is best known for its reds and ports. Pick up a copy of the free Mudgee and Gulgong visitor's guide, from the information centre in Mudgee, for directions and details of opening times.

A centre for small farming, (Mudgee hosts the annual Small Farm Field Days on the third weekend in July) and a bit of a mecca for Sydneysiders seeking an inland sea change, many farmers are specialising in gourmet and boutique food products. There are three different gourmet food and wine trails you can follow (maps available at the visitor's centre) where you can try olives, local venison, fish, honey and of course, lots of wine.

www.mudgee-gulgong.org

Orange/Cowra

The Central West area of NSW is the new hot spot for cool climate wines. The regional town of Orange has matured into a cosmopolitan urban centre. The surrounding area is the state's largest supplier of apples and pears, a major producer of stone fruit and vegetables, beef and lamb, as well as more than 50 wine-growers. There are some 23 cellar doors for your tasting pleasure. Already known for great chardonnay, cabernet sauvignon and shiraz, Orange is now seeing pinot noir and merlot rising through the ranks. Time your visit for the annual FOOD (Food of Orange District) Week in early April, or early spring when the surrounding hills are covered in cherry and apple blossom. Just over an hour away, Cowra and Canowindra are also opening new cellar doors, with chardonnay the best seller.

www.visitnsw.com.au

Hastings River

Think Port Macquarie and most people think sun, sand and sea. Long a favourite summer holiday destination, the area around Port Macquarie and the Hastings River is fast becoming a new wine region. The main wine style is the red table wine, chambourcin, and there are five wineries in the area. Cassegrain was the first to open their cellar door and is still the largest wine maker in the district. Nearby Bago Vineyard has a Jazz in the Vineyard concert on the second Sunday of the month. Head out to Ellenborough River Olives west of Wauchope to taste some local oils or hit the monthly Hastings Farmers Markets (also at Wauchope) on the third Saturday of each month for the best of local produce.

www.portmacquarieinfo.com.au

Riverina

The sun-parched plains around Griffith and Leeton in the far south-west of the state are, thanks to the Murrumbidgee Irrigation Scheme, one of the largest wine producing areas in NSW. First established by the McWilliam family in 1912, and then by waves of European migrants after WWII, the Riverina produces some good white wines, particularly semillon, and fortified wines. When you're not sampling the wine, try one of the many fine Italian restaurants, tour the historic towns, explore the national parks or visit one of the several pioneer museums.

www.griffith.nsw.gov.au/GriffithVisitorsCentre

Around Canberra

The Poachers Trail is a great way to explore Canberra's surrounding regions of Hall, Murrumbateman, Gundaroo and Yass. Along the way, you'll enjoy cool climate wines, tempting food and lovely rural scenery.

The cool climate wines of the Canberra district are coming of age with more than 140 vineyards and 30 cellar doors open to the public, and eateries such as the Poachers Pantry are redefining the Capital's culinary landscape. Try some gourmet smoked meats and taste their wines at the Pantry's Smokehouse Café or head to the Royal Hotel in Gundaroo for a menu uniquely focused on the Canberra district, showcasing the best local fresh farm produce and probably the world's largest Canberra district wine list.

www.canberratourism.com.au www.poacherstrail.com.au

Yarra Valley's Yering Station barrel cellar. *(Tourism Victoria)*

victoria

King Valley/Milawa

Milawa, around two and a half hours north of Melbourne, and just a short side trip from the beginning of the Great Alpine Road touring route, is foodie heaven. Brown Bros Winery has long been a Milawa gourmet institution, but add the winery's Epicurean Centre, Milawa Mustards, the Milawa Cheese Factory with its new bakery and Factory restaurant, the Olive Shop, Blue Ox Blueberry Farm, Whitehead's Mead and Honey farmgate and Merlot Restaurant at the new five-star country house hotel Lindenwarrah, and you've got all the makings for a gourmet country capital.

Head to nearby Whitfield and the King Valley for more food and wine. The produce of this valley is strongly influenced by the Italian and Mediterranean families who settled here after World War II, originally farming tobacco but these days producing fine Italian-style wines. Varieties such as sangiovese, nebbiolo, verduzzo, pinot grigio and berbera all grow well here in these cool climate vineyards.

www.milawagourmet.com

King Valley, Victoria. *(Tourism Victoria)*

Yarra Valley

The Yarra Valley, around an hour's drive from Melbourne, is one of the best cool climate wine districts of the world with the most widely produced wines being chardonnay, sauvignon blanc and pinot noir. There are more than 50 wineries open for tastings and cellar door sales, ranging from stunning multi-million dollar tourism ventures to the warm welcome of boutique family winemakers. Combine all that with the lovely scenery, great food, and lots to see and do and it is easy to see why it is a favourite weekend gourmet destination for Melbournians.

Follow the Yarra Valley Regional Food Trail, which criss-crosses the entire region, taking in the Yarra Valley, Warburton Ranges, The Dandenongs and Marysville. It's easy to follow and each stop displays the distinctive blue and orange Yarra Valley Food Trail sign. Along it, you'll find dozens of producers whose food features on local and city restaurants–free range eggs, honey, fruit, berries, herbs and cheese, game, pasta, preserves, trout, clotted cream, chocolates and ice cream. Before you set out, check the opening days of the local markets, where stalls are piled high with local foods, much of it organic.

www.yarrarangestourism.com

Mornington Peninsula

The Mornington Peninsula is one long beach–a 100km boot-shaped peninsula jutting into the ocean on the eastern edge of Port Phillip Bay, 80km south of Melbourne. On a sunny day crowds head for the sun, sand and sea, finishing off the afternoon in a sunny beer garden in one of the beach-side pubs or restaurants. Drop in for a wine tasting at one of the Peninsula's 40 wineries producing sleek chardonnays, full-flavoured cabernet sauvignons, pinot noir and increasingly, pinot gris; or visit Sunny Ridge Strawberry Farm, the largest strawberry producer in Australia. Pick your own (November to April), take a farm tour, sample the fruit wines or an afternoon tea in the café.

Take the car and passenger ferry across Port Phillip Bay from Sorrento to Queenscliff on the Bellarine Peninsula for some great fish and chips and more wineries around Geelong, gateway to the Great Ocean Road.

www.visitvictoria.com.au

Macedon Ranges and Daylesford

Mount Macedon, just an hour from Melbourne, is the place to escape the summer heat–or snuggle up in front of a roaring winter-time fireplace. There are more than 20 wineries in the area, with shiraz and sparkling wines among the best varieties. The region is full of award-winning restaurants, such as Lake House in Daylesford, cafes and a vast range of specialist growers and local producers, offering everything from fresh vegetables and smallgoods to chocolates and olive oil.

www.macedonandspa.com

Pyrenees, Grampians and goldfields

The Great Grape Road touring route is a sign-posted scenic circuit through the Pyrenees, Grampians and Ballarat wine regions of western Victoria. Producing some of Australia's finest cool-climate wines–most notably shiraz–the mountainous country around the Grampians area has some of the oldest shiraz vines in the world, planted in 1863. There are 12 wineries open to the public in the nearby Pyrenees region around Redbank and Avoca, originally selected by the French Remy Martin group in the 1960s for the production of brandy, eventually eclipsed by the production of sparkling wines. To the south, the nine goldfields wineries around Ballarat turn out some very good chardonnay and pinot noir.

www.visitvictoria.com.au

Mildura and north-west Victoria

Home to one of Australia's most celebrated chefs, Stefano de Pieri, Mildura on the banks of the Murray River is a centre for fine produce. The Mediterranean climate and sophisticated irrigation systems nurture vast orchards, citrus and olive groves, vineyards and grain fields producing a huge range of fruits, nuts and vegetables. It is the centre of Australia's citrus and dried fruit industries; the river provides fresh-water fish including yellow belly perch, red fin, yabbies and the famed Murray cod; and more recently, salt is being commercially harvested. The huge wineries in this area produce much of the bulk table wines sold in casks (Australia's unique wine-in-a-box) in bottle shops around the country, with chardonnay the principal white grape variety, while rich and ripe reds come from cabernet sauvignon and shiraz vines.

www.visitvictoria.com.au

Rutherglen and Beechworth

This historic wine growing area of Rutherglen is famous for its unique rich, fortified tokays and muscats and the unique Australian sparkling red wine. It was established in the 1850s by German winemakers from the Barossa Valley and many of those first vineyards are still in operation today. Nearby Beechworth has also been producing wines since 1856 when the first vines were planted. Today the region's small vineyards produce chardonnay, pinot noir and other cool climate varieties. Beechworth is one of the Victoria's best preserved gold-rush towns and the locals produce world-class cheeses, preserves, breads and berries. Try the local strawberry wine at Schmidt's Strawberry Winery, pick your own berries at High Grove Chestnuts and take home some freshly baked bread from the award winning Beechworth bakery.

www.visitvictoria.com.au

Gippsland wines. *(Tourism Victoria)*

Gippsland

One of the largest wine regions in Victoria in terms of area, The Gippsland wine region begins in the Great Dividing Range and includes the Strzelecki Ranges, huge tracts of lush dairy pastures and kilometres of unspoilt coastline. Around 100 vineyards and about 30 small, family-owned wineries call this area of south-eastern Victoria home, with pinot noir and chardonnay the principal varieties grown. The lush Gippsland pastures also produce some of the countries best cheese and dairy products. Follow the Gourmet deli trail, where you can pick your own berries, try some of the famous local cheeses and enjoy delicious venison and, trout and seafood. Pick up a trail map from local visitor information centres.

www.gippslandgourmetcountry.com

south australia

Barossa Valley

Despite is larger-than-life reputation in the wine world the Barossa Valley is a snug collection of country towns surrounded by vineyards that is very easy to explore on a day trip from Adelaide. The Barossa has been famous for its rich, big-bodied shiraz for many years–as a repository of the world's oldest Shiraz vineyards, the Barossa's shiraz is unique. Other wines to taste are the crisp rieslings, chardonnays and semillons, grenache and cabernets, as well as the region's foundation wines–the tawny and vintage fortifieds, and sweet dessert wines. The Lutheran pioneers who settled in the region 160 years ago have left not only a legacy of beautiful churches but a bounty of wonderful small meats, sausages, preserved fruits, cheese and delicious breads, all unique to the valley. Most restaurants and cafes pride themselves on serving as much local produce as possible–look for the cork on a fork Food Barossa logo and check out the weekly Farmers Markets in Angaston each Saturday morning.

Clare Valley

The Clare Valley, 90 minutes from Adelaide, has more than 40 wineries, all within 15 minutes drive from each other. The Clare is another of Australia's oldest wine regions. The first settlers to the area were from England, Ireland and Poland, producing a rich architectural heritage, most of which remains, although the original village houses now tend to house restaurants and galleries. The first vines were planted in 1842 by James Green, servant to the district's pioneer John Horrocks. Since then, the industry has grown and the Clare is now one of the best producing wine regions in the country. All sorts of grapes are grown here, but the valley is most well known for its riesling: follow the Riesling Trail–a 27km sealed walking and cycling path that links the villages of the valley.

www.clarevalley.com.au

Fleurieu Peninsula

Just 40 minutes drive south of Adelaide, the stunning rural and coastal scenery and even better food and wine make the Fleurieu Peninsula a much-loved gourmet getaway among local South Australians. All over the peninsula you'll find seriously good wine country (there's more than 50 cellar doors in McLaren Vale alone) and roadside stalls sell local produce in season. McLaren Vale is the most famous wine region, but there's also Southern Fleurieu, Currency Creek and Langhorne Creek. The rich pastures also produce great cheese: visit McLaren Vale's Blessed Cheese and buy a specially packaged hamper of cheeses to take with you on the wine and cheese trail–a progressive picnic matching some of South Australia's finest artisan made cheeses with wines from some of the region's best wineries.

www.fleurieupeninsula.com.au

Kangaroo Island

More well known for its rugged national parks and wildlife–the island is home to 4000 penguins, 6000 fur seals, 600 rare Australian sea lions, 5000 koalas, 15,000 kangaroos, 254 species of birdlife and some-

Barossa Valley, SA. (SATC)

where in between 500,000 and one million tammar wallabies. Kangaroo Island is also home to some great gourmet producers. Clifford's Honey Farm offers free tastings and sales of honey made from pure Ligurian bees–the only pure strain in the world; you can watch sheep being milked at the Island Pure Sheep Dairy and taste their delicious cheeses; visit Gum Creek Marron Farm and learn about yabby and marron (freshwater crayfish) farming, view the aquariums and buy some for a picnic in the bush-like grounds; or drop into Sunset Winery, the only one of the island's wineries that is open for cellar door tastings.

www.tourkangarooisland.com.au

Adelaide Hills

A quick half-hour drive out of Adelaide will take you to Hahndorf in the Adelaide Hills. Settled in 1839 by Prussian and East German immigrants, Hahndorf is Australia's oldest surviving German settlement. It is the ideal place to buy traditionally made wursts and German smallgoods, stop for an afternoon tea break at The German Cake Shop or head out to Beerenberg Farm to pick your own strawberries (October to May) and buy some of their delicious jams, home-style pickles, chutneys and sauces. The surrounding hills are home to wineries and orchards, many of which are open for tastings and sales or sport farm-gate stalls piled with seasonal fruits. At Melba's Chocolate Factory in Woodside you can watch chocolate being made on historic machinery and then taste and buy the finished goods, and next door is the Woodside Cheesewrights, who make a range of high-quality hand-crafted cheeses.

www.visitadelaidehills.com.au

Houghtons Winery, WA. (LA)

western australia

Swan Valley

Just a cork's pop from Perth, less than 30-minutes drive, The Swan Valley, Western Australia's oldest wine growing region, and the neighbouring Perth Hills district, are both often overlooked in favour of their big brother in the wine stakes, the Margaret River. But the 40 or so wineries in this pretty valley cut through by the lazy Swan River and on the slopes of the Darling Scarp produce some very good sparkling, chardonnay, shiraz, chenin blanc, verdelho and fortified wines. Wineries tend to be smaller and more personal than those of the south west, and you'll usually be talking to the winegrower themselves when tasting the wines. To explore the valley follow the 32km loop Swan Valley Drive from Guildford, take a Swan River Cruise form Perth to Sandalford Estate or follow the Bickely Valley Wine Trail, a pretty signposted trail that winds through the Perth Hills visiting 11 wineries.

www.swanvalley.info

Margaret River

The Margaret River region, a wild knob of land jutting into the sea off the bottom corner of WA, is home to some of Australia's finest sauvignon blanc and chardonnay (and plenty of terrific cab savs and shiraz). Caves Road, a 110km scenic drive that stretches from Cape Leeuwin to Cape Naturaliste, is the best way to explore the area. Highlights include the Boranup Karri Forest, beautiful beaches and world famous wildflower displays in spring. With more than 70 wineries in the district, The Margaret River has a wine to suit every taste and many wineries feature innovative architecture, extensive formal gardens, art galleries and excellent restaurants as well as an extensive range of merchandise in the tasting room boutiques. Further south, the area surrounding Mt Barker, Frankland and the Porongurup National Park is rapidly becoming another premier wine region and there are also a number of olive groves in the area.

www.margaretriver.com or www.australiassouthwest.com

Cool climate wines. *(TQ)*

queensland

The Granite Belt

Queensland's Granite Belt, just north of the NSW border in the foothills of the Great Dividing Range around three hours' drive from Brisbane, is the Sunshine State's premier wine growing district. Stanthorpe is the main commercial centre, and the roads south and north lead to picturesque villages and forgotten hamlets and more than 30 wineries, most with cellar door sales. Along with luscious stone fruit, the Granite Belt produces a wide range of cool climate wines, with the stand-out styles being shiraz, cabernet sauvignon and semillon. The annual Apple and Grape Harvest Festival in March celebrates the region's wine and produce with events such as the famous Grape Crushing competition, a wine fiesta and street carnivals and parades.

www.stanthorpe.com

Salamanca Market, Hobart. *(LA)*

tasmania

Almost anywhere you go in Tasmania is a gourmet experience and you'll find plenty of organic and boutique food producers making and selling anything from farmhouse cheeses, herb vinegars and mustards to bush honeys and organic fruit and vegetables. A must is a visit to Salamanca Market, held every Saturday in Hobart, for a great introduction to some of the local fresh produce. Take a tour of the oldest operational brewery in Australia at Hobart's Cascade Brewery, relive your Willy Wonka fantasies on a tour of Cadburys Chocolate Factory or indulge in some succulent shellfish at Barilla Bay Oysters just near Hobart Airport.

The east coast is the place to go for fresh seafood and south of Hobart, the Derwent, Coal River and Huon valleys are producing some terrific cool climate wines. Take a river cruise down to Peppermint Bay for a long lunch, taste sheep's cheese at Grandvewe Farm Cheesery and visit some of the Huon's famous apple orchards.

In the north, the Tamar Valley Wine Route is a triangular loop drive from Launceston along the banks of the wide Tamar River and across to George Town and back via Pipers River. There are 21 wineries along the way, producing some of the state's best cool climate wines, with pinot noir, sauvignon blanc and chardonnay the main varietals you'll find, although aromatic gewurztraminers, reislings and pinot gris are making an appearance on more cellar door release lists and many wineries feature top-class restaurants with long views and food just as fine.

The rich pastures of King Island produce famous beef and cheeses. A legacy, according to local legend, from straw mattresses containing dried grass seeds that floated ashore from early ship-wrecks–it is believed that the grass seeds then took hold in the island's rich soils and resulted in a unique style of grass on which the cows of King Island graze.

www.discovertasmania.com.au

australian wildlife

Many species of unique fauna are found in Australia and nowhere else in the world as a result of millions of years of geographic isolation.

Fraser Island dingo. *(TQ)*

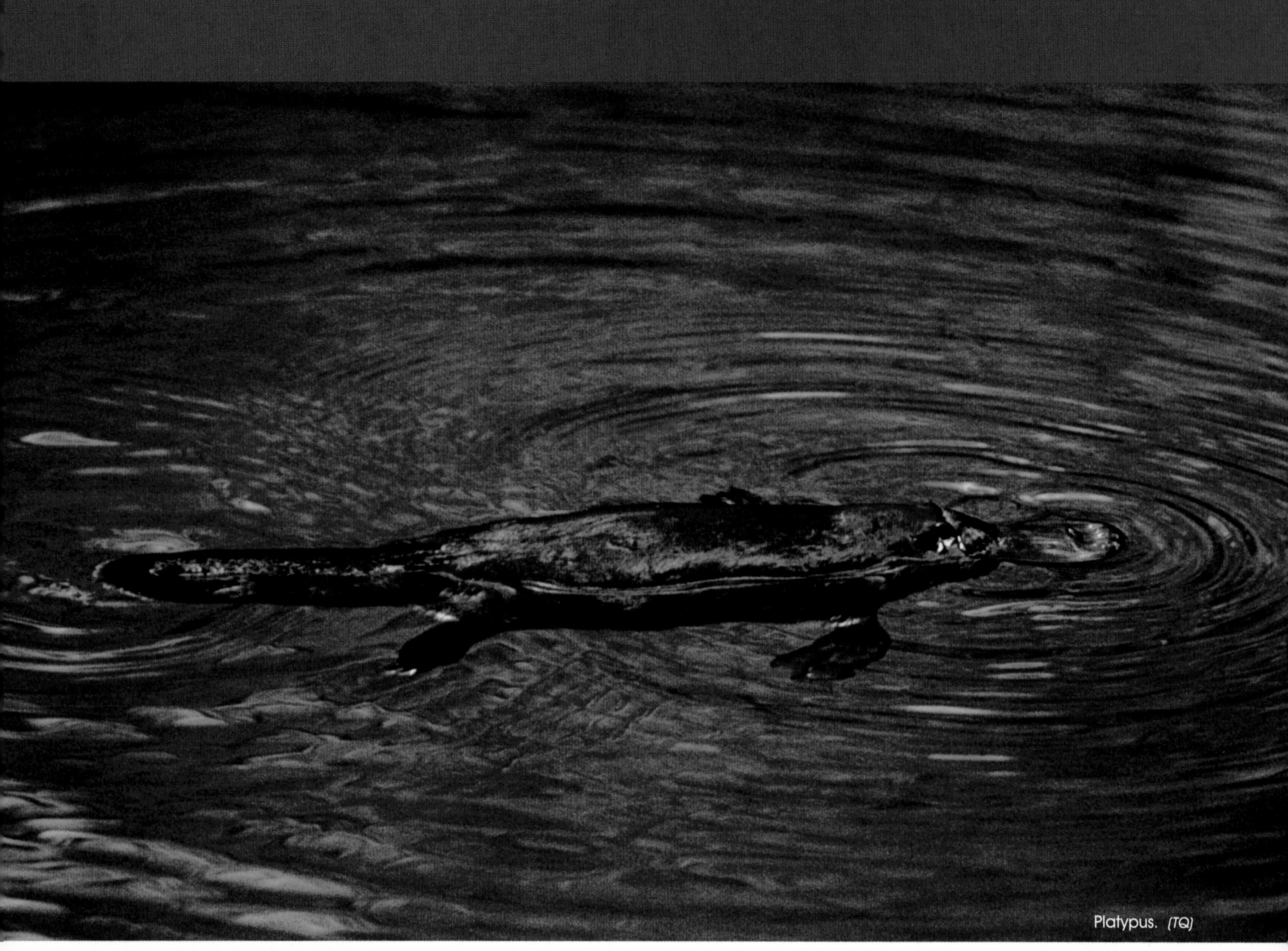
Platypus. *(TQ)*

monotremes

The platypus and the echidna (spiny anteater) are the world's only monotremes, an extremely rare group of egg-laying mammals. The platypus is unique to Australia while the echidna is also found in Papua New Guinea. The word monotreme means these animals have only a single opening for reproduction and for eliminating body waste. Some of their bones are like a reptile's and they lay reptile-like eggs.

Echidna

There are two species, one specific to the New Guinea highlands while the other, smaller species is found both there and throughout Australia. All have sharp spines covering the back of their short, stocky bodies. Their colour can vary from light brown in hot northern locations becoming darker and thicker in the cooler south, even black in Tasmania. Echidna eat ants, tasty grubs and insects found while rummaging through bush litter, among tree roots and in hollow logs and holes. They are also called 'spiny anteater'.

Where to see them: Adelaide Hills or Kangaroo Island in South Australia

Platypus

The Platypus is a unique and remarkable creature, with a sleek furry body, like that of an otter, but with webbed feet and a wide bill worthy of Daffy Duck (hence the common name 'duck-billed platypus). Platypus are about the size of a domestic cat and live in long burrows dug into riverbanks throughout the permanent river systems and lakes of eastern Australia. They forage on riverbeds for shrimp, tadpoles, worms and larvae. The mature male can eject venom from a spur on the heel of each hind leg. The poison is potent enough to kill a dog.

Where to see them: David Fleay Wildlife Park, off the Pacific Hwy at West Burleigh Rd, Burleigh Heads, Gold Coast, Queensland

☎ (07) 5576 2411

Warrawong Earth Sanctuary, 25 minutes drive from Adelaide

www.warrawong.com ☎ (08) 8370 9197

marsupials

Marsupials are mammals with external pouches in which their young develop. They are Australia's dominant native mammals, the best known of which are kangaroos, koalas and possums.

Most of the 140 species of marsupial living in Australia are found nowhere else. They are grouped into 13 distinct families, which include marsupial moles and bandicoots, gliders and wombats, kangaroos and the koala. The red kangaroo, a herbivore, is Australia's largest marsupial. The largest meat-eating marsupial is the Tasmanian Devil. The smallest is the Pilbara Ningaui, which weighs only a few grams yet preys on centipedes and cockroaches sometimes bigger than itself.

Bettong

This small mammal with a long tail eats underground fungi along with seeds, roots, bulbs and insects. The brushtailed bettong, inhabiting grasslands in south-west Australia and east into New South Wales, is greyish-brown with an almost bald muzzle and tail. The northern bettong, found in Queensland, is grey with large hind legs. Bettong in Tasmania are brown-grey with white underparts. The burrowing bettong lives year round in a burrow and is resident only on the Barrow, Dorre and Bernier islands off WA's northwest coast.

Bilby

Australia's answer to the Easter Bunny is also known as the rabbit-eared bandicoot because of its proportionately huge ears. A protected creature, it has a long pointed snout, a small body and a black and white tail. Like all bandicoots, the bilby is nocturnal. An omnivore and a solitary animal, it lives in long burrows in desert, dry forest and grassland areas. Australia has 19 species of bandicoot. They have backward-facing pouches to prevent dirt getting in when digging.

Where to see them: Kanyana Wildlife Rehabilitation Centre, 70 Kalamatta Way, Gooseberry Hill, Perth, Western Australia

www.kanyanawildlife.org.au ☎ (08) 9293 1416

Dingo

Australia's wild dog is found in all states except Tasmania. Dingos are a medium-sized dog with a bushy tail and a reddish-yellow coat, although the desert dingo is a pale sandy colour. They do not bark but will howl. Primarily a meat eater, the dingo will eat reptiles and any other food it can find if necessary. It can hunt in groups and eat larger animals such as kangaroos. Some states classify dingo as vermin. Hunting, baiting and crossbreeding with feral dogs is reducing the number of pure dingo, which now face extinction in the wild.

Where to see them: spend the night in a B&B and hear dingos howl at dusk at the Dingo Discovery Centre at Toolern Vale, about 40 minutes drive from Melbourne.

http://clix.to/dingodiscoverycentre ☎ (03) 5428 1245

Dugong

Also known as the sea cow, this marine mammal grazes on sea grasses. It can grow to about 3m and weigh up to 400kg. The dugong must surface to breathe and does not remain underwater for long periods. Most of the world's dugongs live in northern Australian waters between Moreton Bay in Queensland and Shark Bay in Western Australia. Sadly, dugong numbers in the Great Barrier Reef area have declined dramatically over the last 40 years.

Koala. *(SATC)*

Dunnart

A mouse-like nocturnal marsupial with wide face, big eyes, pointed nose and fat tail. The dunnart lives in a burrow or nests in secure places, such as hollow logs, in dry areas. It eats spiders and small insects. In times of scarcity it draws on fat reserves stored in its tail.

Fruit bat (Flying fox)

Australia has over 60 kinds of bat. Eight types, fruit-bats or flying-foxes, feed only on fruit and flowers. It's one of the world's largest bats, weighing as much as a kilogram with a wing span of a metre or more.

Where to see them: Sydney's Botanical Gardens near the Sydney Opera House where the bats can be seen hanging upside down from the trees during the day. Each evening they fly off to forage for food.

Kangaroos and wallabies

Macropods are marsupials that are 'large footed'. They vary in size but most have very large hind legs and a long, powerful tail, such as kangaroos, wallabies and their close relatives. Some are browsers and others are grazers. The difference between kangaroos and wallabies is simply one of size. The six biggest species are called kangaroos. The red kangaroo is dominant in drier regions. The eastern and western grey kangaroo usually inhabit woodlands. This trio are close relatives to 11 smaller wallabies and wallaroos. All look similar, with small front legs and large, powerful hind legs and strong tail.

The wallaroo is a stockily-built rock kangaroo, smaller than the red or grey kangaroo but larger than wallabies. The western sub-species of wallaroo is known as the euro. The pademelon is a rainforest kangaroo with thick soft fur and short thick tail. The quokka is a small wallaby with a proportionately shorter tail which lives mainly on Rottnest Island off the Western Australia coast.

Koala

This iconic Australian marsupial is cuddly-looking yet is probably the country's most boring creature to observe. Mostly nocturnal, the koala does little other than sit slumped in a tree fork, sleeping as much as 18-20 hours a day. It's extremely fussy about its food, eating only a few types of gum leaves. As a result, it's confined to eucalypt forests and low eucalypt woodlands in eastern Australia and some islands off the southern and eastern coasts.

Where to see them: Lone Pine Koala Sanctuary, Jesmond Road, Fig Tree Pocket, Queensland

www.koala.net ☎ (07) 3378 1366

Numbat

A small, endangered marsupial that feeds almost entirely on termites, it has reddish-brown fur crossed with white bands and a bushy tail about the same length as its body. The numbat is active during the day and Western Australia is the only state where it's found in the wild. Also known as banded anteater or walpurti.

Where to see them: Dryandra Woodland, 164km south east of Perth. (Accommodation available)

☎ (08) 9884 5231

www.calm.wa.gov.au/tourism/dryandra_woodland_splash.html

Perentie

Australia's largest monitor lizard, growing up to 2.5m in length with a strong lashing tail, sharp claws and teeth, is a fearsome predator of snakes, lizards, birds and small mammals. It lives in arid regions of Western Australia, the Northern Territory, South Australia and Queensland, escaping the heat by digging burrows or in shady areas amid rocky terrain. The perentie hibernates between May and August.

Where to see them: Uluru-Kata Tjuta National Park, Northern Territory

Possum

Australia has many species. The most common one is the brushtailed possum, often seen in trees in suburban gardens. It's a herbivore about the size of a cat with pointed snout and pink nose and usually black or grey. The ringtail possum occurs along the entire length of the eastern seaboard, in the south-west of Western Australia and in Tasmania and, unlike the brushtailed, is strictly arboreal. The rare Leadbeaters possum is found only in Victoria. There are only two known populations of the tiny mountain pygmy possum, one in NSW, the other in Victoria.

Potoroo

The long-footed potoroo is also known as the rat kangaroo. It feeds mainly on a variety of underground and partially underground fungi. There are just three known populations in Australia; in New South Wales, east Gippsland and the Great Dividing Range. Equally rare is Gilbert's potoroo, Australia's most endangered mammal, only known from a single, small population on Mt Gardner, near Albany in Western Australia. The long-nosed potoroo lives in Tasmania.

Quoll

A small marsupial with fur covered in white spots. It eats small animals, lizards, birds, insects and carrion as well as plants and fruit. There are four species; the spotted-tailed quoll, western quoll, eastern quoll and northern quoll. The eastern quoll is found only in Tasmania, the northern quoll in tropical north Queensland, the western quoll in southern Western Australia and the spotted tailed quoll along the east coast.

Sugar glider

The sugar glider is the best known of several similar possums, each of which have a flap of loose skin connected to front and back feet that extends to enable them to 'fly' between trees. As the name suggests, sugar gliders like sweet things. They eat insects but prefer flower nectar, acacia gum and eucalypt sap.

Echidna. *(SATC)*

Tasmanian devil. *(Tim Dubb)*

Tasmanian Devil

The world's largest surviving carnivorous marsupial is about the same size as a large cat and has extremely powerful jaws and teeth. It's black with a white band on chest and hindquarters and has hairless pink ears. Found all around Tasmania, it's nocturnal and spends the daytime secreted in a den, sometimes occupying old wombat burrows. Like the wombat, the female Tasmanian Devil has a backward-opening pouch. It's primarily a scavenger, so will eat anything available including small mammals, birds, reptiles and carrion. This creature can make a variety of sounds, including snarls and an unnerving screech.

Where to see them: Tasmanian Devil Park, 5990 Port Arthur Highway, Taranna

www.tasmaniandevilpark.com ☎ 1800 641 641

Wombat

The koala's nearest relative is a tough, stocky, strictly terrestrial and generally solitary animal. The wombat has a rotund body and weighs about 24–27kg when mature. There are two types; the Common Wombat and the Hairy-nosed Wombat, the latter separated into northern and southern Hairy-nosed. The only remaining northern Hairy-nosed live in Epping Forest in Queensland. The southern variety inhabit the coastal areas of South Australia and parts of Western Australia.

The Common Wombat lives mainly in Tasmania, eastern NSW and eastern Victoria. All are superb diggers and inhabit large burrows preferably dug in damp, well-forested areas. Females have a backward-opening pouch so dirt is kept out while digging. Wombats are nocturnal grazers, feeding mainly on grasses and roots. They can be brown, black or grey. All about wombats:

www.wombania.com/wombats/

Wombat.

reptiles

Salt water crocodile–see Dangerous Creatures

Frill necked lizard. *(Tourism NT)*

FRESH WATER CROCODILE

Found on the north coast of Australia ranging from Queensland's coast to Broome in Western Australia. It has a long and much narrower snout than the saltwater crocodile. Mature freshwater crocodiles grow to about 1.5 metres on average although some more than 3m have been recorded. The freshwater crocodile eats fish and small vertebrates, crustaceans and even turtles. It is not considered dangerous to humans.

FRILL NECKED LIZARD

This little reptile is another Australian icon. It grows to between 70–90 cm in length and has a 'frill' around its head. It spends most of its time up trees. When frightened the lizard opens its mouth and expands its frill, making it larger and more fearsome than it is. This is one of its defences against predators. It can also run very fast on its two hind legs. The lizard inhabits hot tropical parts of Australia and feeds on all sorts of small insects.

Where to see them: Kakadu National Park, Northern Territory

GOANNA

Also known as the lace monitor, this very large lizard can reach 2m in length and eats insects, reptiles, birds and small mammals. It can climb trees and can bite. They are generally dark-coloured on their back with yellowish-white scales underneath.

THORNY DEVIL

An amazing little creature only about 20cms in length with a skin that seems to be covered in thorns, hence its name. Despite its alarming appearance, the thorny devil is harmless and, like the chameleon, can change colour. Thorny lizards inhabit the arid lands and deserts of central and western Australia. When it rains, the water falling on its back is cleverly channelled to its mouth via its weird body contours. It eats a wide variety of ants, snapped up with its tongue like an anteater.

Where to see them: Uluru—Kata Tjuta National Park, Northern Territory

dangerous creatures

Saltwater crocodile. (WATC)

Saltwater Crocodile

A protected species in Australia, the world's largest reptile is found along the northern coastline and 100km or more inland. Averaging 4m long but known to reach 7m. Crocodiles have been successful predators since primeval times and are extremely dangerous. Never swim in rivers, pools, the ocean or any body of water unless you are absolutely certain there are none in the vicinity.

Great White Shark

The most infamous hunter of the seas is found on all Australian coasts. It's a solitary predator that can grow from 3.5m to about 7m long, weighing 1300kg or more. Females are larger than males. The Great White is also 'the great bite', its huge mouth filled with rows of ragged, triangular-shaped teeth. It can detect traces of blood in the water from a great distance.

Box Jellyfish

This extremely venomous creature inhabits the ocean off north-eastern Australia and along the Great Barrier Reef coast. Box jellyfish are usually found in estuaries and river mouths and not often above coral reefs or sea grasses. Extreme toxins are expressed from stinging cells located along its many dangling tentacles. If enough venom is transmitted then death can occur within minutes unless proper treatment is administered. The pain of being stung can send a victim into shock, which could result in drowning.

Irukandji

A tiny jellyfish about the size of a thumbnail, which is very difficult to see in the water. Irukandji occur in northern waters from the end of October to early May. It is related to the box jellyfish but has a single tentacle hanging from each of the four corners of its flotation bell. The initial sting is not all that painful, but victims soon succumb to irukandji syndrome: severe backache or headache, shooting pains in the muscles, abdomen and chest along with nausea, anxiety and vomiting. An antivenom is under development.

Blue-Ringed Octopus

Blue-ringed octopus are found in south-west Australia to southern Queensland and also northern Tasmania. The smaller, more common species is seen in shallow rock pools beside the ocean. When at rest, the octopus is pale brown to yellow, but when alarmed it displays pulsating blue rings. Never pick one up! The neuromuscular venom present in its saliva can kill within minutes. There's no known antidote and the only chance of surviving is many hours of mouth-to-mouth resuscitation and heart massage while the poison slowly works itself out of the victim.

Stone Fish

This deadly marine creature inhabits shallow coastal waters and is well camouflaged, being speckled brown and looking like a rock, hence its name. It has 13 sharp spines along its back that contain extremely toxic venom capable of inflicting death within hours. Most poisonings occur when someone steps unwittingly on the fish.

spiders

Wolf spider in Simpson Desert. *(Getty Images)*

FUNNEL-WEB

The country's most venomous spider is found in eastern Australia including Tasmania, and as far west as the Gulf Ranges in South Australia. Dark brown or black, the spider grows to about 4.5cm in body length. It burrows in sheltered places in the bush or urban gardens. Its burrow has irregular silk 'trip-lines' radiating from the entrance. A funnel-web bite can cause serious illness, even death. Most incidents occur during the summer–autumn mating season when the male spider leaves its burrow to seek females. Antivenom is available.

RED-BACK

Australia's best-known dangerous spider is found throughout the country and is common in urban and suburban areas. It is small and black with a distinctive red or orange stripe on its abdomen. The red-back lives under bricks, rocks, logs, in empty pots, in sheds and outdoor toilets. Only the bite of the female is dangerous to humans. It can cause serious illness and sometimes death. Antivenom is available. The red-back is closely related to the American black widow spider.

WHITE-TAIL

Found all over Australia, particularly in urban areas, the white tail spider can be up to 1.5cm in body length, is dark grey and has a distinctive white spot on the end of its abdomen. It lives in crevices, under bark, litter and indoors. A bite usually results in localised pain followed by an itchy swollen lump. Available evidence questions the common belief that a white tail bite results in a skin ulcer or necrosis.

Brown snake. *(Getty Images)*

snakes

Australia has many venomous snakes, of which the most dangerous are:

Taipan

Australia has two species. The western or inland taipan (aka fierce snake) produces the most toxic venom of all snakes and, therefore, tops the list of the world's deadliest snakes. It's purportedly limited to a small area of western Queensland although sightings elsewhere mean its true range is unknown.

Its cousin, the coastal taipan, is aggressive, highly venomous, and ranked fourth on the deadliest list. Found along the coast of northern Australia and as far south as the Kimberleys in Western Australia, it has the longest fangs (13mm) and is also the longest venomous Australian snake, measuring up to three metres. It will react fiercely if cornered or threatened. Taipan venom causes severe paralysis and blood clotting.

Brown Snake

Ranked second on the most deadly list, this reptile is found in eastern Australia, but not in Tasmania. The brown snake averages about 1.5 metres although longer specimens have been recorded. Brown snake venom can kill a human relatively quickly if the bite is untreated.

Tiger Snake

The tiger snake is ranked fifth on the deadly list. It's found in eastern and southern Australia, and in suburban areas. It has striped markings and can grow to 1.5 metres. These markings may change according to season and age.
A tiger snake will attack if disturbed or threatened. Its venom can kill but deaths are quite rare since antivenom became available.

Death Adder

Found throughout most of Australia and ranked 10th on the world's most deadly list. It has a broad triangular head, short, thick body and hides under leaves, in sand or gravel in order to ambush its prey. The death adder is mainly nocturnal. Because it does not necessarily slink away when humans approach it can inadvertently be stepped on or accidently disturbed. Its venom affects the nerves, resulting in paralysis. Antivenom is available.

australia's diverse underwater world

Green turtle. *(TQ)*

Whale shark.

Ningaloo Reef, WA

On the remote shores of Coral Bay and Exmouth in Western Australia you can step from an arid desert into a mass of coral and underwater life, sometimes just 50m from shore. The Ningaloo Reef starts south of Coral Bay and stretches 260km to the North West Cape near Exmouth. Its remoteness shelters it from the crowds but what people tend to overlook is that this reef is in fact much more accessible than the Great Barrier Reef due to its proximity to the coast.

From March to June each year visitors have the chance to swim with the oceans' largest fish, the whale shark. Dive operators work with spotter planes to locate the sharks and groups of people with snorkels swim beside these ocean giants, witnessing their awesome beauty. It is a humbling experience. Whale sharks can grow up to 14m and their sheer enormity tends to make you feel like a tiny remora hugging the underbelly of an enormous fish.

Although whale sharks are Ningaloo's drawcard, there are many other spectacular dive and snorkelling opportunities. Manta rays are prolific and you can snorkel and interact with at least 30 different mantas in just one afternoon.

Another good dive in the Exmouth Gulf is the 300m Navy Pier that opens up a world of astonishing underwater life. Because of the large tides however, visibility isn't always great and it can only be dived on low or high tide. Nearby a drift dive along the Sponge Gardens is another notable site among the many on offer.

TIP on a good day the whale sharks move slowly, interacting with you at you speed. Sometimes, however, they swim quickly through the area and humans need to swim quite frantically to keep up with them. Confidence in swimming is a must.

Montague Island, NSW

The waters of Montague Island Nature Reserve, 9km offshore from Narooma on the NSW south coast, are rich in marine life and offer a diverse choice of dive sites and animal encounters, most notably the opportunity to swim with playful fur seals.

From June to December, hundreds of Australian fur seals live here with smaller numbers sighted year round. Above thick kelp forests young seals perform barrel rolls, somersaults and swoop past you to stare. With whiskers and bulging eyes just centimetres away, they present divers and snorkellers with an unforgettable adventure.

Montague Island is home to a large colony of Little Penguins and breeding grounds for 15 bird species. Nearby you can dive the recently discovered wreck of *The Lady Darling,* covered in jewel anemones, beautiful sea fans and exquisite sponges. at a depth of 25-30m.

TIP young seals can be overly friendly but adult seals are very protective of their young.

Frolicking fur seal.

Shipwreck.

Yongala Shipwreck, Townsville, Qld

In 1911 the coastal steamship SS *Yongala* went down in a cyclone 90km south-east of Townsville near Cape Bowling Green. Now this 110m structure lies on a sandy seabed and attracts such a prolific variety of marine life that it is considered one of the world's greatest dives.

The wreck lies in 15–30m of water and on your descent you will see what makes this location so famous. Myriad ocean life blocks your view. Eagle rays, sea snakes, queenfish, turtles, cobia, giant Queensland gropers, batfish and schools of trevally are just a few of the things you will see. There is also a huge diversity of corals growing on the skeleton of this elegant and well-preserved ship. This dive is a showcase of our fish species in the Australian Coral Sea.

TIP the *Yongala* wreck is located in open water so very susceptible to weather conditions. Quite frequently there are moderate to high currents with choppy surface conditions and poor diving visibility. It is therefore recommended for confident and experienced divers.

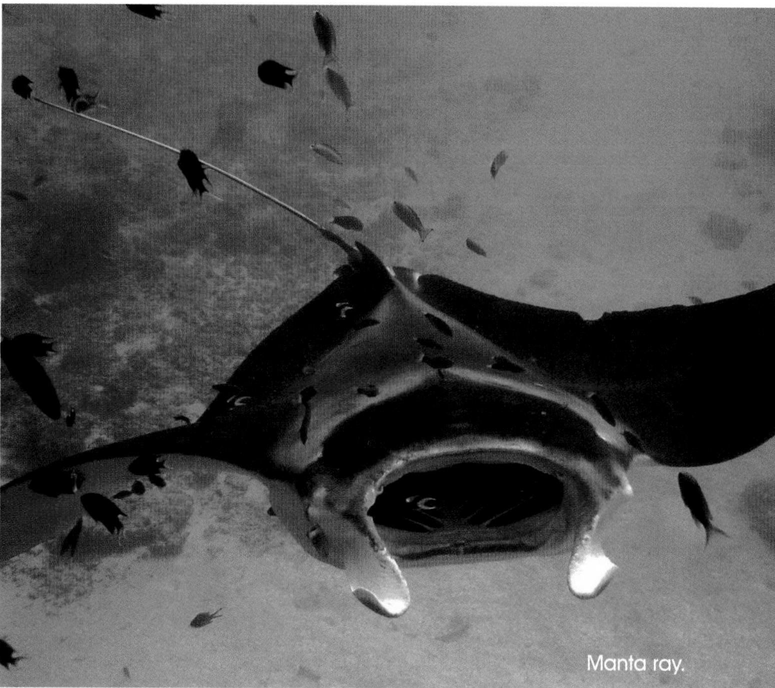
Manta ray.

Heron Island, Great Barrier Reef, Qld

Heron Island is located in the Capricorn Group of islands, 72km off the coast of Gladstone and is easily accessed by a 30-minute flight with Australian helicopters or a two-and-a-half-hour journey on the Heron Island launch.

This small, pretty coral cay makes a perfect base to explore the surrounding coral reef system and offers easy and relaxed diving conditions with the majority of sites just 5–15 minutes from the island. Diving is therefore perfect for beginners, including the more advanced with all of the delicacies of the Great Barrier Reef right here at your fingertips.

Between the months of October and March the island becomes a breeding ground for turtles which are seen in large numbers both above and below the water. Locations such as the Heron Bommies act as the area's cleaning station. Turtles, manta rays, wrasse and sharks along with other large creatures congregate here to be cleaned by the smaller fish.

Blue Pools is another favourite Heron dive site. Here it appears as if a bite has been taken out of the reef, forming a sheltered semicircle where dives start at just 5–6m and snorkelling is popular.

TIP Heron Island offers a selection of more than 30 dive sites and is the perfect spot to complete your open water dives to become fully certified. Complete your theory and pool sessions prior to your arrival on Heron and then utilise the areas exotic marine life environment to practise your newly acquired skills.

Because of the calm conditions, many of these sites can also be enjoyed while snorkelling. If you are a beginner, first practise over sandy areas away from the coral to gain buoyancy control.

Other island stays on the Great Barrier Reef renowned for excellent snorkelling and diving are Lady Elliot Island and Lizard Island.

The Rowley Shoals, WA

The pristine Rowley Shoals is a group of three coral atolls, Mermaid Reef, Clerke Reef and Imperieuse Reef, rising up 400m from the ocean floor and teetering on the edge of one of the widest continental shelves in the world. Located 280km north-west of Broome prevailing weather conditions prevent the area from being visited except between September and December when boating conditions are considered more savoury. The area is accessed via live-aboard vessels and is approximately a days steam out of Broome.

For your efforts, virgin reefs will adorn the windows of your mask displaying giant clams, spectacular coral gardens and thousands of fish. It is not unusual to have water visibility up to 60m where more than 200 species of corals flourish in their masses and up to 700 species of fish thrive. Mackerel, tuna, trevally, giant potato cod and maori wrasse are likely to be your companions as you drift dive through these exquisite blue lagoons, coral bommies, caves and sheer walls covered with gorgonians, soft corals, sea whips and large sponges.

TIP be careful at dusk when sharks are active and feeding. Treat them with respect and remember they are attracted mostly by movement.

If you would like to dive The Rowley Shoals in style, step onboard the luxury vessel True North complete with smaller boats on board and private helicopter. visit **www.northstarcruises.com.au**

Respected operator Mike Ball has been in the industry since 1969 when he first opened 'Dive School' in Townsville. Mike Ball Expeditions have trips that cover many of Australia's favourite spots including the Cod Hole, Coral Sea, Minke Whale and Great White Shark expeditions.

www.mikeball.com

LEARN TO DIVE

PADI Open Water Diver certification courses take approximately four days to complete. They are split into three parts. The first two days involve pool and classroom training made up of five theory sessions and five pool sessions. After this you need to do four training dives.

Many people like to do the classroom side of their course in their home town, utilising their local dive shop. After this they choose an exciting dive destination to complete their four training dives. This option is known as a 'referral' and many operators around Australia accommodate divers in this manner. After completion of the four training dives, you are now an Open Water Certified Diver.

A medical is required for all Learn to Dive courses but generally, if you are in good health and are comfortable in the water, there is no reason why you cannot take the plunge. You must be over the age of 14 years.

PADI Jr Open Water Diver courses are available for children 10–14yrs. They must dive at all times with a PADI professional or certified parent/guardian and not exceed a maximum depth of 12 metres.

Great Barrier Reef. *(TQ)*

THE GREAT BARRIER REEF

It is impossible to know where to start when talking about the Great Barrier Reef and Coral Sea. It is the world's largest reef and extends for 2300km from Bundaberg to the northern tip of Queensland. This huge expanse presents an overwhelming choice of dive sites with more than 2800 reefs accessible from many coastal points along the Queensland coast.

The opportunities are endless so you must first identify how much time you have and what type of exploring suits your needs. Are you looking for a day trip scub dive or snorkel? Do you want to base yourself on an island or maybe charter a vessel, seaplane or helicopter? To see the best the Great Barrier Reef has to offer you should consider spending a few nights onboard a live-aboard vessel that travels to the pristine outer reefs.

North of Cairns 10 coral reefs string together to form the Ribbon Reefs and offer spectacular coral garden diving and abundant fish life. This is the home to the world famous dive site, the Cod Hole, where a family of huge, friendly Potato Cod (Groper) are the star attractions. Live-aboards to the Ribbon Reefs leave from Cairns and Port Douglas. Osprey Reef and Holmes Reef are also popular live-aboard destinations out of Cairns. Day trip sites are also plentiful. Hastings, Michaelmas, Moore, Norman and Agincourt Reefs are among the more frequented.

Flinders Reef, approximately 200km east of Townsville, offers spectacular dive sites such as Watanabe Bommie and Scuba Zoo. At Scuba Zoo two shark cages are anchored to the seabed and divers have the opportunity to observe up to 50 sharks circling them on a 30 minute dive and shark feed.

The Whitsunday Islands offer all the facilities of world-class resorts and have diving and snorkelling opportunities outside their doors. The main reef however is some two hours away by charter boat and Hook and Hardy Reefs are very popular.

The beauty of the Great Barrier Reef can be seen in all of these areas and in thousands more unlisted. The true beauty remains in the fact that there is still so much more left undiscovered.

Australia is one of the best places for whale watching. A variety of species are easily seen on their annual migration along the coast, from Antarctica to warmer waters, between May and November.

Coastal headlands are good vantage points for whale spotting, but boat-based whale watching has grown rapidly in recent years, offering close encounters with these magnificent creatures.

Humpbacks and southern right whales are the most common large whales in Australian waters, although orcas, sperm, pilot, fin, sei, Bryde's, minke and blue whales are also seen.

whale watching in australia

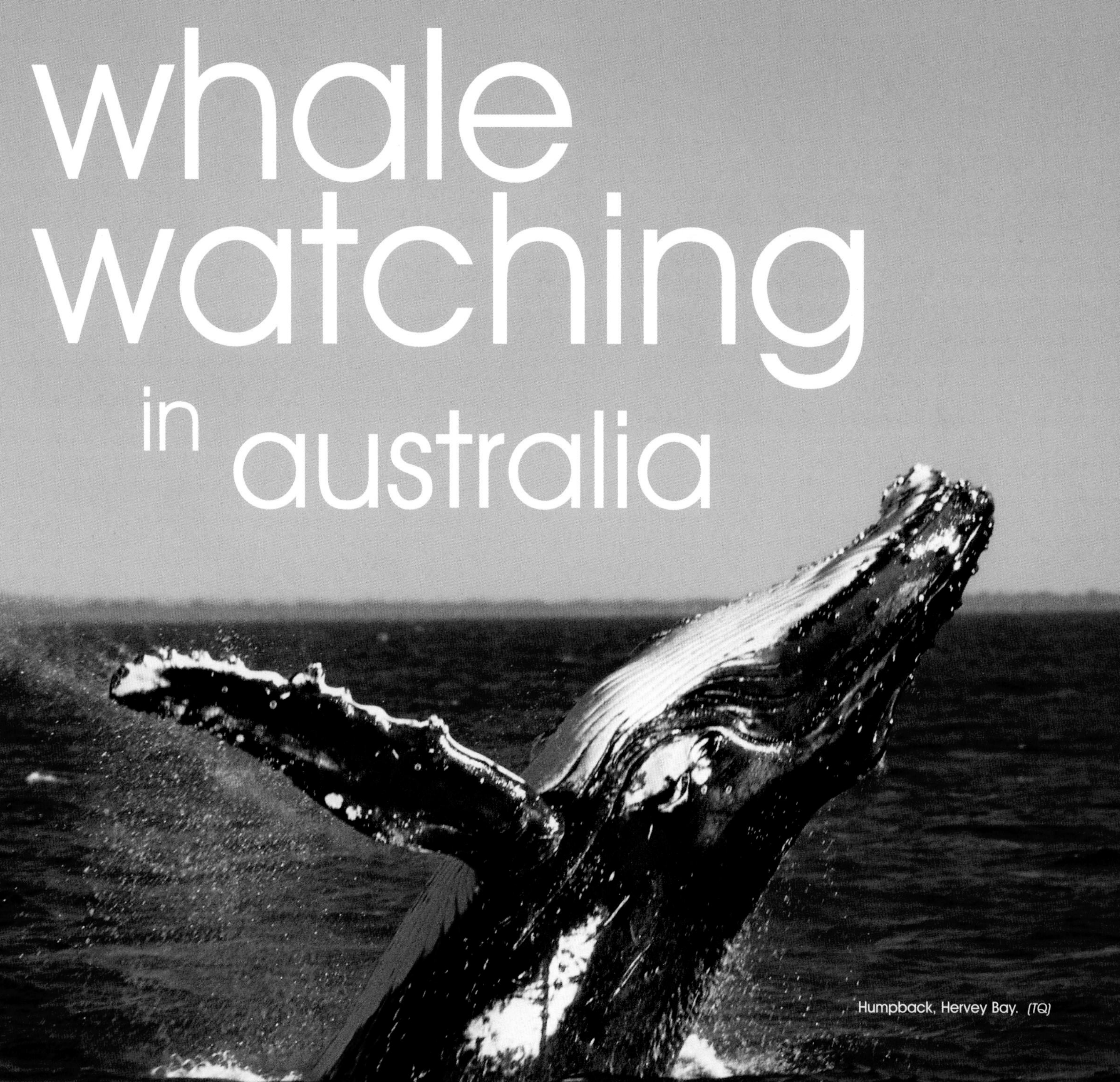

Humpback, Hervey Bay. *(TQ)*

Byron Bay tail wave, NSW. *(TNSW)*

Queensland

Hervey Bay, 300km north of Brisbane, has been called the 'Whale Watch Capital of Australia'. Between July and November, the World Heritage-listed Fraser Island provides a sheltered area for humpback whales to give birth and rest in preparation for their long migration south. A number of commercial whale watching operators are located in Hervey Bay.

Further north, the warm and protected waters of Airlie Beach (1275km north of Brisbane) and the high vantage points from many of the islands in the Whitsundays are ideal for spotting humpbacks. Most boat trips depart from Shute Harbour or Abel Point Marina on Airlie Beach.

The cliff face below the lighthouse at Cape Moreton on Moreton Island (just off Brisbane) is a spot often used by researchers conducting population surveys of humpback whales.

Cairns (1717km north of Brisbane) and the Great Barrier Reef is one of the only places in the world where it is possible to join a research expedition and swim with minke whales. The expeditions operate in June and July.

www.herveybay.qld.gov.au www.whalewatching.com.au
www.minkewhale.org

New South Wales

Humpback whales and southern right whales can often be seen very close to Sydney. Both North and South Head at the entrance to Sydney Harbour are good locations, and on occasion inquisitive whales have been known to swim right into the harbour! Cape Solander, overlooking Botany Bay, is a favourite spot for dedicated whale-watchers. The northern beaches are also prime sites, particularly Barrenjoey Head at Palm Beach.

The most easterly point on the continent, Cape Byron at Byron Bay, 830km north of Sydney, is one of the best sites in Australia to see humpback whales from land, with uninterrupted views far along the coastline.

Coffs Harbour, Port Macquarie, Port Stephens, and Newcastle, north of Sydney and Wollongong, Jervis Bay, Batemans Bay, Narooma and Merimbula in the south, are all renowned whale watching locations. Cliffs and headlands all along the coastline provide excellent lookouts.

Twofold Bay at Eden, 476km south of Sydney, was the site of one of the most productive whaling stations in Australian history. Sperm whales and orcas (killer whales) may be seen on boat trips out beyond the continental shelf, and if lucky, there may be a chance to catch a rare glimpse of a blue whale–the largest animal on earth. There is a Killer Whale Museum located in Eden and every year in October the town hosts a whale festival.

In northern New South Wales the best months for whale watching are July to September, while in the south of the state it's best at the beginning (May–June) and end (November–December) of their migration.

www.nationalparks.nsw.gov.au www.sapphirecoast.com.au
www.killerwhalemuseum.com.au

Breaching humpback whale off Fraser Island, Qld. *(Getty Images)*

Whale watching, Hervey Bay, Qld. *(TQ)*

Victoria

Whale watching in Victoria is based mainly along the west coast. The species most often seen is the southern right whale, so named by whalers because they were the 'right' whales to hunt, being slow swimmers and their high blubber content kept them afloat.

Warrnambool, 260km south-west of Melbourne, is a southern right whale nursery. Between June and September female southern right whales calve or bring their calves close to shore at Logans Beach, where a viewing platform has been constructed on the beach.

Further west along the coast, Port Fairy was the base for the local whaling industry in the early 1800s. It is sometimes possible to spot blue whales near Portland (362km west of Melbourne) as nearby Cape Nelson is one of only a few known blue whale feeding areas in the world. They generally arrive in December and remain until May.

www.visitvictoria.com

South Australia

Each year, from June until September, southern right whales gather at the Head of Bight (1000km west of Adelaide) on the Nullarbor to calve and to breed and can be watched from platforms built along the cliffs. The southern rights were such easy game that by 1935 only a few hundred remained from an estimated population of more than 200,000. They became protected in 1935, but were still illegally hunted until the 1980s.

Victor Harbor, 85km south-east of Adelaide, is also an excellent land-based site for viewing southern right whales. The South Australian Whale Centre is located here and provides information on where to see whales as well as interactive displays on Australia's whaling history and marine environment.

www.sawhalecentre.com

www.tep.com.au/region/head_of_bight.htm

Flinders Bay, near Augusta, WA. *(WATC)*

Western Australia

Western Australia's impressive stretch of coastline facing the Indian Ocean provides spectacular views of migrating southern right whales and humpbacks.

The southern shores of the state are visited by southern right whales between May and October. In June and July, humpback whales head north, returning southwards between September and November.

Albany (410km south of Perth) is the site of an old whaling station where the last whale hunted in Australia was processed in 1978. A museum now occupies the site as an important reminder of the country's whaling history.

Exmouth (1270km north of Perth) is the gateway to the Ningaloo Marine Park and provides a sheltered bay for humpbacks and calves to rest on their southward migration during winter and spring. The lighthouse on Vlamingh Head offers sweeping views over North West Cape and Ningaloo Reef.

Humpbacks that migrate along the west coast often calve in the waters off the north-west of Australia that extend from Broome to the top of the Kimberley. Peak sighting times are August and September.

www.whaleworld.org www.exmouth.wa.gov.au

Tasmania

In Tasmania southern right whales and humpback whales can be seen at east coast vantage points such as Great Oyster Bay and Coles Bay where the Freycinet Peninsula (210km north of Hobart) provides a protected inlet. As the two species have quite different migration patterns they are seen at different times. Humpbacks migrate during May-July and then return south in October-December. Southern right whales arrive at their breeding grounds in Tasmanian waters in June and stay until October before migrating south again.

While most species migrate some distance off the continental shelf, the humpback and southern right whale come sufficiently close to the coast to allow regular sightings from land.

At the peak of the whaling boom, there were enough whales migrating through Tasmanian waters to support 45 whaling stations, nine of which were in or around Hobart. Southern right whales are occasionally sighted between May and October in the sheltered waters of the Derwent River and humpbacks have been seen feeding at the mouth of the river.

Occasionally orcas can be seen in Adventure Bay off Bruny Island, 35km south of Hobart.

www.parks.tas.gov.au/wildlife/mammals/whales.html

Boat-based Whale Watching

If you are planning on taking a whale-watching cruise, it is worth seeking out an operation that has a knowledgeable naturalist or researcher on board who can help spot the whales, identify the species and any behaviour you are seeing. The most responsible operators will put the welfare of the animals first and contribute some of their profits to whale conservation and research.

There are strict guidelines in Australia governing whale watching operations and vessels are not permitted to approach within 100m of a whale, or 300m if a calf is present. Some craft such as jet skis and motorised watercraft are prohibited from approaching whales at all, and swimming and diving with whales

is also regulated. Heavy fines apply for breaches of the law so it's best to familiarise yourself with the rules if planning to charter your own boat.

Land-based Whale Watching

Watching whales from the shore is the most non-invasive way to observe whales in their natural habitat, and often enables a range of natural behaviours to be observed, uninhibited by the presence of motorised craft.

The best choice is a headland between 30 and 50 metres above sea level. Any lower and you can't see out to sea, but if the headland is too high it will be difficult to make out dorsal fins against the background. Cliff tops where lighthouses are located are a good starting point.

WHALE WATCHING EQUIPMENT

- A good set of eyes and a big supply of patience—whales are not on a timetable and they don't perform on demand!
- Binoculars are useful for sighting a 'blow' in the distance, the first sign that whales are about. The characteristic blow is formed when the whale exhales at the surface of the water.
- A camera with a telephoto lens can come in handy for capturing those spectacular whale moments.
- Water—even though its winter, you will need to ensure you have plenty of liquids to drink as you will be outdoors for several hours. Don't forget sunscreen and a hat.
- Plan to spend at least three to four hours at the observation site.

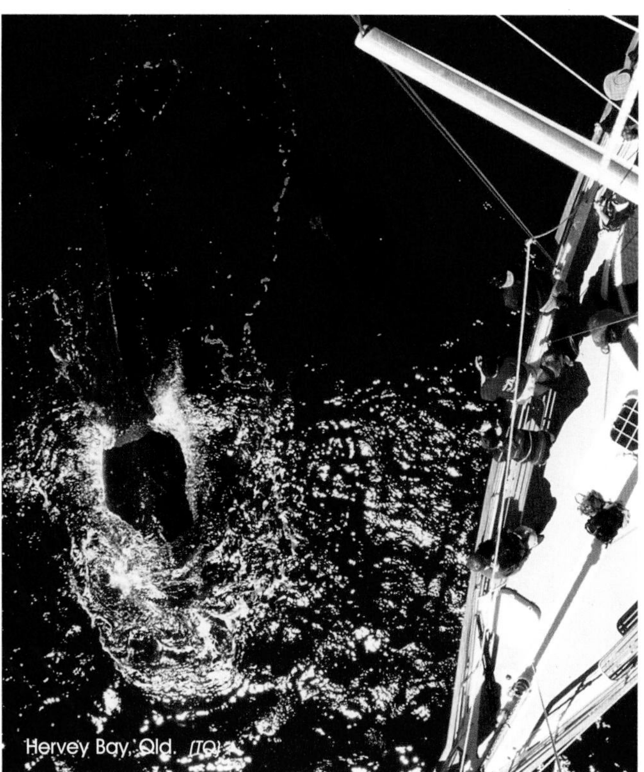

Hervey Bay, Qld. (TQ)

WHAT TO LOOK FOR

Usually the first thing you will most likely see when you spot a whale is the distinctive 'blow', a spout of air that can be seen above the surface of the water when the whale exhales. On clear days this can be visible from quite some distance. Each species of whale has a different shaped blow, and the size, shape and angle is often used to help with identification. Other ways to identify whales include size, tail shape and the size and position of the dorsal fin.

Common behaviours that may be observed include:

- **Breaching:** one of the most spectacular behaviours, where the whale leaps into the air, twists its body and crashes down into the water on its back, sometimes repeating the action over and over again. This behaviour is most commonly seen in humpback whales. The exact function of breaching is unknown, but possibilities include dislodging parasites, communicating with other whales, or taking visual bearings. It may also be performed for the sheer fun of it.
- **Tail Slapping or 'Lobtailing':** one of the behaviours noted in many whales, including killer, sperm and southern right whales, is where the whale raises its tail fluke in the air and slaps it down forcefully on the surface of the water. The sound can often be heard for kilometres around and may indicate threatening behaviour or social communication.
- **Spy hopping:** the whale lifts its head and throat above the surface and takes a look around—equivalent to an 'up periscope' action. The purpose of spy hopping may be to get a bearing from nearby headlands, but it could also signal curiosity about nearby vessels.
- **Flipper slapping:** many whale species lie on their sides or backs and slap one or both of their flippers onto the surface with a distinctive splash. This may be a form of courtship display, a way of signalling across great distances underwater or to indicate that the whale feels threatened.

bird watching in australia

Australia offers unlimited opportunity for birdwatchers, making it very difficult to compile a brief list of species. We have the largest number of endemics in the world, with more than 800 species in total. Ask 100 different bird watchers and you would get 100 different lists. However in creating this list we have tried to keep to the better-known species and have chosen nature destinations that give the traveller the opportunity to appreciate wildlife of all kinds, as well as the area's natural beauty.

Kookaburra. *(Isabelle Quartly)*

Bush stone-curlew. (IQ)

northern territory

Egrets, Cormorants and Herons in Kakadu National Park

Kakadu National Park is Australia's largest national park and considered one of the world's best. Habitat is diverse with fresh and salt water mangroves, billabongs, rivers and swamps, making it a paradise for waterbirds. At Yellow Water Lagoon egrets, cormorants and herons can all be viewed with little effort. There is a camping ground at the lagoon, but with no facilities apart from toilets.

Litchfield NP for the Bush Stone-curlew

The strange wailing calls of the Bush Stone-curlew (Bush Thick-knee) are enough to scare anyone into believing stories of murderous bunyips. Sadly the Bush Stone-curlew has become rare in southern areas of Australia, although you can still find it in the north in places like Litchfield National Park. They come out to feed only at night so try spotlighting for it along the park's roads.

Sulphur-crested cockatoo. (IQ)

new south wales

Parrots in the Blue Mountains

The Blue Mountains is located only a few hours from Sydney and is home to numerous parrots including the Australian king parrot, gang-gang and sulphur-crested cockatoo, crimson rosella and galah. Information on the many walks in the region is available from the visitors centre at Echo Point, site of the Three Sisters, but for an easy one try the 2km walk from the visitors centre to Katoomba Cascades.

Australian Pelicans at The Entrance

The Australian pelican will do almost anything for a free feed. At The Entrance on the Central Coast of NSW, a large group of wild Australian Pelicans are fed daily rain, hail or shine. This tradition started more than 20 years ago when the local fish shop gave the pelicans their leftovers. On days they had none, the pelicans would cross the road to the fish shop to 'demand' food. The daily feeds are now used for pubic education and to check the birds for fishhooks.

Tawny Frogmouth at Royal National Park

The tawny frogmouth is a nocturnal bird found throughout Australia. Although often called an owl, they are actually not even closely related. One of the best chances of seeing the tawny frogmouth is spotlighting in Sydney's Royal National Park, especially along Lady Carrington, Sir Bertram Stevens and Lady Wakehurst drives. With almost 200 species, birders are guaranteed to see a variety of interesting birds, as well as the opportunity to enjoy the park's undeveloped coastline.

Fairy Penguins. (TV)

victoria

Laughing Kookaburra in the Grampians

No doubt the laughing kookaburra has one of the world's most distinctive calls, which has come to signify the Australian bush. At Halls Gap in the Grampians National Park laughing kookaburras are a common sight in picnic areas and caravan parks, you may even get your lunch stolen! The Grampians is Victoria's largest national park and is popular with tourists for both its natural beauty and diversity of flora and fauna.

Superb Fairy-wren at Wilsons Promontory

Wilsons Promontory is mainland Australia's southern most point and one of Victoria's most popular reserves. It is also one of the best places in Australia to see the superb fairy-wren and over 250 other species. Tidal River is the site of the park's visitor's centre and accommodation, as well as the starting point for many walks. To find the superb fairy-wren, try the track that leaves from the car park just north of Tidal River.

Fairy Penguin at Phillip Island

Also called the little bblue penguin, this is the smallest penguin species and is found only in southern Australia and New Zealand. It weighs about a kilogram and stands between 30 and 40cm tall. The Australian fairy penguin differs from those in New Zealand by having white feathers on its tail and flippers. It lives in burrows, foraging at sea for fish, squid and crustaceans by day and returning to its nest at dusk, often in groups, giving rise to the popular 'penguin parade' attraction.

Black Swans. (IQ)

tasmania

Black Swans at Moulting Lagoon

Moulting Lagoon has been listed as a RAMSAR site, which means it is a wetland of international significance. It is the main breeding ground for the Black Swan in Tasmania with a population of up to 8000 in the breeding season. Unfortunately public access to the lagoon is limited, so you may need to take a tour.

Gulls on Bruny Island

Bruny Island, off the east coast of Tasmania, is popular with birders because all 12 of Tasmania's endemics can be found on this one island. However, Bruny Island is also one of the few places in Australia where you will see both the Pacific Gull and Kelp Gull together. Although the two are similar in appearance, the Kelp Gull has a red spot on its lower bill only, whilst the Pacific Gull has red on both its upper and lower bill.

BIRD WATCHING TIPS

- Research the species and the areas you want to see before you arrive at your destination. Joining a specialised tour may help in finding specific species.
- Always carry a good field guide to help with identification (such as *The Slater Field Guide to Australiian birds*, New Holland). Sometimes taking notes or photographing a bird can help identify similar species at a later time.
- Optical equipment such as binoculars or spotting scope is almost essential for bird watching, as many species will not allow you to approach at close range. A magnification between 25X and 50X is recommended. It is probably worth investing in equipment that is dust proof and water resistant as you will encounter a vast range of environmental conditions in your travels.
- Try to avoid approaching birds too close to their nests or 'chasing' them after they have moved off, as this will cause stress to the bird.
- Finally, take the time to enjoy observing each bird you encounter, try not to become too obsessed with ticking off a checklist of species as you will miss out on their beauty and uniqueness.

Don't forget your binoculars. *(IQ)*

Sacred kingfisher. *(IQ)*

queensland

Australian Brush-turkey in Lamington National Park

The Australian Brush-turkey is unusual because the female lays her eggs in a mound of vegetation that generates heat as it decays. It is the male who is responsible for maintaining the temperature, by varying the amount of vegetation, until they hatch. Lamington National Park is a great place to find the Australian Brush-turkey, you will find them in abundance at both O'Reilly's Guest House and Binna Burra Lodge.

Kingfishers at Daintree National Park

The Daintree is home to almost 430 species of birds including seven different species of kingfisher. Although most of this World Heritage listed area is inaccessible, seeing the kingfisher is possible by taking a specialised bird watching cruise along the Daintree River. Another place you are likely to see them, especially the Little and Sacred Kingfisher, is on the Marrdja Botanical Walk in the mangroves.

Cassowary in far north Queensland

Australia's second largest bird lives in the cool shade and seclusion offered by the dense rainforests of far north Queensland. It can be up to 1.8m tall and has a distinctive grey-brown crest (casque) on its head which, along with its neck, is blue and featherless. A flightless bird, it has three toes with sharp claws on each foot and powerful legs which allow it to run at high speed. The cassowary mostly eats fruit but will also chomp snakes, frogs and other small animals, insects and forest fungi.

Osprey chicks. (IQ)

south australia

Ospreys on Kangaroo Island

Ospreys often return to the same nest each year for breeding, their nests are made of sticks and are added to each year until they grow quite large. Ospreys can be seen along most of the Australian coast, but a good place to start is Ballast Head on Kangaroo Island.

Ducks at Bool Lagoon

Bool Lagoon is the best spot in South Australia for waterbirds, especially during breeding season or in times of drought. There are numerous species of duck including freckled and Pacific black duck, Australian shelduck, chestnut teal, hardhead and plumed whistling-duck. It is worth contacting the ranger before making a trip as some years the area dries up completely and the birds have to go elsewhere.

Emu. (IQ)

western australia

Purple Swamphen and Dusky Moorhen in Perth

With more than 50 lakes in the metropolitan area, Perth is one of the best places in Western Australia to see waterbirds. To find the Purple Swamphen and Dusky Moorhen try the lakes in King Park. Only a few minutes from the centre of Perth this park has a tree-top walk and nature trail, which is a good place to see many of the 80 other species of birds in the area.

Emus in the Kimberley

Found throughout most of the mainland, the emu is Australia's largest bird. Unlike most birds, emus are curious of people and are sometimes known to approach at close range. The Kimberley is a region of great contrasts and is one of Australia's last frontiers and, with 300 species of birds, it is a prime bird-watching destination. To see emus, take a drive along some of the area's more deserted roads.

Eastern yellow robin. (IQ)

ACT

Canberra for Eastern Yellow Robins

The Eastern Yellow Robin is probably the easiest of the robins to see. It is often found looking for handouts from picnickers, although its natural diet is insects. Taking a walk along the tracks of the Australian National Botanic Gardens in Canberra you are likely to see this robin in a more natural setting. Informative ranger-guided tours depart every Sunday from the car park at 10am and 2pm.

ZOOS

BIRDS OF PREY IN 'FREE FLIGHT' BIRD SHOWS

Birds of prey can be found Australia wide, but one way of getting close is by seeing a free flight bird show. Taronga Zoo in Sydney and Currumbin Wildlife Sanctuary and Australia Zoo in Queensland all have good shows. Some of the species you are likely to see are the wedge-tailed and white-bellied sea eagle, barking owl and peregrine falcon.

White-bellied sea eagle. *(IQ)*

sport fishing in australia

Port Philip Bay snapper. *(A McGlashan)*

Australia is a massive country and despite being mostly semi arid it is still loaded with fishing opportunities. The diversity is amazing and extends from trout in snow-lined high country lakes to barramundi in mangrove-lined tropical creeks and beyond to the cobalt blue waters that are home to oceanic apex predators. It doesn't seem to matter what style of fishing you like, be it fly fishing or big game fishing, there are numerous places to go.

With so many endless fishing opportunities, selecting the best is no easy chore. After much painstaking thought we have chosen what we think are the six of the best fishing spots in the country. Having said that there is no reason why this book won't inspire you to go and find another eight hot spots!

Giants of Cairns

When it comes to big fish nowhere else on earth can compare to Cairns. More thousand-pound marlin (known as granders) are caught in the waters off this far north Queensland town than anywhere else in the world. If you want to catch the biggest fish in the world then Cairns is the place to be.

Every spring black marlin congregate along the outside edge of the famous Great Barrier Reef north of Cairns to spawn. Ranging in size from 100kg to well over 500kg in weight they are seriously massive fish that require heavy tackle. For this reason it is not a place for the faint-hearted where 60kg chair rods go hand-in-hand with professional charter boats and some of the best crews in the world. Catching a fish that could weigh more than five times as much as you is very much a team effort.

The standard technique is to troll two dead baits and work along the outside edge of the reef in the cobalt blue waters of the Coral Sea. For the first timer seeing the deckhand rig up a 10kg tuna as bait is something that takes a bit of time to get used to!

The greatest part of fishing for these giants is not actually fighting them but just seeing them exploding out of the water like a missile. The only downside to this type of fishing is that the grounds are well offshore and the only way to access them is by live-aboard charters, which is expensive. However on the same note living on the reef only adds to uniqueness of this amazing adventure.

Touring the Tiwi Islands

Found north of Darwin in the Arafura Sea these two remote islands are surrounded by fish-rich waters. Not only are there dozens of mangrove-lined creeks but the coastal waters are loaded with endless reefs as well. An amazing array of fish call this area home, from the energetic queenfish through to aggressive mangrove jacks. However of all the sportfish available, it is the barramundi (or barra as the locals call them) that is the biggest drawcard.

Found in large numbers in the creeks the barra often stack up around snags and creek junctions ambushing bait fish that make the mistake of swimming too close. There are a number of techniques employed to catch these chrome-plated estuary dwellers but the most exciting way to catch them is with lures. Casting in tight against the snags with deep diving lures like RMGs can produce some explosive strikes, especially if you retrieve the lure with jerky stop-start action. Barra can be caught year round but are most active during the warmer months from October through to May.

If you get tired of catching barra then you can cast poppers (surface lures) around the headlands and bommies for explosive action on trevally and queenfish. These hard pulling species are both exciting and challenging to catch. Further offshore there are numerous reefs and ledges that are loaded with bottom fish like monster black jewfish and sweet tasting golden snapper.

City snapper

Not all the best fishing spots are far flung locations; in fact some are right under your nose. Port Phillip Bay is surrounded by Melbourne's sprawling suburbia, yet despite this it sees a huge influx of snapper every year. As the wattle trees begin to bloom the snapper, drawn by the urge to spawn start to migrate into the bay. By November their numbers have swelled into the thousands and as the water temperature rises they suddenly come on the chew.

Primarily a boat fishery, anglers use their depth sounders to locate the snapper schools and then once located they anchor up. It's also primarily a bait fishery and anglers use multiple rods to increase their chances. Being surrounded by suburbia you rarely have the Bay to yourself so always use super fresh bait!

Ranging in size from barely a kilo to more than 10kg the snapper are best targeted with 4-8kg spin tackle. When a snapper picks up the bait use the Baitrunner mode on your spinning reel to let it run for a second then crank the handle and set the hook. Snapper are stubborn fighters so take it easy and just use constant pressure to bring them to the boat.

Potato cod, Great Barrier Reef. *(TQ)*

Clarence canoeing

The Clarence River is one of the few rivers that is still flowing completely unobstructed from its source in the Great Dividing Range to where it meets the sea on the New South Wales north coast. Unhindered by dams this river and its tributaries not only offers fantastic fishing but also some fantastic wilderness canoeing as well.

The main species targeted is Australian bass which migrate upstream in spring after spawning down in the estuarine reaches. Holding in the deeper pools the bass will aggressively attack any lure that comes within striking distance. Small deep diving lures, such as Tilsans or spinnerbaits that probe the depths work best during the day while surface lures can work a treat during the hotter months.

Ranging in size from barely a few hundred grams to a few kilos in weight bass are tough little fish that are best targeted with 4-6kg baitcaster outfits spooled up braid line. Navigating through granite strewn pools in the shadows of forest-covered mountains is certainly a pleasant place to fish.

Remote Rowley Shoals

Isolated by a 180 nautical miles Rowley Shoals are surrounded by the aqua blue waters of the Indian Ocean. Found east of Broome the Shoals–three individual atolls–have no permanent land and as a result are still largely untouched. Renowned for its fishing and diving, the Shoals are only accessible by long range live-aboard charters.

Dropping away into more than a hundred fathoms of water there is a multitude of species found in the waters beyond the reef. Sailfish, yellowfin tuna, barracuda and wahoo will all happily swipe at your lures; alternately if you pull up and drop baits down to the bottom then just about anything is a possibility from a huge dogtooth tuna to stubborn red bass or even colourful coral trout.

Fishing inside the lagoons is even more exciting. Drifting amongst the brilliantly coral bommies casting surface lures about can cause explosive strikes from a wide ranging species including bluefin trevally, emperor and even Maori wrasse.

Being isolated means the only time to visit the shoals is during the dry season when there is no chance of a cyclone. Late winter to early spring is the season with the calmest weather, however, the best fishing is usually early in the middle of winter. Considering the long run out, most trips to the shoals are at least five days.

LICENSED TO FISH

Each state and territory has different fishing rules and licence requirements. See below for details and where to find out more on how and where you can get a fishing licence.

- **NT fisheries:** www.fisheries.nt.gov.au (no licence required)
- **WA fisheries:** www.fish.wa.gov.au (no licence required)
- **SA fisheries:** www.pir.sa.gov.au (no licence required)
- **VIC fisheries:** www.dpi.vic.gov.au (licence required)
- **TAS fisheries:** www.fishonline.tas.gov.au (licence required for freshwater only)
- **NSW fisheries:** www.fisheries.nsw.gov.au (licence required)
- **QLD fisheries:** www.dpi.qld.gov.au (permit required for some stocked dams only)

Fly fishing for trout. *(AMcG)*

Tasmania's Central Highlands

An inhospitable yet beautiful place, Tasmania's Central Highlands are loaded with lakes, tarns and streams. Cold for most of the year these waterways are ideally suited to trout and the brown trout, in particular, has flourished to create a world-class fishery.

Although most forms of fishing are permitted, it is fly fishing and spinning with lures that are the most productive. The best time to fish is during the warmer months when the insect life is prolific and the fish are actively feeding. The fact that the weather is a bit more stable is just another bonus!

One of the big advantages of this fishery is that a boat isn't essential and anglers patrolling the banks can often spot fish tailing in the shallows. In fact the Western Lakes, which is a massive area, can only be accessed by hiking in and is also renowned for its trophy-sized trout.

A boat will certainly be an advantage on all the larger lakes giving you access to more areas. Using your Polaroid lenses to spot fish–as they cruise along looking for food–is a challenging and very exciting way to fish. Alternately–if you are into lure casting–drifting through the drowned timber can be very productive for the persistent angler.

Found in huge numbers most the trout are around the kilo mark and are ideal for a six weight fly rod or a 2-4kg spin rod. The weather in the Central Highlands is notorious and can turn from bright blue skies to a ranging storm in the blink of an eye so always be prepared for the worst Mother Nature can throw at you.

skiing in australia

Mt Hotham, Vic.

Even though Australia's mountains are low-altitude on a world scale, facilities including lifts and snow-making are world-class, as are services such as ski instruction, slope grooming and specialist installations like half-pipes and terrain parks for snowboarders and new-school skiers.

The ski touring in areas like the Snowy Mountains in New South Wales and the Bogong High Plains in Victoria is also stunning with steep mountain faces and vast snowy plains calling to adventurers.

Resort skiers and snowboarders have five main players vying for their business—Thredbo and Perisher Blue in New South Wales and Falls Creek, Mount Buller and Mount Hotham in Victoria. Each state has some smaller areas to cater for beginners, families or cross-country skiers and Tasmania also has two minor skifields.

Falls Creek, Vic.

new south wales

Perisher Blue

In the numbers game of Australian skiing, Perisher Blue is the clear winner–a huge area that has a huge following.

Its altitude gives it the country's most reliable cover of good quality snow and its size means it has a lot of choice for skiers and boarders at every level.

There are four main centres. Perisher itself has some very good beginner terrain on its Front Valley, which also hosts a half-pipe for boarders and skiers that is generally regarded as one of Australia's best. Perisher's more challenging terrain is at North Perisher and Mount Perisher.

Smiggin Holes is a mainly beginner area which is very good for young families–most of the slopes are highly visible so parents can keep an easy eye on children.

Blue Cow and Guthega were developed as resorts in their own right and both have a balance of terrain, with Blue Cow's Kamikaze area home to some of Australia's most steep and challenging.

Both these areas have base facilities, but the main centres for accommodation, eating and entertainment are at Perisher Valley and Smiggin Holes.

- **Village elevation:** 1720m
- **Highest lifted point:** 2034m
- **Total vertical:** 355m
- **Number of lifts:** 50
- **Terrain split:** Beginner 22%; intermediate 60%; advanced/expert 18%

www.perisherblue.com.au

Thredbo

Two of the most important ingredients in a snow resort are vertical drop and reliability of snow cover–the first gives you the terrain variety and length of run, the second means you can enjoy it on your skis or snowboard.

Thredbo puts the two together very nicely, with the greatest vertical drop in Australia, consistently good quality snow on the upper mountain and, thanks to snowmaking, reliable snow cover on the lower mountain's main trails.

While many of a lesser standard enjoy the long groomed runs, Thredbo attracts a core of very good skiers and boarders with an eager eye for powder snow on the mountain and some favourite places to find it–like the Golf Course Bowl or the Bluff.

Thredbo's Friday Flat area is a good choice for beginners because it so easily accessed and has very even, encouraging terrain, although crowding can be a problem. There is also a very good children's centre based at Friday Flat.

Thredbo has a reputation for sophistication and it is well earned with a beautiful, well-run village with a range of restaurants, bars and ski shops.

- **Village elevation:** 1365m
- **Highest lifted point:** 2037m
- **Total vertical:** 672m
- **Number of lifts:** 14
- **Terrain split:** Beginner 16%; intermediate 67%; advanced/expert 17%

www.thredbo.com.au

SMALLER NSW AREAS

Charlotte Pass is like an island in the snow—deep in the heart of the Snowy Mountains beyond Perisher Blue, the only winter access is by oversnow vehicle. Removing the urban features makes for a very different snow holiday and with its gentle slopes it can be very good for families, especially younger ones with developing skiers and boarders.

Selwyn Snowfields is another good destination for families and people still learning the basics. At the western side of the Kosciuszko National Park, it offers good value, with facilities for tobogganing and snowplay as well as skiing and boarding.

www.charlottepass.com.au www.selwynsnow.com.au

NSW SKI TOURING

The Snowy Mountains has world-class terrain for alpine tourers, with the more accomplished taking on seriously steep terrain on the likes of The Sentinel or Tom Thumb.

The best access for the Main Range slopes is from Charlotte Pass, although tourers also often head out from Guthega on the far side of Perisher Blue.

For trail skiing, there are well planned and well maintained networks around Perisher and also near Selwyn Snowfields.

One spectacular but only moderately challenging touring run is from Thredbo's highest lifted point along the Ramshead Range and then through the snow gums to Dead Horse Gap (a car needs to be staged at the gap for the return to Thredbo).

Snowbiking, Perisher, NSW.
(Getty Images)

Perisher Blue, NSW. *(Getty Images)*

victoria

Falls Creek

It is generally agreed that the two most beautiful mountain villages in Australia are Falls Creek and Thredbo and, if Falls Creek has an edge, it is because the village roads are usually snow-covered and closed to conventional traffic during winter. That gives the resort an intimacy and, with the slopes in view of the village, a strong alpine flavour.

Falls Creek has very good intermediate terrain with reliable snow cover, some steep trails and some beautiful, long and challenging runs that wind their way through the snow gums.

Over recent seasons it has also become popular with snow-boarders and younger skiers for the spectacular half-pipe and adventurous terrain park constructed by resort staff.

- **Village elevation:** 1600m
- **Highest lifted point:** 1842m
- **Total vertical:** 360m
- **Number of lifts:** 15
- **Terrain split:** Beginner 17%; intermediate 60%; advanced/expert 23%.

www.fallscreek.com.au

Mount Hotham

With its village perched on the ridge top above most of the slopes, Hotham is unique in the snow world and the location delivers some spectacular views.

The nature of the terrain also means Hotham has some of Australia's most challenging skiing and boarding, with some of its steepest slopes getting the double black diamond rating.

That terrain tends to attract and develop some very good skiers and boarders who remain fiercely loyal to Hotham and get to know its qualities very well–newcomers could do worse than tag along with a local to uncover the mountain's best qualities.

Beginners have some good terrain at the area and while there is extensive terrain rated as intermediate, much of it is at the higher end of the scale.

Hotham has come a long way over the past few years, with new apartments and chalets and refurbished commercial lodges. The range of restaurants and bars is still limited but respectable.

Nearby Dinner Plain village is another base for accommodation, eating and entertainment and it also has some limited facilities for skiers, boarders and cross-country skiers.

- **Village elevation:** 1750m
- **Highest lifted point:** 1845m
- **Total vertical:** 395m
- **Number of lifts:** 13
- **Terrain split:** Beginner 20%; intermediate 40%; advanced/expert 40%.

www.mthotham.com.au www.hotham.com.au

Mount Buller

Proximity is one thing that underpins Buller's popularity–depending on their suburb, Melbournians can be on the mountain and skiing within about three hours of leaving home. Another appealing factor is the variety of terrain, especially for very good skiers and especially when there's a full cover of snow. Beyond that expert terrain, Buller has been able to build some reliability on its intermediate runs by investing extensively in snowmaking and concentrating it on long cruising runs like Little Buller Spur.

Its main beginner run, Bourke Street, is well-named–after one of the busiest strips in Melbourne's CBD–and while the pitch is good for beginners, the crowds can be a problem. Buller was initially a club mountain, but now has commercial accommodation for most budgets with interesting bars and restaurants.

Aerial skiing is one of the mountain's highlights, with the annual World Cup events in September a stage for Australia's winter Olympians.

- **Village elevation:** 1600m
- **Highest lifted point:** 1780m
- **Total vertical:** 405m
- **Number of lifts:** 25
- **Terrain split:** Beginner 25%; intermediate 45%; advanced/expert 30%.

www.mtbuller.com.au

SMALLER VICTORIAN AREAS

Mount Baw Baw, on the Gippsland or coastal side of Victoria's Alps often gets good snow falls early in the winter. Terrain is gentle and the scope limited by that fact and generally low altitude, but it is a good area for beginner and developing skiers and boarders. There are also some good ski touring prospects beyond Baw Baw and at nearby Mount St Gwinear.

Mount Buffalo, in Victoria's north east near Bright, has slopes similar in standard to Baw Baw's—possibly the main attraction of the Buffalo plateau is the ski touring, with some beautiful trails winding over snow plains, through snow gum forests and past huge granite boulders.

www.mountbawbaw.com.au www.mtbuffalochalet.com.au

VICTORIAN SKI TOURING

The main Victorian ski areas have significant trail networks for cross country skiers. Falls Creek, host of the Australian leg of the World Loppet cross country race series has the most extensive.

Falls Creek and Mount Hotham are Victoria's best launching points for accomplished tourers venturing into the Alpine National Park to tackle extreme peaks like Mount Feathertop or tour the Bogong High Plains.

Victoria has two mountains dedicated to cross country skiers. Lake Mountain, only two hours from Melbourne, has a 38km trail network, most of them groomed during winter.

Mount Stirling, neighbouring Buller, has a 75km trail network with enormous variety in the challenge of its terrain. Stanley Bowl on the southern side has some steeper, open terrain that appeals to alpine tourers and adventurous snowboarders. Both Stirling and Lake Mountain are suitable for those who want a simpler snow experience—tobogganing or building snowmen.

www.lakemountainresort.com.au www.mtstirling.com.au

Ben Lomond National Park, Tas. *(Tourism Tasmania, Owen Hughes)*

tasmania

The commercial base for Tasmanian skiing is Ben Lomond–a beautiful mountain plateau that suffers from a lack of altitude with a highest point of 1572m.

That translates to short runs in a typically short season, but there is no lack of enthusiasm in the heart of Tasmanian skiing. Ben Lomond has a vibrant village with about 450 beds, some of them commercial, but most in club lodges.

Ben Lomond is about an hour's drive from Launceston and two and a half hours from Hobart.

Mount Mawson, within the Mount Field National Park is theoretically closer to Hobart, but a 30-minute walk through forest from the car park to the skifield makes the overall time difference for the trip marginal.

Mawson's four rope tows are operated by a network of clubs that have the only accommodation on the mountain. Some additional commercial accommodation is available nearby in the national park.

The rule for skiers and snowboarders in Tasmania is simple–when the snow's on the ground, don't waste any time, it may not stay for long.

Short runs and mainly gentle terrain mean Tasmania is best suited to beginners, but the state can still offer an enchanting mountain experience.

www.ski.com.au/resorts

bushwalking in australia

Jim Jim Falls, Northern Territory. *(Tourism NT)*

A country of vast distances best covered by car or plane, Australia is also a land of tropical landscapes, stony desert and forested mountains, best explored on foot. Every state has thousands of kilometres of walking tracks in national and state parks. Picking the best is impossible, instead we have chosen six regions to highlight the country's diversity. Don't be surprised, though, if hiking in any of these places inspires you to walk in other areas covered in this book.

High Country

The Great Dividing Range, which runs down eastern Australia from the tip of Cape York to Gippsland, reaches its physical and scenic peak around the New South Wales/Victoria border. Mt Kosciuszko (2228m), Australia's tallest mountain, is the centrepiece of Kosciuszko National Park in southern New South Wales, and Victoria's highest, Mt Bogong, tops 1986m in Alpine National Park.

Many of these and neighbouring parks are the winter playgrounds of skiers and snowboarders, but snow melt reveals walking tracks that follow ridges, lead to precipices, traverse high plains carpeted with wildflowers and meander among twisted snow gums.

There is a track suitable for every fitness level, from easy nature trails to multi-night pack walks that demand high energy, good equipment, self sufficiency and alpine experience. Best bushwalking is from October to April, but even at the height of summer High Country weather can change suddenly so always carry a rain jacket, warm clothes, sun hat and water.

Mountains to Shore

Australia's island state has more than its fair share of great walks. Whether you prefer mountains or coast, remote fitness tests or nature rambles, there is a Tasmanian trail for you.

The most popular walking area is Cradle Mountain-Lake St Clair National Park, one of seven parks and conservation areas in the Tasmanian Wilderness World Heritage Area, and the six-day Overland Track is a renowned walk in spectacular but fragile alpine country. Greater challenges, for experienced hikers only, in Southwest National Park include epic walks to Federation Peak in the Eastern Arthurs and along the remote South Coast Track.

Elsewhere there are wonderful day and overnight walks on Freycinet and Tasman peninsulas, Maria Island (a 19th century penal settlement) north-east of Hobart, and mountainous Flinders Island, off Tasmania's north coast, home to tens of thousands of sea birds.

The best walking in the wilderness area is December to March, and even then you should be prepared for snow. The walking season elsewhere can be longer but check weather reports before heading out.

Coast

The third largest island off mainland Australia (after Tasmania and Melville), Kangaroo Island in South Australia has spectacular shores, abundant wildlife, and invigorating sea air.

The many natural and man-made attractions walkers can see include historic lighthouses, platypus pools, sand dunes, and the truly remarkable Remarkable Rocks in Flinders Chase National Park. Also in this park is Snake Lagoon Hike, a wonderful 2-hour walk to the isolated bay where tea-brown Rocky River meets the Southern Ocean. Signs warning of 'freak waves' are not just for show.

An 8km circuit walk further north in the Ravine des Casoars Wilderness Protection Area snakes through a ravine to limestone cliffs above another remote beach, and there are views over Investigator Strait and Yorke Peninsula from the remote Western River area on the north coast.

Winter on Kangaroo Island can be cold and windy but with appropriate equipment you can walk at any time.

South Coast Track, Tasmania. *(Tourism Tasmania)*

Arid Outback

Eroded by time from once great heights, the ancient MacDonnell Ranges run east and west of Alice Springs, in the Northern Territory's Red Centre, like arms reaching into the desert. Walking here reveals the colours and textures that inspired renowned Aboriginal painter Albert Namatjira–chalky ghost gums, buckled red rock, the purple wash of dusk and dawn–as well as a surprising array of plants and animals.

Short tracks meander up often dry rivers to permanent waterholes that can be dangerously cold for swimming, and longer ones follow ridges between gorges and climb the range for sweeping views.

Snaking 250km through the West MacDonnells, the Larapinta Trail is one of Australia's classic long-distance walks. It is divided into twelve sections graded easy to hard and all accessible by vehicle for day and overnight walks. Four companies run guided Larapinta walks. Others provide transport and food drops for independent hikers.

Spring and summer are the best walking seasons here; winter nights can be bitterly cold and summer days unbearably hot. Whatever the season or walk, carry more than your normal water load.

Sandstone Country

For a visual feast of inland Australian plants and birds and Aboriginal art in a spectacular setting, nowhere compares with Carnarvon Gorge in outback Queensland. Part of the much bigger and mostly inaccessible Carnarvon National Park, the gorge was cut by Carnarvon Creek, which now runs between soaring white sandstone walls.

The main walking track meanders 9.3km upstream to Big Bend, crossing the creek on stepping stones dozens of times (look out for azure kingfishers). Side trails lead to a dripping moss garden, natural amphitheatre, miniature water falls, rare king ferns, and two galleries of Aboriginal stencils and engravings.

Give yourself at least two days to explore the gorge. You could see most of it in two long day walks, but bush camping at Big Bend (maximum 20 people, bookings required) allows time to climb Battleship Spur for a bird's eye view of the gorge system and park. There is another great view from Boolimba Bluff, a 6.4km return walk-climb from the car park.

Rainforest

Covering the steep slopes of the McPherson Range, in the Gold Coast Hinterland, Lamington National Park is part of the Central Eastern Rainforest Reserves (Australia) World Heritage region. Hiking here reveals the sometimes subtle differences between subtropical, warm temperate and cool temperate rainforest.

You can do dozens of day walks from the two walking centres, Green Mountains and Binna Burra, and the 21.4km Border Track linking them is one of Australia's best forest trails. A highlight is two majestic Antarctic beech trees, mossy giants believed to be several thousand years old. With close relatives in South America and New Zealand and fossils in Antarctica, this species convinces many scientists that the four continents were once linked. There are also fabulous views from Border Track lookouts of Mt Warning (the volcanic core of a massive caldera) and the Tweed Range, across the border in New South Wales.

As you walk, listen–and look–for the green catbird, which makes a disconcerting cat-like cry.

Rain can flood Lamington creeks and make tracks slippery so check trails at the National Park office and wear footwear with ankle support and good grip.

The Bibbulmun Track

The Bibbulmun Track is one of the world's great long distance walk trails, stretching nearly 1000kms from Perth to Albany, through the heart of the scenic south-west of Western Australia. Boardwalks, well positioned lookouts and footbridges all form part of the trail through jarrah and karri forest, across wide plains, granite outcrops and occassional swamps and wetlands. Finally walkers reach the coast with its dense forest of miniature salt-resistant bush.

Western Australia is dry and hot, so do not rely on finding water in streams and watercourses shown on maps. It is important to carry water. In summer, this is at least four litres or more, per person, per day. There are 48 campsites along the track, spaced a day's walk apart, which contain a basic shelter, water tanks and toilets.

www.bibbulmuntrack.org.au

BEST FOOT FORWARD

- Never walk alone; three is a good group for safety.
- Pick walks suitable for the least experienced member.
- Tell someone where you are going and when to expect you back.
- Stay on marked tracks; short cuts are dangerous and cause erosion.
- Be prepared for changes in weather, no matter how short the walk.
- Carry a basic first-aid kit; also a whistle and notebook and pencil in case you get lost.
- Australia is one of the world's driest countries and ground water in even remote areas can be unsafe to drink without treatment. Carry plenty of drinking water.
- Bring out all litter you take in.
- Use only fuel stoves for cooking, unless fires are permitted and wood provided or available.
- Never feed the wildlife.

Franklin River forest. *(Tourism Tasmania)*

surfari around australia

Australians don't mind being called sons (or daughters) of beaches. They know they are spoiled when it comes to great surfing and windsurfing spots. Any time of year you will find surfers flinging their bodies, surfboards, wave skis, longboards, body boards, surfboats, kitesurfers and windsurfers onto anything that resembles a wave. At the heart of this obsession is the simple magic of being thrust shorewards on the great free-ride energy of ocean and wind.

Surfing and wanderlust seem to be inseparable bedfellows and the Australian coast has an enormous number of lures, ranging from unridden breaks on the outer Barrier Reef to the cyclone-season swells of Broome. Here is a quick whip-around of the best.

Shredding Margaret River, WA. *(Getty Images)*

Snapping off the lip, Esperance, WA. *(John Carter/Starboard)*

QUEENSLAND

Kitesurfers and windsurfers can blast off almost anywhere in the 'Sunshine State'. For Queenslanders, Tannum Sands at Gladstone is a favourite. At Seventy Five Mile Beach on Fraser Island they have the water to themselves and rarely have to avoid bathers or surfboard riders.

In the right swell Noosa National Park's waves are legendary. Along with the Gold Coast's dramatic, right-hand point breaks like Burleigh Heads they are some of the most heavily surfed waves in the country.

The Gold Coast starts on the Queensland-NSW border (the 'Banana Curtain') with the quiver of Coolangatta sandbanks that link up at times into one stupendous break known as the Superbank whose waves can barrel half a kilometre from Snapper Rocks almost to Kirra.

NEW SOUTH WALES

When the classic point surf at Byron Bay in northern New South Wales is pumping you can almost walk on water, from surfboard to malibu longboard to body board ('shark biscuit') to ski ('goat boat'), such is the intense competition for the take-off slot. Hardly a daylight metre of surfable swell goes unridden here.

Head south to Broken Head Reserve's untrammelled beaches or 18km further to Lennox Head, fabled for its powerful right-handers. The shore break rocks can be merciless on your board, but howling across those big, blue walls makes it all worthwhile.

The NSW north coast has its share of sacred surf sites. The most venerated–and well attended–of these 'green cathedrals' are at Angourie, south of Yamba. A steep take-off straight towards the rocks immediately sorts out the internal fortitude players from the wannabes.

Long lines of swell fan around Crescent Head east of Kempsey, making this ideal for longboards. Further south, Newcastle's beaches like Merewether, Cowrie Hole and Nobbys are consistent, while, in a big swell the locals ride a literally 'filthy' wave inside the Hunter River mouth.

Sydney is surf city: stick a pin in the coastal map and paddle out anywhere from Palm Beach to Cronulla. Offshore breaks like Long Reef's are perfect for windsurfers, while spots such as North Narrabeen, Maroubra and Shark Island are world-famous for their quality and competitiveness. Enclosed, wind-swept waters like Botany Bay are excellent for windsurfing and kitesurfing.

Heading south past the scores of beach breaks between Wollongong and Ulladulla, you'll find plenty of little gems such as Wreck Bay, south of Jervis Bay. Known also as Black Rock or Summercloud Bay, this intense left-hand tube is one the east coast's most revered waves.

VICTORIA

Melbourne's windsurfers and kitesurfers can rip in scores of places in both Port Phillip Bay and Western Port Bay. Meanwhile along the west coast, Bells Beach is famed for its right-hand point waves and the world's longest-running professional surfing contest, the Easter Classic.

TASMANIA

Unless you have a death-wish, you don't surf Tasmania's Ship Stern Bluff, south of Port Arthur, for fun–but for its bone crushing, 5m, 'tow-in' waves. On the northwest coast, Marrawah, one of the state's prime surfing breaks, is less life-threatening and renowned for windsurfng due to the prevaling Roaring Forties, a powerful wind current.

SOUTH AUSTRALIA

Adelaide's Semaphore Beach is good for kites and sailboards but surfers have to some head 80km south to Middleton Bay. Meanwhile at Cactus Beach, 800km west of Adelaide, desert waves and no crowds are the big drawcard. Keep an eye out for the white pointer sharks inclined do their Great Australian Bight thing.

WESTERN AUSTRALIA

Western Australia is a surf glutton's feast, from the world famous Margaret River in the south to Exmouth and even Broome in the far north, via Kalbarri and a score of desert reefs, many with fast, heavy lefts. The fabled 'Freemantle Doctor' is the power source for hordes of wind-powered action along WA's coast. Contacio's is just one of Perth's city beaches that's popular with kitesurfers and windsurfers, but the hardcore wind junkies head north to Lancelin, Geraldton or Cervantes. They don't tilt at windmills here, just at the wind. On Hansen Bay at Cervantes, windsurfers howl across the crystal-clear, blue-green water on the afternoon south-westerly, at speeds of up 60km/h.

Kitesurfing Cronulla Beach, Sydney. *(accent)*

Margaret River, WA. *(WATC)*

SO, YOU WANT TO SURF

It all seems easy.

Don't be fooled: that skinny adolescent sashaying across the face of a wave might look like a nautical rap dancer, but it took years for her or him to surf that well.

- If you want to ride waves, consider starting on a body board instead of a surfboard. Do this to learn about the power and behaviour of waves, not to mention your own arm strength.
- If you still have the determination to learn to ride a surfboard, firstly beg, borrow or rent one, then get someone to give you a few pointers.
- Learn to surf on broken waves over sand, not coral or rock, and not at a crowded urban beach. If it's a patrolled beach, observe the 'No surf craft between the flags' signs.
- Surf in the company (but definitely not in the way) of other riders and stay out of the water if it is rough.
- Beginners in surfing are told where to go—in very robust language—should they 'drop in' on a wave on which another surfer is already riding.
- Always stay clear of other riders when they're paddling or standing up. If the cussing doesn't puncture your ego, consider your body being impaled by someone else's hard, sharp surfboard. It happens, it hurts, it injures.
- The best way to start is with a few lessons at a professional surf school.
- How to choose a surf school? Ask around, especially at surf shops, although they'll probably be selling courses at a particular school.
- Check out the operation: do they have 'soft' boards in good condition; do they offer you a rash vest; are their instructors certified? Standing and carving on a board doesn't happen in a day or even a week.
- Give yourself four or five concerted days, if possible, interspersing lessons with plenty of practice. You'll know it when you hit that magical point where balance and 'the knack' come together.
- One fun way to learn is to join a surf bus tour, such as Mojosurf's five-day Learn To Surf trip from Sydney to Byron Bay. In movie terms, it's a bit like Road Trip meets Endless Summer, served with a slice of American Pie. The standard of instruction is high, as are the meals and accommodation. At first there's plenty of flailing about by the L-plate surfers, but the instructors stay in the water for hours, patiently helping each student to paddle and launching them endlessly onto waves. By the end of the trip, everyone is standing, even if briefly, as they surf with P-plates, but are ecstatic.

www.mojosurf.com.au ☎ 1800 113 044

Season: November–May.

cycle australia

At a glance, Australia is a daunting cycling prospect. The national highway is an exhaustive 12000km around with up to 300km between roadhouses and towns. Break this enormous land into parts, however, and you'll discover some of the finest cycling in the world. There's the pleasure of riding on the planet's flattest continent, thousands of kilometres of coastline to explore and just enough lumps and bumps to remind you that you have granny gears for a reason.

Any road or track can be good on a bicycle, but a few stand out as cycling destinations.

Northern Territory ride. *(ROC Tours)*

Great Ocean Road

Famed as one of the world's great scenic drives, the Great Ocean Road is an even better journey by bike. Ridden east to west–Torquay to Warrnambool–cyclists pedal just centimetres from the road's sheer drop into the Southern Ocean (albeit into the prevailing winds). The road is suited to touring or road bikes and is a ride in three distinct parts. Between Torquay and Apollo Bay, the road is winding, undulating and almost hangs over the sea. Out of Apollo Bay it ascends 500m through the lush Otway Ranges, providing one of the stiffest climbs around the mainland coast. From here, it heads west across the open cliff-top plains around the iconic Twelve Apostles.

The road is at times narrow and busy, though traffic is slowed by its serpentine course. To escape the heaviest traffic, avoid cycling during the summer school holidays or on weekends, when it can seem that half of Melbourne is driving to Lorne.

Towns are frequent along the road, and you'll need to ride no more than 70km each day, leaving plenty of time to simply enjoy this spectacular slice of coast.

Mawson Trail

Connecting Adelaide to the Flinders Ranges, the 800km Mawson Trail offers cyclists an opportunity to brush against the outback without going to extreme. This cycling route begins generously–through Australia's flattest capital–but quickly becomes a hilly challenge, climbing on rough tracks into the Adelaide Hills, and then trailing along the Mt Lofty and Flinders Ranges into distant Blinman. At times it is both rugged and steep–expect to push your bike several times–but along the way you'll pedal through two of the country's best wine regions–the Barossa and Clare Valleys–and past the Flinders Ranges' trademark natural feature, Wilpena Pound.

The route is marked with Mawson Trail logos at one-kilometre intervals and at intersections and turn-offs, and utilises fire trails, farm tracks, road reserves and quiet country roads. It's mostly on dirt surfaces, making a mountain bike the smart choice of wheels.

East Coast Tasmania

Tasmania's east coast is the most popular touring route in Australia, propelled to cycling favouritism by the beauty of the coast, the lightly trafficked road, the flat terrain and the short distances between towns–the longest gap is around 50km. Couple this to wonderful detours onto Freycinet and Tasman Peninsulas and vehicle-free Maria Island, and it's little wonder that there can sometimes seem to be as many bikes as cars on the road. Though the route is mostly flat, those who fancy hills (and pancakes) can grind up the 400m climb to Elephant Pass and the Mt Elephant Pancake Barn, near St Marys.

Relatively few cyclists continue around the west coast to complete a Tasmanian circuit, though it is a more spectacular route. What scares cyclists away are the climbs–to return from Hobart to Launceston around the west coast involves more than 4000m of ascent.

Munda Biddi, WA (ROC Tours)

CYCLING ORGANISATIONS

State and territory cycling advocacy organisations offer great features, events and benefits for members.

- **Bicycle NSW:** ☎ (02) 9218 5400. www.bicyclensw.org.au
- **Bicycle Victoria:** ☎ (03) 8636 8888. www.bv.com.au
- **Bicycle Queensland:** ☎ (07) 3844 1144. www.bq.org.au
- **Bicycle South Australia:** ☎ (08) 8232 2644. www.bikesa.asn.au
- **Bicycle Tasmania:** ☎ (03) 6229 3811. www.biketas.org.au
- **Bicycle Transportation Alliance:** ☎ (08) 9420 7210. www.btawa.org.au
- **Bicycle Northern Territory:** bicyclent@hotmail.com

Mountain bikers are represented by:
Mountain Bike Australia: ☎ (07) 4959 1913. www.mtba.asn.au

CYCLING EVENTS

Around the Bay in a Day
Spend a day riding 250km or 210km around Melbourne's Port Phillip Bay, or 100km halfway, held each October.
www.bv.com.au

Sydney to the Gong
Ride 90km or 56km, Sydney to Wollongong, through the Royal National Park and over the Sea Cliff Bridge. Held each November.
www.gongride.org.au

Alpine Classic Ride
A challenging 200km endurance ride across three of Victoria's highest climbs: Mt Buffalo, Mt Hotham and Falls Creek; held each January.
www.audax.org.au/alpine.htm

Simpson Desert Cycle Challenge
Five days, 580km, 750 desert dunes; held each October.
www.sdcc.org.au

Crocodile Trophy
One of the world's most difficult mountain-biking events, covering 1400km across the bumps of Cape York; held each October.
www.crocodile-trophy.com

Murray to the Mountains Rail Trail

Australia has around 70 rail trails open to cyclists, of which almost half are in Victoria. The showpiece trail among them is Murray to the Mountains, an 83km sealed path along the disused railway from Wangaratta to Bright, trailing along at the foot of the Victorian High Country. Following the course of the Ovens River, it provides fantastic views of granitic Mt Buffalo, and can be divided into two days by stopping a night in Myrtleford, 53km out from Wangaratta. Despite its proximity to the High Country, the trail has only one climb of any note, a 4.5km uphill haul out of Bowman to Taylors Gap.

A separate arm of the trail also leaves from Everton, climbing more steeply for 15km into the historic town of Beechworth.

www.railtrail.com.au

The Oaks & St Helena Trail

Descending from the Blue Mountains to the suburban edge of Sydney, these twin trails were once voted Australia's most popular mountain biking rides, which is testimony to cyclists' love of a long downhill run. Beginning at Woodford train station and book-ended by thigh-bursting climbs, The Oaks descends around 450m during its 30km sprint to Glenbrook train station–for most of its latter half it's not even necessary to pedal. About 5km along the track, St Helena Trail departs to the left, offering a more technical descent that includes deep sand and loose ground, rewarded with lots of tight, thrilling singletrack. The steep final climb out from Glenbrook Creek is just about unrideable if you really want to test your mountain bike or mountain-climbing mettle.

www.ozemail.com.au/~dnoble/Sydneyrides.html

Thredbo

In summer, Australian ski fields offer some of the best downhill mountain biking in the country. Foremost among them is Thredbo, at the fall of Australia's highest mountain, Mt Kosciuszko. Thredbo's major trail is the Cannonball Run, descending 600m from the top of the Kosciuszko Express chair-lift to Thredbo village.

This 4.2km trail begins on difficult terrain–a rocky and loose road–but for most of its course you can make the descent as tough or as simple as you want. There are rock gardens to negotiate, ladders to cross, a 'terrain park' featuring a range of jumps and the double-black extreme run through Snakes and Ladders. You can avoid this most difficult of sections by slipping down the leisurely Village Trail.

Before riding the Cannonball Trail it's compulsory to complete the 'Cannonball Initiation' with RawNRG, whose instructors take you over the route to familiarise you before you attack it yourself. Full-face helmets are compulsory on Thredbo and RawNRG can also pad you up like a gladiator; recommended in this rocky terrain.

www.rawnrg.com.au ☎ (02) 6457 6282

Downhill madness. *(Getty Images)*

Munda Biddi Trail

One of Australia's most ambitious cycling projects is also set to become one of its finest cycle routes. The Munda Biddi Trail is a dedicated 900km cycling path through south-west Western Australia, paralleling the famous bushwalking trail, the Bibbulmun Track. Stretching from Mundaring, at Perth's edge, to Albany and passing through some of the highest and most impressive forest in the country, the trail is expected to be completed in 2008. The first stage–332km from Mundaring to Collie–opened in 2004, with a second section through to Nannup completed in late 2006.

The infrastructure along the trail is exceptional, with camp sites established around every 40km, and each one containing water tanks, undercover bike storage and sleeping shelters that can accommodate up to 25 people. The trail is maintained and managed by the Munda Biddi Trail Foundation who have maps for sale and detailed information on their website.

www.mundabiddi.org.au

CYCLING TIPS FOR AUSTRALIA

- Never ride alone; three is a good group for safety.
- Make yourself visible. Bright, reflective clothing, a bright flag on a tall aerial and bright lights—even in daytime—will catch the eye of drivers not always accustomed to finding cyclists on the road.
- Australia's typical weather pattern sees high-pressure systems hovering over the centre of the country. The prevailing winds from these systems make anticlockwise travel most favourable for cyclists.
- When riding in hot conditions—the norm in Australia—a good way to keep your drinking water cool is to place your bottles inside a wet sock. Wind blowing through the sock will chill your water.
- Be particularly careful in the sun. Wear sunscreen that won't run into your eyes. Protect your neck, nose and arms, particularly the back of your hands. The cooling effect of wind can be deceptive and you can easily convince yourself that the burning sensation is due to the physical effort.

sailing in australia

Charter boat in the Whitsunday Passage. *(Tourism Queensland)*

Australia offers enormous variety in sailing destinations, including bustling working harbours, placid lakes and rivers, tropical reef-fringed waterways and dramatic tidal coastlines. Charter boats include skippered or bareboat (skipper yourself) and vessels range from monohulls to catamarans, sleek yachts to luxurious cruisers.

Cruising in style. *(Tourism Queensland)*

QUEENSLAND

The Whitsunday Islands

Australia's most popular cruising destination, the Whitsundays, is situated off Queensland's north-east coast. Covering 30 x 40 nautical miles the 74 islands lie in the tropics, protected from ocean swells by the Great Barrier Reef, and offer safe year-round sailing. All islands are within close proximity allowing visual navigation and keeping island-hopping passages to about two hours.

Most of the coral fringed islands are uninhabited so you can lounge on pristine sandy beaches, snorkel colourful reefs, take an island hike or visit Aboriginal engravings. Combine this with fine dining and entertainment on the seven island resorts that welcome cruisers and you've got the ideal sailing holiday.

TIP To secure specific dates it pays to book well ahead. The local cruising 'bible' is *100 Magic Miles of the Great Barrier Reef* by David Colfelt.

NEW SOUTH WALES

Sydney Harbour

Sailing past the Opera House and under the Harbour Bridge, while dodging ferries, cargo ships, passenger liners and racing skiffs, is an adrenaline-fuelled experience that offers an entirely different perspective of Sydney's spectacular harbour.

As well as city locations like The Rocks and Darling Harbour, there are islands, beaches, rivers and parks to explore, magnificent homes to ogle and waterfront restaurants to visit. You might even get to sail alongside some 'Sydney to Hobart' race contenders. Then go fishing or just anchor in one of the many secluded coves.

TIP Bareboating is for experienced skippers only. Skippered half-day, full-day and overnight charters are available. Consider including New Year's Eve for one of the world's best fireworks shows.

Pittwater and Cowan Creek

Pittwater and Cowan Creek flow into Broken Bay, 16 nautical miles north of Sydney. Pittwater, bordered by suburbia on one side and national park on the other, offers excellent sailing with sheltered beaches.

West of Pittwater, Cowan Creek extends 12 nautical miles into Ku-ring-gai Chase National Park. Almost completely surrounded by sandstone cliffs and bush-clad hills, civilisation feels a million miles away. Rugged natural beauty, native flora and fauna, deep water and protected anchorages makes for relaxed peaceful cruising.

TIP *Cruising Guide to the Hawkesbury River and Cowan, Broken Bay, Pittwater* by John and Jocelyn Powell is available from www.deerubbinpress.com.au

www.cruising-broken-bay.com

VICTORIA Gippsland Lakes

Approximately three-and-a-half hours drive from Melbourne, the Gippsland Lakes are Australia's largest inland waterway, covering $400km^2$. Comprising three lakes, three navigable rivers and numerous creeks and backwaters it offers year-round cruising. Sheltered by sand dunes from Ninety Mile Beach and bordered by national parks and farmlands, the soft-bottomed lakes are suitable for novice boaters.

Sail the expansive lakes alongside playful dolphins or potter around the placid rivers, calling into waterfront towns for supplies or a meal. Try spotting the 140 bird species or visit free-range kangaroos and koalas in the national parks. At night you can nose onto a beach or riverbank and share a bonfire with fellow cruisers.

TIP Local cruising guide is *Creeks and Harbours of the Gippsland Lakes* by Richard Hawkins.

CHARTERING

- No qualifications are required for bareboat chartering in Australia, just some previous sailing experience.
- When selecting charter companies compare their cruising areas, sailing hours, age of boats and back-up services. Look for testimonials or awards.
- Check these charter boat directories:

www.boatingoz.com.au www.charteroz.com
www.charterguide.com.au

WESTERN AUSTRALIA Kimberley Coast

Described as the last great wilderness frontier in Australia, this vast untouched coastline offers spectacular scenery, abundant wildlife and pristine waterways. Located on the northern coast of Western Australia and accessed via Broome the area is largely uninhabited.

Explore mangrove creeks, horizontal waterfalls and inland reefs. Onshore visit rainforests, freshwater rock pools and Aboriginal art. Go bird watching, crocodile spotting and whale watching or just relax and enjoy the stunning rock formations and brilliant sunsets. Fishing, mud-crabbing and oyster collecting provide fresh ingredients for lavish seafood feasts.

TIP Due to the huge tides (up to 12m), unsurveyed coastline and lack of infrastructure, only skippered charters operate here. Season March to October.

www.redsky.com.au www.shorething.com.au

SAILING SCHOOLS

- Some sailing schools offer weekend 'bareboat skipper' courses.
- You could extend existing qualifications on an ocean sailing adventure up Australia's eastern seaboard or polish your racing skills during Hamilton Island Race Week.
- Some sailing schools combine the latter two.

Bareboating the Whitsundays. *(Tourism Queensland)*

rock climbing australia

Clocks, Balls Head, Sydney. *(Simon Carter/onsight.com)*

Australia is arguably the best place in the world for rock climbing. This is the only continent that offers all styles of rock climbing—sport, traditional, bouldering and aid—at a high standard on such varied types of rock with a generally good, consistent, year-round climate. Quality climbs are found in every state and territory, on the coast and in the bush, with new routes opening every day.

A vast wealth of local knowledge is pushing the limits of international rock climbing. Australia is one of the few countries where you can camp at the base of the cliff you are climbing. Journeying to remote locations to be rewarded with classic climbing rekindles the spirit of adventure that first gripped pioneering rock climbers—an experience not often found elsewhere.

VICTORIA Grampians

Nowhere in Australia offers the same quality and quantity of climbing as the Grampians National Park. Two types of rock are found here: orange-red quartzite and sandstone, the latter providing much greater friction. The sheer cliffs and spectacular scenery are spread across 2000km^2, making this a very scenic spot to climb.

TASMANIA Freycinet Peninsula

Probably the most beautiful coastal climbing in Australia is found at Coles Bay. Nearby, 'The Hazards' is famous for its orange granite sea cliffs, which are not crumbly as is often the case on the coast of the mainland. Exposed yet safe, grades vary from 5 to 28, so you can push yourself with a hard climb or take it easy and enjoy the ocean views.

NEW SOUTH WALES Nowra

This is where some of the hardest grades were opened up, with several climbs graded at over 30 and more climbs added every year. Nowra has the best crags for sport climbing–many overhanging at 45 degrees. Most climbs are short and intense; some are less than 15 moves long. South Central and Rosies are two of the best, while Thompson's Point has good roof climbing.

QUEENSLAND Frog Buttress

Many people come here to practise and refine their crack climbing technique on the rhyolite rock, which is easier on your hands than granite or sandstone, but still remember to take your tape. There are more than 300 routes, including plenty of face climbing sport routes.

NORTHERN TERRITORY Ormiston

The West MacDonnell Ranges, 130km west of Alice Springs, has easier climbs to suit the hotter climate. Overlooking a dry riverbed, Ormiston offers about 30 moderate grade routes, all sandstone and under 30m. Be sure you don't climb in sacred Aboriginal areas where climbing is banned.

WESTERN AUSTRALIA Kalbarri

Well-known as the spot for an epic climb, the Z-bend Gorge has very difficult sport climbs and good traditional climbing. Sport climbing is steep and protected with permanent bolts, with varied grades catering for a wide range of ability, from beginner to advanced.

SOUTH AUSTRALIA Moonarie

A remote cliff in a bushy area of the Flinders Ranges, Moonarie has more than 400 routes of all grades. With such a variety of climbs, you can choose a short and pumpy single-pitch climb or test your endurance on a long, exposed, multi-pitch route up to 120m high.

ACT Booroomba

Located in the Namadgi National Park, Booroomba provides a lot of slab climbing on granite to test your balance and the friction of your shoes. Most climbs are moderate but the weather is changeable, which increases the challenge.

Tackling Tasman Island's cliffs. *(Tourism Tasmania)*

SAFE CLIMBING

- Due to the remote locations of many climbs, it is important to never climb alone and to always let someone know where you are going.
- Bring more water than you think you will need—at least three litres each—and something to eat as you may be out for most of the day.

www.climbing.com.au/index.php

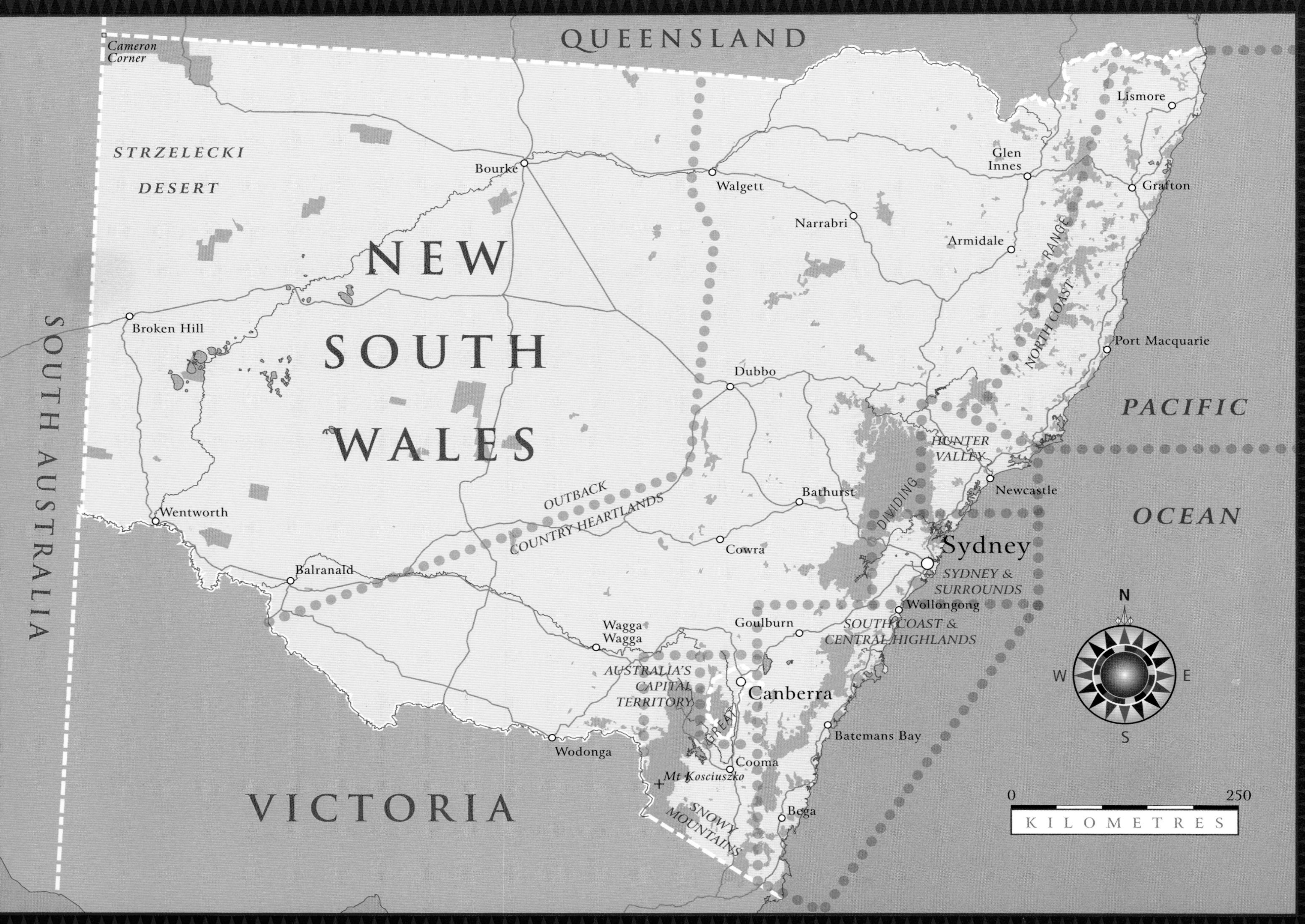
QUEENSLAND
Cameron Corner
STRZELECKI DESERT
Bourke
Walgett
Glen Innes
Lismore
Grafton
Narrabri
Armidale
NORTH COAST RANGE
NEW SOUTH WALES
Broken Hill
Port Macquarie
Dubbo
PACIFIC
OCEAN
HUNTER VALLEY
Newcastle
Bathurst
DIVIDING
OUTBACK
COUNTRY HEARTLANDS
Wentworth
Cowra
Sydney
SYDNEY & SURROUNDS
Balranald
Wollongong
Goulburn
SOUTH COAST & CENTRAL HIGHLANDS
Wagga Wagga
AUSTRALIA'S CAPITAL TERRITORY
Canberra
GREAT
Batemans Bay
Wodonga
Cooma
Mt Kosciuszko
SNOWY MOUNTAINS
Bega
SOUTH AUSTRALIA
VICTORIA
N
W
E
S
0
250
KILOMETRES

new south wales & ACT

Australia's most populous state is also its oldest in terms of European settlement—the First Fleet set up its ragged penal camp on the shores of Port Jackson in 1788 and the country's oldest, largest and most economically powerful city, Sydney, was born. NSW can be roughly divided into four main areas. The narrow coastal strip north and south of Sydney features countless beautiful beaches, coastal waterways, subtropical and temperate rainforests. It is flanked by the Great Dividing Range that runs along the eastern coast of the continent. In the south rise the snow-covered peaks of the Australian Alps, commonly known as the Snowy Mountains. West of the range are dry plains that gradually fade into arid outback and desert in the far western reaches of the state.

Blue Mountains *(Tourism NSW)*

sydney & surrounds

Blue Mountains. *(Tourism NSW)*

Balls Head, Sydney Harbour. *(onsight.com.au)*

▶ AUSTRALIA'S LARGEST CITY, Sydney, is a city that lives on the water's edge. With one of the biggest and most beautiful natural harbours in the world—that's no surprise. Sydney also boasts a string of beautiful, sandy beaches to the north and south while to the west rises the magnificent wilderness of the Blue Mountains.

Sydney is Australia's oldest city, with a wealth of history that lies just beneath the surface, waiting to be discovered. Eighteen years after Captain James Cook claimed the eastern half of the land mass known as New Holland for Britain in 1770, Captain Arthur Phillip, along with the first fleet of 11 English ships carrying convicts, sailed into Botany Bay. He established a struggling penal colony on the shores of Sydney Harbour, then called Port Jackson. Fast forward almost 220 years and the city is now home to 4 million people and welcomes more than 2.5 million international visitors each year.

NEW SOUTH WALES

PARKS/RESERVES

1. Blue Mountains National Park
2. Bouddi National Park
3. Brisbane Water National Park
4. Dharug National Park
5. Ku-ring-gai Chase National Park
6. Royal National Park
7. Sydney Harbour National Park

TAREE 51 KM

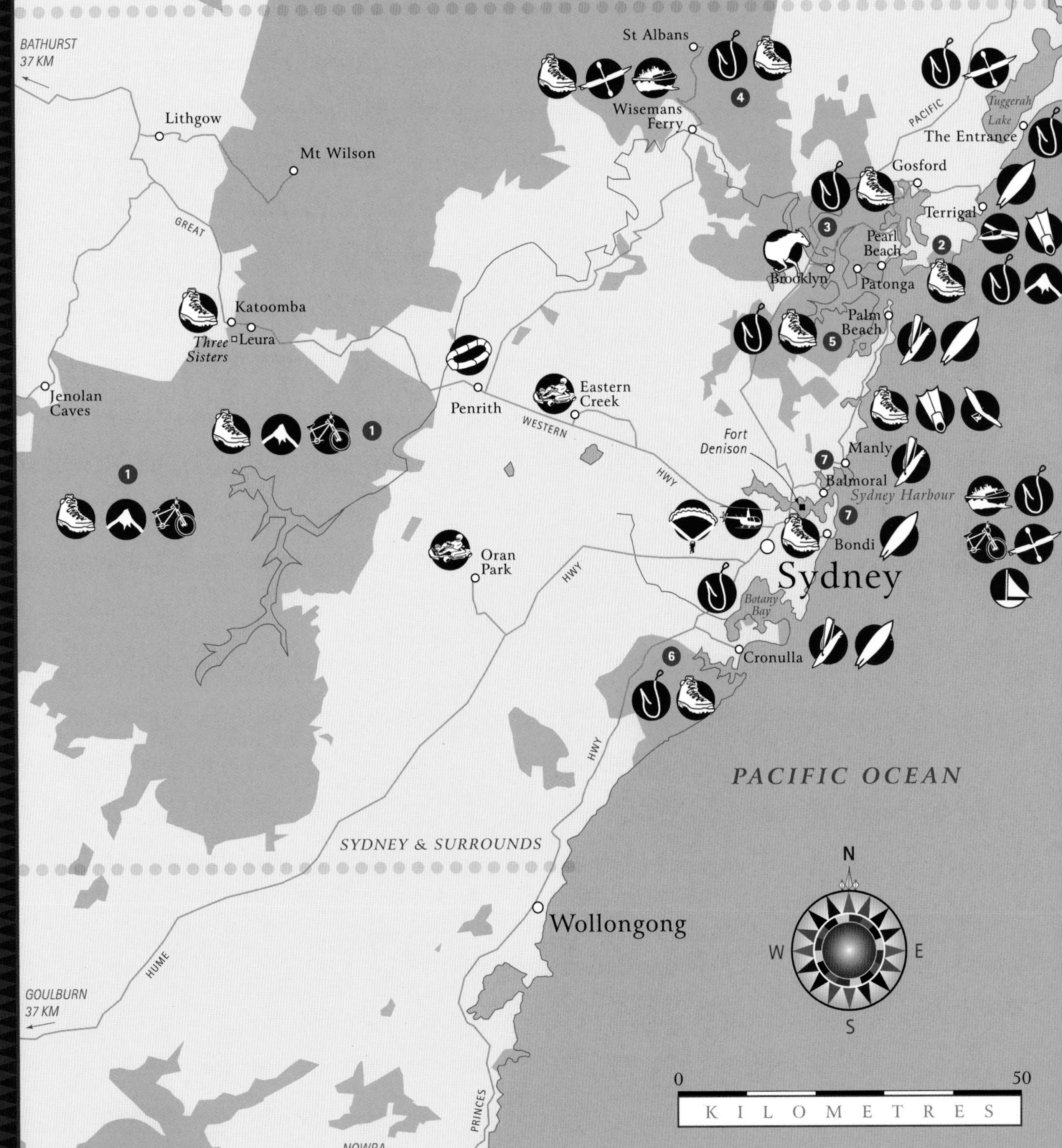

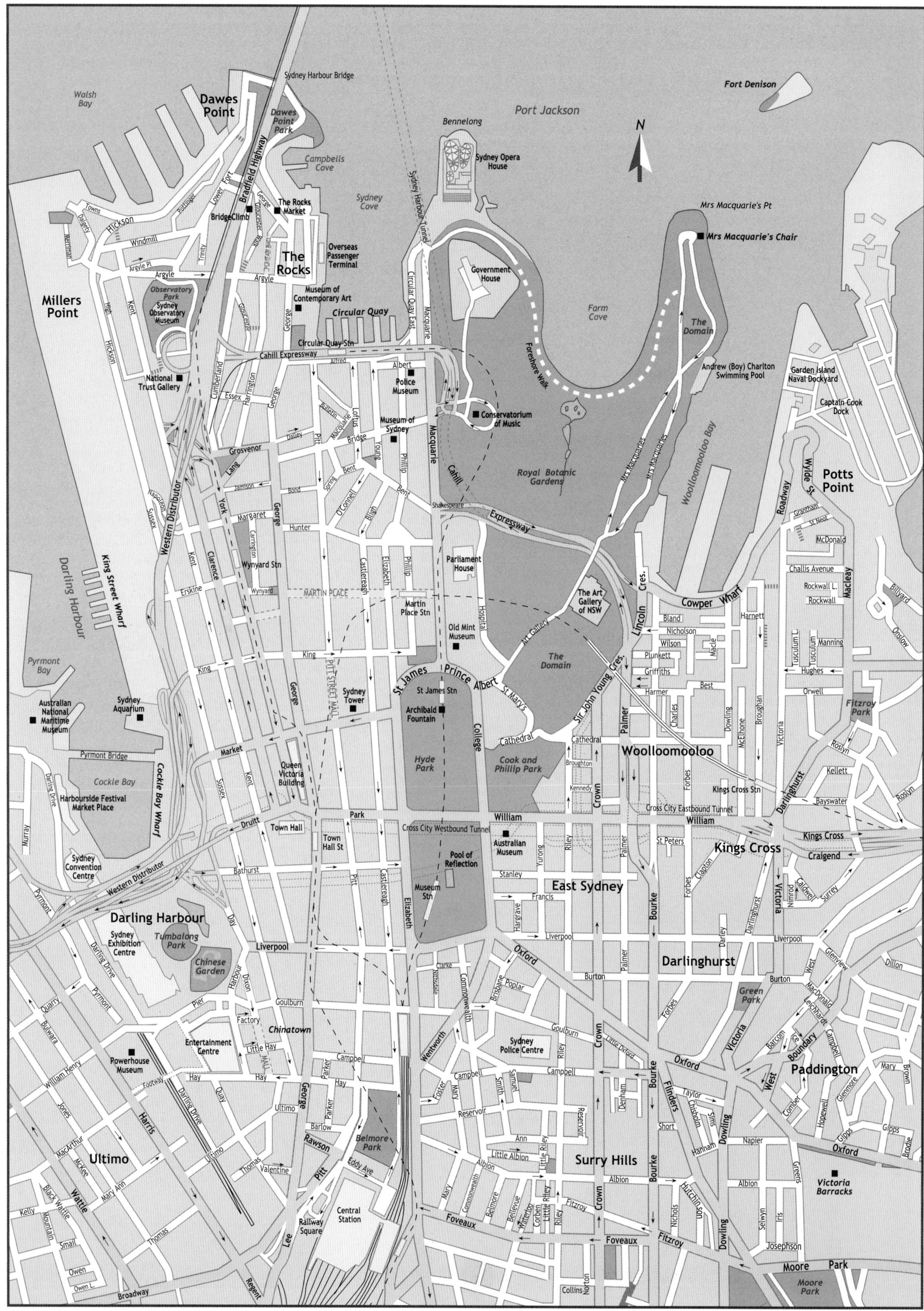

Sydney Harbour Bridge
Fort Denison
Walsh Bay
Dawes Point
Dawes Point Park
Port Jackson
Bennelong
N
Campbells Cove
Sydney Opera House
Sydney Cove
Sydney Harbour Tunnel
Bradfield Highway
The Rocks Market
BridgeClimb
Mrs Macquarie's Pt
Mrs Macquarie's Chair
Overseas Passenger Terminal
The Rocks
Government House
Farm Cove
The Domain
Millers Point
Observatory Park
Sydney Observatory Museum
Museum of Contemporary Art
Circular Quay
Circular Quay East
Foreshore Walk
Circular Quay Stn
Cahill Expressway
Andrew (Boy) Charlton Swimming Pool
Garden Island Naval Dockyard
National Trust Gallery
Police Museum
Conservatorium of Music
Captain Cook Dock
Museum of Sydney
Royal Botanic Gardens
Woolloomooloo Bay
Potts Point
Darling Harbour
King Street Wharf
Western Distributor
Wynyard Stn
Martin Place
Parliament House
The Art Gallery of NSW
Cowper Wharf
Martin Place Stn
Old Mint Museum
Pyrmont Bay
Sydney Tower
St James Stn
Archibald Fountain
Fitzroy Park
Australian National Maritime Museum
Sydney Aquarium
Woolloomooloo
Pyrmont Bridge
Cockle Bay
Queen Victoria Building
Hyde Park
Cook and Phillip Park
Harbourside Festival Market Place
Cockle Bay Wharf
Kings Cross Stn
Cross City Eastbound Tunnel
Town Hall
Town Hall St
Cross City Westbound Tunnel
Australian Museum
Kings Cross
Sydney Convention Centre
Pool of Reflection
Museum Stn
East Sydney
Darling Harbour
Sydney Exhibition Centre
Tumbalong Park
Chinese Garden
Darlinghurst
Green Park
Chinatown
Entertainment Centre
Powerhouse Museum
Sydney Police Centre
Paddington
Belmore Park
Ultimo
Surry Hills
Victoria Barracks
Central Station
Railway Square
Moore Park

The city centre

The central business district is compact and easy to get around on foot, although it is well serviced by trains and buses. It stretches from Central Railway Station and Chinatown in the west, down to Circular Quay on the harbour. Here you'll also find the historic centre known as The Rocks and many of the city's famous icons, including the white sails of the Sydney Opera House and the majestic curve of the Sydney Harbour Bridge, known colloquially as 'the Coathanger'. Most of the city's major museums and art galleries, as well as Government House, the Botanic Gardens and the NSW Parliament are all within a few blocks of each other.

The harbour foreshore and the inner suburbs

Sydney Harbour boasts more than 240km of foreshore and covers over 55km^2. Harbourside real estate is the preserve of the rich, famous and well-heeled, although Sydney Harbour National Park protects numerous quiet bays and most of the harbour's islands, including Fort Denison, a former convict prison known as Pinchgut that is now open for tours (ferries leave from Circular Quay).

Take the ferry to Manly and stroll down the Corso to the surf beach, or head further north winding though the string of beautiful beachside suburbs to Palm Beach. To the east of the city are the world-famous beaches of Bondi, Bronte and Coogee, linked by a spectacular cliff-top walking trail. Inner city suburbs, such as Kings Cross, are famous for their nightlife and restaurants and to the west, the areas around Glebe, Newtown and Leichhardt are popular for their range of cafes, restaurants, eclectic boutiques and cosmopolitan urban village atmosphere.

Blue Mountains

The massive ridge of mountainous wilderness known as the Blue Mountains is around two hours by car or train west of the city. Impenetrable to Europeans for the first 25 years of the colony, the mountains were finally crossed in 1813 by the trio of Blaxland, Wentworth, and Lawson, finally opening up the western hinterland to farming and settlement. It's an area of dramatic mountain scenery, home to the well-photographed Three Sisters rock formations and a great place to do some bushwalking or enjoy the cool mountain air. There are plenty of art galleries, historic houses, wonderful gardens and many delightful coffee shops specialising in homemade scones and Devonshire teas.

Central Coast

Two hours north of the city is an area of beachside villages and towns known collectively as the Central Coast. A favourite weekend destination for Sydneysiders the Central Coast offers a range of accommodation options for every budget, great surfing beaches and national parks with stunning lookouts, picturesque bays and Aboriginal rock engravings. The central hubs are the towns of: Gosford, where you'll find the Australian Reptile Park and Wildlife Sanctuary; the seaside resort of Terrigal, full of visitors and locals enjoying the outdoor cafes, restaurants and boutique shops and, further north, the calm waters of The Entrance, where Tuggerah Lake spills into the ocean, is a favourite with families.

The Hawkesbury

To the northwest, the Hawkesbury River winds its way to Wisemans Ferry and St Albans through rich fertile valleys and rugged sandstone ridges. It's an historic area, full of beautiful convict-built sandstone buildings, ancient (by Australian standards) pubs and sleepy villages. It's a popular place to go on a sunny Saturday or Sunday, where most people while away a large slice of the afternoon over lunch at one of the two historic pubs: Wisemans Ferry Inn or the Settlers Arms at nearby St Albans.

Cascades, Blue Mountains.

NATIONAL PARKS

Sydney Harbour National Park: includes harbour islands, vast swathes of foreshore and contains pockets of rare bushland, once common around Sydney. Highlights, apart from the beautiful views, include convict-built buildings, historic maritime and military installations and Aboriginal sites. Take a ferry to Fort Denison or one of many other islands, a night-time ghost tour of the Quarantine Station, which used to protect Australians from infectious diseases, unpack a picnic at historic Nielsen Park beside Shark Beach, swim inside a shark-netted enclosure or follow one of the many walking trails to beautiful beaches and spectacular lookouts.

Royal National Park: the world's second oldest national park (after Yellowstone in America) was established in 1879. Just 32km south of Sydney, the park features an incredibly diverse range of flora and fauna, riverside picnic areas, surf beaches, cliff-top heathland walks and rainforest cycle tracks.

Ku-ring-gai Chase National Park: on the northern edge of Sydney's suburbs, the Hawkesbury River meets the sea in a tight cluster of secretive, winding creeks, sheltered beaches, hidden coves and wide expanses of deep blue water. You'll find heathlands on the sandstone ridges, dense forests on the slopes, mangroves on the tidal mudflats and a rich Aboriginal heritage.

Blue Mountains National Park: gaze at the spectacular views from the many lookouts, or walk, cycle or drive the cliff-top paths. The park's landscapes range from exposed, windswept plateaus and ridges, to cool, damp canyons and gorges. Highlights include the view from Echo Point—with the famous Three Sisters in the foreground and the Jamison Valley and Mount Solitary behind—the Grand Canyon Track, Blue Gum Forest, historic stone staircases and beautiful forest on Federal Pass track.

Dharug National Park: one of the best parks on the Central Coast. Try the 1.6km Grass Tree Circuit or stroll a section of the convict-built Great North Road. Picnic at Mill Creek or Hazel Dell. Discovery walks, talks and tours are available year round. The park is also good for mountain biking (bikes must be walked up Devines Hill); call the National Parks office in Gosford for details on ☎ (02) 4320 4200.

Brisbane Water National Park: rugged sandstone country bordering the Hawkesbury River. Highlights are wildflowers in season and Aboriginal engravings.

Bouddi National Park: on the northern entrance to Broken Bay, 20km south-east of Gosford. Beautiful beaches beneath forests, steep hills and cliffs. All marine life is protected in its 300ha Marine Extension.

The Skillion, Terrigal. *(Tourism NSW)*

scenic highlights

In the Blue Mountains, follow Cliff Drive along the cliff tops between Leura and Katoomba for good lookout points over the Jamison and Megalong Valleys. Highlights include Leura Cascades, intriguing formations such as Mount Solitary, the Ruined Castle, Katoomba Falls and Cascades and, of course, the Three Sisters at Echo Point in Katoomba. Pack yourself a picnic and head to any one of dozens of perfect picnic spots. Wentworth Falls Lake, Gordon Falls Reserve Leura, Evans Lookout, Govetts Leap and Bridal Veil Falls in Blackheath top the list and have access to lookouts or bush-walking trails. The Three Sisters walk in Katoomba and the Fairfax Heritage Track in Blackheath are suitable for wheel-chairs. Go swimming at Old Ford Reserve, Megalong Valley or visit the Cathedral of Fern at Mount Wilson.

From Gosford, you can head south to the sleepy water-side hamlets of Patonga and Pearl Beach and explore some of the region's five national parks featuring coastal lakes, lagoons, rivers and rugged sandstone country.

Caravan and camping

Camping is prohibited in Sydney Harbour National Park, but there are camping areas in Ku-ring-gai Chase and the Royal national parks.

Popular campsites in Blue Mountains National Park include the Euroka at Glenbrook Gorge. Other good camp spots are Murphys Glen south of Woodford and Perrys Lookdown north of Blackheath.

With five national parks on the Central Coast there are lots of opportunities for camping. A favourite is Putty Beach, where you can set up camp adjacent to the car park. Gas barbecues, water and toilets are provided. You have to carry your camping gear (and your own water) 700m from the car park down to Little Beach, where facilities include gas barbecues and composting toilets. If you really want to get away from it all, the most remote campsite at Bouddi is Tallow Beach, which involves a one-kilometre walk from your car.

Visit the National Parks and Wildlife Service website for detailed information on camping spots in the National Parks around Sydney. They are very popular, especially during school holidays and on weekends, so book a site with the relevant office as early as possible.

www.nationalparks.nsw.gov.au

Commercial caravan parks are available in several locations around the city outskirts and surrounding areas. Visit:

www.visitnsw.com.au

Bushwalks

The 9.5km Manly Scenic Walkway trail starts at The Spit, which can be accessed by a range of buses from Sydney (Wynyard), and finishes at Manly–or vice versa. It hugs the harbour shoreline, taking in beaches, Aboriginal sites, community parks, forests, scrublands and even pockets of subtropical rainforest. Highlights are the sweeping views of the harbour and city skyline and historic Grotto Point Lighthouse.

The 6km Coogee to Bondi walk is a spectacular cliff-top walk that links several of Sydney's most iconic beaches and offers stunning views. See the Top 100 entry on page 30 for more information.

Following the 44km route of the original 1884 bridle track from Katoomba to Jenolan Caves, the Six Foot Track (named for its width, not its length) is a strenuous, but beautiful, walk through the heart of the World Heritage-listed Blue Mountains National Park. See the Top 100 entry on page 30 for more information.

There are dozens of walking tracks in the Blue Mountains National Park ranging from challenging seven-hour walks down gullies and along ridge spines to the 90-minute easy stroll along Prince Henry Cliff Walk, following the line of the cliff edge from Katoomba Cascades in the west to Gordon Falls, near Leura. If you like lookouts, you'll love this walk. The National Pass trail is a difficult four-hour walk that winds its way along a ledge half-way up the sheer cliffs around Wentworth Falls, but well worth doing, as is the three-hour Glenbrook Gorge Track that involves wading and boulder-hopping your way down the beautiful Glenbrook Gorge and the 5km Grand Canyon Track that goes deep into the Grand Canyon. The walk is great in summer, when you can enjoy the shade and cool waterfalls. For more walks in the Blue Mountains go to:

www.nationalparks.nsw.gov.au

On the Central Coast, the Bouddi Coastal Walk is a four-hour walk with fantastic views along the coast, including the distant Sydney skyline.

Those after a longer walk should try the 43km section of the convict-built Old Great North Road from Wisemans Ferry to Mount Manning. It takes two to three days to comfortably walk, but along the way you'll see Clare's Bridge, one of the oldest bridges on the mainland, and Circuit Flat Bridge. You can also walk into Frog Hollow, a volcanic plug. There are basic camping facilities at Ten Mile Hollow and Mogo Creek. Take plenty of water because there is no permanent water supply along the road.

Catch a wave at Dee Why Beach. *(Getty Images)*

DON'T MISS

- **Sydney Harbour Cruises:** no trip to Sydney is complete without a harbour cruise and there are several cruise operators that run cruises of varying lengths and itineraries. Head down to Circular Quay and take your pick, bookings are not normally necessary. Best value though is a trip on one of the many ferries and river cats that criss-cross the harbour to Balmain, the north shore, Manly and Parramatta.
- **Sydney Explorer:** a great way to see all the major sites, the Sydney Explorer bus visits 26 stops, from the Sydney Harbour Bridge and the Opera House to Darling Harbour and Kings Cross, with plenty in between. Onboard commentary details the attractions near each stop for you to explore at your leisure. The Sydney Explorer departs from Circular Quay approximately every 18 minutes, from early morning to late afternoon every day. You can hop on or hop off wherever you like. If you want to stay on the bus, a full circuit will take about 100 minutes. There's no need to book, just jump onboard at any of the distinctive red stops and buy your ticket from the driver.
- **Art Gallery of NSW:** one of the country's major public art galleries, it holds significant collections of Australian, European and Asian art, and presents nearly 40 exhibitions annually. Art Gallery Road, The Domain. Open daily, 10am–5pm. **www.artgallery.nsw.gov.au**
- **Museum of Contemporary Art:** Australia's only museum dedicated to exhibiting, interpreting and collecting contemporary art from across Australia and around the world, with a continually changing programme of exhibitions. 140 George Street, The Rocks. Open daily, 10am–5pm. **www.mca.com.au**
- **Museum of Sydney:** built on the ruins of the house of Australia's first governor-general, Governor Phillip, the Museum of Sydney explores colonial and contemporary Sydney through objects, pictures and new digital media techniques. Cnr Phillip and Bridge Streets. Open daily, 9.30am–5pm. **www.hht.net.au/museums/museum_of_sydney**
- **Powerhouse Museum:** a unique and diverse collection of 385,000 objects spanning history, science, technology, design, industry, decorative arts, music, transport and space exploration. 500 Harris Street, Ultimo, near Darling Harbour. Open daily, 10am–5pm. **www.phm.gov.au**
- **Australian Museum:** Australia's oldest museum, established in 1827, with unique and extensive collections of natural science and cultural artefacts. Free guided tours daily. 6 College Street, Sydney (opposite Hyde Park). Open daily, 9.30am–5pm. **www.austmus.gov.au**
- **Taronga Zoo:** spectacularly sited zoo with terrific views of the city skyline. A range of specialist tours and Sky Safari cable car as well as all the usual animal exhibits. Ferries depart Circular Quay, every quarter past and quarter to the hour. Open daily, 9am–5pm. **www.zoo.nsw.gov.au**
- **Luna Park:** one of Sydney's harbourside icons, the giant grinning face is the entry to a fun park right under the Sydney Harbour Bridge that has been thrilling Sydneysiders since 1935. Open 11am–6pm weekdays and Sunday, until 10pm on Friday night and 11pm on Saturday. **www.lunaparksydney.com**
- **Scenic World:** incorporating Scenic Skyway, Scenic Railway, and the Sceniscender. Cnr Violet Street and Cliff Drive, Katoomba. Open daily, 9am–5pm.
- **Australian Reptile Park and Wildlife Sanctuary:** Pacific Highway, Somersby, near the Gosford turn-off. Open daily, 9am–5pm. ☎ (02) 4340 1146. **www.reptilepark.com.au**
- **Hawkesbury Riverboat Postman:** cruise the river with the postman. Departs from Hawkesbury River wharf at Brooklyn. The Postman leaves at 9.30am Mon–Fri, except public holidays; returns 1.15pm. ☎ (02) 9985 7566 for bookings.
- **Barrenjoey Head:** once home to the indigenous Guringai people, is one of Sydney's most imposing headlands, complete with a spectacular lighthouse.

  Walk the steep track to the summit or climb the Smuggler's Track, built by convict labour, and be rewarded with spectacular views of Broken Bay (Hawkesbury River mouth), Lion Island and Box Head as well as Palm Beach and Pittwater. The National Parks and Wildlife Service offer guided tours every Sunday that allow visitors to climb the winding stairs to the 120-year-old lighthouse balcony for the best view in Sydney. **www.nationalparks.nsw.gov.au**

adventure activities

Adventure caving

Jenolan Caves Reserve trust has a range of adventure caving tours through several of the 280 known caves in the Blue Mountains. Elder Cave, the first 'dark' cave to be entered at Jenolan in 1848, includes several large chambers, some fine crystal and many historical signatures perfectly preserved from the 1800's. The two-hour tour provides a good introduction to the world of caving, with a series of climbs, crawls and squeezes to negotiate. The 'Plughole' is a variation on the Elder cave tour which involves entering the cave at the top of the mountain via a short abseil into a sinkhole before following the Elder Cave to its conclusion in the infamous 'S-Bend' squeeze. Mammoth Cave adventure tours involves spending six hours underground, with extensive climbing and some cave ladder work. Jenolan also offers a half- and full-day adventure abseiling inside some of the caves.

www.jenolancaves.org.au

Sydney Harbour BridgeClimb

BridgeClimb

It's a long way down from the top of Sydney Harbour Bridge (aka the Coathanger), but the view is unbeatable. The climb, which takes three hours, begins with a briefing in BridgeClimb's training centre, where you are provided with a grey climbing suit and a harness that is later linked to a static line once you reach the catwalk. Once ready, it's out on the catwalk to the pylon and climbing up the ladder onto the arch itself. It is an easy walk, just lots of steps. At all times you are attached to the static line and there is always a handrail for extra support. You will need to wear rubber-soled shoes. Bookings are essential.

www.bridgeclimb.com ☎ (02) 8274 7777

Diving with sharks

Oceanworld Manly's main oceanarium holds four million litres of water and is home to seven grey adult nurse sharks. The Aquarium runs diving with sharks programmes for both divers and non-divers where you get inside the tank and up close and personal with huge grey nurse sharks, giant stingrays, sea turtles, wobbegong sharks, moray eels and a vast array of marine life. Bookings necessary.

www.oceanworld.com.au ☎ (02) 8251 7878

Dive with sharks in the open water at Terrigal on the Central Coast. Terrigal Dive Centre runs boat trips to Foggy Cave, an underwater cave about 5km from Terrigal Beach, for experienced divers only as the dive is 40m deep. From March to the end of May, endangered sharks come here to breed and you can see up to eight sharks on any one dive.

You can play with giant stingrays, two metres wingspan, directly in front of the Dive Centre at Terrigal Beach. It's a do-it-yourself adventure if you are a basic qualified diver. Hire the gear and they will point you in the right direction. The stingrays seem happy enough to let you stroke and feed them and are present in the waters most of the year.

www.terrigaldive.com.au ☎ (02) 4384 1219

Fishing

With so many waterways, beaches and bays there are plenty of opportunities for fishing in and around Sydney. Around the harbour there's good fishing from the rocky shorelines and sandy beaches, although dioxin levels can be high in harbour-caught fish and you should not eat more than 150g of Sydney Harbour fish a month. Fish are numerous–particularly flathead, tailor, snapper, mullet, bream and jewfish. Fishing from ocean-side cliffs is dangerous and not recommended. Fishing is not permitted in marine parks, netting and spear fishing are also not permitted in many areas and it is forbidden to collect crustaceans and marine animals from the rocks in national parks. A fishing licence is required in NSW.

☎ 1300 369 365

Helicopter tours

For an unusual view of Sydney, or if you only have time for a 'flying visit', a helicopter tour is a great way to see the city and waterways. Sydney Heli Tours has a range of helicopter tours of the city and surrounds. After a quick safety briefing and weigh-in, you'll climb aboard and are soon skimming over the sands and cliffs of the south-eastern suburbs and then on to the northern beaches. Over the city airspace, the pilot circles the well known landmarks of the harbour. This section of the flight is a photographer's heaven as you snap picture postcard shots in all directions. The Coast Rush tour is a 20–25 minute thrilling flight along Cape Banks, Bare Island, Coogee Beach, Bondi Beach and Wedding Cake Island. Each passenger is guaranteed a 'window' seat (the doors are removed). Other tours include the 30-minute Grand Tour, a 20-minute Harbour Flight and the 25-minute Twilight Flight. Longer tours (two-and-a-half to five hours) are available to the Hawkesbury River, South Coast and Hunter Valley, which include lunch and touring.

www.sydneyhelitours.com.au ☎ (02) 9317 3402

Horse riding

Glenworth Valley is Australia's largest horse riding centre, set on a 3000-acre property surrounded by national park on the Central Coast. Ride to the natural rock pools for a swim or follow the creek as it meanders its way through the valley. There are 50km of wilderness trails–enjoy the freedom of free range riding or take a guided ride. All riders are given individual instruction before leaving the yards. Cattle muster rides, twilight rides, campfire dinners, overnight rides, BBQ and picnic areas and free camping packages are also available. Rides leave at 10am and 2pm weekdays, and 9.30am, 12pm and 2pm on weekends. 69 Cooks Road, Peats Ridge.

www.glenworth.com.au ☎ (02) 4375 1222

Hot laps

If you fancy yourself a bit a race driver head to Oran Park or Eastern Creek raceways and strap yourself in for five hot laps in a V8 Supercar, reaching speeds of around 230km/h down the front straight. Sessions start with a pit lane briefing before getting suited up in race overalls and helmets. Professional drivers then fire up the engine and the 600 horsepower acceleration kicks in! The awesome braking and cornering of the V8 Supercar usually comes as huge surprise, as normal driving experience bares no resemblance to what you get in a pure-bred race car. The Supercar Experience operates at two circuits in and around Sydney at Oran Park and Eastern Creek.

www.thesupercarexperience.com.au ☎ 0428 44 9414

Jet boating

A ride on Sydney's Harbour Jet is not a sightseeing tour. Sure, it's a harbour cruise (of sorts) but if your idea of seeing the sights includes a good dose of thrills and a guarantee of getting wet, then Harbour Jet is definitely the thing to do. The jet boats offer a range of trips, from 35-minute 'jet blasts' to 80-minute 'Middle Harbour Adventures'. They all offer a mixture of high-speed touring (up to 75km/h–which feels really fast when you're in a small boat being bombarded with salt spray!), 270-degree spins, wild fishtails and power brake stops that bury the nose of the boat deep into the water.

www.harbourjet.com ☎ 1300 887 373

Jet fighter and aerobatic flights

LIVE Adrenalin organise aerobatic flights on a Robin 2160 from Bankstown airport. This Canadian-built plane is a perfect vehicle for introductory aerobatics with side-by-side seating and bubble canopy. Learn to fly barrel rolls and loops or go through a full aerobatics routine with your instructor. Flights last about 50 minutes (depending on air traffic) and are one huge roller coaster ride, as wild or as tame as you wish, just let the pilot know. Alternatively, climb aboard a Pitts Special Biplane, a World War I-style open-cockpit aircraft, and hang on to your hat (and stomach) for the medium to high 'G' forces. There is no need for previous flying experience with either of the flights.

www.adrenalin.com.au ☎ 1300 791 793

Kayaking and rafting

The best way to explore Sydney Harbour is at sea level: just you, a kayak and your paddle. Sydney Harbour Kayaks offer full and half-day guided kayaking tours of Middle Harbour, Manly and Garigal National Park. Half-day tours depart Sunday mornings and include all equipment, guide and refreshments. To book, contact Sydney Harbour Kayaks.

www.sydneyharbourkayaks.com.au ☎ (02) 9960 4389

Sydney International Regatta Centre in Penrith is one of the best rowing and sprint kayak courses in the world, winning international acclaim during the Sydney 2000 Olympic Games. It is now a popular water adventure park with competition and warm-up lakes available for rowing, canoeing, sailing, fishing, kitesurfing, swimming, model boating and windsurfing. You must book online at:

www.regattacentre.com.au

Penrith Whitewater Stadium, the competition venue for the canoe/kayak slalom events during the 2000 Olympics, recreates the characteristics of a wild river and is the only whitewater course of its kind in the Southern Hemisphere. Raging white water flowing over a moveable obstacle system provides a challenging and exciting ride for even the best paddlers in the world. Available year round for white water rafting, kayaking, beach volleyball and guided venue tours.

www.penrithwhitewater.com.au ☎ (02) 4730 4333

Megalong Valley. *(Tourism NSW)*

Kitesurfing

Kitesurfing has come from humble beginnings, with a few eccentric sailors trying to propel themselves with a huge kite instead of a sail, to a full blown adrenaline sport. All you need is a wide open beach, eight knots of wind and plenty of room to slash, soar and 'boost' big aerial manoeuvres. Balmoral Kitesurfing School on Sydney Harbour offers tuition, from basic kite flying, line maintenance, safety and body dragging, to full blown boarding and launching huge airs. Equipment included.

www.sailingschool.com.au ☎ (02) 9960 5344

Wakeboarding

Wakeboarding is a relatively new board sport, created from a combination of water skiing, snow boarding and surfing techniques. As in water skiing, the rider is towed behind a boat or a cable skiing setup, but typically at slower speeds. Black Diamond Wakeboarding School is located on the Hawkesbury River and runs half hour and hour-long lessons as well as three and five-day packages.

www.blackdiamondwakeboarding.com.au ☎ (02) 4566 4511

Mountain biking

With its rugged bush setting and numerous hills, Sydney is a mountain biker's ideal playground. All around the city pockets of bush become impromptu off-road tracks as city commuters take to two wheels for several hours of adrenalin-packed adventure.

The Blue Mountains boast hundreds of kilometres of rideable mountain cycling tracks through towering forests, across windswept heath or down precipitous descents. LIVE Adrenalin run mountain biking trips for all levels, from the nervous novice to downhill expert. There are two trail choices: the Oaks trail, a classic Blue Mountains downhill ride from Woodford to Glenbrook railway station with a descent of more than 500m altitude or the Mt York trail, an advanced day for the experienced mountain biker with many long downhill stretches and climbs on single tracks. Bikes are included.

www.adrenalin.com.au ☎ 1300 791 793

Bonza Bikes is a fun way to explore Sydney's beautiful harbour foreshore and a perfect way to see the bits of the city you never see from a bus tour or taxi ride. You will smell the gardens, feel the breeze and hear the chatter of people sitting in coffee shops and strolling the pavements. The fully-guided three-hour leisurely bike ride begins at the Opera House and meanders through some of Sydney's most colourful inner city precincts. Learn about the history and culture of the Rocks and Darling Harbour, before cycling through the buzz of the city and tranquillity of Hyde Park and the Royal Botanic Gardens. Tours meet daily at 10.30am and 2.30pm, are designed for all levels of fitness and experience. Well maintained bikes are included.

www.bonzabiketours.com ☎ (02) 9331 1127

Paragliding and parasailing

Get a bird's eye view of Sydney Harbour parasailing in Manly Cove. Departing from Manly Wharf, you will be winched into the skies above Sydney Harbour on a 150m towline, achieving a maximum height from the water of 100m. Most rides last around 8-10 minutes, for a little added excitement, you can choose to be dipped in the water. The air parasail area extends from Manly Cove to the Watsons Bay side of Sydney Heads. Solo and tandem parasail adventures are available.

www.parasail.net ☎ (02) 9977 6781

Microlight Adventures offer introductory and tandem microlight flights over the beaches and hinterland of the Central Coast from their base in Port Jackson Road, Terrigal.

www.microlight.net.au ☎ 0404 808 853

Rock climbing, abseiling and canyoning

The Blue Mountains is the place to go for rock climbing, abseiling and canyoning; there are thousands of square kilometres of rainforest, canyons, plateaus and sandstone cliff-line. There are almost a dozen operators that run guided tours that include any and all of these three activities.

www.asmguides.com ☎ (02) 4782 2014
www.bluemountainstourism.org.au ☎ 1300 653 408

Central Coast Bushworks run full-day abseiling (rapelling) courses, outdoor top-rope climbing courses and a range of guided bushwalks. All equipment is supplied.

www.bushworks.info

Sailing

Sydney Harbour is a sailor's paradise and there is no better place to learn to sail on a sunny day than Sydney. Sydney By Sail is a Yachting Australia Training Centre that offers introductory level courses, covering the basics of sailing as well as competent crew courses conducted aboard a Hunter 216, a 7m sailing boat. Yachts are also available for bareboat or skippered charter. Sail training courses run all year round on weekends (midweek course can be arranged).

www.sydneybysail.com.au ☎ (02) 9280 1110

Sydney Harbour.

Enjoy morning adventure cruises and evening sunset sightseeing sails on Sydney Harbour, sailing aboard a modern, luxurious yacht with EastSail, based at Rushcutters Bay. No sailing experience required, just relax and enjoy the scenery, or the skipper will show you the basics if you wish to help sail the yacht. If you wish to learn to sail, EastSail also runs Australia's largest sailing school right on Sydney Harbour.

www.eastsail.com.au

Sail back to a more romantic time, cruising the harbour on an authentic, working, tall-masted, sailing ship. The 19th century three-masted iron barque, *James Craig*, is one of only four similar vessels in the world still sailing. It is also one of the few that are available for day trips for landlubbers. The *James Craig* sails every second Saturday. You can choose to become involved in the hauling, heaving and coiling of the ropes if you wish, or simply mooch around the deck, watching the eastern suburbs slip by and marvel at the hearty souls who climb aloft to the top of the masts to haul in the sails.

www.australianheritagefleet.com.au ☎ (02) 9298 3888

Sky diving

Sydney's only self-contained skydiving centre with private airfield is run by Sydney Skydivers. Tandem and accelerated freefall jumps are available and there is a departure lounge to cater for visitors without their own transport located near Central Station.

www.sydneyskydivers.com.au ☎ 1800 805 997

Surfing

With over 60km of surf beaches along the metropolitan coast, Sydney is a world class surfing destination and the training ground of several world champions. From Cronulla in the south to Palm Beach in the north the coast is a serious of wide, sandy beaches separated by wild, rocky headlands. Whatever the swell or wind direction there is always a perfect point break, reef, sand bank or 'bommie' to be found. The water temperatures rarely drop below 15°C, so surfing is comfortable in a light wetsuit, even in the middle of winter. In summer the water temperature rises to over 20° and everyone heads to the beach to enjoy the casual Sydney beach lifestyle, clad in as little as possible. Surf schools are set to teach everyone, from beginners to competition surfers, all along the coast and many run day or week-long surfing trips or *surfaris* to iconic breaks.

www.manlysurfschool.com

Sydney skywalk

Skywalk lets you literally walk across Sydney's skyline–a quarter of a kilometre above the city on top of Sydney Tower's golden turret, twice the height of the Sydney Harbour Bridge. The viewing platforms offer 360-degree views of the Opera House, harbour, surf beaches and all the way to the Blue Mountains, the South and the Central Coasts. Glass-floored viewing platforms overhanging the tower provide an eye-popping perspective of the city below. Skywalkers are anchored to safety rails and escorted by guides during the 95-minute adventure.

www.skywalk.com.au

Surf school, Manly Beach. *(Getty Images)*

Windsurfing

Sydney is a windsurfer's playground with a huge range of sailing locations to suit every skill level. Botany Bay is the slalom sailor's high-speed race course, open to the wind from all directions. For winter westerlies travel to the Kurnell Peninsula for clean wind. Other flat water areas for novices, bump'n'jump sailors or simply blasting around are Pittwater, Narrabeen Lakes and Sydney Harbour, especially Balmoral Beach and Rose Bay. When the summer north-east seabreeze kicks in wavesailors and ocean cruisers have a ball sailing off the ocean beaches. Sailing through the shore break can be daunting for the uninitiated, so sitting and watching others for a while is recommended. Palm Beach is a favourite haunt on the Northern Beaches, along with Newport Reef, Narrabeen and Long Reef, while Cronulla is highly recommended on the south side.

Balmoral Windsurfing School have been teaching people to windsurf and sail for over 10 years. Their centre in Mosman teaches everyone from school age to master instructors as well hiring equipment.

www.sailboard.net.au

MORE INFORMATION

- **Sydney Visitor Centre:** 106 George Street, The Rocks. ☎ (02) 9240 8788. www.visitnsw.com.au
- **Blue Mountains Tourist Information Centre:** Echo Point, Katoomba. ☎ 1300 653 408. www.bluemountainstourism.org.au
- **Central Coast Tourism:** Rotary Park, Terrigal Drive, Terrigal. ☎ (02) 4385 4430. www.cctourism.com.au
- **Hawkesbury Visitor Centre:** ☎ (02) 4588 5895 www.hawkesburyvalley.com.au

weather watch

- January: 17–29°C
- July: 5–18°C
- Winters tend to be dry and cool, while summer temperatures can get into the 30s. Storms, with heavy rain, can occur in summer, particularly February–March.

hunter valley

Gresford countryside. *(Tourism NSW)*

Hunter Valley. *(Tourism NSW)*

► THE HUNTER VALLEY, two or so hours drive north-west of Sydney, is home to some of Australia's best wineries and winemakers. It is also a favourite weekend getaway for Sydneysiders who come here for the guesthouses, hotels and boutique accommodation, good restaurants, gardens, golf and galleries. But the Hunter Valley is not just all wine and roses, it's also home to one of the state's last patches of untamed wilderness, which means it's the perfect place to really lose yourself in the bush.

To the north-east the World Heritage-listed rainforest and wilderness of the Barrington Tops sits at one of the highest points of the Great Dividing Range, high enough for the occasional dusting of snow during cold winters. The Hunter River spills into the sea at Newcastle, the state's second largest city and to the south is the saltwater paradise of Lake Macquarie.

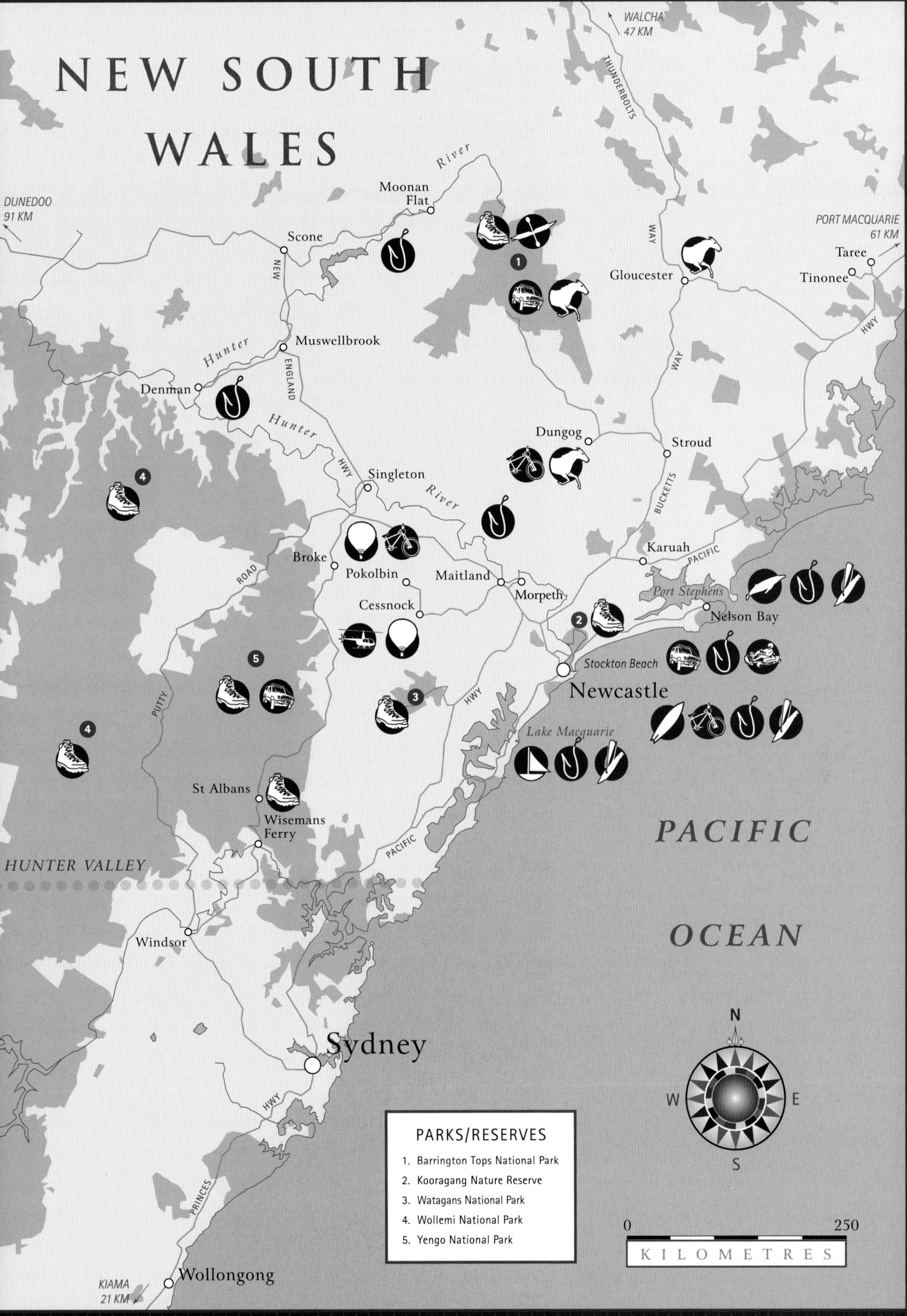
NEW SOUTH WALES
WALCHA 47 KM
THUNDERBOLTS WAY
DUNEDOO 91 KM
PORT MACQUARIE 61 KM
River
Moonan Flat
Scone
NEW ENGLAND HWY
Gloucester
Taree
Tinonee
Muswellbrook
Hunter
Denman
Hunter
Dungog
Stroud
Singleton
River
BUCKETTS WAY
Karuah
PACIFIC HWY
Broke
ROAD
Pokolbin
Maitland
Morpeth
Port Stephens
Nelson Bay
Cessnock
Stockton Beach
Newcastle
PUTTY
Lake Macquarie
St Albans
Wisemans Ferry
PACIFIC
HUNTER VALLEY
OCEAN
Windsor
Sydney
HWY
PRINCES
PARKS/RESERVES
1. Barrington Tops National Park
2. Kooragang Nature Reserve
3. Watagans National Park
4. Wollemi National Park
5. Yengo National Park
N
W
E
S
0
250
KILOMETRES
Wollongong
KIAMA 21 KM

Barrington Tops National Park. *(Tourism NSW)*

NATIONAL PARKS

Yengo National Park: one of the state's great wilderness parks stretches from Wisemans Ferry to the Hunter Valley. It's a wild area of steep gorges and rocky ridges, part of the Greater Blue Mountains World Heritage area. The northern section, near Broke, is one of the state's least known and least visited national parks. Mt Yengo is culturally significant to local Aboriginal communities and the historic Old Great North Road, an intact early 19th century convict road, follows the south-east park boundary.

Barrington Tops National Park: full of contrasts, this rugged high-altitude wilderness—carved out of an ancient volcano—rises from near sea level to 1500m. The valleys contain World Heritage-listed subtropical rainforests with subalpine woodland on the plateau. Great bushwalking trails range from easy half-hour strolls to difficult 10-hour wilderness walks and, like all sub-alpine regions, weather conditions can change quickly, so be prepared. The north of the park has numerous mountain bike trails, but the 4WD trail from Barrington Tops Forest Road to Mount Barrington is only open during summer. The park also features stunning lookouts and several beautiful picnic areas.

Wollemi National Park: is part of the Greater Blue Mountains World Heritage Area and is a maze of canyons, cliffs and undisturbed forest. In 1994 a bushwalker discovered the Wollemi Pine, a rare example of a 200-million-year-old tree species, known from fossil records and presumed extinct. It is now the focus of extensive research to conserve and propagate this species.

Kooragang Nature Reserve: 9km north of Newcastle, this is the largest single estuary wetlands reserve in NSW, a magnet for migratory shorebirds and there are good bird viewing areas near Stockton Bridge. You can also visit the Kooragang Wetlands, a rehabilitation project on Ash Island, and explore the mangroves along the boardwalk.

Watagans National Park: the headwaters of the Congewai, Quorrobolong, Gap and Dora creeks, which flow into the Hunter River and Lake Macquarie, are all in this swath of forest south of Cessnock. Rainforest walks and lookouts are highlights and the many creeks are great places to cool off.

Newcastle

First settled in 1804 as a penal colony for some of the worst Sydney convicts, the camp at the mouth of the Hunter River grew to become one of the colony's most important industrial centres on the strength of its rich coal deposits in and around the surrounding valley and the nearby subtropical forest full of cedar. For most of the 20th century Newcastle was the heart of the Australian steel industry but today, the city has shaken off its heavy industrial image and has emerged as an attractive waterfront city with spectacular beaches and a fabulous collection of historic architecture.

Lake Macquarie and Port Stephens

To the south of Newcastle, Lake Macquarie is a huge expanse of saltwater, four times the size of Sydney Harbour. To the north, 32km of constantly shifting sand dunes separate the city suburbs from Port Stephens, a large harbour home to a resident pod of around 160 bottlenose dolphins and a prime koala habitat. The calm blue waters and sandy beaches of both areas offer plenty of water activities, from boating and fishing to surfing and swimming.

Barrington Tops

The rugged cliffs and cool-temperate and subtropical rainforests of the Barrington Tops and Gloucester Tops are part of the Mount Royal Range, which runs north-south and reaches a height of 1577m at Polblue. The pretty country towns of Gloucester and Dungog are the two main gateways. The green foothills that surround both towns are studded with wilderness retreats that offer extensive horse riding trails and the rivers have some great white water sections good for kayaking and rafting when water levels are high enough.

Lower Hunter

The Lower Hunter Valley area around Cessnock and Pokolbin is one of the most important and best known wine producing areas in the state, and this is where you'll find the bulk of the Hunter's wineries, guesthouses, restaurants and other tourist attractions. But it wasn't always about the wine. Beneath the fertile soils that nurture the grapes are rich coal seams that are still mined today. Maitland, established in the 1820s to service the surrounding farms and coal mining villages, is full of beautiful historic buildings and nearby Morpeth's historic buildings house a collection of art and craft galleries and gift shops that are very popular on weekends.

Nobbys Head, Newcastle. *(Tourism NSW)*

DON'T MISS

- **Wineries:** see www.winecountry.com.au for detailed listings of more than 120 wineries. Most are open for tastings and sales daily, 10am–5pm.
- **Hunter Valley Gardens:** 8km of pathways to wander among the 12 themed gardens, including a storybook garden for the kids. Open daily, 10am–5pm. **www.hvg.com.au**
- **Hunter Valley Cheese Factory:** watch cheese being made, go on a cheese making tour, or simply browse the well stocked produce room for just about anything you need to build a picnic. McDonalds Road, Pokolbin. Open daily, 9am–5.30pm.
- **Campbell's Store:** 13 speciality craft shops at 175 Swan Street, Morpeth. Open Thu–Sun, 10am–5pm. ☎ (02) 4933 1407.
- **Royal Australian Infantry Corps Museum:** lots of guns, but also some great exhibits giving charming snapshots of the human side of the infantry. Singleton Army Camp, Lone Pine Barracks, Singleton. Open Wed–Sun and public holidays, 9am–4pm. Closed November.
- **Hunter Valley Harvest Festival:** various venues throughout the Hunter Valley during March and April. **www.winecountry.com.au**
- **Fighter World:** aviation museum located next to the entrance to Royal Australian Air Force Base at Wiliamtown, the home of Australia's Strike/Fighter Force. Open daily, 10am–4pm. **www.fighterworld.com.au**
- **The Newcastle Police Station Museum:** inside the Hunter Heritage Centre building which functioned as a Police Station from 1861 until 1982. 90 Hunter Street, Newcastle. Open Fridays and Saturdays, 11am–3pm.
- **Newcastle Region Art Gallery:** more than 3300 works of art, presenting a comprehensive overview of Australian art from colonial times to the present day. Laman Street, Newcastle. Open Tue–Sun, 10am–5pm.
- **Fort Scratchley:** a former military fort overlooking Nobbys Beach built between 1881 and 1886 that was used to defend Newcastle in 1942 when a Japanese submarine surfaced shelling the city. It's now a maritime museum. Open Tue–Sun, 10.30am–4pm.
- **The Wetlands Centre:** wetland rehabilitation project in the lower Hunter incorporating coastal freshwater lagoons and marshes and non-tidal freshwater forested wetlands. Activities include bushwalking, canoeing and birdwatching. Sandgate Road, Shortland. Open daily, 9am–5pm. **www.wetlands.org.au**
- **Walka Water Works:** restored pump house classified by the National Trust on the outskirts of Maitland. Built in 1887 it is one of the oldest water works in NSW. Inside the ornate brick building there is a working model of the original pump and a teahouse. Beside the lake there are barbecues and picnic tables. 55 Scobies Lane, Maitland. Open daily.
- **Maitland City Art Gallery:** specialises in exhibiting local artists, one of which is Margaret Olley. 230 High Street, Maitland. Open Tue–Sun, 10am–5pm.
- **Maitland Gaol:** 150 year-old gaol closed in 1998 and now open for tours led by ex-inmates, including spooky evening torchlight tours. John Street, East Maitland. Open daily. **www.maitlandgaol.com.au**

scenic highlights

The Bucketts Way

The rolling hills and twisting turns of the Bucketts Way between Karuah and Taree is a country road in its truest sense—there are bits that are more like a goat track than a highway, but most of the time there'll be little traffic and the scenery is some of the prettiest you'll find in country NSW.

First stop is the historic village of Stroud, home of the International Brick and Rolling Pin Throwing Competition each July. Most of the buildings along the main street date from the 1830s and many are convict built.

Gloucester is around half an hour away. The mountains behind the town are known as the Bucketts, and the inspiration behind the road's moniker. From Gloucester, the Bucketts Way continues on to Tinonee, full of local craft shops and art galleries, and Taree.

Barrington Tops Forest Road

The Barrington Tops Forest Road runs from Gloucester along Tourist Drive 29 up over the mountains and through the national park to emerge on the western side of the range at Moonan Flat, not far from Scone and is a must-do day trip when in the area. Although sections of the road are unsealed it is fine for conventional cars. The panoramic scenery along the route is breathtaking as you pass from the grassy foothills into the rainforest and up onto the plateau and there are numerous places along the way to stop at lookouts for short walks and picnics.

Barrington Tops. (Tourism NSW)

Upper Hunter

The Upper Hunter, bounded by Singleton, Denman and Muswellbrook also features great wineries, although not many as the Lower Hunter. Scone is one of the world's largest thoroughbred horse breeding centres, eclipsed only by Kentucky in America. Take a drive around the district and you'll see air-conditioned stables with facilities that rival many of the Hunter's five-star hotels and guesthouses.

Caravan and camping

The most popular camping spots are in Barrington Tops National Park. Polblue camping area is suitable for cars, caravans and camper trailers an hour and a half from either Gloucester (70km) or Scone (76km). It can get chilly at night, but there are some lovely short walks through snow gum woodland, tall eucalypt forest and areas of high-altitude swamp that leave from the campground.

Horse Swamp on Tubrabucca Road and Gloucester River camping ground, off the Gloucester Tops Road, where red-necked pademelons, brush turkeys and lyrebirds wander, are suitable for caravans and camper trailers. There are good swimming spots nearby. Those without a caravan can camp at Devils Hole, with spectacular views over the Barrington wilderness and farmlands.

Four-wheel-drive camping spots include the Gummi Falls camping area on Bullocky Brush Trail, the Junction Pools camping ground, which also has some great swimming holes but, at 1440m the water can be cold, and the Little Murray camping area on the edge of Little Murray Swamp at 1490m. Both campgrounds are off the Barrington Trail, which is closed to all vehicles during winter.

There are also several walk-in campgrounds and you can bush camp anywhere in the park as long as it is at least 200m from any road or track.

You can also camp at Finchley camping ground in Yengo National Park and further south in Watagans National Park. There are also several commercial caravan parks in the region.

Bushwalks

There are literally dozens of good walking trails in the Barrington Tops. Thunderbolts Lookout is a 20-minute easy stroll through snow gum woodland and a small patch of Antarctic beech to a spectacular view on the edge of the escarpment. Polblue Swamp Track is a circuit walk around the Polblue Swamp near the campground that winds in and out of the forest. It's a good walk for spotting grey kangaroos and the occasional wombat. The slightly longer Jerusalem Creek Trail is a one-way downhill walk to Jerusalem Creek Falls. You can return the same way (uphill) or walk 2.5km back along the road to the picnic area. The Antarctic Beech Forest Track starts at the parking area on the Gloucester Tops Road and is a pleasant 90-minute loop through cool temperate rainforest full of Antarctic beech and tree ferns and beside mossy creeks. Keep an eye out for the rufous scrub-bird, one of Australia's rarest birds. Link three short walks (Antarctic Beech Forest Track, Gloucester Falls Track and River Track) for a four-hour Gloucester Tops circuit.

The 7km Carey Peak Trail is a one-way walk over the plateau to Careys Peak from the Barrington Trail following the rim of the escarpment. If you like a challenge, try the 20km, 10-hour Corker Trail from Lagoon Pinch to Careys Peak, a long, steep climb to the Barrington Tops Plateau and down again. It's a serious walk through the Barrington Wilderness–you need to be fit, well prepared for weather changes, carry topographic maps, compasses and your own water.

The Tops to Myalls Heritage Trail is a 220km walk that begins at Lagoon Pinch and finishes at the seaside town of Tea Gardens. If you can cope with the 9km ascent along the Carey's Peak trail, the rest of the walk is mainly downhill. The track has 10 designated campsites and takes 11 days to walk.

adventure activities

Redhead Beach, Lake Macquarie. *(Tourism NSW)*

Aerobatic flights

Action Aerobatics will take you into the wild blue yonder on an aerobatic scenic flight in an open cockpit Pitts Special Biplane. There are also Trojan Fighter Bomber flights available and you can even train to become an aerobatic pilot here.

www.aerobatics.com.au

Ballooning

Like many of Australia's popular wine-growing and weekend getaway areas, the Hunter is a popular place to go hot air ballooning and there are several operators who offer dawn flights over the valley. Almost all include champagne breakfasts afterwards and transport to and from the launch/landing place. Balloon Aloft is one of the longest running ballooning outfits, originally flying in Canowindra, the country's ballooning capital in the central west of the state, while Cloud 9 Balloon Flights offer flights over Sydney and the Hunter Valley.

visit www.balloonaloft.com ☎ 1800 028 568

www.cloud9balloonflights.com

Cycling

Enjoy the freedom of cycling in beautiful vineyard surrounds. Bicycle tours are a popular way to tour the Hunter's wineries, sample the fresh air and burn off a few calories. Hunter Valley Cycling organise a Wine and Wilderness, self-guided bicycle tour that covers 50km over two days including tandem or mountain bike hire, luggage transfers, accommodation, dinner, maps and road-side assistance, should you run into trouble–or sample too much wine.

www.huntervalleycycling.com.au

Grapemobile Bicycle Hire operate from their Grandvin Estate in the heart of the Pokolbin vineyards. Their Mountain to Valley adventure is a picturesque downhill run from Pokolbin Mountain Lookout, high above the vineyards, to your choice of vineyard for wine tasting, cheese sampling, chocolate gorging and other indulgences. You can devise your own itenary, letting Grapemobile supply the bikes, maps helmets and sunscreen, as well as wines at wholesale prices. Pedal to a local restaurant for lunch or simply take a picnic along a quiet country lane.

www.grapemobile.com.au ☎ 0418 404 039

Newcastle has a number of cycle tracks along the foreshore and throughout the city. The new Fernleigh Track is a shared cycleway that follows a former railway corridor, complete with the restored (and illuminated) railway tunnel, originally opened in 1892. You can also ride from the mangroves at Carrington via the convict timber yard to Nobbys Breakwater at the mouth of the Hunter River. For bike hire contact Fishers at Honeysuckle: ☎ (02) 4926 2722. You can download cycle trail maps from the Newcastle Visitors Information Centre.

http://www.newcastletourism.com/pages.asp?code=53

The Dungog Pedalfest is an annual three-day cycling event in and around the Williams Valley forest and farmland near Dungog–a celebration of cycling and sociability over the second weekend in September. Events include guided tours through the history of the valley, music, dancing and food at the historic Bandon Grove School of Arts, a film night at the Dungog Picture Theatre, local markets and an assortment of cycling activities for all ages and abilities.

www.pedalfest.org.au

Dolphin and whale watching

Port Stephens is home to some 160 bottlenose dolphins so there's a good chance you'll spot some of one of the many dolphin and whale watching cruises that visit the harbour year round.

Whale watching season is from June to November all along the east coast. You can see humpbacks, minke, southern right, sei and brydes whales passing on their annual migration to the warm northern waters to breed. Because the islands and headlands off Port Stephens extend so far east, the whales come in very close to the mainland.

The best way to see the whales is on the water, but they can also be seen close to the shore from Fingal to Anna Bay. Look for the whale blow as they come up to breathe. On a good day, whales can be seen as far away as 2km, surfacing for four or five breaths every four to eight minutes. Watch these enormous mammals wave their tails or jump nearly clear of the water as they breach. You'll never forget the sound and splash as a 40 ton humpback slam dunks. A number of companies offering dolphin and whale watching cruises, ranging from simple day trips to evenings of luxury with dinner and drinks.

www.imaginecruises.com.au www.moonshadow.com.au

Fishing

Port Stephens is a popular summer fishing spot good for both land and boat-based fishing, with luderick (blackfish) one of the most common catches, especially around estuaries and rock walls. Other catches include flathead, whiting and bream. Head to Broughton Island for good snapper fishing. Stockton Beach is also popular, especially for those searching for pipis. Thousands of the clam-like shellfish live in the sands here, thanks to strict bag limits. You may dig pipis for bait if you are fishing on the beach, but remove even one beyond the high-water mark and you'll face an on-the-spot fine of $500 and up to six months in prison. The stringent rules protect both pipis and humans as the shellfish are particularly susceptible to contamination by the naturally occurring algal blooms in the water, can be toxic to humans and must be tested before consumption.

The rivers of the Upper Hunter contain both rainbow and brown trout, the rainbows are the most commonly caught.

Off-road driving

The Barrington Trail 4WD track runs off Barrington Tops Forest Road, to Little Murray Camping Area, Mount Barrington and a walk-in campsite at Junction Pools. The trail leaves Barrington Tops Forest Road 1.7km east of Polblue Swamp. The carpark, information shelter and gate are just off the main road. The trail is closed 1 June to 30 September and may be closed at other times due to weather conditions. Some 4WD tour companies specialise in the Barrington and Gloucester areas. Contact the Gloucester Visitor Information Centre for details.

The 4WD-only Old Settlers and Yengo tracks in the northern section of the Yengo National Park wind their way along the tops of two sandstone ridges above steep rocky gorges. There are some great Aboriginal rock carvings, lots of wildlife and extensive wilderness views. The track is well marked, but finding the right access into the park is difficult due to a lack of roadside signs and a deep creek crossing just inside the gate. Contact the National Parks and Wildlife Service for detailed directions and track information before you go.

www.npws.nsw.gov.au ☎ (02) 4320 4200

Horse riding

The mountain forest trails near Gloucester and Dungog and around the Hunter offer some of the prettiest horse riding in the state. Dozens of properties combine guided trail rides with overnight accommodation, ranging from rustic farm stays to five-star wilderness retreats. Contact the closest visitor information centre for more details.

Kayaking and rafting

The Barrington River offers great whitewater kayaking, especially for novices, with rapids to grade 3. Barrington Outdoor Adventure Centre runs one and two-day mountain biking, canoeing, and kayaking tours. Canoe Barrington also run tours as well as canoe and kayak hire.

www.boac.com.au www.canoebarrington.com.au

The Steps Wilderness Retreat offer accommodation options from four-star to camping beside the Barrington River, run guided river trips and hire inflatable kayaks, if you want to go it alone.

www.thesteps.com.au

Upper Hunter Valley. *(Tourism NSW)*

Snorkelling at Port Stephens. *(Tourism NSW)*

Sailing

Australia's largest coastal lake, Lake Macquarie is a favourite sailing spot with good smooth water sailing. Budget Sailing School specialises in courses for backpackers, including a two-day mid-week Lake Macquarie cruise on a veteran 10m yacht. Snorkel, fish, swim and sunbathe while you learn to handle the sails, steer the boat and much more. They also have one-day introductory sails and a range of courses from competent crew to yachtmaster.

www.budgetsailingschool.com

Master Class Sail Training provide full-day, half-day and twilight cruises on Lake Macquarie aboard a luxury modern 13m yacht. They will provide full catering or you can bring your own. Full weekend cruises are also offered.

www.winddancer.com.au

Windsurfing

Lake Macquarie, the Myall Lakes and Port Stephens provide fantastic flat-water sailing experiences, with beaches and bays that can be sailed in winds from every direction. Port Stephens is the top spot to harness a roaring winter westerly. Wavesailing beaches around Newcastle are famous for their variety and sweet ramps. For helpful information, lessons and board hire try Board Crazy in Belmont.

www.boardcrazy.com.au ☎ (02) 4947 7131

Sandboarding

Stockton Beach, with 32km of immense sand dunes that spill into the ocean from Newcastle to Port Stephens is the place for sandboarding. Sandboarding employs the same principal as downhill snowboarding, but on sand. If you snowboard or skateboard then sandboarding should be an easy cross-over for you. If you have never boarded before, sitting, rather than trying to stand on your board is just as much fun.

Surfing

As the training ground for four-time world surfing champion, Mark Richards, Newcastle and surrounding beaches offer an abundance of prime surfing breaks catering for all levels of ability. Newcastle's surf is pretty consistent. The morning offshore breeze seems to reliably funnel down through the Hunter Valley. Spots like Merewether can be incredible on their day, behind the baths, peeling way down the beach. If you haven't surfed before, or want to hone your skills, the Newcastle Surf School has classes teaching beginners how to ride a surfboard, surf awareness and surf safety while intermediate surfers can learn how to turn, to take off and drop down a forming wave and surfing manoeuvres. Advanced classes include technique improvement with video, contest strategies and fitness training under the guidance of Daniel Frodsham, a former competitor on the World Qualifying Series.

www.pacificdreams.com.au ☎ 0405 500 469

Quad biking

For fun on four wheels join a quad-biking tour of Stockton Beach's sand dunes. Sand Safaris runs tours, for beginner and experienced quad bikers, of the dune system on rider-friendly Honda TRX 350 quad bikes. Each tour covers 30–40km of terrain, taking in environmental and historical sites of significance, including WWII defence lines, sea birds and the largest shipwreck washed up on the east coast of Australia. Advanced riders can take a specialised tour through some of the most intense dune sections.

www.sandsafaris.com.au

MORE INFORMATION

- **The Wine Country Visitors Information Centre:** Main Road, Pokolbin. ☎ (02) 4990 4477. www.winecountry.com.au
- **Gloucester Visitor Information Centre:** 27 Denison Street, Gloucester. ☎ (02) 6558 1408. www.barringtons.com.au
- **Newcastle Visitor Information Centre:** 361 Hunter Street, Newcastle. ☎ (02) 4974 2999. www.newcastletourism.com
- **Port Stephens Visitor Centre:** Victoria Parade, Nelson Bay. ☎ 1800 808 900. www.portstephens.org.au

weather watch

- January: 18–31°C
- July: 6–17°C
- The Hunter Valley has a temperate climate with temperatures rarely reaching extremes, though it can be very humid in January. March and April is harvest time and there are lots of special events, winemaker's dinners and vintage parties, festivals and fairs.

north coast

Dorrigo . (Tourism NSW)

Cape Byron. (Tourism NSW)

▶ THE COASTLINE OF NORTHERN NSW, from north of Newcastle to the Queensland border, is classic beach holiday territory. A string of beautiful beaches, punctuated by rocky headlands and patches of national park wilderness, backed by rainforest-clad mountains, picturesque rolling hills and farmlands cut through with wide, sometimes raging, rivers draws thousands of holiday makers to its sunny shores each summer. Travel through the area in winter though, when days are sunny and mild, and you'll more than likely have the beaches and parks all to yourself.

The first Europeans to move into the region were convicts, with a penal settlement established in Port Macquarie in 1823. Cedar cutters who were initially stationed around the Hunter region followed the convicts north, reaching the Macleay in 1837, the Clarence in 1838 and moving further north to the Richmond River in 1842. Logs transported on the rivers were intercepted at ports downstream before being shipped to Sydney. Once the cedar was logged out, farmers moved in, farming cattle, dairy, crops and sugar cane.

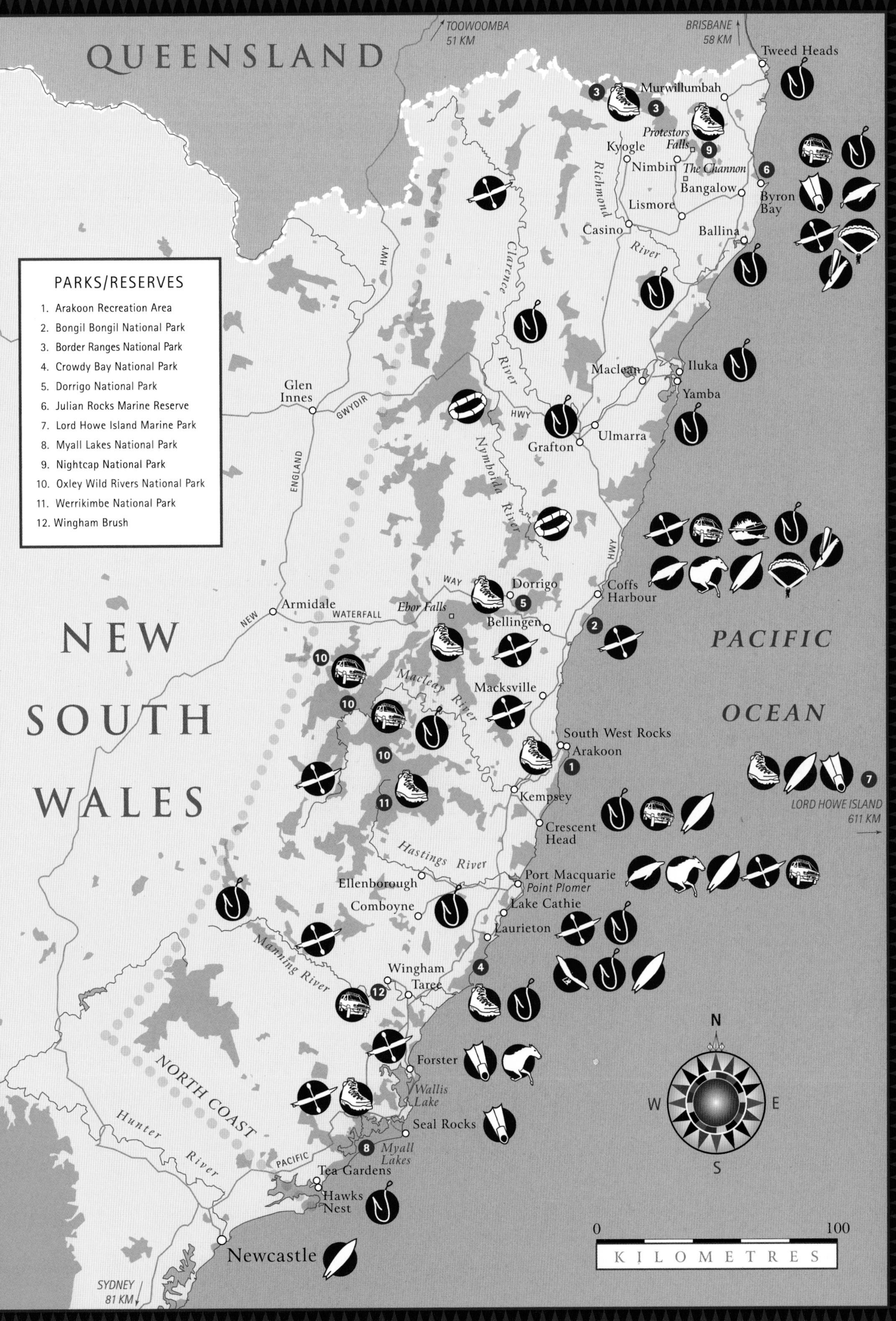

QUEENSLAND
TOOWOOMBA 51 KM
BRISBANE 58 KM
Tweed Heads
Murwillumbah
Protestors Falls
Kyogle
Nimbin
The Channon
Bangalow
Byron Bay
Lismore
Casino
Ballina
Richmond River
Clarence River
HWY
PARKS/RESERVES
1. Arakoon Recreation Area
2. Bongil Bongil National Park
3. Border Ranges National Park
4. Crowdy Bay National Park
5. Dorrigo National Park
6. Julian Rocks Marine Reserve
7. Lord Howe Island Marine Park
8. Myall Lakes National Park
9. Nightcap National Park
10. Oxley Wild Rivers National Park
11. Werrikimbe National Park
12. Wingham Brush
Maclean
Iluka
Yamba
Glen Innes
GWYDIR
HWY
Ulmarra
Grafton
ENGLAND
Nymboida River
HWY
WAY
Dorrigo
Coffs Harbour
Armidale
NEW
WATERFALL
Ebor Falls
Bellingen
NEW SOUTH WALES
PACIFIC OCEAN
Macleay River
Macksville
South West Rocks
Arakoon
Kempsey
LORD HOWE ISLAND 611 KM
Crescent Head
Hastings River
Port Macquarie
Point Plomer
Ellenborough
Comboyne
Lake Cathie
Laurieton
Manning River
Wingham
Taree
N
W
E
S
Forster
Wallis Lake
NORTH COAST
Hunter River
Seal Rocks
Myall Lakes
PACIFIC
Tea Gardens
Hawks Nest
0
100
KILOMETRES
Newcastle
SYDNEY 81 KM

NATIONAL PARKS

Myall Lakes National Park: in spring, the heath lands are ablaze with scented wildflowers, banksias, flannel flowers, lilies and flowering gums. Despite the annual human invasion there is an abundance of wildlife: kangaroos, wallabies, possums, bandicoots, gliders, echidnas, goannas and ample birdlife. Great for camping, swimming, bushwalking, boating, about 20km from Hawks Nest.

Wingham Brush: nature reserve and home to 100,000 grey-headed flying fox *(Pteropus poliocephalus)* at Wingham.

Crowdy Bay National Park: the sculpted rock formations of Diamond Head tower 100m above Crowdy Bay near Laurieton. Australian author Kylie Tennant lived and wrote beneath the headland, and her hut has been restored. At low tide explore the rocks and pools below the cliffs. There's good fishing, birdwatching and headland walks with abundant wildlife.

Sea Acres Nature Reserve: the second largest coastal rainforest reserve in NSW. A 1.3km boardwalk lets you walk through the rainforest without harming sensitive eco-systems. Pacific Drive, just north of Lighthouse Beach, Port Macquarie.

Arakoon State Recreation Area: beachside picnic and camping area, Trial Bay Gaol and access to Smokey Cape Lighthouse. 3km east of South West Rocks near the village of Arakoon.

Dorrigo Rainforest Centre: interpretive centre and gateway to the national park. Includes Skywalk canopy boardwalk and the Canopy Café. Dome Road (off the main road to Coffs Harbour), Dorrigo National Park.

Nightcap National Park: 35km north of Lismore. World heritage rainforest saved by a determined group of conservationists, including Protestors Falls. The Mt Nardi and Minyon Falls areas are easily reached by car and offer breathtaking views. Whian Whian Forest Drive (unsealed) is off the Lismore-Mullumbimby road. Camping is prohibited.

Border Ranges National Park: World Heritage rainforest park on the rim of a vast, ancient volcano. Enjoy views and tall forests on the walking track network. The Tweed Scenic Drive (unsealed), a loop from Murwillumbah to Kyogle and Lismore, is a highlight. There is car-based camping at Sheep Station Creek or Forest Tops. To get there drive 38km west of Murwillumbah off the Summerland Way or Kyogle Road.

Julian Rocks Marine Reserve: this marine reserve off Byron Bay provides resting and nesting grounds for many seabirds, such as seagulls and cormorants, and is a great diving spot where you'll see grey nurse sharks, docile leopard sharks, wobbegong sharks, turtles, cuttlefish, schools of white spotted eagle rays, egg-cowry shells, moray eels, banner fish, giant guitar fish and shovel-nose rays.

Lord Howe Island Marine Park: the marine park surrounding Lord Howe Island contains the world's southernmost barrier coral reef, 300 species of algae (around one-tenth of which are unique to the area), 450 species of fish (also around one-tenth unique to the area) and 120 species of mollusc. Green and Hawksbill turtles are common in summer, but may be observed throughout the year. Lord Howe is the only place in Australia where such a diversity of fish, coral, algae and associated creatures can be seen by snorkelling just a few metres from the beach.

Nightcap National Park. *(Tourism NSW)*

Myall Lakes

The twin towns of Tea Gardens and Hawks Nest are around three hour's drive north of Sydney. There is a koala sanctuary here and you'll often spot koalas around the village streets, as well as a resident pod of dolphins that is often seen from the beaches. Forster, where Wallis Lake meets the sea, is a busy holiday resort town but you can still find moments of peace, like eating local oysters or fish and chips with the pelicans on the wharf outside the fish co-op.

Mid-north coast

The mid-north coast, nicknamed the Holiday Coast, is bordered by Taree on the Manning River to the south, through to beachside Port Macquarie at the mouth of the Hastings River and north to Coffs Harbour, also right on the coast. All three are large, but pretty, towns that swell to several times their normal population during the summer holiday season. Beyond these three regional centres, the somewhat sleepier villages of Crescent Head (famous for its right-hand surf breaks) and South West Rocks boast great beaches and Bellingen in the valley behind Coffs is a great place for browsing and eating in the cafes and galleries that line the main street.

Far north coast

Byron Bay is the most popular holiday spot on the far north coast, full of cafes, restaurants and boutiques that attract year-round holiday crowds. It's Australia's most easterly point and watching a sunrise from the lighthouse is a rite of passage for many young Australians, especially on New Years Eve. It is also a great place to watch whales between June and October. At Easter, Byron is home to the East Coast Blues Festival, one of the biggest Blues Festivals in the country.

In the surrounding hinterland, The Channon is home to the famous its craft markets on the second Sunday of each month. If you miss them, most stall holders move with the markets between Byron

Lord Howe Island. *(Tourism NSW)*

Bay, Nimbin, Bangalow and The Channon on alternate weekends. To the north is Tweed Heads, to the south is Ballina, straddling the mouth of the Richmond River and the pleasant inland towns of Lismore, Casino and Grafton, famous for its Jacaranda trees which paint the town purple each October. The historic 19th century river port of Ulmarra has a collection of galleries, antique shops and craft shops, and nearby Maclean calls itself 'the Scottish town in Australia'–many of the shops and street signs highlight the Scottish heritage of the village.

Lord Howe Island

Around 550km east of Port Macquarie, Lord Howe Island is one of the east coast's best kept secrets. Just 11km long and barely 2km at its widest point, the World Heritage-listed island is home to the world's most southerly coral reef, pristine beaches where king fish swim around your ankles (Ned's Beach was named the cleanest beach in Australia in 2005 by the Keep Australia Beautiful Council), beautiful kentia palm forests, a vast array of rare birdlife and one of the most challenging bushwalks in Australia, the climb to the summit of Mount Gower. Lord Howe is a two hour flight from Sydney, Brisbane or Coffs Harbour.

Caravan and camping

Mungo Brush in Myall Lakes National Park is very popular with campers and caravanners so you'll need to book:

☎ (02) 4984 8200

Car-based and caravan camping is available at Diamond Head, Indian Head and Kylies Beach. Fees apply. Bring your own drinking water, firewood is sold on site.

The Hastings Forest Way is a wonderful drive that provides access to several terrific camping sites including: Wild Bull camping area on the banks of the Wilson River, and Bluff Picnic Area where there are several secluded campsites.

In the far north there are not a lot of wilderness camping options in the popular national parks but Border Ranges National Park has some great camping spots with nice swimming. There is car-based camping at Sheep Station Creek or Forest Tops.

Caravanners are spoilt for choice: there are caravan parks in almost every town in the region, many are right on the beach, but you will need to book ahead in the summer holiday season. See local visitor information centres for details.

DON'T MISS

- **Tobwabba Arts:** Aboriginal art co-op. 10 Breckenridge Street, Forster. Open Mon–Fri, 9am–5pm. **www.tobwabba.com.au**
- **Timbertown:** Pioneer village. Oxley Highway, Wauchope. Open daily.
- **Norfolk Punch:** herbal drinks, gardens, wildlife refuge and kitchen museum. Batar Creek Road, Kendall. **www.norfolkpunch.com.au**
- **Koala Hospital:** Macquarie Nature Reserve, Lord Street, Port Macquarie, Open daily. Feeding times are 7.30am and 3pm.
- **Trial Bay Gaol:** built in 1877, closed in 1903 and reopened in 1915 to hold internees from Germany during WWI, who were allowed out onto the beaches during the day but locked up at night, this is a gaol with a view. It's now a museum. Arakoon State Conservation Area near South West Rocks. Open daily, 9am–4.30pm.
- **Lighthouses:** there's a string of lighthouses along the northern NSW coast. Worth looking at Sugarloaf Point lighthouse in Myall Lakes National Park, Crowdy Head north of Taree at the fishing village of Harrington, Tacking Point Lighthouse at Port Macquarie, Smoky Cape at South West Rocks and Cape Byron on Australia's most easterly point.
- **Bowraville Folk Museum:** High Street, Bowraville, Wednesday and Friday 10am–11.30pm, Tuesday and Saturday 10am–3pm, Sunday 11am–3pm, daily 10am–3pm during school holidays.
- **Bunker Cartoon Gallery:** Australia's only gallery of cartoons housed in a WWII bunker. Cnr Hogbin Drive and Albany Street, Coffs Harbour. Open daily, 10am–4pm.
- **Coffs Harbour Regional Art Gallery:** Cnr Coff and Duke streets. Open Wed–Sun, 10am–4pm.
- **The Big Banana:** Australia's first 'big thing'. Guided plantation tours and toboggan ride. Pacific Highway, Coffs Harbour. Open daily, 9am–5pm. **www.bigbanana.com**
- **Pet Porpoise Pool:** kiss a sea lion and see porpoises, sharks and penguins. Orlando St, Coffs Harbour. Shows 10.30am and 2.15pm daily.
- **Thursday Plantation:** Tea Tree plantation, factory, visitor's centre, shop and sculpture garden. Pacific Highway, Ballina. Open daily, 9am–5pm. **www.thursdayplantation.com**
- **Lismore Regional Art Gallery:** 131 Molesworth Street, Lismore. Open Tue–Fri, 10am–4pm, Sat–Sun, 10.30am–2.30pm.
- **The Nimbin Museum:** a nostalgic and slightly off-beat look at hippie culture. Cullen Street, Nimbin.

Nimbin shop. *(Lee Atkinson)*

scenic highlights

Nymboida River. *(Tourism NSW)*

Take the coast road to Mungo Brush deep inside Myall Lakes National Park. This shady, lakeside camping and picnic spot is one of the most popular spots in the park. The road rejoins the main Pacific Highway at Bulahdelah, but don't stay on it for long—the Lakes Way to Forster winds through Bulahdelah State Forest and along the shores of Myall, Smiths and Wallis Lakes. Turn-off to the surfing mecca of Seal Rocks, a sleepy fishing village where fishermen sell shells outside their boat-houses and the pace of life is gently quiet. Walk up to Sugarloaf Lighthouse, on the point overlooking the beach, swim and sunbake on the soft sandy beach or play in the rock pools.

Port Macquarie hinterland

To explore the hinterland follow Tourist Drive 8 from Taree to Wingham to walk through Wingham Brush with its resident flying foxes and then on to Ellenborough Falls. You can take the 642 steps to the bottom or follow the much easier walk through the rainforest to view the falls from the other side of the gorge.

The village of Comboyne is perched high on an open plateau and surrounded by lush farmland and rain-forest, and if it wasn't for the distinctly Australian bird calls ringing out of the bush, the green patchwork hills could be in Yorkshire, England. From Comboyne, the road winds its way back down the mountain rainforest towards Wauchope.

Ocean Drive

Take the coast road from Kew through Laurieton to Port Macquarie. It cuts through heath-covered sand dunes, over headlands with views along endless beaches and skirts the shores of Lake Cathie (pronounced 'cat-eye'). In spring the land is carpeted in Christmas bells and flannel flowers. In Laurieton, the lookout at North Brother Mountain has views over the Camden Haven and its expanse of waterways and beaches.

The Waterfall Way

This classic drive starts on the mid-north NSW coast at the banana-rich, beach resort town of Coffs Harbour and coils its way through lush rainforest of the Great Dividing Range to the New England Tablelands and finishes in Armidale. Highlights include Bellingen with its strip of cafes, galleries and alternative markets; mountain-top Dorrigo, smothered in rainforest with its spectacular skywalk over the rainforest canopy; and the high plateau gorge country. Of waterfalls there are plenty, with the pick of the bunch being Dorrigo's Dangar, Ebor, Wollomombi (the highest in Australia) and Apsley.

The northern rivers hinterland

From Murwillumbah head south-west to Nimbin, capital of the 'Rainbow Region', so-called for the rainbows often seen in the area (it's a high-rainfall district) as well as the alternative lifestyle of many locals in this area that was the heart of the 1970s hippie movement. Shopfronts in the main street are deco-rated with colourful murals and a range of craft shops sell new-age goods. Take a short drive out from The Channon to Protestors Falls, site of one of the first conservationist protests in Australia. It's a 15km drive along a gravel road that tunnels through the rainforest. There is a maze of local roads that wind through the valleys, in and out of pockets of rainforest, along ridge tops and through sleepy villages in this area. The views are fabulous and there are plenty of roadside stalls selling fresh fruit, vegies and macadamias.

Summit of Mount Gower, Lord Howe Island. (Lee Atkinson)

Bushwalks

With so many national parks in the region there are hundreds of great bushwalks.

The Miners Beach Walking Track is a pretty walk from Town Beach to Lighthouse Beach at Port Macquarie with timber walkways over two rocky outcrops, a timber staircase down onto the beach and a whale watching vantage point on the headland.

In Dorrigo National Park the Dorrigo Skywalk is a dramatic boardwalk above the rainforest canopy that leads out over the edge of the escarpment for spectacular views across the rainforest and down to the coast. The Wonga Walk is a two-and-a-half-hour walking track that takes in stunning sections of rainforest, waterfalls and views.

The climb to the summit of Mount Gower on Lord Howe Island is not for the unfit or those with a fear of heights or dodgy knees. It's a 10-hour return climb from sea level to 875m at the summit and involves lots of ropes and narrow ledges, but, if you're at the top when the clouds break, it really is like being on top of the world. Walk is only open to those who go with a licensed guide.

In Mount Warning National Park you can walk to the summit. It's a challenging trail particularly in the hotter months, because most of it is steep. The return trip can take four to five hours so be sure to leave enough time to get back before sunset. Near the top you'll find a chain to help you up the last of the climb. Keep in mind that under local Bundjalung law, only certain people can climb Mount Warning. Consider respecting the Bundjalung people's wishes.

In the Border Ranges National Park the Pinnacle Walk is a 20-minute walk and one of the highlights of the park. No other walk in the region offers such a dramatic encounter with the Mount Warning crater. The first part of the walk is through subtropical rainforest. Closer to the escarpment edge you emerge out of the rainforest into a stand of New England blackbutt. The track finishes at a lookout platform perched at the edge of the escarpment. From here you have spectacular views of Mount Warning and the Tweed Valley 1000m below. It's one of the best locations in Australia to watch the dawn–the silhouette of Mount Warning against the rising sun should not be missed.

Protestors Falls in Nightcap National Park is a 45-minute easy walk that winds its way through bangalow palms to the base of Protestors Falls at Terania Creek Picnic Area. Swimming is not permitted in the area as it is home to the endangered Fleay's barred frog.

adventure activities

Humpback Whales on annual migration.

Camel Safaris

Port Macquarie Camel Safaris will take you on a camel ride along beautiful Lighthouse Beach in Port Macquarie. Rides are usually 20 minutes or an hour. Ask at the visitor information centre for more details.

www.portmacquarieinfo.com.au

Diving and snorkelling

Fix yourself a date with a nurse and dive the Pinnacles near Forster–swim with large grey nurse sharks, schooling king and jew fish and large bull rays. Visibility is up to 30m and temperature a balmy 18-24°C. Dive Seal Rocks for fantastic shark encounters plus the wreck of the SS *Satara*. At 125m in length this is the biggest diveable ship wreck in NSW. Hailed as one of the best 10 dive spots in Australia, Fish Rock Cave near South West Rocks has an amazing diversity of life, as well as superb visibility and water temperature that is good all year round. Close to the continental shelf, you'll see turtles, spotted eagle rays, huge schools of pelagic fish, coral forests, grey nurse sharks and more.

www.southwestrocksdive.com.au www.fishrock.com.au

Julian Rocks Marine Reserve near Byron is another great diving spot.

With the most southerly coral reef in the world, 90 species of coral and 500 species of fish, Lord Howe Island is a premier dive and snorkelling spot. For those that prefer to stay dry there are also a number of glass bottom boat tours available.

Dolphin and whale watching

Whale season is May to November and there are countless good vantage points from beaches and headlands along the coast. The Water Rats in Port Macquarie specialise in whale-watching expeditions on a high-speed, high-powered Special Forces boat. Outside of whale season there's still lots of thrills while dolphin and bird watching.

www.aquaticbluecharters.com.au ☎ (02) 6583 8811

Also in Port Macquarie, Port Venture Cruises run two-hour tea cruises and four and five-hour barbecue cruises. Boom nets tow you behind the boat while dolphin spotting. Whale and dolphin watching cruises are also available in Coffs Harbour and Byron Bay.

www.portventure.com.au ☎ 1300 795 577

Fishing

The entire north coast is a fisho's paradise. Along the Camden Haven River there are many boat ramps, fish cleaning tables and picnic areas. Chat to the locals along the break wall about the best fishing sites. Yamba is another great fishing spot. According to the locals 'virtually every fish you can catch' can be caught around here, in the river, off the beach or along the rock wall. Together, Yamba and the village of Iluka across the wide river mouth, is home to one of the biggest fishing fleets in the state. Hook yourself a monster from the deep on a deep sea fishing charter off Crowdy Head, Port Macquarie, Coffs Harbour or any of the towns further north. Your catch of the day could include snapper, marlin, dolphinfish, pearl perch, kingfish and jewfish.

Fishing at Yamba. *(Tourism NSW)*

Off-road driving

Best off-road wilderness opportunities are to be found in the Werrikimbe National Park near Wauchope. The Racecourse Trail links the east and west sides of the park and Coachwood Road gives 4WD access to the north. From these trails you can reach the Youdales Hut Visitor Area in Oxley Wild Rivers National Park, which is just north of Werrikimbe National Park. There's also a great 4WD-only road from the North Shore of Port Macquarie following the coast to Point Plomer past fantastic picnic spots and surfing beaches to Crescent Head.

If you don't have your own 4WD vehicle, join one of the many 4WD tours run out of Port Macquarie, Coffs Harbour and Byron Bay that explore the mountainous hinterland beyond the coast.

Hang-gliding, paragliding and microlighting

Soar like an eagle over spectacular mountain rainforest and white sandy beaches of the Camden Haven, south of Port Macquarie, with High Adventures in their fleet of paragliders and microlights. You can fly alone or in tandem.

www.highadventureparagliding.com ☎ 0429 844 961

Further north, the Byron Bay Gliding Club operate joyflights and trial instructional flights in powered gliders (MotorFalkes, G109, Dimona H36), flying over Byron Bay Lighthouse and beyond to Mt Warning. Their courses are designed to take the new pilot to solo stage in the shortest possible time.

www.byrongliding.com ☎ (02) 6684 7627

Horse riding

Clarendon Forest Retreat offers rainforest rides to residents and visitors through 40,000 acres of the Kiwarrak forest in the hills behind Forster. Most levels of riding ability–including children from six years upwards–are catered for, with challenging rides for the more experienced. Coates Road, Possum Brush.

www.cfr.com.au ☎ (02) 6554 3085

Bakers Creek Station, a 1000-acre property on a tributary of the picturesque Nambucca River, also offers two-hour horse rides through spectacular rainforest in the mountains and valley as does Valery Horse Trails and Bushland Trail Rides, both on the Coffs coast.

www.coffscoast.com.au

Kayaking and rafting

There are lots of places to put a kayak into the water on the north coast. Top spots include the magnificent waterways of Wallis, Smiths and Myall lakes, including the Bombah Broadwater or sea kayaking off the beaches. If you don't have your own kayak or canoe you can hire one from most of the larger towns or take a kayaking tour from Coffs Harbour, Port Macquarie and various other places along the coast. The Valley of the Mist Wetlands Canoe and Gourmet Bushtucker Brunch tour near Macksville will introduce you to a huge variety of water birds in the Congarinni wetlands and Bongil Bongil National Park; see what really does come out to play when there's a full moon on a Bellinger River Full Moon canoe tour; and at Byron Bay you can combine dolphin

Surf rafting, Coffs Harbour. *(Tourism NSW)*

watching and kayaking with Dolphin Kayaking, using two-person, sit-on-top kayaks visiting local dolphins and other marine life in the shallow coastal waters of Byron Bay.

www.dolphinkayaking.com.au ☎ (02) 6685 8044

The Nymboida River has some of the best white water rafting anywhere in Australia. Try a full day tour down the Nymboida, or a half-day adventure on Goolang Creek. There are a number of rafting companies to choose from, you'll find more details at the Coffs Harbour Visitors Centre.

www.coffscoast.com.au

Not sure if you'd rather go rafting or surfing? For the best of both worlds try surf rafting–white water rafting on the ocean–on the beaches at Coffs Harbour.

www.surfrafting.com

Sky diving

Coffs City Skydivers offer tandem skydives and Accelerated Freefall (AFF) first jump courses at Coffs Harbour and Byron Bay Skydiving Centre is just five minutes north of the Byron Bay town centre on Tyagarah airstrip. Take in the coastal and hinterland views as you plummet to the ground on a tandem jump or the solo course.

www.coffsskydivers.com.au ☎ (02) 6651 1167
www.skydivebyronbay.com ☎ (02) 6684 1323

Surfing

Many of Australia's best surfers learnt to ride the waves on a north coast beach or point break. Summer for Sydney residents often means a trip to the coastal beaches for a seaside holiday. Once they become independent, Aussie teenagers head off on the obligitory surfari to Meccas such as Byron Bay, Seal Rocks and Scotts Head. Crescent Head is famous for its swell and there are great beaches up and down the length of the coast–take a drive and take your pick. If you've never surfed before sign up at one of the numerous learn-to-surf schools at One Mile Beach near Tomaree National Park, Port Macquarie, Scotts Head, Coffs Harbour or Byron Bay. There are campsites close to many surf beaches, but booking is essential during school holidays.

Experience the thrill of surfing a wave with Surfing Byron Bay surf school, who cover Byron Bay, Lennox Head and Brunswick Heads. Running courses of half a day to five days, they teach surfing basics, how to assess the conditions–rips, currents and wave conditions–and how to choose the right equipment.

www.gosurfingbyronbay.com

Windsurfing and kitesurfing

The beaches and breaks that are so loved by Australian surfers are also ideal playgrounds for windsurfers and kitesurfers, especially when the summer seabreezes crank in from the north east. Lennox Head, Coffs Harbour and Byron Bay are favourites with wavesailors, but flat-water sailors and novices are spoiled for choice too. Lake Ainsworth is an

Beachside Paragliding. (Tourism NSW)

ideal learning spot with camping on site at Lennox Head. Smiths and Wallis Lakes offer wide-open shallow water for blasting slalom runs, freestyle training or just exploration. The water is seldom more than waist deep, warm and totally shark free.

The harbour and river at Ballina is also a prime sailing spot when the breeze is pumping, but beware of the fast moving current and practice your self-rescue technique before launching.

Jordan's Boating Centre and Caravan Park, located on the beautiful Hastings River at Port Macquarie, teach windsurfing and sailing and of hire equipment, including kayaks and catamarans.

www.jordans.com.au ☎ (02) 6583 1005

weather watch

- January: 18–27°C
- July: 7–19°C
- These temperatures are for the coast. The hinterland has slightly greater extremes, and can get quite cold at night in winter. The far north coast enjoys a year-round subtropical climate with an average temperature of 25° Celsius.

MORE INFORMATION

- **Taree and Manning Valley Visitor Information Centre:** Manning River Drive, Taree North. ☎ 1800 801 522. **www.manningvalley.info**
- **Port Macquarie Visitor Information Centre:** Clarence Street, Port Macquarie. ☎ (02) 6561 8000. **www.portmacquarieinfo.com.au**
- **Coffs Coast Visitor Information Centre:** cnr of Marcia Street and the Pacific Highway, Coffs Harbour. ☎ 1300 369 070. **www.coffscoast.com.au**
- **Kempsey Visitor Information Centre:** Pacific Highway, South Kempsey. ☎ (02) 6563 1555, Freecall 1800 642 480. **www.kempsey.nsw.gov.au**
- **Lord Howe Island: www.lordhoweisland.info**
- **Lismore Information Centre:** cnr Ballina and Molesworth Streets. ☎ (02) 6622 0122.
- **Ballina Information Centre:** cnr River Street and La Balsa Plaza. ☎ (02) 6686 3484.
- **Grafton Information Centre:** Pacific Hwy. ☎ (02) 6642 4677.
- **Byron Bay Visitor Information Centre:** 80 Jonson Street, Byron Bay. ☎ (02) 6680 8558. **www.tropicalnsw.com.au**

south coast & southern highlands

Cathedral Rocks, Minnamurra. *(Tourism NSW)*

Skydive the beach.

▶ THE STRETCH OF COASTLINE south of Sydney to the Victorian border is one of the prettiest in the country with fine, white sand beaches punctuated with rugged, rocky headlands and backed by rainforest-clad mountains, lakes, rivers and fertile farmlands. Having managed to so far escape the worst of coastal development, it's a place of simple pursuits like surfing and fishing from the beaches, bushwalking, camping by the sea and browsing through the antique shops and art galleries in historic country villages.

First settled by whalers and timber getters in the 19th century, the forests and annual whale migration are now two of the region's biggest drawcards. Every town and village seems to have its own fishermen's co-op selling fresh catches of the day, the lush dairy farms in the hills produce some fantastic cheeses and the fertile fields yield an amazing array of fresh fruit and vegetables and some very good wines. So grab yourself a blanket, an empty picnic basket, and head south.

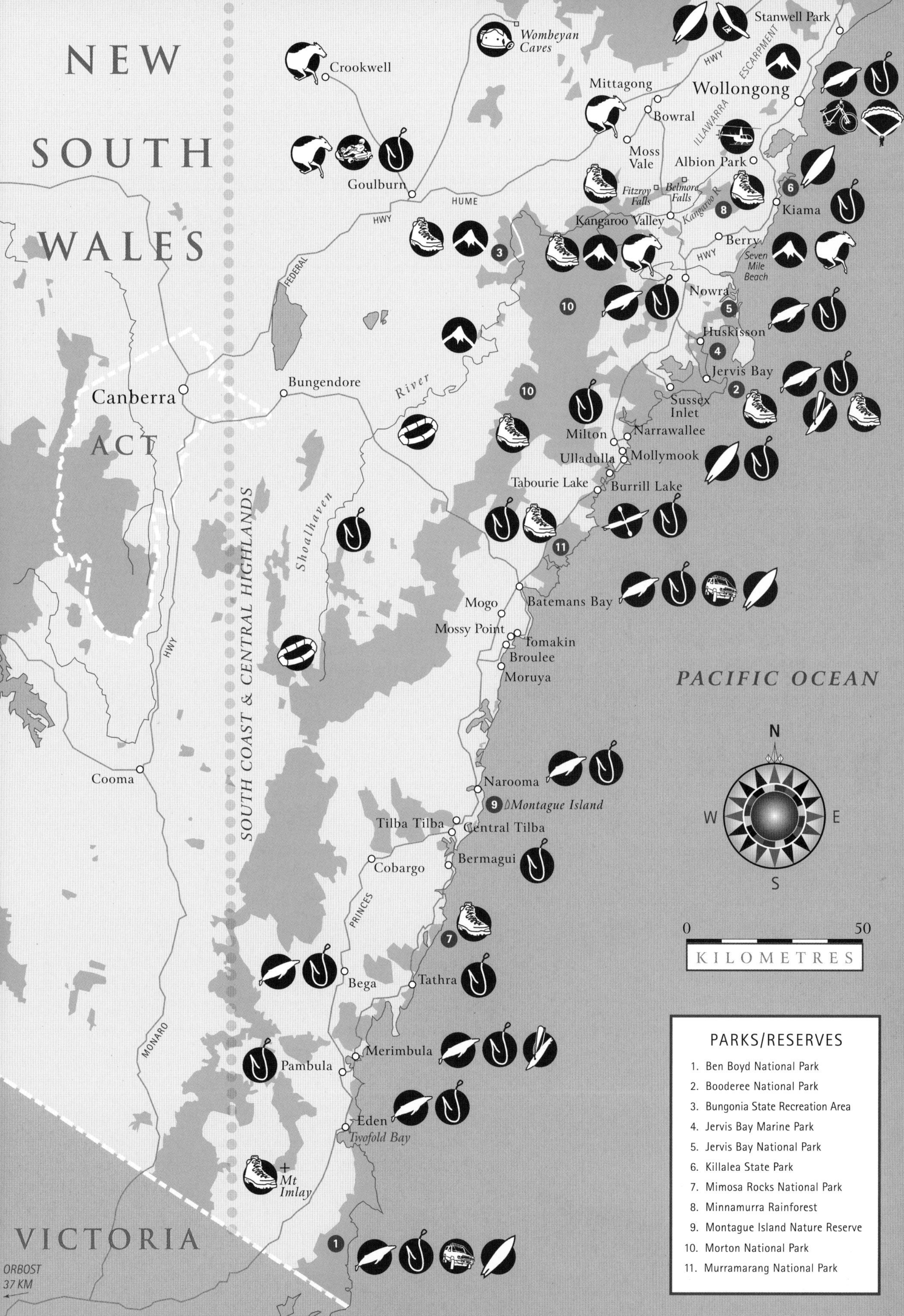
NEW SOUTH WALES
ACT
VICTORIA
SOUTH COAST & CENTRAL HIGHLANDS
PACIFIC OCEAN
Canberra
Bungendore
Crookwell
Wombeyan Caves
Goulburn
HUME HWY
FEDERAL
Mittagong
Bowral
Moss Vale
Stanwell Park
HWY
ESCARPMENT
ILLAWARRA
Wollongong
Albion Park
Fitzroy Falls
Belmora Falls
Kangaroo R.
Kangaroo Valley
Kiama
Berry
HWY
Seven Mile Beach
Nowra
Huskisson
Jervis Bay
Sussex Inlet
River
Shoalhaven
Milton
Narrawallee
Ulladulla
Mollymook
Tabourie Lake
Burrill Lake
Batemans Bay
Mogo
Mossy Point
Tomakin
Broulee
Moruya
HWY
Cooma
Narooma
Montague Island
Tilba Tilba
Central Tilba
Bermagui
Cobargo
PRINCES
Bega
Tathra
MONARO
Merimbula
Pambula
Eden
Twofold Bay
Mt Imlay
ORBOST 37 KM
N
W
E
S
0
50
KILOMETRES
PARKS/RESERVES
1. Ben Boyd National Park
2. Booderee National Park
3. Bungonia State Recreation Area
4. Jervis Bay Marine Park
5. Jervis Bay National Park
6. Killalea State Park
7. Mimosa Rocks National Park
8. Minnamurra Rainforest
9. Montague Island Nature Reserve
10. Morton National Park
11. Murramarang National Park

NATIONAL PARKS

More than 30 national parks are strung along the south coast hinterland. A few highlights are:

Bungonia State Recreation Area: 30km east of Goulburn, features the deepest limestone gorge in Australia with a network of limestone caves, waterfalls, river canyons and spectacular lookouts. One of NSW's oldest conservation reserves, sections were first protected as a water reserve in 1872. Canoeing, canyoning and caving are popular activities in the park, and there are five designated walking tracks ranging from 90 minutes to four hours.

Morton National Park: sandstone scenery on a grand scale in the mountains behind Nowra. To the south, George Boyd lookout, Little Forest Plateau and Pigeon House Mountain offer views of the coast and Budawang wilderness areas. Tianjara lookout, on the Nowra-Braidwood road, gives views of Tianjara Falls. To the north, Fitzroy Falls and Belmore Falls plunge off the plateau into rainforest gullies. To the west, at Tallong, are wonderful views of the Shoalhaven Gorge from Badgerys and Longpoint lookouts.

Jervis Bay National Park and Marine Park: fringes Jervis Bay, St Georges Basin and ocean beaches. The area is rich in Aboriginal heritage, includes wetlands, Lake Wollumboola and borders Booderee National Park. Activities include swimming, bushwalking, surfing, scuba diving and dolphin and bird watching. The bay offers beaches, rocky platforms, reefs, extensive sea grass beds, estuaries, deep-water cliffs and caves.

Murramarang National Park: the rugged coastline here between Batemans Bay and Ulladulla is popular in summer with great swimming beaches, rock platforms, spotted gum forests, rainforest gullies and beautiful Durras Lake. There's beachfront cabin accommodation, good snorkelling and a range of bushwalks including popular Pigeon House Mountain. Murramarang Aboriginal Area protects what is regarded as the largest midden on the south coast. Keep an eye out for kangaroos on the beaches.

Montague Island Nature Reserve: a granite lighthouse stands sentinel above the island 9km offshore from Narooma, watching over colonies of Australian and New Zealand fur seals and numerous little penguins. Crested terns, silver gulls and three different species of shearwaters reside here during the nesting season and it's a great spot to watch whales between September and November. The National Parks and Wildlife Service (NPWS) run tours to the island, where you'll learn the history of the island and lighthouse, Aboriginal heritage and wildlife. Night-time tours include penguin watching. Tours depart Narooma Wharf daily at 9.30am; and evenings two hours before sunset. ☎ (02) 4476 2881.

Mimosa Rocks National Park: beaches and bushwalking are popular in this long, narrow park, stretching from Tathra north towards Bermagui. Highlights include natural volcanic sculptures, rugged coastal headlands, cliffs and rock stacks.

Ben Boyd National Park: pristine, bush-flanked stretches of coastline near Eden with fantastic rock formations, heaths and banksia forest. Highlights are Boyd's Tower, built for whale-spotting, Green Cape Lightstation and the Pinnacles, white sand cliffs.

Southern Highlands

The southern highlands and tablelands, around two-hours drive south-west of Sydney is a predominately rural area studded with historic towns and pretty hamlets that do a brisk weekend trade in antiques and local art, especially in winter when the cool highland temperatures are conducive to long fireside lunches. Visit historic Goulburn, full of grand Victorian architecture; the charming town of Crookwell, perched atop the Great Dividing Range; the gold mining village of Tuena and the craft shops and galleries of Bungendore, Mittagong and Bowral, famous for their spring time flower displays.

Wollongong and the Illawarra

The Illawarra Escarpment tumbles into the sea just north of Wollongong and is a favourite spot for hang-gliders and paragliders. Wollongong, the third largest city in NSW and a major coal, iron and steel producer is also one of the most attractive seaside cities in the country. Explore the horseshoe-shaped cove of Wollongong Harbour with its lighthouse, fishing fleet, fish markets and wonderful city beaches. Linger over coffee in one of the many cafes along the foreshore, admire the colonial architecture of the sandstone courthouse or stockpile some inner harmony at the eight-story Nan Tien Buddhist Temple–the largest Buddhist temple in the Southern Hemisphere. Further south there are more beautiful beaches and the dramatic wave-soaked blowhole at Kiama.

Shoalhaven

The Shoalhaven is the area roughly between Berry in the north to the fishing community of Ulladulla in the south. One of the most beautiful spots is Jervis Bay with a resident pod of dolphins, great national and marine parks and Hyams Beach, reputed to have the whitest sand in the world. Berry draws weekend crowds to its eclectic range of antique shops, galleries, boutiques and nearby wineries; Kangaroo Valley in the hinterland is the place to hire a canoe and paddle through the waterways of the lush valley and to the south, the holiday coastline encompasses the rural town of Milton and the seaside towns of Sussex Inlet, Ulladulla, Mollymook, Narrawallee, Burrill Lake and Lake Tabourie.

Eurobodalla

Eurobodalla means 'land of many waters' and the 130km stretch of coastline and hinterland between Batemans Bay and Narooma has more beaches, rivers and ocean waterways than you can count. Batemans Bay is a bustling holiday town close to mountains, national parks and the gorgeous Clyde Valley. Seaside villages such as Tomakin, Mossy Point and Broulee are full of laid back charm and the very photogenic towns of Central Tilba and Tilba Tilba are both heritage listed. The vibrantly painted wooden houses and shopfronts look much the same as they would have at the turn of last century. Narooma is famous for its fishing and Montague Island Nature Reserve, 9km offshore, is home to a large colony of little penguins and seabirds. Seals, dolphins, turtles and even whales are regularly spotted in the waters around the island.

Sapphire Coast

The most southerly coastal region of NSW has Bega as its main hub–a large country town famous for its rich dairy farming industry and some of the best cheeses in Australia. The historic wooden wharf at Tathra is a popular spot to drop a fishing line, Bermagui is good for game fishing and fantastic beaches and further south you can enjoy the beaches and lakes at picturesque Merimbula and Pambula. In the hinterland, Cobargo is renowned for its crafts and antiques and the old whaling town of Eden is located on beautiful Twofold Bay. Don't miss nearby Boydtown and Mount Imlay behind Eden for sweeping views of the Sapphire Coast to the north and south to the Victorian border.

Caravan and camping

Camping and caravanning is one of the most popular accommodation choices on the south coast during the summer months and school holidays, especially in late December and throughout January, when you'll need to book well in advance if you want to secure a place. Most of the national parks have camping grounds, and almost every town along the coast has a commercial caravan park.

Camping and caravan sites are available in Bungonia State Recreation Area with hot showers, flush toilets and a communal kitchen. The camping ground can hold about 200. There's more car-based camping and caravan sites at Gambells Rest campground in Moreton National Park near Bundanoon, at Green Patch in Booderee National Park and at Pebbly Beach, Pretty Beach and Depot Beach in Murramarang National Park. In Ben Boyd you can camp at Bittangabee Bay and Saltwater Creek and at Aragunnu, Middle Beach, Gillards Beach and Picnic Point in Mimosa National Park.

For more camping and caravanning information, and to book a site, visit:

www.nationalparks.nsw.gov.au

Bushwalks

The climb to the top of Pigeon House Mountain is one of the most popular walks on the coast. Graded as difficult, it's a four-hour return climb that includes ladders at the top. Your reward is magnificent panoramic views of the rugged cliffs and gorges carved by the Clyde River and its tributaries. On a clear day, you can see the coastline from Point Perpendicular in the north to Mount Dromaderry in the south.

The wheelchair accessible boardwalk in Minnamurra Rainforest (part of Budderoo National Park near Jamberoo) that leads from the Minnamurra Rainforest Centre to through subtropical and temperate rainforest areas to Minnamurra Falls is very popular with families.

The Light to Light walk in Ben Boyd National Park is a three-day, 30km easy walk along the coast from Boyd's Tower to Mowarry Point.

Shorter walks include the 2km White Sands Walk along the coast to Hyams Beach in Jervis Bay, and the very pretty four-hour walk from Pretty Beach to Pebbly Beach in Murramarang National Park that takes you through rainforest to the top of Durras Mountain, with spectacular views of the ocean and offshore islands.

Grey kangaroos on Pebbly Beach. *(Getty Images)*

scenic highlights

Wombeyan Caves. *(Tourism NSW)*

NSW's answer to Victoria's Great Ocean Road, the Grand Pacific Drive (aka Lawrence Hargrave Drive), runs along a man-made cliff-hugging ledge between the pounding surf and towering escarpment north of Wollongong, now complete with the new Sea Cliff Bridge. Hargrave made aviation history by rising five metres strapped to a huge box kite in 1894 at Stanwell Park. Today hang-gliders and paragliders ride the air currents that rise up the escarpment.

Another spectacular drive is from Mittagong to Wombeyan Caves, through High Range (25km sealed road) mountains and valleys (40km dirt road), all suitable for ordinary cars except in extreme wet weather. Points of interest include a man-made tunnel, views over the Burragorang Valley and a delightful picnic spot and swimming hole at Goodman's Ford.

Kangaroo Valley is one of the state's prettiest valleys. Take the scenic drive from Berry to Moss Vale in the Southern Highlands over Barrengarry Mountain and visit Fitzroy Falls in Morton National Park, which tumble 82m to the floor of the ravine and can be viewed from an easily accessible lookout. Take a short detour to Manning Lookout for dramatic views over the valley and drive over historic Hampden Bridge. Built over the Kangaroo River in 1898, this is the oldest suspension bridge in Australia. Follow the Upper Kangaroo River through dairy country, stop for a swim at Flat Rock or have a picnic on the river bank near the old hall. The last section of the road is gravel but is well maintained.

A scenic alternative to the Princes Highway between Tilba and Tathra is Tourist Road 9, which follows the coast and traverses lush dairy country, the fishing village of Bermagui, and the forests of Mimosa National Park. Keep your windows open and you'll be serenaded by bell-birds almost the entire way, although you'll need to close them for the 20km unsealed section.

DON'T MISS

- **Bradman Museum:** located next to the Bradman Oval and near the former home of the great cricketer Don Bradman. The museum contains memorabilia and displays of Bradman's career and of the history of the Ashes. St Jude Street, Bowral. Open daily, 10am–5pm. **www.bradman.org.au**
- **Nan Tien Buddhist Temple:** in the suburb of Berkeley near Wollongong is the largest Buddhist temple in the Southern Hemisphere, offering weekend retreats and accommodation as well as a fascinating insight into modern Buddhism with classes on Tai Chi, meditation, calligraphy and the indispensable skill of lotus flower folding. Open daily, 9am–5pm except Mondays. **www.nantien.org.au**
- **Kiama blowhole and lighthouse:** a sea-cliff cave that periodically blows water as high as 60 metres in the air, most spectacularly when the wind and water are coming from the south-east. It is floodlit until 9.30pm each night. The 1887 lighthouse is nearby.
- **Bundanon:** gifted to the Australian people by artist Arthur Boyd, Bundanon is an historic sandstone homestead on 1000 acres of land adjacent the Shoalhaven River near Nowra. Boyd's former home and studio features includes a collection of art and craft works by four generations of the Boyd family, plus other famous Australian artists. Open to the general public every Sunday, 10.30am–4pm. Due to a single access road, arrival time is from 10.30am–1pm and departures between 1.30pm–4pm. **www.bundanon.com.au**

Sea Cliff Bridge, Lawrence Hargrave Drive. (Tourism NSW)

- **Australian Museum of Flight:** a large collection of historic military aircraft and memorabilia, including vintage aircraft and engines, photographic and art displays, weapons, models, uniforms, and aviation equipment. 489A Albatross Road, 8km south-west of Nowra. Open daily, 10am–4pm. **www.museum-of-flight.org.au**
- **Mogo Zoo:** dedicated to the conservation of exotic animals this private zoo's collection includes Nepalese red pandas, golden lion tamarins (one of the most endangered mammals on Earth), jaguars, lions, snow leopards, Syrian brown bears and both Sumatran and Bengal tigers. This is a great place to spend a couple of hours, particularly if you have children, who can follow the keepers around the zoo as they feed and talk about the animals under their care. Tomakin Road, Mogo, 10km south of Batemans Bay. Open daily, 10am–5pm. **www.mogozoo.com.au**
- **ABC Cheese Factory:** tastings of its famous Club and Tilba cheeses, Central Tilba. Open daily, 10am–4.30pm; peak times (school holidays) 9am–5pm.
- **Foxglove Spire Gardens:** Corkhill Drive, Tilba Tilba. Open daily.
- **Umbarra Aboriginal Cultural Centre:** interpretive centre and tours, Bermagui Road, Wallaga Lake. Open Mon–Fri, 9am–5pm; weekends 9am–4pm. **www.umbarra.com.au**
- **Bega Cheese Factory and Heritage Centre:** museum, craft shop, factory viewing platform, cheese tastings, cafe and sales. Lagoon Street, Bega. Open daily.
- **Killer Whale Museum:** details the history of Eden and the role whales have played in the town's fortunes. One of the most interesting stories is that of Old Tom, leader of a pack of killer whales (orcas) who, in a strange example of human and animal symbiosis, would help the whalers hunt and kill the huge baleen whales in the harbour by rounding them up and directing them towards the whalers waiting with harpoons in exchange for unwanted whale scraps. There are also displays on shipping, fishing and associated maritime industries as well as local history. Imlay Street, Eden. Open Mon–Sat, 9.15am–3.45pm, Sun 11.15am–3.45pm. ☎ (02) 6496 2094. **www.killerwhalemuseum.com.au**
- **Davidson Whaling Station:** another legacy of the whaling era is this historic site, in Ben Boyd National Park, just south of Eden. Just around the bay is Boyd's tower, a huge square tower built by Ben Boyd in 1846. It was originally intended to be a lighthouse, but the Government would not give permission to use the privately-owned structure as a light so it was used as a lookout for whales. Ben Boyd National Park. Open daily 10am–5pm.
- **Green Cape Lightstation:** the 1883 lighthouse stands on headland that juts out unexpectedly from the coastline, which many ships would hug in order to avoid the strong East Australian Current. The nearby bay, aptly named Disaster Bay, is littered with wrecks—there is a good lookout on the road in to the lighthouse. Just below the lightstation car park is a cemetery with the graves of some of the 71 people drowned when the *Ly-ee-Moon* was wrecked here in 1886 (inexplicably, the lighthouse was operating at the time). Ben Boyd National Park, Lighthouse tours daily. For accommodation and tour bookings ☎ (02) 6495 5000.
- **Gabo Island:** take a tour to Gabo Island to see more than 40,000 nesting penguins that live in burrows around the island—the largest known colony of little penguins in the world. Gabo Island tours depart from Merimbula airport and include two scenic flights, lighthouse and island tour and gourmet lunch. **http://mas.asitis.net.au/gabo.html**

adventure activities

Surfing the South Coast. *(Getty Images)*

Abseiling and canyoning

The sandstone cliffs of the Shoalhaven River, the lush rainforest canyons of the Berry and Kangaroo Valley escarpments and the deep limestone gorges of Bungonia State Recreation Area east of Goulburn offer some great opportunities for abseiling, rock climbing and canyoning. Mild to Wild, based in Berry, run a range of abseiling and canyoning tours.

www.m2w.com.au

Caving

Wombeyan Caves, between Goulburn and Mittagong along a largely unsealed road, are among the most beautiful caves in the country featuring vast caverns adorned with striking and delicate formations. There are five caves open for inspection on a range of guided and self-guided tours, as well as adventure caving tours of the largely vertical Bullio Cave, which involves steep ladders of up to 20m, crawl holes, squeezes and an underground streamway. Visit the Jenolan Caves Reserve Trust website for more details on Wombeyan Caves.

www.jenolancaves.org.au

Cycling

Wollongong's legendary Sydney to the Gong Bike Ride has long been a favourite with hard-core cyclists, but the new 15km City Cycleway caters for cyclists of all abilities. The 15km route starts in the CBD and follows the shoreline north to the coastal village of Thirroul and offers wonderful views of the Pacific Ocean on one side and the brooding Illawarra Escarpment on the other and is lined with restaurants and cafes–just in case you need a breather.

Dolphin and whale watching

100 years ago, Eden, on the shores of Twofold Bay, was one of the most important whaling centres in the country. Today it is one on the best places to watch whales between September and November and boasts the Killer Whale Museum which includes the skeleton of 'Tom' the Killer Whale that once hearded other whales into the bay for the hunters. Other good whale watching spots along the south coast are Merimbula, Batemans Bay, Nowra, Wollongong and the Shoalhaven. You can join a whale watching tour or cruise in most of these towns.

Jervis Bay is home to a resident pod of around 80 bottlenose dolphins and several operators run dolphin and whale watching tours out of Huskisson.

www.whalecruises.com.au www.dolphinwatch.com.au

Fishing

The waters off the south coast of NSW are renowned for their excellent fishing. Great catches are made in the estuaries and on the offshore reefs of table species such as snapper, flathead, morwong, kingfish and many other local varieties. Further out on the edge of the continental shelf, you can fish for the big game fish–marlin, yellowfin tuna, shark and others. The fishing can be good in the local waterways, off the beach or from the many rock shelfs along the coast, or try your luck with a snorkel and a speargun from the many beach and headland locations. Visitor information centres will have details on fishing charters.

Fly fishing is popular in inland rivers and streams of the southern highlands. Gundowringa Homestead runs fly-fishing courses near Goulburn.

http://members.ozemail.com.au/~gundowringa/

Fitzroy Falls. *(Tourism NSW)*

Off-road driving

There are some great 4WD tracks around Batemans Bay, but you won't find them on most tourist maps. Specialist maps are published by State Forests of NSW; call the Batemans Bay office. On these will you find the positions of logging tracks and fire trails.

☎ (02) 4472 6211

Alternatively, join a 4WD tour (or tag-along tour).

www.southcoast.com.au/oztrek4wdtours/

Hang-gliding and paragliding

Bald Hill at Stanwell Tops just north of Wollongong is Australia's best spot for hang-gliding and paragliding. The site is about 150m above sea, providing spectacular ocean views with the Royal National Park to the north and the escarpment to the south, and makes for fantastic flying when the winds are from the south/south-east. There are a number of companies offering tandem and instructional flights.

www.hangglideoz.com.au www.hanggliding.com.au

Horse riding

Explore the beautiful hills, valleys and rainforests of the south coast hinterland on horseback. There are a number of horse riding operations offering trail rides for all riding abilities. Ask at the local visitor information centre for more details.

Jet fighter flights

Take to the skies above the Illawarra on a kidney-rattling 900km/h aerobatic jet fighter flight in a L39-C Albatros or A-37 Dragonfly. Flights depart from Illawarra Regional Airport, Albion Park and include rolls, loops and other high-speed manoeuvres that will do their best to dislodge your lunch.

www.topgunflights.com.au

Kayaking and canoeing

With so many beautiful rivers, lakes and waterways there's lots of places that are perfect for a paddle. Kangaroo Valley Safaris specialise in self-guided overnight canoe and kayak safaris on the Kangaroo River, Lake Yarrunga and the spectacular Shoalhaven Gorge. Sea kayaking is also very popular. Ask at local visitor information centres for details on other companies that hire canoes and kayaks.

www.kangaroovalleycanoes.com.au

Sky diving

The only place in NSW where you can sky dive the beach with the drop zone right on the beach in north Wollongong. Experience the ultimate rush from 14000ft over the beautiful coastline of the Illawarra with great mountain and coastal views. Tandem freefall jumps available daily, weather permitting.

www.skydivethebeach.com

Surfing

Good surf beaches are everywhere on the south coast. The wide expanse of Seven Mile Beach near Gerroa is a popular surfing spot, and Land's Edge Surf School offers group beginner lessons, two- and

Stanwell Tops paragliding. *(Tourism NSW)*

four-day surf packages, plus private lessons with fully qualified and experienced instructors. The more experienced should try The Farm in Killalea State Park, which attracts surfers from around Australia and the world.

www.landsedge.com.au

Wakefield Park

If you have ever wondered what it would be like to be a racing car driver head for Wakefield Park on the Braidwood Road, 13km south of Goulburn. It's one of the few privately owned motor racing circuits in Australia. You can also drive your own car around the track on special No Speed Limit Days. For those of us who don't own a racing car, you can ride a few laps with a professional driver in a V8 Supercar or V8 Auscar, or drive one yourself behind a pace car. Helmets and racing suits are provided.

www.wakefieldpark.com

White water rafting

A number of rafting companies run full-day rafting trips on the Shoalhaven River. Although not as well known as other rafting rivers such as the Nymboida on the mid-north coast or the Tully and North Johnstone in north Queensland, the Shoalhaven has some great white water. There are 12 rapids to be run in all. Run your eye over their names–Frustration Falls, Gobler's Trench, The Pimple, Rodeo Falls, Double Falls and Powerline Rapid–and you'll have a good idea of the type of action you can expect. Although some of the rapids are challenging, beginners will have no problems.

www.bushsports.com.au/whitewater.html

MORE INFORMATION

- **Goulburn Visitor Information Centre:** 201 Sloane Street, Goulburn. ☎ (02) 4823 4492. www.igoulburn.com
- **Southern Highlands Visitor Information Centre:** 62–70 Main Street, Mittagong. ☎ 1300 657 559. www.southern-highlands.com.au
- **Tourism Wollongong:** 93 Crown Street, Wollongong. ☎ 1800 240 737. www.tourismwollongong.com
- **Batemans Bay Visitor Information Centre:** cnr Princes Highway and Beach Road, Batemans Bay. ☎ 1800 802 528. www.naturecoast-tourism.com.au
- **Narooma Visitor Information Centre:** Princes Highway, Narooma. ☎ 1800 240 003. www.naturecoast-tourism.com.au
- **Bega Information Centre:** Princes Highway, Bega. ☎ 1800 633 012. www.sapphirecoast.com.au/bega.htm
- **Sapphire Coast Tourism Booking Service & Merimbula Visitor Information Centre:** Beach Street, Merimbula. ☎ 1800 150 457. www.sapphirecoast.com.au/merimbula.htm
- **Eden Information Centre:** Princes Highway, Eden. ☎ (02) 6496 1953. www.sapphirecoast.com.au/eden.htm

weather watch

- January: 16–23°C
- July: 6–16°C
- Temperatures are moderate most of the year. March is usually the wettest month.

country heartlands

Glen Innes. *(Tourism NSW)*

▶ BEYOND THE SANDSTONE CURTAIN of the Great Dividing Range is a place of subtle beauty, a place of wide open landscapes under a huge clear sky, endless fields dotted with grazing sheep and cattle, parched hills and dry river beds in summer and cool, crisp days in winter. The central plains and north-western tablelands hide a wealth of Australian pioneer and gold mining history, and to the south, the rich farmlands of the Riverina produce some of the country's finest produce.

Explorers Blaxland, Wentworth and Lawson became the first Europeans to catch a glimpse of the fertile western slopes and plains when they crossed the Blue Mountains in 1813. They were quickly followed by government surveyors who opened up the land for grazing and farming and the country's first inland city, Bathurst, was established in 1815. In 1851, the first payable gold in the country was found at nearby Ophir, sparking a gold rush that transformed not only the colony of New South Wales but the entire country, bringing settlements to far flung areas of the state.

Today the rivers, lakes and dams of the central western plains and Riverina attract keen anglers and water sport lovers of all ages and the World Heritage-listed national parks in the rugged slopes and northern highlands offer great opportunities for bushwalking, caving, abseiling and other adventure sports.

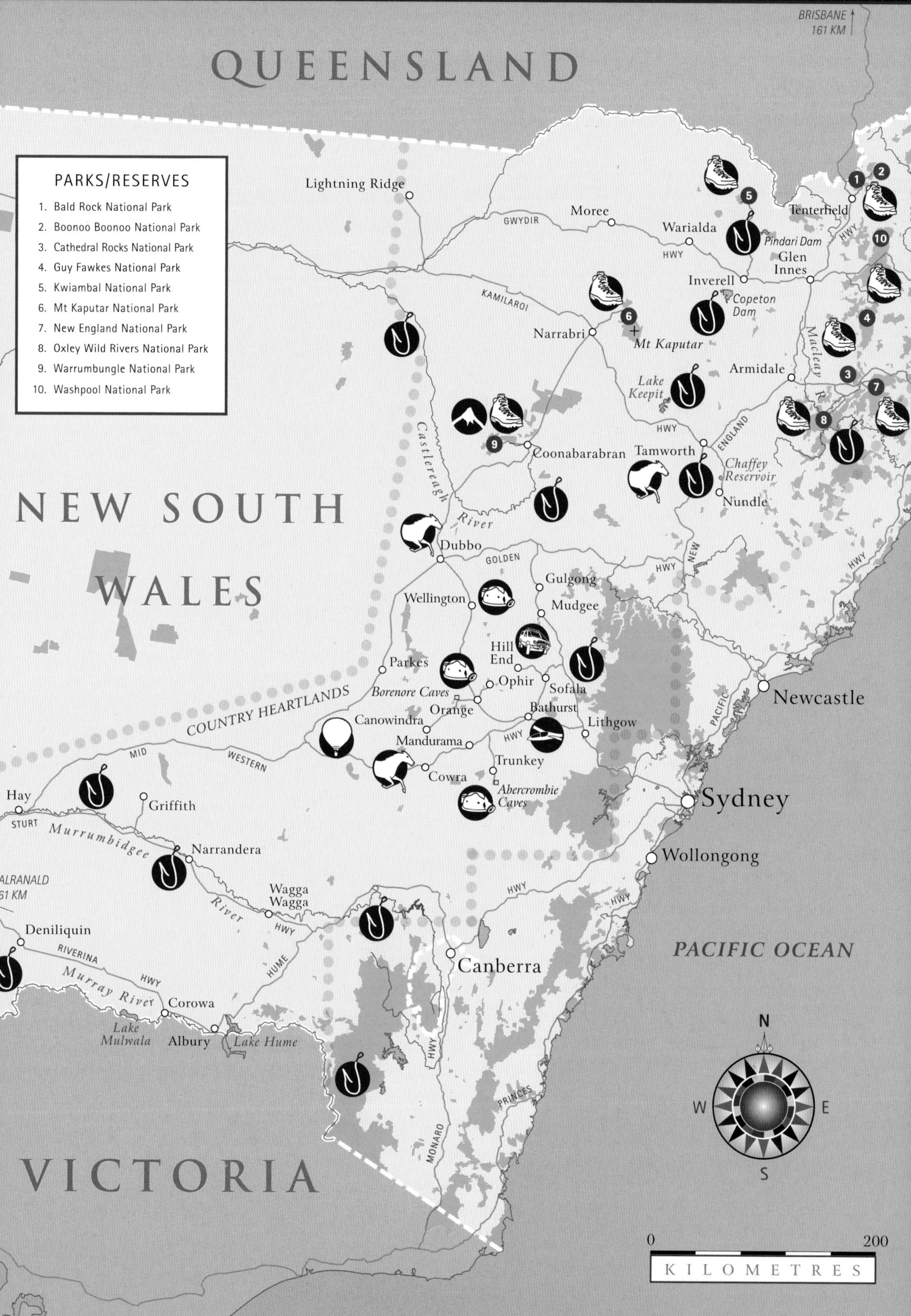
QUEENSLAND
NEW SOUTH WALES
VICTORIA
PARKS/RESERVES
1. Bald Rock National Park
2. Boonoo Boonoo National Park
3. Cathedral Rocks National Park
4. Guy Fawkes National Park
5. Kwiambal National Park
6. Mt Kaputar National Park
7. New England National Park
8. Oxley Wild Rivers National Park
9. Warrumbungle National Park
10. Washpool National Park
BRISBANE 161 KM
Lightning Ridge
Moree
GWYDIR
Warialda
HWY
Tenterfield
Pindari Dam
Glen Innes
Inverell
Copeton Dam
KAMILAROI
Narrabri
Mt Kaputar
Macleay R.
Armidale
Lake Keepit
HWY
ENGLAND
Castlereagh River
Coonabarabran
Tamworth
Chaffey Reservoir
Nundle
Dubbo
GOLDEN
NEW
HWY
HWY
Gulgong
Wellington
Mudgee
Parkes
Hill End
Ophir
Sofala
Borenore Caves
Orange
Bathurst
Lithgow
COUNTRY HEARTLANDS
Canowindra
Mandurama
HWY
PACIFIC
Newcastle
MID
WESTERN
Trunkey
Cowra
Abercrombie Caves
Hay
Griffith
Sydney
STURT
Murrumbidgee
Narrandera
Wollongong
BALRANALD 161 KM
Wagga Wagga
HWY
River
HWY
HWY
Deniliquin
RIVERINA
HUME
PACIFIC OCEAN
Canberra
HWY
Murray River
Corowa
Lake Mulwala
Albury
Lake Hume
HWY
N
W
E
S
PRINCES
MONARO
0
200
KILOMETRES

NATIONAL PARKS

Kwiambal National Park: 90km north of Inverell is one of the most pristine and enjoyable parks in NSW. On the junction of the Macintyre and Severn rivers, the large, shady camp site next to the Severn River has great fishing and swimming holes. There is good swimming at the Junction (8km easy walk) and at Macintrye Falls (lots of steps but worth it).

Bald Rock National Park: the water-streaked dome is the largest granite rock in Australia. Climb to the summit for great views into Queensland or walk through the park's granite landscape.

Boonoo Boonoo National Park: pronounced bunna bunoo, from a local Aboriginal term for big rocks, with a 210m-high waterfall of the same name. Cool off in one of several swimming holes, but be warned, even in summer the water is icy cold.

Mt Kaputar National Park: the Nandewar Range is a dramatic landscape of lava terraces, volcanic plugs and ring dykes. The highest peak, Mt Kaputar is 1200m with superb views from the summit. Sawn Rocks, a 40m basalt cliff face, features perpendicular-octagonal shaped rocks, resembling a series of giant organ pipes.

New England National Park: a landscape of cliffs and world heritage rainforests, fast creeks, occasional snowfalls and mist that spills over the edge of the Great Escarpment. Point Lookout, Banksia Point and Wrights Lookout all offer wilderness views and walks.

Cathedral Rocks National Park: a wild and rugged landscape of giant boulders, sculpted rock and distinctive granite tors. Explore the rock formations on the Cathedral Rock track, an easy three-hour circuit, or the longer Woolpack Rocks walk.

Washpool National Park: steep gorges, clear waters and expansive World Heritage rainforest protect some of the most diverse and least disturbed forest in NSW, including the world's largest stand of coachwood trees.

Guy Fawkes National Park: large and secluded wilderness area of rugged and scenic river systems with limited facilities. There are some lovely walking trails for well-equipped, experienced bushwalkers.

Oxley Wild Rivers National Park: one of the most beautiful parks in NSW. It is the sixth largest wilderness area in the state with the largest area of dry rainforest in NSW and easily accessible by conventional cars. Situated on the Great Escarpment which divides the tablelands from the coast, the New England Plateau drops into the rugged gorges carved out by the Aspley and upper Macleay rivers. There are 13 major waterfalls, although many run only after local rains.

Warrumbungle National Park: one of the state's most popular parks with forested ridges, rocky spires and domes, deep gorges and plenty of camping and visitor facilities. The volcanic cliffs are popular with rock climbers, which is permitted everywhere except the Breadknife and Chalkers Mountain, and there are several excellent bushwalking tracks. The park is also famous for its clear atmosphere and views of the night sky are exceptional.

Western slopes and central plains

The western slopes and plains are characterised by the rich volcanic soils that support sheep, cattle and crops as diverse as grapes, wheat and cotton. This once restless land has produced some fantastic rock formations, such as the rocky spires known as the Warrumbungles near Coonabarabran, one of the state's premier bushwalking destinations. The clear night skies are also good for star gazing and there are major observatories in Coonabarabran and the legendary 'dish' radio telescope near Parkes that was instrumental in the *Apollo 11* moon landing of 1969.

Major towns include historic Bathurst with its colonial and Victorian architecture; graceful Orange, a city of cherry and apple blossoms, stately homes and cool-climate wines; Dubbo, with its famous open-range zoo; Mudgee, a centre for small farming and gourmet food and wine; Cowra with its beautiful Japanese Gardens, while historic gold rush towns like Hill End, Sofala and Gulgong look much they same as they did 100 years ago.

The Riverina and Murray

To the south of the western plains lies the area known as the Riverina, one of Australia's richest agricultural regions, kept green by the waters of the Murrumbidgee River and vast irrigation systems. Settled predominately by European farmers in the late 19th and early 20th centuries, the area has a distinct Mediterranean flavour and produces more than 60 per cent of all grapes grown in New South Wales.

Wagga Wagga, on the banks of the Murrumbidgee, is one of the State's largest inland cities and has many fine buildings, tree-lined streets, parks and gardens, as well as one of the largest stockyards in Australia. Griffith is the main regional town and is earning a reputation for gourmet food and wine, while the pioneer farming town of Hay is a welcome diversion in the centre of a large expanse of dusty flatlands known as the Hay Plains.

To the south, Australia's most important river, the 2750km-long Murray, forms the border between NSW and Victoria and has always been an important trade route and farming centre. Albury has Lake Hume, one of the country's biggest artificial lakes and a haven for water sports; Corowa is an archetypal country town with wide verandahs lining the main street and was the place where the Federation movement was kick-started at a conference in 1893; and pretty riverside Deniliquin holds several Guinness World Records when 20,000 ute (utility vehicle) enthusiasts from all around the country flock here each September/October for the annual ute muster.

New England and the north-west

At almost 1000m above sea level the northern tablelands of the New England district enjoys its own distinct micro-climate with warm, dry summers, colourful autumns and chilly winters. One of the world's richest gem areas, the region was opened up by hopeful fossickers and gold miners in the latter half of the 19th century, paving the way for privileged squatters who established expansive selections of prime grazing and farming land.

The bustling city of Tamworth is dubbed the country music capital of Australia with its giant golden guitar, guitar-shaped swimming pools, halls and walks of country music fame, memorials and museums dedicated to the music and its makers and of course, the annual Country Music Festival in January. Armidale, a university town full of beautiful National Trust-listed buildings is home to the New England Regional Art Museum, Australia's most significant regional art collection; dusty Lightning Ridge is famous for its opals; Moree is the place to go for a dip in thermal hot springs and Tenterfield is known as 'the birthplace of the nation' where Henry Parkes first advocated Federation.

Murray River campsite. *(Tourism NSW)*

Caravan and camping

Almost all the national parks in the region have good camp grounds and camping is generally allowed anywhere in the parks you can walk to. If you are visiting outside of holiday season, you'll more than likely be sharing the campground with just a couple of others.

In the north, you can't go past Hanging Rock for a campsite with a view–11km from Nundle and 1100m above sea level. You can camp (summer is best) at Sheba Dams, built by miners in 1888, and in the state forests further along the road.

For those with a caravan, Copeton Waters State Park at Copeton Dam is a nice place to stay if you have a boat and Kwiambal's shady riverside camp ground is delightful. There are also plenty of good camping sites near waterfalls in Oxley Wild Rivers National Park at Wollomombi Gorge (caravan access for smaller vans), Dangars Falls, Apsley Gorge and Tia Gorge.

The most popular camping destination in the central west is undoubtedly in the Warrumbungles, although Mount Kaputar also has some good car-based camping spots.

For more camping and caravanning information, and to book a site, visit:

www.nationalparks.nsw.gov.au

Bushwalks

The Grand High Tops Track in the Warrumbungles is a terrific walk that takes you to the base of the Breadknife, a narrow rock sliver formed when magma forced its way through a long crack in the bedrock beneath the ancient Warrumbungle volcano, and the most famous feature of the national park. It's a five-hour, 12.5km walk that is graded medium in terms of difficulty, but the rewards for the strenuous climb make it all worthwhile. The track begins from Pincham car park, following the shaded valley of Spirey Creek, lined with colourful wildflowers in spring. It's a steep climb up to the base of the Breadknife and beyond to the Grand High Tops, where you'll get a panoramic view of the Warrumbungles and beyond from the ridge. The route back down to Spirey Creek follows the other side of the Breadknife with close-up views of its western face.

There are numerous good short walks to lookouts and waterfalls in Oxley Wild Rivers National Park including Tia Falls, Apsley Gorge and Apsley Falls as well as several good gorge walks.

In Mount Kaputar National Park you can climb to the summit of Mt Kaputar for great sunrise and sunset photos, explore some of the gorges or follow the shady creekside track to Sawn Rocks. The one-hour walk is along an easy, well-graded track, but it does include a couple of short sections with steps. The best time for photography is after midday, when the sun shines on the cliff face.

scenic highlights

The Fossickers Way, from Glen Innes and Inverell south to Warialda and Nundle, snakes its way along the western slopes of the New England plateau and passes through some of the world's richest gem areas. Seventy per cent of the world's sapphires come from Australia, and almost 70 per cent of those come from the Inverell area. Other finds along the way, if you are lucky, could include zircon, jasper quartz, agate, ironised woods, pyrites, malachite, jasper, red, brown and yellow quartz and gold. A scenic highlight is the drive from Tamworth, following the very pretty Peel River to Nundle at the foot of the Great Dividing Range. Originally a gold rush town, it retains much of its heritage in the buildings of the main street, many of which have now been transformed into galleries, shops and a guesthouse. Take the drive up to Hanging Rock for fantastic mountain views and an icy dip at Sheba Dam.

Explore more of our goldmining past in the historic gold-rush villages of the central west. Head towards Mudgee, turning off the Great Western Highway just west of Lithgow. Follow this road past the massive water vapour stacks of Wallerawang and over the range 70km to Ilford and turn left to Sofala. This is the start of Tourist Drive 4, which ultimately branches off to Bathurst or Mudgee. Sofala is 27km down the road, which includes a short unsealed section that is in good condition—dusty but easy to drive. An alternative 45km sealed road runs from Bathurst. Sofala claims to be the oldest surviving gold town in Australia, dating from the beginnings of the gold rush in May 1851. The main street once stretched for 16km and the population numbered tens of thousands. Today, Sofala is a sleepy little village on the banks of the Turon River, where the café is also the souvenir shop and post office and your sandwiches have to wait until the mail's been sorted. The river is a good place for fossicking for gold. You can buy fossicking equipment at the souvenir shop or pick up a free leaflet detailing an historical town walk and some local drives.

Hill End. *(Tourism NSW)*

Like Sofala, Hill End, 38km west on an unsealed road, is a ghost of its former grandeur. It was once one of the largest inland towns in New South Wales. In 1872, Beyers and Holtermann discovered the largest single mass of gold found in Australia and Hill End became a place where fortunes were made overnight. By 1874 there was a mile of shops, 28 hotels, five banks, several opium dens, an oyster bar, two newspapers and a brewery. The town population climbed to more than 8000, with more in outlying areas. Today the population numbers about 100, many of whom are descendents of original Hill End goldminers and fossickers. It is now a national historic site, managed by the National Parks and Wildlife Service. Most of the buildings date back to the 1870s, when the gold rush was at its height. Wander through the village streets and read the various interpretive boards detailing what once stood on each spot. The National Parks Centre is in the old hospital building and includes a museum filled with village artefacts and photographs of Hill End in its halcyon days, as well as a 15-minute video telling the history of the town through a series of original photographs.

With its crooked, narrow streets overhung with wooden verandahs trimmed with iron lace, Gulgong, 25km north of Mudgee, is instantly recognisable (for those old enough to remember) as the town portrayed on the old paper $10 note. The town's claim to fame is its close association with poet and storyteller Henry Lawson who went to school in nearby Eurunderee, about midway between Mudgee and Gulgong along Henry Lawson Drive—although there is nothing left of the old bark school these days except for a commemorative plaque. Nearby is a picnic area memorial to the writer at the site of his old home—although the only relic left is the fireplace and chimney.

Gulgong was established during the gold rush when Tom Sunders discovered gold lying on the ground at nearby Red Hill in 1870. The town's life and times has been preserved not only in the many old buildings along the main street, but in the photographs of Charles Bayliss and Beaufoy Merlin. These photographs, known as the Holtermann Collection, consist of more than 500 original negatives taken in Gulgong and Hill End and accurately portray life in these two boomtowns at the height of the gold rush in 1872. You can view some of these photographs at Gulgong Pioneers Museum.

DON'T MISS

- **Australian Standing Stones:** the only standing stones erected outside the British Isles in the past 3000 years, were erected in 1992 as a National Monument to the Celts at Glen Innes.
- **DeJon Sapphire Centre:** see sapphires from ground to gem. Fossicking, gem centre and retail showroom. Open daily. 19km from Inverell on the Gwydir Highway.
- **Cranky Rock:** nature reserve, picnic and camping area and swimming hole near Warialda.
- **Moree artesian hot springs:** take a dip in the healing hot mineral springs naturally heated to 41°C.
- **Golden Guitar Tourist Centre:** wax museum, 12m Golden Guitar, café and gift shop with good local country music CD collection. 2–8 Ringers Road, Tamworth. Open daily 9am–5pm.
- **Country Music Festival:** Tamworth, last two weeks in January.
- **Mount Misery Mine:** underground gold museum. Oakenville Street, Nundle. Open daily 10am–5pm.
- **New England Regional Art Museum:** home to more than 3,500 works of art including the Howard Hinton and the Chandler Coventry collections of Australian art, featuring works by Arthur Streeton, Tom Roberts, Margaret Preston, John Coburn, George Gittoes and Ann Thomson. Kentucky Street, Armidale. Open Tue–Sun 10.30am–5pm. **www.neram.com.au**
- **Aboriginal Centre and Keeping Place:** permanent Aboriginal collection which focuses on arts and artefacts from the New England region. There is also an extensive collection of works from artists from regional NSW. The centre includes a well-stocked shop selling Koori artworks, didgeridoos, artefacts, jewellery and clothes, made by local and regional artists. Kentucky Street, Armidale. Open daily 9am–5pm.
- **Saumarez Homestead:** 10-hectare grazing property established in1830s includes 20 buildings dating from the 1860s–1910, is now a national Trust property. Take a guided tour, stroll through the gardens or explore the farm area with Thomas House and its interpretative display, stables, poultry yard, slaughter house and old timber buildings. Saumarez Road, Armidale. Open daily 10am–4pm. Closed mid-June until 1 Sept.
- **Hill End Visitor Centre:** displays on goldmining and the town in its 1872 heyday, and is the base for a number of tours. The shop has souvenirs and gold samples. Open daily, 9.30am–12.30pm and 1.30pm–4.30pm (closed Christmas Day).
- **History Hill Museum:** learn about goldmining and explore an underground mine at Hill End. Open Wed–Sun. **www.historyhill.com.au**
- **Henry Lawson Centre:** tells the history of Lawson and his career, his family and his association with the area. It is the largest collection of Lawson material outside the Mitchell Library in Sydney. The centre is host to the annual celebration of Lawson's birthday in June. Mayne Street, Gulgong. Open Wed–Sat 10am–3.30pm, Sun–Tue 10am–1pm.
- **Gulgong Pioneers Museum:** this huge museum includes tools and firearms, needlework and clothing, goldmining equipment, an old hotel bar, old shops, vehicles and coaches, war memorabilia, a school house and a settler's cottage—and is worth spending a few hours ferreting among the displays. Herbert Street, Gulgong. Open daily 9am–5pm.
- **Windamere Dam:** fishing, sailing, waterskiing, caravan and camp ground, 34km south of Mudgee.
- **Wellington Caves:** limestone caves and restored phosphate mine full of fossils. Also at the complex are several galleries and the Wellington-Osawano Japanese Garden. Mitchell Highway, 8km south of Wellington. Open daily, except Christmas Day.
- **Western Plains Zoo:** one of the best open-range zoos in Australia, 3km south of Dubbo on Obley Road. Open daily 9am–5pm, but no admission after 4pm. Early-morning zoo walks available on selected days, starting at 6.45 am. **www.zoo.nsw.gov.au**
- **Dundullimal Slab Homestead:** one of the oldest homesteads in western NSW. 2km past the zoo on Obley Road, Dubbo. Open daily 10am–5pm.
- **Old Dubbo Gaol:** restored gaol with extensive displays of animatronic models and artefacts. Macquarie Street, Dubbo. Open daily 9am–4.30pm.
- **Dubbo Regional Art Gallery:** unique collection of 'animal art' and regular touring exhibitions. Opposite Victoria Park at 165 Darling Street, Dubbo. Open daily (except Mon) 11am–4.30pm.
- **Siding Springs Observatory:** Australia's largest optical telescopes, including the 2.3m Advanced Technology Telescope, the world famous 3.9m Anglo-Australian Telescope, the 2m Faulkes Telescope, the 1.24m UK Schmidt Telescope, two Boller & Chivens Cassegrains 1m and 0.6m telescopes, the 0.5m Automatic Patrol Telescope and the 0.6m Uppsala Schmidt Telescope. 20 minutes from Coonabarabran on National Park Road. Open Mon–Fri 9.30am–4pm, weekends and public holidays, 10am–2pm. Guided tours Mon–Fri 11am. **www.sidingspringexploratory.com.au**
- **Parkes Telescope:** famous for its role in relaying *Apollo 11* telemetry and television pictures from the Moon on 21st July, 1969, the giant 64-metre dish used to examine a wide range of radio energies from our galaxy and other parts of the universe. 20km north of Parkes on the Newell Highway. Open daily 8.30am–4.15pm (except Christmas and Boxing Day). **www.outreach.atnf.csiro.au**
- **The Australia Telescope:** an array of six 22m antennas used for radio astronomy at the Narrabri Observatory. 25km west of Narrabri. Call (02) 6790 4070 for best times to visit. **www.outreach.atnf.csiro.au**
- **Pioneer Park Museum:** outdoor museum. Remembrance Drive, Griffith. Open daily, 9am–4.30pm.
- **Cowra Japanese Gardens:** five-hectare garden follows the Kai-yu Shiki style of the Edo era that flourished in the 1600s. Binni Creek Road, Cowra. Open daily 8.30am–5pm. **www.cowrajapanesegarden.com.au**
- **Shear Outback:** modern museum complex that includes the Australian Shearers' Hall of Fame; the Shear Outback Exhibition; the historic Murray Downs Woolshed and a special exhibition gallery. Take on Jackie Howe's legendary blade-shears record, see inside a working handpiece, take part in live shearing demonstrations several times daily, and more. Corner Sturt & Cobb highways, Hay. Open daily, 9am–5pm. **www.shearoutback.com.au**

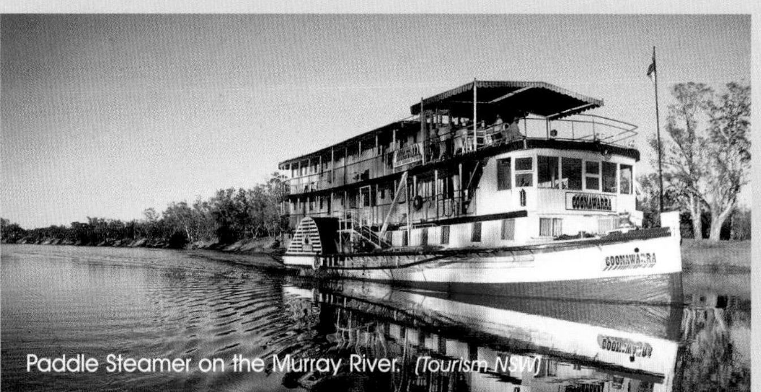
Paddle Steamer on the Murray River. *(Tourism NSW)*

adventure activities

Ballooning

Canowindra (pronounced Ca-noun-dra), roughly midway between Cowra and Orange, is the ballooning capital of Australia. For years hot air balloon enthusiasts have found the climate and topography, not to mention the scenery of Canowindra perfect for ballooning. Every April, 20,000 people descend on the small country town for Marti's Balloon Fiesta, one of the biggest hot air balloon spectaculars in the Southern Hemisphere.

www.aussieballoontrek.com.au

Caving

Wellington Caves Reserve, near Dubbo, has two show caves–Cathedral and Gaden caves–and a series of smaller limestone caves. They boast wonderful stalagmites and stalactites, including what is reputed to be the world's largest stalagmite, 'the alter', and a restored phosphate mine, which apart from a few palaeontologists looking for fossils, has remained virtually untouched for the past 80 years. The first visitors to the cave were ancient bats who left behind tons of droppings or guano, rich in phosphates. The NSW Phosphate Company began mining the cave in 1913. By the time the mine was abandoned five years later, 6000 tonnes of phosphate had been removed for fertiliser. The walls of the Bone Cave in the eastern loop of the mine are embedded with thousands of fragments and fossils. Lit by ultra-violet light, the ancient bones glow eerily in the darkness. The 350m-long mine cave has been developed with easy access in mind so it is accessible for wheelchairs and strollers. Most tours take around an hour and a half.

Borenore Caves are 17km from Orange. These undeveloped caves do not have guides or tours, but are accessible all the time. Highlights include the Tunnel and Arch Caves–take a torch and some commonsense and be prepared for adventure. Contact the Orange Visitors Information Centre for information on the fossil evidence located behind the caves and walking trails.

Abercrombie Caves, 11km south of Trunkey in the state's central west also have spectacular formations. The largest feature in the cave system is 'the Archway' which is 221m long and 60m wide at both ends. On a self-guided tour you'll find a wooden dance floor that was built by gold miners more than 100 years ago. Guided tours of the four caves run everyday. Some tours involve steps, climbing up ladders and squeezing past formations, but they are a lot of fun for those tired of larger, more sedate, cave tours. Children love the Bushranger's Cave with its many tunnels that was once used as a hideout for the Ribbon Gang in 1830, long before the reign of more well-known bushrangers like Ben Hall or Ned Kelly and before the caves were 'officially' discovered in 1842.

www.jenolancaves.org.au

Fishing

The inland rivers of western NSW offer great fishing opportunities. The cool rivers of the New England region are home to brown and rainbow trout; try the Aspley, Styx, Serpentine and Wollomombi rivers. There is also good fishing in major dams and lakes such as Chaffey, Keepit, Copeton and Pindari. Fish the warmer inland rivers, like the Macquarie and Castlereagh, for Murray cod, golden perch, silver perch, European carp and catfish. The Murray and Murrumbidgee around Wagga Wagga, Narrandera and Hay are good for goldens, cod and redfin. Lake Mulwala is one of the best Murray cod fisheries in the country. The Turon River behind the Royal Hotel in Sofala is the place to cast a line for some trout between October and June. And if the fish don't bite–at least the pub's not too far away.

Off-road driving

Hill End is the end point of one of the NSW's classic bush tracks–The Bridle Track. The track runs from Duramana, north-west of Bathurst, to the old mining town of Hill End. It is approximately 60km long, and in 4WD terms, can be graded 'easy'. Driven carefully, a conventional vehicle could manage the entire distance, though extreme care would be required on some of the steeper, shaly sections of the road. You'll need a 4WD with a snorkel if you want to check out some of the better, more isolated camp sites on the other side of the river.

Gliding

The Bathurst Soaring Club offers joy flights and gliding instruction at Pipers Field airfield. 20-minute flights are available. Call the airfield or just drop in (weekends and public holidays only) to arrange a flight.

www.bathurstsoaring.org.au ☎ (02) 4757 1824

Horse riding

Like all rural areas there are plenty of places that offer horse-riding. Millamolong Station at Mandurama have numerous trails on their 5000-hectare sheep and cattle property beside the Belubula River.

www.millamolong.com

The Western Plains Riding Centre at Dubbo also run trail rides on gentle horses with experienced escorts with riding lessons available for beginners. 8R Merrilea Road, Dubbo.

☎ (02) 6884 3155

Most of our great outback tracks started life as a droving trail, where stockmen would ride for days guiding mobs of cattle or sheep from remote stations to towns or railheads. These days, road trains have replaced much of the traditional droving way of life but there are a few places where you can still taste for yourself the life of an outback drover. Try Mountain Cattle Drives, based near Tamworth in country NSW. Here, novice and experienced riders alike spend five days in the saddle moving cattle through the stock routes and camping in the foothills of the New England Ranges.

www.mountaincattle.com.au

Jillaroo and Jackaroo schools

Learn how to rope and ride a horse, muster cattle and myriad other farm-based skills at a jackaroo or jillaroo school. For the uninitiated, a jackaroo is a cross between a cowboy and a 'jack of all trades', and jillaroo is, of course, the female equivalent. The 10-day Bellandre Rural

Gliding at Lake Keepit. *(Tourism NSW)*

Discovery course at Molong in the central west of NSW is both a holiday and an adventure. The course covers some of the basics of farm living including cattle and sheep handling, chainsaws, fencing and mustering. Try your hand at motorbike and 4WD vehicle operation as well as take part in sheepdog and whip cracking demonstrations. There is also the opportunity to take a trip to nearby Dubbo where you can visit a sheep and cattle sale and participate in wine tasting of award-winning local vintages.

☎ 1300 666 292

Leconfield Jackaroo and Jillaroo School near Tamworth also runs courses where you learn to catch and saddle horses and natural horsemanship riding; horse-shoeing; bush survival and local bush tucker; whip cracking and lassoing; mustering sheep on horseback; sheep health and husbandry and, for the non-vegetarians, how to slaughter and butcher a sheep; fencing and yard building; wrestling, branding and marking calves and a number of fun things like barrel racing horseback games.

www.leconfield.com

Motor racing

The Mount Panorama racing circuit at Bathurst has been the home of motor racing since 1938. The National Motor Racing Museum is situated at the end of Conrod Straight and the Hall of Fame has captured the history of the mount from the early days of the dirt track to the current days of speed up to 290km/h. For most of the year the track is a public road and it's great fun to drive (slowly, normal speed limits apply) around all the famous landmarks.

Rock climbing

The Warrumbungles has some of the country's best and most adventurous long climbing routes (100–450m). There are four main climbing areas–Crater Bluff, Belougery Spire, Touduron and Bluff Mountain. The grades of the routes range from 8 to 24 but most are between 14 and 21. You'll need to register at the visitor centre before you start. Climbing is permitted everywhere except the Breadknife and Chalkers Mountain. Camp at Balmor Hut, a 1.5-hour walk uphill from the Camp Pincham car park. Best in autumn and spring.

www.climbing.com.au/crags/guide.php?page=warrambungles

MORE INFORMATION

- **Hill End: National Parks & Wildlife Service and Visitor Information:** ☎ (02) 6337 8206.
- **Bathurst Visitor Information Centre:** 1 Kendall Avenue, Bathurst. ☎ 1800 681 000. www.bathurst.nsw.gov.au
- **Orange Visitor Information Centre:** Byng Street, Civic Gardens, Orange. ☎ 1800 069 466. www.orange.nsw.gov.au
- **Mudgee Visitor Centre:** 84 Market Street, Mudgee. ☎ 1800 816 304. www.mudgee-gulgong.org
- **Wellington Visitor Information Centre:** Cameron Park, Wellington. ☎ 1800 621 614. www.wellington.nsw.gov.au
- **Dubbo Visitor Centre:** corner of Newell Highway and Macquarie Street, Dubbo. ☎ (02) 6884 1422. www.dubbotourism.com.au
- **Cowra Visitor Information Centre:** Olympic Park, Mid Western Highway, Cowra. ☎ (02) 6342 4333. www.cowratourism.com.au
- **Griffith Visitor Centre:** corner Banna and Jondaryan avenues ☎ 1800 681 141. www.griffith.nsw.gov.au
- **Armidale Visitor Information Centre:** 82 Marsh Street, Armidale. ☎ 1800 627 736. www.armidaletourism.com.au
- **Glen Innes Visitor Information Centre:** New England Hwy, Glen Innes. ☎ (02) 6732 2397. www.GlenInnesTourism.com
- **Inverell Tourist Information Centre:** Campbell Street, Inverell. ☎ (02) 6728 8161. www.inverell-online.com.au
- **Warialda Tourist Information Centre:** Hope Street, Warialda. ☎ (02) 6729 0046.
- **Bingara Information Centre:** 64 Maitland Street, Bingara. ☎ (02) 6724 0066.
- **Tamworth Visitor Information Centre:** corner Peel and Murray streets, Tamworth. ☎ (02) 6755 4300. www.tamworth.nsw.gov.au
- **Nundle:** www.nundle.info

weather watch

- January: 16–31°C
- July: 1–14°C
- Distinct seasons—hot summers, cold winters, very pleasant autumn and spring. Expect very cold nights and occasional snowfalls in winter in the New England highlands.

outback

Outback rodeo. *(Getty Images)*

► THE FAR NORTH-WESTERN CORNER OF NEW SOUTH WALES is a great introduction to the outback, where endless red dust plains studded with salt bush and mulga seem to stretch on forever under cloudless blue skies, and mobs of kangaroos, emus and cackling galahs are the only signs of life. Rain out here is rare, but when it does fall, unsealed roads quickly become rivers of thick, glue-like mud that can be impassable for days, so always check road conditions before setting out. Travelling on roads that have a 'closed road' sign, even if you are in a 4WD vehicle, may incur a substantial fine of up to $1000.

The region is rich in indigenous culture and history, but remains sparsely populated. Mining and sheep farming are the main industries, although tourism is becoming more popular in larger towns such as Broken Hill which has a thriving arts scene.

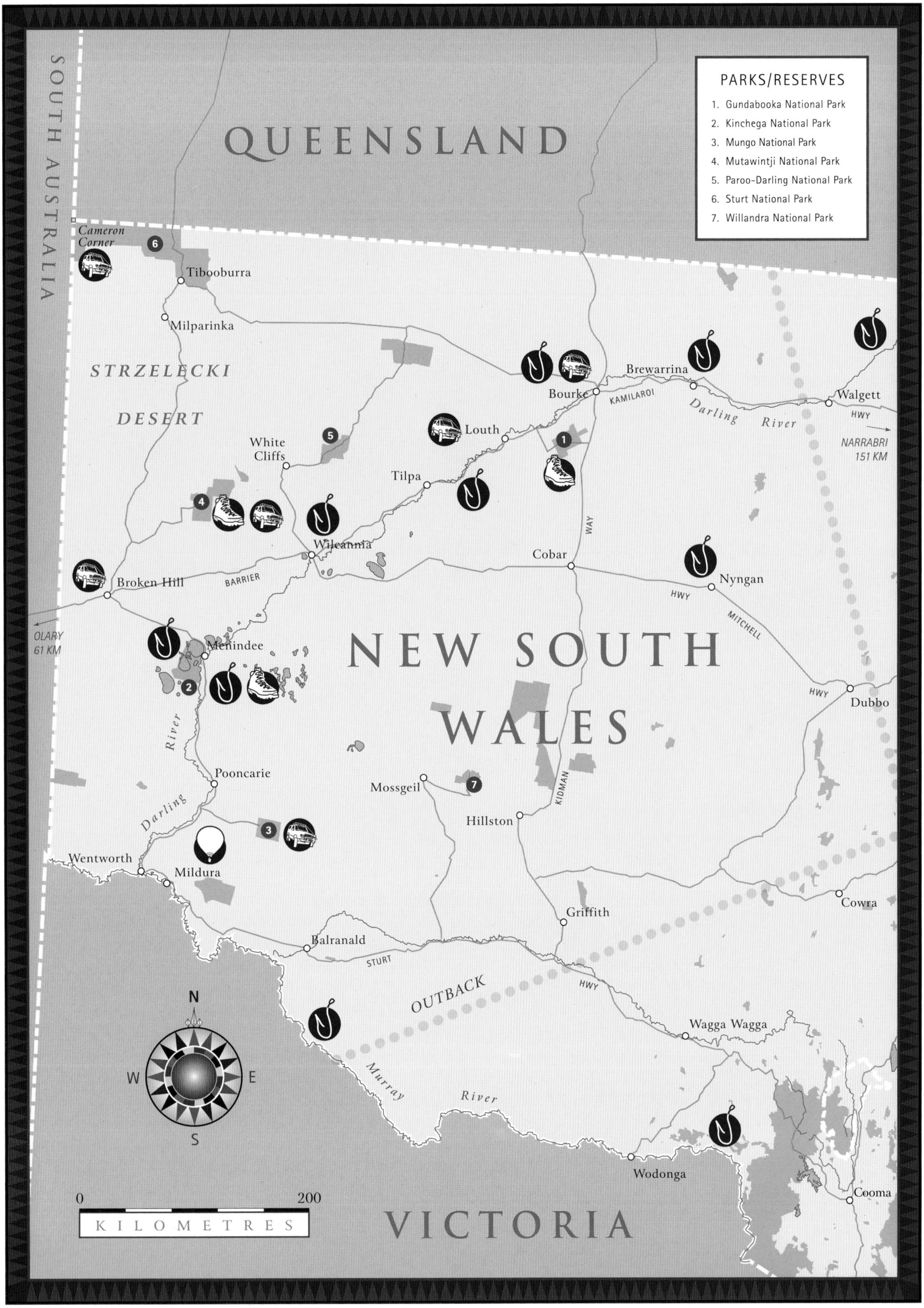

QUEENSLAND

SOUTH AUSTRALIA

PARKS/RESERVES

1. Gundabooka National Park
2. Kinchega National Park
3. Mungo National Park
4. Mutawintji National Park
5. Paroo-Darling National Park
6. Sturt National Park
7. Willandra National Park

Cameron Corner
Tibooburra
Milparinka
STRZELECKI DESERT
White Cliffs
Louth
Bourke
Brewarrina
KAMILAROI
Darling River
Walgett
HWY
NARRABRI 151 KM
Tilpa
WAY
Wilcannia
Cobar
Nyngan
Broken Hill
BARRIER
HWY
MITCHELL
OLARY 61 KM
Menindee
NEW SOUTH WALES
HWY
Dubbo
River
Pooncarie
Mossgeil
KIDMAN
Hillston
Darling
Wentworth
Mildura
Cowra
Griffith
Balranald
STURT
HWY
OUTBACK
Wagga Wagga
Murray River
N
W
E
S
Wodonga
Cooma
0 200
KILOMETRES
VICTORIA

NATIONAL PARKS

Mungo National Park: 15,000 years ago this vast, flat plain was a huge lake. Along the eastern edge is a 22km crescent-shaped wall of sand and clay eroded into weird and fantastic formations. Called the Walls of China by Chinese station workers in the 19th century, the lunette has preserved countless Aboriginal campfires, cooking hearths and burials. It was here that the oldest recorded cremation in the world was found—an Aboriginal woman more than 40,000 years old—along with skeletons of ancient megafauna and Tasmanian tigers. Take a short walk from the car park to a viewing platform at the Great Walls, or take a 60km sign-posted drive around the park through Mallee country.

Kinchega National Park: here the Darling River flows into the Menindee Lakes, forming three huge bodies of water. Much of the park was originally Kinchega Station, and you can visit the original 62-stand woolshed, built in 1875. There are two great drives around the lakes and along the Darling River inside the park. Sunsets over the lakes are spectacular and birds and wildlife are prolific.

Mutawintji National Park: spectacular gorge country. The Mutawintji Local Land Council conducts tours explaining Aboriginal rock art dating back over 8,000 years, as well as the significance of the area and the many uses of its flora and fauna. Take a self-guided tour of the Homestead Creek Gorge to Wright's Cave to see more engravings and stencils, or the longer walk to Old Mootwingee Gorge, a delightful swimming hole surrounded by towering red cliffs.

Sturt National Park: this outback park features dramatic jump ups, flat mesa-like mountains that rise dramatically from the surrounding plains. After rain, the dry plains transform into a sea of green with kangaroos and emus everywhere. The NPWS information centre in Tibooburra has information on the various self-drive tours you can do in the park.

Willandra National Park: Willandra Station, between Hillston and Mossgiel, was once famous for its wool. Today it offers an insight into the pastoral history of the region. The restored homestead, built in 1918 and surrounded by gardens and overlooking peaceful Willandra Creek, offers accommodation. The grasslands and coolibah-lined creek beds to the west of the homestead are home to kangaroos, emus and ground-nesting birds.

Paroo-Darling National Park: a relatively unknown park near White Cliffs, the Paroo River wetlands is one of the most regularly flooded systems of the arid catchment zones. Peery and Poloko lakes and their associated wetlands form part of the Paroo River overflow, the only unregulated river in the Murray-Darling Basin and have sustained Aboriginal life for many thousands of years. The middens at Peery Lakes contain mammal and fish bones and are the most extensive bone midden deposits in NSW.

Gundabooka National Park: near Bourke, this park features rugged cliffs, gorges and hills formed from rust-coloured rocks more than 385 million years old. The main feature is the Gunderbooka Range which rises 500m from the surrounding plains.

Sculpture Symposium, Broken Hill. *(Tourism NSW)*

The western plains

West of Dubbo, the countryside becomes increasingly flatter and arid, wheat fields giving way to enormous sheep stations. The inland rivers of the western plains, particularly the Darling, were once the lifeblood of the area and the main transport route for paddle steamers that once plied the waterways taking wool down the river to Adelaide and Melbourne. The river traffic is now long gone, but visit riverside towns like Brewarrina and Wilcannia and you'll find plenty of reminders of those halcyon days of the late 19th century when they were boom towns, riding the sheep's back to good fortune, the prosperity of the age reflected in the graceful architecture and impressive courthouses and public buildings. Bourke, the most famous of these outback river ports, has become synonymous with the outback, thanks largely to its immortalisation in the stories of Henry Lawson.

Broken Hill and beyond

Closer to Adelaide than Sydney, Broken Hill is the hub of the outback and the base for most of the essential services, such as the Royal Flying Doctor Service (RFDS) and School of the Air that service the outlying stations and communities. Nicknamed the Silver City, Broken Hill made its fortune on the wealth of silver and zinc buried beneath the surface that was first discovered in the 1880s.

In the past decade or so, Broken Hill has become one of the state's most important arts centres, the unique outback light and landscape attracting artists from all around the world. There are almost 30 galleries in town and at nearby Silverton. Don't miss Pro Hart's gallery, the Broken Hill City Art Gallery and the Sculpture Symposium in the Living Desert reserve on the outskirts of town.

Amid the vast arid plains, Menindee, 110km east of Broken Hill, is a veritable desert oasis where the Darling River flows into the Menindee Lakes. The constant presence of water attracts an amazing wealth of birdlife–flocks of pelicans, groups of ibis, herons, whistling kites, great egrets, and countless others. Explorer Charles Sturt camped at Menindee on his search for the inland

sea and, in 1860, Burke and Wills stayed at Maidens Hotel at the beginning of their ill-fated trip that ended at Cooper Creek. William Wright, the man who has been blamed for a large part of the tragedy, was a station manager at Kinchega before he joined their party.

The opal mining town of White Cliffs is 245km to the north-east, where most of the hopeful fossickers live underground in dug-outs. Spend a night or two in the underground motel or B&B, tour the galleries and fossick at the opal fields. Follow the Darling River south and watch the countryside change from dry mallee scrub to lush farming lands of the Sunraysia area near Wentworth, rich with vineyards, orchards and agriculture. A pretty historic port town with many heritage buildings, Wentworth has the distinction of the being the town where two of our greatest rivers, the Darling and the Murray, converge. From the lookout tower in Junctional Park you can see the differently-coloured waters eddy together beneath the cruising houseboats and paddle steamers that take passengers on lunch or tea-and-coffee river cruises.

Corner country

315km north of Broken Hill along a mostly unsealed road is one of the last true frontier towns, Tibooburra. This is harsh country and there are plenty of reminders of fortunes made and lost, such as the ghost town of Milparinka, 39km south of Tibooburra, where you can wander around the historic courthouse and buildings that stand empty in the now almost deserted town.

From Tibooburra, you can head north-west to Cameron Corner, where NSW, South Australia and Queensland meet amongst the red dunes and wide brown gibber plains of the Strezlecki Desert. If you are lucky enough to be here after the rain has been and gone, the dunes are carpeted in yellow and white daisy-like wildflowers. There's not much at Cameron Corner–just the Corner Store on the Queensland side. But like all good corner shops it sells everything–fuel, basic mechanical gear, food supplies, snacks, cold beer and souvenirs. Stop and chat awhile with the owners, who can fill you on local road conditions and good places to camp.

Caravan and camping

The campsites along the bank of the Darling River in Kinchega National Park are some of the best in the state. Facilities are basic, but the campsites are spread along the bank out of sight of each other. Lakeside camping in this park has the best sunset show around. There is also good camping in Sturt and Mungo. Homestead Creek camping ground in Mutawintji has (unpowered) caravan sites. There's a small camping and picnic area at Dry Tank at the foot of Gunderbooka Range in Gundabooka National Park and several good campgrounds in Willandra, although they are not suitable for caravans.

Bushwalks

The best walks in this area are in Mutawintji National Park. Old Mootwingee Gorge Walk is a 3km walk of medium difficulty into one of the park's most picturesque gorges, ending at a peaceful rock pool enclosed by towering rusty red cliffs. The longer and more difficult Sunset Ridge Trail is a five-hour walk that includes several steep sections that takes you to the top of a ridge overlooking the vast desert plains and beautiful Bynguano Range. It's wonderful at sunset, but the walk can take up to two hours to complete and night falls quickly, so take a torch. The Homestead Gorge Trail is a leisurely three-hour walk between the craggy cliffs of Homestead Creek, and into the Homestead Gorge. Keep an eye out for Aboriginal engravings.

scenic highlights

The Kidman Way runs almost 800km through outback New South Wales and is a great introduction to the wide open expanse of western NSW, particularly for those who prefer to stay on the bitumen. Along the way you can visit the scene of some of bushranger Ned Kelly's more notorious raids, enjoy the wineries and restaurants of cosmopolitan Griffith and the surrounding Riverina region, learn about the true story behind the legend of the 'black stump', discover a rich local history at the copper mining town of Cobar and explore the town that has become synonymous with the bush and the outback, Bourke.

A more adventurous trip is the Darling River Run, which follows the river from Bourke to Wentworth along largely unsealed roads through tiny outback settlements like Louth and Tilpa, both famous for their annual picnic horse races, visiting riverside ports such as Wilcannia, Menindee Lakes and finally Pooncarie and Wentworth.

Windmill service, Pineview Station, Broken Hill. *(Getty Images)*

Camel trek, Silverton. *(Tourism NSW)*

DON'T MISS

- **Wentworth river cruises:** contact the visitor centre in Wentworth for details of paddle steamer and other river cruises. ☎ (03) 5027 3624.
- **Old Wentworth Gaol:** historic cells and museum. Beverley Street, Wentworth. Open daily, 10am–5pm. ☎ (03) 5027 3337.
- **Australian Inland Botanic Gardens:** 122-acre native gardens and historic Garnpang homestead. River Road, Mourquong. Open daily, 10am–4pm except Saturday and days over 36°C. www.austinlandbotgardens.org
- **Broken Hill School of the Air:** listen to the children do their lessons on air. Bookings must be made the day before at the Tourist Information Centre. Lessons: Mon–Fri, 8.30am.
- **Royal Flying Doctor Service:** tour the headquarters and visit the museum. Broken Hill Airport. Open Mon–Fri 9am–12noon and 1–5pm. ☎ (08) 8080 1777.
- **Art galleries:** Broken Hill has become a major arts centre. There are many galleries in town and at nearby Silverton. Top three are Pro Hart's gallery, the Broken Hill City Art Gallery and the Sculpture Symposium at the Living Desert. The Broken Hill Visitor Information Centre has details on the many other art galleries.
- **White's Mineral Art Gallery and Mining Museum:** imaginative art made from minerals and ingenious models explaining how mining is carried out—in the past and today. Open daily 9am–5pm. ☎ (08) 8087 2878.
- **Geo centre:** interactive museum of minerals. Open Mon–Fri, 10am–4.45pm, weekends 1–5pm. ☎ (08) 8087 6538.
- **Ned Kelly Post Office:** visit the scene of one of the Kelly Gang's most notorious raids. Powell Street, Jerilderie.
- **Great Cobar Outback Heritage Centre:** local and mining history. Barrier Highway, Cobar. Open Mon–Fri, 8am–5pm; Sat–Sun, 10am–5pm.
- **Mt Grenfell Historic Site:** good examples of ancient Aboriginal rock art by the local Wongaibon people as well as scarred trees, ochre pits and a waterhole. No camping or dogs. 72km north-west of Cobar. ☎ (02) 6836 2692.
- **Fort Bourke Stockade:** although explorer Sturt passed through the area in 1829, when he discovered the Darling River and Mt Oxley, Surveyor Major Mitchell was the first to 'settle' at Bourke, when he erected Fort Bourke Stockade in 1835. You can tour the stockade site where there is a replica and a commemorative cairn. Directions are available from the Visitors Information Centre in the old railway building in Bourke.
- **Back O'Bourke Exhibition Centre:** tells the story of the Darling River and the region beyond with frontier and pioneer stories. Kidman Way, Bourke. www.backobourke.com.au
- **Fort Bourke Hill Lookout and New Cobar Open Cut Gold Mine:** the historical site of Cobar's first gold mine and the New Cobar Gold Mine. Peak Gold Mines (Rio Tinto) has commenced open cut mining operation at Fort Bourke and you can look down upon the mine from the viewing platform. Limited access to the lookout by contact with the Cobar Heritage Centre on ☎ (02) 6836 2448.
- **Peak Gold Mine:** a viewing platform gives a view of a modern-day working mine site. The Golden Walk takes you past the Conqueror mine shaft and the remains of an old 1890s stamper battery used to crush gold-bearing ore. 8km south of Cobar, on the Kidman Way.
- **Perry Sandhills:** just on the outskirts of Wentworth, these rolling, red sandhills are in stark contrast to the surrounding irrigated fields and are now a popular film and television backdrop, but they were once a favoured Aboriginal hunting and camping ground. The sandhills are constantly shifting as the wind picks up and redeposits the sand, and have uncovered the skeletal remains of giant kangaroos and wombats. Ask at the visitors centre for directions. ☎ (02) 6845 1733 or 1800 621 614.

adventure activities

Camping in Menindee Lakes. (Tourism NSW)

Ballooning

Hot air ballooning for sleepy heads. Balloon flights daily at dawn (depending on the weather), but as Mildura is at the western end of the eastern standard time zone, wake up times and call out times are later in Mildura than anywhere else in eastern Australia. Flight packages include a wake up call, collection to and from your accommodation, one-hour scenic flight, champagne celebration after landing, gourmet restaurant breakfast and souvenir certificate, and returned to your accommodation.

www.milduraballooning.com.au

Bird watching

The Menindee wetlands are a bird watchers paradise as the constant presence of water attracts an amazing wealth of birdlife. Geoff Looney, Menindee's resident birdlife and fishing expert, calls the wetlands around here "the Kakadu of the South". Disappointed that we turned up at midday for our birdwatching tour on Lake Wetherell, he muttered that "you won't see anything out here at this time of day." One hour later, we had identified more than 20 different species of birds, all of which were in plentiful numbers–flocks of pelicans, groups of ibis, herons, whistling kites, great egrets, plovers, spoonbills, cormorants, honeyeaters, willy wagtails, ducks, darters, bee eaters and tree martins.

☎ (08) 8091 4437

River Lady Tours run cruises aboard the flat-bottomed *River Lady* from the Main Weir on Lake Wetherell every Monday, Tuesday and Wednesday or on request.

☎ (08) 8088 5404

Camel safaris

Explore the outback in the mode of explorers Burke and Wills–on a camel. Barrier Range Camel Safaris is located at Silverton and offer rides from half an hour up to full day and overnight safaris along dry creek beds and through the rocky landscape.

On longer safaris you will tour through the Silverton township, past the old cemetery, Penrose Park, the old Silverton railway line, abandoned mines and Mundi Mundi Plain, a popular filming location. The camels are all very friendly and quiet and are suitable for all ages and camel riding experience. They also sell camels, just in case you have the burning desire to take one home. They are, apparently, great weed eaters.

www.silvertoncamels.com

Sturt National Park. *(Tourism NSW)*

Fishing

The Darling River at Bourke is a great place to do some inland fishing. The best spots are on the other side of the riverbank to the town and under the North Bourke Bridge. Fish to catch are yellow-belly, catfish, black bream, European carp and Murray cod. There's good yabbies when the Paroo and Warrego Rivers run. A fishing weekend starts each Easter Friday with the weigh-in on Sunday.

Another great spot to fish is the regulator at Menindee Lakes, where golden perch can congregate in large numbers.

Off-road driving

The outback is 4WD nirvana. While the majority of main roads in outback NSW are fine for conventional vehicles, most of the minor roads and station tracks are 4WD only. There are numerous tour companies that run guided and tag along 4WD tours in and around Broken Hill and along the Darling.

Local visitor information centres all have lists of good local tour operators. Alternatively, many of the local farms and sheep stations will provide you with a mud map so you can explore the farm tracks on your own.

www.cornercountryadventure.com.au www.tristate.com.au
www.outbacktours.net

Harry Nunya Tours

Mungo National Park is an important place for local Aboriginal groups, with a history of Aboriginal occupation in the area going back more than 40,000 years. The best way to gain an insight into the cultural significance of the area is to join one of the Harry Nanya tours. These tours explain how the original owners of this land lived and hunted as well as the dreamtime creation stories associated with the area. There are a range of full and half-day tours as well as sunset tours–the park is particularly beautiful in the evening when the white sand lunette changes colour and glows in the light of the setting sun.

☎ (03) 5027-2076

Outback mail runs

Join the local postie on his mail run to really get a glimpse of how the locals live and just how far away their nearest neighbours really are. The Bush Mail Run is a mail delivery operating every Wednesday and Saturday from Broken Hill, travelling over more than 55km of bush roads by four-wheel drive. The full day trip includes a visit to an outback homestead for morning tea and meet third generation landowners Gordan and Val Gillett at Budgeree Station, lunch on the banks of the Darling River, a stop to see Woolcunda Lake which only fills twice a century and lots of local wildlife, both native and introduced, including kangaroos, emus, foxes, eagles, goats, occasional wild pigs and other bird life.

email: greenhil@bigpond.net.au ☎ (08) 8087 2164

MORE INFORMATION

- **Wentworth Shire Visitor Information Centre:** Darling Street, Wentworth. ☎ (03) 5027 3624. www.wentworth.nsw.gov.au/tourism
- **Broken Hill Visitor Information Centre:** corner Blende and Bromide streets. ☎ (08) 8087 6077. www.visitbrokenhill.com.au
- **Tibooburra:** ☎ (08) 8091 3308. www.outbacknsw.com.au/tibooburra.htm
- **Great Cobar Heritage Centre:** Barrier Highway, Cobar. ☎ (02) 6836 2448. www.cobar.nsw.gov.au
- **Bourke Visitor Information Centre:** Anson Street, Bourke. ☎ (02) 6872 1222. www.outbackonline.net/BourkeTourism.htm

weather watch

- January: 14–32°C
- July: 5–18°C
- Summer can be very hot and the flies are extremely friendly—winter (although nights can be cold) is the most pleasant time to travel throughout the area.

Alternatively, hitch a ride with Broken Hill's flying postman. Passengers spend the morning helping to deliver the mail to remote outback stations before landing at White Cliffs, where most of the locals live underground in dug-outs for lunch and a tour, before flying back to Broken Hill.

☎ (08) 8088 5702

Station life

Get a taste of the real outback and experience life on a remote outback sheep station living and working on a fully operational grazing property. Kallara Station, near Tilpa was established in 1857 with an area of one million acres. It was one of the original big 'runs' in western NSW and stretched approximately 130km from the Darling River taking in the Cuttuburra and Paroo Rivers. In its heyday, Kallara shore 400,000 sheep and boasted a steam-driven mechanical shearing shed of 44 stands and a riverside wool scour. Stay in luxury and budget river-front accommodation.

www.kallarastation.com.au

Trilby Station, a 130,000 acre working station near Louth also has a range of accommodation options. Farm activities include shearing, crutching, lamb marking, calf branding and mustering depending on what jobs need to be done while you are visiting.

www.trilbystation.com.au

For details of other outback farm stays contact the visitor centres in each town.

Underground mine tours

There are several adventure tours of underground mines available in Broken Hill. At Delprats Mine, the original BHP Mine, you can don a miner's hat and lamp and descend slowly, via a cage 120m down the mine shaft, for a tour of drives, stopes and mining machinery in working order. Any specimens you find are yours to keep. Tours Mon–Fri 10.30am, Sat 2pm. Additional tours during school holidays.

You can also go underground at Day Dream Silver Mine, near Silverton, which gives a subterranean look at mining in the 1880s when most of the miners were eight-year-old boys working with hammers and taps.

Milparinka. *(Tourism NSW)*

snowy mountains

The Snowy River's icy waters. *(Tourism NSW)*

▶ ALPINE NEW SOUTH WALES, or the Snowy Mountains, stretches from the ACT to the Victorian border along the spine of the Great Dividing Range. Kosciuszko National Park encompasses most of the area, protecting not only Australia's highest peak, Mt Kosciuszko, but also some of the country's most fragile alpine environments. In winter the area is a magnet for lovers of snow sports; in summer, fishing, bushwalking and mountain biking reign supreme.

First settled in the mid-19th century by graziers who summered their stock in the high country, and immortalised in Banjo Paterson's epic poem (and subsequent film adaptations), *The Man From Snowy River*, the rugged peaks of the Snowy Mountains hold a significant place in the psyche of most Australians. However, it was not until the second half of the 20th century, with the construction of the Snowy Mountains Hydro-electric Scheme, that the rugged and inhospitable area was really opened up.

The largest engineering project ever undertaken in Australia, the snowy scheme is also one of the largest and most complex hydro-electric schemes in the world, consisting of 16 major dams, seven power stations, a pumping station and 225km of tunnels, pipelines and aqueducts. Just two per cent of the entire construction is visible above the ground. Water from melting snow and rain in the Snowy Mountains that once flowed into the Snowy River is diverted through tunnels in the mountains and stored in dams. The water is then used by the power stations to create electricity and to provide water for farming districts west of the range.

Work on the system started in 1949 and was finished 25 years later in 1974, employing more than 100,000 people from more than 30 countries. Seventy per cent of the workforce were migrants from post-WWII Europe, and the snowy scheme is seen as one of the most influential factors in the shaping of Australia's multicultural society.

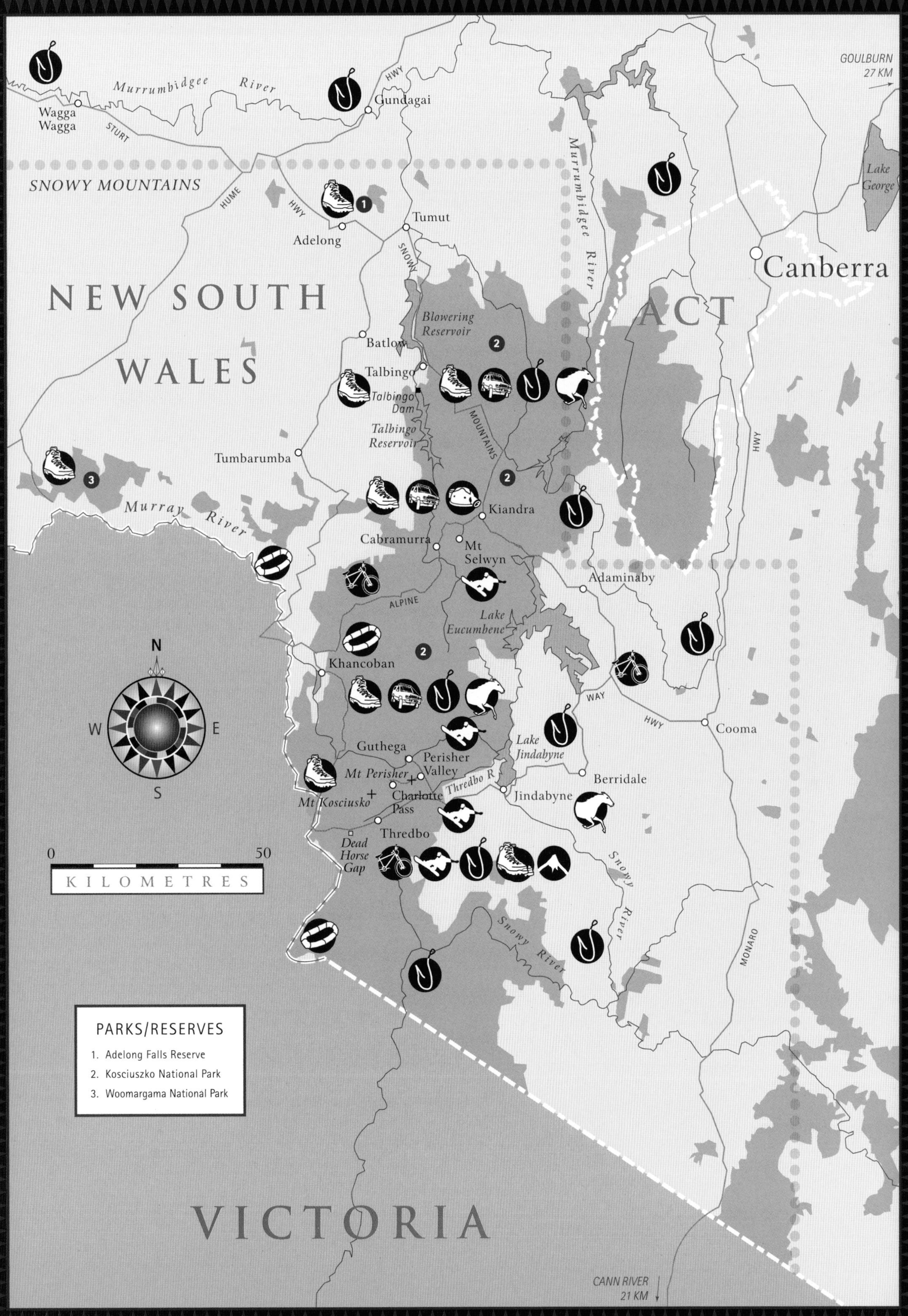

GOULBURN 27 KM
Murrumbidgee River
Wagga Wagga
STURT
Gundagai
HWY
SNOWY MOUNTAINS
HUME
HWY
Adelong
Tumut
SNOWY
Murrumbidgee River
Lake George
Canberra
NEW SOUTH WALES
ACT
Blowering Reservoir
Batlow
Talbingo
Talbingo Dam
Talbingo Reservoir
MOUNTAINS
Tumbarumba
Kiandra
Murray River
Cabramurra
Mt Selwyn
Adaminaby
ALPINE
Lake Eucumbene
Khancoban
WAY
HWY
Cooma
Guthega
Perisher Valley
Mt Perisher
Lake Jindabyne
Berridale
Mt Kosciusko
Charlotte Pass
Thredbo R
Jindabyne
Thredbo
Dead Horse Gap
Snowy River
MONARO
HWY
0
50
KILOMETRES
N
S
W
E
PARKS/RESERVES
1. Adelong Falls Reserve
2. Kosciuszko National Park
3. Woomargama National Park
VICTORIA
CANN RIVER 21 KM

Snowy Creek, Kosciuszko. (Tourism NSW)

NATIONAL PARKS

Kosciuszko National Park: the largest park in NSW and home to the highest mountains in Australia. Highlights include the Snowy River, alpine herb fields, caves and gorges, historic huts, homesteads, scenic drives and of course, all of NSW's ski fields. Activities include both downhill and cross country skiing, bushwalking, caving, mountain cycling, fishing and horse riding.

One of the Australian Alps national parks, this park is nationally and internationally recognised as a UNESCO Biosphere Reserve. It contains six wilderness areas, and its alpine and sub-alpine areas contain plant species found nowhere else in the world. The park is also home to the rare mountain pygmy possum and corroboree frog.

Woomargama National Park: this new park near the Murray River 40km west of Tumbarumba is the largest protected area west of the Great Dividing Range in south-eastern NSW and contains the largest remnant of box woodlands on the south-west slopes. It's an important haven for a large number of threatened and endangered species, such as the regent honeyeater, swift parrot, powerful owl, brown toadlet and carpet python. It's also home to the very rare *Acacia phasmoides* wattle. Parts of the reserve are close to 1000m above sea level, giving stunning views over the Murray River and areas west of the park. Access is via 4WD only and all access roads are closed when wet.

Cooma, Jindabyne and the ski fields

The main town in the Snowies is Cooma, which has a permanent population of around 8000 or so. It is the main headquarters of the Snowy Mountains Authority (SMA) and was once one of the country's most cosmopolitan towns.

Jindabyne is a modern town created after the original settlement was drowned by the Snowy Mountains Hydro-electric Authority in the late 1960s. The man-made lake of the same name, along with nearby Lake Eucumbene is a great spot for trout fishing as well as sailing, windsurfing and water skiing.

Thredbo is a resort village that caters mainly for the winter skiing crowd but is one of the few resorts that offers a range of summer activities. You can take the chairlift to the top of Crackenback and walk the 6km easy track to the top of Mt Kosciuszko, which at 2228m, is Australia's highest peak. It was named in 1840 by the Polish geologist and explorer Count Paul de Strzelecki in honour of General Tadeusz Kosciuszko, a Polish patriot and freedom fighter.

There is a range of guided walks available in Thredbo as well as mountain bike riding, fly fishing, horse riding and the bob sled. The Australian Institute of Sport Alpine Training Centre is open to the public. It has an Olympic-sized swimming pool, fully-equipped gym, squash, basketball, netball and volleyball courts and a running track.

Adaminaby, Talbingo and Tumut

Like Jindabyne, the original township of Adaminaby is now underwater (Lake Eucumbene), and you can still see the remnants of Old Adaminaby if you drive a couple of kilometres out of town towards Kiandra, but most of the buildings were moved to the new site in the mid-1950s. The waters of Lake Eucumbene are a favourite with anglers and you can't miss the 'big trout', a huge fibreglass rainbow trout standing guard over the park in the centre of town.

Gold was discovered at Kiandra in 1859; today all that remains are a few ruins covered by wildflowers and some display boards telling the story. Nearby, the limestone Yarrangobilly Caves are among the most richly decorated in Australia, where there is a thermal pool with water a constant 27°C, bushwalks and picnic facilities.

The birthplace of Miles Franklin (author of *My Brilliant Career*), Talbingo is a pretty village beside Lake Journama in the shadow of the mountains; although much of the town's history is now underwater in order to accommodate the Snowy Scheme. Drive up to Talbingo Dam to a lookout over the dam wall and mountains into the valley below before touring Tumut 3 power station. This is the biggest power station in the scheme and you'll see massive pipes big enough for a double-decker bus to drive through. The 30-minute drive to Tumut–famous for it autumn colours and the annual Festival of the Falling Leaf, held in late April–follows the shoreline of Blowering Reservoir with good views of the lake and mountains.

Adelong, Batlow and Tumbarumba

The historic township of Adelong just west of Tumut was once a bustling town of 20,000 during a gold rush in 1857; it is now a sleepy village of 900. Many of the buildings in the main street are listed by the National Trust. One kilometre out of town is the Adelong Falls Reserve, where Adelong Creek flows by the ruins of the old Reefer Battery that served the gold mines until abandoned in 1910. The creek and hills here are said to have yielded more than 25 tonnes of gold; you can try your luck panning in the creek and there are some pleasant short walks, picnic tables, barbecues and toilets.

scenic highlights

Mount Kosciuszko National Park. *(Tourism NSW)*

The Alpine Way is a very impressive scenic drive which winds a slow but spectacular 111km through the ranges from Jindabyne to Khancoban. The road was originally built in 1955 as an access road during construction period of the Snowy Scheme and was not intended to be permanent, but has been rebuilt to cater for tourist traffic. It is not suitable for caravans, large or articulated vehicles.

From Jindabyne the road begins to climb into the mountains, rising from 930m to 1370m at Thredbo and finally 1580m at Dead Horse Gap. The Alpine Way enters Kosciuszko Park just before Thredbo, around 20 minutes from Jindabyne (park fees apply even if you are only driving through the park). Leaving Thredbo the road snakes its way to Dead Horse Gap, which, according to local legend, got its name from brumbies that were trapped here in severe snow storms and died. During spring and summer the roadsides are lined with masses of white, lemon and pink wildflowers and even in February, there are patches of snow in the mountain crevices. Stop at Pilot Lookout for expansive views of the upper Murray River valley and the NSW/Victoria border. From here the road descends to rest areas at Leatherbarrel Creek and Tom Groggin near Tom Groggin station, home of Tom Riley who was reputedly the original 'man from Snowy River', and Geehi on the banks of the Swampy Plains River. All three rest stops have toilets, fireplaces, picnic and bush camping areas.

Climbing again, the road cuts through the mountains with more stunning views of sheer mountain walls. Rosellas flit through the tree tops and if you're travelling in the morning or late afternoon, you'll probably see a few kangaroos as well. Stop at Scammell's Spur Lookout for spectacular panoramic views of the western face of the main range. Ten kilometres east of Khancoban is the turnoff for Murray 1 power station, the second largest power station in the Snowy Scheme.

Although the Alpine Way officially ends at Khancoban, continue on, turning right to Cabramurra. Winding through lush farmland on the valley floor the road climbs again through the mountains, through dry sclerophyll forest, past Tooma Dam and across the wall of Tumut Pond Reservoir, to reach the SMA township of Cabramurra, about an hour's drive. You can then hook up with the Snowy Mountains Highway back to Cooma or north to Tumut.

Snow chains must be carried between 1 June and 10 October on The Alpine Way between Thredbo and Tom Groggin, the Kosciusko Road beyond Sawpit Creek and the Island Bend/Guthega Road for its full length. Other trouble spots include Kiandra and Talbingo Mountain.

To the south, Batlow is one of the main stone-fruit producing areas in the state and you can buy apples, pears, cherries and other stone fruit from roadside stalls during the season.

Tumbarumba has some great antique shops. Eight kilometres on the Wagga road is the Glenroy Heritage Reserve and the Pioneer Women's Hut, a fascinating museum dedicated to preserving the everyday objects of ordinary women and Paddys River Falls just on the edge of town has a pretty little waterfall with a nice picnic and barbecue area beside the river.

Cabramurra and Khancoban

Cabramurra is Australia's highest township at 1,488m. Built as a construction camp in 1951 it is totally owned and operated by the SMA. There is petrol available and a general store with takeaways but not much else. Tiny Khancoban, on the very scenic Alpine Way, also predominately serves the workers of the SMA although there are some private businesses in town.

High country mountain bike trails. (*Tourism NSW*)

Caravan and camping

Backpack camping is permitted virtually anywhere in Kosciuszko National Park but you'll need to be out of sight of the roads and well away from watercourses. Camping is not permitted near the resorts, in the catchment areas of the glacial lakes, or at Yarrangobilly Caves. Most of the official campgrounds in the park are very basic and do not have drinking water.

Good places to set up camp include Coolamine Homestead, in the northern section of the park, a complex of huts which relate to the earliest days of exploration and settlement of the Snowy Mountains and there are some nice summer camping spots at Tom Groggin on the banks of the Murray and beside Swampy Plain River at Geehi, 31km south of Khancoban. Three Mile Dam, near the Mount Selwyn ski fields in the north of the park, provides good high altitude camping and further north still, Talbingo and Blowering Reservoirs provide exposed camping with good views over the water.

Bushwalks

There are dozens of great bushwalking trails in Kosciuszko National Park but almost every visitor to the aea will walk to the summit of Mt Kosciuszko. You can take the chairlift to the top of Crackenback from Thredbo village and walk the 6km easy track to the top of Mt Kosciusko, which at 2228m, is Australia's highest peak. The walk is easy enough to do on your own, but there are a range of guided walks available including sunset and sunrise tours.

www.thredbo.com.au

If you have all day, you can combine it with the 10km Dead Horse Gap walk that takes you from the chairlift across the mountain and then back to the village through stands of snow gums and along the Thredbo River. Make sure you take water, warm clothing and sunscreen as the weather can change suddenly and the sun can be severe, even when cool.

The Snow Gums Boardwalk is a 15-minute stroll that starts at the Charlotte's Pass lookout and traverses sub-alpine woodland on the Guthrie Range. You will see many of Australia's highest peaks and superb views.

The Summit Walk from Charlotte's Pass to Mt Kosciuszko is a 9km, three-hour difficult walk that follows the old road to Mt Kosciuszko. The walk passes through snow gums, heath and alpine herb fields and provides extensive views of the Main Range and Snowy River. After crossing the Snowy River the track climbs gradually to Seaman's Hut, Rawson's Pass and Mt Kosciuszko's summit.

For those that like a challenge, the two-hour Charlotte's Pass to Blue Lake lookout crosses the Snowy River below Charlotte's Pass before climbing through alpine herb fields past Hedley Tarn lookout to Blue Lake lookout. You can continue on to Mt Kosciuszko climbing Carruther's Peak and along the exposed ridge of the Main Range above Club Lake and Lake Albina until it meets the Summit Walk between Rawson's Pass and Mt Kosciuszko.

In the Kiandra area you can follow the Goldseeker's Track, a 3.5km medium walk that begins opposite the southern entrance to Three Mile Dam. Among its features are snowgrass flats, snow gum woodland and an abandoned ore-crushing battery. The Kiandra Heritage Track is an easy walk around the site of one the shortest gold rushes in Australian history–from November 1859 to March 1861. It has been claimed that by March 1860 there were up to 10,000 people on the diggings. The track begins at the Roads and Traffic depot (former courthouse) and a number of signs along the way provide information about many of the major buildings and life in historic Kiandra.

To the north, in the Talbingo area, the Blowering Cliffs Walk is a two-hour medium walk that starts from the parking area at the bridge over the Snowy Mountains Highway at the Log Bridge Creek picnic area. The track, which goes to Blowering Falls, is quite steep in sections and passes through dense vegetation which grows on the damp, sheltered hillsides. The last section of the walk involves negotiating rock slabs which have fallen from the cliff above.

Old Mountain Road Walk follows the first road up Talbingo Mountain, built in 1860 during the Kiandra gold rush. It starts at the RTA stockpile, which, if you were travelling toward Cooma, is 5.5km

Snowboarding Thredbo. (*Tourism NSW*)

DON'T MISS

- **Eucumbene Trout Farm:** Round Plain Road, via Berridale. Open daily 10am–5pm, NSW school holidays & public holidays and NSW Ski Season (1 June – 30 Sept). Other times by arrangement.
- **Murray 1 power station:** free 45-minute guided tours of the station. 72km from Thredbo, 10km from Khancoban. Open Mon–Fri 9am–4pm, weekends 10am–4pm (closed on weekends in winter).
- **Tumut 2 power station:** underground tours. 12km from Cabramurra. Open Mon to Fri for guided tours. Bookings are essential. Tour Times 1 October – 30 May Mon–Fri 10am, 11am, 12 noon and 1pm; 2pm weekends and school holidays. ☎ 1800 623 776.
- **Tumut 3 power station:** Talbingo. Open daily. Guided tours at 10am, 11am, 12noon, 1.30pm & 2.30pm (closed Good Friday and Christmas Day).
- **Glenroy Heritage Reserve and the Pioneer Women's Hut:** museum dedicated to preserving the everyday objects of ordinary women. Wagga Road, Tumbarumba. Open Wed, Sat and Sun, and most public holidays, 10am–4pm.
- **Fossicking:** enthusiastic gold panners can try their luck at what was once the workplace of thousands of goldminers. Perfect for a picnic, a quick dip on a hot day or quiet reflection in a peaceful setting. There are three walks on the reserve ranging from 15-40 minutes. Adelong Falls Reserve, Wagga Road, Adelong. Tumut Region Visitor Cente. ☎ (02) 6947 7025.
- **Yarrangobilly Caves:** 6.5km off the Snowy Mountains Highway in Kosciuszko National Park. Take a self-guided tour of Glory Hole Cave between 10am–4pm (daily), or join one of the guided tours of the other caves.
- **Kosciuszko Express Chairlift:** the chairlift is 1.8km long and rises 560 vertical metres. The ride takes 15 minutes one way and offers spectacular valley views as you are lifted to the closest access point to Mount Kosciuszko. Chairlift is open 9am–4.30pm daily.
- **Thredbo Valley Distillery:** unique schnapps distillery with cellar door, art gallery (artist in residence), sculpture walk and of course the Wildbrumby schnapps. On the Alpine Way half way between Jindabyne and Thredbo. Open daily.

Snowgum. (Tourism NSW)

past the Talbingo turn-off on the left side of the highway. It involves a steep descent, so organise a car shuttle at the bottom. The first part of the walk provides excellent views of the Bogong Peaks and Jounama Creek valley.

The Hume and Hovell Walking Track stretches more than 440km between Yass and Albury and follows the route of explorers Hamilton Hume and William Hovell on their expedition to Port Phillip in 1824. The track is fully signposted and provides opportunities for numerous day walks, weekend walks or a total walk of around 24 days. The track starts at Cooma Cottage on the outskirts of Yass and finishes at the Hovell Tree on the banks of the Murray River in Albury. It has three trackheads (major access points and are ideal for car-based camping) approximately 100km apart: James Fitzpatrick at Wee Jasper, Thomas Boyd on the Goobarragandra River 23km from Tumut and Henry Angel on Burra Creek near Tumbarumba. The track passes through the towns of Yass, Wee Jasper and Albury and nearby the towns of Tumut, Talbingo and Tumbarumba. It has 17 basic campsites, numerous boardwalks and three major bridges over rivers. For more information contact the NSW Department of Lands.

www.lands.nsw.gov.au

adventure activities

Snowboarder gets air. *(Getty Images)*

Bobsledding

Thredbo Bobsled is a 700m-long luge-style track that twists and turns its way down the mountain whilst you control the speed with a brake on your cart. It's great fun for all the family and open every day of the year, weather permitting.

Climbing and abseiling

The superb granite tors above Thredbo are a spectacular place to try climbing and abseiling. Thredbo Sports run half-day introductory courses. The indoor Traverse Climbing wall at the Thredbo Leisure Centre also gives a fun introduction to climbing.

Fishing

The Snowy Mountains is the premier trout fishery in NSW with good numbers of both brown and rainbows found in the fast flowing rivers and streams, dams and lakes. The NSW Fisheries Gaden Trout Hatchery regularly releases rainbow and brown trout fry and fingerlings into the local waterways to maintain stock levels. Although some of the smaller streams can be affected by low summer flows, the Monaro and Thredbo rivers offers some of the best fly fishing in the world and you can land good Atlantic salmon in Lake Jindabyne, while the rivers of the western slopes have good native populations such as Murray Crayfish, which you'll often hook in the Murrumbidgee.

There are a range of fly fishing schools and guides available that cater for all levels of expertise, from absolute beginners to experienced angler. Contact the nearest visitor information centre for details.

Four-wheel driving

There are some good 4WD tracks in the Kiandra area of Kosciuszko National Park visiting some of the historic huts and homesteads such as Currango Homestead on the Port Phillip Fire Trail, the oldest surviving homestead in the park. It is also the largest and most intact example of permanent settlement above the snowline in the country, and has great historical significance as one of the most important links to the first European settlement of the area. There are 25 remaining buildings and ruins which span 150 years of settlement in the park. Continue down Port Phillip Fire Trail to reach another historic homestead, Coolamine, and a spectacular gorge at Blue Waterholes.

Horse riding

This is *Man from Snowy River* country: the pioneer, hard-riding mountain men providing the inspiration for Banjo Patterson's famous poem and debate still rages today on exactly who was the role model for the famous horseman. Horse riding has always been a way of life in the Snowies and commercial horse treks through the mountains first began in the 1940s, so there are lots of places that offer trails rides and riding trips, ranging from one-hour easy trails across high-country grazing lands and to longer six-day camping trips in and around the back country trails of Kosciuszko National Park.

www.cochranhorsetreks.com.au www.reynellarides.com.au
www.penderlea.com.au

Planet X Winter Extreme games, Perisher Valley. *(Getty Images)*

Mountain biking

Thredbo is the undisputed capital of mountain biking in Australia with a range of trails, from nice easy-riding trails for casual riders to gnarly terrain for the downhill dynamos, as well as regular championship racing events.

Either bring your own bike and pick up a trail map in the village or hire one with any or all of the gear you need from RawNRG who also run a range of guided trips. One of the most popular is the legendary Cannonball Run, which involves taking your bike up to the top of the mountain on the chairlift and hurtling back down as fast as you can. It's for experienced riders only and can only be done after a three-hour instruction session from RawNRG and under their supervision.

Other trails include the Tom Groggin trail along the Alpine Way descending an easy 1000 vertical metres to the Tom Groggin camping ground at the headwaters of the Murray River and the Schlink's Pass Epic ride, an all-day expedition for experienced riders on challenging bike tracks.

www.rawnrg.com.au

Skiing

There are four ski fields in NSW. Thredbo has the highest and longest ski runs and Australia's highest-lifted point, Karel's T-bar at 2037m. You can ski a thigh-aching 5.9km all the way from Karel's to the beginner's area of Friday Flat or stop at Terminal Valley, which is still a good 3.7km run. There's also plenty of cross-country and back country trails to follow. Most of the terrain is suitable for intermediate skiers, and for beginners there's also a purpose-built slope. There's night skiing on Thursdays and Saturdays during July and August, and every Saturday the downhill flare run takes place at 6.30 pm, followed by fireworks.

Perisher Blue is the largest ski field with 50 lifts and 100 groomed trails ranging from incredibly easy to invitingly steep. The longest run is three kilometres. It's good for first-time skiers and popular with cross-country fanatics with its 100km of groomed trails. Freestyle snowboarders like the slopestyle course and wall ride.

Charlotte Pass is Australia's highest and most isolated resort, snowbound for much of the winter season and can cater for just 600 chalet guests. It's popular with families who take advantage of the free child minding. There are no cars or buses, nor are there long queues for the ski lifts, which are right on your doorstep, so you get more time to ski and snowboard.

Selwyn Snowfields at the northern end of Kosciuszko National Park is a drive-in day resort offering all the usual activities such as skiing, snowboarding and tobogganing as well as fun stuff like snowtubing, where you sail down the slopes sitting in a blow-up tube.

Back country skiing in the Australian Alps. *(Tourism NSW)*

Whitewater rafting

Spring rains and snow melt swell the flow of the headwaters of the Murray River to form some of Australia's best white water for rafting. The Upper Murray River has rapids up to Grade 3–4 including the descriptively-named 'Guides Mistake', 'Sharks Tooth' and 'Easy Over'. Rapid Descents, a rafting company based in Khancoban, runs one and two-day rafting trips for all levels during spring and summer, beginning the first weekend of September and rafting through to the end of January.

www.rapiddescents.com.au

Upper Murray River rafting. *(Tourism NSW)*

MORE INFORMATION

- **Snowy Mountains Authority Information Centre:** Yulin Avenue, Cooma. www.snowyhydro.com.au
- **Snowy Region Visitor Centre:** provides information, day and annual passes, books, maps, and clothing. Includes cafe and a cinema where you can watch a free screening of the 15-minute film 'Kosciuszko Reflections'. Wheelchair access provided. Open seven days a week, 8.30am to 5.30pm in winter and 8.30am to 5pm in summer. Closed Christmas Day. Kosciuszko Road, Jindabyne. ☎ (02) 6450 5600.
- **Cooma Visitor Centre:** ☎ 1800 636 525, (02) 6450 1742. www.visitcooma.com.au
- **What's on at Thredbo:** www.thredbo.com.au
- **What's on at Perisher Blue:** www.perisherblue.com.au/

weather watch

- January: 10–25°C
- July: -2–11°C
- Summer can be warm and dry, but nights can get very cold. Expect snow during winter.

australian capital territory

National Library of Australia, Canberra. *(Canberra Tourism)*

► MOST PEOPLE visit the nation's capital to see its amazing range of museums, like the National Museum, the Questacon science museum or the Australian War Memorial; its galleries, such as the National Gallery of Australia or the new National Portrait Gallery in Old Parliament House; or come in spring time for the month-long flower festival Floriade when Commonwealth Park erupts in a blaze of colour with more than 1.5 million bulbs and annuals in bloom. But the thing that really sets Canberra apart from our other capital cities is that it is a city surrounded by bush, including the wild and rugged peaks of the snowy mountains wilderness.

Unlike most other Australian cities that grew organically around pioneer settlements, Canberra was born of a political decision to build a new city in order to appease rivalries between Sydney and Melbourne as to which city should be the capital of the newly federated nation at the turn of the 20th century.

Prior to Federation in 1901, Canberra was little more than a large sheep station called 'Canberry'. Post-Federation debates on possible locations for the new seat of Government raged for a number of years, and the final decision to site the capital in Canberra, roughly mid-way between Sydney and Melbourne, was made in 1908 by the new Commonwealth Parliament.

In 1911 an international competition to design the new capital city of Australia was held. More than 130 entries were received in the competition and the winning entry was submitted by American architect Walter Burley Griffin and his partner and wife, Marion Mahony Griffin, a design based on a series of geometrically precise circles and axes. The Australian Capital Territory was declared on 1 January 1911. It became a self-governing territory in 1989.

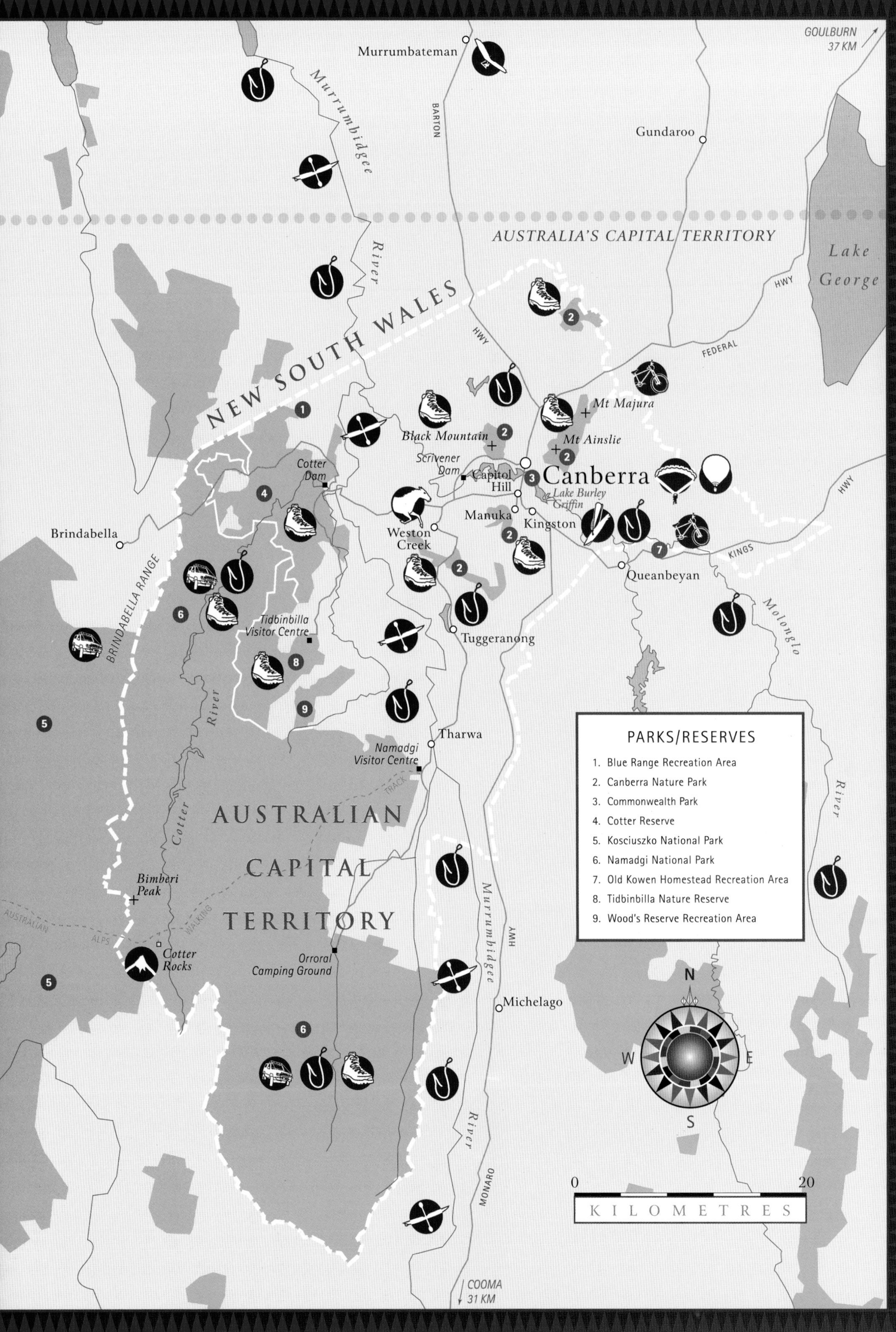

Murrumbateman
GOULBURN 37 KM
BARTON
Murrumbidgee
Gundaroo
AUSTRALIA'S CAPITAL TERRITORY
Lake George
River
NEW SOUTH WALES
HWY
FEDERAL
Mt Majura
Black Mountain
Mt Ainslie
Cotter Dam
Scrivener Dam
Capitol Hill
Canberra
Lake Burley Griffin
Manuka
Kingston
Brindabella
Weston Creek
KINGS
HWY
Queanbeyan
BRINDABELLA RANGE
Tidbinbilla Visitor Centre
Tuggeranong
Molonglo
River
Cotter
River
Tharwa
Namadgi Visitor Centre
TRACK
AUSTRALIAN CAPITAL TERRITORY
Bimberi Peak
AUSTRALIAN ALPS WALKING
Cotter Rocks
Orroral Camping Ground
Murrumbidgee
HWY
Michelago
River
MONARO
COOMA 31 KM
N
W
E
S
0
20
KILOMETRES
PARKS/RESERVES
1. Blue Range Recreation Area
2. Canberra Nature Park
3. Commonwealth Park
4. Cotter Reserve
5. Kosciuszko National Park
6. Namadgi National Park
7. Old Kowen Homestead Recreation Area
8. Tidbinbilla Nature Reserve
9. Wood's Reserve Recreation Area

Snow gum, Namadgi National Park, *(Lee Atkinson)*

NATIONAL PARKS

Namadgi National Park: Namadgi is the Aboriginal word for the rugged mountains south-west of Canberra, and the park is 105,900 hectares, making up more than half of the Australian Capital Territory. Bimberi Peak, at 1911m, is the park's highest feature, only 318m lower than Mt Kosciuskzo and snowfalls are common during winter. The north-west section of the park lies just to the south of Canberra's outlying suburbs. To the south-west, the park joins Kosciuszko National Park and the Bimberi and Scabby Range nature reserves with Brindabella National Park on the north-eastern border.

The central Namadgi ranges, with their bold outcrops of granite, are of great importance to Aboriginal people, who have lived and roamed this country for more than 21,000 years. There is a network of public roads within the park that pass through the majestic mountain country. The unsealed roads are narrow and can be slippery when wet or frosty. Much of Namadgi's beauty, however, lies beyond its main roads and picnic areas. There are 170km of marked walking trails in the park, but you will need to be well-prepared if you are going to walk into the more remote areas. Before you depart, make sure you sign one of the bushwalking registers located at the visitor centre and elsewhere in the park. The main entrance and visitors centre are located on Naas Road. Follow the main highway south onto Tharwa Drive at Tuggeranong. Corrin Dam can be accessed via Corrin Dam Road off Tidbinbilla Road.

Tidbinbilla Nature Reserve: wedged between the Tidbinbilla and Gibraltar Ranges, Tidbinbilla Nature Reserve is a 40-minute drive from the city centre along Tourist Drive 5. Tidbinbilla features walking trails, ranger-guided activities and prolific wildlife including koalas, the endangered brush-tailed rock wallaby and the northern corroboree frog. Camping, fishing, horse riding, car rallies, off-road 4WD activities and trail bike riding are prohibited in the reserve, as are pets.

Canberra Nature Park: a series of 30 bushland locations and hill-top nature reserves around the city including Black Mountain (home of the Telstra Tower); Mount Majura and Mount Ainslie, which has one of the best lookouts over the city.

Parliamentary Triangle

Canberra's central focus point is Lake Burley Griffin, an artificial lake around which are most of the country's more culturally and politically significant buildings–Capital Hill with Australia's most expensive building, Parliament House, and the much smaller (in comparison) Old Parliament House, today home to the National Portrait Gallery; the National Archives; National Library; National Gallery; High Court of Australia; the National Science and Technology Centre (Questacon) and the Australian War Memorial. Known as the Parliamentary Triangle, the precinct is formed by Commonwealth, Kings and Constitution avenues, with Capital Hill at the apex, the City Hall and city centre and Defence Headquarters at Russell at the other two points.

Walter Burley Griffin's plan was for a garden city, and the area is characterized by streets lined with large deciduous trees, and buildings set in expanses of grassed parkland and of course, Commonwealth Park, home of the annual free Floriade festival. What this means for the visitor is that all of the country's most important buildings, and the city's most popular tourist attractions, are all within a few minutes of each other.

City Centre

Compared to other capital cities, the CBD is quite small, but, like the Parliamentary Triangle, it is studded with major league attractions, such as the National Museum of Australia; the CSIRO Discovery Centre and the Australian National Botanic Gardens. On the outskirts of the city you'll find the National Aquarium and Canberra Zoo and just a few minutes drive away is Black Mountain crowned with the spire of Telstra Tower, a 195m-high communications tower with a viewing platform, restaurant and exhibition hall.

Southern suburbs

The inner southern suburbs are home to official residences, including the Lodge, the official residence of the Prime Minister and Yarralumla, the Governor's residence; the diplomatic precinct, the Royal Australian Mint and many beautiful Art Deco bungalows and cottages. The inner suburbs of Manuka and Kingston are the place to go for boutique shopping and the best restaurants and cafes.

As the city grows the suburbs creep ever southwards into the foothills of the Brindabella Range. Ravaged by bushfires in 2003, the once densely pine-forested hills are home to the historic Mount Stromlo Observatory, tragically destroyed by the fires but in the process of being rebuilt; Canberra Deep Space Communications Complex at Tidbinbilla, Tidbinbilla Nature Reserve and Cotter Dam and Reserve–a popular weekend spot for bushwalking, swimming, picnics and camping.

Floriade. *(Lee Atkinson)*

scenic highlights

Namadgi National Park in winter. *(Canberra Tourism)*

Tourist Drive 5, with its distinctive bright orange '5' markers is a great way to explore the best attractions and surrounding countryside around Canberra. This loop drive, that begins and ends in the heart of the city, offers nature, art, craft, history, wildlife and science—depending on where you choose to stop.

Begin at Capital Hill in the heart of the city, where you'll find all the city's attractions quite close together. These attractions take a day alone to explore, so once you're done, head west on Adelaide Avenue and then Cotter Road towards Cotter Dam. On the way, you'll drive through the remains of the pine plantations of the Stromlo Forest, badly burnt during the devastating 2003 bushfires but now slowly regenerating again, and Stromlo Observatory. On the way, detour to the right on Tourist Drive 2 for a trip out to Scrivener Dam and the Molonglo River which cuts its way through dense bushland, surprisingly close to city outskirts.

Cotter Reserve, near the Cotter Dam, is 22km west of Canberra and is a popular spot for picnics and bushwalking at the artificial lake that was the original water reservoir built in 1915 to serve the new capital. Take the path over the suspension bridge to the top of the dam wall for some good views. The best place for swimming is at the large pool shaded by river oaks at Casuarina Sands on the Murrumbidgee River on the drive in just before you get to the dam.

Tourist Drive 5 now follows Paddy's River, through more pine plantations. Take a short detour to visit the Canberra Deep Space Communication Complex, where you'll find Canberra's answer to the 'Dish'. It's one of only three active NASA tracking stations in the world. Next stop is Tidbinbilla Nature Reserve and as you follow the loop around its most southern edge, the road skirts Namadgi National Park. Stop at the small town of Tharwa, one of the oldest settlements in the ACT, and drop into the Cuppacumbalong Craft Centre for some terrific modern Australian craft, wander the gardens or eat at the restaurant—a great place to linger over lunch or coffee beside the roaring open fireplace. Not far from Tharwa is the turn off to Lanyon Homestead, an authentic reflection of life in the 19th and 20th century, and next door the Nolan Gallery has a superb collection of paintings by Sir Sidney Nolan.

The final stage of the drive takes you to Rose Cottage, a former shearing station and tavern built in the 1870s. Now a fully licensed restaurant and bar, the main property is surrounded by a mini village of craft shops reminiscent of a small country town.

From here, simply follow Tourist Drive 5 back to centre of Canberra.

The Australian War Memorial, Canberra. *(Australian Capital Tourism)*

DON'T MISS

- **National Museum of Australia:** Australia's newest national museum housed in an innovative purpose-built building that profiles 50,000 years of indigenous heritage, settlement since 1788 and key events including Federation and the 2000 Sydney Olympics. Five permanent galleries and changing exhibitions. Lawson Crescent, Acton. Open daily 9am–5pm. **www.nma.gov.au**
- **National Gallery of Australia:** Aboriginal and Torres Strait Islander art, Asian art, Australian art, photography, sculpture garden and international art, including blockbuster exhibitions. Parkes Place, Parkes. Open daily 10am–5pm. ☎ (02) 6240 6502. **www.nga.gov.au**
- **National Portrait Gallery:** portraits of people who have had a significant impact on the country. Old Parliament House, King George Terrace, Parkes. Open daily 9am–5pm. ☎ (02) 6270 8236. **www.portrait.gov.au**
- **Australian War Memorial:** military relics and exhibitions, including the Hall of Memory and the Tomb of the Unknown Australian Soldier. Treloar Crescent. Top of ANZAC Parade, Campbell. Open daily 10am–5pm. 9am–5pm ACT and NSW school holidays. ☎ (02) 6243 4211. **www.awm.gov.au**
- **Parliament House:** see parliament in action during Question Time at 2pm each sitting day. Capital Hill. Open daily 9am–5pm, later when Parliament sits. **www.aph.gov.au**
- **Old Parliament House:** beautiful 1920s building and home of the Australian Parliament for 61 years, with much of the interior offices left just as they were when the tenants left to move up to the big house on the hill. King George Terrace, Parkes. Changing exhibitions and guided tours every 45 minutes, 9.30am–3.15pm. Open daily 9am–5pm.
- **National Library of Australia:** collections of the personal papers of many famous Australians, rare books, maps, photographs, sheet music and other historic documents. Changing exhibitions, café and bookshop. Parkes Place, Parkes. Open daily, 9am–5pm. **www.nla.gov.au**
- **Questacon—the National Science and Technology Centre:** making science fun, this interactive museum is a hit with both kids and adults. King Edward Terrace, Parkes. Open daily, 9am–5pm. **www.questacon.edu.au**
- **Screen Sound Australia:** the national screen and sound archive holds 100 years of Australian film, radio and television history. McCoy Circuit, Acton. Open 9am–5pm Monday to Friday, 10am–5pm weekends and public holidays.
- **National Archives of Australia:** a treasure trove of fascinating records and documents. Queen Victoria Terrace, Parkes. Open daily 9am–5pm.
- **Australian Institute of Sport:** take a tour with an elite athlete and test your athletic skills in the Sportex exhibition. Leverrier Crescent, Bruce. Public tours operate daily (except Christmas Day) at 10am, 11.30am, 1pm and 2.30pm.
- **Canberra Deep Space Communication Complex:** one of three NASA Deep Space Network antennas. Includes the new Satellite Laser Ranging Observatory and Space Research Centre researching the problems caused by man-made space debris. Tidbinbilla, about 40km south-west of the city. Open daily, 9am–5pm (6pm Summer time).
- **Lanyon Homestead and Nolan Gallery:** Lanyon is one of Australia's most historic grazing properties. The homestead dates from the 1850s and has been beautifully restored and furnished and is set in superb gardens. The Nolan Gallery displays important works by renowned Australian artist, Sir Sidney Nolan. Lanyon, Tharwa Drive, Tharwa. Open Tue–Sun and most public holidays: 10am–4pm.

Northern suburbs

Just a few minutes to the north of the city centre is the Australian Institute of Sport, the elite training centre for the county's top athletes; Cockington Green, a miniature recreation of an English village that is very popular with kids; Gold Creek village with the privately-owned National Dinosaur Museum, Australian Reptile Centre and the Bird Walk, a walk-in aviary; and historic Ginninderra Village, first settled in 1883 with many Heritage-listed buildings still remaining.

Caravan and camping

Namadgi's the place to go if you want to really get out in the bush for a while. There are three designated campsites within the park: Orroral Valley, Honeysuckle Creek and Mt. Clear. All have only basic facilities including pit toilets, picnic tables and fireplaces. Water must be boiled before consumption. There are no caravan services.

Bush camping is allowed anywhere within the park away from roads. Camping permits are required when camping in the Cotter catchment (as it is part of Canberra's water supply), and some areas are totally banned. Permits can be obtained from the Namadgi Natioinal Park offices during working hours. Banned areas include within 1km of Corin Dam and within 500m of the Cotter River. Cotter Hut, a service residence, is locked to the public and the rangers request that you camp at least 1km from it. The regulations for camping within the catchment are detailed on the back of the permit.

www.environment.act.gov.au/bushparksandreserves/namadgi.htm

Gibraltar Rock. *(Australian Capital Tourism)*

There are also several good campsites in the ACT Forests. The Blue Range Recreation Area is centred around the Heritage-listed remains of a WWII Italian internment camp. Facilities include wood fired and gas barbeques, picnic tables, pit toilets and the historic hut, the original galley for the internment camp. Blue Range Recreation Area is located in Uriarra Forest on Blue Range Road, approximately 2.6km from the turn-off on the Brindabella Road.

Wood's Reserve Recreation Area on the banks of Gibraltar Creek, off the Corin Road, 5.4km from the Tidbinbilla Road turn-off. Facilities include wood-fired barbeques and gas barbeques, a picnic shelter, picnic tables, water (from the creek), flushing toilets, hot showers and a washing up area. It is popular with school groups.

The Old Kowen Homestead Recreation Area was developed after the fires in January 2003 destroyed many of the recreational sites around Canberra. It has become one of Canberra's hidden treasures and is available for camping, picnics and barbeques. Facilities include wood-fire pits and a gas barbeque, picnic shelter with tables and a pit toilet with tank water. Please remember to bring your own drinking water. It can also be booked exclusively for specific functions and events. The Old Kowen Homestead site is situated in Kowen Forest Pine Plantation off Sutton Road to the north-east of Canberra on the way to Queanbeyan. Kowen Forest is a locked forest so bookings are essential in order to obtain approval and access to the area.

For all ACT Forest campsite bookings book online or call:

☎ (02) 6207 2486

Commercial caravan parks are available in several locations in an around the city. Contact the visitor centre for detailed lists.

www.visitcanberra.com.au

Bushwalks

Australia's bush capital has plenty of bushwalking opportunities in and around the city. Within the Canberra Nature Park you can walk to the summits of Mt Majura, Mt Ainslie, Black Mountain, Red Hill, Mt Painter, Mt Taylor, Burnt Stump and Old Joe in Goorooyaroo Nature Reserve, Wanniassa Hills, McQuoids Hill, Urambi Hills, Cooleman Ridge, and Tuggeranong Hill.

Within the sprawling wilderness of Namadgi National Park there are 170km of marked walking trails throughout the park. Leaflets describing some of the walks are available from the Namadgi National Park visitors centre, 3km south of Tharwa on the Naas Road. One of the best is the 6km short trail to Yankee Hat, great for family trips with kids or grandparents in tow. The trail meanders through open grasslands past mobs of eastern grey kangaroos and along boardwalks skirting the edge of the Bogong Swamp to end at the lower slopes of Yankee Hat Aboriginal Rock Art Site where you'll find an excellent rock art gallery of ancient art depicting human figures, kangaroos, wombats, koalas, dingos and birds.

Also worth doing is the 8km return walk through sub-alpine forest and snowgum woodlands to Square Rock, a fantastic outcrop of large boulders and great views of the Tidbinbilla Ranges.

adventure activities

Lake Burley Griffin and the National Museum of Australia. *(Australian Capital Tourism)*

Ballooning

Each March, Canberra hosts the Canberra Balloon Fiesta when some 50 novelty balloons from around Australia and overseas take off from the lawns in front of Old Parliament House. Throughout the year you can take to the skies most mornings, weather permitting, with one of several one-hour balloon flight operators. Flights leave at dawn, drifting over the slumbering city, usually waking dogs in almost every backyard you glide over. It's a great way to get a birds-eye view of the radiating lines of Walter Burley Griffin's original city plan.

www.dawndrifters.com.au www.balloonaloft.com

Fishing

The main angling species in the ACT are Murray cod, golden perch, trout, redfin and carp. Open fishing waters include Murrumbidgee River, downstream from the junction with the Gudgenby River, Molonglo River below Scrivener Dam and urban lakes. You can fish in open fishing waters all year. If you catch Murray cod or trout in these waters out of season they must be returned to the water unharmed.

Namadgi National Park has good trout fishing in its rolling hills and scattered forests. You can fish the lakes all year round for trout–most rivers in the ACT have a closed season for trout from June to September. The Murray cod season is closed August to November. Fish with a professional guide and his licence will cover you too.

Off-road driving

Namadji National Park is popular for off-road driving although vehicles are generally restricted to public access roads. There are, however, several roads suited to four-wheel driving in the north of the park: Mt Franklin Road as far as the Ginnini gate access road to Bendora Dam, Two Sticks Road which travels across the top of the Brindabella Ranges to Mt Coree, Old Mill Road and Warks Road. During periods of total fire ban or after heavy snowfalls in winter, road closures are common.

Capital 4WD Tours run tag-along and guided tours in the Brindabella Mountains beyond the city, including two-day camping trips. Highlights are the views from Mt Coree and river crossings.

☎ 0427 778 725

Horse riding

Canberra offers 22km of bushland equestrian trails. The historic National Equestrian Centre has 1500 acres of picturesque rolling countryside along Murrumbidgee River overlooking the foothills of the Brindabella Range. It offers activities from trail rides to holiday riding programs. A short drive from Canberra, the centre has programs for regular or casual riders. 919 Cotter Road, Weston Creek, Canberra.

www.neqc.com.au

Kayaking and rafting

From September to December the Murrumbidgee River offers white-water rafting and kayaking close to Canberra. Rapids like Junkyard, Super Move, Shredder, Horseshoe get the adrenalin pumping. Spectacular Red Rocks Gorge is for experienced paddlers only.

www.realfun.com.au

Mountain Biking

With hundreds of kilometres of off-road bike trails and paved cycle-ways in and around the city Canberra is a great place for cycling. With so many nature reserves and bushland close to the city, it's also a mecca for mountain biking with Mt Majura pine plantation and Kowen Forest the most popular. Check out Canberra Off-Road Cyclists.

www.corc.asn.au

R.E.A.L Fun runs mountain bike trips into the mountains with a guide and support vehicle, leaving you free to enjoy the ride. The bikes are fully equipped and even offer gel seat covers. No experience required.

www.realfun.com.au

On the water

Canberra's lakes are a great place to spend a day messing about on the water. You can hire paddleboats, surf skis, canoes and windsurfers at Acton Park and take to the water of Lake Burley Griffin, the largest of Canberra's three artificial lakes. Windsurfing and special events are held on Lake Tuggeranong and Lake Ginninderra, but they are small and too shallow in parts for sailing larger boats. Power boats are not permitted on Canberra's lakes, apart from a charter operator, water police and boats operated by the sailing and rowing clubs. Canberra Yacht Club and the YMCA Sailing Club offer learn-to-sail programs.

www.visitcanberra.com.au

Paragliding

The Australian Paragliding Centre, full-time professional paragliding and paramotoring school, operates all year at Murrumbateman, 30 minutes north-west of Canberra. Courses range from tandem flights for beginners to full license and two-day introductory courses. Expect anything from dynamic ridge soaring to thermalling up to cloudbase and flying cross country. If you like power and are experienced, try a paramotor 'tester day' when you can strap a paramotor on your back and take-off from the small field down the road. Open daily.

www.australianparagliding.com

Rock climbing and abseiling

If politicians make you want to climb the wall, head to Canberra Indoor Rockclimbing, 38 Essington Street, Mitchell, and climb all you like.

www.canberrarockclimbing.com.au

If you prefer your thrills outside, R.E.A.L Fun run half-day abseiling adventures at Cotter Rocks. Start the day with a safety briefing and practice on the ground before moving to the abseil wall. The 20m abseils are challenging and great fun. You can even try abseiling face first. After afternoon tea you can try climbing back up the rocks while attached to a safety rope.

www.realfun.com.au

Sky diving

Canberra is a great place to jump out of plane–the weather is suitable all year and there's acres of space to land. Jump! Australia offers tandem skydives for first-timers that include a 30–40 second adrenalin-packed freefall from 12,000 feet and five to eight minutes of soaring parachute ride–plenty of time to learn the 'ropes' with your Tandem Instructor and practice steering, forward speed and even high-speed downward spirals (only recommended for those with strong stomachs!). The trip includes a 25–30 minute scenic flight over Canberra and the Brindabella Ranges as you climb to jump altitude, but you'll probably be too nervous to really take in the view. You can also sign up for 10-jump solo freefall course covering basic skydiving and parachute handling.

www.jump.com.au

MORE INFORMATION

- **Canberra and Regions Visitors Centre:** 330 Northbourne Avenue, Dickson, Canberra. ☎ (02) 6205 0044 or 1300 554 114. www.canberratourism.com.au

Learning the ropes at Cotter Rocks. *(Tourism NSW)*

Zoo Venture

The National Zoo and Aquarium runs daily behind-the–scenes tours where you can get up close and personal with many of the animals in the zoo. The two-hour ZooVenture Tour lets you hand feed tigers, lions, bears and is one of the most hands-on animal tours in the country. You are separated from the big cats by a fence, but when you look a 110kg Sumatran tiger in the eye as they leap on the fence, stand tall above you, take a piece of meat from your hand, have a tiger roar inches from your face or a brown bear lick honey off your hand–inside their den, the adrenalin is guaranteed to flow. There is also a 'Meet a Cheetah' programme that takes you inside the cheetah's enclosure and allows you to touch the fastest land animal in the world.

www.zooquarium.com.au

weather watch

- January: 12–26°C
- July: 0–10°C
- Canberra has a temperate climate. Be prepared for cool evenings in summer and snow and sub-zero temperatures in winter.

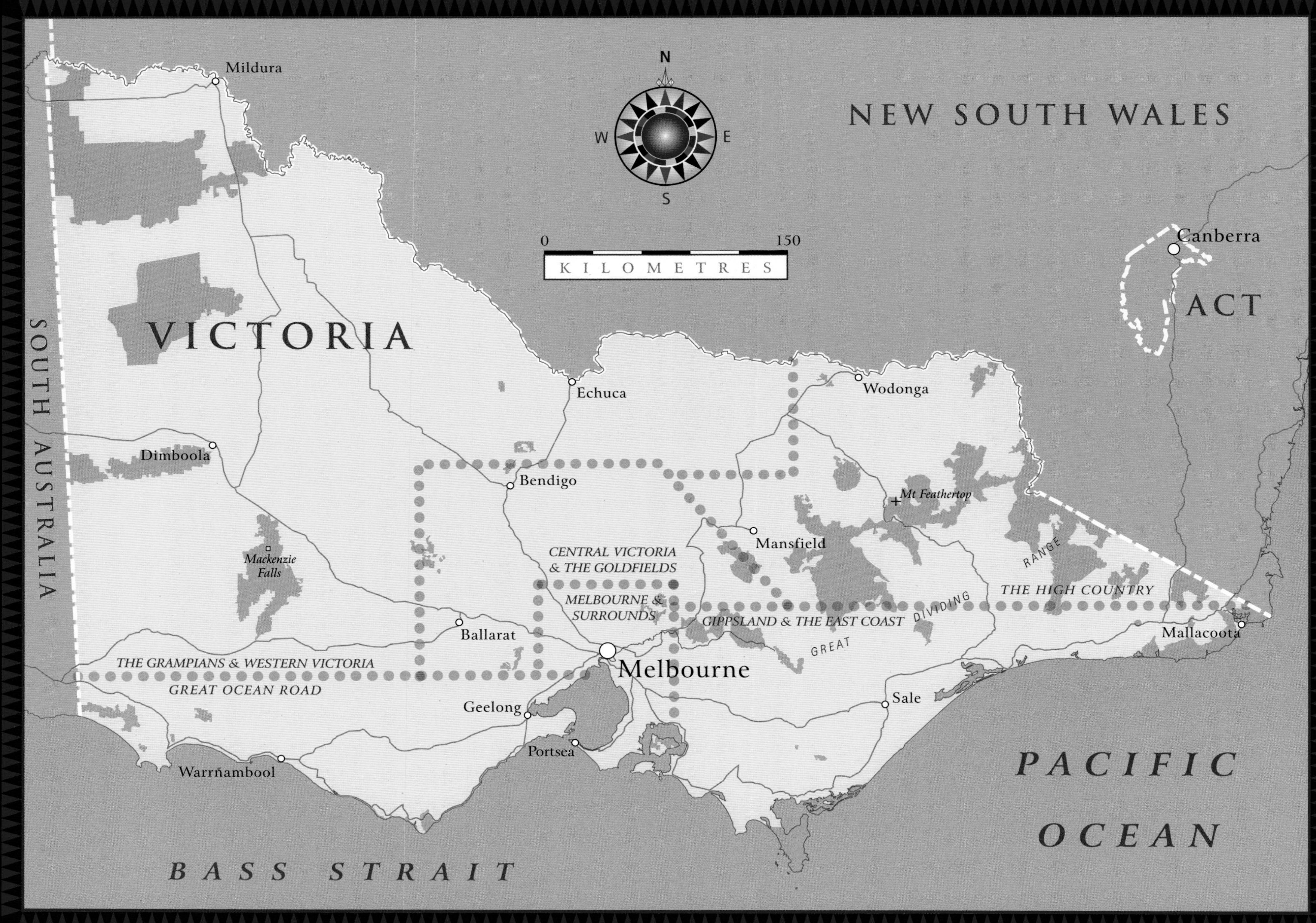
N
W
E
S
NEW SOUTH WALES
0
150
KILOMETRES
Canberra
ACT
Mildura
VICTORIA
SOUTH AUSTRALIA
Echuca
Wodonga
Dimboola
Bendigo
Mt Feathertop
Mansfield
CENTRAL VICTORIA
& THE GOLDFIELDS
Mackenzie
Falls
RANGE
THE HIGH COUNTRY
MELBOURNE &
SURROUNDS
DIVIDING
GIPPSLAND & THE EAST COAST
Ballarat
Mallacoota
GREAT
THE GRAMPIANS & WESTERN VICTORIA
Melbourne
GREAT OCEAN ROAD
Sale
Geelong
Portsea
Warrnambool
PACIFIC
OCEAN
BASS STRAIT

victoria

Victoria is Australia's smallest mainland state, and the most populated. It is bordered by the Murray River in the north and a rugged coastline to the south. The southern tip of Great Dividing Range runs across the state from east to west, separating a vast volcanic plain from the drier Mallee and Wimmera areas that border South Australia.

melbourne & surrounds

Melbourne's autumn colours. *(Tourism Victoria)*

▶ ART LOVER, history buff, culture vulture, movie fiend or just plain sports mad, Australia's second largest city, Melbourne, is a city with something for everyone, and a museum or gallery to suit every passion.

Located on the shores of Port Phillip Bay with the Yarra River running through the heart of the city, Melbourne is all wide tree-lined streets, elegant buildings and beautiful public gardens. Although originally surveyed during the 1830s, it was during the height of the mid-19th century gold rush in central Victoria—when the diggers who struck it lucky built grand houses and founded cultural institutions with their newfound wealth—that the foundations of this sophisticated city were really established.

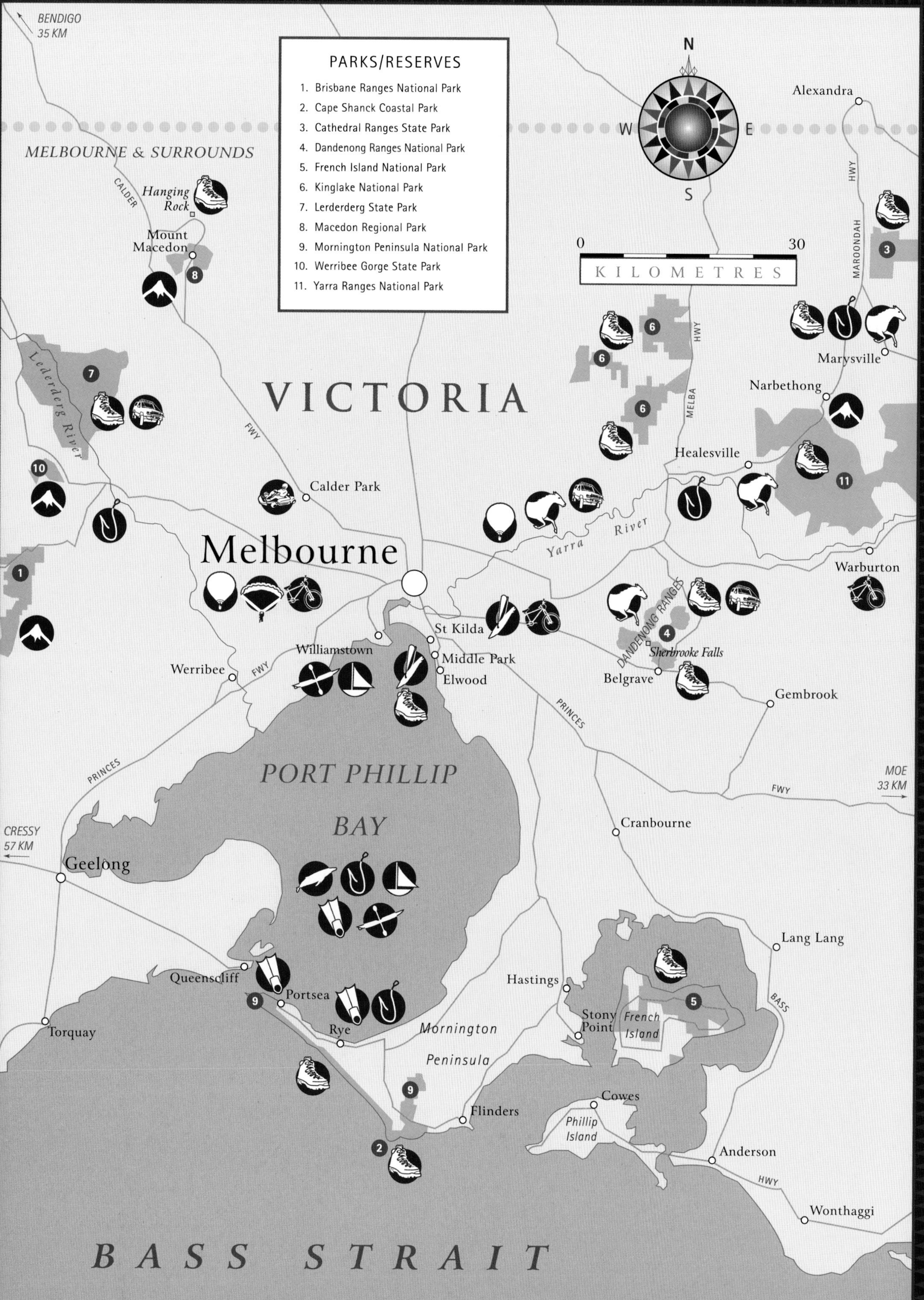

MELBOURNE & SURROUNDS
PARKS/RESERVES
1. Brisbane Ranges National Park
2. Cape Shanck Coastal Park
3. Cathedral Ranges State Park
4. Dandenong Ranges National Park
5. French Island National Park
6. Kinglake National Park
7. Lerderderg State Park
8. Macedon Regional Park
9. Mornington Peninsula National Park
10. Werribee Gorge State Park
11. Yarra Ranges National Park
N
W
E
S
0
30
KILOMETRES
BENDIGO 35 KM
VICTORIA
Melbourne
PORT PHILLIP BAY
BASS STRAIT
Hanging Rock
Mount Macedon
Lerderderg River
Calder Park
Alexandra
Marysville
Narbethong
Healesville
Warburton
Yarra River
DANDENONG RANGES
Sherbrooke Falls
Belgrave
Gembrook
St Kilda
Williamstown
Middle Park
Elwood
Werribee
MOE 33 KM
CRESSY 57 KM
Cranbourne
Geelong
Lang Lang
Queenscliff
Portsea
Hastings
Stony Point
French Island
Torquay
Rye
Mornington Peninsula
Flinders
Cowes
Phillip Island
Anderson
Wonthaggi
CALDER
FWY
PRINCES
HWY
MELBA
MAROONDAH
BASS

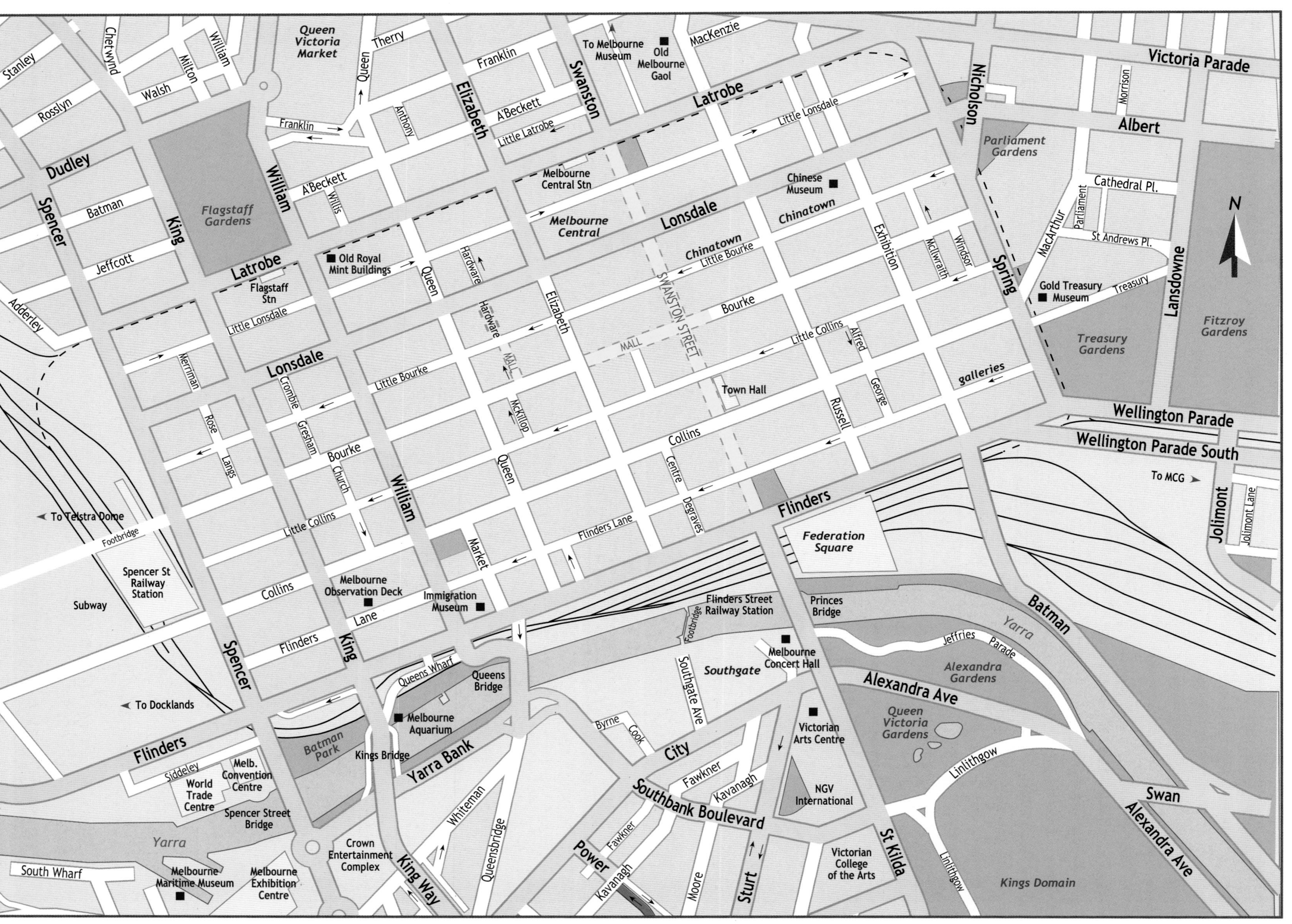
N
Victoria Parade
Nicholson
Albert
Morrison
Parliament Gardens
Cathedral Pl.
Parliament
St Andrews Pl.
MacArthur
Lansdowne
Fitzroy Gardens
Gold Treasury Museum
Treasury
Treasury Gardens
Spring
Wellington Parade
Wellington Parade South
To MCG
Jolimont
Jolimont Lane
Queen Victoria Market
Therry
Queen
Franklin
Stanley
Chetwynd
Milton
William
Walsh
Rosslyn
Dudley
Spencer
Batman
Jeffcott
King
Flagstaff Gardens
William
A'Beckett
Willis
Anthony
Elizabeth
Little Latrobe
Swanston
To Melbourne Museum
Old Melbourne Gaol
MacKenzie
Latrobe
Little Lonsdale
Melbourne Central Stn
Melbourne Central
Lonsdale
Chinese Museum
Chinatown
Chinatown
Little Bourke
SWANSTON STREET
Exhibition
McIlwraith
Windsor
Old Royal Mint Buildings
Flagstaff Stn
Hardware
Adderley
Merriman
Crombie
Gresham
Rose
Langs
Bourke
Church
Little Collins
MALL
Alfred
George
galleries
Town Hall
Russell
McKillop
Collins
Centre
Degraves
Flinders
Flinders Lane
Market
Federation Square
To Telstra Dome
Footbridge
Spencer St Railway Station
Subway
Melbourne Observation Deck
Lane
Immigration Museum
Flinders Street Railway Station
Princes Bridge
Batman
Yarra
Jeffries Parade
Alexandra Gardens
Melbourne Concert Hall
Southgate
Southgate Ave
Alexandra Ave
Queen Victoria Gardens
Queens Wharf
Queens Bridge
Melbourne Aquarium
To Docklands
Batman Park
Kings Bridge
Yarra Bank
Byrne
Cook
City
Victorian Arts Centre
Linlithgow
Swan
Siddeley
Melb. Convention Centre
World Trade Centre
Spencer Street Bridge
Whiteman
Fawkner
Kavanagh
Southbank Boulevard
NGV International
Alexandra Ave
Crown Entertainment Complex
King Way
Queensbridge
Power
Moore
Sturt
Victorian College of the Arts
St Kilda
Kings Domain
South Wharf
Melbourne Maritime Museum
Melbourne Exhibition Centre

The city centre

Laid out on a simple grid system Melbourne is an easy city to find your way around. The heart of the city contains all the major cultural institutions, such as the National Gallery of Victoria, the Arts Centre, Federation Square and countless smaller galleries and museums. The city centre is criss-crossed with a maze of back lanes and alleyways where locals in the know head for designer shopping, cosy restaurants and elegant bars.

On the southern side of the river is Southgate, an attractive kilometre-long stretch of upmarket shops, cafes and restaurants and the Crown Entertainment Complex. Across St Kilda Road is a huge swathe of parkland, including the Royal Botanic Gardens and the MCG, home to the 2006 Commonwealth Games.

A first-time trip to Melbourne isn't complete without a ride on a Melbourne icon: the tram. The free City Circle Tram circles the downtown city area: Fitzroy Gardens, State Parliament, Old Melbourne Gaol, Spencer Street Station, the National Gallery of Victoria, St Pauls Cathedral and all the city sights.

Inner city suburbs

Bayside St Kilda was once better known as the red light district of town, but today, although still bold and brassy, St Kilda offers everything from fine dining to 24-hour takeaway food, most of which can be found on Fitzroy Street.

Melbourne is one of the world's great multicultural cities and the northern inner-city of Carlton is Melbourne's Italian quarter: Lygon Street is alive with Italian restaurants and cafes, Italian clothes, Italian groceries and, of course, great Italian coffee. Victoria Street, Richmond is known as little Saigon, where countless Vietnamese restaurants emit aromatic invitations. Walk around the block to Bridge Road or Swan Street, which are both overflowing with Greek restaurants. Shopping and eating mix easily in Fitzroy, on colourful Brunswick Street, full of eccentric street art and an eclectic mix of tastes from all around the world. Speciality bookstores, second-hand furniture, art galleries, alternative lifestyle shops, floral artistry, over-the-edge clothing and off-the-wall gifts jostle for space with outdoor cafes and fine restaurants of all flavours, from Afghan to Mauritian.

The Dandenong Ranges and Yarra Valley

An hour or so to the east of the city rise the Dandenong Ranges, where towering mountain ash forests and fern gullies frame historic cool-climate gardens. It's a favourite weekend escape for Melbournians and historic cottages have been transformed into romantic B&Bs and art galleries. Puffing Billy is a century-old steam train still running on its original mountain track from Belgrave to Gembrook through the rainforest.

Further north, the pretty Yarra Valley is one of the best cool climate wine districts of the world, specialising in sparkling wines, chardonnay and pinot noir. There are more than 50 wineries open, ranging from stunning multi-million dollar tourism wineries to the warm welcome of boutique family winemakers.

Macedon Ranges

In the 19th century, wealthy Melbournians would escape the summer heat in the Macedon Ranges, just an hour or so to the north-west of the city, where they built impressive mansions and created some of Victoria's finest gardens in the rich volcanic soil. Ancient volcanic eruptions also created the picturesque Hanging Rock, north of Mount Macedon. It is the setting for Joan Lindsay's famous novel, *Picnic at Hanging Rock,* a work of fiction so popular that many people come here believing the mystery of the missing schools girls to be fact.

Mornington Peninsula. *(TV)*

NATIONAL PARKS

Dandenong Ranges National Parks: lush fern-filled gullies, forests of mountain ash (one of the tallest trees in the world) and more than 300km of walking tracks. Good barbecue and picnic areas.

Yarra Ranges National Parks: tall forests with many walking tracks, waterfalls, lookouts and scenic drives that wind through the mountain ash forest with panoramic views of the countryside. The Rainforest Gallery at Mount Donna Buang has a treetop observation platform set among 300-year-old heritage trees and a rainforest walkway.

Kinglake National Park: this park on the slopes of the Great Dividing Range boasts forests, fern gullies, beautiful waterfalls and several scenic lookouts with dramatic views of the Melbourne skyline, Port Phillip Bay, the Yarra Valley and across to the You Yangs.

Lerderderg State Park: a wilderness park with rugged river gorges and spectacular scenery. The Lerderderg River has cut a 300m-deep gorge through sandstone and slate, bisecting the park. There's a wide variety of vegetation and wildlife, interesting goldmining relics as well as good walking, off-road driving, cycling, riding and camping.

Cathedral Ranges State Park: spectacular 7km-long ridge of rock with walking tracks and views of the forest and farmland in the valley below.

Mornington Peninsula National Park: includes Cape Schanck's basalt cliffs, 133-year-old lighthouse, the former quarantine station and military fort at Point Nepean, spectacular surf beaches and Greens Bush native bushland, a great place to see kangaroos.

French Island National Park: a 10-minute passenger ferry ride from Stony Point, French Island has Victoria's largest population of koalas: so many that 200 are transferred to reserves in other parts of Victoria every year. The island also supports a large population of long-nosed potoroos. The wetlands, mangroves and salt marshes provide habitat for water birds, including sea eagles. French Island Marine National Park is one of the most extensive areas of saltmarsh and mangrove communities in the state. The seagrass beds are nursery areas for fish, including commercially and recreationally important species such as King George whiting, bream and mullet.

scenic highlights

The Yarra Ranges has two of the most beautiful short scenic drives in Victoria. The Black Spur between Healesville and Narbethong is a narrow 10km section of the Maroondah Highway that winds its way up into the Great Dividing Range through towering mountain ash and lush green fern forests. Continue on to Marysville and visit Steavenson Falls, Victoria's highest cascades. If you are staying overnight, come back after dark when the falls are floodlit.

From Marysville, take Lady Talbot Forest Drive, a round trip of 46km into the Yarra Ranges National Park. There are several walking trails that will lead you through old-growth myrtle beech forest to waterfalls tumbling over huge granite boulders and through dense rainforest. It's a dry weather road only, unless you have a 4WD.

Return to Melbourne via the Woods Point Road, which runs east from Marysville through the Yarra Ranges National Park and along the Yarra River to Warburton. Detour along the way to drive up to Lake Mountain for spectacular views of the Victorian Alps to the east and Melbourne to the west.

Marysville. *(TV)*

Steavenson Falls. *(TV)*

Macedon Gardens. *(TV)*

DON'T MISS

- **NGV International:** Australia's oldest public art museum and home to one of the country's most important art collections, with everything from Egyptian and Roman antiquities and Asian art, through to Renaissance, Baroque and everything up to and including contemporary art. 180 St Kilda Road. Open daily except Tuesdays, 10am–5pm. **www.ngv.vic.gov.au**
- **The Australian Centre for Contemporary Art:** photography, video, electronic imaging, painting and sculpture as well as new developments in sound, movement and popular culture. 111 Sturt Street, Southbank. Open Tue–Sun, 11am–6pm. **www.accaonline.org.au**
- **The Ian Potter Centre, NGV Australia:** the world's first major gallery dedicated exclusively to Australian art, with more than 20 galleries presenting the history of Australian art from the Colonial period through to contemporary art. It encompasses photography, prints and drawings, fashion and textiles, decorative arts and includes a suite of galleries dedicated to Aboriginal and Torres Strait Islander art. Federation Square. Open daily, 10am–5pm. **www.ngv.vic.gov.au**
- **Australian Centre for the Moving Image:** the first centre of its kind in the world, dedicated to the moving image in all its forms—from early cinema to the latest digital media. Two multi-format cinemas, the world's largest dedicated screen gallery with changing exhibitions, movie/art installations, hands-on public activity, education and production zones. Federation Square. Open daily, 10am–5pm (until 6pm on weekends). **www.acmi.net.au**
- **Champions, Australian Racing Museum:** befitting of a city that is host to the Melbourne Cup, the 'race that stops a nation', the museum is home to the nation's finest collection of racing memorabilia and the Australian Racing Hall of Fame, immortalising some the of the most significant moments in racing history. Federation Square. Open daily, 10am–6pm. **www.racingmuseum.com.au**
- **Melbourne Museum:** largest museum in the Southern Hemisphere. Highlights include the Science and Life Gallery; *Bunjilaka*—a living cultural centre for the Koori community of south-eastern Australia—and the Australia Gallery, focusing on the vibrant history of Melbourne and Victoria, including the kitchen set from the *Neighbours* television show. The Forest Gallery is a living interpretation of Victoria's tall temperate forests, which features around 8000 plants from more than 120 different species. It's also home to more than 20 different vertebrate species, including snakes, birds, fish, frogs and hundreds of different insects. 11 Nicholson St, Carlton. Open daily, 10am–5pm. **www.melbourne.museum.vic.gov.au**
- **Immigration Museum:** housed in the historic old Customs House offering the personal stories of immigrants through a variety of interpretive techniques, including multimedia, interactive displays, historical objects, footage and photos. 400 Flinders Street. Open daily, 10am–5pm. **www.immigration.museum.vic.gov.au**
- **Chinese Museum:** established in 1985 to document, preserve and display the history of Chinese Australians since the mid 1800s. The four levels of galleries showcase artefacts and photographs depicting the stories and culture of Chinese Australians. Highlights include the 'Finding Gold' time tunnel in the basement and *Dai Loong*, the world's largest dragon. In the heart of Chinatown at 22 Cohen Place. Open daily, 10am–5pm.
- **Gold Treasury Museum:** houses three permanent exhibitions, Built on Gold, Making Melbourne and Growing Up in the Old Treasury. Old Treasury Building, Spring Street. Open Mon–Fri, 9am–5pm, weekends and public holidays, 10am–4pm.
- **AFL Hall of Fame:** traces the history and heritage of Australian Football and pays tribute to the legends and inductees of the Australian Football Hall of Fame and clubs from the VFL/AFL competition. 292 Swanston Street. Open daily, 9am–6pm. **www.aflhalloffame.com.au**
- **Mazes:** Ashcombe Maze and Water Gardens is Australia's oldest and largest hedge maze and circular rose maze. Open daily 10am, Shoreham Road, Shoreham. Arthurs Seat Maze has a farmland nursery and themed gardens as well as traditional hedge maze and a maize maze. 55 Purves Road, Arthurs Seat. Open daily 10am–6pm.
- **Mornington Peninsula Regional Gallery:** changing program of exhibitions by Australia's leading artists. Civic Reserve, Dunns Road, Mornington. Open Tue–Sun, 10am–5pm.
- **Yarra Valley Wine Touring Guide:** self-guided trail visiting many wineries in the region. Brochures available from visitor centres throughout the area.
- **Gulf Station:** the most complete 19th-century farm complex in Victoria. Operated by the National Trust of Australia. Melba Highway, Yarra Glen. Open Wed–Sun and public holidays 10am–4pm.
- **Healesville Sanctuary:** more than 200 species of native birds, mammals and reptiles, displayed in a beautiful bushland setting. Badger Creek Road, Healesville. Open daily, 9am–5pm. **www.zoo.org.au**
- **Puffing Billy:** century-old steam train running on its original mountain track from Belgrave to Gembrook in the Dandenong Ranges. Trains operate daily. **www.puffingbilly.com.au**
- **Museum of Lilydale:** exhibitions on the history of the Yarra Valley and opera singer Nellie Melba. 33 Castella Street, Lilydale. Open Wed–Sun, 11am–4pm.
- **Art at Mount Macedon:** changing exhibits of contemporary artists in painting, sculpture, prints, drawings, photography and ideas. 789 Mount Macedon Road, Mount Macedon. Open Thu–Sun, 11am–6pm. ☎ (03) 5426 3798.
- **Hanging Rock Reserve:** said to be the best example of a volcanic plug or mamelon in the world, consisting mainly of soda trachyte rock (*solvsbergite*). South Rock Road, Woodend.

Lake Mountain. *(TV)*

Marysville canoeing. (TV)

Mornington Peninsula

The Mornington Peninsula is one long beach–a 100km boot-shaped peninsula jutting into the ocean on the eastern edge of Port Phillip Bay–just 80km south of Melbourne with more than 260km of coastline. Colonies of seals and bottle-nosed dolphins cruise and frolic in the bay and lines of brightly-coloured wooden beach 'bathing boxes' jostle for space at the edge of the sand, behind which grand Victorian mansions and hotels compete for the best water views. Behind them, rolling green farmland gives way to thick and fragrant tea-tree bush. The Cape Shanck Coastal Park, with its windswept dunes and steep cliffs, stretches along the peninsula's Bass Strait foreshore (the foot of the boot) from Portsea to Cape Shanck. It's home to grey kangaroos, southern brown bandicoots, echidnas, native rats, mice, reptiles, bats, and many forest and ocean birds.

Caravan and camping

In the Dandenongs and Yarra Valley area you can camp at Upper Yarra Reservoir Park and in the towns of Warburton and Marysville. You can also camp at three sites in Cathedral Ranges State Park (Neds Gully, Cooks Mill and the Farmyard) and there are five designated camping areas in the Bunyip State Park including Mortimer Picnic Ground, Dyers Picnic Ground, Camphora Picnic Ground, Forest Road Picnic Ground, and Kurth Kiln Park. Take your caravan to Cooks Mill, which has areas suitable for a small number of caravans.

In the Macedon Ranges the best camping is in Lerderderg State Park at O'Briens Crossing. You can bush camp anywhere else you can walk to in the park.

You can camp at Fairhaven on the west coast of French Island. No camping is allowed in Mornington Peninsula National Park, although you can pitch a tent on one of the many stunning foreshore reserves all along the coasts of the Mornington Peninsula that offer beautiful settings with bay views. They are generally open only during summer periods and are very popular so early bookings are recommended. You'll find reserves at Dromana, Rosebud, Rye, Sorrento, Balnarring Point Leo and Shoreham.

Bushwalks

Sherbrooke Falls Trail is a gentle half-hour walk to Sherbrooke Falls and a good introduction to the Dandenong Ranges. The track begins near the main entrance on Sherbrooke Road and winds past rough and smooth tree ferns. Along the way you'll see the region's finest sassafras and mountain ash, some of them up to 200 years old.

The Beeches is a lovely 5km medium walk that begins at The Beeches picnic site on Lady Talbot Drive near Marysville. It follows streams and rivers, past waterfalls and through stands of some of the region's oldest and most impressive beech trees. Most of the track passes through cool temperate rainforest with myrtle beech, southern sassafras, blackwood and soft tree ferns, as well as a section of eucalypt forest dominated by tall mountain ash trees, which are also known as Victorian ash.

The two-hour Steavenson Falls Walk follows the Steavenson River upstream through tall tree ferns and luxuriant vegetation to the spectacular Steavenson Falls, one of Victoria's highest waterfalls. The falls drop 82m in three stages into the steep-sided river valley below.

Lake Mountain Summit Walk in Yarra Ranges National Park takes in landscapes of snow gums and alpine heath as well as panoramic views of the Victorian Alps, Melbourne and the Great Dividing Range.

At Hanging Rock you can climb through the rocky maze that winds around the mound of massive granite tors, made famous by the classic Australian novel, *Picnic at Hanging Rock*. It's riddled with caves, tunnels and overhanging boulders, its shapes and acoustic echoes enhancing its already spooky reputation. The 718m summit provides a good view over the surrounding plains and farmland as well as the nearby Macedon and Cobaw ranges.

Forest Ecotourism Walking Trail is an easy one-hour family interpretive walk through the native forests of the Macedon Ranges that loops past the peaceful tree-fringed Sanatorium Lake.

On the Mornington Peninsula the Fort Nepean Walk is an easy 90-minute one-way walk to the tip of the peninsula. The walk passes Cheviot Beach, where Prime Minister Harold Holt disappeared in 1967, and The Rip, the treacherous divide between Point Nepean and Point Lonsdale that has claimed many ships since European settlement.

The 6km Bushrangers Bay Trail starts at the historic 1859 Cape Schanck Lighthouse and offers sweeping views of the wild coastline and, at the point of Bushrangers Bay, an impressive spire called Elephant Rock.

Two Bays Trail, from Dromana on Port Phillip Bay to Bushrangers Bay near Cape Schanck, is the Peninsula's longest continuous track: the 26km walk will take around 10 hours to complete. It is a moderate-graded trail with boardwalks, bridges and steps making it safe and enjoyable. The surface ranges from steep gravel sections around Arthurs Seat to undulating grass paths through Greens Bush.

adventure activities

Abseiling and rock climbing

The Brisbane Ranges, just beyond Melbourne's western suburbs, offer good places for abseiling and rock climbing. Falcons Lookout in the Werribee Gorge State Park and the spectacular Camels Hump Lookout in the Macedon Regional Park are also popular abseiling and climbing spots. Access the lookout from the Ballan-Ingliston Road. Both these sites are within easy access of Melbourne and tour operators offer beginner and more advanced climbs at both. Live Adrenalin run one-day introductory courses at Staughton Vale from January to June and at Werribee Gorge during the months of July to December.

www.adrenalin.com.au

Ballooning

Stable weather and breathtaking scenery make the Yarra Valley the state's most popular year-round hot air ballooning spot. On most still mornings you can see several hot air balloons drifting over the valley's vineyards. Balloon flights depart just after dawn for a sunrise float over a panorama of forests, farms and corridors of vines before setting down for a breakfast of sparkling wine and local produce at a local winery. There are several ballooning companies. Contact the visitors information centre for more details or visit:

www.hotairballooning.com.au www.globalballooning.com.au

You can also fly over Melbourne in a balloon. Although launch and landing sites vary, the main meeting point is in the city's Royal Botanic Gardens and, after a one-hour flight watching the city wake up and come to life, tuck into a celebratory champagne breakfast at the Observatory Café in centre of the gardens.

www.balloonovermelbourne.com.au

Canoeing and kayaking

Hire canoes and rowing boats from boathouses along the Yarra, which also offer afternoon tea after your paddle. SeaKayak Australia runs half and full-day sea kayaking tours on the waters of Port Philip Bay. Paddle to Williamstown, cross the shipping channel to the West Gate Bridge–and the confluence of the Yarra–and explore the Williamstown docks by water. They also run paddling trips along the Yarra River.

www.seakayakaustralia.com

Cross-country skiing

Lake Mountain, near Marysville, is Australia's premier cross-country ski resort and is one of the southernmost sub-alpine areas of the Australian continent. Its highest point is 1530m and, for several months of the year, Lake Mountain plateau (undulating between 1330-1490m) is blanketed in snow. There are 40km of well-marked ski trails through snow gum woodland, ranging from trails suitable for the first-time skier to the most advanced, which become popular walking tracks and challenging mountain bike trails in spring and summer.

www.lakemountainresort.com.au

Yarra River. *(TV)*

Cycling

Melbourne is a great city for cycling. The Main Yarra Trail is a 33km, five-hour scenic riverside cycling path from Templestowe in Melbourne's eastern suburban fringe to the CBD, ending at Southbank.

Another great ride, the Bay Trail, starts at St Kilda Pier and heads past historic Luna Park before dropping in at a bustling Acland Street café for cakes and coffee, past the colourful St Kilda Marina, parks, restaurants and sports grounds to finish in Brighton, 6km or 40 minutes later. If you want to walk it will take around two hours.

The 29km Capital City Trail is a loop from Southbank that links the city's most famous landmarks, historic properties, parks and gardens on an easy ride through peaceful river landscapes.

The Warburton Rail Trail is a 38km trail–along the old 1901 Lilydale-Warburton railway line–through beautiful bush, lush fern gullies and grazing properties on the fertile Yarra River flood plains, past wineries, flower farms, the Yarra River and the Yarra Ranges National Park and state forest. It starts at Queen Rd in Lilydale, finishes at the Warburton Water Wheel and Visitor Centre and will take around three hours one way.

Diving

The underwater world of Port Phillip Bay includes more than 60 19th century shipwrecks and submarines sunk during WWI, as well as a wealth of marine life that includes: sea dragons, seahorses and gardens of soft corals. Popes Eye is a former fort that is now a ring of rocks and a sanctuary for many species of marine life including fish, birds and seals. Kelp Beds Reef features underwater cliffs, ledges and caves. Port Phillip Heads are home to some of the most spectacular wall dives in Australia, which start at a depth of about 12m and extend beyond 90m. The caves, ledges and overhangs of these walls are adorned with marine life and are quite spectacular.

The *Eliza Ramsden* hit Corsair Rock in Port Phillip heads and stuck fast on the reef in 1875. The bow and parts of the hull still remain intact and can be dived to at slack water (between the tides) when there is no shipping traffic. There are four scuttled WWI 'J Class' submarines outside Port Phillip Heads in water from 26–40m. These dive sites are deep and special training is required to penetrate the wrecks, but two other subs lie in shallow water inside the bay, making them very accessible to divers. The Ships Graveyard is located about 20 minutes from Port Phillip Heads by boat. There are many ships in the Graveyard with depths ranging from 40–70m, giving technical divers an ideal playground to explore. There are wrecks in the Graveyard that are still to be found, including *The Pioneer* (50m), *The Euro* (48m) and *VHB Barges*.

Portsea Pier at the end of the Mornington Peninsula is the home of Victorian diving. Most diver training takes place here and the site is a popular shore dive for its sea dragons, rays and nudibranchs. To the left of the pier is a reef system that stretches out under the boat moorings. Rye Pier is home to Victoria's first underwater trail, suitable for snorkelling and diving and takes you on a marine life tour.

Diving with sharks

Dive with the sharks–even if you are a non-diver–inside Melbourne Aquarium's 2.2-million-litre Oceanarium. The tank holds grey nurse sharks, gill sharks, Port Jackson and gummy sharks as well as stingrays and myriad other marine life. There are two shark dives available: the Shark Dive for Certified Divers and the Shark Dive for Non-Certified or Beginner Divers, which includes an introductory 'resort' dive course. Melbourne Aquarium is on the corner of Queenswharf Road and King Street, Melbourne.

www.melbourneaquarium.com.au

Dolphin swims

The Mornington Peninsula is a popular destination for dolphin watching, with the number of local dolphins on the rise. There are now approximately 150 bottlenose dolphins living in the bay, with up to 60 of them frequenting the southern end of Port Phillip. Polperro Dolphin Swims is an award-winning eco-tourism operation that runs summertime trips into the bay to swim with dolphins and Australian fur seals. Swimmers float in the water–behind the boat, holding onto a rope–while dolphins and seals approach, so all contact is dictated by the marine animals. They are usually friendly, inquisitive and playful and will often come very close to swimmers.

www.polperro.com.au

Fishing

The Mornington Peninsula fronts some of Victoria's most productive fishing grounds and you'll always see hopeful anglers on the dozens of piers that dot the shores of Port Phillip, Hobsons, Corio and Westernport bays. Catches include whiting, gummy and school shark, squid, salmon, flathead and elephant fish. The best fishing is usually in the warmer months when good-sized snapper can be caught from boats and occasionally from piers, jetties and rocky groynes. Popular fishing beaches include Rye Back Beach, Gunnamatta and Point Leo.

There are lots of charter boat operators who will take you to local fishing spots as well as deep-sea ocean fishing in Bass Strait for larger sharks, southern bluefin tuna and smaller mackerel tuna.

For a river so close to a city the size of Melbourne, the Yarra has a surprisingly healthy population of brown and rainbow trout–head to the river at Warburton, the Steavenson River and streams near Marysville. The Lerderderg River in the Lerderderg State Park contains plenty of trout, but access to the river is limited by the surrounding rugged gorge country. The best access points are at McKenzies Flat, Blackwood and O'Brien's Crossing.

Diving with sharks. *(Getty Images)*

Yarra Ranges. *(TV)*

Off-road driving

The Yarra Valley and Dandenong Ranges have some good off-road tracks–through towering mountain ash forest in the Toolangi and Murrindindi State Forests and along the higher ridges–that include lots of dips full of water and river crossings. Other parks with off-road tracks include the Bunyip State Park, Yarra Ranges National Park and Lerderderg State Park, which has some difficult tracks with steep gradients and rocky sections. Bacchus Marsh to Trentham via O'Briens Crossing is a medium track of 73km. Woodend to Daylesford via O'Briens Crossing is an easier track of around 82km. Both are dry-weather roads only. Many roads in the Lerderderg State Park are closed between June and the beginning of November as the park is within a water catchment area.

Horse riding

The Yarra Valley and Dandenong Ranges have some gorgeous horse riding trails through the forests and mountains. Popular spots include Christmas Hills, Chum Creek near Healesville, Warburton and Marysville. The Dandenong Ranges National Park also has a designated horse trail. In the Macedon Ranges there are trails in the Wombat State Forest, Mt Disappointment State Forest, Lerderderg State Park and the Gisborne Ranges. One of the most popular places to go horse riding, however, is the long sandy stretch of Gunnamatta Beach on the Mornington Peninsula, perfect for a nice long gallop. Details of horse riding centres in and around Melbourne, Yarra Valley and Mornington Peninsula at:

www.visitvictoria.com

Hot laps

Strap yourself in for a few 'hot laps' in a high-performance race car at Calder Park Thunderdome–the only Superspeedway track built outside America–reaching speeds of up to 250km/hour. Ride with a professional driver in a NASCAR, Formula One or drive yourself in an AUSCAR or V8 Supercar VX six-speed manual Commodore. Contact Calder Park Raceway:

www.motorsport.com.au ☎ (03) 9217 8800

Kitesurfing and windsurfing

With the great Southern Ocean on the city's doorstep, onshore winds make Melbourne a great location for windsurfing. Elwood and Middle Park beaches are very popular with windsurfers and, on a windy summer day, you can often find dozens of windsurfers on the bay with St Kilda and Brighton among the most popular spots. You can hire windsurfers or take lessons at Elwood and Sandringham.

http://rpstheboardstore.com

Sailing

Yachting is one of Melbourne's most popular sports, with about 20 clubs lining the shores of Port Phillip, many of which welcome visitors who volunteer to crew on racing boats. Larger clubs include the Royal Melbourne Yacht Squadron in St Kilda, Royal Brighton Yacht Club, Sandringham Yacht Club and Hobsons Bay Yacht Club at Williamstown. You can charter yachts to sail yourself, sailed by someone else or learn to sail at one of the learn-to-sail organisations.

Portsea. (TV)

The schooner *Enterprize* is a replica of the ship that first brought settlers to Melbourne. One-hour sails from Williamstown and Docklands, overnight adventure sails and extended voyages are also available.

www.enterprize.com.au

The Yarra River also offers plenty of boating opportunities, from taking out a barbecue boat and lunching on the water to a gondola trip.

Skydiving

For inner city skydiving try Sky Dive City where you can jump into Royal Park (near the zoo), just one kilometre from the city centre. Enjoy a scenic flight over Melbourne's skyline and thrill to the spectacular view of skyscrapers by day or city lights by night.

www.skydivecity.com.au

MORE INFORMATION

- **Melbourne Visitor Centre:** Federation Square, corner of Flinders and Swanston streets, Melbourne. ☎ (03) 9658 9658. **www.visitmelbourne.com**
- **Yarra Valley and Dandenongs:** ☎ 13 28 42 or visit **www.yarravalleytourism.asn.au** or **www.yarrarangestourism.com**
- **Mornington Peninsula Visitor Information Centre & Booking Service:** 359B Point Nepean Road, Dromana. ☎ 1800 804 009 or visit **www.visitmorningtonpeninsula.org**

weather watch

- January: 13–25°C
- July: 3–14°C
- Expect slightly colder temperatures in the ranges, with the occasional dusting of snow in the Dandenongs, especially in the upper reaches around Lake Mountain. Summer is mild, winter is more likely to be wet.

great ocean road

Loch Ard Gorge. *(TV)*

▶ TOP OF ANY LIST OF GREAT AUSTRALIAN DRIVES is Great Ocean Road. Built between 1919 and 1932, the cliff-hugging road was hewn from the rock by 3000 returned World War I soldiers using picks, crowbars and shovels. They dedicated the 14-year project as a memorial to their colleagues who died in the war.

The Great Ocean Road officially begins in Torquay and stretches 195km to Warrnambool, but many people continue along the coast to Port Fairy or even Portland. Although it can be done in a day, plan to spend at least three days exploring the varied landscapes and attractions along the way.

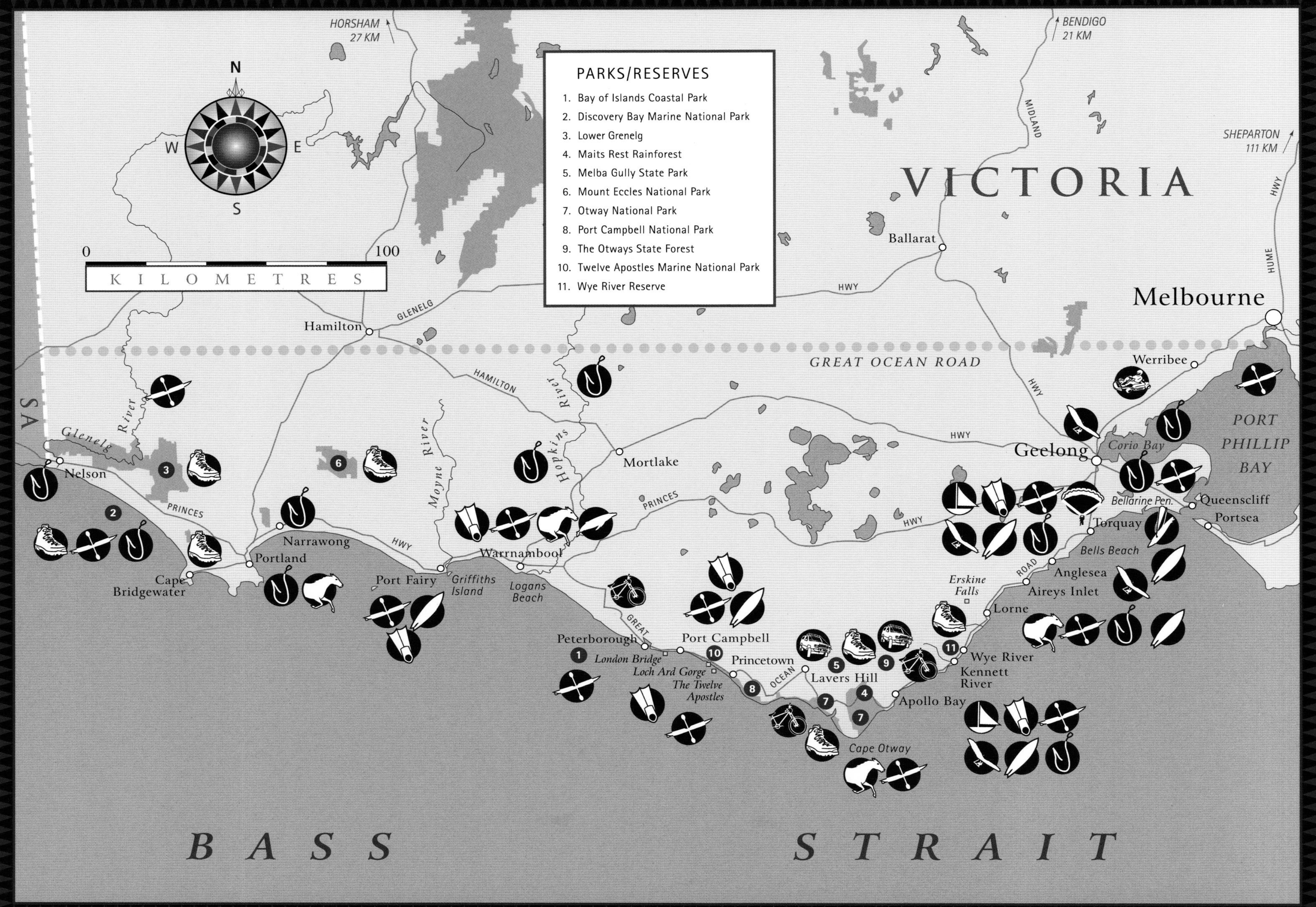
VICTORIA
PARKS/RESERVES
1. Bay of Islands Coastal Park
2. Discovery Bay Marine National Park
3. Lower Grenelg
4. Maits Rest Rainforest
5. Melba Gully State Park
6. Mount Eccles National Park
7. Otway National Park
8. Port Campbell National Park
9. The Otways State Forest
10. Twelve Apostles Marine National Park
11. Wye River Reserve
0
100
KILOMETRES
N
S
E
W
HORSHAM 27 KM
BENDIGO 21 KM
SHEPARTON 111 KM
Melbourne
Ballarat
Hamilton
Mortlake
Geelong
Werribee
PORT PHILLIP BAY
Corio Bay
Bellarine Pen.
Queenscliff
Portsea
Torquay
Bells Beach
Anglesea
Aireys Inlet
Erskine Falls
Lorne
Wye River
Kennett River
Apollo Bay
Cape Otway
Lavers Hill
Princetown
Port Campbell
Loch Ard Gorge
The Twelve Apostles
London Bridge
Peterborough
Warrnambool
Logans Beach
Griffiths Island
Port Fairy
Narrawong
Portland
Cape Bridgewater
Nelson
SA
GREAT OCEAN ROAD
MIDLAND
HUME
HWY
GLENELG
HAMILTON
PRINCES
GREAT
OCEAN
ROAD
Glenelg River
Hopkins River
Moyne River
BASS STRAIT

NATIONAL PARKS

Otway National Park: this huge park covers much of the tall forests and steep slopes of the Otway Ranges as well as the rugged, largely inaccessible coastline around Cape Otway and west to Princetown. Highlights include the Cape Otway Lightstation, Maits Rest rainforest boardwalk, giant mountain ash gums, fern gullies and many coastal and rainforest walking tracks.

Port Campbell National Park: the most photographed section of Great Ocean Road is in Port Campbell National Park and includes the Twelve Apostles, rock towers (there are actually only eight left) carved the out of the surrounding cliffs by wind and wave erosion. The cliffs rise to nearly 70m in some places and the highest Apostle is around 50m from base to tip. Other attractions include Loch Ard Gorge—the site of a tragic shipwreck in 1878 that left just two survivors—and London Bridge, which dramatically lost one of its arches in 1990 stranding two startled sightseers on the newly formed tower.

Twelve Apostles Marine National Park: located 7km east of Port Campbell, this is Victoria's second largest marine national park, covering 7500 hectares along 17km of coastline. The park extends out from the Twelve Apostles and includes some of Victoria's most spectacular underwater scenery with dramatic underwater arches, canyons, fissures, gutters and deep sloping reefs.

Bay of Islands Coastal Park: stretching from Peterborough almost to Warrnambool in a 32km long narrow strip, this park offers spectacular views, accessible bays and secluded beaches.

Discovery Bay Marine National Park: a majestic 50km sweep of ocean beach, huge dunes, Aboriginal middens and coastal lakes. Attractions include mainland Australia's largest breeding colony of fur seals at Cape Bridgewater, blowholes, a sand-petrified forest and the highest coastal cliffs in Victoria, 130m above sea level. The Bridgewater Lakes, 16km west of Portland, are popular for picnics, swimming, boating, waterskiing and surf fishing.

Melba Gully State Park: one of the wettest places in the state with an annual rainfall over 2000mm, the gully is a dense rainforest of myrtle beech, blackwood and tree ferns with an understorey of low ferns and mosses. The 'Big Tree' is more than 300 years old. In holiday periods there are guided night walks to see glow worms.

Lower Glenelg National Park: the Glenelg River is the central feature of this park in the south-western corner of Victoria where the river has carved a spectacular gorge up to 50m deep through limestone. River erosion and the action of rainwater have created some remarkable caves including the richly decorated Princess Margaret Rose Cave.

Mount Eccles National Park: stands at the western edge of the volcanic plains that stretch from Melbourne to Port Fairy. Highlights are extensive lava flows, lava caves, scoria cones and crater lakes.

Geelong and Bellarine Peninsula

Victoria's second largest city, Geelong is 75km from Melbourne, on the shores of Corio Bay, and is the major gateway to the Bellarine Peninsula and Great Ocean Road. More than 100 National Trust-listed buildings make this a pleasant city to stroll around. The waterfront precinct is decorated with brightly-painted bollards that chronicle characters from the city's past and present, including 1930s life-savers, footballers, sailors, fishermen and ladies in neck-to-knee bathing costumes.

To the east is the Bellarine Peninsula, full of stately Victorian-era mansions transformed into restaurants and guesthouses. At the entrance to Port Philip Bay, just a short ferry ride from the Mornington Peninsula, Queenscliff started as a fishing village, became a fashionable holiday destination for Melbourne's elite in the late 19th century and still attracts thousands of holidaymakers to the beaches, galleries and boutiques each year.

Torquay to Apollo Bay

The Great Ocean Road starts at Torquay, surfing mecca and the birthplace of Rip Curl and Quiksilver, two of the world's leading surf-wear and fashion brands. Visit Surfworld, an interactive museum dedicated to the art and culture of wave riding, shop for surf wear at Surfcoast Plaza or check out the waves at Front Beach. Bells Beach, one of the most famous surf beaches in Australia and home of the world's longest running professional surfing event, the Rip Curl Pro, is a short detour away.

From Torquay head south along the 'surf coast' through Anglesea, where the road hits the coastline and you see the first of the long stretches of dramatic coastal views that the Great Ocean Road is famous for. Lorne is a stylish resort town, its main street opposite the beach lined with boutiques, cafes and restaurants, as is Apollo Bay, although it is also home to a lively fishing industry. Watch the fleet unload its catch at the wharf or buy some of the local speciality, crayfish or lobster, at the fisherman's co-op at the edge of the wharf to munch on the beach.

Touring the Great Ocean Road.

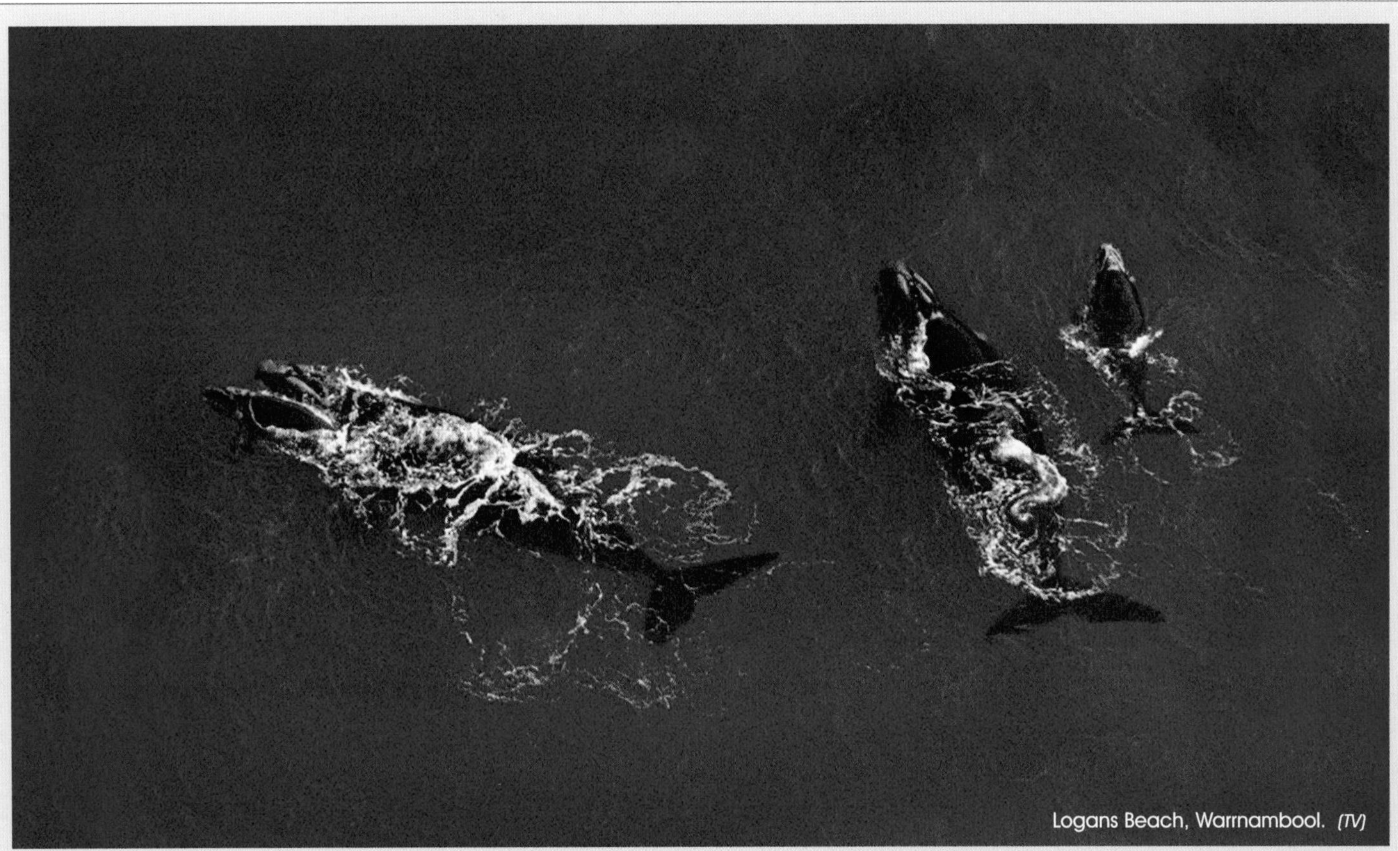

Logans Beach, Warrnambool. *(TV)*

DON'T MISS

- **Werribee Open Range Zoo:** Open range zoo with a range of activities including slumber camping safaris and 2.5-hour, fully-guided canoe safaris along the Werribee River. K Road, Werribee. Open daily, 9am–5pm. ☎ (03) 9731 9600. www.zoo.org.au
- **Werribee Park:** 1870s mansion, 10 hectares of exquisite formal gardens, the internationally acclaimed Victoria State Rose Garden, contemporary sculpture walk, natural riverine, original farmyard and ShadowFax winery. Open daily, 10am–5pm. www.parkweb.vic.gov.au
- **National Wool Museum:** Australia's only comprehensive museum of wool, showcasing wool's enduring impact on Australia social and economic life. Housed in a century-old (1872), refurbished bluestone wool store, the museum uses unique objects and innovative displays to tell the story of the Australian wool industry from early settlement to the present day. 26 Moorabool Street, Geelong. Open daily, 9.30am–5pm.
- **Surfworld:** a celebration of Australia's surfing and beach culture. Interactive exhibits, memorabilia, Surfing Hall of Fame and lots of surf art and kitsch. Located at Surf City Plaza in Torquay, home to several surf-wear outlet stores. Open daily 9am–5pm. www.surfworld.org.au
- **Otway Fly:** get close-up views of the rainforest on the elevated boardwalk, 25m above the ground with a 47m lookout tower. Open daily. www.otwayfly.com
- **Cape Otway Light Station:** built in 1848, is one of the best groups of historic lighthouse buildings in Australia. There are daily tours of the lighthouse, and accommodation in the historic keeper's quarters can be arranged by contacting the lighthouse on ☎ (03) 5237 9240. Open daily. Tours at 11am, 2pm and 3pm, self-guided tours at other times.
- **Twelve Apostles:** towering rock stacks rising from the sea, these, along with the neighbouring rock stacks and arches of the Bay of Islands, are one of the main attractions of Great Ocean Road. Nearby is Loch Ard Gorge, scene of a shipwreck disaster in 1878 when 52 crew and passengers of the *Loch Ard* were lost, with just two survivors.
- **Helicopter flights:** there are two helicopter charter companies who offer joy flights over the Twelve Apostles. Premiair Helicopter Services is located behind the Interpretive Centre at the Twelve Apostles. www.premiairhelicopterservices.com
- **Flagstaff Hill:** created around the original 1859 lighthouses and fortifications that established Warrnambool, Flagstaff Hill is an open air museum: a recreated 1850s coastal village. The Great Circle Gallery tells the story of the more than 180 shipwrecks along this section of coast. Star exhibit is the Loch Ard Peacock, a priceless statue recovered from the wreck of the *Loch Ard*. The nightly sound and laser show, Shipwrecked, tells the story of the *Loch Ard* disaster. Merri Street, Warrnambool. Open daily 9am–5pm. www.flagstaffhill.com
- **Whale nursery:** each year, between June and September, female southern right whales arrive at Logans Beach near Warrnambool to give birth.

scenic highlights

Port Campbell National Park. *(TV)*

The Great Ocean Road starts at Torquay and hugs the coastline. At Aireys Inlet climb up to the lighthouse for fine views of the coastline. At Eastern View, a few kilometres on, is the Great Ocean Road Memorial Arch: a good place for a souvenir photo.

Wedged between the coast and the Otway forests, Lorne is a good base for short excursions into the hinterland. Erskine Falls are a few minutes drive from the village centre along well-made walking tracks though the rainforest, past the falls, huge tree ferns and towering trees.

Apollo Bay is an hour's drive from Lorne. The road hugs the coast the whole way, passing through the pretty hamlets of Wye and Kennet River and pull over at Cape Patton Lookout for a fantastic coastline view and another great photo.

At Apollo Bay, the road leaves the coast to cut through lush farmland then dense rainforest in Otway National Park, before emerging on the the coast again at Port Campbell National Park. Take the turn-off to tour Cape Otway Lighthouse, one of the best-preserved groups of lighthouse buildings in Australia. Keep your eyes open as you will often see koalas crossing the road or asleep in the trees beside the road.

The road cuts across a heath-covered plateau to Princetown, where the high plain falls into the sea over sheer cliffs, sometimes just metres from the road. Highlights include the Twelve Apostles, Loch Ard Gorge, London Bridge and the Bay of Islands Coastal Park. All of these major natural attractions are well signposted and offer good lookout points and boardwalks.

After Peterborough the road meanders through beautiful pastoral lands before meeting the coast again at Warrnambool. Port Fairy, a picturesque town with many historic buildings housing restaurants, boutiques and art galleries, is 30 minutes away.

Warrnambool. *(TV)*

Warrnambool and Port Fairy

The largest town on the south-west coast, Warrnambool is a port town with a colourful seafaring heritage. Flagstaff Hill is an open-air maritime museum–a recreated 1850's coastal village and museum–telling the story of the more than 180 shipwrecks along this section of coast, including the *Loch Ard* disaster. Between June and September, head for Logans Beach where you might be lucky enough to see one of the many female southern right whales that come here each year to give birth.

Port Fairy is a picturesque town with many historic buildings housing restaurants, boutiques and art galleries. Take a stroll along the Moyne River boardwalk to see what the fishing boats have brought in and out to the sheltered harbour or to the lighthouse and shearwater colony on Griffiths Island. If you are there in March make time to visit the annual Port Fairy Folk Festival.

www.portfairyfolkfestival.com

Caravan and camping

Some good camping spots along the Great Ocean Road include Cumberland River Reserve, 7km west of Lorne–a lovely grassy camping area set beside the river and beachfront–and Kennet River Foreshore Reserve beside the Kennett River between Lorne and Apollo Bay. Also good is the Wye River Reserve, 15km south of Lorne, and Allenvale Mill Site in Angahook-Lorne State Park, a basic but secluded camping area beside the George River on Allenvale Road, 2km south-west of Lorne. There is also a large camping area beside the river at Steavensons Falls.

In Otway National Park, at Blanket Bay near Cape Otway, campsites are on the edge of a good swimming beach but get very busy during school holidays. Other good camping spots in the park include the mouth of the Aire River, behind the sand dunes at Johanna Beach, on the river bank at Dandos and at Lake Elizabeth.

Sunset over the Twelve Apostles. *(TV)*

West of Warrnambool you can camp at Lake Surprise in Mt Eccles National Park where you can see extensive lava flows, lava caves, scoria cones and crater lakes. Lake Monibeong camping area in Discovery Bay Coastal Park has tent sites only.

In Lower Glenelg National Park you can camp at Battersby's camping area beside the river and Forest Camp South on the south side of the Glenelg River.

Bushwalks

Maits Rest Rainforest Trail in Otway National Park is a 30-minute boardwalk stroll through beautiful rainforest, where giant myrtle beeches tower above a delicate understorey of tree ferns, lichens and moss. Madsens Track Nature Walk in Melba Gully State Park is another delightful half-hour walk that gives a good introduction to the features of the Otway forest.

Great Ocean Walk is a 91km (eight day) coastal walk linking Apollo Bay to the Glenample Homestead, near Port Campbell and includes many of the prime attractions of the Great Ocean Road. It passes through the dense mountain forests and spectacular coastal margin of the Otway Ranges and Otway Plain through the Otway and Port Campbell National Parks, coastal reserves and road reserves. Highlights include all the coastal formations (Bay of Martyrs, Loch Ard Gorge, Twelve Apostles and London Bridge) as well as Maits Rest rainforest boardwalk, giant mountain ash gums, fern gullies, rugged, inaccessible beaches and the historic, 150-year-old Cape Otway Lighthouse. Many of the beaches along the walk are exposed to tides, rips and reefs and are not patrolled. The safest time to walk along them is during low tide. Check tide times before setting off.

Cape Bridgewater Seal Walk is a moderate two-hour-return walk with striking views across Cape Bridgewater, once a volcanic island that is now joined to the mainland by calcified sand dunes. The viewing platform at the end of the trail looks out over rock platforms and on to a colony of about 650 Australian fur seals. You can continue through a petrified forest–the limestone remains of huge trees that once covered the sea cliff to the blowholes.

The 10-day, 250km Great South West Walk is a loop that winds inland from Portland to Nelson via the Cobboboonee Forest and the Glenelg River then returns along the rugged coastline. Twenty shorter walking tracks will take you to most of the major attractions of the Great South West Walk. There are 16 campsites dotted along the way and all feature a pit toilet, fresh water and a wood barbecue or stone fire ring. Highlights include Cape Bridgewater, the beaches of Bridgewater Bay and Cape Nelson, spectacular ocean views, rivers, forests and fern-filled gullies. Register at the Portland Visitor Information Centre or with local police before attempting an overnight leg of this walk.

Crater Rim Nature Walk is a 2km easy walk in Mt Eccles National Park that includes a lava cave and Lake Surprise, a 700m-long lake fed by underground springs. The track climbs to the summit of Mt Eccles for panoramic views over the Western Volcanic Plain, including the classic volcanic cone of Mt Napier to the north. Watch for koalas sleeping or feeding in the manna gums near the track. A shorter loop track follows the shoreline of Lake Surprise within the crater.

adventure activities

Anglesea. (TV)

Canoeing and kayaking

The Great Ocean Road by sea kayak is even more breathtaking than the drive, taking in Torquay and Bells Beach, Lorne, Wye and Kennet River villages, Apollo Bay, the seal colony at Henty Reef, The Cape Otway lighthouse and the secluded beaches along the 'shipwreck' coast to the Twelve Apostles at sea level. There are a number of tour operators at Anglesea, Lorne and Apollo Bay that cater for all levels of experience, skills and adventure tastes and offer lessons as well as tours. Meridian Kayak Adventures offer kayak hire and range of sea kayaking tours. Go Ride a Wave run sea and surf kayaking trips from Anglesea.

www.meridiankayak.com.au www.graw.com.au

For some of Australia's finest flat water canoeing, make a trip up the coast to the Glenelg River near Nelson. The river offers striking scenery from upriver snags, through rolling bushland and ancient gorges to the sweeping estuary, with well maintained campsites every five to 10km. Grampians Adventure Services offer canoe and kayaking tours of the Bridgewater Lakes and Glenelg River.

www.g-adventures.com.au

Cycling and mountain biking

The Great Ocean Road is even more personal and just as grand an experience from a bike as it is from a car, but if you want to get off the main road the place to go is the Otways. The beautiful Old Beechy Rail Trail–where a narrow gauge railway once ran from Colac via Beech Forest to Crowes through the Otway Ranges–will take you across open farmlands, into dense forest, through fern gullies and tall timbers. Contact Bicycle Victoria for more information:

www.bv.com.au

Join a tour with one of the local operators and enjoy a ride from the top of the range through lush rainforests and breathtaking views down to the ocean. Otway Expeditions Mountain Bike Tours has a two to three-hour tour (mostly downhill) or you can request a custom designed tour. Their six and eight-wheel drive Argo buggies can go almost anywhere.

☎ (03) 5237 6341

Diving

Some of Australia's best, but least known, dive sites are along the Great Ocean Road, along with giant kelp forests, abundant fish and underwater caves. They don't call it the shipwreck coast for nothing: the SS *Casino* lies in 9m of water, around 400m from shore near Apollo Bay; the *Fiji* which ran aground in 1891 is near Moonlight Head and the famous *Loch Ard* wreck is in Port Campbell. You can still see its cargo such as lead ingots, lead shot, tiles, bottles and crockery, even a marble headstone. On the Peterborough side of Port Campbell more shipwrecks include the *Newfield* and the *Shomberg*. Near Peterborough is the wreck of the *Falls of Halladale*, nearly 100m long and home to lots of fish. The *Labella* lies about 250m off the breakwater at Warrnambool and is a great dive with lots of fish, plant growth and crayfish.

Local dive operators run tours to many of these spots and most conduct diving courses for all levels.

www.divevictoria.com.au

Fishing

Corio Bay near Geelong and the Bellarine Peninsula offer good all-year snapper fishing, especially off piers and jetties. Lorne and Apollo Bay also have good pier fishing, with catches including mullet, garfish, trevally, Australian salmon and barracouta. Good catches of silver trevally, snapper, shark, King George whiting, Australian salmon and flathead are common in inshore areas. For offshore fishing, try Ingoldsby Reef off Anglesea. There's bream in the estuarine reaches of the Hopkins River near Warrnambool or take a charter at Port Fairy for southern bluefin tuna and other offshore game fish. Portland offers great fishing: offshore, in the harbour, from the beaches or off the breakwall. Beach fishing is good at Narrawong, best in the evening. Discovery Bay, between Cape Bridgewater and the Glenelg River, is renowned for producing large salmon, gummy shark, snapper and mulloway. The Glenelg estuary provides salt-water habitat far upstream for a wide range of fish, including mulloway, bream, mullet, salmon trout and estuary perch, making it a popular fishing destination.

www.gonefishing.com.au

Off-road driving

The Otways State Forest has the some good off-road tracks from Forrest to Lavers Hill. You'll need a detailed map of the area, but try the Cowley track, Goat track, Noonday track, Number One Spur track, West Barwon track, Tuntons track, Delaney's Road and Curtis Road. All of these tracks are driveable in a standard 4WD when it is dry, but you'll need mud tyres and a winch in the wet. Many tracks are closed during the wetter months to avoid damage to the forest. For a challenging drive around Forrest try Number One Spur track or Noonday track in wet weather conditions. Cowley's Drop Off, which isn't on the map, links Goat track and Cowleys track but is worth checking out. Tracks in the Lavers Hill area include Egan track, Mount McKenzie Road, Number Nine Ridge track, Holy Water track, Bennets track and Heffernan track. Lavers Hill is generally wet.

www.parkweb.vic.gov.au

Hang-gliding and paragliding

For a bird's eye view of the Great Ocean Road it's hard to beat a hang-glider or paraglider. Adventure Airsports provide half-hour tandem soaring flights between the Lighthouse at Aireys Inlet and Moggs Creek at Fairhaven. They also run one and two-day introductory paragliding and hang-gliding course on the foreshore and sand dunes and coastal ridges of Torquay.

www.adventureairsports.com.au

Wingsports Flight Academy at Apollo Bay also offers tandem flights in a paraglider, hang-glider or powered hang-glider.

www.wingsports.com.au

Horse riding

There are a number of tour operators offering horse riding trips in and around Great Ocean Road, including rides along beaches, along coastal cliff tops and through bushland to spectacular river settings. Blazing Saddles runs beach and bush rides between Anglesea and Lorne. Wild Dog Trails does one to three-hour beach rides during the day and at sunset at Apollo Bay. Bimbi Park Adventure Camp is a family park featuring playgrounds, discovery walks, pony and horse trail rides at Cape Otway and Rundells Horse Riding offers lessons and trail rides for beginners to experienced riders on trail rides through the forest as well as day beach rides and one to four-night beach and forest safaris near Portland (bush) and Warrnambool (beach).

Wild Dog Trails	☎ (03) 5237 6441
Bimbi Park Adventure Camp	☎ (03) 5327 9246
www.blazingsaddlestrailrides.com	☎ (03) 5289 7322
www.rundellshr.com.au	☎ (03) 5529 2303

Hot laps

Try an Australian Rally Championship 4WD. Live Adrenalin run full and half-day rally driving lessons on a dirt circuit at Werribee, driving a WRX STi and the 'King of Evos', the WRC Group N Ralliart EVO6. You don't need to know how to drive a rally car, as teaching you the skills is what the day is all about, but the cars all have manual transmission, so some prior experience driving a manual is essential.

www.adrenalin.com.au

Kitesurfing and windsurfing

Torquay's Point Danger is the home training ground of world champion windsurfer Jason Polakow and is one of Australia's iconic wavesailing spots. Point Danger is in the middle of Torquay, just a two minute walk from the caravan park. It's a beautiful cross-shore south westerly and there are a different breaks for people of differing expertise levels to try. Strapper Surfboards are the best local windsurfing shop:

☎ (03) 5261 2312

Mark Occhilupo during the Rip Curl Pro at Bells Beach. *(Getty Images)*

Torquay is also ideal for kitesurfing when the wind is onshore or southerly. Learners should head for Geelong's Point Henry, which works well in northerly wind conditions and has shallow water for easy learning. Airsports Kite Surfing in Torquay offers hire and lessons.

www.airsportskitesurfing.com.au

Sailing

Sea Spirit Yacht Charters depart daily from the Apollo Bay wharf for seal and bay sailing tours. For bookings and enquiries:

☎ 0438 240 257

The Apollo Bay Sailing Club operate learn to sail courses.

www.greatoceanroad.com.au/sailing

Sky diving

For thrill-a-minute views you can't beat skydiving and the Parachute School offers tandem jumps at Torquay with one minute of freefall and a more peaceful canopy ride for 6–8 minutes when you can take in the views over the scenic surf coast and the Great Ocean Road. Flights depart from Tiger Moth World Adventure Park where you can also take a scenic or aerobatic joy flight in a restored 1930s open-cockpit tiger moth biplane.

www.skydivingassoc.com.au www.tigermothworld.com

Surfing

The Great Ocean Road is one of the country's best-loved surfing destinations. Dozens of good surf breaks along its coastline draw a steady stream of seasoned surfers all year round. Experienced surfers head to Bells Beach, an icon of Australia's surf scene, where the Rip Curl Pro, part of the ASP World Championship Tour, is held every Easter. For beginners the region is also a great place to learn how to surf. There are a number of excellent surfing schools along the coast and most beginners find themselves standing on a board by the end of a two-hour session. Check out the local visitor information centres for details of surf schools.

MORE INFORMATION

- **Great Ocean Road Visitor Information Centre:** Apollo Bay. ☎ 132 842. www.greatoceanrd.org.au

weather watch

- January: 14–21°C
- July: 4–13°C
- Summers are dry and warm, most rain falls during winter when temperatures can be very chilly.

Port Campbell. *(TV)*

gipsland & the east coast

Thompson River. *(TV)*

▶ THE NORTH-EASTERN CORNER of Victoria is a vast coastal wilderness, fed by Australia's largest system of inland waterways. Alpine rivers tumble into the sea from the high country to the west, feeding a series of large lakes and a very long beach, making this area a favourite holiday destination with a wealth of sailing, fishing and other water sports on offer. Coastal villages serve up delicious freshly-caught seafood. National parks with more than 100km of pristine coastline are great places to go bushwalking or surfing and the many islands are home to large colonies of koalas, seals and penguins.

Beyond the coastal strip are lush farmlands—gourmet deli country—and pretty historic timber-getting and gold rush villages. Try some famous Jindi or Tarrago cheese at Yarragon, browse the weekend farmers' markets or pick your own fresh produce at fruit and berry farms.

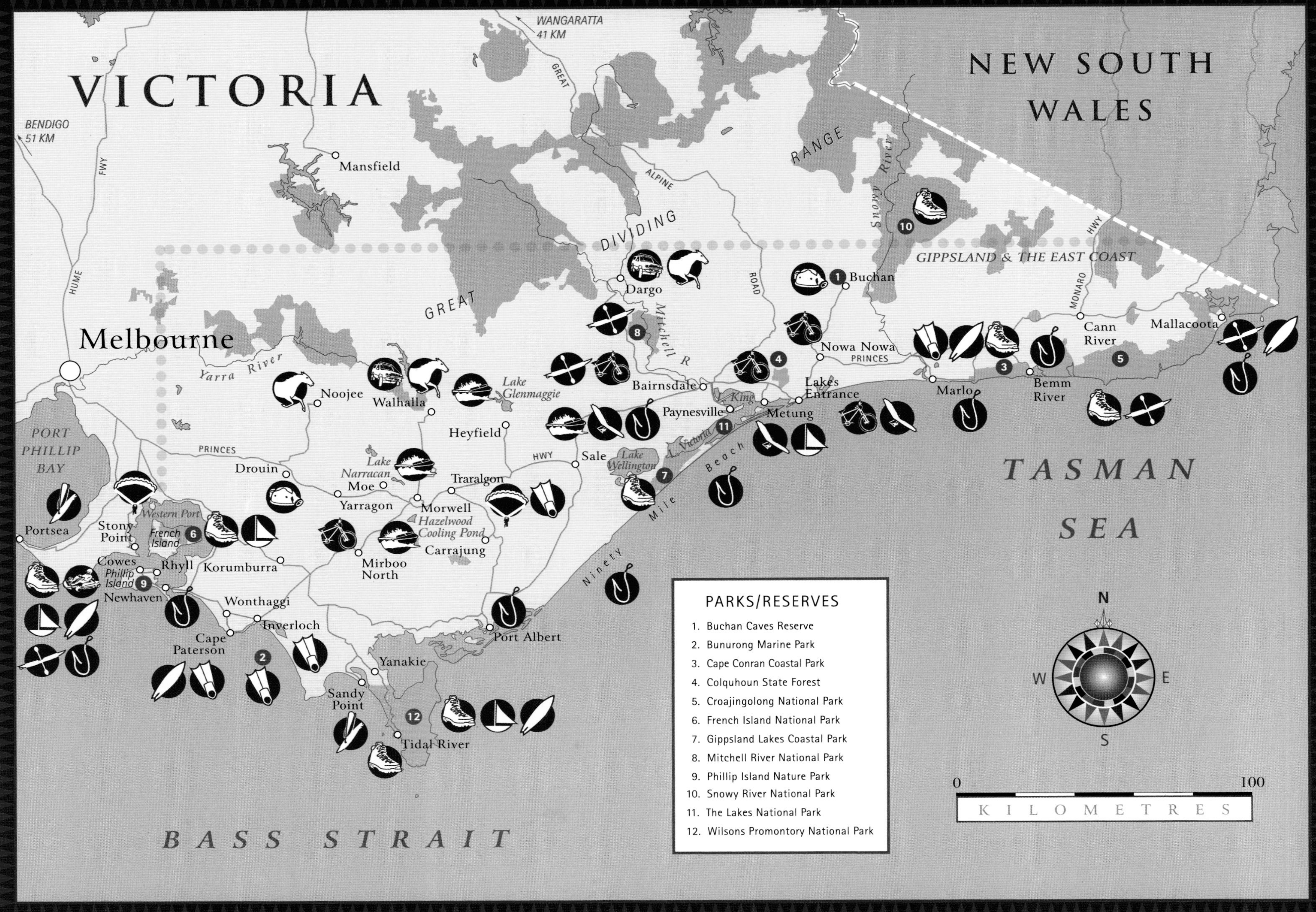
VICTORIA
NEW SOUTH WALES
GIPPSLAND & THE EAST COAST
BENDIGO 51 KM
WANGARATTA 41 KM
Mansfield
Melbourne
Yarra River
Noojee
Walhalla
Lake Glenmaggie
Heyfield
Dargo
Mitchell R
Buchan
Snowy River
GREAT DIVIDING RANGE
ALPINE ROAD
GREAT
HUME FWY
PRINCES HWY
MONARO HWY
PORT PHILLIP BAY
Portsea
Stony Point
Western Port
French Island
Cowes
Phillip Island
Rhyll
Newhaven
Korumburra
Wonthaggi
Inverloch
Cape Paterson
Drouin
Lake Narracan
Moe
Yarragon
Traralgon
Morwell
Hazelwood Cooling Pond
Carrajung
Mirboo North
Sale
Lake Wellington
Bairnsdale
Paynesville
King
Lake Victoria
Metung
Lakes Entrance
Nowa Nowa
Marlo
Bemm River
Cann River
Mallacoota
Ninety Mile Beach
Port Albert
Yanakie
Sandy Point
Tidal River
TASMAN SEA
BASS STRAIT
N
S
E
W
0
100
KILOMETRES
PARKS/RESERVES
1. Buchan Caves Reserve
2. Bunurong Marine Park
3. Cape Conran Coastal Park
4. Colquhoun State Forest
5. Croajingolong National Park
6. French Island National Park
7. Gippsland Lakes Coastal Park
8. Mitchell River National Park
9. Phillip Island Nature Park
10. Snowy River National Park
11. The Lakes National Park
12. Wilsons Promontory National Park

NATIONAL PARKS

Croajingolong National Park: extending for 100km along the wilderness coast of Victoria's East Gippsland, this park—a Unesco World Biosphere Reserve—features remote beaches, tall forests, heathland, rainforest, estuaries and granite peaks.

Wilsons Promontory National Park: one of the state's most popular parks. The 130km of sparkling coastline is framed by granite headlands, mountains, forests and fern gullies and contains the largest coastal wilderness area in Victoria. Tidal River is one of the most popular spots for swimming and Mt Oberon has one of Victoria's most stunning panoramic views. Surrounding waters are part of a marine national park with spectacular underwater scenery and granite cliffs plunging below the surface. Wilsons Promontory is the northernmost exposed link in a chain of granite mountains that continue across Bass Strait to eastern Tasmania. On land, explore intertidal life in the rock pools formed by granite boulders at many of the beaches. The park includes islands that are home to penguins and seabirds. Others are breeding grounds for Australian fur seals.

Gippsland Lakes Coastal Park: a narrow coastal reserve covering a portion of the Ninety Mile Beach from Seaspray to Lakes Entrance with lakes, wetlands, fishing and boating opportunities. The park also includes Lake Reeve, several islands and the Boole Poole Peninsula.

Cape Conran Coastal Park: near Marlo in East Gippsland this park features heathlands, wild ocean beaches and banksia woodlands brimming with nectar-feeding birds.

Mitchell River National Park: the Mitchell River passes between high cliffs forming several gorges lined with remnants of temperate rainforest and some of Gippsland's best forest country.

French Island National Park: accessible only by 30-minute passenger ferry ride, the 11,100ha park supports a large population of the long-nosed potoroo, as well as the most significant population of koalas in Victoria, which reproduce so successfully that each year that more than 200 are transferred to reserves in other parts of Victoria. Wetlands, mangroves and salt marshes provide habitat for water birds, including sea eagles and waders that forage along the coast at low tide.

Snowy River National Park: magnificent river scenery, spectacular deep gorges and forests of grey gum, alpine ash, messmate and native pine. McKillops Bridge is one of the few places in the park with access to the Snowy River by conventional vehicle. The Deddick River meets the Snowy just upstream of the bridge and wide sandy beaches with shallow rock pools between the rapids make this a great swimming spot. This is also the best canoe-launching place. Little River Gorge, Victoria's deepest gorge, is to the west of McKillops Bridge and downstream from the junction of the Little River and Snowy River.

The Gippsland Lakes

More than 400km^2 of lakes, rivers and lagoons combine to form Australia's biggest and most beautiful expanse of inland waterways, the Gippsland Lakes, separated from the ocean by Ninety Mile Beach, a strip of coastal sand dunes. The three main lakes, Lake King, Lake Victoria and Lake Wellington include many small islands, which are reached by ferry or water taxi from Paynesville. Raymond Island is home to a large koala colony and Rotamah Island is famous for its bird life.

Lakes Entrance at the head of the lakes is a popular holiday town, while the larger towns of Bairnsdale–on the banks of the Mitchell River–and Sale further inland, service the surrounding rural communities.

Mallacoota

North, towards the NSW border, Croajingolong National Park protects an area of magnificent coastal wilderness and dense forests. The low-key resort town of Mallacoota is surrounded by beaches, cliffs and lakes and offers great sailing and fishing and beautiful sunsets.

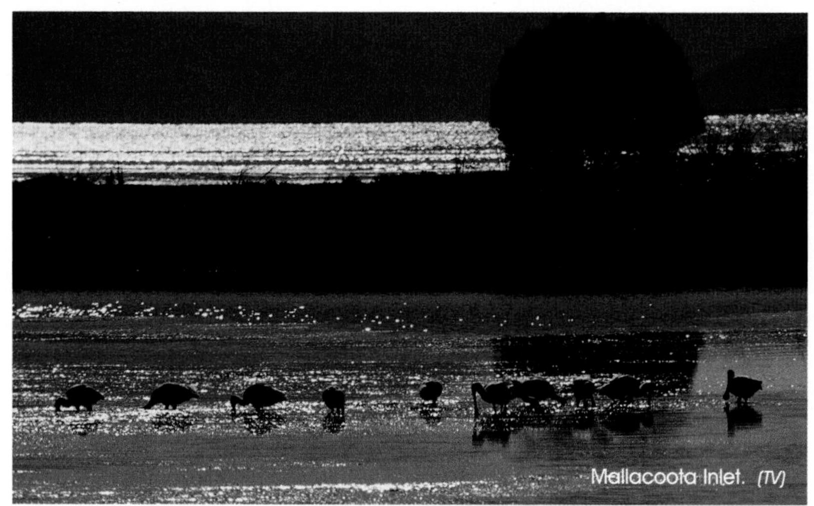

Mallacoota Inlet. *(TV)*

Wilsons Promontory

At the southernmost tip of mainland Australia, the Prom, as it is fondly called by locals, is famous for its abundance of flora and fauna, wild ocean beaches and mountain views, and is a favourite wilderness escape for Melbournians offering some fantastic walking trails.

Phillip and French islands

Waddling penguins and fast bikes and are the two major attractions on Phillip Island in Western Port, both of which draw thousands of international visitors to the island each year. Each night at the Phillip Island Nature Park a parade of penguins head up the beach to the delight of onlookers. The island is also home to Australia's largest colony of fur seals. At the island's Koala Conservation Centre treetop boardwalks take you nose-to-nose with the koalas.

At the opposite end of the spectrum the World Superbike Championship hits the track in April, followed by the Australian Motorcycle Grand Prix in October and V8 Supercars in November.

French Island, a 30-minute ferry ride from Stony Point on Western Port, is home to Victoria's healthiest koala population. You'll also see potoroos, sea-eagles and wading birds.

Tarra-Bulga National Park, swing bridge. *(TV)*

DON'T MISS

- **Krowathunkoolong Keeping Place:** Aboriginal cultural museum. Guided tours, cultural talks, displays, exhibitions, art and craft. 37–53 Dalmahoy Street, Bairnsdale. Open Mon–Fri, 9am–5pm.
- **Coal Creek Heritage Village:** depicts life in a coal mining town from 1870–1920s, using many buildings sourced from the region or recreated. South Gippsland Highway, Korumburra. Open daily, 10am–4.30pm. **www.coalcreekvillage.com.au**
- **State Coal Mine:** take a guided tour through Victoria's last original black coal mine. Above ground visit the mining museum, Garden Street, Wonthaggi. Open daily.
- **Point Hicks Lightstation:** Point Hicks was the first part of Australia's east coast sighted by Captain Cook in 1770. Point Hicks Road, Cann River. Tours of the 38m-high lighthouse on Friday, Saturday, Sunday, and Monday at 1pm.
- **Walhalla Goldfields Railway:** unique narrow gauge train winds its way through the spectacular Stringers Creek Gorge from Thomson Station to the township of Walhalla and back.
- **Long Tunnel Extended Gold Mine:** take a guided tour underground to see the original workings of the Long Tunnel Extended Gold Mine (LTEM), one of Walhalla's richest mines. Main Road, Walhalla. Tours of the mine daily.
- **PowerWorks:** the Latrobe Valley is the centre of Victoria's brown coal mines and power stations, responsible for generating 85 per cent of Victoria's electricity. Off Commercial Road, East Morwell. Tours of the mines and power stations depart daily. ☎ (03) 5135 3415.
- **Bataluk Cultural Trail:** extends from Sale through Stratford, Mitchell River National Park, Bairnsdale, Metung, Lake Tyers, Buchan and Orbost to Cape Conran. It follows the trails and trading routes of pre-colonial days and focuses on elements of Koorie history and culture, including Dreamtime stories, traditional lifestyles, the Den of Nargun, Legend Rock, Aboriginal Keeping Places, archaeological sites such as canoe trees and shell middens, cultural centres of the region, and aspects of European invasion, colonial settlement and present-day existence. The trail is well signposted and literature is available at visitor information centres. **www.ramahyuck.org/bataluk/bataluk.html**
- **Gippsland Regional Maritime Museum:** showcases the regions coastal history, including the many shipwrecks that occurred on the rugged South Gippsland coast. Tarraville Road, Port Albert. Open weekends and school holidays.
- **Gippsland Armed Forces Museum:** 1500 items in a military collection showcasing the rich Army, Navy and Air Force history of Gippsland. Raymond Street, Sale. Open Fri–Mon.
- **Gippsland Heritage Park:** pioneer township with authentic buildings furnished with original décor. Princes Highway, Moe. Open daily.
- **Penguin Parade:** approximately 26,000 little penguins live in the waters around Phillip Island, 4500 of which have their burrows around Summerland Beach on the far south-western point of the Island. See the little penguins make their way up the beach to their burrows at the nightly Penguin Parade in Phillip Island Nature Park, Main Tourist Road, Cowes. **www.penguins.org.au**
- **Koala Conservation Centre:** come face-to-face with koalas dozing in their treetop homes as you wander along the elevated boardwalk at the Koala Conservation Centre, also in Phillip Island Nature Park.
- **Churchill Island:** historic island farm with Heritage buildings and gardens, walking tracks, part of Phillip Island Nature Park.
- **Phillip Island Circuit:** different eras of motor racing through to the present day, with photos and vehicles on display. Tour the race control tower, podium and pits to see where all the action happens. Back Beach Road, Cowes, Phillip Island. Open daily. **www.phillipislandcircuit.com.au**

scenic highlights

Wilsons Promontory. *(TV)*

The Grand Ridge Road is a 132km scenic tourist drive that covers the entire length of the Strzelecki Ranges and features some of the most spectacular views in Victoria. The Grand Ridge Road starts at Carrajung, about 15km south of Traralgon, and runs west and north across the spine of the mountains, through magnificent mountain ash forests and steep, lush fern gullies to Mirboo North, with beautiful views of emerald farmlands and the Latrobe Valley along the way. Some sections of the road are unsealed. Continue south to Wilsons Promontory across undulating farmland. Beyond the township of Yanakie, the landscape becomes increasingly rugged as you head deeper into the national park towards the main camping area and information centre at Tidal Flat. Watch out for wildlife along the way as wombats, kangaroos, wallabies, echidnas and koalas are prolific. Side roads spear off leading to beaches and bushland.

Walhalla

This well-restored historic town was one of Australia's richest towns following the discovery of gold in the area in 1863, particularly the two-mile-long Cohen's Reef. Walhalla's Long Tunnel Mine operated between 1865 and 1914 and was Victoria's most profitable single mine. Today there are just 20 people living in the township.

Caravan and camping

The Tidal River camping area at Wilsons Prom has 450 camping and caravan sites near the beach and river. There are also 11 remote walk-in sites located within the park. You'll need to book during holiday periods and a ballot is held to allocate sites for summer. Contact Parks Victoria on:

www.parkweb.vic.gov.au ☎ 131 963

In Gippsland Lakes Coastal Park there are 20 large free camping areas between Golden Beach and Seaspray on Ninety Mile Beach. Sites are located behind the primary dune, 50–100m from the beach and are perfect for fishing, swimming or walking.

Wingan Inlet camping area in Croajingolong National Park has secluded campsites set in tall bloodwood forest near the shores of the inlet and the Peachtree Creek camping area on the banks of the Cann River is another good spot to camp. Other good spots to camp in the park include the Mueller River camping area where there are eight campsites located on the banks of the Mueller Inlet; Thurra River camping area near the mouth of the Thurra River, the largest camp ground in Croajingolong with 46 campsites between the river and the ocean beach (bookings essential for the Christmas and Easter holidays) and Shipwreck Creek camping area where there are five sites set in tall forest above rocky headlands at the mouth of Shipwreck Creek.

Bushwalks

Wilsons Promontory is one of the most popular bushwalking locations in the state with more than 30 walks along 130km of tracks varying in length and difficulty. The Tidal River to Squeaky Beach Trail is a pretty 90-minute riverside trail that becomes a gentle bay walk featuring coastal plants, wonderful panoramas and, of course, the famous white (and noisy) sands of Squeaky Beach. The Mt Oberon Summit walk follows a moderate to steep track to the summit, but the 360-degree views at the summit are well worth the effort. Wilsons Prom Circuit Trail is a three-day, 44km loop from Tidal River that winds through a landscape of beaches, bays, mountains, forests and fern glades. Prom Lighthouse Trek is a ranger-guided 38km walk to the southernmost part of the Australian mainland and includes a stay at the heritage-listed light station in a refurbished lightkeeper's house.

☎ (03) 5680 9555

On Phillip Island the Cape Woolamai Trail is an 8km sandy track winding along the sheer cliff tops on the Island's southerly point. Keep an eye open for the burrows of the Cape's short-tailed shearwaters (mutton birds), small migratory birds that fly to Alaska each April. The George Bass Coastal Walk is another good cliff top walk (easy, 7km) that heads east toward Kilcunda.

The Wilderness Coast Walk extends 100km from Sydenham Inlet in Croajingolong National Park, to Wonboyn in the Nadgee Nature Reserve in NSW. If you want to complete an overnight section, you must obtain a permit and detailed information from Parks Victoria prior to departure.

adventure activities

Canoeing and kayaking

The Mitchell River near Bairnsdale has good canoeing through tranquil pools and turbulent rapids down to the Gippsland Lakes. It provides challenging grade 3 and 4 rapids and the best time to paddle is July to December. The Snowy River offers thrilling canoeing or rafting with rugged gorges, rapids, flat sections with sand bars and beautiful scenery. The best time to go is in spring (August–September) when snowmelt swells river levels.

For a gentler paddle, launch a canoe or kayak on the Gippsland Lakes or further along the coast at the Mallacoota Inlet. You can also canoe on the tranquil waters of the Genoa and Wallagaraugh rivers that lead into the Mallacoota Inlet or the Thurra and Mueller rivers in the Croajingolong National Park and sea kayaking is also popular in this region. You can also paddle the many calm bays and inlets around Phillip Island, including Swan Bay, Rhyll Inlet and Churchill Island and take in the scenery, colonies of migratory waterbirds and other wildlife. Canoe and kayak hire is readily available from most major centres.

Caving

Buchan Caves Reserve, near the township of Buchan, has guided tours of Royal Cave and Fairy Cave. Both caves are lit and have walkways. Royal Cave has beautiful calcite-rimmed pools; Fairy Cave has elaborate stalactites and stalagmites. Tours to 'wild' unlit caves can be arranged for small groups. You can also book tours of some of the other caves that have been opened, including the less accessible Murrindal Caves, just north of Buchan.

www.parkweb.vic.gov.au ☎ 131 963

Live Adrenalin runs adventure caving trips exploring the wild Labertouche Cave near Drouin, a granite boulder infill cave formed when a large mass of granite weathers to form a huge jumble of boulders with linked gaps forming tunnels and caverns. The entrance and exit to the caves involve the use of ladders and ropes so tours entail lots of crawling, climbing and getting dirty!

www.adrenalin.com.au

Cycling and mountain biking

There are a number of good bicycle and rail trails in the Gippsland area. The East Gippsland Rail Trail is a gently undulating 50km trail alongside farmland and forest between Bairnsdale and Nowa Nowa. Gippsland Lakes Discovery Trail Ride runs from Bairnsdale to Lakes Entrance, through the Colquhoun State Forest, linking the East Gippsland Rail Trail to Lakes Entrance. The Great Southern Rail Trail follows the route of an old railway line through rolling farmland, forested slopes and native bush. It's an easy, two-hour flat ride. Sample the wines of a local winery or rediscover the past at Coal Creek Heritage Village in nearby Korumburra.

Mirboo North-Boolarra Rail Trail is a moderate ride that starts at Railway Park near Boolarra's historic Old Pub. Following the old railway line, it climbs steadily through tall eucalypt forest, lush pastures, sheltered fern gullies and pockets of beautiful rainforest, crossing many small creeks and streams along the way. After an ascent of nearly 240m over 13km from Boolarra, the trail ends at Mirboo North just outside the Grand Ridge Brewery.

Diving

Gippsland's rugged and spectacular coastline is protected by a number of marine parks. The broad rock platforms and underwater reefs of Bunurong Marine Park support a range of habitats along

Fishing at Marlo. *(TV)*

17km of coastline–set out from Eagles Nest, Shack Bay, Cape Paterson, Flat Rocks and Inverloch. Further along the coast, Cape Conran Coastal Park is another popular spot for scuba diving, particularly around West Cape Beach and Salmon Rocks. The rocky headlands, caves, rock pinnacles and rock pools also provide plenty of interest at low tide for snorkellers. Hammers Haven with its many large rock pools and caves is another good spot.

SEAL Diving Services at Traralgon hire equipment and run dive courses and diving trips.

www.sealdivingservices.com.au

Fishing

The vast lake systems of the Gippsland Lakes are a haven for anglers and one of the regions major attractions. You'll catch bream, trevally and flathead in the lakes, rivers and inlets around Paynesville, Marlo, Bemm River and Mallacoota, with boat angling the best choice. The remote beaches of Lake National Park and Ninety Mile Beach provide some of the state's best surf fishing for salmon, tailor and flathead. Port Albert is famous for catches of big snapper between October and March. Inland rivers are good for trout. Flathead, snapper, whiting, salmon, shark and squid are caught off the jetties at Cowes, Newhaven, Rhyll and San Remo on Phillip Island.

Off-road driving

The forests, fern gullies and mountain ranges of the Gippsland region, particularly the high country to the west, have some good 4WD tracks. The most popular tracks are in and around the Wonnangatta Valley near Walhalla with a variety of steep, narrow, rough tracks and river and creek crossings. Carry recovery gear through this region as you will probably need it and make sure you travel with other vehicles. The Myrtleford to Wonnangatta Homestead, near Dargo via Dandongadale and Abbeyard, is a difficult (dry weather only) track. For something a little easier, head to Walhalla. The road between Walhalla and Woods Point follows many ridges, crosses the Aberfeldy River and descends into Woods Point. Some sections are very narrow and make it difficult to pass another vehicle. There are also many offshoot tracks ranging from easy to difficult.

Mountain-Top Experience offers passenger and tag-along 4WD tours around the Gippsland area.

www.mountaintopexperience.com

Horse riding

There's not a lot of beach horse riding on offer, but there are plenty of trails that wind through the foothills of the Great Dividing Range around Noojee, Walhalla and Dargo in Central Gippsland. Trails range from pleasant two-hour rides along quiet bushland trails to more challenging mountain treks over several days, camping out in tents, swags or historic cattlemen's huts.

Noojee Horse Safaris and Trail Rides range from three hours to seven days, including snow rides between July and September (snow permitting).

http://members.ozemail.com.au/~waynewm

Hot laps

Strap in for a few 'Hot Laps' in a high performance HSV V8 with a professional driver at Phillip Island Grand Prix Circuit, except during major event periods and MotoGP and SBK testing periods.

www.phillipislandcircuit.com.au

Sailing

The Gippsland Lakes are nature's gift to novice sailors. There are no rocks, reefs or tides and the navigation is easy, so you are free to concentrate on the techniques of sailing. Riverina Nautic, based at Metung, charters all sorts of boats for all types of messing around and learn-to-sail packages can be incorporated into the standard boat charter. For more information:

www.rivnautic.com.au ☎ (03) 5156 2243

Wildlife Coast Cruises run Seal Watching Cruises along Phillip Island's coastline to Seal Rocks, home to a wild seal colony of up to 12,000 seals. The seal watching season is November to April and tours depart Cowes Pier at 2pm each day. Full-day cruises follow the coast of Wilsons Prom to French Island. Visitor information centres have details of the many charters and sailing cruises available.

www.bayconnections.com.au

Skydiving

Soar over the breathtaking scenery of the Latrobe Valley on a tandem skydive with Aerial Skydives based at Traralgon

www.aerialskydives.com

or take in the waters of Western Port with Commando Skydivers, who offer Static Line training (parachute opens automatically as you jump) progressing to solo freefall, where you pull your own ripcord.

www.skydiveworld.com/commandos

Surfing

Experienced surfers should head to Cape Paterson, Venus Bay and Waratah Bay or Red Bluff at Lake Tyers Beach, Salmon Rocks at West Cape Beach in the Cape Conran Coastal Park and Bastion Point Beach in Mallacoota. Phillip Island has one of the most consistently reliable and varied surf locations in Australia. More advanced surfers can find world-class beach breaks at Cape Woolamai and Cat Bay while safe surfing for learners can be found at Smiths Beach and YCW Beach. Other good beaches for novices are Inverloch and Lakes Entrance which have gentle uncrowded waves ideal for beginners.

There are a number of surf schools on the east coast and on Philip Island. The Offshore Surf School will teach anywhere along the Victorian south-east coast from Cape Paterson to Wilsons Promontory on beaches ideal for beginners. Lessons are conducted daily. 45 Beach Avenue, Inverloch.

☎ (03) 5674 3374

Wilsons Promontory Surf School caters for all age groups and ability levels, especially beginners. Contact the post office at Tidal River.

☎ (03) 9598 3114

Sailing off Metung on the Gippsland Lakes. (TV)

Waterskiing and parasailing

The Gippsland Lakes offer excellent waterskiing at a number of spots such as Bunga Arm, Newlands Arm or North Arm, but you can ski almost anywhere on the lakes. In Central Gippsland, Lake Glenmaggie near Heyfield, Lake Narracan at Moe and the Hazelwood Pondage at Morwell are among Victoria's best-kept secrets for waterskiers, with deep fresh water and open space for skiing, wakeboarding and biscuiting. Clint's Ski School at Paynesville runs lessons for all levels, from beginners to advanced, and also has ski tubes or kneeboards.

☎ (03) 5156 6518

Parasailing Victoria offers rides at Lakes Entrance, Metung and Paynesville from spring to autumn. Using winch boat technology and parasail deployment you lift from the back deck of the boat to a height of 70m. Landings are dry, with a gentle touchdown on the rear deck, allowing safe flights for all ages, including those in wheelchairs with advance notice. Fly with a friend or fly solo.

Windsurfing

Sandy Point, near Wilsons Prom attracts windsurfers from around the world with its flat, protected waters and south-westerly winds. It was here that Mal Wright broke the world short course speed sailing record with his windsurfer in 1989 and, in 1993, the *Yellow Pages* sailing team broke the world record. There is now an annual speed week for serious wind junkies held here. Surf, wind, wave and tide reports are posted, along with other useful information, in most surf shops in the region.

MORE INFORMATION

- **Phillip Island Information Centre:** Phillip Island Tourist Road, Newhaven. ☎ 1300 366 422. www.basscoast.vic.gov.au
- **Prom Country Visitor Information Centre:** South Gippsland Highway, Korumburra. ☎ 1800 630 704. www.promcountrytourism.com.au
- **Lakes Entrance Visitor Information Centre:** Corner Marine Parade and Esplanade, Lakes Entrance. ☎ 1800 637 060. www.lakesandwilderness.com.au

weather watch

- January: 14–24°C
- July: 5–15°C
- The Gippsland area of enjoys a year-round temperate climate, with mild summers and relatively warm winters.

central victoria & the goldfields

Main Street, Sovereign Hill, Ballarat. *(TV)*

► THE GOLDFIELDS of central Victoria were once the richest goldfields in the world, attracting hundreds of thousands of hopeful fossickers and miners to the district. In just one decade, from 1851–1861, the population of Victoria swelled from 97,000 to almost 540,000. During the same period, the diggings yielded almost 2.6 million ounces of gold each year.

The discovery of gold more than 150 years ago has left a rich and lasting legacy of grand hotels and public buildings along the main streets of Ballarat and Bendigo as well as historic gardens, homesteads and quaint shopfronts and miners' cottages in townships such as Maldon, Castlemaine and Clunes.

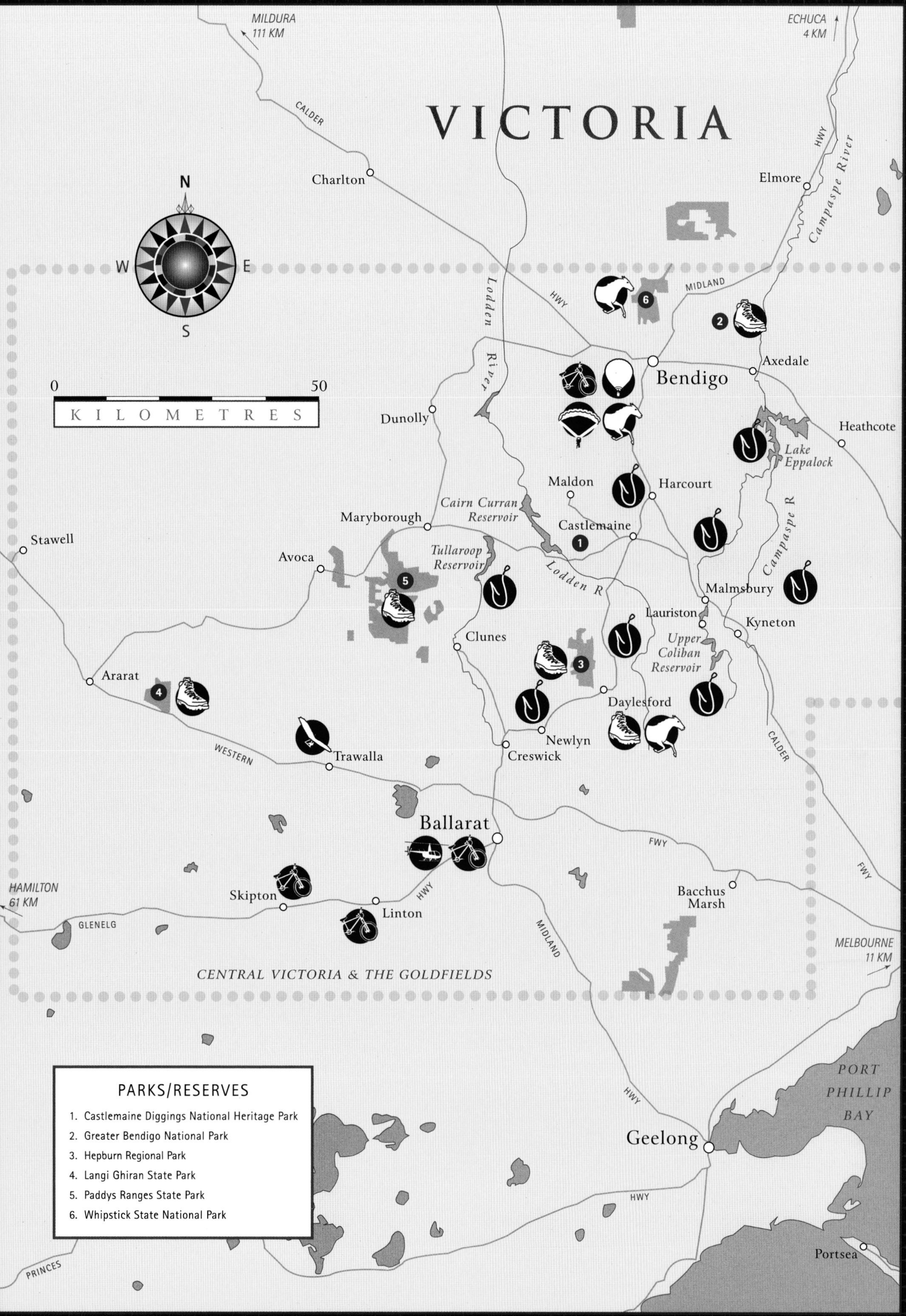
VICTORIA
MILDURA 111 KM
ECHUCA 4 KM
CALDER
HWY
Charlton
Elmore
Campaspe River
N
W
E
S
Loddon River
MIDLAND
HWY
Bendigo
Axedale
0
50
K I L O M E T R E S
Dunolly
Heathcote
Lake Eppalock
Maldon
Harcourt
Cairn Curran Reservoir
Maryborough
Castlemaine
Campaspe R
Stawell
Avoca
Tullaroop Reservoir
Loddon R
Malmsbury
Lauriston
Kyneton
Clunes
Upper Coliban Reservoir
Ararat
Daylesford
WESTERN
Trawalla
Newlyn
Creswick
CALDER
Ballarat
FWY
HAMILTON 61 KM
Skipton
Linton
HWY
Bacchus Marsh
GLENELG
MIDLAND
MELBOURNE 11 KM
CENTRAL VICTORIA & THE GOLDFIELDS
PORT PHILLIP BAY
HWY
Geelong
HWY
PRINCES
Portsea
PARKS/RESERVES
1. Castlemaine Diggings National Heritage Park
2. Greater Bendigo National Park
3. Hepburn Regional Park
4. Langi Ghiran State Park
5. Paddys Ranges State Park
6. Whipstick State National Park

Mount Franklin. *(TV)*

NATIONAL PARKS

Paddys Ranges State Park: just south of Maryborough this park has many relics of the goldmining era and is well known for its spring wildflower displays, especially at the Settling Ponds Track/Possum Gully Track junction, along Whipstick Track, and in the Wildflower Reserve. The park is also home to more than 140 native birds, including the rare Painted Honeyeaters and Swift Parrots.

Castlemaine Diggings National Heritage Park: Australia's first National Heritage Park, the park has an extensive network of roads, fire trails and walking tracks. Highlights include the 22m Garfield Water Wheel, Spring Gully and Eureka Reef, ruins of an old Welsh village and other ruined house sites and mineral springs at Vaughan.

Greater Bendigo National Park: spanning some 17,007 hectares, the park contains some of the highest quality box-ironbark forest in the Bendigo area, along with broombush mallee, grassy woodlands and Kamarooka mallee. There are also many significant relics of gold mining and eucalyptus oil industries in the park.

Langi Ghiran State Park: abuts the Western Highway 80km west of Ballarat and 14km east of Ararat. The park contains two distinct land types—rugged granite peaks and gentle sloping open woodland. Mt Langi Ghiran rises to 949m above sea level.

Hepburn Regional Park: natural mineral springs and relics of the gold mining era. Other highlights of the park include the Blowhole, an artificial diversion tunnel on Sailors Creek was built by gold miners in the early 1870s, and the extinct volcanic crater of Mount Franklin.

Ballarat

Gold was first discovered in Ballarat in 1851 and it didn't take long for the pretty little valley with its meandering stream and surrounding ironbark forests to be transformed into a sea of mud, tree stumps and canvas tents. By 1854, ongoing grievances at the unfair license system and government corruption, coupled with the murder of one of the diggers, sparked Australia's first armed rebellion–the Eureka Stockade. The events leading up to the short-lived battle are masterfully retold each night in the spectacular outdoor sound and light show, *Blood on the Southern Cross*, at Sovereign Hill, a huge outdoor museum that recreates Ballarat in the decade between 1850 and 1860.

The legacy of the riches that poured into the town is a stunning streetscape of grand Victorian buildings and it is worth spending some time wandering the main streets in the centre of town. The Ballarat Fine Art Gallery is one of the best regional art galleries in the country.

Clunes and Maldon

North of Ballarat, Clunes is a sleepy little town which was once the fifth largest town in the colony, but has remained pretty much unchanged for the past 100 or so years. Most visitors to the area miss Clunes, which is a shame as it is one of the most authentic 19th-century settlements in the country–a glimpse of real gold rush heritage without the glitz of tourism. The bakery is a good place for coffee and light lunch.

Maldon, like Clunes, is a town that time seems to have forgotten, and miner's cottages stand cheek-by-jowl with restored mansions and the shopfronts along the crooked main street look like they have come straight from a movie set. Unlike Clunes however, Maldon's historic buildings host a number of cafes, galleries, antiques stores and other shops, and is very popular with browsing shoppers on weekends.

Bendigo

Bendigo is built on gold–quite literally. More gold has been found in Bendigo than anywhere else in Victoria: a colossal 22 million ounces since 1851, worth around nine billion dollars by today's standards and there's plenty left. Bendigo Mining estimates there's at least 12 million ounces still waiting to be extracted. After Kalgoorlie, Bendigo is the second highest producing goldfield in Australia and is ranked seventh in the world.

At the height of the rush lavish public buildings were constructed with the new found wealth and they lined Bendigo's thoroughfares with ornate sandstone facades, a testimony to the city's wealth and power. Today, Bendigo has one of the finest collections of Victorian buildings of any inland city in Australia. The wide streets are lined with majestic, richly-decorated buildings, theatres and shopfronts, and in the centre of the city, a fountain dedicated to Queen Victoria's daughter-in-law, Princess Alexandra, sits in the middle of the main street.

Like most of the Australian gold fields, the Bendigo diggings attracted thousands of Chinese prospectors, but it is here that their legacy is the strongest. Each Easter the city celebrates with a festival program of fireworks, arts, food and wine and, on Easter Monday, a parade with Sun Loong, the world's longest (more than 100m) Chinese Imperial Dragon. Bendigo is home to five dragons, including Loong, also the world's oldest Imperial dragon, who made his first appearance on Bendigo streets in 1892. All five are displayed in the Golden Dragon Museum, which explores the Chinese history and culture of the city and surrounding goldfields.

Lake Daylesford. (TV)

scenic highlights

The Goldfields Touring Route takes in most of the towns and villages that feature in the history of the Victorian goldfields, and includes Ballarat, Creswick, Castlemaine, Maldon, Bendigo, Dunolly, Avoca, Stawell and Ararat. It is well signposted with distinctive golden 'G' signs along the loop, which takes in important heritage sites, cities, villages and wineries.

The Great Grape Road is an established touring route or scenic circuit through the Pyrenees, Grampians and Ballarat wine regions of western Victoria.

The wines produced in these regions are renowned as some of Australia's finest cool-climate wines. The shiraz in particular has a well-deserved international recognition.

It's recommended that you take three days to follow the Great Grape Road, allowing plenty of time to visit the wineries, which range from sophisticated tasting rooms to barrel-side tastings in underground tunnels.

Daylesford

Daylesford is the centre of spa country. This area has the highest concentration of mineral springs in the country, but the lord of the springs is Hepburn Spa, which has been spruiking the benefits of the local mineral water since 1894. They say that the sulphate purifies your liver; that the calcium is good for your bones; the bicarbonate balances the PH in your bloodstream; the magnesium is good for your kidneys; the silica will help strengthen your bones; the sodium helps prevent stomach disorders; the iron will help carry oxygen to your brain and that your mind and muscles will thank you for the potassium. Of course, the best way to get all this goodness is to drink it–bring lots of empty water containers with you and fill them up at one of the many roadside springs. It's plentiful and free.

Caravan and camping

There is a bush camping ground located along Karri Track in Paddy Ranges State Park, which leads to a walking track loop which also links up with the day picnic area. You can also camp at Vaughan Mineral Springs in Castlemaine Diggings National Heritage Park. Camp amongst candlebark gums at the end of Kartuk Road or at the popular sites beside Hidden Lagoon between the peaks in Langi Ghiran State Park. Facilities include toilets, fireplaces, picnic tables and water. Remote, dispersed camping is permitted in the mountainous section of the park.

In the Daylesford area you can camp at Mount Franklin in Hepburn Regional Park (fireplaces, toilets and washing water provided).

Bushwalks

The 3.5km Eureka Trail follows the footsteps of the government troops as they marched to the brief but bloody battle with rebellious miners on the Ballarat goldfields in 1854. Recreated from historical maps and records of the time, the trail begins amid the majestic Victorian architecture of Lydiard Street, and winds along the banks of the Yarrowee River, through historic residential areas to the site of the original Eureka Stockade. See examples of intact miners' cottages and picnic under the shade of willows beside the river. Interpretive signs along the trail explain the major features and historic sites.

The 70km Federation Track from Ballarat to Lake Daylesford is part of the Great Dividing Trail, a superb 260km walking trail that connects the towns of Ballarat, Bendigo, Daylesford and Bacchus Marsh. Also part of the Great Dividing Trail, the 57km Dry Diggings Track stretches from Castlemaine to Lake Daylesford, past a diverse series of historic mining landscapes.

The Tipperary Walking Track is a 16km walk that takes you past the remains of water races used by gold miners in the last century, through native bush and stands of European trees and past mineral springs in Hepburn Regional Park. It runs from Lake Daylesford to the Hepburn Mineral Springs Reserve, following Sailors Creek and Spring Creek through foothill forest for most of the way. The 16km track takes five to six hours and is quite easy walking. There are also shorter sections between Lake Daylesford and Bryces Flat on both sides of Sailors Creek.

Shorter walks include the 6km Lake Wendouree Trail that winds around the edge of Lake Wendouree in Ballarat and the 2km Eureka Reef Walk through the Mount Alexander Diggings near Castlemaine.

DON'T MISS

- **Sovereign Hill:** outdoor museum recreating a goldfields township set over 60 acres on the site of the world's richest alluvial gold mine. The park depicts Ballarat's first 10 years after the discovery of gold in 1851 with more than 60 buildings and 200 costumed volunteers. Highlights include the Sovereign Quartz Mine (c1880), craftsmen at work in traditional 1850's trades, the underground Red Hill and Quartz Mines, gold museum with a daily demonstrations of $50,000 of liquid gold being poured and the spectacular nightly outdoor sound and light show, *Blood on the Southern Cross* depicting the events of the Eureka stockade and rebellion in 1854. Open daily 10am–5pm. Bookings essential for *Blood on the Southern Cross*, ☎ (03) 5333 5777. **www.sovereignhill.com.au**
- **Ballarat Fine Art Gallery:** established in 1884, Australia's largest and oldest regional gallery housing major collections of Australian art. Centrepiece is the original Eureka Flag. 40 Lydiard Street, Ballarat. Open daily 10.30am–5pm. Free guided tours at 2pm. **www.balgal.com**
- **Eureka Centre:** located in East Ballarat next to the site of one of the most significant events in the evolution of Australian democracy—the Eureka Rebellion, this interpretative centre tells the story and ideals behind the uprising. Cnr Eureka and Rodier Streets, Ballarat. Open daily 9am–4.30pm. **www.eurekaballarat.com**
- **Bendigo Art Gallery:** permanent collections of 19th century European and Australian art, as well as travelling exhibitions. 42 View Steet, Bendigo. Open daily 10am–5pm. Free guided tours at 2pm.

Bendigo Pottery. *(TV)*

Bendigo Pottery: Australia's oldest working pottery. Interpretative museum, potters workshop, kids play clay, throwing lessons and sales gallery. Midland Highway, Epsom. Open daily 9am–5pm. **www.bendigopottery.com.au**

- **Central Deborah Gold Mine:** descend 20 stories underground for tours of historic mine. 76 Violet Street, Bendigo. Open daily 9.30am–5pm. **www.central-deborah.com**
- **Golden Dragon Museum:** explores the Chinese history and culture of Bendigo and surrounding goldfields and home to Sun Loong, the world's longest Chinese Imperial dragon and Loong, the world's oldest Imperial dragon. The museum complex also contains a Chinese tea room, classical Chinese gardens and a Guan Yin Temple. 5–13 Bridge Street, Bendigo. Open daily 9.30am–5pm. **www.goldendragonmuseum.org**

Lavendula. *(TV)*

Lavendula Lavender Farm: working farm producing lavender, olives, chestnuts and wine. Homemade produce, lavender body products, gardens, fully licensed cafe and farmyard. Shepherd's Flat, 10 minutes from Daylesford. Open daily 10.30am–5.30pm, but weekends only in winter Jun–Sep. School holidays 10.30am–5.30pm daily. **www.lavandula.com.au**

- **Talking Tram:** one-hour vintage trams tours of Bendigo with taped commentary of the history of Bendigo and the significance of the many grand Victorian buildings as you pass by. Tours depart on the hour, 10am–4pm, departing from Central Deborah Gold Mine. **www.central-deborah.com/tram**
- **Buda:** historic home and gardens built in 1861 and home of noted silversmith Ernest Leviny. Highlights are the family's art and craft collections and extensive gardens. 42 Hunter Street, Castlemaine. Open Wed–Sat, noon–5pm, Sun, 10am–5pm. **www.budacastlemaine.org**
- **Spas:** there are nine spa resorts and/or facilities in the district. The place where it all began is Hepburn Spa Resort in the Mineral Springs Reserve at Hepburn Springs. There are a range of treatments available. Reservations are essential for all private facilities. ☎ (03) 5348 2034. **www.hepburnspa.com.au** and **www.macedonandspa.com**

adventure activities

Ballooning

Weather permitting, Bendigo Ballooning offers hot air balloon rides daily over Bendigo and the surrounding goldfields towns. Most flights depart just after dawn to take advantage of calm conditions, although half-hour afternoon and evening flights are sometimes possible, particularly in late autumn and winter. Morning flights include a celebratory champagne breakfast. Afternoon and evening flights are no-frills, apart from sparkling wine and chocolates, but are generally less expensive, although they can only be booked on the day once weather conditions are ascertained.

www.bendigoballooning.com.au

Cycling and mountain biking

The 53km Ballarat-Skipton Rail Trail is a rough but flat track between the historic gold mining towns of Ballarat and Skipton. The trail passes the former Chinese settlement site at Nintingbool, numerous railway remains and picturesque timber trestle bridges. Allow some time to wander around some of the small towns along the trail, such as Linton, with its 19th century church and local craft markets. Wildflowers are prolific in spring.

The Bendigo Bushland Trail is a six-hour, 65km moderate ride that meanders through Bendigo's rural fringe, starting and finishing at the Visitor Information Centre. Highlights include wildflowers, abundant wildlife, heritage buildings and relics of the gold rush past. Mountain bikes are recommended for sections of the trail.

The O'Keefe Rail Trail is a two-hour, 19km trail from Lake Weeroona in Bendigo to Axedale, a leisurely ride among gum and box trees, tea tree and wattles, as well as wildflowers, especially in late winter and spring, but is best suited to mountain bikes.

In the wine district around Bendigo there are four winery cycling trails: the 21km Mandurang Valley Wine Trail weaves through the rolling hills of beautiful Mandurang and highlights four wineries; the 35km Harcourt Valley Wine Trail circles around the granite slopes of Mt Alexander, through the fruit bowl and profiles seven wineries; the 33km Big Hill Wine Trail meanders through rich farmlands, magnificent Box-Ironbark forests and visits four wineries and the 50km Loddon Valley Wine Trail takes in the stunning wildflower bushlands and highlights five wineries including one of Bendigo's oldest. Maps of the winery trails are available from Bendigo Visitor Information Centre.

Fishing

With a climate cooler than surrounding areas, Goldfields trout fishing is good year round. There are more than 1000 private and public trout lakes in the greater Ballarat area, and all produce brown and rainbow trout–some weighing in at up to six kilograms. Lake Wendouree receives about 3000 brown trout from the local hatchery each year and other lakes such as the Upper Coliban, Lauriston, Tullaroop, Cairn Curran, Malmsbury, Andersons, Newlyn and Harcourt are popular choices with trout anglers.

Flyfishing. (TV)

There are also a number of private fishing retreats (Sherwood Grange, Millbrook Lakes Lodge and Tuki Trout farm) where you can catch trophy-sized fish. For river fishing, head to the Campaspe River from Lake Eppalock to Axedale. For Murray cod or golden perch, try Lake Eppalock, near Bendigo or Heathcote. The Loddon River and Elmore Weir on the Campaspe River also provide great fishing as well as spectacular scenery. In addition to the sought after species such as brown trout, rainbow trout and redfin, some local waters also carry roach, crucian carp, tench and eels.

Gold prospecting

Hire a metal detector from one of the many gold prospecting stores in the region and try your luck! The Mining Exchange Gold Shop in Ballarat can arrange a prospector tour tailored to your needs.

☎ (03) 5333 4242

The Bendigo Goldfields Experience runs guided tours searching for gold and gold relics with all equipment supplied and includes gold panning lessons–bookings essential:

☎ (03) 5448 4140

At Castlemaine's Forest Creek Historic Gold Diggings you can take a tour or go gold panning on a surviving section of an 1850s diggings. Open Sundays and Mondays, Pyrenees Highway, Castlemaine.

☎ (03) 5470 6200

Hang gliding

Dynamic Flight offer a range of hang gliding courses, from tandem flights to full-day introductory courses at their 1500-acre flight park at Trawalla west of Ballarat. Using tow straps that can launch gliders up to 1000 feet, gliders can take off whatever the wind direction, so the sport is less weather dependent than at other popular hang gliding locations around the country. Tandem flights are usually around half

Riding the trails. *(Getty Images)*

an hour or so, depending on flying conditions. The full-day training course includes a virtual reality simulator, a joy flight on a Dynamic simulator where the glider is tethered to a moving platform, and a tandem flight in a powered hang glider where the pilot may hand over the controls if you are up to it.

www.dynamicflight.com.au

Horse riding

Boomerang Holiday Ranch is a family-owned and operated Camp located 2km from the main centre of Daylesford and surrounded by Hepburn Regional Park. They offer trail riding through native bushland, with all rides supervised, but mainly cater for groups and schools. Ironbark Riding Centre is five minutes from Bendigo and offers trail rides for all levels through Ironstone Reserve and the many tracks and trails of the Whipstick State National Park. Packages range from half-hour rides to full-day rides through historic gold mining fields to historic bush pubs and weekend rides with accommodation.

www.bwc.com.au/ironbark www.boomerangranch.com.au

Jet fighter flights

Australian Jet Adventures, based at Ballarat Airport operate adventure flights over the goldfields in Yak-52 and Strikemaster jet fighter planes. Packages include aerobatics and air combat manoeuvres including inverted flight, weightless flight (0 Gs), barrel rolls, loops, victory rolls, derry turns, wing overs and combination manoeuvres. Operating up to 12,000 feet. Flight times vary between 20 minutes and one hour and are tailored to suit the passenger with mild to wild air combat and aerobatic manoeuvres.

www.austjetadv.com

Skydiving

Airsports Skydiving Academy offers courses for that first solo jump as well as tandem jumps at their Bridgewater on Loddon facility near Bendigo.

www.airsports-skydiving.com.au

MORE INFORMATION

- **Ballarat Tourism:** corner of Sturt and Albert streets, Ballarat. ☎ 1800 44 66 33 or visit **www.ballarat.com**
- **Bendigo Tourism:** corner of Pall Mall and Williamson Street. ☎ 1800 813 153. **www.bendigotourism.com**
- **Daylesford Visitor Centre:** 98 Vincent Street, Daylesford. ☎ (03) 5321 6123. **www.macedonandspa.com**

weather watch

- January: 10–25°C
- July: 3–10°C
- Summers are temperate, most rain falls during winter when temperatures can get very cool.

Taking the leap near Bendigo. *(Getty Images)*

the high country

Mountainous Victoria. *(TV)*

► THE HIGH COUNTRY of north-eastern Victoria is home to some to the country's best winter skiing and, when the snows melt in summer, is an adventure playground. The first Europeans in the area were explorers, Hume and Hovell, in 1824, but before that the mountains were the traditional meeting and hunting grounds for tribes of Aborigines who came here each summer to feast on the Bogong moths. Gold was discovered in the mid-19th century, cattlemen moved into the high alpine grazing fields and bushrangers such as Ned Kelly roamed the foothills, while Italian farmers planted hops, tobacco and grapes in the fertile valleys.

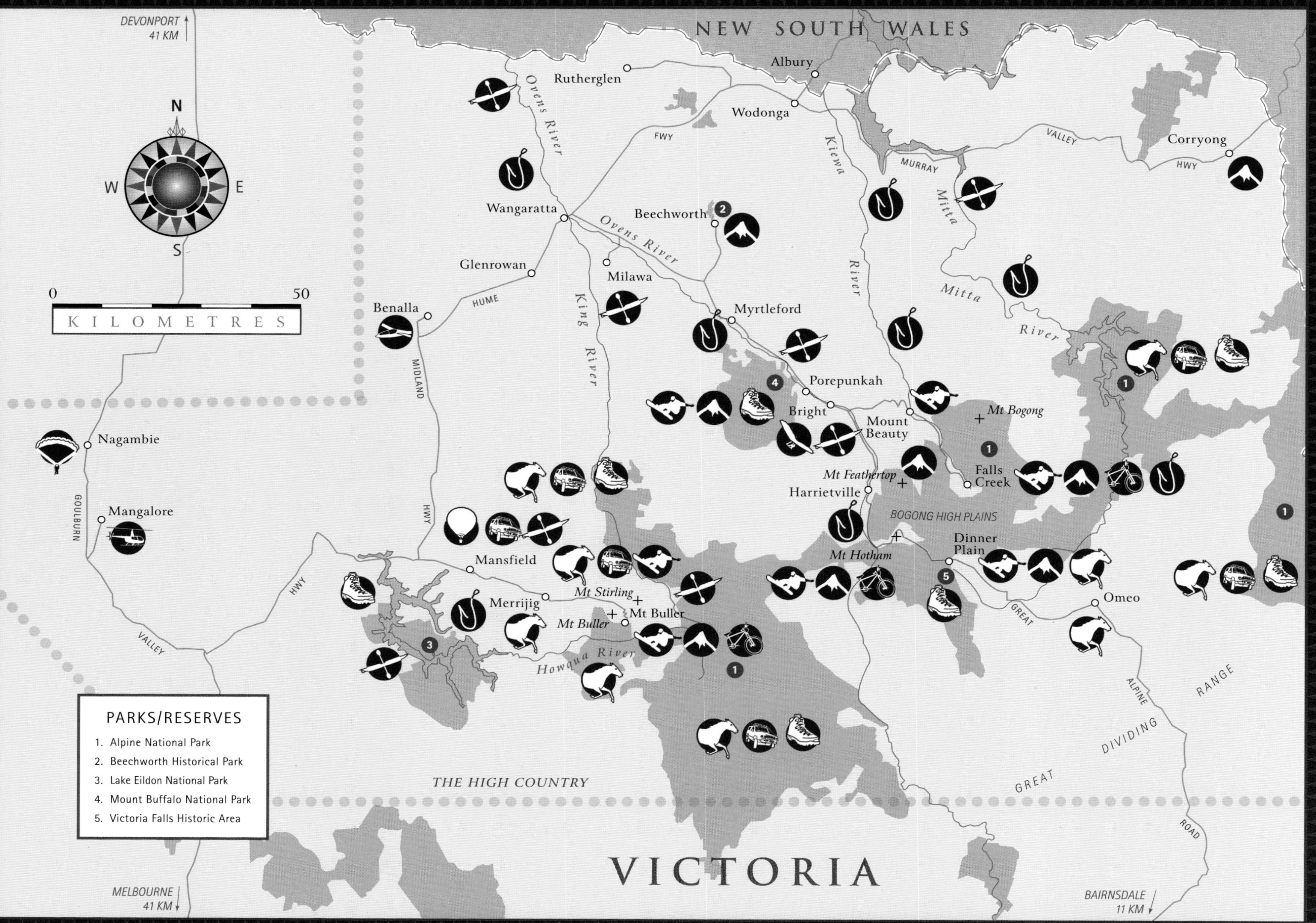

NEW SOUTH WALES
VICTORIA
THE HIGH COUNTRY
DEVONPORT 41 KM
MELBOURNE 41 KM
BAIRNSDALE 11 KM
N
S
E
W
0
50
KILOMETRES
Rutherglen
Albury
Wodonga
Corryong
Wangaratta
Beechworth
Glenrowan
Milawa
Myrtleford
Benalla
Porepunkah
Bright
Mount Beauty
Mt Bogong
Falls Creek
Mt Feathertop
Harrietville
BOGONG HIGH PLAINS
Mt Hotham
Dinner Plain
Omeo
Nagambie
Mangalore
Mansfield
Merrijig
Mt Stirling
Mt Buller
Mt Buller
Ovens River
Ovens River
King River
Kiewa River
Mitta Mitta River
Howqua River
FWY
HUME
MIDLAND
HWY
GOULBURN
VALLEY
HWY
MURRAY
VALLEY
HWY
GREAT
ALPINE
ROAD
GREAT
DIVIDING
RANGE
PARKS/RESERVES
1. Alpine National Park
2. Beechworth Historical Park
3. Lake Eildon National Park
4. Mount Buffalo National Park
5. Victoria Falls Historic Area

Mount Buffalo. (TV)

NATIONAL PARKS

Mount Buffalo National Park: features include fantastically shaped granite boulders and cliffs, waterfalls, alpine lakes and snow gum woodlands. In summer there is a huge range of walks as well as canoeing, swimming, horse riding, bike riding, abseiling, rock climbing and hang gliding. In winter it is a popular tobogganing, downhill and cross-country skiing area.

Alpine National Park: Victoria's largest national park. With adjoining national parks in NSW and the ACT, it forms a protected area that covers almost all of Australia's high country. Extensive snowfields are the main winter attraction; spring and summer bring stunning wildflower displays and opportunities for bushwalks, four-wheel driving and horse riding.

Beechworth Historic Park: one of the best preserved gold towns in Victoria, Beechworth has more than 30 buildings classified by the National Trust. Outside the town, a number of significant goldmining sites are incorporated in sections of the Historic Park, which also includes museums, a powder magazine, the ceremonial Chinese burning towers, and the courthouse where bushranger Ned Kelly stood trial.

Lake Eildon National Park: in the northern foothills of Victoria's Central Highlands, the park offers good access to the Lake Eildon for all types of water activities including boating, skiing, fishing and swimming.

Bright

Bright is famous for its autumn display, when the many stately trees that line the streets in town are ablaze with colour. There are some nice parks in town beside the Ovens River for a roadside rest or picnic.

Wangaratta

At the junction of the Ovens and King rivers, Wangaratta is one of the main centres for the surrounding rural area, and also where you'll find the grave of Dan 'Mad Dog' Morgan, one of Australia's most notorious and brutal bushrangers. His head was taken to Melbourne after he was shot dead in 1865 to be used in a study of the criminal mind.

Wangaratta is also the beginning of two unique touring routes. Cycle or walk a section of the Murray to the Mountains Rail Trail or drive the Great Alpine Road, which extends from Wangaratta across the Alps to Bairnsdale and the Gippsland Lakes.

Milawa and the King Valley

Milawa is home to three great gourmet institutions: Brown Bros Winery, Milawa Mustards and the Milawa Cheese Factory. All are open daily for tastings and sales and are great for stocking up on picnic supplies.

The nearby King Valley, was once one of the country's most important tobacco growing areas, but has been steadily replanted in the last few years with the more lucrative grape vines. Keep an eye out for the oddly-shaped tobacco curing sheds that still dot the countryside. Other crops you'll see (and taste at roadside stalls in season) around here are chestnuts, walnuts and blueberries.

Beechworth

In the 1860s Beechworth was the administrative centre of the rich Ovens Valley goldfields and the many grand buildings in town attest to the town's prosperity. The main street is lined with impressive buildings of which 32 are classified by the National Trust. It's also Ned Kelly Country. In his younger days Ned spent time at Beechworth Gaol and after his capture at Glenrowan he was sent to Beechworth before being tried in Melbourne. You can visit his cell in the basement underneath the shire offices.

Downtown Beechworth. (TV)

scenic highlights

High country 4WD tracks. *(TV)*

The Great Alpine Road is one of Australia's great mountain drives. It begins in pastoral northern Victoria, takes you high into the ski fields of the Australian Alps and finally brings you out a stone's throw from the coast in east Gippsland.

Take the Ovens Highway out of Wangaratta towards Myrtleford and Mount Buffalo through hop fields and vineyards. If you are planning to drive further during winter, Myrtleford, or the smaller village of Porepunkah, are the places to get your wheel chains—it is compulsory to carry chains during the snow season—Queen's Birthday weekend in early June to the first weekend in October.

Take the turn-off to Mount Buffalo National Park at Porepunkah. The park is a massive granite mountain, and here you'll see fantastically-shaped granite boulders and cliffs, waterfalls, alpine lakes and snow gum woodlands.

From Bright, The Great Alpine Road snakes its way through the valley via little villages such as Smoko, once set amongst fields of tobacco. Mount Feathertop dominates the scenery and soon after Harrietville the road begins to climb. This is a terrific piece of road—sharp bends through forests of mountain ash and stringy bark before traversing the ridgeline for 30km, giving superb views on both sides of the road.

The road passes through the ski villages of Mount Hotham and Dinner Plain before it begins to descend, winding its way through extensive forests, following various rivers and streams, almost all the way to Bairnsdale on the Gippsland coast.

An alternative route in summer is to travel from Bright to Omeo via Mount Beauty and Falls Creek across the Bogong High Plains. About 37km of this road is unsealed between Falls Creek and the junction with the Omeo Highway, and it closes in winter, but the views of Mt Bogong, Victoria's highest mountain, and the Kiewa Valley, as well as the wind-swept high plains, are worth it.

Rutherglen

The fertile land and mild climate around Rutherglen has been producing great wines since the early 1800s, making this one of the oldest wine-growing areas in Australia. It's most well known for its unique rich, fortified tokays and muscats. Once a major gold mining town, the historic buildings now house boutiques, antiques shops, tea rooms and restaurants.

Glenrowan

One of the most famous towns in Australia, Glenrowan was site of the famous siege where bushranger, Ned Kelly, and his gang took 60 hostages in the Glenrowan Inn on Saturday, 27 June 1880 before being wounded and captured in a bloody gun fight with police. There are a variety of Ned Kelly attractions in town, including a giant 6m-high effigy of Ned in the main street, a memorial museum and Kellyland, an animated theatrical portrayal of the Kelly Gang's final stand that uses original props including an authentic handgun once owned by Kelly.

Albury Wodonga

Straddling the border between NSW and Victoria, the twin towns of Albury and Wodonga form the largest regional centre in north-western Victoria. The Murray River, once a busy trade route for paddle steamers, flows between the twin cities, which both boast a number of heritage buildings and some lovely parks and well-established gardens.

Bushwalking in Mount Buffalo National Park. *(TV)*

Omeo

Omeo, in the heart of rolling cattle-grazing land, is a small town that dates back to the gold rush days of 1851. There are some historic buildings in town, including the courthouse where author Rolf Boldrewood (*Robbery Under Arms*) whose real name was TA Browne was once magistrate. Just out of town is the Oriental Claims Historic Area, one of the largest gold-sluicing operations in the world. It is unique for the alluvial workings that were mined for more than 50 years. Alluvial gold is usually worked out first and quartz mines provide payable gold for longer periods. There is a 45-minute work called Ah Fongs Loop, one of the richest sites in the area.

Caravan and camping

The Buckland River Valley (signposted at Porepunkah) is a good place to camp–but take your own wood. About 40km from Dinner Plain the Victoria Falls Historic Area is a nice bush camping area beside the Victoria River. Anglers Rest near Omeo is a beautiful setting beside the Mitta Mitta River and can be reached from the Omeo Highway between Omeo and Glenvalley. Lake Catani at Mount Buffalo is set amongst the snow gums, and is open from the beginning of November until the end of April. A popular camping spot on the King River with pebble beaches and clear fresh water is located at the 'Edi Cutting' on the Whitfield Road. At Lake Eildon you can camp at Jerusalem Creek, Big River and the Fraser camping area.

Bushwalks

There are literally hundreds of good walking trails that criss-cross the national parks in the high country. The Horn Trail is a 30-minute steep climb to a magnificent lookout at the highest point on Mt Buffalo. An easier walk is the one-hour Gorge Heritage Walk around the top of the Buffalo Gorge, with towering granite cliffs, tumbling waterfalls and views over the surrounding countryside.

The 6km Wallaces Hut to Cope Hut Trail is an easy loop that visits two of Victoria's best-known cattlemen's huts on your way to one of the highest peaks on the Bogong High Plains. The Mt Bogong via Staircase Spur Trail is a steep four-hour walk to the summit of Mt Bogong–Victoria's tallest mountain–and the Mt Feathertop via Razorback Trail is another demanding four-hour walk from Mt Hotham to the summit of Mt Feathertop–the state's second highest mountain–following the sharp, craggy spine of the ridge above the treeline.

Longer walks include the Howqua River Bluff Trail, a strenuous but rewarding two-day trek to the rocky escarpments of the Bluff, featuring breathtaking mountain views, alpine meadows and historic cattlemen's huts and the 650km-long Australian Alps Walking Track, which starts in the old goldmining town of Walhalla in Gippsland and finishes at Namadji near Canberra, traversing the ridges and high plains.

adventure activities

Abseiling and rock climbing

The sheer granite face of The Gorge and North Wall at Mount Buffalo are popular places for rock climbing and abseiling. Mt Hotham has some small boulder areas in the resort area and also a reasonable climbing site at Mount Smyth. There is an abseiling area at Dinner Plain, ice climbing at Australia Drift (below Hotham) and mountaineering on Mount Feathertop. Falls Creek has good beginner abseiling and some limited top rope climbing at Strawberry Saddle. There is also an abseil site below the Howmans Gap Alpine Centre. Mount Buller has small outdoor climbing areas, an indoor climbing wall and an outdoor abseiling tower. La Trobe University provides tuition on the indoor climbing wall and the outdoor tower and will take you to rock faces at the summit and behind Chamois Tun. The university also offers ice-climbing tuition in winter.

☎ (03) 5733 7000

At Corryong there is a good abseiling site on Mount Mittamatite and Beechworth has two great climbing areas at Mount Pilot and Mount Stanley. Abseiling locations are available at Mount Pilot and also at the Beechworth Gorge. There is also an abseiling site near Eldorado.

Adventure Guides Australia run abseiling adventures on some of the largest cliffs in Victoria at Mt Buffalo with beginner abseils off

Mount Buffalo. *(TV)*

DON'T MISS

- **Airworld:** aviation museum at Wangaratta airport. Largest collection of vintage aircraft and aviation memorabilia in Australia. Open daily 9am–5pm. ☎ (03) 5721 8788.
- **Exhibitions Gallery:** changing exhibitions of social history, fine arts, architecture, photography, sport and design. Ovens Street, Wangaratta. Open Sun–Tue, noon–5pm, Wed–Sat 10am–5pm. ☎ (03) 5722 0865.
- **Milawa Mustards:** mustard tastings and sales. Old Emu Inn, Milawa crossroads. Open daily 10am–5pm, except Wednesdays.
- **Burke Museum:** regular changing exhibitions plus Aboriginal artefacts, exhibits on the goldfields, the Beechworth Chinese community, a natural history collection, and a re-created street of 19th century shops. Next to Town Hall Gardens, open daily 10.30am–3.30pm, 10am–4.30pm during school holidays.
- **Beechworth Historic Courthouse:** original goldfields court and the place where many bushrangers, including Ned Kelly, were tried. Open daily, 10am–4pm.
- **Historic Murray Breweries and Museum:** 1865 beer and stout brewery. 29 Last Street, Beechworth. Open daily, 10am–4pm.
- **Carriage Museum:** National Trust collection of 19th and early 20th century horse drawn vehicles. In the old railway goods shed, Railway Ave, Beechworth. Open daily, 10am–noon, 1pm–4pm (1–4pm only Feb and Aug).
- **Mt Pilot:** Yeddonba Aboriginal art site. Boardwalk and platform to view rock artwork. 12km from Beechworth via the Chiltern Road.
- **Bright & District Museum:** local history and memorabilia. Old Railway Station, Bright. Open Tue, Thu, Sun 2–4pm.
- **Bright Art Gallery and Cultural Centre:** permanent collection of paintings, porcelain and designer glass. 28 Mountbatten Avenue. Open during school holidays on Wed and weekends, 2–4pm.
- **Oriental Claims Area historic site:** self-guided walking trails through historic gold fields. 3km south of Omeo on Great Alpine Road.
- **Kelly Land:** semi-live theatre production recreating Kelly's Last Stand. Gladstone Street, Glenrowan. Open daily. ☎ (03) 5766 2367. **www.nedkellysworld.com.au/glenrowan**
- **Costume and Pioneer Museum:** collection of exhibits from the region's past including well preserved costumes that date back as far as 1770. 14 Mair Street, Benalla. Open daily, 9am–5pm. **www.benallamuseum.org**
- **Benalla Regional Art Gallery:** includes Sir Sidney Nolan's magnificent Glenrowan tapestry, which depicts the capture of Ned Kelly. Bridge Street, Benalla. Open daily, 10am–5pm.
- **Albury Regional Art Gallery:** collection of local, regional and national art, including collection of contemporary Australian photography and works by Sir Russell Drysdale. 546 Dean Street, Albury. Open Mon–Fri 10.30am–5pm, Weekends 10.30am–4pm.
- **Corryong Man from Snowy River Folk Museum:** celebrates the pioneering efforts of the people who worked and lived in the High Country. Hanson Street, Corryong. Open 10am–12noon and 2–4pm daily, all year except during winter. ☎ (02) 6076 1363.

Victoria's north-east. *(TV)*

cliffs ranging from 10m through to cliffs of 250m. For those keen to try an abseil free fall there is the exhilarating 45m abseil adventure off the 'Dragon' site with exposure into the Mt Buffalo Gorge. For the ultimate adventure experience book a 300m full-day North Wall of Mt Buffalo Gorge Abseil Expedition. The first pitch alone is 160m.

www.adventureguidesaustralia.com.au

Ballooning

See the high country from the air on a one-hour dawn flight over Mansfield and Lake Eildon with Global Ballooning. After the flight, enjoy a breakfast with sparkling wine at Highton Manor just outside of Mansfield.

www.globalballooning.com.au ☎ 1800 627 661

Canoeing, kayaking and rafting

The Mitta Mitta River flows through one of Australia's most spectacular granite ravines, providing numerous grade 3 and 4 rapids as it squeezes past 18km of rock formations.

The King is another excellent whitewater-rafting river, with more than 40 rapids from grade 2 to grade 4. Adrenalin White Water Rafting is a local, family-owned company, based in the King Valley who offer one and two-day rafting trips on both rivers as well as 'raft, dine and wine' packages.

www.whitewaterrafting.com.au ☎ 1800 800 445

The beautiful Howqua and Delatite rivers outside Mansfield are popular with canoeists, kayakers and rafters in summer. Both rivers are rated from easy to challenging according to water levels. High water means high rapids and these should only be tackled by experienced paddlers.

Rio's Alpine Centre in Porepunkah near Bright run ripple rafting trips to Bright Canyon over lots of gravel races and a few small rapids. They also hire canoes and kayaks and run guided paddling tours down the Ovens River.

http://rios.netc.net.au ☎ (03) 5756 2208

Cycling and mountain biking

Like many winter skiing areas, during the summer the ski runs make for some great mountain biking. There are bike tracks around the Horse Hill Chairlift on Mount Buller of varying difficulty, from easy terrain to the 'Abominable Downhill' track that crosses Chalet Creek and is one of the most difficult in the country. During peak holiday times in summer and over Easter, chairlifts are available to lift mountain bikers at Falls Creek and Mount Hotham. Another area with an excellent reputation for mountain biking is Mount Beauty and the Bogong High Plains.

The Murray to Mountains Rail Trail is a 94km trail that follows the course of a decommissioned regional rail line from Wangaratta, through Beechworth, Myrtleford, Porepunkah and Bright. It's the longest trail of its type in Australia, and to do it all takes around three days. The trail winds its way through fertile farmland,

vineyards, small villages and historic country towns–past cellar doors, farm gate stalls (great for provisions), old tobacco kilns and traces of the gold rush. Even though it's in the Alpine High Country, those old trains weren't very good at hauling heavy loads up steep hills, so most of the climbs and descents are gradual.

The High Country Rail Trail will eventually extend to 112km from Bandiana to Cudgewa but currently runs for around 30km around Albury Wodonga's Lake Hume.

www.highcountryrailtrail.org.au

Fishing

The high country is a great fly fishing destination for brown and rainbow trout, with popular spots including the Ovens River between Myrtleford and Harrietville and the Kiewa River. Rocky Valley Reservoir and the smaller Pretty Valley Reservoir, both near Falls Creek, are two of Australia's best trout fishing lakes. Also worth fishing are the lower Mitta Mitta River, Lake Dartmouth, Upper Murray River, Swampy Plains River, Nariel Creek, Geehi River and Tooma River, where you'll find some of the largest river-dwelling trout in mainland Australia. Lake Eildon offers good fishing for both trout species, golden perch and Murray cod.

Off-road driving

There are a number of good 4WD tracks in the Alpine National Park. One of the most popular is the track to Craig's Hut on Mount Stirling, built specifically for the movie film *The Man from Snowy River*, although the materials were salvaged from old, ruined mountain huts in the area. Even though it is not an authentic mountain hut–any of the locals will tell you that a real mountain man would not build a home on such an exposed peak–it hasn't stopped the legend and it is now one of the biggest tourist attractions in the area.

The Craig's Hut tour begins 20km from Mansfield at Sawmill Settlement. The entire 139km trip, which is a circuit, takes around three to five hours, but allow more time for stops along the way.

Other 4WD tracks include: Mount Stirling, which also visits Craig's Hut, Bindaree Falls, Mount Timbertop and the Howqua River; two-day trip to The Bluff which includes several bushwalks and fishing side-trips; and the two-day Mitchell's Flat tour which takes in a pioneer homestead, disused slate mine, rivers and old growth forest. Tracks are closed during winter and are dry weather roads only.

Horse riding

If you've ever harboured secret thoughts of emulating *The Man from Snowy River*, galloping across the high country plains, then the Victorian High Country is the place to do it. Dinner Plain Trail Rides, which has a summer stables in the ski-resort village, offers a range of guided horse treks–for an hour or two, a full day, or up to five days.

www.dinnerplaintrailrides.com

Bogong Horseback Adventures offer packhorse adventures of up to seven days into the Alpine National Park and Mount Bogong as well as two and three-hour and full-day trail rides.

www.bogonghorse.com.au

High Country Horses run shorter rides through the foothills of Merrijig and the Dead Wood Forest (as featured in *The Man from Snowy River*) and extended camp-out rides up the headwaters of the Delatite River over the Summit of Mt Stirling, to Craig's Hut or into the Howqua Valley, Mt Howitt, Wonangatta Valley and beyond.

www.highcountryhorses.com.au

Charlie Lovick was Master of Horse for the two *Man from Snowy River* movies and he has taught and advised on many feature films and documentaries. Lovick's High Country Adventure run a range of trips varying from two to nine days, from weekends in the Howqua Valley to the more challenging four, five, six and nine-day rides through wilderness and high peaks.

www.lovicks.com.au

Packers High Country Horse Riding, based at Anglers Rest north of Omeo, offers horse riding treks from one hour to fully catered five-day safaris following along routes that were once used by Aborigines, early explorers, goldminers and cattlemen. Riders are accommodated in a mud brick house with huge decks overlooking superb views.

www.horsetreks.com

For details of other horse riding operators contact the local visitor information centre.

Jet fighter and aerobatic flights

Live out your Top Gun fighter pilot fantasies on a 20-minute jet combat air patrol flight or a 35-minute jet low-level strike mission and air combat manoeuvres flight that includes a dog fight and simulated weapons release. Jet Fighter Flights leave Mangalore airport, one and half hours north of Melbourne.

www.jetfighterflights.com

Microlighting, hang-gliding and paragliding

Soar like an eagle in a tandem microlight with the Eagle School of Microlighting and Hang Gliding. Based at Porepunkah at the base of Mt Buffalo near Bright, the flying school offers tandem instructional flights for beginners in a microlight–a hang glider with a small engine

Microlight at Bright. *(TV)*

Mount Buller. *(TV)*

and propeller attached to the back. It only takes a short run off and, before you know it, you are climbing into the air and soon circling over the township of Bright and the mountains and forests surrounding the town. Twin flights are available so you and a friend can fly together-wingtip to wingtip.

www.eagleschool.com.au

Alpine Paragliding offer tandem flights from Mystic Hill, 500m above Bright. Choose between a 500m-high glide from Mystic with a flight time of 10 minutes or take an extended 20-30-minute thermalling flight above Mystic. No experience is necessary and tandem flights are open to all ages and the disabled. They also have a two-day introductory course that will have you flying solo on 500m-high flights from Mystic.

www.alpineparagliding.com

For fixed wing flying, the Gliding Club of Victoria, the largest gliding club in the Southern Hemisphere, offers joy flights to visitors from its base at Benalla airport. The area is ideal for thermal soaring, with open plains to the north and west. On passenger glider flights a powered 'tug' aircraft will tow the glider to release height for a 'silent flight' back to base, where you can, if you wish, get some hands-on flying experience as your instructor shows you the basics.

www.gliding-benalla.org

Skiing

Falls Creek is the largest ski and boarding resort, with the good cross-country skiing terrain on the Bogong High Plains and is also home to some of Australia's steepest and deepest slopes at Mt McKay. Special tours include a skidoo transfer to the slopes for a 40-minute night Kassbohrer ride and snow bikes available for riding every Wednesday and Saturday nights during winter.

www.fallscreek.com.au

Mt Buller has the most chairlifts of all the Victorian resorts with the capacity to lift 40,000 skiers per hour and has 80km or resort trails suitable for skiers and snow boarders as well as snow tubing, tobogganing and cross-country trails.

www.mtbuller.com.au

Mount Hotham is known as the 'powder capital' and holds the record for the highest annual snowfall of any Victorian resort over the past decade. Hotham offers 320 hectares of ski area, including 35km of tree-lined cross-country trails and a network of 13 lifts-the longest run is 2.5km long.

www.mthotham.com.au

Dinner Plain, Mount Buffalo, or Mount Stirling all feature good cross-country trails across snow-clad landscapes. Mount Buffalo hosts a small selection of downhill runs and as well as well groomed cross-country trails, and Mount Stirling provides excellent cross-country skiing with many well marked trails taking you through beautiful forests of alpine ash and snow gum.

Skydiving

Skydive Nagambie offer the longest free-fall time in Victoria and are also the only drop zone in Victoria certified to jump through cloud-which looks amazingly solid when you are hurtling towards it in freefall-and at that height, the chances of jumping through cloud are high. Every jump is from 14,000 feet, out of Victoria's largest jump plane, which takes up to 17 people at a time so you can jump with your friends. Both tandem jumps and skydiving lessons are available.

www.skydivenagambie.com

Paragliding near Bright. (TV)

MORE INFORMATION

- **Wangaratta Visitor Information Centre:** cnr Tone Road and Handley Street, Wangaratta. ☎ 1800 801 065. www.visitwangaratta.com.au or www.milawagourmet.com
- **Bright Visitors Centre:** 119 Gavan Street, Bright. ☎ 1800 500 117.
- **Beechworth Visitor Information Centre:** Town Hall, Ford Street, Beechworth. ☎ 1300 366 321. www.beechworthonline.com.au or www.greatalpineroad.info

weather watch

- January: 15–31°C
- July: -2–14°C
- The Great Alpine Road is fully sealed and is open all year. However, expect snow and ice in winter.

the grampians & western victoria

MacKenzie Falls. *(TV)*

▶ RISING FROM THE WESTERN Victorian plains like a hulking primeval giant, the wild and rugged Grampian Range is one of the most popular places in Victoria for a weekend escape from the city. Most of the densely-forested mountains are national park and are criss-crossed with walking trails, lookouts, clear streams cascading down some of the state's largest waterfalls and provide good places for rock climbing, abseiling and other adventure activities.

To the north, is the semi-arid wilderness of the Mallee country and, on the Murray River, are the vast vineyards of the Mildura and Swan Hill region that produce almost a third of all Australian table wines.

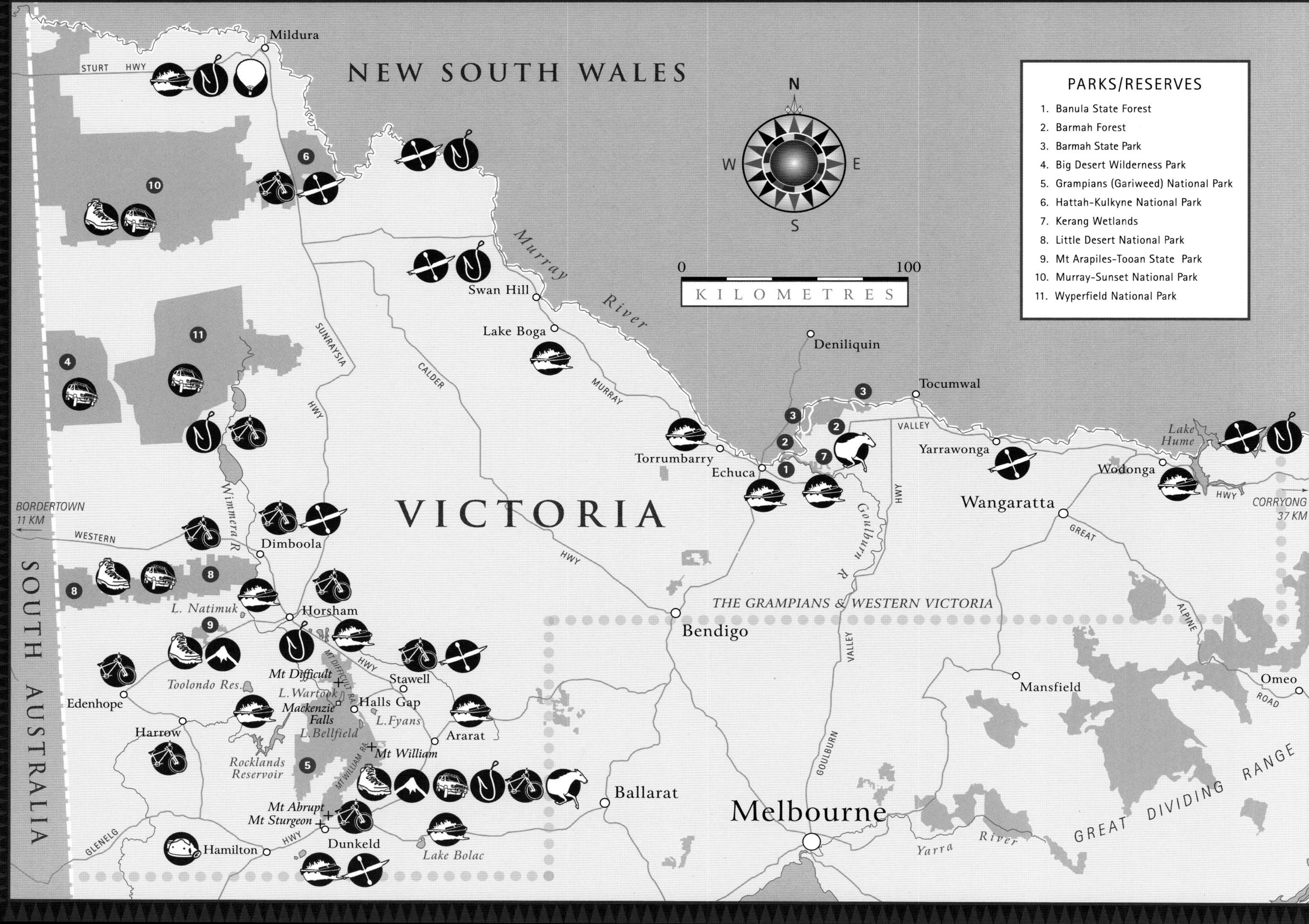

PARKS/RESERVES
1. Banula State Forest
2. Barmah Forest
3. Barmah State Park
4. Big Desert Wilderness Park
5. Grampians (Gariweed) National Park
6. Hattah-Kulkyne National Park
7. Kerang Wetlands
8. Little Desert National Park
9. Mt Arapiles-Tooan State Park
10. Murray-Sunset National Park
11. Wyperfield National Park
N
W
E
S
0
100
KILOMETRES
NEW SOUTH WALES
VICTORIA
SOUTH AUSTRALIA
Mildura
STURT HWY
Murray River
Swan Hill
Lake Boga
Deniliquin
Tocumwal
Torrumbarry
Echuca
Yarrawonga
VALLEY
Lake Hume
Wodonga
HWY
CORRYONG 37 KM
Wangaratta
GREAT
SUNRAYSIA HWY
CALDER
MURRAY
BORDERTOWN 11 KM
WESTERN
Wimmera R
Dimboola
HWY
Goulburn R
L. Natimuk
Horsham
THE GRAMPIANS & WESTERN VICTORIA
Bendigo
ALPINE
VALLEY
Mt Difficult
MT DIFFICULT RA
Stawell
Mansfield
Omeo
ROAD
Toolondo Res.
L. Wartook
Mackenzie Falls
Halls Gap
L.Fyans
Edenhope
Harrow
L. Bellfield
Ararat
Rocklands Reservoir
MT WILLIAM RA
Mt William
GOULBURN
Ballarat
GREAT DIVIDING RANGE
Mt Abrupt
Mt Sturgeon
Melbourne
GLENELG
Hamilton
HWY
Dunkeld
Lake Bolac
Yarra River

NATIONAL PARKS

Gariweed National Park (Grampians Ranges): the 167,000-hectare park is made up of four spectacular sandstone ridges running north to south with steep and craggy slopes on the eastern side and gentler slopes to the west. Famous for its bushwalking (it has more than 160km of tracks), rock climbing, plant life (including 970 native species and brilliant spring wildflowers) and wildlife (more than 200 species of birds have been recorded) it is a landscape of peaks and valleys, with panoramic lookouts and a number of pretty waterfalls.

A highlight in the park is the collection of Aboriginal art sites—approximately 60 rock art sites, containing more than 4000 different motifs have been identified in the park to date. Shelters in the park where you can see ancient art work include Bunjil's Shelter, one of the most important Aboriginal rock art sites in the region depicting Bunjil, the traditional creator of the land, and his two dingoes; the Gulgurn Manja Shelter which displays small handprints in red ochre; Ngamadjidj Shelter depicting the dancing spirit with white painted figures and Bilimina Shelter, a massive rock overhang covered with more than 2500 motifs.

The park is accessible from Halls Gap—turn left off the Western Highway at Stawell. The southern area of the Grampians National Park is accessible from Dunkeld, north-east of Hamilton.

Mt Arapiles-Tooan State Park: Mt Arapiles, a spectacular formation that rises sharply from the Wimmera Plains, is considered to be the best rock climbing area in Australia. The park includes Mitre Rock, adjacent to Mt Arapiles and the Tooan Block.

Wild flowers, Mount Arapiles. (TV?)

Little Desert National Park: a desert in name only, this semi-arid park abutting the South Australian border supports an amazing array of arid vegetation and animals that can survive with little water. Visit between late winter and early summer when the temperatures are comfortable and the park is full of blossoms and wildflowers. Keep an eye out for the shy mallee fowl.

Big Desert National Park: Victoria's first declared wilderness area, its inhospitable terrain has been left largely untouched by Europeans. More than 50 species of lizards and snakes and 93 species of birds have been recorded in the park including the extremely rare western whipbird.

Wyperfield National Park: a chain of lake beds connected by Outlet Creek, the northern extension of the Wimmera River is the central feature of this huge park in the flat, semi-arid north-western corner of Victoria. The lakes only fill when Lake Hindmarsh overflows with water fed from the Wimmera River. When it rains the semi-arid landscape is transformed by tiny desert plants that form a carpet of flowers.

Murray-Sunset National Park: named for its spectacular sunsets and one of the few remaining semi-arid regions in the world where the environment is relatively untouched, this is the state's second largest national park. A highlight are the Pink Lakes, which turn pink during late summer when a red pigment, carotene, is secreted from the alga. They are best seen early or late in the day or when it is cloudy. The lakes evaporate over summer leaving concentrated salt crusts over black mud.

Barmah State Park: on the floodplain of the Murray River between Tocumwal, Deniliquin and Echuca, the Barmah Millewa Forest is the largest red gum forest in the world and has more than 180 Aboriginal sacred sites. The area is frequently flooded and the resulting wetlands are home to almost 900 species of wildlife.

Halls Gap and Dunkeld

The main town in the Grampians is Halls Gap, which is situated in a tight valley between the southern tip of the Mt Difficult Range and the northern tip of the Mt William Range, just beyond the border of the Grampians National Park (Gariweed).

The pretty village of Dunkeld at the southern entrance of the Grampians stands in the shade of Mt Sturgeon and Mt Abrupt, the highest mountain in the southern Grampians. Stop for lunch in the Royal Mail Hotel, with beautiful views over Mount Sturgeon.

The southern Grampians sits atop one of the largest volcanic plains in the world. Although dormant, there are plenty of traces of past eruptions. The Volcanoes Discovery Trail (maps available from any of the local visitors centres) explores the volcanic past of the area. Highlights include trekking up to the crater of Mt Napier, going underground in the lava tubes near Byaduk and climbing tumuli, or lava blisters, in the nearby paddocks.

Stawell

A short drive to the east of Halls Gap, the bustling regional centre of Stawell is the home of the famous 120m dash, the annual Stawell Gift. The foot race has been run each Easter since 1898 and is one of the richest professional foot races in the world. Gold was discovered here in 1853 and is still mined in Victoria's largest operating mine.

Hamilton

To the south, Hamilton, one of the first areas of pastoral settlement in Victoria, claims to be the wool capital of the world–roughly six million sheep graze within an 80km radius of the town. For the full story on the local industry, visit the Big Wool Bales in Coleraine Road.

Mallee country and the Murray

The north-western corner of the state is known as Mallee country, a semi-arid region watered by the Murray River through vast irrigation systems first established in 1900. The river, which forms the border between NSW and Victoria, was once an important transport corridor and the gracious towns along the banks on both side of the border have a rich riverboat heritage. Mildura is a green oasis of orchards and vineyards with a strong Mediterranean flavour thanks to the wave of Italian immigrants who settled in the area early last century. To the east, Swan Hill is home to the Pioneer Settlement, a recreated port town of the paddle steamer era and Australia's oldest open air museum.

Caravan and camping

There are five main camping areas in Grampians National Park, all with toilets, fire places and picnic tables–the large camping ground at the base of Mount Stapylton in the northern Grampians which offers good walking opportunities; the Old mill site near the MacKenzie Falls; Borough Huts by Fyans Creek near the Wonderland Ranges in the Central; Jimmy Creek on the Wannon River in the south-east and Buandik, a forested area on Billimina Creek near a number of Aboriginal sites in the south-west of the park. All areas get busy at Easter, long weekends and during summer holidays. You can also bush camp in other areas of the park.

There's a good campsite at the base of Mount Arapiles that is popular with rock climbers. In the Little Desert National Park you can camp at Horseshoe and Ackle Bend along the banks of the Wimmera River near Dimboola and at Kiata Sanctuary east of Nhill. In Big Desert National Park there are campsites at Big Billy Bore, the Springs, Moonlight Tank and Broken Bucket Reserve along the Nhill-Murrayville Road.

Around Mildura there are several sandy beaches on the Murray River where you can camp including Merbein Common, Bruces Bend and Green Point, most of which have boat ramps. In Swan Hill there is bush camping along the banks of the Murray River in the Nyah State Forest, Vinifera State Forest and at The Loddons Floodway.

Bushwalks

There are more than 50 marked walking trails in the Grampians National Park, but if you only have time for a short one, choose the half-hour descent to MacKenzie Falls. 265 steps later you'll emerge at a beautiful waterhole at the foot of the falls. One of the most popular walks in the park is the five-hour Wonderland Walk, a loop from Halls Gap around the spectacular Pinnacle Lookout. Highlights include the high-walled Grand Canyon, the sandstone rock face named 'Elephant Hide' and the Venus Bath Rock Pools. Mt Abrupt Trail is a steep 90-minute climb to the top of Mt Abrupt (Mt Murdadjoog, 827m), one of the park's finest lookouts.

The Desert Discovery Walk is a four-day, 84km hike through the Little Desert National Park while the Pink Lakes Trail is a gentle 90-minute stroll around the lakes of the same name in Murray-Sunset National Park and in Swan Hill, the two-hour flat and easy River Walk trails along the river banks has plenty of interpretive signs detailing the history of the area, the paddle steamers and the Aboriginal heritage.

scenic highlights

Grampians National Park. *(TV)*

The road from Dunkeld to Horsham via Halls Gap, called the Grampians Tourist Road, cuts right through the heart of the Grampians National Park, alongside the Serra Range. It takes in most of the major highlights of the park, such as MacKenzie Falls, Boroka and Reed lookouts, several Aboriginal shelters and numerous good picnic sites.

MacKenzie Falls. *(TV)*

The Murray River. *(TV)*

DON'T MISS

- **The Volcanoes Discovery Trail:** self-guided touring route exploring the volcanic history of the Grampians area. Free map available from any of the local visitors centres.
- **Brambuk Aboriginal Living Cultural Centre:** adjacent to the Grampians National Park Visitor Centre. It offers an excellent introduction to the area's Aboriginal history and accessible rock art sites. Open daily 10am–5pm.
- **Hamilton Art Gallery:** see the famous collection of silver, glass, porcelain and oriental ceramics, many of which were gifts from country homesteads around Hamilton. The permanent collection of more than 7000 items is complemented with a program of temporary exhibitions. Open Mon–Fri, 10am–5pm; Sat, 10am–noon and 2–5pm; Sun 2–5pm.
- **Horsham Regional Art Gallery:** collection of Australian art and photography. 80 Wilson Street, Horsham. Open Tue–Fri 10am–5pm, weekends 1–4pm.
- **Sir Reginald Ansett Transport Museum:** commercial aviation pioneer Sir Reginald Ansett lived in Hamilton. His relocated company hangar is now a museum showcasing the earliest days of commercial flight. Open daily 10am–4pm.
- **Seppelt Great Western:** the birthplace of Australia's greatest sparkling wines, cellared in an intricate system of tunnels dug by gold miners in the 1860–70s. Moyston Road, Great Western. Open daily for tours and tastings. **www.seppelt.com.au**
- **Gum San Chinese Heritage Centre:** memorial to the Ararat's Chinese founders who found gold at present-day Ararat in 1857. The centre also explores the influence of Chinese culture on the economic, cultural and social development of Australia. 31 Lambert Street, Ararat. Open daily, 10am–4.30pm. **www.gumsan.com.au**
- **Swan Hill Pioneer Settlement:** a re-creation of a riverside port town of the paddle steamer era featuring more than 50 buildings. At dusk a 45-minute spectacular light show illuminates the village. 1 Horsebend Bend, Swan Hill. Open Tue–Sun 9.30am–4pm, daily during school holidays. **www.pioneersettlement.com.au**
- **Red Cliffs Historical Steam Railway:** restored Kerr Stuart No 742 steam train, built in 1901, runs along the Red Cliffs Historical Steam Railway. ☎ (03) 5029 1388.
- **Port of Echuca:** on the banks of the Murray River, the historic Port of Echuca is an authentic operating steam port. One-hour paddle steamer cruises depart from the wharf daily. Take a self-guided Port Tour, wander along the historic red gum wharf, discover the underground bar and escape tunnel at the Star Hotel, see shipwrights and apprentices at work and visit the magnificent Bridge Hotel. Open daily. **www.portofechuca.org.au**

adventure activities

Mount Arapiles. *(TV)*

Ballooning

The stable weather patterns around Mildura make it an ideal place to for hot air ballooning. Each July Mildura hosts the Hot Air Balloon Championships when the skies come alive with the colours of more than 100 hot air balloons from around the world. The 2004 World Hot Air Balloon Championships were held in Mildura. During the rest of the year you can take to the skies on dawn flight over the patchwork of farmlands, vineyards and citrus orchards–following the twists and turns of the Murray River. Pamper yourself with Miludua Ballooning's personalised service.

www.milduraballooning.com.au ☎ (03) 5024 6848

Abseiling and rock climbing

Mount Arapiles in Mt Arapiles-Tooan State Park is one of Australia's premier rock climbing sites with 2500 rock climbing routes marked out across 365m of sandstone cliffs. Climbs range from easy ascents for beginners to level 30 climbs, the most extreme ascents and some of the world's hardest. Arapiles Climbing Guides, based in Natimuk, reckon they know the mountain like the back of their hand–they have been showing people the ropes since 1992–and offer a range of climbing and abseiling programs for all levels, from beginners to advanced and run groups as well as private instruction and guiding.

http://users.netconnect.com.au/~climbacg ☎ (03) 5387 1284

Rock climbing is also one of the main activities in the Grampians National Park, with hundreds of exciting climbs, especially on the rugged cliff faces of Mount Stapylton, at the park's northern end and Mount Rosea, just south of Halls Gap. There are several adventure specialists based in Halls Gap, including Grampians Adventure Services who also run canoeing and kayaking and hire mountain bikes as well rock climbing and abseiling trips.

www.g-adventures.com.au

Canoeing and kayaking

One third of Victoria's lakes can be found in the Grampians area, which is also riddled with streams and creeks so there are lots of opportunities for canoeing and kayaking. Rent a kayak or canoe in Halls Gap and paddle Lake Bellfield, Lake Fyans and Lake Wartook, the channels of Greenhill Lake east of Ararat, or take a canoe down the Wimmera River. Canoes can be launched along the banks of the river near Dimboola and this section is a designated State Heritage river because of its exceptional natural scenery. Lake Hamilton, near the town of the same name, is another good spot for canoeing.

The Murray River is host to the longest canoe race in the world. The annual Murray Marathon in December is a gruelling 404km race taking in the length of the Murray between Yarrawonga and Swan Hill and attracts more than 6000 participants each year.

The Lower Murray River has some great flat water canoeing and there are plenty of places to stop at a shady riverside clearing beneath the red gums for a picnic. The Murray Gates section of the Upper Murray near Corryong has grade 5 rapids, especially after spring rains and snow melt swell water levels. Contact Rapid Descents White Water Rafting for details of one and two-day white water rafting trips.

www.rapiddescents.com.au ☎ 1800 637 486

Hot air ballooning in the Grampians. (TV)

Towards Mildura, the Hattah-Kulkyne National Park and Kings Billabong offer excellent canoeing and the opportunity to see bird life from the water. During spring, when the Barmah Forest (the largest red gum forest in the world) near Echuca is flooded, you can paddle your way around the trees to the sound of birdsong and croaking frogs.

Caving

Byaduk Caves or lava tubes, near Hamilton, are part of a lava flow from Mount Napier, stretching 24km to Mount Eccles. The caves were formed by molten lava flowing beneath the solidified surface. The caves contain wrinkles, stalactites and stalagmites, columns and ropy lava and are the most extensive and accessible set of lava caves in Victoria. Only one cave, Harmans 1, is open to the public, but you'll need to bring a torch as they are unlit. You can also explore the Mount Eccles Lava Tube to the south-west of Hamilton on a series of self-guided walks.

Bentwing bats spend winter in some of the caves. To avoid winter food shortages the bats slow their body systems down in what is known as 'torpor' so that their body temperature matches that of their surroundings. The caves are closed during this period as disturbance during the torpor period can kill them.

www.parkweb.vic.gov.au

Cycling and mountain biking

The Grampians are a great place for mountain biking, with hundreds of kilometres of downhill tracks. Bring your own bike or hire one in Halls Gap–the road from Halls Gap to Dunkeld through the Victorian Valley is a great ride with unsurpassed scenery.

Good rides include the Horsham to Mt Arapiles Rail Trail via Natimuk and return (48km round trip over flat terrain); the 70km roundtrip from Edenhope to Harrow through traditional farming country; the flat and easy 8km cycling route from Dimboola along the banks of the Wimmera River to Horseshoe Bend in the Little Desert National Park and return; Stawell to Halls Gap return via Pomonal, a beautiful 60km scenic ride; and from Cavendish along the Wannon River among River Red Gums to the Grampians Lookout near Dunkeld.

Grampians Adventure Services run guided rides down the mountain range, stopping at both Reeds and Lakeview Lookouts, or you can do your own self-guided downhill run–they will drop you off at one of the two lookouts and you can choose your own way back to town. They also do off-road mountain bike tours in the national park with lots of ups, downs, twist, turns, bumps and jumps and, depending on the weather, lots of mud and sand.

www.g-adventures.com.au

Closer to the Murray you can walk or cycle your way around a series of beautiful billabongs lined by majestic red gums and sand dunes on the 10km Bugle Ridge Track in Hattah-Kulkyne National Park.

Fishing

The Grampians, with all that fresh water about, is a freshwater fishing enthusiast's paradise with plentiful species of brown trout, rainbow trout, the Murray cod, silver perch, golden perch, freshwater catfish, river blackfish, redfin and carp. Popular fishing spots in the national park include Fyans Creek, Lake Bellfield, Lake Wartook and the MacKenzie River. Other good spots in the district include Rocklands Reservoir, the Wimmera River, Green Hill Lake, Natimuk Lake and Lake Hindmarsh.

During summer yabbies are prolific throughout the region and are good fun to catch–for both kids and parents.

The Murray River offers excellent fishing from both the shore or boats and huge Murray cod are frequently caught in the waters around Swan Hill and up to Mildura.

Off-road driving

The mountainous terrain of the north west is perfect for four-wheel driving, with 4WD roads and access tracks criss-crossing the Grampians and all other national and state parks of the region. A favourite track in the Grampians National Park is the Halls Gap to Zumstein via Victoria Valley track, an easy dry-weather only track and the seasonal Victoria Range Road.

Little Desert National Park has almost 600km of tracks across all three blocks of the park, giving access to even the most remote areas near the South Australian border. Most tracks are too sandy for two-wheel drive vehicles and some of the clay surfaces become very boggy after rain. Carry recovery gear.

The Murrayville Track from Nhill to Murrayville across the Big Desert National Park is a sandy 180km track through some of the most remote and inhospitable countryside in the state and the North-South Scenic Route in Wyperfeld National Park is another good off-road track. You'll also need a 4WD to really explore the best of Murray Sunset National Park.

Horse riding

Bridle paths in the Wartook Valley near the Grampians National Park thread through sweeping countryside with the ever-present backdrop of the Northern Grampians escarpment. The Grampians Horse Riding Centre is set on the Grelco Run Estate in the foothills of the park near Halls Gap with 11,000 acres of farmland and forest to explore and offer tours for all riding levels. More experienced riders are able to explore the forest on their own.

☎ (03) 5383 9255

On the Murray, Billabong Trail Rides offer trails rides through the Banyula State Forest near Echuca and along country trails near Kanyapella Basin, Warrigul Creek and the Goulburn and Murray Rivers. Pub rides and overnight rides are also available.

www.grampians.net.au/trides www.justhorses.com.au

Murray River Horse Trails offer trail rides along the banks of the Murray River and in the Barmah Forest.

☎ (03) 5868 2221

Windsurfing and waterskiing

The lakes and rivers around the Grampians provide some great places to swim, windsurf and waterski. Favourite spots include Rocklands Reservoir, east of Balmoral, Lake Hamilton, Taylors Lake and Pine Lake east of Horsham, Natimuk Lake, Greenhill Lake east of Ararat, Green Lake east of Horsham, Toolondo Reservoir south of Horsham, Lake Bolac east of Dunkeld and the Wimmera River.

The River Murray is one of the state's most popular waterskiing destinations. The Club Marine Southern 80, the largest waterskiing race in the world, is held in Echuca each February and attracts up to 40,000 spectators. The Mildura 100 Ski Race is held each Easter, the fastest contestants earning the 'King of the Murray' title.

The best skiing sites are the wider stretches of river at Mildura, Echuca and Torumbarry as well as Lake Boga near Swan Hill. Other favourite destinations for waterskiing and wakeboarding include the extensive lake system in the Kerang Wetlands just east of Echuca, in particular Lake Charm and Kangaroo Lake off the Murray Valley Highway and Gunbower Creek Ski Run off Island Road in Cohuna, as well as Lake Mulwala to the east of Echuca and Lake Hume near Albury Wodonga.

Experienced professionals in the area offer waterskiing lessons in the calm waters of the river. Contact the Mildura and Visitors Information Centre for details.

Cycling in the Southern Grampians. *(TV)*

MORE INFORMATION

- **Halls Gap Visitor Information Centre:** Grampians Road, Halls Gap ☎ 1800 065 599. **www.visitgrampians.com.au**
- **Mildura Visitor Information Centre:** 180–190 Deakin Avenue, Mildura. ☎ 1800 039 043. **www.visitmildura.com.au**
- **Swan Hill Region Information Centre:** Corner McCrae and Curlewis Streets, Swan Hill. ☎ 1800 625 373. **www.swanhillonline.com**

weather watch

- January: 13–29°C
- July: 4–12°C
- Summers are dry and warm, most rain falls during winter when temperatures can get very chilly. Expect higher summer temperatures in the north west.

Torres
Strait
Islands
N
W
E
S
0
500
KILOMETRES
GULF OF
CARPENTARIA
Cape York
Peninsula
Cooktown
Palmer River
Roadhouse
PACIFIC
OCEAN
Cairns
Mt Bartle Frere
Karumba
Burketown
FAR NORTH QUEENSLAND
OUTBACK & GULF COUNTRY
GREAT
Riversleigh
Townsville
Mount Isa
Hughenden
THE WHITSUNDAY COAST
DIVIDING
Mackay
QUEENSLAND
NORTHERN TERRITORY
Tropic of Capricorn
Rockhampton
Emerald
Blackall
THE FRASER & CAPRICORN COAST
RANGE
SIMPSON
DESERT
Birdsville
Hervey
Bay
Charleville
Roma
THE SUNSHINE
COAST
SOUTH
AUSTRALIA
BRISBANE &
SURROUNDS
Brisbane
Cunnamulla
THE GOLD COAST
NEW SOUTH WALES

queensland

Flanked by the Great Barrier Reef and a string of tropical islands is Australia's favourite holiday destination. The Gold Coast, south of the capital Brisbane, is a beach-front high-rise resort strip, more neon than natural. In the far north, Cairns is a busy travellers centre and a popular spot for diving adventures. In between a string of beaches, towns and islands offer almost any holiday adventure you can think of, including rainforest wilderness. West of the Great Dividing Range the vast outback has isolated communities and large cattle stations, including one of the county's most famous and isolated towns, Birdsville.

(Tourism Queensland)

brisbane & surrounds

Brisbane from Kangaroo Point. *(BM)*

► AUSTRALIA'S THIRD-LARGEST CITY Brisbane, is also, as you would expect from Australia's only sub-tropical capital city, a green city. Almost 25 per cent of its area is bushland-with 9500 hectares of bush and 1500 parks and public gardens. The Brisbane River winds though the city's office towers and the wide streets are lined with overhanging Moreton Bay fig trees, providing shady places to sit and watch the world go by.

Like its southern sister, Sydney, Brisbane began life as a penal settlement in 1824 and was not opened to free settlement until 1842. By 1859, when Brisbane became capital of the self-governing colony of Queensland, almost all traces of convict occupation had disappeared making way for grand public buildings like Old Government House and Customs House.

GYMPIE 17 KM
N
W
E
S
Pomona
PACIFIC OCEAN
QUEENSLAND
0 50
KILOMETRES
Maroochydore
BRUCE
Kilcoy
Woodford
Lake Somerset
Brisbane R
PARKS/RESERVES
1. Blue Lake National Park
2. Boondall Wetlands Reserve
3. Bribie Island National Park
4. Brisbane Forest Park
5. D'Aguilar National Park
6. Daisy Hill State Forest Park
7. Moogerah Peaks National Park
8. Moreton Bay Marine Park
9. Moreton Island National Park
10. Mount Coot-tha Reserve
11. Mt Mee Forest Reserve
12. St Helena Island National Park
Bribie Island
HWY
Mount Mee
Somerset Dam
Caboolture
Pumicestone Channel
Tangalooma
Moreton Island
Esk
Lake Wivenhoe
Mount Glorious
Mount Sampson
Mount Nebo
Wivenhoe Dam
Moreton Bay
Brisbane
Toowong
Brisbane R
North Stradbroke Island
Toowoomba
Gatton
LOGAN
Cleveland
LOCKYER VALLEY
Ipswich
HWY
Russell Island
HWY
FASSIFERN VALLEY
PACIFIC
Pimpama
Fassifern
Boonah
CUNNINGHAM
BRISBANE & SURROUNDS
Nerang
HWY
Warwick
Coolangatta
TENTERFIELD 71 KM
NEW SOUTH WALES
BALLINA 51 KM

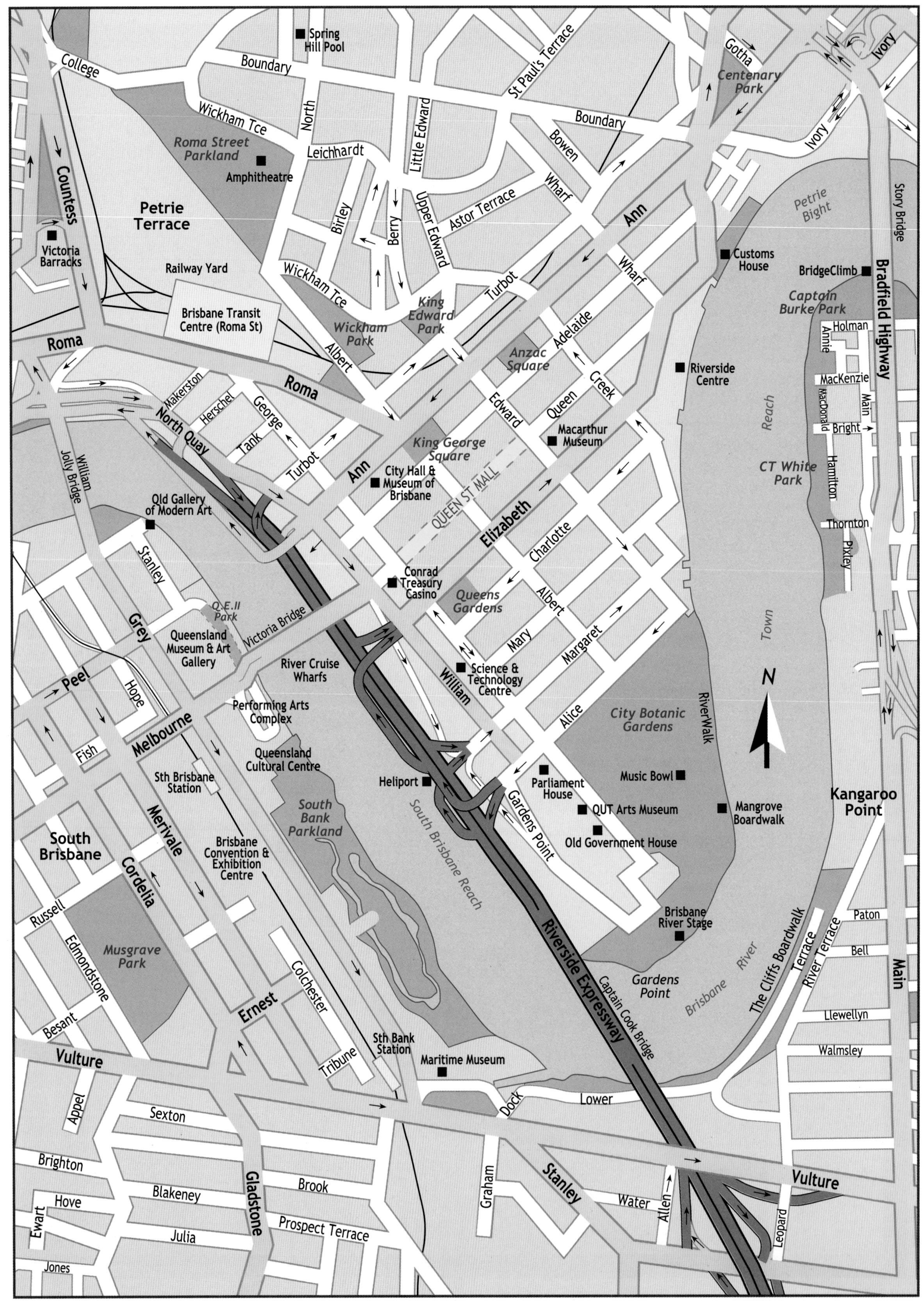

Spring Hill Pool
College
Boundary
Wickham Tce
North
Little Edward
St Paul's Terrace
Boundary
Gotha
Centenary Park
Ivory
Ivory
Roma Street Parkland
Amphitheatre
Leichhardt
Bowen
Wharf
Astor Terrace
Upper Edward
Berry
Birley
Countess
Petrie Terrace
Victoria Barracks
Railway Yard
Wickham Tce
Ann
Wharf
Turbot
King Edward Park
Wickham Park
Brisbane Transit Centre (Roma St)
Albert
Roma
Roma
Adelaide
Anzac Square
Creek
Queen
Edward
Customs House
Petrie Bight
Story Bridge
BridgeClimb
Bradfield Highway
Captain Burke Park
Holman
Annie
MacKenzie
MacDonald
Main
Bright
Riverside Centre
Reach
Makerston
Herschel
George
Tank
North Quay
Turbot
Ann
King George Square
City Hall & Museum of Brisbane
Macarthur Museum
QUEEN ST MALL
William Jolly Bridge
Old Gallery of Modern Art
Elizabeth
Charlotte
CT White Park
Hamilton
Thornton
Pixley
Stanley
Conrad Treasury Casino
Queens Gardens
Albert
Q.E.II Park
Grey
Queensland Museum & Art Gallery
Victoria Bridge
Mary
Margaret
Town
River Cruise Wharfs
Science & Technology Centre
William
Peel
Hope
Performing Arts Complex
Alice
City Botanic Gardens
RiverWalk
N
Fish
Melbourne
Queensland Cultural Centre
Sth Brisbane Station
Heliport
Parliament House
Music Bowl
South Bank Parkland
South Brisbane Reach
Gardens Point
QUT Arts Museum
Mangrove Boardwalk
Kangaroo Point
Merivale
South Brisbane
Cordelia
Brisbane Convention & Exhibition Centre
Old Government House
Brisbane River Stage
Russell
Edmondstone
Musgrave Park
Colchester
Riverside Expressway
Captain Cook Bridge
Gardens Point
Brisbane River
The Cliffs Boardwalk
Terrace
River Terrace
Paton
Bell
Main
Llewellyn
Walmsley
Besant
Ernest
Tribune
Sth Bank Station
Maritime Museum
Vulture
Appel
Sexton
Dock
Lower
Brighton
Graham
Stanley
Vulture
Brook
Hove
Blakeney
Gladstone
Water
Allen
Leopard
Ewart
Julia
Prospect Terrace
Jones

The city centre

Brisbane's CBD is huddled on a fat peninsula of land framed by the meandering loops of the Brisbane River. Queens Street Mall is the heart of the shopping district while the city foreshore is home to waterfront restaurants and cafes. City Botanic Gardens claim absolute river frontage at the tip of the peninsula while, at the northern end of the CBD, the Roma Street Parklands are the largest subtropical city garden in the world, featuring 16 acres of spectacular horticultural displays, distinctive architecture, sweeping views and unique artwork.

Across the river are the South Bank Parklands where you can wander or cycle along a winding pathway through the park, past South Bank Beach, Australia's only artificial inland city beach complex, complete with swimming and wading pools. Continue past Kangaroo Point cliffs and towards the iconic Story Bridge, designed by the same man that designed Sydney's famous Harbour Bridge, Dr J Bradfield. Opposite Kangaroo Point is Fortitude Valley, the city's favourite place to play once the sun goes down, home to Brisbane's best, and seediest, nightlife and an eclectic range of restaurants, cafes and shopping.

South-east Queensland is home to the largest concentration of native koalas in Australia. The Brisbane Koala Bushlands, a large area of relatively undisturbed bushland in the south-eastern suburbs, cover more than 800 hectares of parks and is part of south-east Queensland's Koala Coast network which protects between 3000 and 5000 koalas, as well as many other native animals.

Moreton Bay

The Brisbane River empties into the sea in Moreton Bay, a short ferry ride from the CBD. Moreton Island, one of the largest sand islands in the world, is 38km long, 98 per cent National Park and a popular place for sandboarding, quad biking, four-wheel driving and wreck snorkelling. You can hand-feed wild dolphins at Tangalooma Wild Dolphin Resort each evening. North Stradbroke Island, another large sand island at the southern end of Moreton Bay is accessible by vehicle ferry (barge) and water taxi from Cleveland. With spectacular scenery, white sandy beaches and freshwater lakes it is a popular weekender and holiday spot.

Brisbane hinterland

The mountainous hinterland 20 minutes drive north-west of Brisbane is a largely untouched swathe of bushland and rainforest that belies the notion that a bustling city metropolis is just a stone's throw away. A short drive through Mt Nebo and Mt Glorious, along the Northbrook Parkway to the quiet country towns of Kilcoy and Woodford takes you into a rugged mountain wilderness that is perfect for long lazy picnics and short bushwalks.

Toowoomba and Darling Downs

On the rim of the Great Dividing Range, Toowoomba, 127km west of Brisbane, is a gracious city full of historic buildings, beautiful parks and gardens, famous for their flower displays, especially in September during the annual Carnival of Flowers. The surrounding Darling Downs is the heart of south-east Queensland's agricultural district, with rich volcanic black soils producing grapes, fruit, wheat and fat cattle.

South Bank parklands. *(TQ)*

NATIONAL PARKS

Brisbane Forest Park: is one of the largest tracts of bushland near a major capital city in Australia, and contains Brisbane's closest and most accessible rainforest—28,500 hectares of national parks, state forests and council reserves, including D'Aguilar National Park. Good picnic areas, great views and numerous bushwalking tracks.

Mt Mee State Forest and Forest Reserve: contains beautiful open forests, scribbly gum forests, rainforest remnants, hoop pine plantations and picturesque creek scenery.

Moreton Island National Park: a large sand island with freshwater creeks and lakes, coastal heath, rocky headlands, paperbark swamps, a historic lighthouse and ruined coastal forts. Mt Tempest is the highest stable coastal sand dune in the southern hemisphere. Migrating wading birds flock to the island from September to April, nesting turtles occasionally come ashore in summer and migrating humpback whales pass by in late winter and spring. The adjacent waters are protected in Moreton Bay Marine Park.

Bribie Island Recreation Area: linked to the mainland by road bridge, 65km north of Brisbane, Bribie Island offers beautiful coastal scenery, low-key bush camping spots, popular boating and fishing areas in Pumicestone Passage, excellent birdwatching opportunities and spring wildflowers.

St Helena Island National Park: stone ruins of a brutal penal settlement on a pretty island in Moreton Bay. Accessible by boat from Manly or New Farm.

Blue Lake National Park: on North Stradbroke Island, this national park protects coastal wallum and a freshwater lake of special significance to the local Quandamooka people. Blue Lake or 'Karboora' is a window lake formed in a hollow in the island's water table. Tortoise Lagoon, a small seasonal swamp, is a perched lake, located above the water table.

Daisy Hill Forest Reserve: on the Brisbane's south-eastern outskirts includes the Daisy Hill Koala Centre, where you can see koalas up close as well as learn about their life cycle and how they've adapted to the changing Australian environment.

Boondall Wetlands Reserve: Brisbane's largest wetlands, on the edge of Moreton Bay between Nudgee Beach, Boondall and Shorncliffe and includes more than 1000 hectares of tidal flats, mangroves, salt marshes, melaleuca wetlands, grasslands, open forests and woodlands.

scenic highlights

Head north-west out of Brisbane via the The Gap along Route 31, signposted Mt Nebo/Mt Glorious. No sooner have you left the last of the suburbs behind than you are climbing along the spine of mountains in D'Aguilar National Park and Brisbane State Forest Park. Stop at Jolly's lookout for views of the Glass House Mountains and, on a clear day, Brisbane city, Caloundra and Moreton Bay Islands.

Northbrook Parkway, as the road is now called, winds its way up through tall eucalypt forests before cresting the mountain range. The blink-and-you'll-miss-them villages of Mt Nebos and Mt Glorious both have cafes where you can sit outside admiring the views while being serenaded by the colonies of bellbirds that live in the tall forest trees.

The Parkway twists its way down the mountain through dense dark rainforest and stands of palm trees in a steep descent that is not suitable for caravans. Another good spot for a picnic along the way is Wivenhoe Lookout, which looks west over Lake Wivenhoe and the valley floor below.

Once down the mountain the valley opens up into rich grazing lands. Travel on past Somerset Dam, where you can picnic and camp beside the water, to the towns of Kilcoy and Woodford. Follow the loop back to Brisbane via tourist drive 29 through Mt Mee State Forest along the top of D'Aguilar Range and through the Samford Valley.

Picnic Point. *(Tourism Queensland)*

Caravan and camping

There are two small camping areas in Mt Mee State Forest: Neurum Creek, 6km from the Gantry picnic, and beside Neurum Creek at Archer camping area, 16km from the Gantry picnic area along Loveday's Rd You'll need a camping permit and a permit to traverse the forest beforehand. Both camping areas are unsuitable for caravans or camper trailers. You can also bush camp in Brisbane Forest Park, but you'll need a permit from Park Headquarters on Mt Nebo Road.

☎ (07) 3300 4855

On Moreton Island you can camp at Blue Lagoon, Eagers Creek, Ben-Ewa, the Wrecks or Comboyuro camping areas or specific sites along the beach. (Check with the rangers before setting up camp on the beach.) Be prepared for busy holiday times, especially Christmas, New Year and Easter. Both camping areas are unsuitable for caravans or camper trailers. Camping and caravan sites are available at Somerset Dam. On Bribie Island there are 4WD only campsites at Poverty Creek (open grassy sites and shady trees suitable for camper-trailers and groups) or you can bush camp at Ocean Beach just behind the dunes and at Gallaghers. Mission Point is a good campsite for those with a boat. You need a camping permit and a vehicle service permit to travel to 4WD-accessible camping areas.

www.epa.qld.gov.au ☎ 13 13 04

Bushwalks

River Walk is a pedestrian walkway that runs for approximately 3km along the Brisbane River and connects with more than 20km of pathways, roads, bridges and riverside parks. One kilometre of the walkway floats on the river surface and is located approximately 20m from the shoreline.

In Brisbane Forest Park the 20-minute Golden Boulder Track that winds past old mine shafts and the Turrbal Circuit Trail (50 minutes), highlights Aboriginal heritage of the area. The 8km Thylogale Walking Track connects Boombana to Jolly's Lookout through tall eucalypt forest and rainforest and the Morelia Walking Track (6km return) passes through eucalypt forest and small patches of rainforest before reaching Mt Nebo Lookout, with views of Samford Valley and Moreton Bay. Westside Track is a three-hour circular track that starts from the picnic area on the western side of Mt Glorious and follows the top of the cliffs before descending steeply to a level track perched on the side of steep slopes. Mt Coot-tha Aboriginal Art Trail is an easy 45-minute stroll featuring contemporary Australian Aboriginal art, including tree carvings, rock paintings and etchings, and a dance pit. The 5km Greene's Falls Track at Maiala takes you through cool, dark rainforest to a small, cascading waterfall.

Good walking tracks on Moreton Island include the two-hour Mt Tempest Track, the seven-hour Rous Battery Track and the 16km, six-hour Old Telegraph Road.

At Blue Lake National Park on North Stradbroke Island the Neembeeba Lookout Track is a 6km return walk to Neembeeba Lookout with magnificent views over the southern part of North Stradbroke Island, the Pacific Ocean and the Gold Coast. The Karboora track is a 5km return walk through wallum woodlands with stunted eucalypt trees, wallum banksias and a flowering heath understorey to Blue Lake.

Bribie Island's three bicentennial bushwalks (Banksia, Palm Grove and Melaleuca) begin near the Community Arts Centre on Sunderland Drive and are an easy one-hour walk through eucalypt forests, paperbark wetlands and wallum heathlands.

Hinterland art gallery. *(TQ)*

DON'T MISS

- **Queensland Art Gallery:** the permanent collection includes one of the world's largest collections of Asian and Aboriginal art. Melbourne Street, South Brisbane. Open Mon–Fri, 10am–5pm, weekends 9am–5pm. www.qag.qld.gov.au
- **Queensland Museum:** includes a dinosaur garden, *Mephisto* (a German World War I tank captured by a Queensland battalion) and the interactive Sciencentre for kids. Grey and Melbourne streets, South Bank. Open daily, 9.30am–5pm. www.qmsouthbank.museum.qld.gov.au
- **The Museum of Brisbane:** on the ground floor of Brisbane's iconic City Hall in King George Square this museum explores Brisbane's contemporary culture, heritage and people. Displays combine social history, visual arts, craft and design. Between Ann and Adelaide streets. Open daily 10am–5pm. Free tours on Tuesdays, Thursdays and Saturdays at 11am.
- **Queensland Police Museum:** learn how the police solve crimes and details of some of the city's most notorious crimes at police headquarters at 200 Roma Street, Brisbane. Open Mon–Fri, 9am–5pm.
- **Queensland Maritime Museum:** features the warship *Diamantina*, the steam tug *Forceful*, the South Brisbane Dry Dock, and a large collection of exhibits. South Bank near the Goodwill Bridge. Open daily, 9.30am–4.30pm. www.maritimemuseum.com.au
- **MacArthur Museum:** includes the actual office occupied by General Douglas MacArthur when he directed the Allied Forces World War II Pacific campaign in 1942. 201 Edward Street. Open Tue, Thu and Sun 10am–3pm. www.macarthurmuseumbrisbane.org
- **Queensland State Parliament:** experience the theatrics of the State's leaders from the visitors' gallery or take a half-hour tour of the old Parliament House and its treasure trove of antiques. Tours are run throughout the year except public holidays. On sitting days tours only run at 10.30am and 2.30pm. For Parliament sitting times call ☎ (07) 3406 7111.
- **Wild Koala Ecotours:** the Australian Koala Foundation (AKF) operates the 'Wild Koala Ecotours' in co-operation with Bushwacker Ecotours departing from Brisbane daily. Spend half a day with a trained scientist, learning all about koalas, other wildlife and how to ensure the future survival of koalas. Bookings required. www.savethekoala.com ☎ 1800 456 252
- **Brisbane's Vineyard:** winery with a view specialising in antioxidant-boosted wines containing olive leaf and grape extracts, ginger, citrus skin and ellagic acid. 1076 Mt Nebo Road, Mt Nebo. Cellar door sales and tastings daily 10am–7pm.
- **Australian Woolshed:** Australiana theme park with sheep shearing, working dog displays and native animals. 148 Stamford Road, Ferny Hills. Open daily, 8.30am–4pm.
- **Samford District Historical Museum:** local history and artefacts. Station Street, Samford. Open Sun 10am–4pm.
- **Old Petrie Town:** historical village with replica and original pioneer buildings. Meet the crafts people and local growers every Sunday at the Country Market 8am–2pm. North Pine County Park, Dayboro Road, Kurwongbah. Open Tue–Sun.
- **Woodford Folk Festival:** local and international musicians and performers bring in the new year with six days and six nights of concerts, workshops and debates in late December–early January each year. www.woodfordfolkfestival.com

adventure activities

Aerobatic joy flights

Flying Fighter Adventures, based at Archerfield airfield, has a collection of 22 lovingly-restored fighter planes ranging from vintage Tiger Moths to Vietnam era bombers. The 30-minute Trojan T-28 combat mission combines simulated combat (an attack run on the unsuspecting Mt Cotton Winery) with high-speed, high-adrenalin aerobatics and fighter evasion manoeuvring that includes barrel rolls, loops and heart-stopping airshow tricks in an American Navy bomber. You haven't flown until you've flown upside down!

www.flyingfighters.com.au

Abseiling and rockclimbing

The city's most popular rockclimbing and abseiling spot is the Kangaroo Point cliffs opposite the heart of the city. The cliffs are about 20m in height and offer great views of the city. Riverlife Adventure Centre in the old Naval Stores at Kangaroo Point offer introductory abseil and rockclimbing courses that will have nervous first-timers hanging over the ledge in no time.

www.riverlife.com.au

More experienced rock climbers should head for Mt French in Moogerah Peaks National Park, 90 minutes south-west of the city. Hailed as one of the best climbs in the world, Frog Buttress has more than 300 climbs for experienced climbers.

Ballooning

Fly Me To The Moon offer gourmet breakfast balloon flights daily over Brisbane with one of Australia's most highly awarded balloon pilots, Steve Griffin. In 1994, Steve was the first person to fly a balloon solo across Australia. In 1999, he broke the Australian balloon altitude record (31,000ft). In 2004 he broke the AX2 World duration record in a balloon that he designed and built himself. He has held numerous other ballooning world records and won the highest international award in ballooning–the 'Montgolfier Diploma'. Tours depart Toowong and the flight will take you over the river for unparalleled views of the Brisbane CBD and surrounding suburbs. Most in-flight views extend north beyond the Glass House Mountains and south to the Border Ranges, with Moreton Bay and the islands visible to the east. Complimentary pick-ups can be arranged from city accommodation.

www.flymetothemoon.com.au

Floating Images take you on a spectacular balloon ride over Ipswich CBD and its scenic surrounds, followed by champagne breakfast.

www.floatingimages.com.au

Balloons Above will float you over the patchwork fields of the Locker Valley, followed with a French-style champagne breakfast on the verandah of their classic Queenslander.

www.balloonsabove.com.au

Flying a jet fighter over Brisbane.

Bridge climb

The new soft adventure experience is one of only three bridge climbs in the world (the others are Sydney and Auckland). The two-and-a-half-hour climb that takes you out onto the eastern side of the Story Bridge, up the steep rise to the summit approximately 80m above sea level for breathtaking views over the river city. It's then down again and across to the middle of the bridge where you can watch six lanes of traffic whiz by just below your feet and then back up and down again along the western arm of the bridge.

www.storybridgeadventureclimb.com.au

Canoeing and kayaking

The Brisbane River is perfect for a paddle and there are plenty of places along the river where you can launch a canoe or kayak. The Riverlife Adventure Centre in the old Naval Stores at Kangaroo Point offers a range of activities including paddling your way up the Brisbane River in a kayak or motorised inflatable boat. On top of all this, the Riverside Bikeway that runs right past the front door is ideal for cycling, kick bikes (like a scooter with a seat), electric scooters, unicycles and rollerblading, and you can hire them all at the Riverlife Centre.

www.riverlife.com.au

Adventure Island Kayak Tours, based on Russell Island lead guided tours to Moreton and South Stradbroke islands.

www.russellisland.biz/BAZ_1.htm

BayDogs Kayak and Canoe also run paddling tours of Moreton Bay, including a twilight paddling trip on the Brisbane River as the city lights up.

www.baydogs.com.au

Cycling and mountain biking

Brisbane is great place for cycling with more than 500km of bikeways across the city. The Bicentennial Bikeway, built in 1988, follows the river from the CBD along Coronation Drive to Toowong. If you only feel like cycling in one direction, hop on the CityCat ferry at either the University of Queensland or North Quay to make the return journey. Other popular cycleways include the Wynnum-Manly Esplanade exploring southern Moreton Bay along the Wynnum-Manly foreshore between Elanora Park and Fig Tree Point at Lota and the Sandgate Foreshores along Moreton Bay from Decker Park at Brighton to Cabbage Tree Creek at Shorncliffe, winding past tidal flats full of birds and crabs. From Shorncliffe, the new Kerry Fien Bikeway takes you to Boondall Wetlands via Curlew Park and the Brisbane Entertainment Centre. You can access the foreshores from Redcliffe by cycling across the old Hornibrook Bridge.

Brisbane Forest Park has several good trails for mountain biking, with favourites being the Mt Nebo Firetrail which follows Mt Nebo Rd (steep in places but a good downhill run on the return stroke) and has many trails leading from it; the scenic Centre Road and the ride from Mt Nebo to Mt Glorious, a very hard ride with fast downhills and steep climbs. Mount Coot-tha Reserve and Daisy Hill Forest Reserve also have good networks of mountain bike trails.

Bushranger bikes runs a variety of half and full-day mountain bike tours in and around Brisbane.

www.bushrangerbikes.com.au

Diving

Brisbane is an offshore playground for those keen on donning a mask, flippers and a wetsuit. Point Lookout at the northern end of Stradbroke Island is home to grey nurse sharks during winter and huge manta rays and leopard sharks in summer. Caves and ledges often hide huge cod and groper at nearby Boat Rock.

Tangalooma dolphins. *(TQ)*

Moreton Island offers good shallow wreck diving and snorkelling at Tangalooma Wrecks, where 15 hulks were scuttled to form a small craft anchorage and at Curtin Artificial Reef (formed with the scuttled wrecks of 19 vessels and one tram) home to giant Queensland gropers, tusk and parrotfish. Comboyuro Point on the north-western corner of the island is one of the best sites for drift diving. On the ocean side of the bay is Henderson Rock, China Wall, Cherubs Cave and north is colourful Flinders Reef, Smiths Rock and Hutchison Shoal. For the wreck diver the St Paul and Cementco lie just off Moreton Island. Aqua X-treme runs both day trips and weekend trips to all these sites.

www.aquax-treme.com.au

Dolphin and whale watching

You can hand-feed wild dolphins at Tangalooma Wild Dolphin Resort on Moreton Island. Each evening the dolphins, varying in numbers from five to nine, swim into the shallow well lit area adjacent to the resort jetty to be hand fed their favourite fish. Full day trips are available that return to the city after the dolphins have been fed.

www.tangalooma.com

Between June and November southern humpback whales congregate in Moreton Bay on their migration route to and from Antarctica. Moreton Bay Whalewatching operates tours from Redcliffe on the purpose-built 30m, 300-passenger catamaran *Eye-Spy* with six outdoor viewing decks and indoor floor-to-ceiling glass viewing areas.

www.brisbanewhalewatching.com.au

Fishing

Brisbane's semi-tropical climate and warm currents are home to a mix of temperate and tropical fish with good coastal, estuary, reef and offshore fishing. Moreton Bay offers good fishing all year: from small whiting through to big game fish such as sailfish and black marlin. The famous 'Tailor Run' occurs from August to December as these hard-fighting fish migrate north for breeding then run back down along Moreton Islands' beaches. The Brisbane River is good for bream which can be caught from city wharves, rock walls and river banks and the hinterland dams, such as Somerset, are well stocked with bass and golden perch.

Off-road driving

The sand islands of Moreton Bay (Moreton, Bribie and North Stradbroke) offer some great places for four-wheel-driving on sand. Indeed a 4WD is essential to reach many recreational and camping spots on the islands. Check tides before driving on the beach and reduce tyre pressure to improve traction in soft sand, but if you do, don't forget to re-inflate your tyres on harder sand or surfaces. Normal road rules apply on beaches.You need a permit for all three islands. Permits available on the barges to Moreton and Stradbroke islands.

ww.epa.qld.gov.au ☎ 13 13 04

Kangaroo Point. *(BM)*

Black Duck Valley, 40km South of Gatton, is a private 4WD and motocross park with more than 90 maintained tracks and trails that wind and weave through 1000 acres of spectacular mountain scenery that takes you from easy terrain for the novices, to the heart pumping extreme for the more experienced.

www.blackduckvalley.com

Gliding

Boonah Gliding Club, Fassifern Valley south of Ipswich, offers a range of 'Air Experience Flights' on Friday, Saturday, Sunday and public holidays. Flights range from 20-minute flights to aerobatic glider flights involving loops, stall turns, barrel rolls, and inverted flight and a full-day package for those who want to get some real hands-on experience. By the end of the third flight you will be flying! Flights operate all day, but you'll get a smoother, clearer flight earlier in the day.

www.boonahgliding.com.au

Horse riding

Daisy Hill Forest Reserve and Brisbane Forest Park both have a network of forest roads throughout the park for horse riding. In Daisy Hill horse riding is allowed along unsealed tracks starting from the upper picnic area where parking for horse floats and a corral are provided. Cyclists and horse riders can also share the Stringybark and Spotted Gum trails with walkers.

You must obtain a permit to ride in Brisbane Forest Park, call the Queensland Parks and Wildlife Service

☎ (07) 3227 7800

Welcome Horse Riding operates on 500 acres of undulating pastures, mountain streams and the slopes of Mount Samson, 35 minutes from Brisbane city. They offer guided trail riding, riding lessons and tailored programs.

www.welcome.net.au

Hot laps

WRX Experience, located at Pimpama around half way between Brisbane and the Gold Coast has a purpose-built track and a rally spec Subaru Impreza WRX STi rally car. The adventure starts with a safety briefing and a run down on the principles of rally driving, then you're strapped into the car with a professional rally driver by your side who helps you work your way around the track. By the sixth lap, you'll be flinging yourself (safely) around the track as you drift and slide your way around the circuit, thankful that the 'trees' you keep ploughing over are, in this instance, plastic traffic cones.

www.thewrxexperience.com

Part of the same complex, Buggy Mania keeps kids of all ages happy on a 600m-long dirt track in 10 horsepower, off-road twister buggies. The wheels spin and the mud flies as you drift, slide and spin your way around the track at speeds over 50km/h.

Ipswich Motorsport Precinct (40 minutes west of Brisbane), home of the Queensland and Willowbank raceways is a theme park for 'rev heads', offering hot laps in V8 race car, super bike, Formula 1 race car or dragster. Alternatively, watch the pro's go through their paces.

www.queenslandraceway.com.au

Windsurfing and kitesurfing

Live Adrenalin run two-hour kitesurfing lessons on the warm flat waters of Moreton Bay covering essential skills such as site assessment, equipment selection and setup, flying the kite, body dragging and self rescue. The exact location of lessons on the bay depends on wind and tidal conditions. Lessons are mostly held in the afternoon up until sunset, but may occasionally be scheduled as early as 9am and are available from September through to April when the winds are most favourable.

www.adrenalin.com.au

Quad biking

Moreton Island, at 38km long and 19,000 ha in area, is one of the largest sand islands in the world. Ninety eight per cent of the island is national park and supports an amazing array of vegetation, wildlife, freshwater lakes, wetlands, forests and achingly beautiful coastline. Tangalooma Resort runs guided quad bike tours through the bushland and around a specially designed course in the dunes. All tours include

Moreton Island. (TQ)

instruction on how to operate the all-terrain motorbikes and a practice run along the beach before heading up, down, over and around the dunes. It's the most fun you can have on four wheels.

www.tangalooma.com

River cruise

Ocean Xplorer boasts that it is 'the city's hottest new ticket out of town, blasting you from South Bank in the city heart to the pristine beaches of Moreton Island in just 50 exhilarating minutes'. Don a life vest and spray jacket then climb aboard the rigid inflatable (think zodiac with a hard bottom), straddle the bicycle-seat-style stool and hold on tight as you zoom up the Brisbane River, stopping only to check out some dolphins and for a slice of cake. Then it's out into the open sea, bumping and crashing over the waves until, spray-soaked and wind-ravaged, you slide onto the white sands of Tangalooma Wild Dolphin Resort on Moreton Island. The ride takes just less than 50 exhilarating minutes.

www.oceanxplorer.com

Sailing

Moreton Bay Escapes 'Solo Sailing' experience offers a full day trip to Moreton Island including a three-hour sail on the famous yacht *Solo* the only four-time winner of the Sydney to Hobart yacht race and three round-the-world circumnavigations. Pick up the basics of sailing such as manning the helm or helping set sail *Solo's* magnificent masts. There's also always the option of 'helping to navigate' (also known as sitting back, relaxing, enjoying a chilled glass of wine and taking in the scenery). Once at the island, tours include snorkelling in summer and sand tobogganing in winter as well as ski tubing.

www.moretonbayescapes.com.au

weather watch

- January: 17–25°C
- July: 9–15°C
- Summer can be warm and humid, winter is temperate and drier.

Sand tobogganing

There's nothing quite like speeding down a giant sandhill clinging onto a waxed up toboggan, and Moreton Island is the place to do it. For the real thrill seeker, the big sandhills reach up to 80m in height and speeds have been clocked up to 50km per hour, while for the not-so-daring and the kids, the small sand hills and The Desert are perfect for giving this fun sport a try. Tobogganing boards are available from Bulwer Bait and Tackle on the island for $4.95, or are included in many of the guided tours.

Skydiving

Brisbane Skydiving Centre offers solo or tandem jumps for first-time beginners as well as fully certified skydiving courses for gaining your international 'A' licence. Situated near Ipswich, the Willowbank drop zone is the closest drop zone to Brisbane city and all tandem jumps include a 25-minute scenic flight to an exit height of 12,500 feet incorporating 6000 feet of free fall. Tandem dives are also available from Archerfield for a skydive over the city.

www.brisbaneskydive.com.au

Waterskiing

The Brisbane River is a popular spot for waterskiing and wakeboarding on weekends, but if you don't have your own boat, Cable Ski Logan is a cable waterski and wakeboard lake for beginners or experienced skiers 30 minutes south of Brisbane. Open daily from 10am–7pm with high-speed sessions available from 9am–10am on Saturday mornings.

Waterskiing is also popular on Wivenhoe and Somerset dams.

www.cableski.com.au

MORE INFORMATION

- **Brisbane Visitor Information Centre:** Corner Albert & Queen Streets, Brisbane. ☎ (07) 3006 6290 or visit **www.ourbrisbane.com/visitors** **www.queenslandholidays.com.au/brisbane**

the sunshine coast

Aussie Sea Kayaks off Noosa. *(TQ)*

Rainbow Beach. *(TQ)*

▶ BEAUTIFUL BEACHES and close-to-perfect summer and winter weather have earned the section of the coast from Caloundra north to Cooloola the moniker 'Sunshine Coast'. It takes in beautiful hinterland including the Glass House Mountains, Blackall Range, Noosa hinterland and the Mary Valley; as well as more than 100km of beaches stretching through the coastal towns of Caloundra, Kawana, Mooloolaba, Maroochydore, Coolum Beach, Noosa and Rainbow Beach.

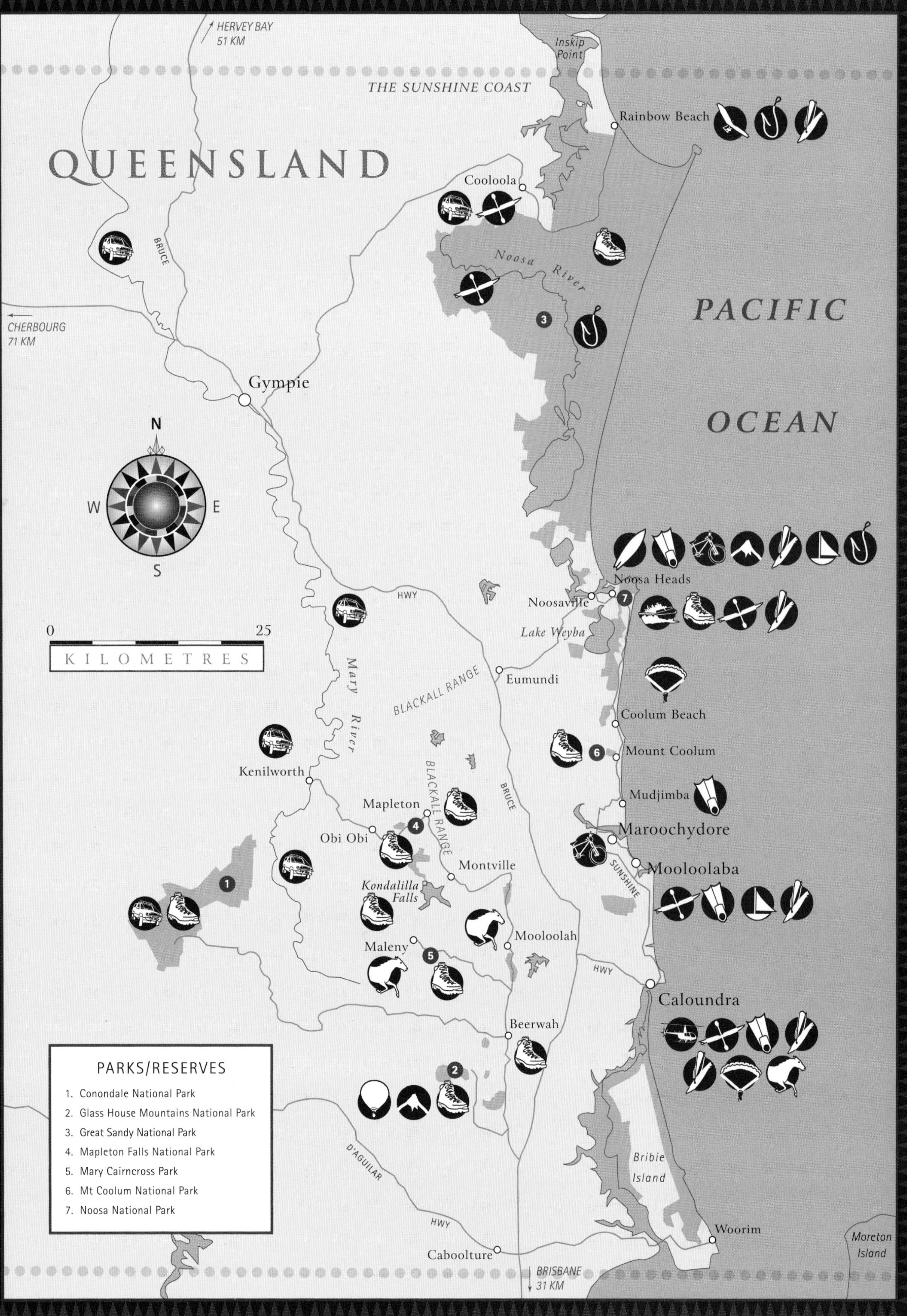
HERVEY BAY
51 KM
Inskip
Point
THE SUNSHINE COAST
Rainbow Beach
QUEENSLAND
Cooloola
BRUCE
Noosa River
PACIFIC
OCEAN
CHERBOURG
71 KM
Gympie
N
W
E
S
Noosa Heads
Noosaville
HWY
0
25
KILOMETRES
Lake Weyba
Mary River
BLACKALL RANGE
Eumundi
Coolum Beach
Mount Coolum
Kenilworth
BLACKALL RANGE
BRUCE
Mapleton
Mudjimba
Maroochydore
Obi Obi
Montville
SUNSHINE
Mooloolaba
Kondalilla
Falls
Mooloolah
Maleny
HWY
Caloundra
Beerwah
PARKS/RESERVES
1. Conondale National Park
2. Glass House Mountains National Park
3. Great Sandy National Park
4. Mapleton Falls National Park
5. Mary Cairncross Park
6. Mt Coolum National Park
7. Noosa National Park
D'AGUILAR
HWY
Bribie
Island
Woorim
Moreton
Island
Caboolture
BRISBANE
31 KM

Glass House Mountains. *(LA)*

NATIONAL PARKS

Noosa National Park: a short stroll from the cafes and boutiques of Noosa's main street. It includes Noosa Heads, parts of Lake Weyba (a large, shallow, saltwater lake in the Noosa River system), Emu Mountain and coastal lowlands extending south towards Coolum and some of the most picturesque coastline in south-east Queensland. Most of the park is covered in open woodlands and low wallum heath, although there are small pockets of rainforest with hoop and kauri pines and koalas are common in the park. Due the popularity of the park and its proximity to town, there have been serious assaults in the park and QPWS advises to always walk with a group or in sight of a group, to stay on marked walking tracks and walk in daylight hours only.

Great Sandy National Park (Cooloola Section): high sand dunes, coloured sand cliffs, sweeping beaches, sandblows, freshwater lakes, tall forests, paperbark swamps and wildflower heath plains make this a spectacular section, which also extends across the Great Sandy Straits to cover much of Fraser Island. The park protects the headwaters of the Noosa River, the only coastal river in Queensland with most of its catchment protected, along with many plants and animals threatened by coastal development such as the rare Cooloola acid frog and ground parrot. It is also home to one of the few remaining emu populations in coastal Queensland.

Conondale National Park: in the heart of the Upper Mary Valley, features luxuriant rainforests, tall eucalypt forest, plantation forests, waterfalls, boulder-strewn creeks and spectacular scenery in the rugged Conondale Ranges.

Mapleton Falls National Park: mountainous park featuring remnants of warm subtropical rainforests, tall open eucalypt forest and pretty waterfalls. At Mapleton Falls Pencil Creek cascades 120m over a steep escarpment into the Mary River catchment.

Glass House Mountains National Park: protecting nine of 16 eroded volcanic plugs known collectively as the Glass House Mountains. There are several good bushwalking tracks, some involving challenging climbs to summits.

Mt Coolum National Park: this park contains most of the dome-shaped Mt Coolum, which rises 208m above the surrounding sugar cane fields. After rain, waterfalls cascade over the craggy cliffs on its sides.

Southern towns

The towns of Caloundra, Mooloolaba and Maroochydore are all an easy hour or so drive from Brisbane and are popular holiday destinations, particularly for families, with patrolled surf beaches and protected lakes and rivers for swimming, boating and fishing, as well as a range of family-friendly attractions such as UnderWater World.

Noosa

The undisputed jewel in the Sunshine Coast crown, Noosa Heads, along with nearby Noosaville, is one of the most popular beachside holiday destinations in the country. With a beautiful swimming beach in the heart of the town, flanked by a strip of exclusive boutiques, excellent restaurants and luxury hotels, a superb national park within walking distance of the cafes and a beautiful river running through it all, it's easy to see why it has retained its popularity for so long.

Cooloola Coast

North of the Noosa River is a large expanse of relatively undisturbed sandy beach, Rainbow Beach, backed by a river and lagoon system rich in bird and wildlife. Much of the area is part of Great Sandy National Park and only accessible by 4WD or boat, and it is most famous for its coloured sands, rising in 200m-high multi-coloured cliffs stained by oxidation and vegetation dyes, although Aboriginal legend has it that the colours are the result of the slaying of the Rainbow Serpent. Rainbow Beach also provides barge access to the southern end of Fraser Island at Inskip Point.

The hinterland

The Sunshine Coast's best keep secret is its hinterland. It's an area of lush dairy country with green rolling hills punctuated by pockets of rainforest and dotted with small villages with thriving arts and crafts. It's home to one of the country's most famous weekly markets, great restaurants and beautiful scenery and includes famous landmarks such as the Glass House Mountains–which on a clear day can be seen from as far away as Brisbane–and Australia Zoo, the one time home to celebrity crocodile hunter, the late Steve Irwin.

Caravan and camping

You can camp at Coochin Creek 9km east of Beerwah in Glass House Mountains National Park and at several sites (camping and caravan) in the Kenilworth State Forest and Conondale National Park. You can also camp at Peach Trees camping and picnic area in Jimna State Forest, 45km north-west of Kilcoy and in the Amamoor State Forest with tent and caravan sites at the Cedar Grove camping area and Amamoor Creek camping area, where there are wheelchair-accessible toilets and cold showers, taps, gas barbecues and a public phone. This is the only camping area where dogs are permitted. If you plan to camp here in August contact the Kenilworth park office first as the entire camping area is used for the annual Country Music Muster, a major event that runs for one week in August.

www.epa.qld.gov.au ☎ 131 304 weekdays

The Cooloola Section of Great Sandy National Park also offers some great camp sites at Harrys, Fig Tree Point, Freshwater (caravan sites and cold showers), along the Noosa River or along Teewah Beach. Take insect repellent. The Cooloola Wilderness Trail has bush camping areas without facilities at Neebs and Wandi waterholes. There is a commercial campground at Elanda Point.

Shelley Beach, Caloundra. *(TQ)*

DON'T MISS

- **UnderWater World:** Queensland's largest oceanarium and aquarium with 14 shows and presentations daily. Get wet as you roll up your sleeves and feel life beneath the waves or feed stingrays and sharks. See playful otters in the Otter Encounter and chill out in the Cold Water Exhibit, dive with sharks and swim with seals. Parkyn Parade, Mooloolaba. Open daily, 9am–6pm. **www.underwaterworld.com.au**
- **Big Pineapple:** 16m-high, fibreglass pineapple with tours of tropical fruit plantations and sugar cane fields, animal nursery, wildlife park and family adventure rides. Nambour Connection Road, Woombye. Open daily, 9.30am–5pm. **www.bigpineapple.com.au**
- **Queensland Air Museum:** collection of historic aircraft. Caloundra Aerodrome 7 Pathfinder Drive, Caloundra. Open daily, 10am–4pm. **www.qam.com.au**
- **Australia Zoo:** created by the late Crocodile Hunter, Steve Irwin. Australian wildlife park with crocodile feeding and snake handling demonstrations. Glass House Mountains Tourist Route, Beerwah. Open daily, 9am–4.30pm. **www.crocodilehunter.com**
- **Noosa Ferry Cruise:** $13.50 buys you an all day (and evening) ticket on the wooden ferry that plies the waterways between Hastings Street, Noosaville and Tewantin. Take the 90-minute return trip, or hop on and off as often as you like.
- **Ikatan Balinese Spa and Gardens:** a little piece of Bali tranquillity in the Noosa hinterland. Take a friend and go for the Noosa Dua package, one and a half hours of massage, mini facial and foot pampering. Bookings essential. **www.ikatanspa.com** ☎ (07) 5471 1199.
- **Eumundi markets:** check out the best of local produce, art and craft at Eumundi markets, every Wed and Sat morning.
- **Design Works Galleria:** eclectic range of high quality Australian art, furniture, woodwork, pottery, jewellery and sculpture. 12 Maple Sreeet, Cooroy. Open Mon–Fri, 9.30am–5pm, Sat 9.30am–3pm.
- **Kenilworth Country Foods:** cheese factory with viewing platform and free cheese tasting. 45 Charles Street, Kenilworth. Open Mon–Fri, 9am–4pm, weekends and public holidays, 10.30am–3.30pm.

Eumundi markets. *(TQ)*

scenic highlights

Noosa. (TQ)

Head west out of Noosa to Eumundi where every Saturday and Wednesday morning people from all over the district flock to the local markets to browse the huge array of local produce, art and crafts. The markets kick off around 6am—parking spaces can be hard to get, so aim to get there early rather than later. If you are not in town on market day there are several good art galleries and craft studios to browse in the main street.

From Eumundi drive south to Nambour and then cut west to Mapleton along the spine of the Blackall Range to Montville and Maleny for great views of the coast and hinterland. Montville is packed with boutiques, arts, crafts and trinket shops: nearby Maleny is less frenetic and also has several good galleries and lots of cafes and restaurants.

Take the short loop drive out of Maleny along Mountain View Road for more views and a boardwalk stroll through Mary Cairncross Park, a 130-acre rainforest reserve.

The late Steve Irwin's Australia Zoo is 30 minutes down the road at Beerwah. Although the world famous Crocodile Hunter himself is no longer with us, you can still watch fearless keepers feed huge crocodiles, have your photo taken with a giant python wrapped around your neck and see lots of Australian wildlife.

Stop at the Glass House Mountains Lookout for spectacular views of the mountains named by Captain Cook (who thought the jagged rock peaks resembled the glass furnaces of his native Yorkshire) which rise dramatically from the valley floor below.

Maleny is deep in the heart of rich dairy country—wind your way down the mountains along the Maleny–Kenilworth road, via Conondale, to taste some cheese at the Kenilworth Cheese Factory. One of the last remaining privately-owned cheese factories in Queensland, it was saved from closure in 1980s when six employees pooled their resources and bought the bulk cheese factory. The handcrafted cheeses are now made using traditional methods.

From Kenilworth you can cross the beautiful Obi Obi Valley that follows the meandering course of the Obi Obi Creek to climb the steep, mountain-hugging ascent back up the range (not suitable for caravans) to Mapleton, stopping at Mapleton Falls to look out over the waterfall or stretch your legs on the one-hour circuit walk.

An alternative route if you are towing a caravan is to continue north from Kenilworth through open grazing country to Eumundi via Belli Park and Eerwah Vale.

Lake Cootharaba. *(TQ)*

Bushwalks

There are more than 15km of walking tracks in the headland section of Noosa National Park. For beautiful coastal scenery you can't beat the three-hour coastal track that skirts the shoreline around the headland and provides access to several pretty beaches. Lookouts along the way provide spectacular views and the track ends on a high bluff at Hell's Gates. The 20-minute Palm Grove circuit passes through rainforest with hoop pines and piccabeen palms and the more difficult three-hour Tanglewood Track meandering through rainforest and woodlands to Hell's Gates, are both sheltered walks good for hot days.

Cooloola Wilderness Trail in Great Sandy National Park is a three-day 46km trail which joins Elanda Point in the south to East Mullen car park on Rainbow Beach Road in the north. Some sections are flooded in the summer and early autumn so check conditions before you go.

The Sunshine Coast Hinterland Great Walk is a 58km walk through the Blackall Range. Highlights include gorges, waterfalls, rock pools and views and it links Kondalilla and Mapleton Falls National Parks, Maleny and Mapleton Forest Reserves, and Delicia Road Conservation Park. Allow four to six days.

A rough 800m trail on the eastern side of Mt Coolum leads to the summit to its isolated volcanic dome, but it is tough going–allow two hours for the return hike. Ecologically, Mt Coolum is one of the most important square kilometres in Australia. The diversity of plant life within such a confined area is unequalled. Geologically the mountain has striking columnar/crystal jointing patterns clearly visible both on the main cliffs and the faces of the disused quarry. South of Caloundra, there is a challenging walk to the summit of Mt Beerwah (3.5 hours return) and a gentle 30-minute loop through open eucalypt forest at Glass House Mountains Lookout.

In the hinterland there are some good walks at Kondalilla Falls, where you can swim or follow two easy circuit rainforest walks. The four-hour Obi Obi Gorge Circuit has some steep sections, but the reward is some spectacular views of the meandering Obi Obi Gorge, carved by water over millions of years. At Mapleton Falls there is a pretty one-hour rainforest walk along the Woompoo Circuit and at Mary Cairncross Park a wheelchair accessible track winds through the rainforest, with good views of Glass House Mountains.

adventure activities

Rainbow Beach. *(TQ)*

Abseiling and rockclimbing

There are a number of good abseiling locations around the hinterland of the Sunshine Coast, particularly in the Glass House Mountains. Adventures Sunshine Coast offer abseiling and rappelling courses at a range of locations including Pt Glorious with its stunning views over the Sunshine Coast, the awesome 100m drop at Mt Tinbeerwah, or the Glass House Mountains where a climb/scramble to the top of one of these famous Sunshine Coast landmarks is followed by a few hours of abseiling and then a swim in mountain rock pools.

www.fameconsulting.com/adventures

KSA in Noosa also offer climbing adventures on Mt Tinbeerwah.

www.kite-surf.com.au/climbing.asp

Aerobatic joy flights

Take a scenic joy flight over the beaches around Caloundra and the Glass House Mountains in an open-cockpit 1944 Tiger Moth. You can also add on aerobatics to the half-hour flights or learn to fly in the Tiger Moth. Flights depart from Caloundra Aerodrome.

www.flywithsmithy.com

Ballooning

Take a dawn flight over the Glass House Mountains with Skydrifter Ballooning. Flights are between 45-60 minutes and include a celebratory breakfast afterwards.

☎ (07) 5438 7003

Camel safari

The Camel Company offer camel safaris on Noosa's north shore: ranging from one or two-hour beach and bushland trips along 40 Mile Beach to the Coloured Sands or Laguna Bay, overnight camel camping trips on Teewah Beach and six-day Fraser Island trips, camping each night in a different location on the west coast of Fraser Island.

www.camelcompany.com.au

Canoeing and kayaking

The waterways of the Sunshine Coast present a host of canoeing and kayaking opportunities. Blue Water Kayak Tours at Caloundra run full and half-day kayaking tours of the Pumicestone Passage and Moreton Bay Marine Park, paddling to Bribie Island including a leisurely walk in the Conservation Park or time to relax on the beach.

www.bluewaterkayaktours.com

The Aussie Sea Kayak Company in Mooloolaba hire kayaks as well as taking guided paddling trips through the Noosa everglades, the Great Sandy Straits between Fraser Island and the mainland and Mooloolaba Bay past coastal headlands and mangroves.

www.ausseakayak.com.au

Cooloola is one of the best canoeing spots in Australia. The tannin-stained water of the upper Noosa River is famous for its spectacular reflections and ideal for paddling, birdwatching, photography and swimming, with tunnel-like tree canopies overhead, mangroves, tangled vine forests and scenic stretches of calm water.

Noosa Ocean Kayak Tours & Hire run daily Noosa National Park and Noosa Riverways tours or you can explore on your own. Kanu Kapers Australia offers half-day and one-day kayaking tours and adventure healing retreats in Cooloola.

www.kanukapersaustralia.com

Pedal & Paddle Adventure Treks, also in Noosa, have guided two-hour kayaking trips along the Noosa River and through nearby mangroves and lakes or you can combine a morning downhill mountain bike run from the top of Mt Tinbeerwah with kayaking in the afternoon.

www.pedalandpaddle.com.au

Elanda Point Canoe Company hires canoes, kayaks and all camping gear for 'do it yourself' expeditions through the Noosa everglades as well as half-day guided Everglades Canoe Safaris every Friday and Saturday, and the Sandpatch Overnight Gourmet Guided Canoe Safari every Saturday. The five-day Noosa Canoe Trail trips feature magnificent canoeing through the entire Upper Noosa River including side walks to the spectacular Cooloola Sandpatch and to Teewah Coloured Sands.

www.elanda.com.au

Cycling and mountain biking

Noosa Bike Hire & Mt Bike Adventure Tours have mountain bikes, road bikes, children's bikes, tandems and babyseats for hire with a free delivery and pickup service in Noosa. They also run a range of mountain biking tours, including a half-day, downhill mountain bike adventure through creek beds and rainforest pockets and a helibiking tour which includes a 20-miunte flight from Maroochydore into the mountains for a challenging descent and flight back to Maroochydore. You'll need good MTB skills before attempting this tour. Other tours include self-guided beach tours and a two-hour night ride through the forest.

www.bikeon.com.au

Bugsports Adventures also offer guided off-road mountain bike tours in the hinterland through old growth rainforest along everything from gentle fire trails to steep single tracks. Choose from half-day, full-day, full moon or night tours under lights.

www.bug.com.au

Pedal & Paddle Adventure Treks also have a two-hour downhill mountain bike run as well as combined kayaking tours.

www.pedalandpaddle.com.au

Diving

Just beyond Noosa Heads is a system of reefs covering more than 20 hectares of ocean floor, a maze of rocky ridges and canyons, sandy patches, coral and sponge-encrusted boulders. The most popular spot for divers is Jew Shoal, about 2km north of the heads, but the system also includes Halls and North Halls Reefs and Sunshine Reef, all stretching to form a north-south arc around Noosa Heads.

The HMAS *Brisbane*, a decommissioned vessel was sunk in 2005 to create an artificial reef at nearby Mudjimba Island. Divers can explore the 133m-long warship and view different areas of the ship. Access holes allow passage into the forward engine room, boiler room and the ship's interior, where divers can view living and sleeping quarters used by the crew during the ship's service from 1967 to 2001. Divers also have the chance to explore the growth of the artificial reef as new marine communities inhabit the wreck and surrounding area. Commercial dive operators are located in Noosa, Mooloolaba and Caloundra.

Both certified divers and non-divers can dive with the resident sharks and rays at the UnderWater World aquarium with one of Scuba World's instructors. Feel your adrenalin rush as you come within centimetres of large grey nurse sharks as well as leopard sharks, whitetip reef sharks, shovel nosed and the sleek whaler sharks and get face to face with black bullrays, coachwhip rays, giant groper, spangled red emperors, sweetlip, snapper, bream, remoras and wobbegongs.

www.scubaworld.com.au

Fishing

The Sunshine Coast has good fishing all year round. There is a great mixture of temperate and tropical species available in the offshore reefs and in rivers and from rocks and beaches. Fish for bream, flat-head, whiting and dart in the surf along Rainbow Beach. In spring, the estuaries produce some of the biggest flathead in Australia, up to 80cm long. There are a number of deep sea fishing charters available in Noosa and other major centres. Noosa River Fishing & Crab Tours run half-day fishing and crabbing trips on the Noosa River and include a meal of freshly caught mudcrabs for lunch.

☎ (07) 5449 8405

Ex-HMAS *Brisbane*. (Stephen Davison)

Sunshine Coast Skydivers. *(SCS)*

Off-road driving

The forests of the Upper Mary Valley around Kenilworth, Jimna and Conondale offer good four-wheel driving, as do the sandy tracks of Cooloola and Rainbow Beach towards the northern end of the park, but be warned, this is a notorious stretch of beach that claims more than 70 vehicles a year. Lower your tyre pressure and check tides before you go–even at low tide you'll sometimes have to drive through axle-deep water. Noosa Nature Tours offer half-day 4WD Sand Safaris in Cooloola. Beyond Noosa run 4WD trips to the Coloured Sands, Rainbow Beach, Carlo Sand Blow and Double Island Point.

www.naturetours.com.au www.beyondnoosa.com.au

Go karts

The Big Kart Track in Landsborough is the largest in the country: 1200m long with sweeping bends, challenging chicanes, hair-raising hairpins and super-charged straights. There are 60 go-karts, a kids track and the Bungy Bullet that shoots you 50m in the air at speeds of up to 400km/h and experiencing 4Gs. Night racing is also available.

www.bigkart.com.au

Horse riding

A range of horse riding adventures are available on the Sunshine Coast. The well-mannered horses at Clip Clop Treks on the Weyba Downs near Caloundra will take you on trail rides from two hours to a full day or longer for the more experienced with varying routes though the shallow Lake Weyba and hinterland rainforest.

www.clipcloptreks.com.au

Mooloolah Valley Riding Centre has horses and ponies to suit all riders in the Mooloolah Valley.

www.mooloolahvalley.com

Wattle Gully Trail Rides wind through native bushland, crossing creeks and gullies around Maleny and include a cool dip in a mountain creek to finish off your ride.

www.wattlegully.com

The Animal Farm at Maleny has 380 acres of horse trails over rolling green hills with creeks, spring-fed dams and cascading waterfalls.

www.malenyaccom.com.au

Kitesurfing

Noosa is one of Australia's top kitesurfing destinations, particularly on the Noosa River. Kitesurf Australia at Noosaville offers sales, lessons and hire. Lessons range from one-hour basics to four-hour self-sufficiency courses as well as private one-on-one lessons.

www.adventuresports.net.au www.goactiv.com.au

Golden Beach Hire, in Caloundra, hire catamarans, windsurfers, double kayaks and single paddle skis. Fully qualified instructors teach sailing, catamaran, windsurfing as well as kitesurfing. Introductory lessons are two hours, but four or eight hour lessons are recommended to consolidate kitesurfing technique and safety.

www.goldenbeachhire.com www.kiteaction.com.au

Paragliding

Paraglide over the Coloured Sands on Rainbow Beach and Tewah Beach with Paragliding Rainbow Australia. Tandem flights last up to 30 minutes and travel up to 40km along a spectacular dune system. You can also enrol in eight-session novice pilot courses to fly solo.

www.paraglidingrainbow.com

Sailing

Learn to sail in the luxury of a magnificent sailing yacht with a qualified skipper to sail you around your chosen cruising area at your own pace with the Sunshine Coast Sailing Academy in Mooloolaba. While you plan your itinerary, they will advise you on the best snorkelling spots, sheltered anchorages and local attractions and your Skipper can provide sailing instruction for novices and help you brush up your navigational skills, or you can just sit back, relax and soak up the sunshine. On a smaller scale, Noosa Beach Catamarans in Hastings Street have catamarans for hire and also offer sailing lessons.

www.learn2sail.com.au

Skydiving

Sunshine Coast Skydivers at Caloundra offer one of the few beach drop zones in Australia: landing right on the beach. Skydive over the coast with a choice of 10 seconds freefall from 6000ft, 45 seconds from 12,000ft or 65 seconds from 14,000ft before floating serenely through the sky under a parachute built for two to a soft, beach landing. They also offer night jumps from 12,000ft with spectacular views of the coast lit up below, again with a beach landing. No experience is needed–you'll be safely fastened to an expert instructor.

www.jumpscs.com

Skydive Ramblers at Coolum Beach also offer beach landings. Jump from 14,000ft with 60 seconds freefall and a five-minute parachute ride. All jumps are videoed so you can watch it before you buy.

www.ramblers.com.au

Surfing

The Sunshine Coast is famous for its waves. Noosa's Surf Festival each March draws the surfers from all over the world and the Noosa Blue Water Swim in May is a 2km race at Noosa's Main Beach. Former world champion surfer Merrick Davis runs Noosa Learn to Surf and guarantees that you will be standing upright on the board on your first lesson.

www.learntosurf.com.au

Noosa Longboards hire old-fashioned boards (Malibus are a speciality) and offer surfing lessons as well.

www.noosalongboards.com

Windsurfing

The Sunshine Coast is Queensland's most popular windsurfing destination. Only an hour's drive north of Brisbane, Golden Beach, Caloundra, offers a great day's sailing as do other great beaches and bays along the coast. Golden Beach is the best flat-water beach for freeriding, slalom and speed runs as it handles all wind directions except west and south-westerlies. Bulcock Beach/Happy Valley offers good bump'n'jump and waveriding in a south-easterly (watch the ebbing tide). Some 40km of open beaches from Caloundra to Noosa are perfect for windsurfing, with good swell and waves. Popular offshore spots are North Caloundra (Dicky Beach and Ann St), Kawana, Mooloolaba (the spit), Maroochydore Surf Club, Mudjimba, Coolum, Perigian and Sunshine Beach. Noosa also has flat water beaches along the river. The best freeride/bump'n'jump spot is at the river mouth in a north-easterly. Lake Cootharaba offers great lake sailing with good camping spots. Sunshine Coast Sailboards are the one-stop shop for both windsurfing and kitesurfing gear, rentals and instruction.

www.windsurfing.com.au ☎ (07) 5492 4344
www.goldenbeachhire.com ☎ mob: 0404 372 703

Sunshine Coast kitesurfer. *(accent)*

MORE INFORMATION

- **Noosa Information Centre:** Hastings Street, Noosa. ☎ 1800 448 833. www.tourismnoosa.com.au
- **Caloundra City Tourist Information Centre:** 7 Caloundra Road, Caloundra. ☎ 1800 700 899. www.caloundratourism.com.au
- **Maroochy Tourism & Travel:** Cnr First Ave & Brisbane Road, ☎ 1800 882 032. www.maroochytourism.com www.tourismsunshinecoast.com.au

weather watch

- January: 17–25°C
- July: 9–15°C
- Summer can be warm, wet and humid, winter is temperate and drier.

the gold coast

Surfers Paradise. *(TQ)*

Hinterland trail riding. *(TQ)*

► Golden beaches, a green mountain hinterland and the most varied theme park attractions in Australia make Queensland's Gold Coast the country's most popular holiday playground. Sixty-five kilometres south-east of Brisbane, the region's 42km coastline stretches from Southport to Coolangatta and basks in more than 300 days of sunshine each year.

Originally settled by timber getters in the 1850s. Once the prized cedar was logged out the area was transformed into a green swathe of dairy farms and sugar cane fields. By the turn of the 20th century, the beautiful beaches were increasingly popular with tourists and, in 1933, the area was named Surfers Paradise. The 1950s and 60s saw a beachside high-rise development boom and, by the 1970s, Surfers Paradise and the Gold Coast were entrenched as the country's holiday metropolis.

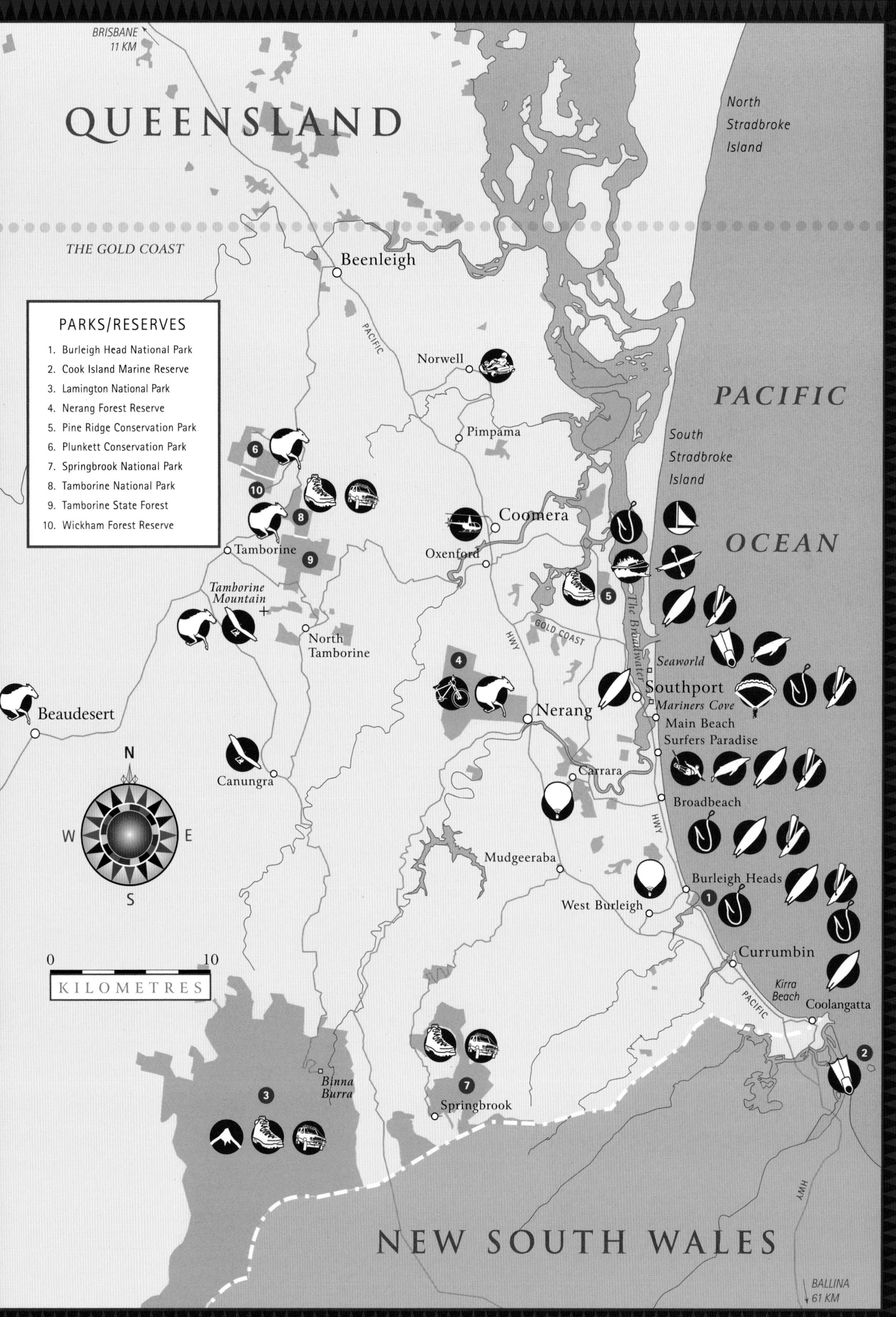
BRISBANE
11 KM
QUEENSLAND
North
Stradbroke
Island
THE GOLD COAST
Beenleigh
PARKS/RESERVES
1. Burleigh Head National Park
2. Cook Island Marine Reserve
3. Lamington National Park
4. Nerang Forest Reserve
5. Pine Ridge Conservation Park
6. Plunkett Conservation Park
7. Springbrook National Park
8. Tamborine National Park
9. Tamborine State Forest
10. Wickham Forest Reserve
PACIFIC
Norwell
PACIFIC
Pimpama
South
Stradbroke
Island
Coomera
OCEAN
Oxenford
Tamborine
Tamborine
Mountain
North
Tamborine
GOLD COAST
HWY
The Broadwater
Seaworld
Southport
Mariners Cove
Main Beach
Surfers Paradise
Beaudesert
Nerang
N
Canungra
Carrara
Broadbeach
W
E
HWY
Mudgeeraba
Burleigh Heads
S
West Burleigh
0
10
KILOMETRES
Currumbin
Kirra
Beach
Coolangatta
PACIFIC
Binna
Burra
Springbrook
HWY
NEW SOUTH WALES
BALLINA
61 KM

NATIONAL PARKS

Springbrook National Park: part of the Scenic Rim, a chain of mountains stretching across the Queensland–New South Wales border with a spectacular landscape of cliffs, gorges and waterfalls and panoramic views. One of the most popular attractions is the Natural Arch, where a waterfall cuts through a rock bridge.

Lamington National Park: protecting one of the largest remaining tracts of subtropical rainforest in Australia, Lamington is also part of the Scenic Rim. Highlights include waterfalls, stands of 15,000-year-old Antarctic beech trees and more than 160km of walking tracks and the treetops canopy walk, a 20m-high suspended walk amongst the rainforest canopy. O'Reilly's Guesthouse inside the park has restaurant and bar facilities.

Tamborine National Park: the park is split into several sections of subtropical rainforest and open forest on and around the slopes of Tamborine Mountain plateau. Queensland's first national park was established at Witches Falls in 1908. There are 22km of graded walking tracks, with most walks taking less than half a day. Palm Grove, Witches Falls and The Knoll have spectacular views, and Zamia Grove has ancient cycads, relics of plants which flourished 150 million years ago.

Burleigh Head National Park: in the heart of the busy Gold Coast, this small park protects remnants of littoral rainforest, mangroves, windswept open grasslands and a headland called Jellurgal by the local Kombumerri people. Tumgun Lookout is a good place to watch for passing whales and dolphins.

Pine Ridge Conservation Park: one of the last wallum remnants on the Gold Coast. It has open eucalypt forest with bloodwood trees, wallum banskia woodland, heath and paperbark swamp forest.

Binna Burra. *(TQ)*

Gold Coast lifesavers. *(New Holland Image Library)*

Surfers Paradise and beaches

The heart of the Gold Coast is in the built up areas around Surfers Paradise, Broadbeach, Main Beach and Southport, with the most popular beaches being Surfers Paradise, Broadbeach, Burleigh Heads, Currumbin and Coolangatta. This is also where you find the concentration of shops, restaurants and family theme parks and tourist attractions.

www.goldcoasttourism.info

The hinterland

In sharp contrast to the beachside bling and bluster, to the west of the chrome and glass towers is an area of rugged volcanic ridges in a national park wilderness with World Heritage rainforests and cool mountain-top villages such as Tambourine Mountain and Canungra and, in the valleys beyond, the rural centre of Beaudesert.

Caravan and camping

There are a host of commercial caravan parks on the Gold Coast, ranging from basic to luxurious four-star tourist parks. However, if you want to camp, best bet is to head to one of the hinterland national parks. Camping is permitted in the Green Mountains section of Lamington National Park and you can bush camp in the park between February and November. All campsites must be booked and paid for three weeks in advance through the Green Mountains office or online.

www.epa.qld.gov.au

Binna Burra Lodge has powered and unpowered caravan sites.

www.binnaburralodge.com.au ☎ 1800 074 260

In Springbrook National Park you can camp at Purling Brook Falls, but campsites are limited and bookings are essential. The campground has very basic facilities (no showers or bins) and is unsuitable for caravans.

Snapper Rocks, Coolangatta. *(TQ)*

DON'T MISS

- **Sea World:** daily exhibition of stunt water skiing, the tiger sharks of Shark Bay, seal and dolphin presentations, Australia's only polar bears, the chance to swim with dolphins, or if you're really game, sharks, plus exciting rides like the Corkscrew Roller Coaster and Bermuda Triangle. Sea World Drive, Main Beach. Open daily, 10am–5.30pm. www.seaworld.com.au
- **Dreamworld:** home to the tallest, fastest thrill rides in the world, Tiger Island, The Australian Wildlife Experience, Big Brother, Nickelodeon Central and Wiggles World. Dreamworld Parkway, Coomera. Open daily, 10am–5pm. www.dreamworld.com.au
- **Wet 'n' Wild Water Park:** Australia's largest water theme park with slides, pools, rides and entertainment. All pools and slides are heated during the cooler months of the year (April through to September). Pacific Motorway, Oxenford. Open from 10am daily, closing times vary. www.wetnwild.com.au
- **Warner Bros. Movie World:** movie-related theme park with behind-the-scenes action, comedy stunts and exhilarating rides and shows. Pacific Motorway, Oxenford. Open daily, 10am–5.30pm. www.movieworld.com.au
- **Currumbin Wildlife Sanctuary:** 27 hectares of landscaped surrounds and bushland with more than 1400 Australian native mammals, birds and reptiles. 28 Tomewin Street, Currumbin. Open daily. www.currumbin-sanctuary.org.au
- **Tropical Fruit World:** tropical fruit farm growing more than 500 different varieties of rare and exotic tropical fruits. Tours and rides available. Duranbah Road, Duranbah. Open daily, 10am–4.30pm. www.tropicalfruitworld.com.au
- **Ripley's Believe It or Not! Museum:** 12 themed galleries featuring hundreds of the world's most unbelievable exhibits, movies, magic, and fun interactive displays. Cavill Avenue, Surfers Paradise. Open daily, 9am–11pm. ☎ (07) 5592 0040.
- **Canungra Valley Vineyards:** vines encircle historic *Killowen* homestead, which is now a restaurant and cellar door. On Sundays there's live jazz or you can buy a gourmet picnic basket and some wine to eat beside the creek. Lamington National Park Road., on the outskirts of Canungra. Open daily, 9am–5pm. www.canungravineyards.com.au
- **Heritage Wines:** family-owned winery and restaurant with views of the Gold Coast. Cnr The Shelf and Bartle Road, Mount Tamborine. Open daily, 10am–4pm.
- **Tamborine Mountain Distillery:** local fruits are fermented and distilled in a small 'Pot Still' to create liqueurs, schnapps, vodkas, and liqueur chocolates. 87 Beacon Road, North Tamborine. Open Wed-Sun, 10am–4pm for tastings and sales.
- **Thunderbird Park:** a geological centre featuring the world's largest thunder egg mine (20 million year old egg-shaped lava cut with a diamond saw to reveal semi-precious minerals). Activities include horse-riding, massage, wildlife sanctuary and bird feeding. Cedar Creek Lodge, Mount Tamborine. Open daily, 9.30am–4pm.
- **The Gallery Walk:** Long Road. between the villages of North Tamborine and Eagles Heights is home to several galleries, craft shops, coffee shops and antique stores.

scenic highlights

Curtis Falls. *(TQ)*

The beauty of south-east Queensland is that, no matter where you are, even in the middle of the glittering high rise strip of the Gold Coast, you're never far from the wilder side of life. Just one hour from Brisbane, half an hour from the Gold Coast, is an altogether different world—mountains, rainforest, valleys, wide plains and World Heritage wilderness—the green behind the gold.

Known as the Scenic Rim it's a chain of craggy mountains and high plateaus cut through with rich, fertile river valleys, dotted with historic townships and magnificent rainforests. It roughly curves around Brisbane and includes 21 national parks, but you'll need more than a day to explore it all. If you've only got one day, then your best bet is to head south.

First stop should be Tamborine Mountain—around an hour's drive south of Brisbane. The air up here is cooler and the views from the plateau are fantastic, but the drive is steep, winding and narrow. Stop and explore the villages of Mt Tamborine, Tamborine Village, North Tamborine and Eagle Heights. Shoppers should head for Gallery Walk on Long Road, a string of galleries, craft shops, antique stores, cafes and eateries.

Head south to Lamington National Park. Highlights of the park include some of the 150 waterfalls and stands of 15,000-year-old Antarctic beech trees as well as the treetops canopy walk. There are two entrances to the park. The Green Mountains entrance is 115km south of Brisbane via Canungra; or 70km from Surfers via Nerang and Canungra. Binna Burra is 107km from Brisbane via Canungra and 55km from the Gold Coast. Both routes are fully sealed, but the road to Green Mountains is too steep and winding for caravans.

If you prefer wining and dining to bush-walking you can also follow the Scenic Rim wine trail. There are nine wineries on the trail, six in the Canungra/North Tamborine triangle. Maps are available from visitor centres in the area.

Bushwalks

The Gold Coast Hinterland Great Walk is a 38km-long walk linking the Green Mountains section of Lamington National Park with Springbrook National Park and is expected to open in late 2006. Highlights will include spectacular views, ancient Antarctic beech forests, waterfalls and geological formations, extensive views of erosion-carved cliffs, Mt Warning (an extinct volcanic core) and sweeping views of the Tweed and Limpinwood Valleys.

There are more than 160km of walking tracks in Lamington National Park. The Treetops Canopy Walk at O'Reillys is a 20m-high suspended walk amongst the rainforest canopy and was the first of its kind to be built in Australia. The 22km Border Track forms the back-bone of most of the trails in the park and connects Binna Burra and Green Mountains. It's a difficult track but rewarding as it winds its way through rainforest and patches of Antarctic beech forest with lookouts along the way providing spectacular views of the Lamington area, Mt Warning and the Tweed Range. Other good walks include the 20km Albert River Circuit with waterfalls, stunning temperate rain-forest featuring Antarctic beech and coachwood and great views into northern NSW; the 11km Box Forest Circuit featuring enormous 1500-year-old brush box trees, beautiful creek scenery, swimming holes and waterfalls, including Elabana Falls; the 18km Coomera Circuit with lots of waterfalls including Coomera, one of the most spectacular in the park, and the 13km Dave's Creek Track, which is a good walk for wildflowers during spring.

In Springbrook National Park the 4km loop to Purling Brook Falls is the most popular walk and the 90-minute Twin Falls circuit is a good introduction to the park with rainforest, open forest and montane heath, waterfalls and scenic views. It's an easy 30-minute stroll to the Natural Arch, where a waterfall cuts through a rock bridge. The longer Warrie Circuit (17km) features many waterfalls along the route and a wide variety of vegetation–start the walk from Tallanbana picnic area or Canyon Lookout.

In Tamborine National Park the 30-minute Cedar Creek Falls Track is an easy stroll to a lookout with views of waterfalls, cascades and rock pools and the one-hour Palm Grove Rainforest Circuit winds through piccabeen palm groves and rainforest with emergent strangler figs. On the 30-minute Curtis Falls Track you walk through rainforest and descend steep stairs to a large pool at the base of Curtis Falls for an impressive view of the falls and surrounding columnar basalt rockface and the one-hour Sandy Creek Circuit, offers scenic views, rainforest and tall trees and a cliff-edge section. The 3km Witches Falls Circuit zigzags down the steep mountainside through open forest with banksia trees and into rainforest with huge strangler figs, past seasonal lagoons to Witches Falls, which flow only after rain.

adventure activities

Abseiling and rockclimbing

Binna Burra Mountain Lodge in Lamington National Park offers one-day abseiling courses that begin with a rappel down a 10m volcanic escarpment before moving on to tackle specially selected 40m or 90m cliff-face. They also have a 160m flying fox on which you can fly through the rainforest canopy.

www.binnaburralodge.com.au

Aerobatic joy flights

Tiger Moth Joy Rides offer heart-stopping aerobatic flights viewing the Gold Coast upside down from 4000ft as part of their range of scenic joy flights in a restored 1931 open-cockpit Tiger Moth bi-plane that flies along the Gold Coast high-rise strip. Formation flights are available for those who want to fly with a friend. Flights depart from Albatros Airfield, Abraham Road, Coomera.

www.tigermothjoyrides.com.au

Barnstormers Australia offer scenic and aerobatic joy flights over the Gold Coast and hinterland in a new Super Waco, a reproduction of the classic 1935 bi-plane. The twin cockpit has room for two passengers.

www.barnstormers.ws

Amphibious tours

Behind the beaches of the Gold Coast there are nine times more man-made canals and waterways than Venice. Adventure Duck and Aquaduck Safaris both offer land and water tours of the Gold Coast roads, canals and waterways in amphibious buses, taking in all the major sites as well as a close up view of the millionaires houses and yachts along the canals and in the marinas.

www.adventureduck.com www.aquabus.com.au

Ballooning

The Gold Coast is a great place to go hot air ballooning, especially for keen photographers, as you can expect views from Brisbane to Byron Bay and early morning silhouettes of the high rise buildings of Surfers Paradise and coastline, floating over rural farmland, golf courses, rain-forests and waterfalls. Balloon Down Under, based at Burleigh West, and Balloon Aloft, based at Carrara, both offer one-hour sunrise balloon flights over the Gold Coast hinterland, high-rise strip and canals, followed by champagne breakfasts.

www.balloondownunder.com.au www.balloonaloft.net

Bungy jumping

Take the plunge at Bungy Australia's 37m-high tower in the heart of Surfers Paradise. Originating in the Pentecost Islands as an initiation ritual into manhood, bungy jumping has grown into one of the world's most popular high adrenalin experiences. For something a little different try the after dark Bungy. Bungy Australia is the only bungy jump in the southern hemisphere offering nightly evening jumps.

www.bungyaustralia.com.au

Lamington National Park (TQ)

Canoeing and kayaking

Splash Safaris Sea Kayaking Adventures run regular full-day adventure tours across the Broadwater and to South Stradbroke Island that include kayaking, snorkelling, guided walks and kayak sailing if winds are favourable, as well as half-day paddling trips to Wavebreak Island.

www.seakayakingtours.com

Australian Kayaking Adventures also run similar tours, including morning dolphin tours.

www.australiankayakingadventures.com.au

Cycling and mountain biking

The V1 Bikeway is a 35km-long cycleway that stretches from Smith Street at Gaven to the Logan River at Beenleigh, linking local parks, major theme parks such as Dreamworld and Movieworld and some of the local tourist attractions like the Strawberry Farm at Pimpama. In Nerang Forest Reserve there are several good mountain bike trails, including the short, but pretty, Casuarina Grove track through the dry open forest and along the creek. Tracks are challenging with tight twists and turns, creek crossings and full of roots and ruts. One of the most popular trails is the Three Hills Climb. You will need a permit to explore the forest tracks.

☎ (07) 3227 7800

Diving

Dive with sharks at Seaworld's Shark Bay–the world's largest man-made lagoon system for sharks and home to some of the most awe-inspiring of the species. Scuba dive or snorkel amongst Shark Bay's whitetip and blacktip reef sharks and join in an exhilarating shark feeding session. The one-hour adventure includes approximately 20 minutes in the water accompanied by a dive escort to ensure your safety at all times. All shark scuba participants must have (and present on the day) a current diving certification. Alternatively, you can also take a snorkelling tour with the sharks.

Sea World also offers non-divers a unique underwater dolphin experience: The Dolphin Helmet Dive, using a helmet device.

www.seaworld.com.au

Local dive sites include the 100-year-old shipwreck *Scottish Prince*, and several reefs with tropical fish, leopard sharks and large pelagic fish. Cook Island Marine Reserve has a range of dives from caves and tunnels to gradually sloping ledges ideal for exploring. Advanced divers should try Nine Mile Reef's Shark Alley with grey nurse sharks in winter and leopard sharks and bullrays in summer and the Canyons, a deep dive along a spur of reef with big splits and caves joining most of them. For more local dive sites visit:

www.oceandive.qld.ms

Dolphin and whale watching

From June to November humpback whales cruise past the Gold Coast on their annual migration. Many whale-watching tours are available.

www.whalewatchinggoldcoast.net.au

www.spiritofthebay.com.au

You can also get up close and personal with dolphins at Sea World as part of the Dolphin Aqua Adventure Program, interacting with dolphins on a submerged platform in a deep-water lagoon pool. The trained dolphins are quite comfortable with the human interaction and will often perform tricks for you–driving up from below to leap through your outstretched arms, floating on their backs while you stroke their bellies or posing with you while you hug them for a photograph. Group sizes are limited to 12 and can only be booked upon arrival at Sea World, on a first come basis. You can buy tickets at the Dolphin Encounters sales booth located at the main entrance of Sea World from 9am until sold out. All guests, including children, wishing to participate in a program must be present when purchasing tickets.

www.seaworld.com.au/entertainment/animal_interactive.cfm

☎ (07) 5588 2222

Fishing

The Gold Coast waters between Coolangatta and Southport provide good estuary and offshore fishing with bream runs in winter and large summer flathead. The Broadwater is good for whiting and offshore reefs are often frequented by snapper. The area is becoming increasingly well-known for big game fish, including marlin, and there are several fishing charter companies available for day trips.

Off-road driving

Most of the good 4WD tracks in the Gold Coast hinterland are private roads, so the best way to get off road is to join a commercial off-road tour. 4WD Mountain Trek Adventures specialise in full and half day tours to Lamington National Park, Tamborine Mountain Plateau and Springbrook Plateau, travelling through prime beef and farming land and rainforests, visiting cascading waterfalls, spectacular scenery and unique wildlife.

www.bigvolcano.com.au/custom/mtntrek

Horse riding

The Beaudesert and Gold Coast region has a network of more than 200km of horse riding trails in and around Plunkett Conservation Park and the boundaries of Wickham and Tamborine Forest Reserves and along unformed gazetted roads, easements, council lands and along the boundaries of Nerang and Clagiraba forest reserves.

There are also a number of farms and stables throughout the hinterland that offer trail rides. Fellcrag Appaloosa Trail Rides at Bromelton near Beaudesert have rides ranging from one hour to an all-day experience to the top of the nearby range with 360-degree views out to the Scenic Rim, Mt Tamborine and the skyscrapers of Brisbane.

www.fellcrag.com

Tamborine Mountain Trail Rides offer easy rides for beginners that wind through the rainforest as well as the more exciting one-hour Mine Ride down one of the world's largest volcanic rock mines and the adventurous Roller Coaster Ride, an exhilarating up and down ride through the forest.

www.horseridingqld.com

The Tally Park Riding Ranch, in a beautiful valley five minutes' drive from Palm Beach, provides horse riding lessons as well as trail rides.

www.tallypark.com.au

Hot laps

The Holden Performance Driving Centre at Norwell is a driver training facility with a 2km circuit, skidpan, offroad track and 'The Turntable', a unique skid simulator. The centre uses a range of training vehicles and courses range from introductory, for new licence holders, through to the CAMS Motorsport Licence Course for budding racers.

Strap in for four very fast Hot Laps in a V8 SS Commodore with one of the centre's professional instructors; or drive a V8 Supercar yourself at the V8 Super School, where you can sign up for classroom and in-car instruction with professional race drivers in performance vehicles and drive 12 laps (three lots of four-lap sessions) in your choice of either a Holden or a Ford.

www.performancedriving.com.au

Jet boating

Take a high-speed cruise of The Broadwater in a supercharged jet boat travelling at speeds of up to 80km/h. Experience fish tails, wave surfing, beach blasting, massive sideward slides and incredible 360-degree spins, weaving around Wavebreak Island and across the Gold Coast Seaway before blasting along the fringe of pristine white beaches and down the Western Channel. Jet boat rides are between 30 and 45 minutes, depending on the tour.

www.ozjetboating.com www.extremejetboating.com

www.paradisejetboating.com.au

Hang-gliding and Paragliding

The high peaks of the Gold Coast hinterland around Mount Tamborine and Beechmont are Queensland's major centre for hang-gliding and paragliding. The Paragliding Centre of South East Queensland offer two-day introductory and full licence training courses, along with tandem instructional flights in the Canungra-Mt Tamborine area. Courses run weekdays and weekends, but bookings are essential.

www.paraglidingcentre.com.au

The Canungra Hang Gliding Club has details of local competitions and instructors.

www.chgc.asn.au

Sailing

Take a cruise on the tall ship *Sir Henry Morgan* or *Maranoa* to a range of Gold Coast destinations, including McLarens Landing Homestead, a unique $2 million privately-owned resort on South Stradbroke Island. Tours vary, but options include speed boat and paraflying off the ship, rainforest tours, and resort activities such as the golf driving range, jet skiing, wind surfing, mountain bikes and sail boats.

www.tallship.com.au

Sky diving

Sky Dive Queensland offer two choices for novice skydivers–a tandem parachute jump from 14,000ft over the beautiful Kooralbyn Hotel Resort in the Gold Coast hinterland, or for something unique, a tandem skydive from a helicopter over Surfers Paradise beaches, the only place you can jump from a helicopter in Australia. Taking off from Mariners Cove, you jump from the helicopter as it hovers at 10,000ft over the ocean, landing right by SeaWorld.

www.skydivequeensland.com.au

Surfing

They don't call it Surfers Paradise for nothing–the Gold Coast is home to some truly spectacular beaches and surfing is a major sport on the Gold Coast, attracting some of the world's best competitors. Duranbah, Burleigh Point, Kirra and South Stradbroke are just four of the many great surfing spots, providing pumping surf and great barrels. The Gold Coast has played host to international championships such as the Billabong Pro and Broadbeach is home to Kurrawa Surf Life Saving Club, host of the annual Australian Surf Lifesaving Titles each March. Most weekends there will be a surf carnival at one of the local beaches.

For beginners there are literally dozens of learn to surf schools on the coast, many run by former champions. Brad Holmes Surf Coaching is the first surfing coach qualified for the disabled, and can handle nearly every type of intellectual and physical disabilities.

www.bradholmessurfcoaching.com

See Surfing Australia for a comprehensive list of registered surf schools in Queensland and around the country.

www.surfingaustralia.com

Zorbs on the Gold Coast.

Zorbing

A zorb, the latest adventure import from New Zealand, is a 3.5m-tall inflated clear plastic ball with another ball suspended inside. Zorbing is the art of strapping yourself inside that ball in a harness and rolling down a hill at speeds of up to 50km per hour. A 700mm cushion of air between you and the ground keeps you safe as you hurtle down the slope–if you are dry zorbing. Otherwise, wet zorbing, or hydro-zorbing, is just you (and maybe some friends) loose in the zorb with 25 litres of water. Try it out at Zorb Gold Coast on the Old Pacific Highway at Pimpama.

www.zorb.com

MORE INFORMATION

- **Surfers Paradise Visitor Information Centre:** Cavill Avenue, Surfers Paradise, ☎ 1300 309 440.
- **Gold Coast Tourism Bureau:** ☎ (07) 5592 2699 www.verygc.com

weather watch

- January: 17–26°C
- July: 8–17°C
- Summer is temperate, with the ranges being much cooler than the coast. Winter is more likely to be dry and sunny.

the fraser & capricorn coast

Lake Wabby Lookout. [TQ]

▶ STRADDLING THE TROPIC of Capricorn, the Fraser and Capricorn Coast stretches from the famous whale watching playground of Hervey Bay and World Heritage-listed Fraser Island north to Rockhampton, Australia's beef capital.

Agriculture, farming and tourism seem to co-exist happily along this stretch of coast that offers beautiful beaches, endless fields of sugar cane, diverse national parks and untamed bushland and friendly towns without the blight of over-the-top coastal development.

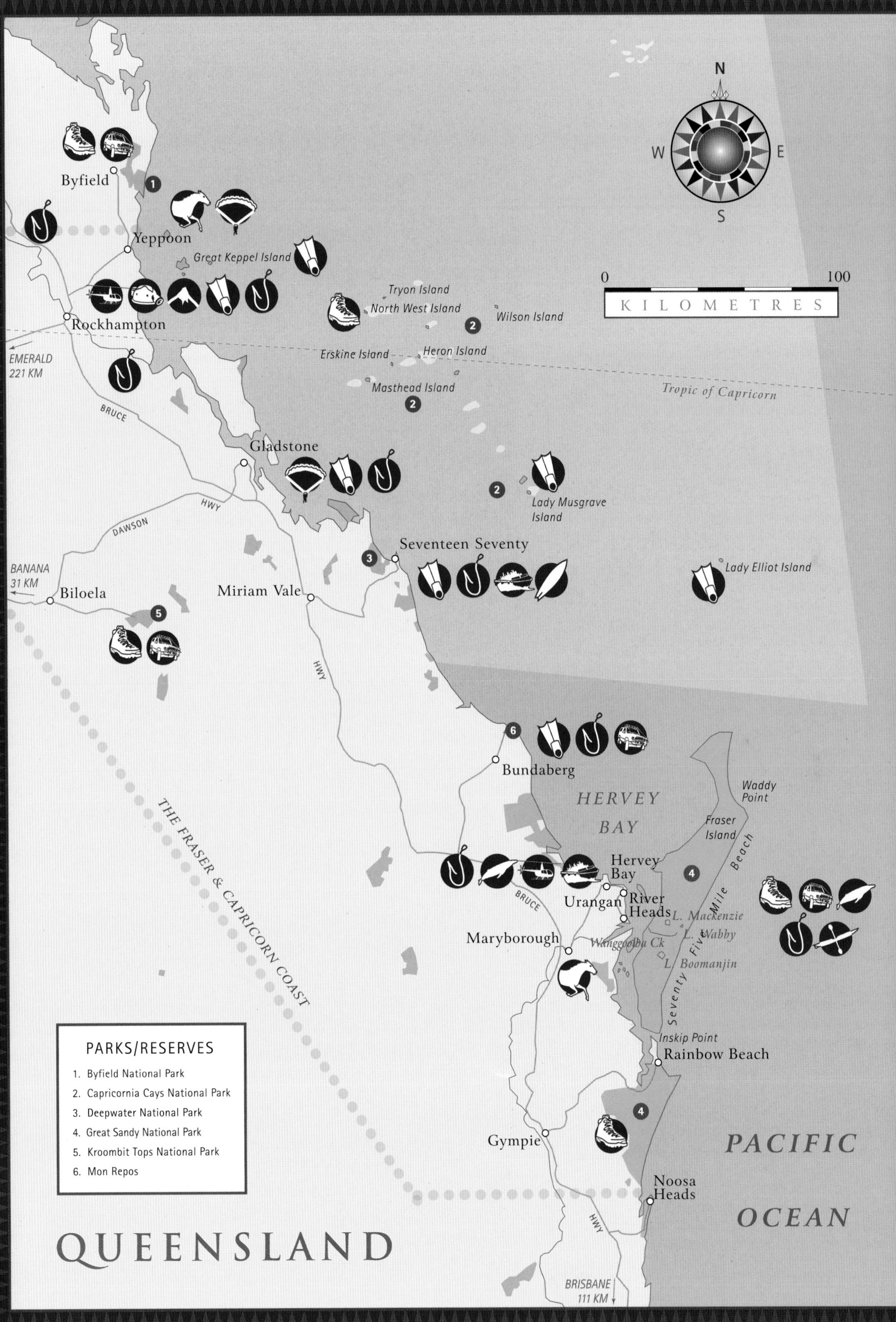

N
W
E
S
0
100
KILOMETRES
Byfield
Yeppoon
Great Keppel Island
Rockhampton
EMERALD 221 KM
BRUCE
Tryon Island
North West Island
Wilson Island
Erskine Island
Heron Island
Masthead Island
Tropic of Capricorn
Gladstone
HWY
DAWSON
Lady Musgrave Island
Seventeen Seventy
BANANA 31 KM
Biloela
Miriam Vale
Lady Elliot Island
HWY
Bundaberg
HERVEY BAY
Waddy Point
Fraser Island
Hervey Bay
Urangan
River Heads
BRUCE
L. Mackenzie
L. Wabby
L. Boomanjin
Wanggoolba Ck
Maryborough
Seventy Five Mile Beach
THE FRASER & CAPRICORN COAST
Inskip Point
Rainbow Beach
Gympie
Noosa Heads
PACIFIC OCEAN
HWY
BRISBANE 111 KM
PARKS/RESERVES
1. Byfield National Park
2. Capricornia Cays National Park
3. Deepwater National Park
4. Great Sandy National Park
5. Kroombit Tops National Park
6. Mon Repos
QUEENSLAND

NATIONAL PARKS

Fraser Island (Great Sandy National Park): a World Heritage wilderness with towering rainforest, massive sandblows, beautiful freshwater lakes and continuous beach. It is the only place in the world where tall rainforests grow on sand dunes over 200m and has half the world's perched dune lakes (40 on the island). These lakes form when organic matter—leaves, bark and dead plants—gradually builds up and hardens in depressions created by the wind. There are also barrage lakes, formed when moving sand dunes block a watercourse, and window lakes, formed when a depression exposes part of the regional water table. Dingos on the island are regarded as the most pure strain in eastern Australia. Most of the island is only accessible by 4WD or boat. Hire and tours are readily available.

Mon Repo Conservation Park: 14km east of Bundaberg, is the rookery for the largest number of nesting loggerhead turtles on mainland eastern Australia. Between November and March, you can watch one of nature's fascinating spectacles—the annual onshore pilgrimage of sea turtles as they come ashore to lay their eggs—and the subsequent hatching of young sea turtles eight weeks later and their return to the sea. The best time to see turtles laying eggs is after dark from mid-November to February. Hatchlings usually leave their nests to begin their journey to the sea at night from mid-January until late March. If you visit in January you might be lucky enough to see both adults and hatchlings. From 6pm–6am, public access to Mon Repos Beach is restricted. Turtle viewing is through the Mon Repos Information Centre from 7pm–1am. Ranger guided tours operate nightly from November to late March. For bookings ☎ (07) 4153 8888.

Capricornia Cays National Park: Capricorn and Bunker are 22 reefs sprinkled across the Tropic of Capricorn at the southern end of the Great Barrier Reef. The national park protects eight vegetated coral cays and part of Heron Island. The islands are only a few metres above the high water mark, except North West Island, which rises to 6m at its eastern end. You can walk around North West and Masthead islands in a few hours and Lady Musgrave in 45 minutes. Seasonal closures to protect breeding seabirds or high tides can restrict walks. The islands are accessible only by boat. Gladstone, Bundaberg and 1770 are the closest towns.

Byfield National Park and Conservation Park: north of Rockhampton features outstanding coastal scenery. The southern section is mainly massive parabolic sand dunes, the oldest reaching 5–6km inland. In the north, the rugged granite pinnacles of The Peaks and Mt Atherton dominate the landscape. Large areas of coastal heath grow on the low-nutrient dune sands. In sheltered areas you'll find eucalypt woodlands and rainforest. Birdlife is prolific.

Kroombit Tops National Park and Forest Reserve: this 800–900m-high plateau is a large erosion caldera up to 40m across, formed by past volcanic activity. Highlights include rugged mountain scenery, sandstone cliffs and gorges, creeks, waterfalls, woodland, subtropical and dry rainforest.

Sandy Cape lighthouse, Fraser Island. *(New Holland Image Library)*

Hervey Bay and Fraser Island

Hervey Bay is one of the best places to see humpback whales; they stop here on their trip south to Antarctica taking advantage of the calm waters in the shelter provided by Fraser Island. The largest sand island in the world, 123km long and 22km wide, Fraser Island is the northernmost in a string of sand islands along the southern Queensland coast that includes Moreton Island near Brisbane and North and South Stradbroke Islands off the Gold Coast, formed over hundreds of thousands of years as winds, waves and ocean currents have carried sands from the eastern river systems of Australia out to the continental shelf and in towards the land again. The highest dune on the island is 244m, but most rise to between 100 and 200m above sea level and drilling shows that the sand extends to 100m below sea level in places.

Access to Fraser Island is via barge at Inskip Point on the northern end of Rainbow Beach and River Heads or ferry from Urangan Boat Harbour. All roads on the island are 4WD only.

Maryborough

On the banks of the Mary River, this gracious provincial city is one of Queensland's oldest and best preserved towns, full of beautiful heritage buildings and lovely old Queenslander-style homes. Take the self-guided heritage walk though the town to the original settlement site.

Bundaberg

One of Queensland's most prosperous coastal cities, Bundaberg is at the centre of the state's sugar industry and fields of cane surround the town. The town's name has become synonymous with one of the country's most popular drinks, Bundaberg (Bundy) Rum, which is distilled here. You can tour the distillery, visit offshore coral cay islands such as Lady Musgrove or Lady Elliot, Mon Repos turtle rookery or wander around the impressive historic buildings in the centre of town.

Rockhampton and the gem fields

Rockhampton, just a few kilometres north of the Tropic of Capricorn on the banks of the Fitzroy River, is Australia's beef capital; more than two million cattle graze the surrounding countryside. The city is full of elegant historic buildings with 30 listed as historically significant. To the west are some of the world's richest gem fields, the names of surrounding towns of Emerald, Rubyvale, Sapphire and Willows Gemfields give a clue to the gems found here, while Blackwater is the centre of the Queensland's coal mining industry.

Caravan and camping

Fraser Island has eight campgrounds: Central Station, Dundubara and Waddy Point, Lake Boomanjin, Waddy Point Beachfront, Ungowa, Lake Allom and Wathumba. Each has water taps or tap stations, and toilets. Most have gas barbecues, deep sinks for washing dishes and information displays. All campgrounds have a 9pm noise curfew and generators are not permitted. There are informal camping areas with no facilities behind the foredunes on the Eastern Beach and Western Beach offering quiet, wilderness experiences. Many are accessible by boat, but permits are still required. Generators are permitted in these areas, but please consider others and only use them between 9am and 9pm. There are also small, walk-in camping areas along the Fraser Island Great Walk set away from main campgrounds but they have few facilities. Walkers' camps are at Jabiru Swamp, Lake Boomanjin, Lake Benaroon, Central Station, Lake McKenzie, Lake Wabby (not situated near the lake), Valley of the Giants, Lake Garawongera and Dilli Village.

☎ (07) 4127 9130

Dingos are a threat to young children. If you are camping with children under the age of 14, camp only in fenced campgrounds, available at Lake Boomanjin, Central Station, Dundubara, Waddy Point (top campground) and Dilli Village.

You can also camp on three islands in the Capricornia Cays National Park, but you will need to purchase a camping permit in advance and book a site.

www.epa.qld.gov.au ☎ 13 13 04

Bookings can be made up to 11 months in advance and school holiday periods are often fully booked soon after bookings open. Lady Musgrave Island has space for 40 people at any one time and camping is permitted from the start of the Easter school holidays until the end of the summer school holidays in January. Masthead Island, a rookery for green and loggerhead turtles which breed on the island during spring and summer, has camping for up to 50 people from the start of the Easter school holidays to 15 October. No facilities are provided. North West Island, the second largest coral cay in the Great Barrier Reef has space for 150 campers from the start of the Easter school holidays until the end of the summer school holidays in January. Composting toilets, information displays, fuel storage and a compressor bunker are provided.

In Byfield National Park you can camp at Five Rocks visitor area, the park's only campground with facilities (picnic tables, toilets, cold showers and water) or you can beach camp at Nine Mile Beach in the 4.5km camping zone south of Freshwater Creek. Or bush camp Waterpark Point, which is only accessible by boat.

Most of Kroombit Tops is rugged wilderness but you can bush camp at The Wall along the circuit drive or at Griffiths Creek along the forest drive. Campfires are allowed but no facilities are provided.

scenic highlights

Eli Creek, Fraser Island

Whether you drive yourself or take a tour, Fraser Island is not to be missed. Lake Boomanjin is the largest perched lake in the world, covering almost 200ha. Its waters are stained brown by tannins leached from the vegetation. Central Station has several good walks though the rain-forest including the Wanggoolba Creek board-walk along a creek with water so clear it is almost invisible. Visit peaceful Basin Lake or stand among some impressive satinay trees in Pile Valley or in the aptly named Valley of the Giants.

One of the most popular sites is Lake McKenzie with white sand and clear, blue water and fantastic swimming. Lake Wabby, at the advancing edge of the Hammerstone Sandblow, is the deepest lake on the island. You can walk across the sand dunes to Ocean Beach, but the shadeless white sands can make for very hot walking in summer—go early in the morning and carry lots of water. Eli Creek is a crystal clear freshwater creek that flows right out to the beach and is very popular place to swim as you can walk the boardwalk then float with the current to the beach. The wreck of the *Maheno* lies slowly deteriorating on the water's edge, about 10km north of Happy Valley. The trans-Tasman liner, bound for a Japanese wrecking yard, was driven ashore during a cyclone in 1935.

Waddy Point headland, at the northern tip of Ocean Beach, offers great views of beach and ocean and you can often see sea turtles, sharks and stingrays in the water below. Champagne Pools, where the surf crashes over a series of rock walls into calm but bubbly rock pool below the headland, is another popular swimming spot.

Wonggoolba Creek, Fraser Island. (TQ)

Bushwalks

Fraser Island Great Walk is a 90km track that winds between Dilli Village and Happy Valley, passing iconic sites such as Lake McKenzie, Wanggoolba Creek, Lake Wabby and Central Station, as well as some of the island's most popular spots like the Valley of the Giants. There are also several short walks from Central Station, Kingfisher Bay Resort, Lake McKenzie, Lake Wabby, Lake Boomanjin and Eurong. Additional walking tracks link the Great Walk to the island's main barge landings, accommodation and supply centres.

There are short walking tracks across North West and Lady Musgrave islands or you can reef walk with care on the reefs surrounding all the Capricornia Cays. Walk in sand channels and avoid stepping on live corals–they are easily damaged and will cause nasty cuts.

In Kroombit Tops, a 700m return track, off the 4WD scenic drive, leads to the site of a WWII American bomber crash. *Beautiful Betsy*, a B-24D Liberator, disappeared on a flight from Brisbane's Eagle Farm in 1945, but the wreckage of it was only discovered in 1994, when a park ranger saw something glinting in the sunlight on the western side of the plateau. Informative signs explain the history of the incident. You must obtain a permit before driving through the forest.

See the subtropical rainforest and cool temperate rainforest just past the lookout. Rough tracks lead to other features but should only be attempted with Ranger advice. Be prepared for leeches if you walk through the rainforest.

The Queen Mary Sandblow is a difficult walk along an undefined track at the southern end of Nine Mile Beach in Byfield National Park. To access the beach you can take either Nine Mile Track or the Southern Track from Five Rocks visitor area. From the beach you will need to scramble over a sand cliff for about five metres. A sign on this dune's peak marks the start of a distinct walking track, which begins with a 500m walk through beach scrub and dune vegetation. Once on the sandblow it is quite exposed and the track is not defined. There are panoramic views from the peak. Take plenty of water and wear sun protective clothing.

DON'T MISS

- **Hervey Bay Historical Museum:** 14 historical buildings housing more than 3000 exhibits from the Fraser Coast and Wide Bay area, including a fully-furnished slab cottage built in 1898, the Goodwood Railway Station, the first Dundowran Hall, a fully equipped blacksmith shop, school and music room and Hervey Bay's original Methodist Church, built in 1901. 13 Zephyr Street, Scarness. Open Fri, Sat, Sun and public holidays,1–4.30pm.
- **Hervey Bay Natureworld:** Australian wildlife park in natural settings. Spotlight tours view nocturnal animals. Maryborough Road, Pialba. Open daily, 9am–5pm.

Bundaberg water tower. *(TQ)*

- **Neptune's Reefworld:** natural reef aquarium with living coral display, colourful fish, sharks, turtles and rays. Turtle pats, seal kisses and reef walks. Dayman Park, Pulgul Street, Urangan. Open daily, 9.30am–4.30pm.
- **Bundaberg Railway Museum:** Bundaberg's first railway station, built in 1881 as an outlet for the Mt Perry railway bringing copper from the mines, is now preserved as a railway museum and houses a wide variety of railway items past and present. 28 Station Street, Bundaberg North. Open Tue and Fri 9am–3pm and Sat 8am–4pm.
- **Bundaberg Rum Distillery:** take a guided distillery tour and taste your way through the rum production process that finishes with a few samples in the bar of a variety of Bundy mixes and rum liqueur based drinks. Whittred Street, Bundaberg. Open daily, tours on the hour Mon–Fri, 10am–3pm, weekends and public holidays, 10am–2pm. **www.bundabergrum.com.au**
- **Flying High Bird Habitat:** two-acre, 7m-high free-flight aviary with more than 1500 birds which can be observed at the different feeding stations along a 300m walking track. Bruce Highway, Corner Old Creek Road, Apple Tree Creek. Open daily, 9.30am–3.30pm.
- **Hinkler House Memorial Museum:** museum dedicated to Australian pioneer aviator, Squadron Leader Bert Hinkler, born in Bundaberg in 1892. Hinkler flew solo from England to Australia in 1928 in a small plane, *Ibis*, which he designed and built in the backyard of his English house. The house has been relocated to Bundaberg and is now the museum in the Botanic Gardens in North Bundaberg. Mt Perry Road, Botanic Gardens, Bundaberg. Open daily, 10am–4pm.
- **The Mystery Craters:** 35 craters in a massive slab of sandstone that have baffled teams of international geologists. 28km from Bundaberg on the Gin Gin Highway.
- **Snakes Down Under:** 90-minute venomous snake-handling show each Tue, Fri and Sat at 10am. 51 Lucketts Road, Childers. **www.snakesdownunder.com**
- **Gladstone Regional Art Gallery and Museum:** permanent and changing exhibitions. Goondoon Street, Gladstone. Open Mon–Sat, 10am–5pm.
- **Rockhampton Art Gallery:** Australian art collection including works by Sir Joshua Reynolds, Grace Cossington Smith, Charles Blackman, Arthur Boyd, John Coburn, Russell Drysdale, James Gleeson and Fred Williams. 62 Victoria Parade, Rockhampton. Open Mon–Fri, 10am–4pm; weekends, 11am–4pm.
- **Rockhampton Botanic Gardens and Zoo:** tropical gardens with excellent specimens of palms, cycads and ferns, some more than 100 years old. The zoo has Australian fauna, as well as some exotic species. Spencer Street, Rockhampton. The zoo is open every day of the year 8am—5pm.
- **Koorana Saltwater Crocodile Farm:** commercial crocodile farm and restaurant with guided tours including Spotlight Dinner Tours. See crocodile hatchings between March and May. Crocodile meat and skin products are available. Coowonga Road, Coowonga, near Emu Park, Rockhampton. Open daily, 10am–3.30pm. **www.koorana.com.au**
- **The Big Sapphire:** fossick for sapphires. 1 Anakie Road, Anakie. Open daily, 8am–6pm. **www.bigsapphire.com.au**
- **Miners Heritage:** walk-in gemstone mine at Rubyvale. 97 Heritage Road, Rubyvale. Open daily, 9am–5pm.

Hervey Bay beach scene. (TQ)

adventure activities

Aerobatic joy-flights

Hervey Bay Air Adventures offer scenic joy flights and aerobatic flights over Hervey Bay and Fraser Island in a Tiger Moth or brand new Super Decathlon, one of the best aerobatic trainers and designed to operate from +6 G to -5 G. They also offer scenic flights over the Hervey Bay foreshore, Woody Islands and Fraser Island in a Trike/Microlight for the ultimate 'wind-in-your-face' joy-flight. Adventure flights available for 15, 30, 45 and 70 minutes.

www.airadventures.com.au

MIG Jet Adventures, in Rockhampton, run aerobatic flights over the coast and Great Keppel Island in a Polish-built Mig-15. After takeoff the aircraft climbs out at an incredible rate of climb putting some height between the Mig-15 and the ground, before performing some aerobatic manoeuvres at about 400 knots (800kph). After these have been completed successfully, it's down to ground level for some low-level strike mission manoeuvres, then back home for a landing.

www.migjet.com.au

Amphibious tours

Jump aboard the pink Army LARC (Lighter Amphibious Resupply Cargo vessel) on a Ride the LARC tour at the town of 1770. The full-day Paradise Tour crosses four tidal creeks in Eurimbula National Park travelling to historic Bustard Head Lightstation across deserted sandy beaches, crystal clear waters and pristine estuaries. Tour includes picnic lunch with billy tea in the shade of a casuarina grove overlooking picturesque Jenny Lind Creek where you can go for a stroll or have a swim before sand boarding down the towering dunes of Middle Island. The one-hour Sunset Cruise travels down Round Hill Creek in Eurimbula National Park for magnificent views of Round Hill Head and the coastline.

www.1770larctours.com.au

Canoeing and kayaking

The rangers at Kingfisher Bay Resort on Fraser Island run guided canoe paddles into Dundonga Creek, a freshwater creek that runs into the ocean close to the resort and has an excellent mangrove colony. Dolphins, dugong, turtles and rays can often be seen, along with pythons which often swim from tree to tree as you glide past.

www.kingfisherbay.com.au

Caving

The spectacular Capricorn Caves are a unique system of above-ground caves in a limestone ridge 23km north of Rockhampton. Discovered in 1882 they are the only privately-owned show caves on freehold land in Australia. Tours range from easy walking, wheelchair accessible caves to wild caving adventure tours with descriptively-named features such Fat Man's Misery, the Rebirth Hole, Entrapment and the Commando Crawl. Challenges range from tight squeezes to surface ridge walking across the limestone karst and bats are more likely to be seen on these tours as they prefer the quieter, darker caves. No caving experience is necessary.

You can also abseil at the caves with a man-made climbing wall for beginners, the intermediate level Sky Window, a 20m drop down a natural rock face and the advanced Summer Solstice Shaft, a natural 14m vertical shaft from the surface ridge into a dark cave below.

www.capricorncaves.com.au

Diving

The Capricorn Coast lies at the southern-most tip of the Great Barrier Reef, so the there are some excellent spots for snorkelling and diving.

Lady Elliot Island is the first coral cay on the Great Barrier Reef. One of the most popular dive sites is the Blow Hole, a large opening in the reef with a main cavern around 20m long with lion fish, manta shrimp, wobbegongs and the unique gnome fish. There are several good bommies and coral gardens and large numbers of manta rays, some four metres from tip to tip, haunt the waters around the island.

First time snorkellers and divers should head for Lady Musgrave Island's lagoon, where the surrounding ring of reef provides a barrier against outside currents. Patch reefs and bommies adorned with corals rise vertically from the lagoon's sandy floor, providing shelter for lots of reef creatures. Best snorkelling is near the reef edge.

There are a number of wrecks in the waters off 1770, including the *Karma, Cetacea, Barcoola, Shannon II,* and *Nautilus* and all are home to a stunning collection of marine life. Fitzroy Reef is a relatively unvisited dive and snorkelling spot off the coast of 1770.

Great Keppel Island off the coast of Rockhampton also has some good diving spots, with good coral gardens and amazing fish life. Egg Rock is a site of undisturbed beauty that is great for underwater photography, with wall dives to 30m and fish up to 60-70kg in weight: coral trout, large clown fish, sea snakes, huge cod and schools of pelagic fish.

Local dive operators are based in Gladstone, Rockhampton, Bundaberg and 1770.

Fishing

Sport and game fishing charter boats go out from Hervey Bay to fish the offshore and outer reefs for snapper, red emperor, sweet lip, wahoo, spanish mackerel, tuna, tusk fish, queen fish and dolphin fish. The fishing is excellent in the calm waters of Great Sandy Strait where the good fishing grounds are the small natural coral reefs off the northern tip of Big Woody Island, the channel ledges around Moon Point, the sand flats near mangroves and the Roy Rufus Artificial Reef. This artificial reef is the largest in the southern hemisphere and was built to help stop the decline of the local fish population. Since 1968, some 2500 car bodies, 800 tonnes of concrete rubble, 12,000 car tyres and seven large vessels have been dumped. It is now home to reef fish, including large groper, coral trout, sweetlip, red emperor, parrot fish and cod.

On the western side of Fraser Island you can catch reef fish, wahoo, mackerel, mack tuna, trevally, black kings, amberjack, tailor, jewfish, whiting, bream, flathead, tarwhine and swallowtail. Crab pots put down in the mangrove areas trap the much-prized

Whale watching, Hervey Bay. *(TQ)*

Queensland mud crab. The whiting fishing is regarded as the best in Queensland and the season runs from July to March. The tailor season runs through the winter months and mackerel abound during the summer months. The sand flats along the western side of the island south of Moon Point are a top salt water fly fishing area, the clear water over the sandy shallow flats home to big golden trevally and bone fish which can be caught by wading off the beach or casting from a boat with experienced local guides. Beach fishing is popular on the eastern side of the island where surf gutters along the ocean beaches provide all-season angling. Whiting and bream are plentiful in the gutters in warmer months and swallowtail can be caught all year round. All the usual rock species can be caught off the headlands from Indian Head to Waddy Point. Offshore, both northern coral and southern reef species can be found.

Further north, the mangrove swamps around Tannum Sands north of 1770 are home to gigantic mud crabs and north of Gladstone you can start catching barramundi, with some good-sized specimens regularly caught in the Fitzroy River near Rockhampton.

Off-road driving

The Capricorn Coast is nirvana for off road driving enthusiasts, with many places only accessible by 4WD. Roads on Fraser Island are 4WD only. The tracks in the centre of the island are soft sand and in dry and/or busy periods can deteriorate quickly. Engage 4WD as soon as you start driving on sand and lower tyre pressure. Normal road rules apply. Most inland tracks are wide enough for just one vehicle, so you will need to pull over frequently to let oncoming traffic pass; those down hill should give way. Most people head to 75 Mile Beach on the eastern side of the island, where driving on hard sand is much easier and access to various highlights is quicker. It is however, inaccessible two hours either side of high tide, so check tide charts before you set off.

Inland, the Central Lakes scenic drive (30km, around two hours) meanders through tall open forest. Highlights include Pile Valley's impressive stand of tall, straight satinay trees, Lake McKenzie and Lake Wabby lookout for a view of Lake Wabby and Stonetool Sandblow. In peak periods (summer holidays and Easter) the road through Lake McKenzie can become very congested and parking may not be available. The Southern Lakes scenic drive (30km, around two hours) is through hoop pine plantations, native tall forests and open forest with extensive areas of banksia

woodland, wallum heathlands and reedy swamps. Lake Garawongera scenic drive (15km, 1 hour) is a very rough inland track and for experienced 4WD users only, as is the remote Northern Forests scenic drive (36km, around 2.5 hours).

In the Bundaberg area between Biggenden and Coalstoun Lakes, there is a good off road track to Coongarra Rock and Falls with rocky outcrops, caves and rock pools. Look for Lords Road, the turn off to Coongarra Rock. The road goes to within a short distance of this spectacular outcrop. It is possible to climb the rock but should only be attempted by fit and experienced bush-walkers. The road to the falls branches off the road to Coongarra Rock and goes within walking distance of the top of the falls.

Tracks through Byfield National Park are suitable for 4WDs, but you'll need some sand driving experience and a permit from Livingstone Shire Council in Yeppon and from Capricorn Coast Tourism in Yeppoon

☎ (07) 4939 4888

In the Sandy Point Section, you can drive along Farnborough beach between Bangalee and Sandy Point. Keep to the boarded track across Sandy Point Spit as endangered little terns nest here, mainly between September and January.

Kroombit Tops also has some good 4WD tracks to the site of a WWII plane crash on the western side of the plateau. A 4WD road from Cania Gorge is another scenic drive for day-trippers.

Horse riding

Susan River Homestead near Maryborough offers horse riding for all levels of experience on their Hervey Bay property. Mounting times are twice daily at 9.30am and 2pm.

www.susanriver.com

Capricorn Coast Trail rides at Yeppon offer one-, two- and three-hour trails, which take the rider over the foothills of Mt Wheeler, amongst unique grass tree forests and iron bark scrub and each of the rides includes a scenic lookout over the Capricorn Coast area and its volcanic plugs.

www.cctrailrides.com.au

Jet boating

Bullamakanka Thrill offer jet boat rides in Hervey Bay. While the eco tours are leisurely, the high-adrenalin Bull Ride is all about getting airborne, jumping waves and conquering high speed turns.

☎ 1800 115 440

Oceanrunners run fast tours of the bay to Bustard Head, near the town of 1770 in a Gemini Waverider RIB powered by two 175Hp Mercury outboards. Rides are structured to quickly get your adrenalin pumping, then pausing to feel the ocean lap beneath boat, recover your composure, shoot a photo or two, and then zoom off again with lots of turning, burning and moving fast.

www.oceanrunners.com.au

Sky diving

Skydive Capricorn Coast at Yeppon offer tandem skydives over the Coral Sea from 10,000 feet in two locations; Yepoon and Gladstone. Take in the fantastic views of the coast and islands such as Great Keppel Island before coming in for landing on the beach.

www.skydivecapricorncoast.com.au

Surfing

1770 has the northern-most surf beach in Queensland. Reef 2 Beach Surf Shop has daily one-hour surf schools, weather permitting, on the town beach at Agnes Water. They are conducted by fully qualified Surfing Queensland State Registered Surf Coaches and bronze medallion holders. This is a good, safe beach for learning.

www.reef2beachsurf.com

1770 Holidays also run two-hour trips to the outer reef for experienced surfers where there are three surf breaks off the reef that work on north-east through to south swells and offshore north-west through to south-east winds.

www.1770holidays.com

Whale watching

Each year some 3000 whales migrate from the cold Antarctic waters to the warmer tropical seas along Australia's east coast to give birth and many stop to rest in the sheltered waters of Hervey Bay before returning south. The mothers use the rest to teach the newborn calves the necessary skills for their calves' survival in the deeper, colder waters of the Antarctica. Between August and November it is one of the best places in the country to see humpbacks with their calves as sightings are almost guaranteed and the whales are active with lots of spectacular displays of breaching, tail flapping and pectoral slapping. There are dozens of whale watching operators who run cruises in the bay during the whale watching season. Other marine life which can be seen during a day's whale watching include dolphins, turtles, and occasionally dugong, the world's only plant-eating marine mammals.

MORE INFORMATION

- **Hervey Bay Visitor Information Centre:** corner of Maryborough/Hervey Bay and Urraween roads, ☎ 1800 811 728. **www.herveybay.qld.gov.au**
- **Bundaberg City Visitor Information Centre:** 186 Bourbong Street, Bundaberg. ☎ (07) 4153 8888. **www.bundabergholidays.info**
- **Rockhampton Tourist Information Centre:** 208 Quay Street, Rockhampton. ☎ (07) 4922 5339. **www.rockhamptoninfo.com** **www.capricorntourism.com.au**

weather watch

- January: 22–32°C
- July: 9–23°C
- Summer can be hot, wet and humid; winter is typically dry with very little rain.

the whitsunday coast

Bareboating in the Whitsunday Islands. *(TQ)*

► THE WHITSUNDAY COAST stretches through the mid tropics of northern Queensland from just south of Mackay north to Townsville. First settled by gold diggers in the 1870s and then by cattlemen and cane growers, cattle and sugar are still the main industries today, along with tourism. The entire coast is a holiday paradise with dozens of unspoiled bays and beautiful beaches and a great place to explore the magic underwater gardens of the World Heritage Great Barrier Reef Marine Park.

Stretching 2300km along the coast from Bundaberg to north of Cooktown, the Great Barrier Reef is the world's largest and most complex expanse of living coral reefs and home to more than 1500 species of fish, about 400 species of corals and a host of sponges, anemones, worms, crustaceans, shells and sea stars. It is one of the world's most significant turtle breeding grounds and whales, dugongs and dolphins are also found in the area. Humpback whales visit each year between June and October to give birth to their young.

Discovered by Captain Cook on Whit Sunday in 1770, the waters around the 74 Whitsunday islands are a sailing paradise that lies between the mainland and the reef. Of the reef's 900 islands, only 22 have resorts or accommodation that cater for tourists—almost half of those resorts are along this stretch of coast.

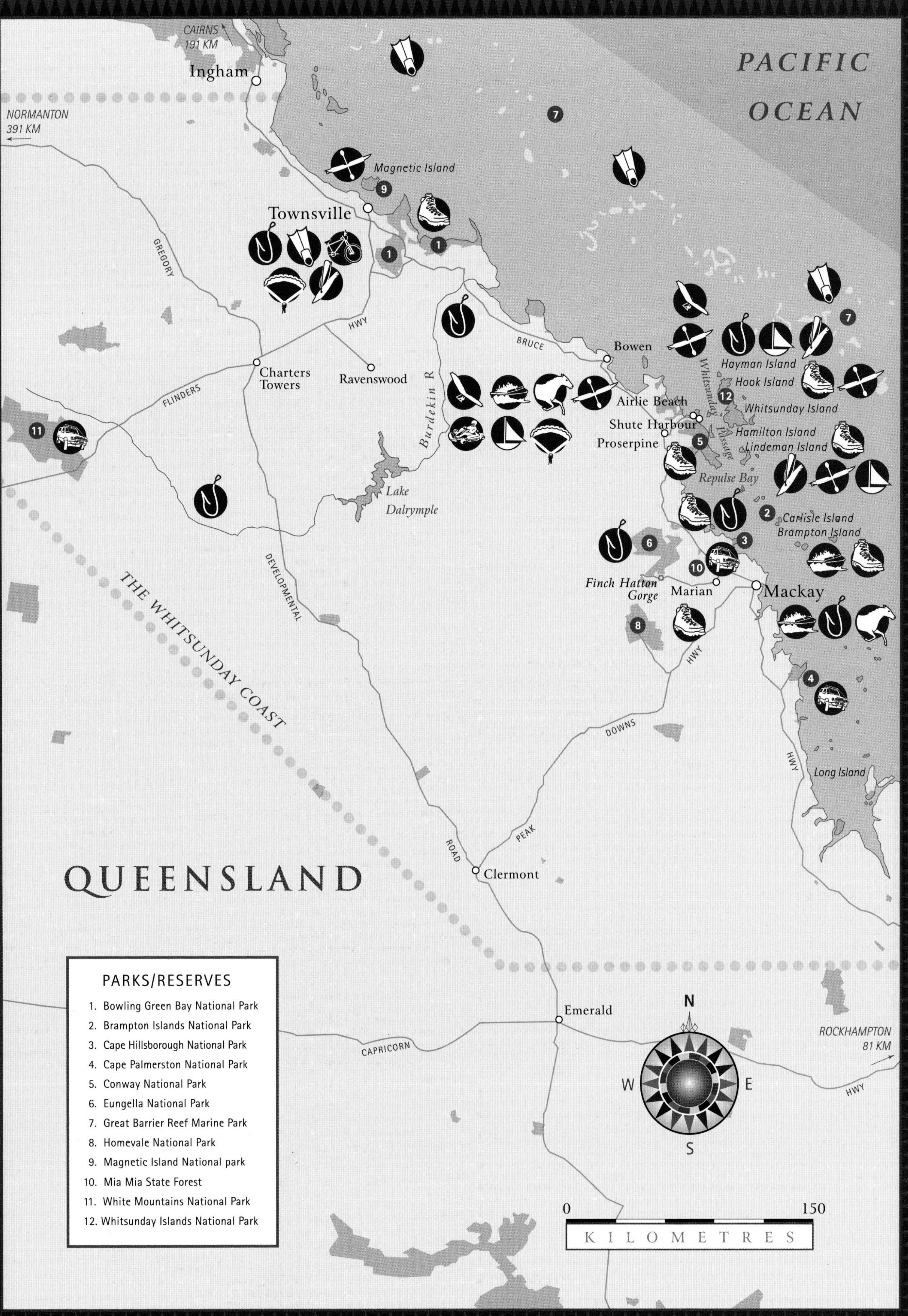

PACIFIC OCEAN
CAIRNS 191 KM
NORMANTON 391 KM
Ingham
Magnetic Island
Townsville
GREGORY
HWY
BRUCE
Bowen
Charters Towers
Ravenswood
Burdekin R
FLINDERS
Whitsunday Passage
Hayman Island
Hook Island
Whitsunday Island
Airlie Beach
Shute Harbour
Proserpine
Hamilton Island
Lindeman Island
Repulse Bay
Lake Dalrymple
Carlisle Island
Brampton Island
Finch Hatton Gorge
Marian
Mackay
DEVELOPMENTAL
THE WHITSUNDAY COAST
HWY
DOWNS
PEAK
ROAD
Long Island
QUEENSLAND
Clermont
Emerald
CAPRICORN
ROCKHAMPTON 81 KM
HWY
N
W
E
S
0
150
KILOMETRES
PARKS/RESERVES
1. Bowling Green Bay National Park
2. Brampton Islands National Park
3. Cape Hillsborough National Park
4. Cape Palmerston National Park
5. Conway National Park
6. Eungella National Park
7. Great Barrier Reef Marine Park
8. Homevale National Park
9. Magnetic Island National park
10. Mia Mia State Forest
11. White Mountains National Park
12. Whitsunday Islands National Park

NATIONAL PARKS

Eungella National Park: drawing its name from an Aboriginal word meaning 'Land of the Clouds' Eungella's mist-shrouded and forest-clad mountains contain Australia's longest and oldest stretch of sub-tropical rainforest, ranging over 51,700 hectares. Much of the park is wilderness dissected by gorges and is home to many unusual plants and animals, including the Eungella gastric brooding frog, Mackay tulip oak, Eungella spiny cray and Eungella honeyeater. Finch Hatton Gorge, with waterfalls that flow all year round, freshwater swimming holes, walking tracks, Forest Flying and a picnic area is a popular spot.

Whitsunday Islands National Park: part of the Great Barrier Reef World Heritage Area this park protects hilly islands dotting the aquamarine waters of the scenic Whitsunday Passage. Whitehaven Beach on Whitsunday Island is world-renowned for its pure, white, silica sands and crystal-clear waters and the Whitsunday reefs have outstanding coral cover and variety. From May to September the Whitsundays are an important calving ground for migrating humpback whales.

Brampton Islands National Park: part of the Cumberland Group of Islands at the southern entrance to the Whitsunday Passage the national park consists of Brampton and Carlisle Islands. Turtles feed in the surrounding marine park waters and the islands are important turtle rookeries. Brampton Island rises from sea level to 214m at Peak Lookout and has a variety of vegetation types including open eucalypt forest on ridges and sheltered slopes, dense vine forest in gullies and valleys, dry rainforest, native grasslands and coastal scrub and mangroves.
There are 12 beautiful beaches, with seven being easily accessible via walking trails. There is a resort on the island.

Cape Hillsborough National Park: one of the most scenic parks along the central Queensland coast featuring a dramatic coastline with rock-strewn sandy beaches, hoop pine-dotted hillsides plunging towards the sea, subtropical rainforest and mangrove-fringed wetlands.

Magnetic Island National Park: just over half this large island surrounded by marine park waters and fringing reefs is national park. Features include rocky granite headlands dotted with hoop pines, sandy bays and pockets of rainforest. WWII coastal forts are listed on the Queensland Heritage Register.

Bowling Green Bay National Park: rugged granite mountains rise abruptly above the coastal plain between Bowen and Townsville with coastal wetlands, saltpans and mangroves. Tropical rainforest grows towards the summit of Mt Elliot, the highest peak in the park. Alligator Creek flows through the park in a series of cascades, deep pools and waterfalls.

Conway National Park: includes the rainforest-clad Conway Peninsula and protects a large area of lowland tropical rainforest. Rugged, steep, rocky cliffs provide a spectacular 35km-long backdrop to the Whitsunday Passage and islands. Home to two of Australia's mound-building birds, the Australian brush-turkey and the orange-footed scrubfowl.

Mackay

The area around Mackay produces more than 25 per cent of all Australia's sugar and beyond the city limits the countryside is a sea of undulating green cane. First settled in the 1870s it is a prosperous coastal city with a distinctly tropical feel to it with lots of swaying palm trees and tropical flowers brightening the town's wide streets.

Townsville

Gateway to the tropical far north, the city of Townsville is a cosmopolitan mix of magnificently-restored heritage buildings, outdoor cafes, restaurants, shops and galleries, all linked by a beach promenade. Climb Castle Hill for views of the city and nearby Magnetic Island, discover Australia's largest collection of palm species at the Palmetum or wander the Strand & Breakwater–a 2.5km stretch of inner city beachfront lined with restaurants, cafes, recreational facilities, parks, play-grounds, swimming enclosures, picnic and bbq areas.

Whitsunday islands

The 74 Whitsunday islands are essentially the drowned volcanic peaks of a submerged range. The bulk of the resort islands are clustered off the coast near Airlie Beach and Shute Harbour, midway between Mackay and Townsville. Daydream, Long, Lindeman, Brampton, Hayman, South Molle and Hamilton islands all have medium-to-large scale resorts. Hook Island is more low key with a wilderness resort and camping while Whitsunday Island is an uninhabited national park. Beyond the resorts the whole area is part of the Great Barrier Reef Marine Park and the uninhabited islands are all controlled by National Parks and Wildlife.

Charters Towers

Queensland's second largest city during the 1870s gold rush, Charters Towers is a showpiece of the era with many well preserved buildings that flaunted the wealth of its early days. Ravenswood, another gold rush centre to the east of the city, is almost a ghost town. Bowen, established in the 1860s, is the region's oldest town–check out the town's history on the 22 murals detailing people and events from the town's past.

Caravan and camping

There are 33 campsites scattered amongst various Whitsunday Islands including Whitsunday, Hook, Cid and Henning Islands. Some have spectacular views over nearby islands. Facilities vary but are limited to toilets and picnic tables. Campers must be self-sufficient. Take fresh water, a fuel stove for cooking and insect repellent. Open fires and generators are prohibited. Remove all rubbish to the mainland. The Queensland Parks and Wildlife Service Island Camping Guide has details of each of the sites.

www.epa.qld.gov.au

On the mainland you can bush and caravan camp at Smalleys Beach in Cape Hillsborough National Park and at Fern Flat in Eungella National Park you can camp near the creek or picnic area but sites are walk-in only. There is a walk-in bush camp beside a secluded, pebbly beach overlooking Daydream (West Molle) Island at Swamp Bay, a 2.1km walk from the Swamp Bay/Mt Rooper car park in Conway National Park.

Walkers' camps have been established along Whitsunday Great Walk at Repulse Creek and on the coastal ridge above Jubilee Pocket–Bloodwood Camp.

Bushwalks

The 30km Whitsunday Great Walk winds through Conway State Forest, starting at Brandy Creek and finishing at Airlie Beach. It follows sections of old logging roads, at times weaving through giant strangler figs and tulip oaks. Highlights include panoramic views of Shute Harbour, Cannonvale and the Whitsunday Islands, majestic stands of Alexandra palms, seasonal creeks and pools surrounded by lush tropical rainforest. Watch out for the brilliant blue flashes of Ulysses butterflies. The walk has short, easy strolls for day visitors and more challenging and remote routes for well-prepared walkers, who should allow three days to complete the whole track.

The Mackay Highlands Great Walk links Eungella and Homevale National Parks, and passes through Crediton State Forest. It is 50km long and takes four to six days. Short walks through the rainforest are also available. Highlights include deep gorges, steep escarpments, a magnificent rainforest of red cedar, massive Mackay tulip oak, groves of piccabeen and Alexandra palms and dramatic views of the Pioneer Valley. You might even catch a glimpse of a platypus from the cool banks of the Broken River.

Good shorter walks include the five-hour 17km Alligator Creek Track in Bowling Green Bay National Park. Learn about mangroves on the 2.4km boardwalk in Cape Hillsborough National Park, where you can also discover how Aboriginal people use plants along the 45-minute Juipera Plant Trail.

On Whitsunday Island you can walk through woodland from Tongue Bay to a lookout for a fantastic view over Hill Inlet and Whitehaven Beach. A 1km track connects Dugong and Sawmill Beaches. A short walk leads to a rock art site at Nara Inlet on Hook Island and, on Lindeman Island, the 9km walk to Mt Oldfield gives a magnificent view over the islands and the 7km Brampton Island circuit is also worth doing.

Hamilton Island. *(SCS)*

scenic highlights

Cape Hillsborough National Park. *(TQ)*

Explore the tropical green hinterland of the Whitsunday coast through the fertile Pioneer Valley between Mackay and Shute Harbour.

First settled by John Mackay and other cattle farmers in the 1860s, the pretty Pioneer Valley is now one of Australia's richest sugar cane-growing areas. Follow the road through a patchwork of cane fields, past sugar mills, cane railways and charming country towns like Pleystowe, home to Queensland's oldest operating sugar mill, Marian, the former home of opera singer Dame Nellie Melba whose father built a sugar mill here and Mirani with its National Trust timber-and-iron railway station.

Past Finch Hatton with its gorge, year-round waterfalls and swimming holes, Eungella Road twists its way up the steep ranges. Stop at one of the lookouts for spectacular views back over the Pioneer Valley and 80km beyond to Mackay.

Eungella National Park boasts Australia's largest stretch of sub-tropical rainforest wtih over 20km of walking tracks featuring spectacular views. At Broken River there is a viewing deck where you can often spot platypus—one of the few places in Australia you can easily do so.

Head back to Marian and snake your way north, with 590m-high Mt Blackwood and the twin peaks of Mt Juke rising above the cane fields. If you have time,explore the beautiful coastline of Cape Hillsborough.

Back on the Bruce Highway head north, stopping at Midge Point for views over Repulse Bay, then continue across marshlands crossed by pretty creeks, through more cane fields to Proserpine and on to Cedar Creek Falls at the edge of Conway National Park, where a 12m-high waterfall cascades into a beautiful plunge pool. The resort towns of Airlie Beach and Shute Harbour are just a few kilometres further on.

Whitehaven Beach. *(TQ)*

DON'T MISS

- **Greenmount Historic Homestead:** pioneer homestead museum with collection from three generations of the Cook family, prominent pioneers of the Pioneer Valley. Greenmount Road, Walkerston, Mackay. Open Sun–Fri, 9.30am–12.30pm.
- **The Ken Burgess Orchid House:** located in Queen's Park, the orchid house has more than 3000 specimens on display, with many of the 989 species aged between 60 and 70 years. Goldsmith Street, Queen's Park, Mackay. Open Weekdays, 10–11am and 2–2.30pm. Sundays 2–5pm.
- **Artspace Mackay:** art gallery and exhibition space with changing exhibitions. Gordon Street, Mackay. Open Tue–Sun, 10am–5pm. www.artspacemackay.com.au
- **Clermont Museum:** museum and heritage park. Exhibits include an old train, the old Masonic Lodge, old steam engines, a shearing shed and fire engine. Peaks Down Hwy, Clermont. Open Mon and Tue 10am–12 noon, Wed 10am–4pm, Thu and Fri 10am–12 noon and 2–4pm, Sat 2–4pm, Sun 10am–4pm.
- **Proserpine Historical Museum:** learn about the interesting history of this sugar cane and cattle town. 192 Main Street, Proserpine. Open weekends, 9am–4pm.
- **Whitsunday Crocodile Safari:** full-day tour that includes two-hour crocodile watching cruise on Proserpine River, open air, elevated wagon tour through wetlands and natural waterholes, guided nature walk, Queensland mud crab capture and display and barbecue lunch. Glen Isla Road, Proserpine. www.crocodilesafari.com.au
- **Billabong Sanctuary:** interactive wildlife sanctuary where you can hold a koala, hug a wombat, hold a crocodile and wrap a python around your neck. Daily wildlife talks and feeding shows. 17km south of Townsville on the Bruce Highway. Open daily, 8am–5pm. www.billabongsanctuary.com.au
- **Maritime Museum of Townsville:** houses a collection of regional and Australian maritime history, a research library, model ship building room, Townsville Port history displays, bbq and picnic area. 42–68 Palmer Street, South Townsville. Open Mon–Fri, 10am–4pm; weekends 1pm–4pm. www.townsvillemaritimemuseum.org.au
- **Museum of Tropical Queensland:** interactive exhibits on a variety of subjects including life in the tropics, weird and wonderful creatures from the deep, interactive display of the 1791 HMS *Pandora* Shipwreck and tropical science centre. 70–102 Flinders Street, Townsville. Open daily, 9.30am–5pm. www.mtq.qld.gov.au
- **Reef HQ:** the world's largest coral reef aquarium and only living coral reef in captivity—which means you can actually explore the Great Barrier Reef while safely on land. Flinders Street East, next door to the Museum of Tropical Queensland. Open daily, 9.30am–5pm. www.reefHQ.com.au
- **Townsville Palmetum:** botanical garden featuring just one family of plants—the palms. Collection contains around 300 species, many rare and threatened in their natural habitat. University Road, Douglas, Townsville. Open daily, 6am–5pm.

adventure activities

Canoeing and kayaking

The best way to explore this region is at water level. The tropical Whitsunday Islands are arguably the best sea kayaking and sailing waters found anywhere in Australia.

Live Adrenalin offer a six-day guided sea kayaking tour that circumnavigates either Whitsunday Island or Hook Island, crosses the Whitsunday Passage on two occasions and–since they operate in the middle of the annual humpback whale migration–it's good odds that you'll see the whales at close range. Tours include snorkelling, fishing, scuba diving, beachcombing, swimming, hiking and camping at isolated beaches.

www.adrenalin.com.au

Sea Kayaking Whitsundays is based on Hamilton Island, in the heart of the Whitsundays, and offer a range of paddling tours including full-day adventure tours, champagne sunset paddles and full moon tours watching the moon rise through Fitzalan Pass from the northern end of Hamilton Island.

www.seakayakingwhitsundays.com.au

At Airlie Beach, Salty Dog Sea Kayaking have single and double sea kayaks for hire as well as half and full-day trips kayaking around the islands of Shute Harbour and the Molle island group. The three-day trip explores the remote northern islands of the Whitsunday group stopping over at Gloucester and Saddleback islands while the six-day trip sets up camp at Whitsunday and Hook islands.

www.saltydog.com.au

Magnetic Island Sea Kayaks, on Magnetic Island near Townsville, also rent single and double sea kayaks and have a morning eco-tour from Horseshoe Bay to the secluded Balding Bay, accessible only by boat.

www.seakayak.com.au

Cycling and mountain biking

There are some good mountain bike trails in the hills and ranges around Townsville. The Bluewater trail ride up the range can be long and tiring in summer (about 10km) but the downhill run is good. Castle Hill and Mt Stuart both have sealed roads to their summits and good views. The climb to the top of Mt Stuart is steep and continuous and not for the novice or unfit rider, but the steep grades make for an exciting–particularly at night–downhill ride. The Deeragun Ride, starting from the Mt Lousia area, is a 33km round trip with one spot (crossing the Bohle River) where you have to get off and carry your bike. It is a mix of reasonably easy access (powerline) track and moderate single track with a set of small-to-medium roller coaster type jumps. There are several fire-trail rides at Paluma Dam, the Paluma Push Track covers 45km of various riding tracks including hills, rainforest and rocky descents and the western end of Mt Louisa has plenty of cross-country and downhill tracks.

www.rockwheelers.com

Sailing on the *Coral Trekker*. *(TQ)*

Diving

Diving and snorkelling is the number one activity on the Great Barrier Reef and there are literally hundreds of extraordinary dive spots and locations. There are commercial dive operators in most of the towns and resorts in the area that cater for first-time divers and snorkellers and experienced divers. Basic learn-to-dive courses can be completed in just one day, while advanced and open-water courses can vary between three and five days.

Certified divers with a minimum level of six logged dives can dive the wreck of the *SS Yongala* off Townsville, which sank during a cyclone in 1911 with the loss of all on board. It was not until 1958 that the wreck was discovered and due to its remote location it has remained mostly untouched. The wreck begins 14m below the surface and extends to 28m. Since it is the only reef structure in the region, marine life gathers at the wreck providing an unforgettable diving experience that is considered to be one of the best wreck dives in the world. All divers are required to present certification cards and log books on board.

www.dancingwithdolphins.com.au www.adrenalindive.com.au

Surfski exploring.

Fishing

The Whitsundays are a fantastic fishing ground with good bay, beach, jetty, offshore and reef fishing for coral trout, mackerel, queen fish, trevally and sweetlip. Creeks and mangroves along the mainland coast have some of the best barramundi and mangrove jack fishing on the east coast. Offshore there's big game fish such as marlin and tuna.

Mackay Harbour is a good spot for jewfish, mackerel, trevally, bream and tuna. Pioneer River has good spots near the river mouth for trevally, whiting, bream, flathead, grunter and barramundi. Cape Hillsborough and surrounding beaches are also very good.

Eungella Dam is renowned for producing oversized sooty grunter and barramundi, stocked by the Mackay Area Fish Stocking Association. Lake Proserpine, which is also known as Peter Faust Dam, has large barramundi and sooty grunter as does Burdekin River and Dam near Townsville. Townsville Harbour also has good barramundi fishing.

Forest Flying

Get a unique up-close view of the rainforest of Finch Hatton Gorge while forest flying, a new back-to-nature flying fox adventure. Strapped into a safety harness you can fly though the rainforest canopy 30m above the ground hooked up to an overhead cable and pulley system strung among the tree tops. Using your own power and gravity, you can wheel yourself along the cable within inches of the foliage and get a whole new perspective on this endangered habitat. The Forest Flying Tour is a one-to-two hour guided session that includes a guided forest walk with informative talk on rainforest plants and bush tucker, and a ride on the flying fox.

www.forestflying.com

Off-road driving

Cape Palmerston National Park near Mackay has two good inland and beach 4WD tracks. The inland track is 15km and takes nearly two hours to complete. The beach track has soft sand and extreme tides of up to six metres at times and you should check tide times before travelling. The five-hour scenic but challenging trek through the Mia Mia State Forest from Mackay to Eungella can be tricky after rain but travels through some beautiful eucalypt and rainforest. You'll need a 4WD to explore the white sandstone bluffs, gorges and rugged wilderness of White Mountains National Park, south-west of Charters Towers.

Horse riding

Stoney Creek Trail Rides, based at Eton near Mackay, run adventure trail rides through semi rainforest along a historic rugged mountain trail overlooking beautiful waterfalls and swimming holes and include a swim at Pine Tree Falls. Rides vary from one-hour children's rides to three-hour trail rides that include some cantering and galloping to full-day cattle droving and mustering or a 6km ride from Stoney Creek through cane fields to the Eton Pub for a beer and lunch with the locals.

☎ (07) 4954 1177

Learn the skills of Horse Whispering on a two-hour natural horsemanship experience and trail ride with Bush Adventures, just outside of Airlie Beach. Based on trust, respect and co-operation, natural horsemanship teaches you to understand horse psychology, learning how to make your horse follow you without a bridle, ride with just a halter and come when you call. Follow this lesson with a trail ride through the cattle farm and rainforest.

www.bushadventures.com.au

Ocean Rafting

Ocean Rafting offers the fastest tour around the Whitsunday Islands in semi-rigid craft capable of cruising at up to 30 knots. A range of available tours feature an exhilarating ride to famous Whitehaven Beach, pristine snorkelling reefs around Hook and Border Islands and a guided Whitsunday Island National Park walk or a guided walk to the sacred Aboriginal cave at Nara Inlet. Tours depart from Airlie Beach.

www.oceanrafting.com

Parasailing

Get a bird's eye view of the Whitsundays from 100m above sea level in a parasail. Located on the Jetty at the Coral Sea Resort in Airlie Beach, parasailing is available for anybody over the age of 10 for a tandem or a triple trip and to anybody over 14 for a single.

www.whitsundayparasail.com.

Also available at many of the island resorts.

www.hamiltonisland.com.au www.daydreamisland.com

Quad biking

Whitsunday Quad Bike Adventures has a purpose-built adventure track with over 15km of bush trails on their 160-acre cattle farm near Airlie Beach. Choose from two tours: a one-hour guided tour exploring the paddocks and woodlands of the property and the rainforest of the Drylander Range, or the two-hour more advanced tour along rainforest tracks as you climb the mountain to a viewing tower, 300m above sea level, with sensational Whitsunday island and valley views.

www.bushadventures.com.au

Skydiving, Airlie Beach. *(TQ)*

Sailing

Known as 100 Magic Miles, the Whitsundays are the premier sailing destination in Australia for both seasoned sailors, novices or deck candy (those who like to lie around with a drink while someone else does all the work). With many comfortable anchorages and land never out of sight, navigation is easy. The large number of sheltered bays and coves make the Whitsundays an ideal and accessible place to charter a sailboat. Use your charter boat as a base for snorkelling, windsurfing the open water or bushwalking on the uninhabited offshore islands. The most popular bays are now equipped with moorings to prevent anchor damage to the fragile coral, which is rapidly regenerating. There are dozens of bareboat charters–hiring a boat without a skipper or crew–available at all levels of luxury. If you have sailing experience you don't need a boat licence for bareboat cruising, but you will receive the necessary introductory training before you set off. You can provision the boat yourself or have it stocked for you, ready to set sail.

www.rentayacht.com.au www.whitsunday-yacht.com.au

Square-riggers, racing or cruising sailboat tours are all available for uninitiated sailors, whether just for lunch afloat or a week's island hopping. Enjoy the clear waters and see the wildlife without revving engines. Tourist information centres and many agencies have details of sailing tours, learn to sail schools, bareboat and crewed charters.

www.barefootcruises.com.au/coraltrekker.htm

Skydiving

If you want to skydive with a breathtaking view then this is the place to do it. Coral Sea Skydivers in Townsville and Tandem Skydive Airlie Beach both offer tandem jumps and solo skydive courses with some of the most spectacular views of the Whitsundays around.

www.coralseaskydivers.com.au www.skydiveoz.com

Windsurfing and kitesurfing

The Whitsundays offer one of the most enjoyable open-ocean windsurfing experiences in Australia. Strong seabreezes in winter funnel through the passages between islands, providing perfect chop-hopping conditions for experienced sailors. May to October are the best months for sailing-strength winds and are also free of nasty jellyfish. Windsurfing or kitesurfing off beautiful Whitehaven Beach is something everyone must do at least once in their life. Sailing between islands is a great adventure for the competent windsurfer. Take a board on your charter yacht or rent from several resorts around the Whitsunday chain, such as Daydream, Hamilton or Hayman islands.

MORE INFORMATION

- **Mackay Visitor Information Centre:** 320 Nebo Rd, Mackay. ☎ 1300 130 001. www.mackayregion.com
- **Townsville Information Centre:** Flinders Mall, Townsville. ☎ 1800 801 902. www.townsvilleonline.com.au
- **Whitsunday Information Centre:** Bruce Highway, Proserpine. ☎ 1800 801 252. www.whitsundaytourism.com

weather watch

- January: 23–30°C
- July: 13–21°C
- Summer can be warm, wet and humid. Winter is temperate and drier, but windier and the prime season for serious sailors. Stinger season runs every year from October through to May. Swimming is not recommended during this time as Box and Irukandji jellyfish are prevalent in the waters and their stings can cause acute pain and serious illness. Box jellyfish can cause death in healthy humans in as little as three minutes.

far north queensland

Mossman Gorge. *[TQ]*

▶ THERE ARE TWO main reasons that thousands of visitors head to Far North Queensland (FNQ) each year: the rainforest and the reef. The World Heritage Wet Tropics area covers around 900,000 hectares of rainforest wilderness along the eastern escarpment of the Great Dividing Range between Townsville and Cooktown. At Cape Tribulation, north of Port Douglas, two World Heritage areas come together when the reef meets the rainforest along the coast making this area one of the best places to access the reef.

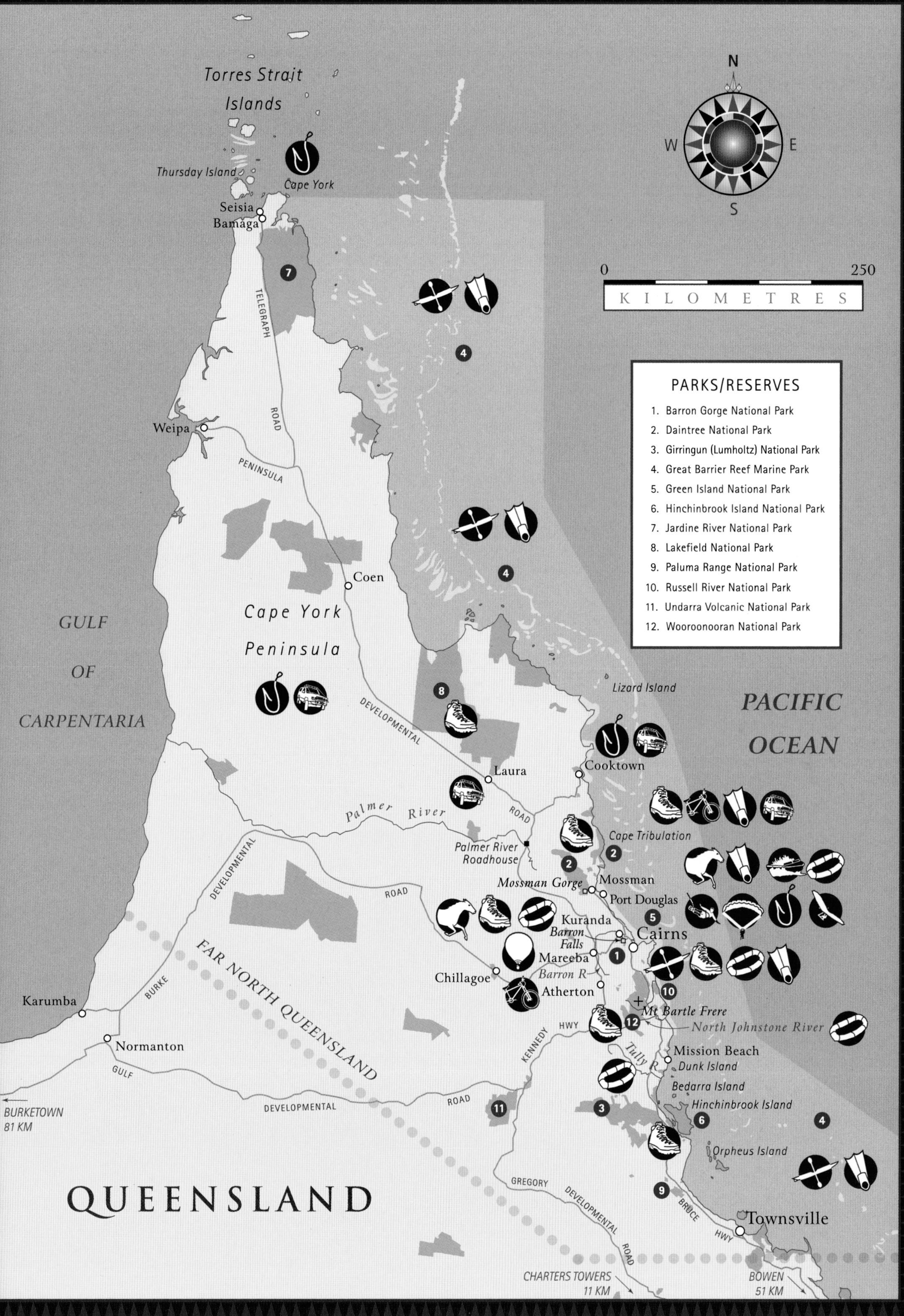

Torres Strait Islands
Thursday Island
Cape York
Seisia
Bamaga
TELEGRAPH ROAD
Weipa
PENINSULA
Coen
Cape York Peninsula
GULF OF CARPENTARIA
DEVELOPMENTAL ROAD
Laura
Cooktown
Lizard Island
PACIFIC OCEAN
Palmer River
Palmer River Roadhouse
Cape Tribulation
Mossman Gorge
Mossman
Port Douglas
Kuranda
Barron Falls
Cairns
Mareeba
Barron R
Chillagoe
Atherton
Mt Bartle Frere
North Johnstone River
FAR NORTH QUEENSLAND
BURKE
Karumba
Normanton
GULF
DEVELOPMENTAL
ROAD
KENNEDY HWY
Tully R
Mission Beach
Dunk Island
Bedarra Island
Hinchinbrook Island
Orpheus Island
BURKETOWN 81 KM
QUEENSLAND
GREGORY DEVELOPMENTAL ROAD
BRUCE HWY
Townsville
CHARTERS TOWERS 11 KM
BOWEN 51 KM
N
W
E
S
0
250
KILOMETRES
PARKS/RESERVES
1. Barron Gorge National Park
2. Daintree National Park
3. Girringun (Lumholtz) National Park
4. Great Barrier Reef Marine Park
5. Green Island National Park
6. Hinchinbrook Island National Park
7. Jardine River National Park
8. Lakefield National Park
9. Paluma Range National Park
10. Russell River National Park
11. Undarra Volcanic National Park
12. Wooroonooran National Park

NATIONAL PARKS

Mossman Gorge, Daintree: Mossman Gorge cuts through dense rainforest. One of the most popular spots in the Wet Tropics World Heritage Area, there is a 2.5km self-guided walking track through the rainforest to riverside picnic areas. Part of the traditional lands of the Kuku Yalanji people, the park is also home to a prolific range of birdlife, the vivid Ulysses butterfly, freshwater turtles and platypus in the creek. Take care around the water as the boulders are often slippery and the river is fast flowing. Camping is prohibited.

Cape Tribulation, Daintree: the rainforest meets the sea in this coastal section of Daintree National Park that features a variety of habitats including rainforests, mangroves, swamps and heath. There are two popular boardwalks: Maardja boardwalk at Oliver Creek and the Dubuji boardwalk at Cape Tribulation. Explore the rainforest along short tracks at Jindalba or walk along Kulki or Myall Beaches. Fit walkers can climb to a lookout over the Daintree coast along the Mt Sorrow ridge trail. Swimming is not recommended as estuarine crocodiles live in the park's creeks and nearby coastal waters. Beware of marine stingers from October to May. Access roads are narrow and winding and not recommended for caravans. Roads may be closed after heavy rain.

Girringun National Park: part of the Wet Tropics World Heritage Area, the park 51km south-west of Ingham, is home to Wallaman Falls, the highest sheer drop waterfall in Australia. It is also the gateway to the Wet Tropics Great Walk and has more than 110km of walking trails.

Paluma Range National Park: the southernmost section of the Wet Tropics World Heritage Area, highlights of the park include the 1000m Mount Spec and Jourama Falls.

Hinchinbrook Island National Park: a beautiful island park with lush rainforests, rugged heath-covered mountains, wetlands, mangroves, woodlands and sandy beaches, which is surrounded by marine park waters where fringing reefs and seagrass beds are home to a variety of marine life including dugong and green turtles.

Barron Gorge National Park: the most accessible rainforest close to Cairns in the highlands near Kuranda. The once-powerful Barron Falls have been harnessed to supply hydro-electric power and only flow after heavy rain. The 34km Kuranda Scenic Railway, one of the most scenic railway lines in the country, was built between 1886 and 1891 and winds its way up from Cairns climbing more than 300m through tropical rainforest, passing through 15 tunnels, around 98 curves and over 40 bridges. Favourite photo stop is the bridge stretching over the Barron River Falls. The Skyrail cablecar is a spectacular 7.5km journey over the rainforest canopy from the top of the escarpment down to Cairns. Enjoy the view over the gorge and falls from Wright's Lookout or the elevated boardwalk through the forest at Barron Falls lookout.

Green Island National Park: this 12 hectare coral cay is the most popular destination on the Great Barrier Reef. The island is covered in tropical vine forest which supports a diversity of birds and insects and the surrounding coral reef is home to many kinds of corals, clams, fish, stingrays and other reef life. Green and hawksbill turtles are often seen offshore.

Wooroonooran National Park: home to Queensland's highest mountains, Mt Bartle Frere (1622m) and Mt Bellenden Ker (1592m), and part of the Wet Tropics World Heritage Area. Highlights include Josephine Falls and the North Johnstone River gorge.

Jardine River National Park: 400,000ha of true wilderness at the remote northern tip of Cape York Peninsula. The park protects much of the catchment of the Jardine River, the largest perennial stream in Queensland, and is bounded by the headwaters of the Jardine River to the south and the mangroves of Jacky Jacky Creek and the Escape River in the north. The park's western boundary follows the historic telegraph line installed in 1887 to provide communications to the remote areas on the Cape. Heath, rainforest and open forest grow on low, broad sandy ridges with intervening swamps while shrub and vine thickets cover the massive coastal dunes. Estuarine crocodiles live in rivers and waterholes in this park, and along the entire coastline and offshore islands.

Lakefield National Park: Queensland's second largest park with large rivers, spectacular wetlands, mangroves and mudflats and home to waterbirds, barramundi and estuarine and freshwater crocodiles. Rivers become a series of waterholes in the dry season but the wet season transforms the park into a vast inaccessible wetland. Visit the restored Old Laura Homestead on the former cattle grazing lease or the site of the former Breeza Homestead where horses were bred for the Palmer River goldfields. See spectacular displays of red lotus lilies and white lilies in the Red and White Lily Lagoons 8km north of Lakefield ranger station.

Cairns

Wedged between the warm waters of Trinity Bay and the rainforest-clad Atherton Tablelands, Cairns, the 'capital' of FNQ, is the natural place to base yourself for a week or two of sun, sand and tropical adventure–there's more accommodation choices than you can count in one sitting, most of it within walking distance to the city's restaurants, cafes, bars, shops, theatres, galleries and nightclubs.

A multi-million dollar foreshore redevelopment project with a 4800m^2 saltwater swimming lagoon has transformed the former mudflat waterfront. Almost 2km of landscaped parkland fringes a busy thoroughfare and restaurant strip on one side and a natural harbour inlet on the other. Relax on the grass, eat at outdoor cafes, walk under the trees or watch the many bird species which come to feed on the tidal zone.

Further afield, you can chill out on the white, palm-fringed sandy beaches just a few kilometres north of town at Palm Cove and Trinity Beach or escape the heat in the rainforest that smothers the mountains west of the city on the drive up to Kuranda, which comes alive with covered markets each day.

Atherton Tableland

South-west of Cairns, thanks to the rich volcanic soils and high rainfall, the 900m-high tableland is a productive farming area producing coffee, peanuts, avocados, mangos and a huge range of exotic fruit and vegetables. Dotted with historic townships, spectacular waterfalls and beautiful sections of rainforest, the tablelands are a popular scenic driving route.

Blencoe Falls. (TQ)

Port Douglas and Cooktown

The Captain Cook Highway between Cairns and Port Douglas is one of the country's most beautiful stretches of road, hugging the coastline for most of the 67km–the views of the rainforest spilling down the mountainside to meet the sea in a necklace of deserted white beaches are magnificent. Further north are the beautiful rainforests of Mossman Gorge, Cape Tribulation and the Daintree before the sealed road runs out and it's 4WD only to Cooktown and beyond.

Captain Cook beached the Endeavour at Cooktown after having accidentally struck the reef off Cape Tribulation in June 1770. The town was not settled until almost a century later when the discovery of gold at Palmer River brought thousands of prospectors to the town.

Cape York Peninsula

Cape York is a vast undeveloped region of wilderness with fewer than 10,000 people calling the entire peninsula home. Cut off by flooding during the wet season, the area is strictly 4WD only and mostly aboriginal land. Weipa on the west coast has the world's largest bauxite deposits and some great gulf fishing. Bamaga, at the tip of the peninsula, is the most northerly town in Australia, an isolated settlement of some 2000 people, most of whom are Torres Strait Islanders.

Torres Strait Islands

The group of 100 or so islands off the northern tip of Cape York are home to Australia's only non-Aboriginal indigenous people. The main island is Thursday Island, which has tours and ferry services from Seisia near Bamaga. The islands include Possession Island where Captain Cook formally took possession of the east coast of Australia in 1770 and Murray Island, the family home of the late Eddie Mabo, famous for his successful 1992 Australian High Court land claim that finally recognised traditional land rights.

scenic highlights

Explore the coast and hinterland on this easy one-day 220km loop drive from Cairns.

Head north out of Cairns, and follow the signs to Kuranda and Mareeba. The road climbs in a series of tight, twisting switchback turns into the rainforest that smothers the mountains west of the city. The air is cooler up here, and once past Kuranda, the traffic is light. Pass fields of sugar cane, macadamia and mango trees, and plenty of orchards of exotic-looking trees.

Ninety per cent of Australian coffee is grown in the Mareeba area. The Coffee Works here and the Australian Coffee Centre at Skybury have tours daily, where you learn about the Australian coffee industry, coffee growing and, best of all, sample the local brews in the terrace cafe. For a taste of another local brew, drop into Golden Pride Winery to taste their mango wines—very FNQ.

There are two ways to Port Douglas: either continue north-west from Mareeba through Mount Molloy to Mossman then turn south to Port Douglas, or north along the coast from Cairns. The drive through Mount Molloy is around 75km through lush farming and grazing country, in contrast to the surf and rainforest steaminess of the coast. Stop for a pie and a beer at the pub in Mount Molloy and soak up some Queensland bush humour at the bar.

The coast road, however, is easily one of the great drives in Queensland. The road hugs the coastline and the views are spectacular—the rainforest spills down the mountainside to meet a never ending series of empty white beaches.

Stop at Hartley's Creek Crocodile Farm, 40km north of Cairns for crocodile feeding, exhibits, crocodile products and a tasty crocodile pie.

Port Douglas has plenty of eating choices on the main street (Macrossan Street). For a real treat try 'Breakfast with the Birds' at the Rainforest Habitat on the edge of town: a buffet-style feast of fruit, bacon, sausages and eggs in a large aviary—but be warned, you may have to fend off the occasional hungry cocky or bush turkey.

Head north to Mossman, through a green sea of waving sugar cane. Stop at Somerset Orchard (4km north of Mossman) and browse the fruit stall. Varieties for sale include red Thai paw paw, jackfruit, black sapote, Malay apples, rowlinnias as well as hands of bananas, pineapples and more common fruit. If you're interested in seeing the trees these mysterious fruits grow on, you can wander the orchard at High Falls Farm, 14km from Mossman.

DON'T MISS

- **Paronella Park:** Spanish castle ruins and rainforest gardens near Mission Beach with guided tours and cultural performances. Japoonvale Road, Mena Creek. Open daily, 9am–6.30pm then from 8pm for the Darkness Falls Tour. www.paronellapark.com.au
- **Cairns Night Zoo:** guided spotlighting tours, dinner and entertainment. Captain Cook Highway, Palm Cove. Mon–Thur and Sat night from 7pm–10pm. www.cairnsnightzoo.com
- **Cairns Regional Gallery:** FNQ's only visual arts museum. Showcases an average of 30 exhibitions per year, and features the work of national and international artists, with a strong focus on local and indigenous works of art. Abbott and Sheild streets, Cairns. Open Mon-Sat, 10am–5pm, Sundays and Public Holidays, 1pm–5pm.
- **Flecker Botanic Gardens:** the only wet tropical botanic gardens in Australia, established in 1886. Collins Avenue, Cairns. Open daily.

Kuranda Scenic Railway. (TQ)

- **Rainforest Habitat:** wildlife park where you can wander through the four different and unique habitats of North Queensland—rainforest, wetlands, woodlands and grasslands—and see more than 180 species that call these ecosystems home. Port Douglas Road, Port Douglas. Open daily, 8am–5.30pm. www.rainforesthabitat.com.au
- **Hou Wang Chinese Temple and Museum:** century-old temple built by Chinese pioneers in the early 1900s. Built from local materials, rainforest timbers and corrugated iron, the temple is the only surviving example of its type and contains a substantial number of its original artefacts handcrafted in China. 86 Herberton Road, Atherton. Open daily, 10am–4pm. www.houwang.org.au
- **Birdworld Kuranda:** largest collection of free flying birds in Australia housed in a tropically-landscaped walk-through aviary. Rob Vievers Drive, Kuranda. Open daily, 9am–4pm. www.birdworldkuranda.com
- **Kuranda Koala Gardens:** Australian wildlife park. Rob Vievers Drive, Kuranda. Open daily, 9am–4pm. www.koalagardens.com
- **Hartley's Crocodile Adventures:** crocodile farm and wildlife park with wetland boat rides and crocodile feeding. 40km north of Cairns at Wangetti Beach. Open daily, 8.30am–5pm. www.crocodileadventures.com
- **Mareeba Wetlands:** protects more than 6000 acres of open savannah woodland, including 350 acres of regionally important wetlands. A great place for bird watching with ospreys, sea eagles, black swans, magpie geese, brolgas, whistling ducks in their hundreds, pelicans, pink-eared ducks and even Australia's only stork, the jabiru seen from the lagoon-side bird hide. Join a Twilight Reserve Safari. Pickford Road, Biboohra via Mareeba. Open Wed–Sun, 10am–4pm (6pm for Twilight Safari guests). Closed January, February and March. www.mareebawetlands.com
- **Tjapukai Aboriginal Cultural Park:** the most awarded Aboriginal cultural attraction in Australia with a stunning theatrical/dance interpretation of local Aboriginal culture from the beginning of time into the future. Kamerunga Road, Smithfield, Cairns. Tjapukai by Day is open daily 9am–5pm, Tjapukai by Night is open every night from 7–10pm. www.tjapukai.com.au
- **Skyrail:** a spectacular 7.5km cablecar journey over the rainforest canopy from the top of the escarpment at Kuranda down to Cairns. Skyrail's Caravonica Terminal is at the corner of Kamerunga Road and Cook Highway, Smithfield. Open daily, 8.15am–5.15pm. www.skyrail.com.au
- **Kuranda Scenic Railway:** one of the most scenic railway lines in the country, the historic railway winds its way up from Cairns to Kuranda on a journey of approximately one hour and 45 minutes. Trips can be combined with Skyrail. Open daily. www.kurandascenicrailway.com.au
- **The Coffee Works:** Mason Street, Mareeba. Open daily, 9am–4pm. Tasting Tours, 10am, 12 noon, 2pm. ☎ (07) 4092 4101.
- **Golden Pride Winery:** Bilwon Road, 10 minutes from Mareeba. Mango wines, open for tastings and sales daily. ☎ (07) 4093 2524.
- **High Falls Farm:** exotic fruit display orchard and restaurant. Old Forestry Road, Whyanbeel (14km north-west of Mossman). Open daily, 10am–4pm Nov–Mar; 9am–4pm Apr–Oct. ☎ (07) 4098 8148.

Snorkelling on the reef. *(TQ)*

Tropical north islands

Like their southern sisters, the northern reef islands are largely uninhabited and protected by national parks, although there are seven that have resort facilities. Orpheus Island north of Townsville, is a small island surrounded by coral reefs and protected by National Park with an exclusive luxury resort, as does Bedarra, which is off-limits to day trippers. The mountainous Hinchinbrook has a small low-key resort and is largely national park, as is Dunk Island, although the resort is much larger and offers more activities. Green Island off the coast of Cairns is popular with day trippers and Lizard and Fitzroy islands have some good camping spots.

Caravan and camping

There are good camping sites at Jourama Falls in a large clearing beyond the second causeway and sites are suitable for both caravans and tents. Drinking water, free gas barbecues, toilets and cold showers are provided. Advance bookings are advisable, especially during school holidays when the campground is very popular. In the Mount Spec section of the park a camping area is provided at Big Crystal Creek with tent and van sites. Camping is only available to those who have booked a site in advance and obtained a booking number.

www.epa.qld.gov.au ☎ 13 13 04

At Wallaman Falls there is a campground next to Stony Creek with gas barbecues, picnic tables, shelter sheds, water and a shower. There are a number of bush camps on Hinchinbrook Island, but once again, you'll need to book. In Wooroonooran National Park you can camp in the rainforest at Henrietta Creek. Tent and caravan sites, toilets, a shelter shed and picnic tables are provided. Take a fuel stove.

Closer to Cairns you can camp at Speewah in Barron Gorge National Park and at Noah Beach, 8km south of Cape Tribulation. Toilets, water and an outdoor shower stand are provided. Take a fuel stove as campfires are not allowed. The camping area is closed in the wet season and after heavy rains.

In Cape York there are a number of remote campsites in Lakefield National Park, including Twelve Mile Waterhole on the Normanby River opposite New Laura Ranger Base, Old Faithful Waterhole, 23km north of New Laura, Mick Fienn and Dingo Waterholes, 33km north of New Laura, Kalpowar Crossing, 3km east of Lakefield Ranger Station, Seven Mile Waterhole, 13km north-west of Lakefield, or Hann Crossing, 6km south-west of Bizant Ranger Station. Kalpowar Crossing has grassy individual campsites, cold showers, tap water, picnic tables, fireplaces and toilets along an 8km stretch of a permanent fresh waterhole. Hann Crossing has individual campsites and pit toilets. At the tip, you can camp beside the Jardine River or at Captain Billy Landing, Ussher Point or Eliot Falls. Only Eliot Falls has facilities (picnic tables, fireplaces and toilets) so visitors must be self-sufficient. Take drinking water, a fuel stove, a screened tent or nets for protection against insects at night.

Bushwalks

Most popular short walks are the 2.5km Mossman Gorge walk and the boardwalk at Cape Tribulation and the various short walks in Barron Gorge National Park, including the 20-minute Barron Falls Lookout track and the one-hour Wrights Lookout to Kuranda track.

There are also some good short walks at both Wallaman Falls and Blencoe Falls, or follow the Wet Tropics Great Walk, a 110km trail that links the two falls.

The Thorsborne Trail is a spectacular 32km trail along the east coast of Hinchinbrook Island. Limits apply to the number of walkers allowed on the trail so you must book at least 12 months in advance during school holidays.

www.epa.qld.gov.au ☎ 13 13 04

In Wooroonooran National Park the historic 18km Goldfield Trail from Goldsborough Valley to The Boulders Scenic Reserve near Babinda will take between 7-9 hours, although bush camping is allowed on the banks of the East Mulgrave River. The Mt Bartle Frere trail leads to the summit from Josephine Falls or the Atherton Tableland. Both routes are 7.5km, steep and very challenging. Allow two days. Bush camping is allowed along the route.

adventure activities

Meeting Queensland's tropical fish. *(TQ)*

Ballooning

Hot Air Cairns has a range of sunrise hot air balloon flights that float above the rainforest and farmlands of the Atherton Tablelands. Hot Air has the biggest range of balloons in Australia, including the world's first Koala Balloon, the Australia Balloon and other Australian-themed balloons. Flights take off and land from Mareeba, but most tours will include pick up from Cairns and Port Douglas. Half hour and one-hour flights available, as well as balloon chase spectator tours, and all tours include a celebratory champagne breakfast.

www.hotair.com.au www.ragingthunder.com.au/ballooning

Bungy jumping

Cairns is the bungy capital of Australia with 15 years jumping behind the success of AJ Hackett's 50m high Cairns Bungy Tower, 15km north of Cairns and surrounded by lush tropical rainforest with panoramic views out to the reef. Night Bungy is available once a month during the famous Full Moon Party–or it can be arranged for groups on request.

Bungy pioneer, Hackett, has also launched the Minjin Jungle Swing, a hang-gliding harness attached to stainless steel cables that allows up to three people to fly through the forest reaching speeds of up to 100km/hour.

www.ajhackett.com.au

Canoeing and kayaking

Coral Sea Kayaking, based in Mission Beach, offer sea kayaking tours, expeditions, private charter and kayak hire within the Great Barrier Reef Marine Park, visiting many of the national park islands in the region, such as Dunk Island, Hinchinbrook Island and the Family Island group.

www.coralseakayaking.com

Live Adrenalin run a Sea Kayaking Tour around Fitzroy Island in a one-day guided paddle to unspoilt areas of Fitzroy Island, which is only accessible by water. Lunch is at Little Fitzroy Island, a small island off main Fitzroy, where you can walk to the lighthouse to admire the spectacular view, go for a snorkel among the tropical fish and colourful coral or just laze around in the sun.

www.adrenalin.com.au

Lake Placid in Barron Gorge National Park near Kuranda is a popular spot for canoeing and you can hire canoes at the kiosk. Technically a wide part of the Barron River, Lake Placid is not far from the base of Barron Gorge and a regular staging post for kayakers or rafters heading for a day in the rapids. It's a good place to try out your equipment and hone your paddling skills.

Cycling and mountain biking

The rainforest hinterland around Cairns has some great mountain bike trails. Dan's Mountain Biking has a range of half and full-day MTB tours including the UCI World Mountain Bike Championship course, both cross country and downhill. The course weaves through tropical rainforest and offers 'interesting' challenges. This course was previously utilised for two rounds of the Grundig World Cup Series. Other tours include an easier ride through the Mulgrave Valley progressing from sealed road to a bush track and following a river to a swimming hole; a wild downhill ride on the Crocodile Trail; a full-day Cape Tribulation ride and rainforest night rides.

www.cairns.aust.com/mtb

Diving and snorkelling

Although the Great Barrier Reef spans more than 2000km of Queensland's coastline, Cairns, Port Douglas and Cape Tribulation are the closest gateways to the spectacular coral beds of the outer reef and there are dozens of snorkelling, diving and glass bottom cruises available. Most trips take a full day and head out to coral cays and islands around 90 minutes to two hours from shore and cater for all levels of swimming abilities. Nearby, Green and Fitzroy islands give you the chance to dive, snorkel or reef walk. If you've always wanted to try scuba diving this is a good place for it, as there are lots of places that offer introductory dive courses for underwater first timers–and all that competition means you're sure to find a trip to suit your budget.

Fishing

From Cairns to Cooktown you'll find great fishing in the creeks, where large barramundi are the main prize and offshore, giant black marlin. Around these parts, catching big fish seems easy, even if you are a beginner. In Cairns, the best fishing is in the heart of town in the tributaries of Trinity Inlet where you'll catch mangrove jack, barramundi, fingermark, trevally, queenfish and threadfin salmon.

Further north, the waters and rivers of the Gulf and Cape York are one of the country's fabled fishing destinations. A wild, last frontier, you really need a boat or to join a charter to get good results, particularly as much of the land is owned by Aboriginals and you will need prior permission to fish in their hunting grounds. There are lots of local guides and charters based in Cairns and other local centres.

www.fishingcairns.com.au

If you are limited for time, try a heli-fishing day trip to the Cape with Cairns-based Brazakka's Cape York Helicopters, who specialise in heli-fishing charters.

www.brazakka.com.au

Off-road driving

All roads north of the Daintree River are 4WD only, and most are closed during the west season. Each year hundreds of 4WD enthusiasts make the trek to the tip of Cape York in what is one of the country's classic adventure drives. The 750km track largely follows the tracks established by builders of the Overland Telegraph Track in the 1880s. It's a tough remote track for experienced four-wheel-drivers only, with many deep and difficult creek crossings (make sure your vehicle is fitted with a snorkel) and is best travelled in a convoy of two or more vehicles if possible. Be careful of saltwater crocodiles when wading through creeks.

Rainforest track. *(TQ)*

For a less extreme four-wheel-driving adventure join a tag-along or guided 4WD tour with one of the many 4WD tour companies based in Cairns and Port Douglas who specialise in day trips through the Daintree wilderness.

Barron River rapid rafting. *(TQ)*

Hang-gliding

Take to the skies with Flying Leap Cable Hang-Gliding Adventures in Cairns, to experience all the thrills but none of the spills. The hang-glider is towed up to the launch area, 300m away, and to a height of 60m, before flying back down with the glider remaining attached to the cable. Speeds reached depend on body weight and wind against you, but 50km/hour is usual.

www.flyingleap.com.au

Horse riding

Springmount Station, west of Cairns on the dry side of the Atherton Tablelands offers half and full-day guided rides though open bush-lands. All riding abilities are catered for and all tours include transfers from Cairns, swimming and a BBQ lunch.

www.springmountstation.com

Blazing Saddles, based in Kuranda, have a stable of more than 70 quiet and gentle horses to suit all levels and ages (minimum age 4 years) and offer half-day adventure trail rides through the rainforest. They also have a large fleet of quad bikes and offer half-day ATV (all terrain vehicles) rainforest tours. Minimum age is 12 years and no license or previous experience is necessary. Combine the two on a full-day adventure.

www.blazingsaddles.com.au

Ride along a beautiful tropical beach with Wonga Beach Horse Rides near Port Douglas who run three-hour rides through the rainforest and along Wonga Beach.

www.beachhorserides.com.au

Motorcycle tours

Cape York Motorcycle Adventures are a specialist motorcycle and dirt bike tour operator. Tour guide, Roy Kunda knows every trail in the region and has taken riders of all ability from backpacker novices to world motorcycle champions. The rides are matched to suit the ability of riders. Provided you have at least a learners license and some experience riding motorcycles, you will be fine. Riding in a group with the comfort of a support vehicle means every contingency from flat tyre to drowned bike will be looked after. Conditions range from jungle trails and creek crossings, to open plain and beach runs.

www.capeyorkmotorcycles.com.au

Skydiving

Paul's Parachuting and Skydive Cairns both have tandem jumps available in Cairns and Mission Beach. Both locations offer stunning views over the ocean, islands, beaches and tropical rainforest.

www.paulsparachuting.com.au www.skydivecairns.com.au

FNQ sunset on the beach. *(TQ)*

Jump the Beach offer tandem jumps over Mission Beach with a choice of skydiving from four different altitudes, depending on your nerve. You can also combine your jump with a tour: with the Skydive Dunk Island package you'll land on the beach near the rainforest resort and spend the afternoon coming down to earth from your adrenalin rush exploring Dunk Island, sunbaking, swimming, relaxing at the bar or enjoying the island's activities before heading back to Mission Beach by water taxi. The two-day Mission Possible tour combines a tandem jump over Mission Beach and a full day whitewater rafting on the Tully River with BBQ lunch.

www.jumpthebeach.com.au

Water skiing and wake boarding

Skii Mee Waterskiing Tours run waterskiing tours from Cairns up to Lake Tinaroo, around an hour's drive from Cairns in the Gillies Range in the Atherton Tablelands. There is a choice of two half-day tours to either Lake Tinaroo or Trinity Inlet. The half day gives you three hours on the water to ski, wakeboard, kneeboard, tube ride and if you're game, barefoot. Full-day tours including a hot lunch and five hours of skiing or boarding on Lake Tinaroo. All transport, equipment and wetsuits are provided.

www.skiimee.com.au

White water rafting

FNQ is a favourite white water rafting spot, with excellent rapids on the Tully River, the Barron River and the North Johnstone River.

The Tully River, near Cairns, is one of Australia's best and most popular one-day rafting trips with rapids up to grade 4. Most trips include the negotiation of more than 45 rapids as you pass through World Heritage rainforest and waterfalls that cascade down the gorge walls.

Barron Gorge is a good introduction to white water rafting with half-day trips near Kuranda and rapids to grade 3, with descriptive names such as 'Rooster Tail', 'Cheese Churn' and 'Hells Gate'. In the calmer sections you will get to enjoy the ethereal beauty of the world's oldest rainforest and waterfalls from a unique waterline perspective.

www.ragingthunder.com.au

More experienced rafters should try a four-day North Johnstone expedition with R'n'R White Water Rafting, with rapids up to grade 5. Rated amongst the world's top 10 rafting tours, helicopter is the only way in; rafting is the only way out. The North Johnstone valley is utterly pristine ancient rainforest. Your group will be the only people within hundreds of square kilometres.

www.raft.com.au

Foaming Fury has a half-day white water kayaking tour down the Russell River, which starts with a trek through the dense rainforest of the Russell River valley, carrying inflatable two-man sports kayaks with you (the lightweight kayaks are deflated and the packs are share carried to the launch point). Rapids range from grade 1 to 4.

www.foamingfury.com.au

MORE INFORMATION

- **Gateway Discovery Centre:** 51 The Esplanade, Cairns www.tropicalaustralia.com.au ☎ (07) 4051 3588

weather watch

- January: 23–37°C
- July: 16–30°C
- Summer is very wet and humid. Winter is warm and sunny with little rain. Stinger season runs every year from October through to May. Swimming is not recommended during this time as box jellyfish and the Irukandji jellyfish are prevalent in the waters and their stings can cause acute pain and serious illness. Box jellyfish can cause death in previously well humans in as little as three minutes.

outback & gulf country

Lawn Hill National Park. (TQ)

▶ WESTERN QUEENSLAND is an immense, sparsely populated area that extends west of the Great Dividing Range through to the Gulf of Carpentaria in the north and across the channel country in the south to the endless red sand hills of the Simpson Desert. It's a place of larger-than-life legends, of iconic bush heroes and rich in fossil fields. It's also a place of ethereal beauty, particularly after rains when the savannah grasslands are lush and green and the dunes are carpeted in wildflowers. Distances are vast, temperatures are extreme and almost anywhere you choose to go out here is an adventure.

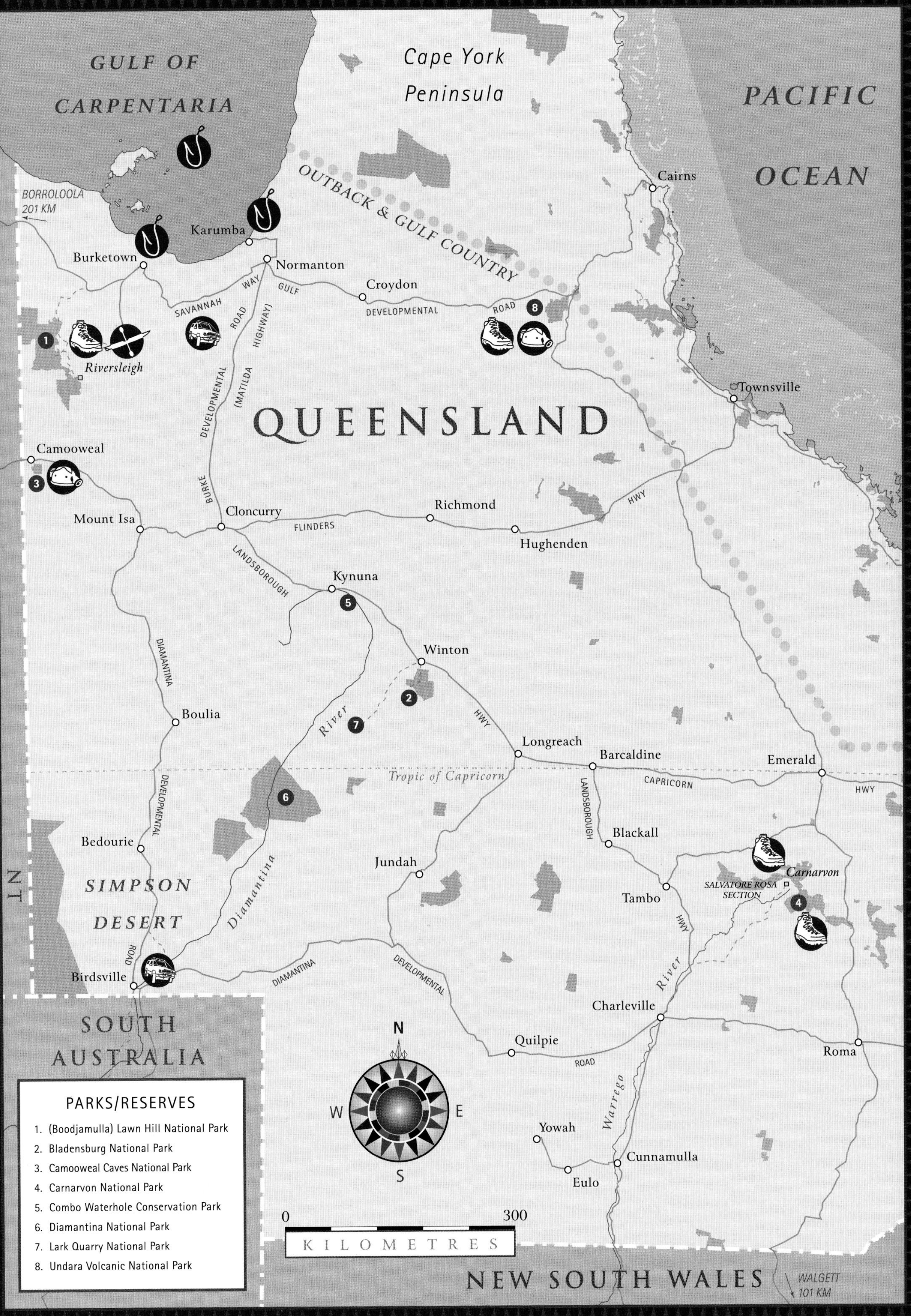
GULF OF CARPENTARIA
Cape York Peninsula
PACIFIC OCEAN
OUTBACK & GULF COUNTRY
BORROLOOLA 201 KM
Cairns
Karumba
Burketown
Normanton
Croydon
SAVANNAH WAY
GULF DEVELOPMENTAL ROAD
BURKE DEVELOPMENTAL ROAD
(MATILDA HIGHWAY)
Riversleigh
Townsville
QUEENSLAND
Camooweal
Mount Isa
Cloncurry
FLINDERS HWY
Richmond
Hughenden
LANDSBOROUGH
Kynuna
DIAMANTINA
Winton
HWY
Boulia
River
Longreach
Barcaldine
Emerald
Tropic of Capricorn
CAPRICORN HWY
LANDSBOROUGH HWY
DEVELOPMENTAL
Bedourie
Blackall
Jundah
NT
SIMPSON DESERT
Diamantina
Carnarvon
SALVATORE ROSA SECTION
Tambo
ROAD
Birdsville
DIAMANTINA DEVELOPMENTAL ROAD
River
Charleville
SOUTH AUSTRALIA
Quilpie
Roma
N
W
E
S
Warrego
Yowah
Cunnamulla
Eulo
0
300
KILOMETRES
NEW SOUTH WALES
WALGETT 101 KM
PARKS/RESERVES
1. (Boodjamulla) Lawn Hill National Park
2. Bladensburg National Park
3. Camooweal Caves National Park
4. Carnarvon National Park
5. Combo Waterhole Conservation Park
6. Diamantina National Park
7. Lark Quarry National Park
8. Undara Volcanic National Park

Carnarvon Gorge. *(TQ)*

NATIONAL PARKS

Combo Waterhole Conservation Park: a string of semi-permanent coolibah-lined lagoons on the Diamantina River south-east of Kynuna, Combo Waterholes are believed to be the site that inspired Banjo Paterson to write *Waltzing Matilda* while on a visit to Dagworth Station in 1895. Day use area only.

Lark Quarry Conservation Park: the world's only known site of a dinosaur stampede where 95 million years ago a large meat-eating dinosaur startled and chased a horde of much smaller dinosaurs on the muddy shores of a lake. The footprints made in the mud have been fossilized. Entry to the park is free but a fee applies if you want to view the trackways. Lark Quarry is 110km or 90 minutes south-west of Winton along the Jundah Road

Bladensburg National Park: this large, remote park south of Winton protects examples of the Mitchell Grass Downs and Channel Country with open plains, rugged ranges, mesa-topped hills and picturesque waterholes.

(Boodjamulla) Lawn Hill National Park: rugged escarpments, gorges and rocky outcrops with sheer red sandstone walls up to 60m high, drop into palm-filled creeks and permanent waterholes. The vegetation is tropical—water lilies, cabbage tree palms and figs; the waters full of freshwater crocodiles and northern snapping turtles. Wallaroos, tiny bats and ringtail possums hide amongst the rocky outcrops and overhangs. The park includes Riversleigh World Heritage site, one of the richest fossil sites in the world, with fossils from 25 million to 10,000 years ago including the remains of giant pythons, carnivorous kangaroos and marsupial lions.

Diamantina National Park: this large, remote park in the Channel Country features sand dunes, claypans, ragged red-capped ranges, and the broad floodplains and braided channels of the Diamantina River, one of the state's longest rivers. See the park along the 157km Warracoota self-guided circuit drive, which takes you past sand dunes, floodplains, claypans, gibber plains and grasslands. Stop at Warracoota Waterhole and visit the old cattle yards, a large constructed dam and an old stock camp.

Undara Volcanic National Park: the Undara lava tubes, which extend more than 160km, were formed around 190,000 years ago, when a large volcano spewed molten lava over the surrounding landscape. The lava flowed rapidly down a dry riverbed, the top outer layer cooling and forming a crust while the molten lava below drained outwards leaving behind a series of hollow tubes. There are 68 separate sections of lava tube that have been identified from more than 300 lava tube roof collapses, and more than 164 volcanoes in the area. Where the tubes have collapsed dense pockets of dry rainforest have formed in the moist, sheltered conditions. You can explore some of the longer lava tubes on one of the daytime tours run by Undara Experience. **www.undara.com.au**

Carnarvon National Park: an oasis in the semi-arid heart of Queensland between Roma and Emerald, Carnarvon Gorge is a steep-sided gorge of towering white sandstone cliffs with narrow, vibrantly coloured and lush side gorges. Boulder-strewn Carnarvon Creek winds through the gorge and the sandstone overhands are adorned with some of the finest Aboriginal rock art in the country, including rock engravings, ochre stencils and freehand paintings at Cathedral Cave, Baloon Cave and the Art Gallery. Other highlights of the park include the sandstone cliffs of Ka Ka Mundi, the Aboriginal rock art of Mount Moffat and the deeply eroded and spectacular rock formations and the Salvator Rosa Section, which has brilliant wildflower displays in spring.

scenic highlights

Combo Waterhole (TQ)

The Matilda Highway is the name of a collection of sealed roads that spear through the heart of outback Queensland, from Cunnamulla near the NSW border north to Karumba on the shores of the Gulf of Carpentaria. It's a long way, almost 1700km, and to really explore the region you'll need at least a week, if not 10 days.

Cunnamulla, on the banks of the Warrego River, is in the heart of wool country, and the first of a succession of down-to-earth country towns, with two-story verandah'd pubs, grand post offices and imposing bank buildings, that you will pass through on this trip. Fossickers keen to try their luck can detour here for the loop to Eulo, Yowah and Quilpie, home of the boulder opal, rejoining the highway at Charleville, where the clear night skies across the plains make for near perfect star-gazing conditions and the Charleville Cosmos Centre is well worth a visit.

From Charleville continue north across the plains through Tambo to Blackall, where shearing legend, Jack Howe, set a world record in 1892 shearing 321 sheep in seven hours and 40 minutes with blade shears. It took another 58 years before anyone could match his feat and that was with machine shears.

From Blackall it's around an hour's drive to Barcaldine on the Tropic of Capricorn, where, just outside the railway station, is the Tree of Knowledge. It was under this ghost gum that striking shearers met in 1891 and the Australian Labor Party was formed. Nearby, the Australian Workers Heritage Centre examines the role of the Australian worker in everything from the shearers' strike to women in the war.

Longreach, the largest town along the Matilda, is home to the Stockman's Hall of Fame. This huge museum depicting all aspects of country life is worth spending a few hours at. Also in Longreach is the Qantas Founders Outback Museum, next to the airport.

Winton is 178km north-west of Longreach, and has long been celebrated as the birthplace of Australia's favourite song, *Waltzing Matilda*. The inspiration for the song was sparked by the suicide of a striking shearer in the Diamantina River in 1895. Banjo Patterson, picnicking with friends at Combo Waterhole, penned the words of a poem about a swagman camped by a billabong. Today Combo Waterhole is little more than a large muddy puddle baking under the relentless sun. A ring of coolibah trees, swarming with bright green budgerigars, provide welcome shade and it is a pleasant picnic spot.

Ninety-three million years ago, the area around Winton was thick with dinosaurs. At Lark Quarry, 110km south-west of Winton, there was a dinosaur stampede, and hundreds of dinosaur footprints have been preserved in the mud of a once prehistoric lake. Most of the footprints were made by a huge carnosaur chasing smaller coelurosaurs and ornithopods and is believed to be the most extensive set of dinosaur tracks ever found in the world.

Cloncurry, the birthplace of John Flynn's Royal Flying Doctor Service, marks the beginning of gulf savannah country, as the road, now the Burke Development Road, continues its run north to the coast. Explorers Burke and Wills passed through the rugged country to the west of here in 1861. The Burke and Wills Junction is a good rest stop before continuing onto Karumba on the Gulf of Carpentaria, the final town on the Matilda Highway.

The Channel Country

The south-west corner of Queensland is a maze of dry waterholes and sandy river beds that fill each year with runoff from the monsoonal rains of the tropical wet season. Towns such as Bedourie and Boulia are little more than a pub and a couple of houses, but are administrative centres, the latter famous for its mysterious Min Min lights which appear after dark. Floating balls of light are said to follow travellers for kilometres before disappearing. According to the legend, anyone who chases the lights and manages to catch one disappears. At the edge of the Simpson Desert, the tiny town of Birdsville is most famous for its annual horse races in September when the town's population swells from 120 to more than 6000.

Mount Isa

Queensland's largest inland town is home to Australia's biggest underground mine, it's the world's biggest single producer of silver and lead and is among the world's top 10 for copper and zinc. It's one of the few places in the world where the four minerals are found in the one spot.

Matilda Country

In 1895 the suicide of a striking shearer became the inspiration for a song that became the unofficial national anthem, *Waltzing Matilda*. Its first public performance is believed to have been on April 6, 1895 at the North Gregory Hotel in Winton. Longreach to the south is the birthplace of the national airline Qantas and home to the Stockman's Hall of Fame. Cloncurry is the birthplace of John Flynn's (Flynn of the Inland) Royal Flying Doctor Service, Blackall was the first town to drill an artesian bore in 1885 allowing vast tracts of the semi-arid outback to be utilised for grazing and Barcaldine on the Tropic of Capricorn was where the Australian Labor Party was formed.

The Gulf

The Gulf of Carpentaria is a fishing paradise, famous amongst anglers for barramundi and other pelagic fish. Karumba, the centre of the Gulf's prawning and barramundi industry, is surrounded by flat wetlands which extend inland for approximately 30km, the meandering saltwater tidal estuaries home to huge saltwater crocodiles and a vast array of bird life. Normanton is home to the historic Gulflander train, Croydon's main street has been listed by the National Trust and little seems to have changed since its gold-rush hey days in the 1880s and Burketown is the self-proclaimed 'barramundi capital of the world'.

Caravan and camping

You can camp at Bough Shed Hole, in Bladensburg National Park. No water supplies are provided, and you must be self-sufficient. In Lawn Hill National Park you can camp near Lawn Hill Creek. Toilets, cold showers, shared fireplaces and water are provided. Take a fuel stove for cooking. Bookings are essential

www.epa.qld.gov.au

Camping is forbidden at Riversleigh but you can camp outside the park at Adels Grove, a commercial camping area where camping/van sites are provided with water, fireplace and BBQ plate, but no power. During June, July and August you'll need to book well ahead for sites. Accommodation with dinner and breakfast is available in pre-erected tents with single beds and clean linen and share amenities close by.

www.adelsgrove.com.au

Camping is prohibited in Undara Volcanic National Park but you can camp at Undara Experience. It offers a range of accommodation options including 100-year-old railway carriages with ensuites; the special Swags Tent Village, off-the-ground permanent tents with lighting and beds (bring your own swag or bedding), six powered caravan sites and plenty of unpowered van and campsites. Individual campsites have campfire pits with firewood available (at extra cost) and there's also a swimming pool, resort kiosk and a licensed bistro.

www.undara.com.au

In the Diamantina you can bush camp at Hunter's Gorge or Gum Waterhole. Take drinking water and a fuel stove. You can camp in the Carnarvon Gorge visitor area only during the Easter, June/July and September/October Queensland school holidays. Booking is essential. There is small hike-in camping area at Big Bend, 9.6km from the information centre. In remote sections of the park, Mt Moffatt has four camping areas, each with a limited number of campsites. Dargonelly Rock Hole and West Branch camping areas are fine for conventional vehicles in dry weather; Rotary Shelter Shed and Top Moffatt camping areas are accessible by 4WD vehicle only. Take your own water. In the Ka Ka Mundi area you can bush camp around Bunbuncundoo Springs and at the Nogoa River camping area in Salvator Rosa.

Bushwalks

There are several good walks you can do in Lawn Hill Gorge. If you only have time for one, the 4km, one-hour Island Stack walk starts with a steep climb before opening up to a circular track that loops round the flat 'table-top' of a large island of rock in the heart of the gorge. This is the best walk for views. You can also add on a short half-hour walk to the Cascades, a delightful pandanus-fringed pool and shallow waterfall. The Waanyi people have lived in the gorge area for at least 17,000 years and know this place as Boodjamulla, or Rainbow Serpent country. Lawn Hill Gorge is sacred to the Waanyi people. The two-hour Wild Dog Dreaming Walk, a semi-sheltered track to the lower gorge where you'll see plenty of crocs, takes you to several Aboriginal rock art sites and past midden heaps. You can also take a self-guided walk around the Riversleigh 'D' Site–read about the fossils in the information shelter at Riversleigh then follow a self-guided interpretive trail, although it does a take a bit of imagination to picture the giant marsupials and strange beasts described from the fragments of bones that are embedded in the limestone hillside.

At Undara a one-hour walk around the rim of Kalkani Crater will give you the best view of the collapsed line of the lava tubes, but if you want to walk through the tubes themselves you will need to join a guided tour. At Undara Lodge there are nine mapped bushwalking trails that you can do, ranging from easy half-hour strolls up to a nearby bluff for views over the volcanic park; to longer walks to 100 Mile Swamp (named for its proximity to the coast, not for the size of

Gold panning. *(TQ)*

DON'T MISS

- **Charleville Cosmos Centre:** enter the world of deep space, watch enormous meteor storms, observe eclipses, and experience many other wonders of the night sky. Qantas Drive (off the Matilda Highway), Charleville. Open daily between 10am–6pm with night shows from 6.30pm. ☎ (07) 4654 7771.
- **Tambo Teddies Workshop:** see sheep-skin teddy bears being created. Each bear is named after a property in the Tambo district. Arthur Street, Tambo. **www.tamboteddies.com.au**
- **Blackall Woolscour:** the only steam-driven woolscour remaining of the 52 which once operated across the country. 20-stand shearing shed attached. Colourful local characters lead guided tours to explain each stage of wool processing. Signposted 4km outside of Blackall. Open daily 8am–4pm for guided tours. ☎ (07) 4657 4637. **http://www.heritagetrails.qld.gov.au/attractions/blackall.html**
- **Australian Workers Heritage Centre:** celebrates the lives and heritage of ordinary working people—telling the stories of the railway workers and blacksmiths, the farmers, nurses and teachers who shaped the nation. Ash Street, Barcaldine. Open daily, 9am–5pm, Sun 10am–5pm. **www.australianworkersheritagecentre.com.au**
- **Stockmans Hall of Fame:** you'll need at least half a day to tour this excellent interactive museum dedicated to the people, pioneers and lifestyle of the outback. Landsborough Highway, Longreach. Open daily, 9am–5pm. **www.stockmanshalloffame.com.au**
- **Qantas Founders Outback Museum:** commemorates the birth of the world's oldest airline. Tour a fully-equipped 747 jumbo jet and enjoy stories of Australia's pioneer aviators. Longreach Airport adjacent to the Australian Stockman's Hall of Fame. Open daily, 9am–5pm. **http://qfom.com.au/**
- **Waltzing Matilda Centre:** this high-tech centre is a tribute to Australia's national song. It features exciting, interactive exhibitions, a Light and Sound Show and a Spectravision presentation by famous Australians. Elderslie Street, Winton. Open daily, 8.30am–5pm. **www.matildacentre.com.au**
- **Royal Flying Doctor Museum:** the RFDS was launched in Cloncurry in 1928. Museum, gallery, outdoor theatre and gardens commemorating the founder of the Service, John Flynn. John Flynn Place, Cloncurry. Open Mon–Fri, 8am–4.30pm, weekends 9am–3pm May–Sep.
- **Birdsville Races:** iconic outback event held annually on the first weekend of September. Two days of horse racing with live entertainment, the AKUBRA Fashions of the Field, Fred Brophy's Boxing Troupe, whipcracking and sideshows. **www.birdsvilleraces.com**
- **Outback at Isa:** former miners lead guided underground mine tours descending to the 1.2km of tunnels in an Alimak cage, lowered from an historic headframe. Complex also includes a multi-media gallery and the Riversleigh Fossils Centre, an interpretive centre for the world heritage listed fossil sites at Riversleigh with displays, museum and Fossil Treatment Laboratory. 19 Marion Street, Mount Isa. Open daily 9am–5pm. **www.outbackatisa.com.au**
- **National Trust Tent Museum:** a timber-framed house with a canvas roof under a free standing galvanised iron roof. This unusual environmental adaptation was once common in Mount Isa as 1930's mining company housing and contains furnishings and objects of historical interest from Mount Isa. Fourth Avenue, Mt Isa. Open daily, 10am–2pm April 1–Sept 30. **www.nationaltrustqld.org**
- **Kronosaurus Korner:** home of the Richmond Marine Fossil Museum displaying more than 400 local fossils from the Cretaceous Inland Sea that covered a large section of Queensland 120 million years ago. Highlight is Australia's best preserved vertebrate fossil, the 4.25m *Richmond Pliosaur*. 91–93 Goldring Street, Richmond. Open daily, 8.30am–4.45pm. **www.kronosauruskorner.com.au**

the swamp); along the route of the historic Gulf telegraph line that was built in the 1870s; and full-day walks across the plains.

Carnarvon Gorge has 21km of walking tracks. The Moss Garden Walk (2–3 hours return) to a gorge wall covered in a vibrant green carpet of liverworts and ferns lapping up a spring as it seeps through the rockface is one of the most popular, as is the half-day Amphitheatre Walk to a hidden crevice accessed by a ladder from the gorge floor to a natural amphitheatre open to the sky, but otherwise enclosed with remarkable acoustics and the Lower Aljon Falls and Ward's Canyon where you will be surrounded by ancient King Ferns, the largest fern in the world. The three-hour (return) climb to Boolimba Bluff provides great views of gorge system from above. The most accessible display of Aboriginal rock art is at the Art Gallery (5km) where, sheltered by an overhanging rock face, you'll find a variety of motifs typical of the region's Aboriginal art. An interpretive display explains their significance. The walk can combine visits to Aljon Falls and the Amphitheatre to make a full-day walk.

In the Mt Moffatt section of the park the Looking Glass is a 1.9km return walk (allow an hour) or part of a 5.8km circuit walk (three hours) to where wind has eroded a cave through an isolated pillar of Precipice Sandstone beside the Maranoa River. Other popular walks are the 20-minute walk to Cathedral Rock and 40-minute walk to The Chimneys where three pillars of rock have been separated from the narrow end of a small bluff of Precipice Sandstone where water has eroded down vertical fractures. The Tombs rock art site is a two-hour return walk to a sandstone shelter with more than 400 stencilled motifs. The Tombs once contained burial chambers for local Aboriginal people where skeletons were wrapped and bound in bark burial cylinders.

adventure activities

Lawn Hill National Park. (TQ)

Canoeing and kayaking

An oasis surrounded by grassy savannah plains, Lawn Hill Gorge is a pleasant place to while away a few hours paddling. You can hire canoes from the camping area in the national park and float for 4km on the calm green waters of the gorge, keeping an eye out for red-winged parrots, egrets, bitterns, kites and lazy crocodiles (the relatively harmless but still scary looking freshwater type) basking in the sun. Indari Falls are a great place to stop for a swim.

Camel safaris

Outback Camel Adventures, based in Winton offer a range of extended camel and camping safaris including a 17-day, 385km camel ride from Winton to Boulia following old coach roads and camping out under the stars. Trips are timed to coincide with the annual Boulia Camel races in July. Other trips include a 10-day trip from Winton to Kynuna exploring the heritage of *Waltzing Matilda*, travelling through the Ayrshire Hills and then onto the Old Dagworth Station and Combo waterholes and a three-day paddle and saddle trek camping beside waterholes, canoeing and fishing.

www.outbackcameladventures.com.au

Caving

Part of the longest lava tube system in the world, the caves of Undara Volcanic Park can only be explored on a guided tour, largely due to naturally-occurring high levels of carbon dioxide found in most of the tubes. There are a range of tours available, including night-time tours to Barker's Cave, home to 40,000 micro bats, and half and full-day tours inside several of the tubes where you'll learn about the geology of the caves and surrounding countryside as well as the local plant and animal life.

www.undara.com.au

Experienced cavers should head to Camooweal Caves National Park, around 20km from the township of Camooweal on the Barkly Tableland. Here, sinkhole openings that dot the landscape give access to an elaborate cave system that lies beneath the surface, where water percolated through 500-million-year-old Cambrian layers of soluble dolomite have created extensive caverns linked by vertical shafts up to 75m deep. Unlike any other cave system in Queensland they are still gradually enlarging as water continues to flow in from the surface and erode away the cave walls during the wet season.

Following the summer rains the water table recedes deep into shafts leaving the caves dry and dusty for the remainder of the year. Exploring the caves should only be considered in the dry season as they can often fill with water during the wet season. Only experienced cavers with appropriate equipment should explore the caves, and should notify the local police or Ranger of arrival and departure times at the caves. The best cave to explore is Great Nowranie that can only be reached after navigating an 18m drop. This cave also has the largest sink hole of 290m long and 70m deep and climbing gear is necessary.

Fishing

The gulf waters are one of the country's most celebrated fishing destinations and it is the main recreation in most of the gulf towns. There are a number of private fishing camps tucked away on remote locations and lots of charter operations. During the dry season the caravan parks of Karumba are full to bursting with hundreds of eager anglers who come here each year for two months of fishing–the shallow waters, rivers and creeks offering prize catches of barramundi, bream, sooty grunter, queenfish, black jewfish, mangrove jack and Spanish mackerel. Burketown is the self-proclaimed 'barramundi capital of the world'. Each April, the tiny town of 235 hosts the World Barramundi Fishing Championships, offering more than $7500 in prize money, with $2600 for the heaviest single catch.

Down south the dams, lakes, rivers and billabongs offer some good fishing for Australian bass, golden perch, Murray cod and silver perch.

Undara lava tube. *(TQ)*

Fossicking

The south-west of Queensland is a rich fossicking area, particularly for boulder opals. At Yowah, around 100km west of Cunnamulla, you can find boulder opal, or Yowah Nuts, an ironstone rock with opal matrix and/or hopefully a crystal centre. Chips of opal or fragments of ironstone matrix can also be found by specking the ground surface or digging in shallow ground. You can also find boulder opal in the spoil dumps of old workings and shallow ground at Opalton, 100km south-west of Winton and around Duck Creek and Sheep Station Creek 100km south south-east of Quilpie. For details on fossicking licences visit:

www.nrm.qld.gov.au

Off-road driving

First established during the 1880s as a stock route between Marree in South Australia and Birdsville in Queensland, the 520km Birdsville Track has become one of Australia's most legendary outback tracks. (See the Outback South Australia chapter, page 352.)

The Gulf Track, now part of the trans-continental Savannah Way that links Cairns to Broome via Katherine, is a well-made dirt road stretching 700km from Normanton to Borroloola in the Northern Territory across the Gulf of Carpentaria. There's a few river crossings, but in the middle of the dry season nothing too dramatic. The golden grass-covered plains of the gulf country savannah are the heart of cattle country, and great Brahmin beasts roam the countryside in unfenced paddocks that stretch for miles, punctuated only by towering termite mounds and the odd gate. Highlights include Burke and Wills' last campsite (camp 119), the fishing town of Burketown, the lush oasis of Lawn Hill National Park and the Lost City at Cape Crawford, a large expanse of tall sandstone columns only accessible by air.

MORE INFORMATION

- **Outback Queensland Tourism Authority:** ☎ (07) 3211 4877 www.outbackholidays.info www.heritagetrails.qld.gov.au

Simpson Desert. *(TQ)*

weather watch

- January: 23–37°C
- July: 7–23°C
- These temperatures are for Longreach. The best time to travel is April to September, when roads in the far north are open and temperatures are less extreme.

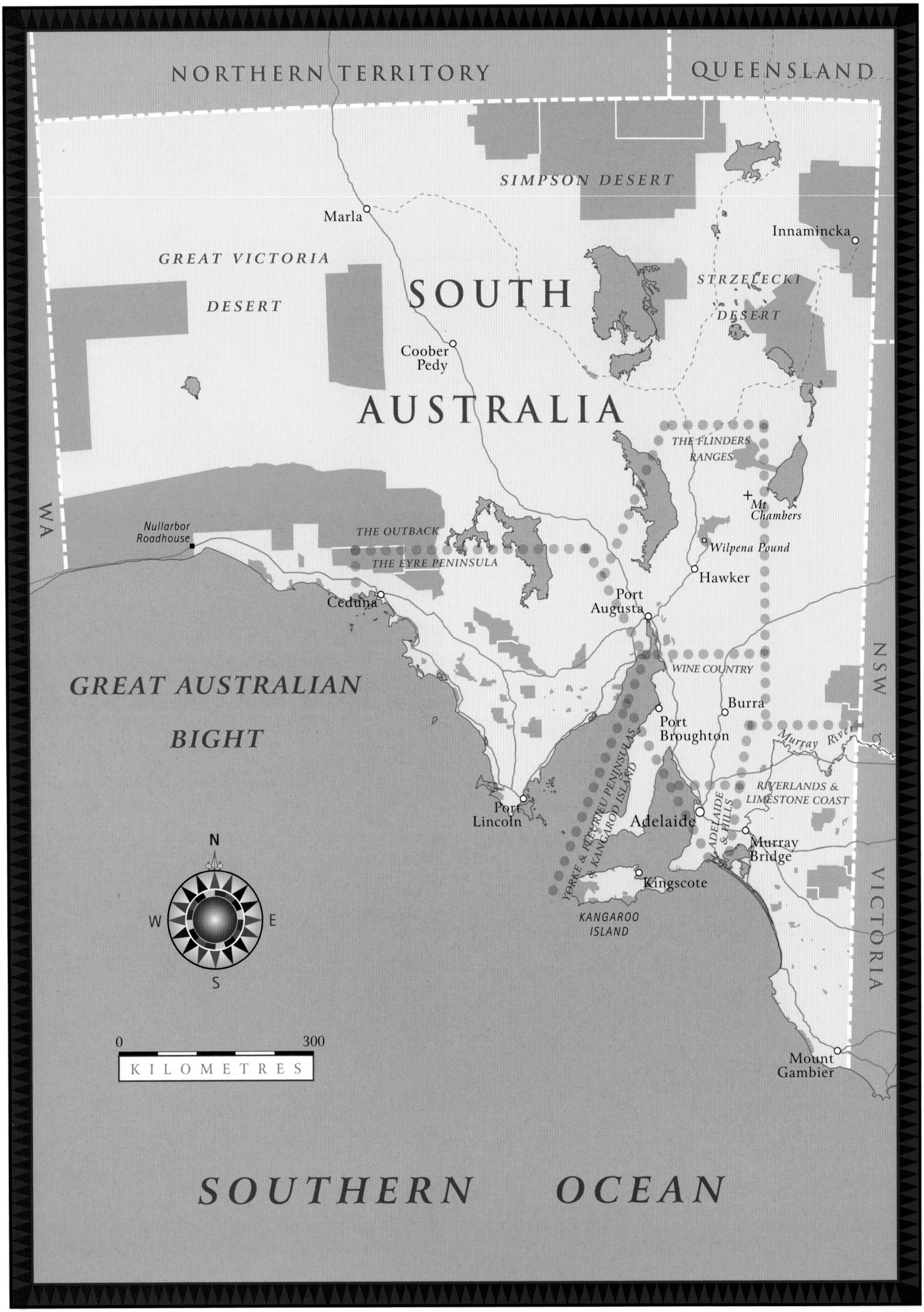

NORTHERN TERRITORY

QUEENSLAND

SIMPSON DESERT

Marla

Innamincka

GREAT VICTORIA

DESERT

SOUTH

AUSTRALIA

STRZELECKI

DESERT

Coober Pedy

THE FLINDERS RANGES

Mt Chambers

Wilpena Pound

Hawker

WA

Nullarbor Roadhouse

THE OUTBACK

THE EYRE PENINSULA

Ceduna

Port Augusta

WINE COUNTRY

NSW

GREAT AUSTRALIAN

BIGHT

Burra

Port Broughton

Murray River

YORKE & FLEURIEU PENINSULAS & KANGAROO ISLAND

RIVERLANDS & LIMESTONE COAST

ADELAIDE & HILLS

Port Lincoln

Adelaide

Murray Bridge

N

W

E

S

Kingscote

KANGAROO ISLAND

VICTORIA

0

300

KILOMETRES

Mount Gambier

SOUTHERN OCEAN

Australia's driest state with the largest proportion of semi-desert, South Australia has some of the most inhospitable landscapes in the country. It also has some of the most fertile—South Australia is renowned for its vineyards and wineries and the lush green valleys north and east of the Adelaide capital produces some of the world's best wines. Australia's longest river, The Murray, spills into the ocean in the east of the state; the peninsulas and islands provide a rugged and beautiful coastline and to the west, the spectacular cliffs of the Great Australian Bight follow the path of the longest, straightest road in the world across the Nullarbor Plain.

south australia

Wilpena Pound *(SATC)*

adelaide & its hills

Bushwalking in the Adelaide Hills – (SATC)

▶ UNLIKE MOST AUSTRALIAN CITIES that grew up haphazardly around early settlements, Adelaide was planned from the start—and it shows. Set beside the River Torrens between the Adelaide Hills and waters of Gulf St Vincent, Colonel William Light's 1837 town plan of broad streets surrounded by parkland has produced a city with next to no traffic jams, a grid-like street system which makes getting lost very hard to do and, best of all, an inner city where everything is within easy walking distance.

The wine and festival capital of Australia, Adelaide is a vibrant, stylish and innovative city with all the buzz, culture and convenience of a big city without the frustrations. The Adelaide Festival of Arts and its fringe festival attract major artists from all over the world. The city centre is a charming blend of historic buildings, wide streets, numerous shops, street cafes and restaurants.

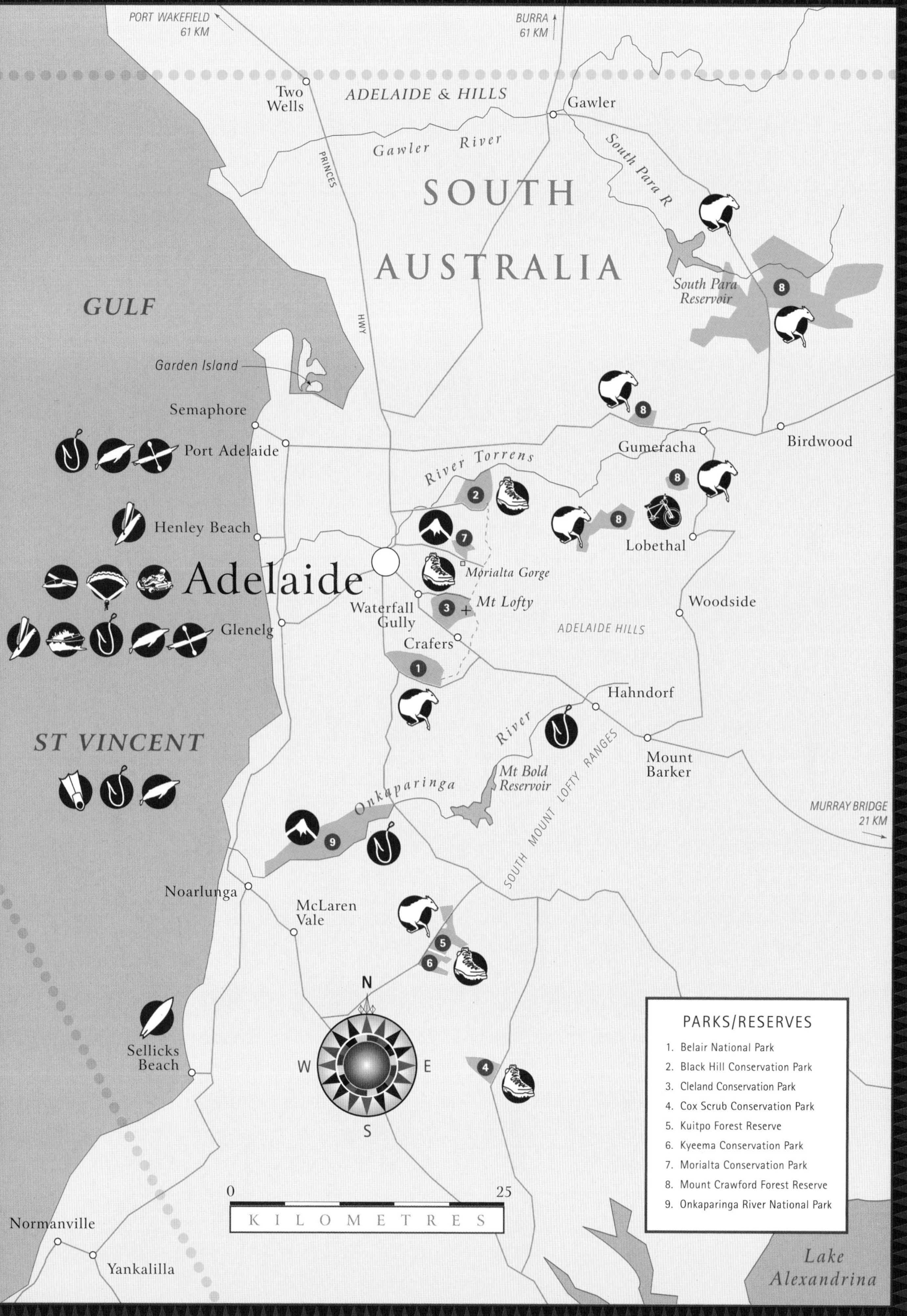
PORT WAKEFIELD
61 KM
BURRA
61 KM
Two Wells
ADELAIDE & HILLS
Gawler
Gawler River
PRINCES HWY
South Para R
SOUTH AUSTRALIA
South Para Reservoir
GULF
Garden Island
Semaphore
Port Adelaide
River Torrens
Gumeracha
Birdwood
Henley Beach
Lobethal
Adelaide
Morialta Gorge
Mt Lofty
Waterfall Gully
Woodside
Glenelg
ADELAIDE HILLS
Crafers
Hahndorf
ST VINCENT
River
Mount Barker
Mt Bold Reservoir
SOUTH MOUNT LOFTY RANGES
Onkaparinga
MURRAY BRIDGE
21 KM
Noarlunga
McLaren Vale
N
W
E
S
Sellicks Beach
PARKS/RESERVES
1. Belair National Park
2. Black Hill Conservation Park
3. Cleland Conservation Park
4. Cox Scrub Conservation Park
5. Kuitpo Forest Reserve
6. Kyeema Conservation Park
7. Morialta Conservation Park
8. Mount Crawford Forest Reserve
9. Onkaparinga River National Park
0
25
KILOMETRES
Normanville
Yankalilla
Lake Alexandrina

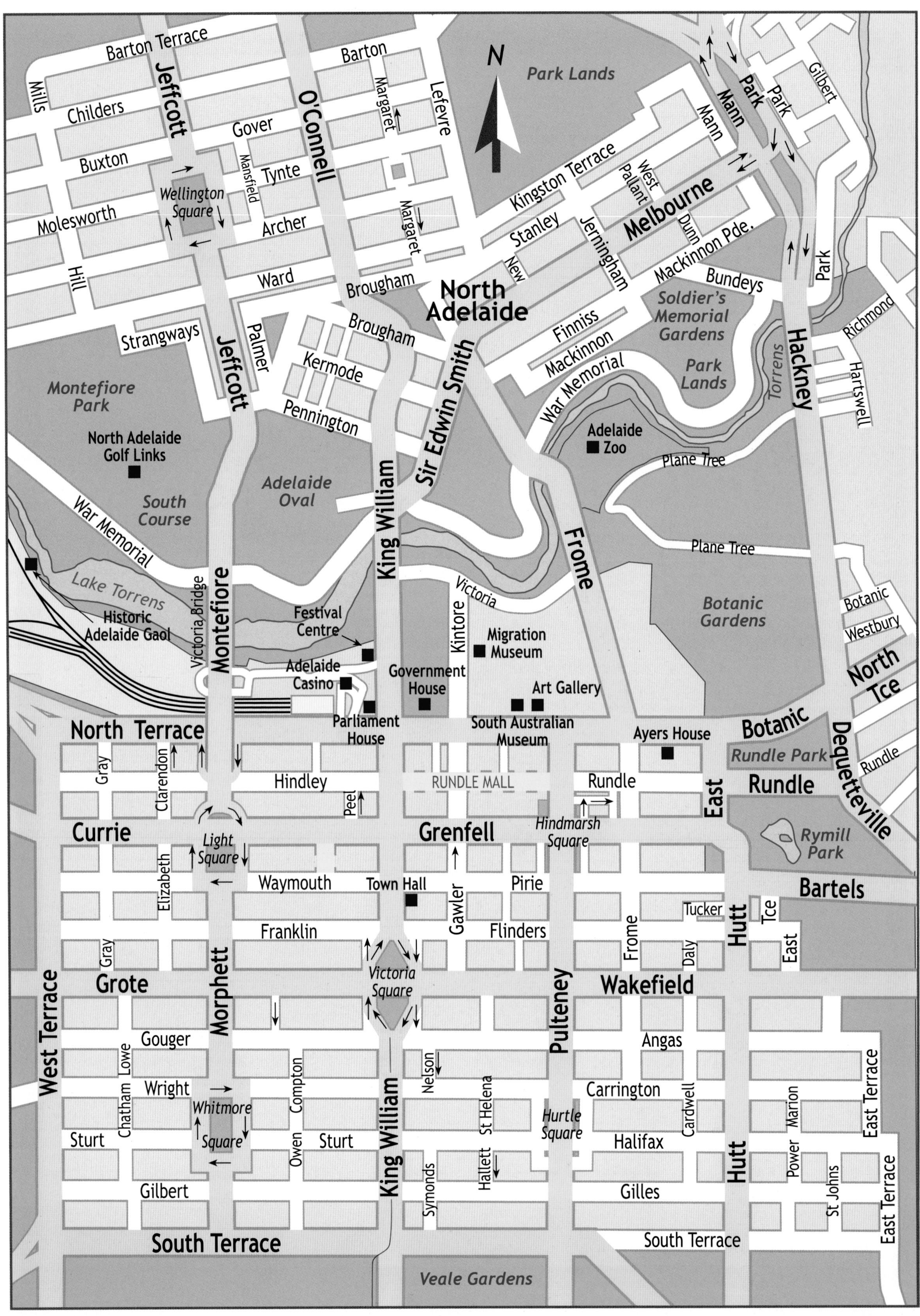
N
Park Lands
Barton Terrace
Barton
Jeffcott
O'Connell
Mills
Childers
Gover
Margaret
Lefevre
Buxton
Tynte
Mansfield
Wellington Square
Molesworth
Archer
Margaret
Kingston Terrace
West Pallant
Stanley
Jerningham
Melbourne
Dunn
Mackinnon Pde.
Mann
Mann
Park
Park
Gilbert
Hill
Ward
Brougham
North Adelaide
New
Bundeys
Park
Soldier's Memorial Gardens
Strangways
Jeffcott
Palmer
Brougham
Kermode
Pennington
Sir Edwin Smith
Finniss
Mackinnon
War Memorial
Park Lands
Torrens
Hackney
Richmond
Hartswell
Montefiore Park
North Adelaide Golf Links
South Course
Adelaide Oval
King William
Adelaide Zoo
Plane Tree
Plane Tree
War Memorial
Frome
Lake Torrens
Victoria Bridge
Montefiore
Historic Adelaide Gaol
Festival Centre
Victoria
Kintore
Migration Museum
Botanic Gardens
Botanic
Westbury
North Tce
Adelaide Casino
Government House
Art Gallery
Parliament House
South Australian Museum
North Terrace
Ayers House
Botanic
Dequetteville
Rundle Park
Rundle
Gray
Clarendon
Hindley
RUNDLE MALL
Rundle
Rundle
East
Peel
Currie
Light Square
Grenfell
Hindmarsh Square
Rymill Park
Elizabeth
Waymouth
Town Hall
Gawler
Pirie
Bartels
Tucker
Tce
Franklin
Flinders
Frome
Hutt
Gray
Daly
East
Grote
Morphett
Victoria Square
Pulteney
Wakefield
West Terrace
Gouger
Angas
Lowe
Nelson
Chatham
Wright
Compton
St Helena
Carrington
Cardwell
East Terrace
Whitmore Square
Hurtle Square
Marion
Sturt
Owen
Sturt
King William
Halifax
Power
Hallett
Symonds
Hutt
St Johns
East Terrace
Gilbert
Gilles
South Terrace
South Terrace
Veale Gardens

The city centre

The geographical heart of the city is Victoria Square, a diamond-shaped island in the middle of the city surrounded by stately government buildings, some of which have been restored and transformed into elegant hotels. On the western side of the square is the Central Market, Australia's oldest produce market which began life as eight produce-laden carts driven by market gardeners in 1869. Today it is a bustling undercover complex with the best range of international foods in Australia.

North Terrace is one of four boundary streets that mark the edge of the city centre and the beginning of the parkland belt that slopes down towards the Torrens River. North Terrace is a gift to visitors of the city. Along its length are all the city's major attractions and museums, which are mostly free.

Seaside suburbs

Just 15 minutes from the city, the waters of Gulf St Vincent wash onto a wide band of fine white sand, which stretches virtually unbroken for more than 30km. The historic tram to Glenelg takes 20 minutes to travel from Victoria Square to the famous seaside suburb with its long pier; grab yourself some fish and chips or an ice cream cone and find yourself a sunny spot on the wooden jetty or sandy beach. Further north around the curve of Gulf St Vincent are the relaxed seaside villages of Henley Beach and Semaphore and eventually, Port Adelaide at the mouth of the Adelaide River. The historic centre for export is still a busy working port but has managed to preserve many of its beautiful historic buildings.

Adelaide Hills

East of the city the Adelaide Hills are a mixture of Australian bushland and European-style farmland, with historic villages and towns such as Hahndorf, settled by Prussian refugees in the 1830s, beautiful gardens, galleries and vineyards. A popular place for weekend getaways there is a wealth of boutique B&Bs and good restaurants.

Caravan and camping

You can camp in the Kuitpo and Mount Crawford Forest Reserves but restrictions apply during summer months. The main camping area in Kuitpo is Chookarloo, set amongst gums along a small creek 1.5km from the information centre on Brookman Road with shelters, rainwater, picnic tables and toilet with access to the Chookarloo and Heysen walking trails. Rocky Creek is popular with school groups. In Mount Crawford, Chalks is a popular campground in a clearing of redgums near the corner of Warren and Forreston Roads, 4km from the information centre, with picnic tables, shelter, toilet, rainwater and a hut with a fireplace. Rocky Paddock is, as the name suggests, a campground with many rocky outcrops in an old pine plantation. The long narrow campground at Centennial Drive is bordered by large radiata pines and a creek and is a short walk from Mount Crawford.

Other parks suitable for camping include Cox Scrub Conservation Park, where camping is allowed at Coles Crossing, and Kyeema Conservation Park which has designated camping areas. Camping is not permitted in either park during the fire season (1 November to 30 April).

Mt Lofty summit. *(SATC)*

NATIONAL PARKS

Greater Mount Lofty Parklands Yurrebilla: stretching 90km north to south across the Mount Lofty Ranges the Greater Mount Lofty Parklands include iconic parks such as Belair National Park and Cleland Wildlife Park as well as the Forest Reserves of Mount Crawford and Kuitpo, and Adelaide's water reserves such as Mount Bold and South Para Reservoirs.

Cleland Conservation Park: conserves an area of natural bushland on the Adelaide Hills face and includes the popular Cleland Wildlife Park, the viewing platform of Mt Lofty Summit and scenic Waterfall Gully. The area has a rich history of Aboriginal occupation and European settlement.

Belair National Park: South Australia's oldest national park established in 1891. An 835 hectacre urban park featuring open woodlands as well as extensive recreational facilities such as sporting ovals, tennis courts, children's playgrounds and picnic areas. In the centre of the park is Old Government House, built on the Government Farm as the official vice-regal summer residence from 1860 to 1880.

Morialta Conservation Park: a spectacular rugged ridge with gully scenery and three waterfalls. The Morialta Gorge and the three waterfalls along Fourth Creek are the best known features of the park: the First and Second falls are the grandest, each cascading over sheer quartzite cliffs (23m and 15m respectively) and Third Falls (13m high). Visit during spring or winter when the water flow is strongest to see the falls at their best.

Black Hill Conservation Park: spectacular rugged ridges and gully scenery. The park gets its name from the low sheoaks, whose foliage gradually matures to a dark rusty, almost black, colour as summer progresses. Looking from the Adelaide Plains, the hill appears to be black.

scenic highlights

Hahndorf parade. *(SATC)*

Lying less than half an hour's drive east of the city, the rugged hill top scenery, vineyards, art galleries and historic towns of the Adelaide Hills make for a great day drive. The best route is a circular one, heading south-east from the city via the freeway and the Heysen Tunnels to Crafers. From there, you can drive the loop, winding up and across the top of the Mount Lofty Ranges, descending into forgotten valleys and meandering creeks towards Gumeracha before heading south to Hahndorf and back to Adelaide.

According to the local Aboriginals, Mt Lofty is one of two ears of the giant *Urebilla*, from the Dreamtime, whose fallen body forms the Mt Lofty Ranges. The summit of Mount Lofty is the place to stop for city views and café, wander the Botanic Gardens with its displays of native and exotic plants and walking trails and the Cleland Conservation Park, also home to Cleland Wildlife Park.

Continue across the range on Marble Hill Road, past Marble Hill Ruins, once the summer home for South Australian Governors until it was destroyed by bushfires in the 1950s. Follow the steep, winding switchbacks down the mountainside, and turn onto Gorge Road, a scenic drive following the course of the Torrens River. At Gumeracha, take a short side trip to Birdwood and spend a couple of hours in the National Motor Museum. Not just for rev heads, this museum examines the social influence of the motor car in Australia and has some great fun, interactive exhibits that the whole family can enjoy as well as displays of hundreds of motor vehicles, motor bikes, buses and trucks.

As you circle back towards Adelaide through Lobethal, past vineyards and orchards, stop for a chocolate fix at Melba's Chocolate Factory in Woodside. Here you can watch chocolate being made on historic machinery and then taste and buy the finished goods.

Hahndorf is the unofficial capital of the Adelaide Hills region, and by far the most popular town with visitors. Settled in 1839 by Prussian and East German immigrants, Hahndorf is Australia's oldest surviving German settlement. The town's main street has many historic buildings housing craft shops, galleries, cellar doors and restaurants.

Make time to visit The Cedars, on the outskirts of town. Home to famous Australian landscape painter Hans Heysen, it is full of family treasures and paintings by Heysen, including many portraits and still life. His studio is just as he left it, and inside the house is the studio of his daughter, Nora, a renowned artist in her own right.

From Hahndorf it is a quick half-hour drive back to the city.

Bushwalks

The Yurrebilla Trail is a 54km-long interpretative bushwalking trail through the Adelaide Hills between Belair National Park and Black Hill Conservation Park in the central Mount Lofty Ranges. The full trail will take three days and is divided into one full-day and four half-day sections: Belair Railway Station to Eagle-on-the-Hill (17.5km); Eagle-on-the-Hill to Summertown (7km); Summertown to Norton Summit (9km); Norton Summit to Morialta (7.5km); Morialta to Ambers Gully (River Torrens) (13km). It passes many of the Adelaide Hills' major attractions, including Waterfall Gully, the Mount Lofty Botanic Gardens, Mount Lofty Summit and Cleland Wildlife Park. The Yurrebilla Trail connects directly with the Heysen Trail (a 1200km walking trail between Cape Jervis in the Fleurieu Peninsula north along the states mountain ranges to Parachilna Gorge in the Flinders Ranges) for 12km, joining between Mount Lofty and Third Falls in the Morialta Conservation Park.

The First Falls Plateau hike in Morialta Conservation Park is a 90-minute steep hike with good views of First Falls and Morialta Gorge's towering cliffs, the Adelaide Plains, city and the coast.

In the city, you can walk from the beachside suburb of Henley Beach to the city's north-eastern suburbs in the River Torrens Linear Park. The trail runs right through the city centre, passing the Adelaide Festival Centre, Adelaide Convention Centre and Adelaide Zoo.

National Motor Museum. (SATC)

DON'T MISS

- **Central Market:** join thousands of people buying, selling and tasting the best of South Australia at the Adelaide Central Market, established in 1869 and now the largest undercover market in the southern hemisphere. Between Victoria Square, Grote and Gouger streets. Open Tue 7am–5.30pm, Thu 9am–5.30pm, Fri 7am–9pm, Sat 7am–3pm. www.adelaide.sa.gov.au/centralmarket
- **Jam Factory Contemporary Craft & Design:** collection of modern art and craft studios and workshops. 19 Morphett Street. Open Mon–Fri, 9am–5.30pm; Sat 10am–4pm. Closed Sundays and public holidays. www.jamfactory.com.au
- **South Australian Museum:** highlights include the natural history section, the remarkable Australian Aboriginal Cultures Gallery and the Mawson Gallery. North Terrace. Open daily, 10am–5pm. www.samuseum.sa.gov.au
- **Art Gallery of South Australia:** permanent and changing exhibitions of Australian and international art. North Terrace. Open daily, 10am–5pm. www.artgallery.sa.gov.au
- **The Bradman Collection:** exhibition dedicated to Australian legend and international hero Sir Donald Bradman, the greatest batsman in the history of cricket. State Library of SA, North Terrace. Open Mon–Thu, 9.30am–6pm; Fri 9.30am–8pm; Sat & Sun noon–5pm. Closed public holidays. www.bradman.sa.com.au
- **Migration Museum:** innovative museum in the former destitute asylum tracing the history of Adelaide's migration, right up to the current situation dealing with asylum seekers and deportation camps. 82 Kintore Ave. Open Mon–Fri, 10am–5pm; Sat, Sun and public holidays 1–5pm. www.history.sa.gov.au
- **Adelaide Botanic Garden:** highlights include several grand avenues and arched walkways crowned in wisteria, the ornate 1868 glass house and the new Bicentennial Conservatory, the largest single span conservatory in the southern hemisphere, which houses tropical rainforest plants and looks like a huge beetle from the air. North Terrace. Open Mon–Fri 8am–sunset; Sat, Sun and public holidays 9am–sunset. www.botanicgardens.sa.gov.au
- **Wine Centre of Australia:** interactive exhibitions on the history of Australia's wine industry and many wine producing regions, tasting rooms and a restaurant. Corner of Botanic and Hackney roads. Open daily, 10am–6pm. www.wineaustralia.com.au
- **Ayers House Museum:** one of the last remaining grand 19th century homes that once lined North Terrace. Open Tue–Fri 10am–4pm; Sat, Sun and public holidays 1pm–4pm. Closed Monday except public holidays. www.nationaltrustsa.org.au
- **National Railway Museum:** train rides, exhibits and displays. Lipson Street, Port Adelaide. Open daily, 10am–5pm. www.natrailmuseum.org.au
- **South Australian Maritime Museum:** historic Bond Stores housing exhibition galleries, lighthouse and floating vessels. 126 Lipson Street, Port Adelaide. Open daily, 10am–5pm. www.history.sa.gov.au
- **South Australian Aviation Museum:** displays and aircraft. Lipson Street, Port Adelaide. Open daily, 10am–4.30pm. www.saam.org.au
- **Mount Lofty Botanic Garden:** large hills garden in a spectacular setting overlooking Piccadilly Valley. Piccadilly Road, Crafers. Open daily.
- **Cleland Wildlife Park:** join animal attendants on the animal feed runs from 10am–3pm daily or on a guided night walk. Bookings are essential for the night walks. Summit Road, Mount Lofty. Open daily, 9.30am–5pm. ☎ (08) 8339 2444.
- **Marble Hill Ruins:** summer residence for the governors of South Australia, built in 1878, destroyed by fire in 1955. Marble Hill Road, Ashton. Open second Sunday of each month noon–5pm.
- **Gorge Wildlife Park:** Australia's largest privately-owned collection of animals and birds, contained in 14 acres of natural bushland. Cudlee Creek. Open daily 8am–5pm.
- **The Toy Factory:** large range of wooden toys. Kids love climbing the giant rocking horse, reputed to be the biggest in the world. Gumeracha. Open daily, 9am–5pm.
- **National Motor Museum:** one of the largest collections of cars, motorcycles and commercial vehicles in the world, with more than 300 vehicles dating from the turn of the century to the present day. Shannon Street, Birdwood. Open daily, 9am–5pm. www.motormuseum.sa.gov.au
- **Melba's Chocolate Factory:** watch (and buy) chocolates and sweets made with historic machinery. Heritage Park, Henry Street, Woodside. Open daily, 10am–4.30pm.
- **The Cedars:** home and studio of renowned Australian artist Sir Hans Heysen and his artist daughter Nora Heysen. Homestead has virtually remained unchanged since the 1930s and is furnished with original artefacts. Heysen Road, Hahndorf. Open Sun–Fri, 10am–4pm.
- **Beerenberg Strawberry Farm:** pick your own strawberries in season and buy a large range of jams and other related products. Mt Barker Rd, Hahndorf. Open daily, 9am–5pm.

adventure activities

Morialta Conservation Park. *(SATC)*

Abseiling and rock climbing

Morialta Conservation Park is the most popular climbing location in the Adelaide Hills and provides many climbs of varying difficulty with a dedicated rock climbing and abseiling area off Norton Summit Road between Second and Third Falls with good solid rock faces, and many secure holdfasts on the Far Crag and Boulder Bridge climbing zones. The area is quite well shaded and the views down the Fourth Creek gully toward Adelaide City are impressive. Descriptions and ratings of each set climb can be found in the Adelaide Hills Rock Climbing book available from most outdoor/adventure shops which stock climbing equipment.

There's also good abseiling and rock climbing in Onkaparinga River National Park, where South Australia's second longest river, the Onkaparinga, enters a steep-sided valley and flows into a magnificent gorge with cliffs up to 50m high and large permanent rock pools. Rock climbing is allowed in a designated area on the southern side of the gorge, 500m north-west of gate 10, which is located on Chapel Hill Road at Blewitt Springs. Bookings are essential to guarantee the site is available for your use.

Live Adrenalin offer combined one-day rock climbing and abseiling courses in Morialta Conservation Park with instruction on rock safety, basic knots, rock sports equipment and techniques.

www.adrenalin.com.au

Canoeing and kayaking

The Garden Island Ships' Graveyard in Port Adelaide and the mangroves of the Port River system provide good paddling experiences in tidal conditions with the chance to see dolphins and marine life. The southern shore of Garden Island in the North Arm of the Port River is one of the largest and most diverse ships' graveyards in the world. Containing vessels dating from 1856, the graveyard is a haven for birdlife and marine creatures. The ships are best seen by canoe or kayak. Diving is also available.

Blue Water Sea Kayaking in Glenelg run half-day guided kayaking tours of the Port River's Dolphin Sanctuary, mangroves and Ships Graveyard Heritage Trail. Tours run from spring to late autumn and are conducted in double sea kayaks. Tours depart from Garden Island boat ramp at Gillman on Monday, Wednesday, Saturday and Sunday from December to February and Saturday and Sunday from March to May.

www.adventure-kayak.com.au

Cycling and mountain biking

One of the most popular cycling paths in the city is the River Torrens Linear Park: a 35km cycling and walking trail that runs from the sea to the Adelaide foothills through the city's CBD. Following the picturesque River Torrens, the trail is ideal for those wanting a short ride that's suitable for children and all fitness levels.

The Westside Bike Path follows the path of the Holdfast Railway for 7km from Richmond to Glenelg. Linked to the River Torrens Linear Park is the 800km Mawson Trail, a good option for mountain-bike riders. Starting at the Adelaide Festival Centre in the heart of the city and travelling to Blinman in the Flinders Ranges, the trail includes little-used country roads, state forest and national park fire trails, farm access tracks and unmade or unused road reserves, and can be ridden in sections or in its entirety.

Closer to Adelaide, the Cudlee Creek Mountain Bike Loop Trails in Mount Crawford Forest offer challenging riding on two 3km downhill tracks plus an 8km cross-country track. There are also three 20km mostly flat loop trails at the end of end of Starkey Road, Mt Crawford.

Cycling to the Great Australian Bight. *(ROC)*

Bike About, based in Lobethal, offers a range of day trips and extended cycling tours and mountain bike camps in and around the Adelaide Hills. Camps and tours range from day trips up to five days or more

www.bikeabout.com.au

Remote Outback Cycletours Australia (ROC) offer a 7-day trip down the Oodnadatta Track, along the Mawson Trail, through the Clare Valley Wine Region, which finishes in Adelaide.

www.cycletours.com.au

Diving

The Adelaide Underwater Heritage Trail includes four shipwrecks off the Gulf of St Vincent: the *Grecian, Zanoni, Star of Greece* and *Norma*. The wrecks represent a variety of vessels associated with trade and development in South Australia during the 19th and early 20th centuries. All the vessels were built in Britain between 1841 and 1893. The trail extends from Port Willunga, around one-hour's drive south of Adelaide, to Ardrossan on the Yorke Peninsula, and the wrecks are marked by underwater plaques. You can also dive the Garden Island Ships' Graveyard Maritime Heritage Trail. Most Adelaide sites are in shallow water (25m or less) making them ideal for novice divers.

www.dive.southaustralia.com/adelaide.html

Dolphin watching

The Gulf of St Vincent is home to over a thousand common and bottlenose dolphins. Temptation Sailing, based at Holdfast Shores Marina in Glenelg, was the first vessel in South Australia to be given a dolphin swim license and has been conducting successful dolphin swims since January 2002. You can choose to get in the water and swim with the dolphins or merely watch them play. Either way, as there are so many dolphins in the water they are able to offer a money back guarantee–if you do not get to swim with the dolphins for whatever reason, they will refund the difference between the watch and the swim. Cruises are aboard the *Temptation*, a 17m sailing catamaran.

www.dolphinboat.com.au

Port Princess Dolphin Cruises offer trips along the Port River, through to the historic Port Adelaide estuary, which is home to a permanent pod of about 30 wild dolphins. Two other dolphin groups reside nearby, one to the north and one to the south. Each group specialises in a different habitat type: sheltered estuary, sandy beaches and muddy mangrove flats, but all three socialise together in the outer parts of the estuary.

www.portprincess.com.au

Fishing

The Gulf St Vincent is home to a variety of good table fish including: King George whiting, snapper, tommy ruff, bream, garfish and mullet. You can also catch snook, flathead, leatherjacket, gummy shark, squid and blue swimmer crabs. The metropolitan foreshore has lots of jetties, wharves, breakwalls and beaches. Two artificial reefs at Glenelg and Grange provide a haven for whiting and snapper. The West Lakes system is heaven for those who like bream and the Port Adelaide River estuary is great for small boat fishing. Inland, the upstream reaches of the Onkaparinga River is popular with fly fishers and has good stocks of redfin, golden perch and both brown and rainbow trout.

Horse riding

The South Australia Trails Network has several good horse riding trails in the Adelaide region. The Tom Roberts Horse Trail is a 20km horse-riding trail that loops through Belair National Park and finishes in Kuitpo Forest. The park is open from 8am to sunset and there is horse float parking adjacent to Sir Edwin Avenue Drive.

The 200km-long Kidman Trail provides a range of trail riding experiences linking McLaren Vale and the Fleurieu Peninsula to the Barossa Valley. Named after Sir Sidney Kidman, a prominent local pastoralist and horse breeder, it utilises existing tracks and trails through Forest Reserves and other accessible public land, quiet roads and unmade road reserves with trail markers indicating the route. There are a number of trailheads providing information on horse yarding, campsites and float parking along the route.

The first section of the trail from Willunga to Echunga is open, with sections to Kapunda in planning and development stages. When completed, the full trail will take between five and seven days to complete, but it can be broken up into the smaller sections and loops. Some sections of the trail may see only one or two riders per day; others are more likely to attract a greater number of regular users.

The Adelaide Hills. *(SATC)*

Hot laps

Live Adrenalin runs introductory racecar courses driving a Formula Ford racing car at Adelaide International Raceway. During the courses you learn to refine your driving skills in either a Van Dieman, Swift or Reynard. High performance driving attitudes, hi-speed car handling techniques such as braking and gear change points, cornering lines, efficient cockpit work, throttle control and safety are all addressed in a session of high speed thrills. You must be able to drive a manual car.

www.adrenalin.com.au

Jet boats

Strap yourself in for a 20-minute offshore thrill on a Hel-a-va jet boat-designed for extreme performance in open seas. It seats 12 passengers in a fully-enclosed cabin. Departs daily (subject to weather conditions) from Holdfast Shores, Glenelg.

www.helava.com.au

Microlight joy flights

Skytrikes offer two-and-a-half-hour microlight adventure packages in the skies above Adelaide. Includes a comprehensive pre-flight briefing, coveralls (if required), helmet and modern communications equipment. Flight time is around 40 minutes, including in-flight tuition and a full scenic route commentary.

www.skytrikes.com.au

Sky diving

SA Skydiving, based at Goodwood, offer tandem sky dives from 10,000 and 12,000 feet. The Drop Zone is around 55 minutes from Adelaide at 'Rollo's' airfield near Monarto. Jumps offer spectacular views of the Adelaide Hills, the Murray River and the Fleurieu Peninsula.

www.skydiving.com.au

Adventure Air also offer tandem jumps from the Lower Light Drop Zone around 40 minutes north of the city on Port Wakefield Road with views of the coastline ranging beyond Adelaide to Rapid Bay and across the Gulf of St Vincent to the Yorke Peninsula.

www.adventureair.com.au

Surfing

Gulf St Vincent protects the beaches of Adelaide from the swells of the Southern Ocean, but there is good surfing less than an hour's drive from the city on beaches like Sellicks and Southport, while beaches around Middleton are good places to learn. Surf and Sun Safaris have full-day learn-to-surf adventure tour from Adelaide that includes two, two-hour surf lessons with all the equipment provided, lunch and sightseeing on the Fleurieu Peninsula and return transport.

www.surfandsun.com.au

Windsurfing

Adelaide boasts conditions as extreme as anywhere in the world and summer brings strong seabreezes, ideal for speed/slalom sailing, as cold water from southern currents flush into the shallow St Vincent Gulf creating temperature differences between land and sea.

Glenelg. *(SATC)*

North Haven is great for slalom blasting inside and good jumps beyond the breakwater.

Less experienced sailors will love the beaches between Semaphore and Largs Bay in a steady seabreeze. The curve of these beaches allows for safe landings and you are almost guaranteed of being blown back to the beach. The shallow bottom allows easy waterstarting and there's plenty of beach room and parking. First timers can tackle West Lakes, a popular location with grassed rigging areas and accessible carparks–excellent for those learning and a good blast for slalom sailors in a howling southerly. Henly Beach or 'Front Yards' or North Glenelg are also popular spots.

www.windsurfing.org/sa

MORE INFORMATION

- **Adelaide Visitor Information Centre:** Ground Floor, 18 King William Street, Adelaide. ☎ 1300 655 276. www.adelaide.southaustralia.com
- **Adelaide Hills Visitor Information Centre:** 41 Main Street, Hahndorf. ☎ 1800 353 323. www.visitadelaidehills.com.au

weather watch

- January: 12–25°C
- July: 5–11°C
- Summers are mild; most rain falls during winter, which can be chilly.

wine country

Bethany Winery, Barossa Valley. (SATC)

▶ THE BAROSSA AND CLARE VALLEYS, just an hour or two from Adelaide, are two of the country's most celebrated wine producing regions. Rich in heritage, these two valleys offer a diverse range of landscapes and activities and are a popular place for a weekend gourmet getaway, with walking and cycling the main adventure activities on offer.

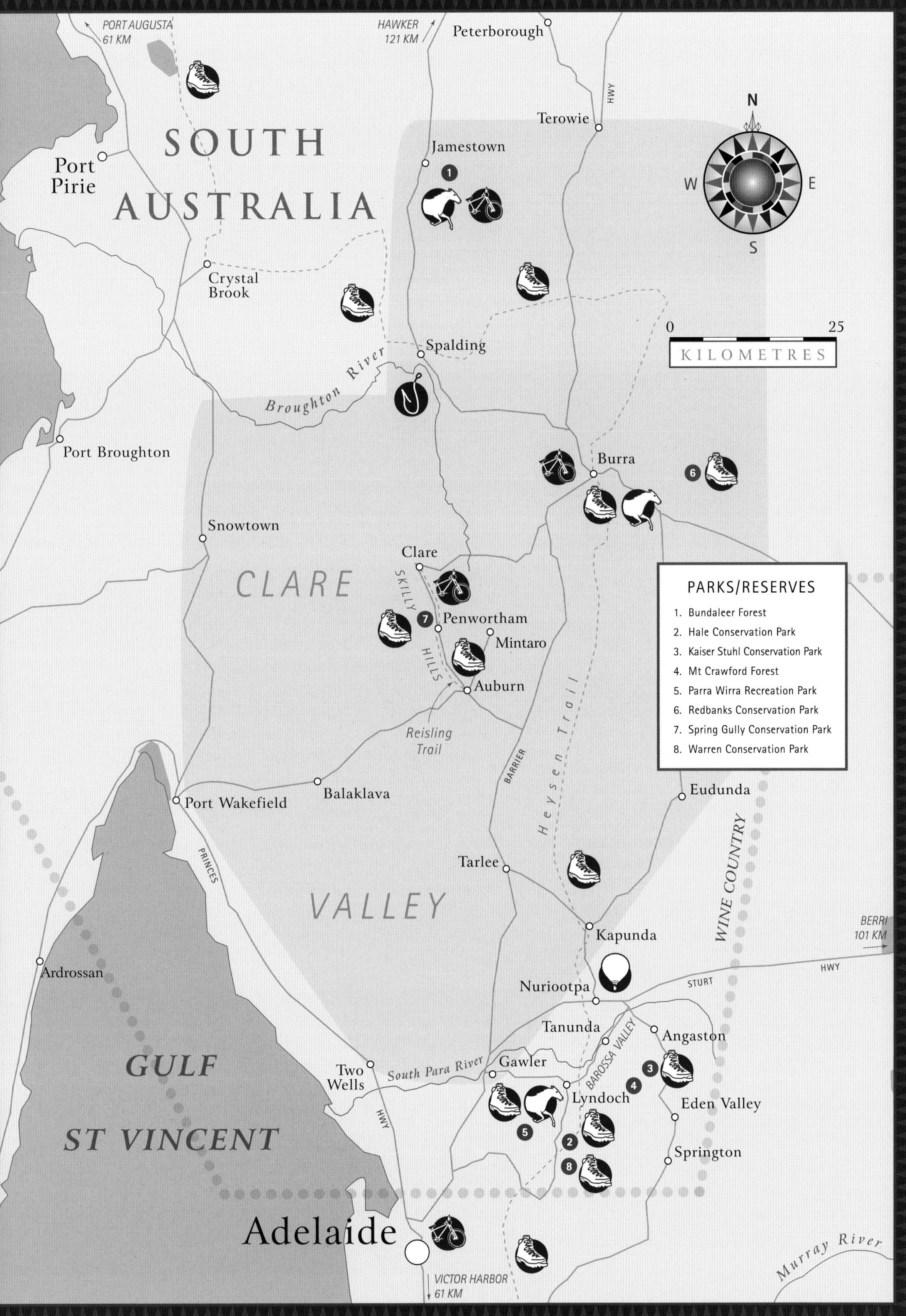
PORT AUGUSTA 61 KM
HAWKER 121 KM
Peterborough
HWY
Terowie
SOUTH AUSTRALIA
Port Pirie
Jamestown
N
W
E
S
Crystal Brook
Spalding
0
25
KILOMETRES
Broughton River
Port Broughton
Burra
Snowtown
Clare
CLARE
SKILLY HILLS
Penwortham
Mintaro
Auburn
Reisling Trail
BARRIER
Heysen Trail
PARKS/RESERVES
1. Bundaleer Forest
2. Hale Conservation Park
3. Kaiser Stuhl Conservation Park
4. Mt Crawford Forest
5. Parra Wirra Recreation Park
6. Redbanks Conservation Park
7. Spring Gully Conservation Park
8. Warren Conservation Park
Balaklava
Port Wakefield
Eudunda
PRINCES
Tarlee
WINE COUNTRY
VALLEY
Kapunda
BERRI 101 KM
Ardrossan
Nuriootpa
STURT
HWY
Tanunda
BAROSSA VALLEY
Angaston
GULF
Two Wells
South Para River
Gawler
Lyndoch
Eden Valley
HWY
ST VINCENT
Springton
Adelaide
VICTOR HARBOR 61 KM
Murray River

Clare Valley Hills (SATC)

NATIONAL PARKS

Parra Wirra Recreation Park: in the northern Lofty Ranges, this park supports more than 100 species of native birds, including emus which often wander about the picnic areas and western grey kangaroos, frequently seen grazing at dawn and dusk. Facilities include gas barbecues, picnic tables, playground, toilets, an oval for cricket or football and walking trails ranging from 800m to 7.5km in length.

Kaiser Stuhl Conservation Park: 12km south-east of Tanunda, this park is great for bushwalking, bird watching and photography at Horsehead Rock and Capped Rock. There are two walking loop trails: the 2.4km Stringybark Trail and 6.5km Wallowa Trail.

Hale Conservation Park: steep rocky ridges popular with birdwatchers, bushwalkers and photographers, when for a few weeks in winter the glorious flame heath lights much of the park with its red blooms. Two rather strenuous walking trails provide spectacular views of the South Para Valley and reservoir.

Spring Gully Conservation Park: 8km south of Clare, this park in the Skilly Hills is the only reserve in South Australia to protect red stringybarks. Walking trails provide magnificent views of the park and surrounding areas. Highlights include the Cascades Walk which leads down to the creek bed of Spring Gully and, after rain, an attractive series of cascades.

Redbanks Conservation Park: red alluvial cliffs, riverflats and meandering gorges covered in mallee scrub and bluebush near Burra are home to wombats, echidnas and euros and the remains of megafauna. The traditional owners of the land, the Ngadjuri people, recently initiated an excavation in the park leading archaeologists to uncover an Aboriginal burial ground. There are also disused gold mine and dugouts in the park.

Barossa Valley

Despite is larger-than-life reputation in the wine world the Barossa Valley is a snug collection of country towns surrounded by vineyards that is very easy to explore on a day trip from Adelaide. Distances between towns are short, and wineries sit next door to each other so it's easy to visit a few in a very short time. Be warned however, with all that good food and wine to taste, it's likely you'll want to stay overnight and indulge.

The Barossa has been famous for its rich, big-bodied shiraz for many years, but the region's heritage of growing, curing, preserving and cooking its own unique foods is less well known. The largely Lutheran settlers who came here 160 years have left not only a legacy of beautiful churches but a bounty of wonderful small meats, sausages, preserved fruits, cheese and delicious breads, all unique to the valley. Most restaurants and cafes pride themselves on serving as much local produce as possible–look for the distinctive cork on a fork Food Barossa logo. Tasting plates with a range of local specialities are served at many cellar doors.

The majority of the vineyards and wineries are centred around the three towns of Angaston, Nuriootpa and Tanunda. On the western edge of the valley, Gawler is a Heritage-listed town with many well-preserved 19th century buildings ranging from mansions to 1840s cottages.

To the south, the elevated Eden Valley is a celebrated cool climate wine growing area.

Clare Valley

The Clare is one of Australia's oldest wine regions, and has more than 40 wineries, all within a 15-minute drive of each other. The first settlers to the area were from England, Ireland and Poland, producing a rich architectural heritage, most of which remains, although the original village buildings now tend to house restaurants and galleries.

Copper was discovered in the district in 1842, just three years after Edward Eyre first explored the area, and soon large mines were established. The mining history is well preserved in Burra and Kapunda where there are numerous sites that recall the 19th century mining boom.

The first vines were planted in 1842 by James Green, servant to the district's pioneer John Horrocks. Since then, the industry has grown and the Clare is now one of the best producing wine regions in the country. All sorts of grapes are grown here, but the valley is most well known for its riesling.

The main towns of the region are Auburn and Clare, service centres for the surrounding wine industry, while the historic towns of Burra and Mintaro are relatively intact 19th-century villages with many buildings featuring the region's unique local slate.

Kapunda. (SATC)

Yalumba. *(LA)*

DON'T MISS

- **Herbig Family Tree:** a giant hollow red gum once home to Barossa settler Friedreich Herbig, his wife Caroline and their 16 children between 1855 and 1860. Main Road, Springton.
- **Seppelt Winery:** established in 1851, the Seppelt family were pioneers in Australian wine making. Taste the wines at the historic cellar door and take a one-hour history tour of the complex, picnic in the gardens and visit the grand Seppelt family mausoleum. Seppeltsfield Road, Seppeltsfield. Open 10am–5pm weekdays, 11am–5pm weekends. Tours 11am, 1pm, 2pm, 3pm weekdays; 11.30am, 1.30pm and 2.30pm weekends. www.seppelt.com.
- **Yalumba:** founded in 1849, the oldest family-owned winery still operating in Australia. Visit the nursery, cooperage and tasting room. Eden Valley Road, Angaston. Open daily, 10am–5pm. www.yalumba.com
- **Barossa Wine Centre:** interpretative wine centre next door to the visitor information centre that tells the story of the Barossa's unique history, people and culture, as well as the wine making process. Murray Street, Tanunda. Open daily.
- **Angas Park:** taste a dazzling array of freshly dried fruits, nuts and other regional gourmet products. Murray Sreet, Angaston. Open daily, 9am–5pm (from 10am on weekends).
- **Farmers Markets:** A 'food only' market with produce associated with the heritage and traditions of the region. Open each Saturday morning from 7.30–11.30am. Situated in the warehouse behind Vintners Bar & Grill, at the corner of Stockwell and Nuriootpa Roads, Angaston.
- **The Whispering Wall:** an acoustic phenomenon at Barossa Reservoir. Whisper a message at one end of the wall and it will carry audibly to the other end, 40m away.
- **Murray Edwards Studio:** browse beautiful and vibrant impressionist-style art works of the Clare Valley and local area at the artist's Corella Hill Studio. Meet the artist and view works in progress. Watervale. Open daily, 10am–5pm. www.murrayedwards.com.au
- **Sevenhill:** founded in the mid-19th century by early Jesuit settlers, the winery offers tastings and sales in the old monastery cellars, as well as tours of the underground cellar, museum, St Aloysius Church, historic cemetery, crypt and shrines. Open daily 9am–5pm, from 10am on weekends. www.sevenhillcellars.com.au
- **Martindale Hall:** historic mansion built in 1881 and located in the 45-acre Martindale Hall Conservation Park. The park is within the original property of 11,000 acres established by Edmund Bowman Snr in 1841 as a sheep station called Martindale station. The station is still intact and active. Open daily, Mon–Fri 11am–4pm; weekends, noon to 4pm. Also available for B&B accommodation. Near Mintaro. www.martindalehall.com ☎ (08) 8843 9088.
- **Burra Heritage Passport:** available seven days a week from the Burra Visitor Centre, the Passport, which comes with a key, enables you to enter eight locked heritage sites, including the mine site, powder magazine, Redruth Gaol—the first gaol built outside Adelaide, Hampton Village and the Unicorn Brewery Cellars, as well as several museums.

scenic highlights

The best way to explore the Barossa Valley is to start at Nuriootpa, about an hour's drive from the city. Take the Barossa Valley Way past Penfolds Winery and head out to Seppeltsfield, past Maggie Beer's Farm Shop and along the avenue of 2000 date palms planted as a work scheme for winery workers during the 1930s Depression.

From Seppeltsfield head to Tanunda, where you should try some of the local bread, pretzels or pastries from Apex Bakery. Many of the valley's best wineries are close by—take a drive along Krondorf Road and drop into St Hallett, Rockford, Charles Melton and Barossa Vines.

Continue down the Barossa Valley Way to Lyndoch for more wines and then double back to Tanunda and take the Bethany Road to Angaston for a very pretty drive through the vine-clad hills. Stop at historic Yalumba with its distinctive clock tower, the oldest family-run operating vineyard in Australia, and take a tour of historic Collingrove, a grand historic homestead that was built for the original Angaston patriarch, John Howard Angas, in 1856.

From Angaston, head back to Nuriootpa to finish the loop, or drive back to Adelaide via the beautiful Eden Valley.

Burra Monster Mine. *(SATC)*

To get to Clare, head north out of Adelaide on the Main North Road to Auburn, the birthplace of CJ Dennis, of *Sentimental Bloke* fame. Auburn has many beautifully-maintained historical buildings, many of which now house good-value, country antique stores. Spear off the main road at Penwortham and travel up through the Skilly Hills. The road is mostly unsealed and deeply potholed in places, but will take you past many wineries, through the Spring Gully Conservation Park and wind through beautiful bush scenery.

You can return home to Adelaide the way you came, but a worthwhile detour is to head east for 43km and spend some time in historic Burra. This quaint little town is one of the world's best preserved colonial mining communities. The best way to really explore the town is with a Heritage Passport—a detailed guidebook and entry ticket to help you follow the 11km heritage trail around the town. There are 47 sites along the trail, including historic cottages, the gaol, churches, museums and the Monster Mine. If that sounds like too much serious history, browse the many antique shops in town.

From Burra, head back to Adelaide via the historic hamlet of Mintaro, South Australia's first proclaimed historic town. Call into the Magpie and Stump Hotel for a cold drink or visit Martindale Hall, a historic mansion built in 1881.

Caravan and camping

Camping is prohibited in most of the national and conservation parks in the area, with bush camping in Redbanks Conservation Park about the only 'wild' option. Best caravanning and camping options are in commercial caravan parks in town centres.

Bushwalks

The most popular walk in the district is the Riesling Trail, a 27km walking and cycling track that follows a disused railway line between Clare and Auburn. It's sealed and suitable for bicycles as well as wheelchairs and strollers. What's more, you don't have to compete with road traffic, so it's great for families and small children.

Named after the grape and wine variety that the Clare Valley is famous for, the Riesling Trail travels past many cellar doors and other visitor attractions, making it ideal for those wanting a leisurely walk with a few distractions along the way. It begins at Auburn before heading through paddocks and vineyards and up through the Skilly Hills. Stop for some refreshment at Sevenhill Winery, founded in the mid-19th century by early Jesuit settlers, and offering tastings and sales in the old monastery cellars, as well as tours of the underground cellar, museum, St Aloysius Church, historic cemetery, crypt and shrines. Clare is just up 6km up the road and the end of the trail.

The 1200km Heysen Trail also passes through both the Barossa and Clare valleys, through the heart of the vineyards and along the Gilbert Valley through the Tothill Ranges to Burra and on into the Flinders Ranges.

In Parra Wirra Recreation Park there are several good short walks including the 90-minute Devils Nose Hike following a ridge top with views of the South Para River with good views of the Barossa Valley: the one-hour Hissey Loop Hike and the 4.5km Goldfields Walk that travels through the historic Barossa goldfields with views of the South Para River and interpretive signs along the trail.

The Stringy Bark Hike in Kaiser Stuhl Conservation Park is a challenging 2.5km loop that crosses Pohlner Creek then passes

Martindale Hall. (SATC)

Behr Creek through rocky outcrops and native vegetation. The Tower Jubilee Hike in Warren Conservation Park and Mt Crawford Forest is a good walk, steep in parts, through dense woodland and open grasslands that will take around four hours.

Hale has two challenging walking trails starting from the Kangaroo Creek car park. The trail to the South Para River passes from the highlands to the river crossing while the trail to the north-eastern boundary of the park follows the creek to emerge in grasslands on the outskirts of Williamstown. Four hours should be allowed for a return walk on both trails.

The Burra Heritage Trail is a pleasant four-hour, 11km stroll visiting many of the historic sites of Australia's earliest and most significant historic mining towns. It contains buildings and structures that date from the mid-19th century when it was the scene of one of the world's great copper mines. The Clare Cascades Walk in Spring Gully Conservation Park is another easy walk (40 minutes return) that meanders through grassy woodlands which often has a carpet of orchids during spring. After rain, water can be seen falling over the rocks at the area known as the 'Cascades'. The Riverton Trails area is a series of five loops in the Gilbert Valley passing through historical sights, including cemeteries, Marshall's Hut and other tourist attractions. They include stunning panoramic views, native vegetation and abundant bird life.

adventure activities

Ballooning

Balloon Adventures, South Australia's longest operating hot air ballooning company, are based in Nuriootpa in the heart of the Barossa and offer hot air balloon flights every morning, weather permitting. Departure points vary depending on prevailing wind conditions, but flight time is an hour and all flights include a celebratory champagne breakfast with some of the Barossa's local sparkling wine and fresh home-cooked produce.

www.balloonadventures.com.au

Cycling and mountain biking

The 27km Riesling Trail following a disused railway line between Clare and Auburn is the most well-known cycling route in the wine country. There are three loop trails along the way for those that want to park and ride. Parking is available at Clare, Sevenhill, Watervale and Auburn. Bike hire available at Clare ☎ 1800 242 132 and free trail maps are available from visitor information centres.

www.southaustraliantrails.com

The Mawson Trail, an 800km bike track from Adelaide to the Flinders also passes through the heart of the Barossa Valley and links up with the Riesling Trail in the Clare before a moderate climb through the Camelhump Ranges with spectacular views over the Valley. The Clare Valley section is 85km and begins at Riverton, finishes at Burra.

Tour the vineyards by bike with Barossa Classic Cycle Tours or hire a mountain bike from Barossa Secrets in Tanunda and ask for copy of local trails. There are also some good mountain bike trails in Bundaleer Forest near Jamestown.

www.bccycletours.com.au

The Riesling Trail. (SATC)

The Jacob's Creek Tour Down Under is one of the most prestigious early season road cycling races on the international calendar, when each January World, Olympic and Tour de France heroes queue to be on the start list for six days of hard fought racing through some of South Australia's most picturesque regions. Starting in the city of Adelaide the race heads through the vineyards of the Barossa and McLaren Vale, the Adelaide Hills and the Fleurieu Peninsula. You can join more than 1000 recreational cyclists on the annual Be Active tour and ride Stage 2 of the Jacob's Creek Tour Down Under just hours before the stars of international cycling hit the road later the same day. Three distance options are designed for various fitness levels.

www.tourdownunder.com.au ☎ (08) 8232 2644

Fishing

The Broughton River in the northern reaches of the Clare Valley near the town of Spalding is regularly stocked with brown and rainbow trout, although access to the river can be difficult as much of it flows through private property.

Horse riding

Burra Trail Rides offer a range of horse riding trail rides for all levels of experience ranging from one-hour trail rides around the scenic Burra hills, half-day trips and longer three-day, two-night rides through the mallee country of the Mount Lofty Ranges and around the northern Clare Valley wilderness, with two nights camping and includes a tour of Mongolata Gold Mine

www.visitburra.com/horse_riding ☎ (08) 8892 2627

The Kidman Trail, a 200km horse riding trail, will eventually link Willunga to Kapunda in the Barossa, although at this stage only the first section from Willunga to Echunga is open. In Para Wirra Recreation Park the 7.5km Mack Creek Trail is open to horse riders as is the 4.6km Bundaleer Forest Scenic Walk in Bundaleer Forest Reserve, Jamestown.

MORE INFORMATION

- **Barossa Wine and Visitor Information Centre:** 66–68 Murray Street, Tanunda. ☎ 1300 852 982. www.barossa-region.org
- **Clare Valley Visitor Information Centre:** cnr Main North Road and Spring Gully Road, Clare. ☎ 1800 242 131. www.clarevalley.com.au

weather watch

- January: 13–29°C
- July: 3–13°C
- Summers are dry and warm, most rain falls during winter.

Balloons over the Barossa Valley. *(SATC)*

the eyre peninsula

Sleaford sand dunes. *(SATC)*

Fowlers Bay. *(Mark Bean)*

► ONE OF THE BEST KEPT BEACH SECRETS in the country is the Eyre Peninsula, the triangle of land jutting into the sea between Adelaide and the Great Australian Bight. It is the outback gone coastal; where vast, undulating wheat fields tumble into the sea over towering, knife-edged limestone cliffs. It is a place, it seems, that tourism has forgotten. In this beautiful and sometimes remote region you'll find beach after beach, visited only by the occasional fisherman, screeching seagulls and very few of the madding coastal crowds you find along the rest of the Australian coast. Campsites are right on the edge of the beach and you're often the only ones there. This is also where you'll find some fantastic four-wheel driving in two stunning national parks, both conveniently close to the resort town of Port Lincoln on the southern tip of the Eyre Peninsula.

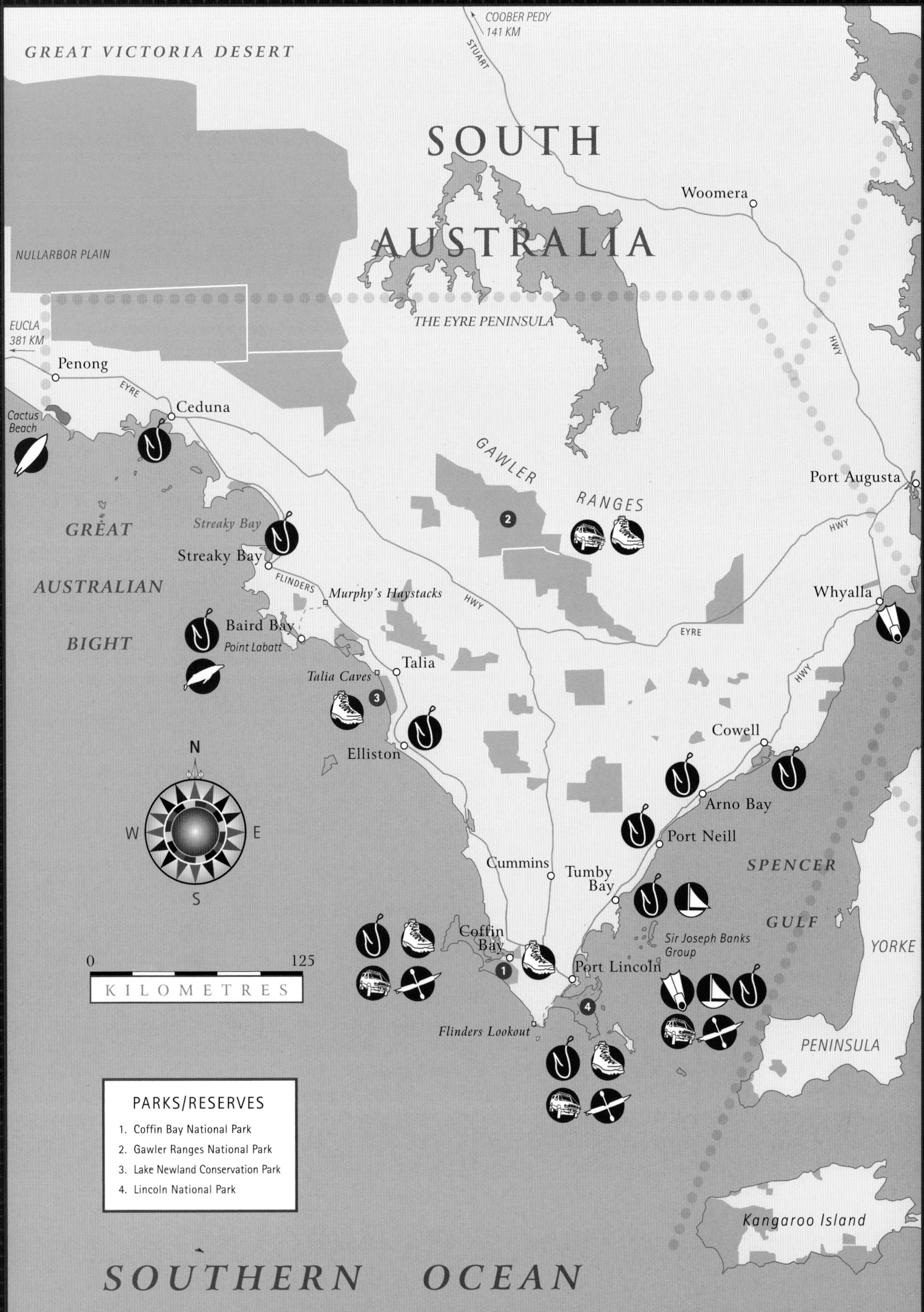

GREAT VICTORIA DESERT
COOBER PEDY
141 KM
STUART
SOUTH
AUSTRALIA
Woomera
NULLARBOR PLAIN
THE EYRE PENINSULA
EUCLA
381 KM
Penong
EYRE
Ceduna
Cactus Beach
GAWLER
RANGES
Port Augusta
HWY
GREAT
AUSTRALIAN
BIGHT
Streaky Bay
Streaky Bay
FLINDERS
Murphy's Haystacks
HWY
Whyalla
Baird Bay
Point Labatt
EYRE
Talia Caves
Talia
Elliston
Cowell
Arno Bay
Port Neill
Cummins
Tumby Bay
SPENCER
GULF
Sir Joseph Banks Group
Coffin Bay
YORKE
Port Lincoln
Flinders Lookout
PENINSULA
0
125
KILOMETRES
N
W
E
S
PARKS/RESERVES
1. Coffin Bay National Park
2. Gawler Ranges National Park
3. Lake Newland Conservation Park
4. Lincoln National Park
Kangaroo Island
SOUTHERN OCEAN

Coffin Bay beach. (LA)

NATIONAL PARKS

Lincoln National Park: a rugged peninsula with vast expanses of coastal mallee, spectacular ocean cliffs and extensive sand dunes, sandy beaches and sheltered camping sites. Highlights include Memory Cove, a pretty beach protected by two headlands, massive wind-sculpted sand dunes, pounding surf and limestone cliffs.

Coffin Bay National Park: diverse coastal landscape with several good beaches and cliff-top lookouts. Home to a resident mob of wild Coffin Bay brumbies. Highlights include four-wheel driving on the beach, beach camping, fishing and swimming.

Gawler Ranges National Park: the park comprises the former Paney Station, and areas of Pine Lodge and Scrubby Peak Stations. Paney was one of the earliest pastoral holdings in the Gawler Ranges. Highlights include the organ pipes, an extensive exposure of volcanic rhyolite, one of the largest in the world. The park is home to about 21 rare and threatened species including the yellow-footed rock-wallaby, central long-eared bat, sandhill dunnart, malleefowl, Major Mitchell cockatoo, honey myrtle, and the locally endemic crimson mallee.

Lake Newland Conservation Park: spring-fed salt lakes separated from Anxious Bay by sand dunes extending to the beach. The lakes extend into a samphire and tea tree community around the fringes with cleared grassland further inland.

Whyalla and the east coast

Wyhalla, a sprawling town built around shipping and the iron ore industry, is the north-eastern hub of the peninsula. To the south, Cowell is famous for its oysters and jade–the local nephrite jade is one of the oldest and largest deposits in the world–and further on is Tumby Bay, via the villages of Arno Bay and Port Neill and past magnificent beaches such as Poverty Beach and Redbanks. Almost every town on the peninsula has a wooden jetty, usually lined with people fishing. Wander along its length and chat to the locals, who'll give you the run down on what fish are biting where, and often try to give away the fish they caught to you as well!

Port Lincoln

Port Lincoln is home to the largest commercial fishing fleet in the Southern Hemisphere. Wander the Lincoln Cove Marina on a guided walking tour to hear the history of fishing in the town and how it grew to become a $300 million a year export industry, see live rock lobster (November to May), or if they are in port, tour a working prawn trawler. You can also take a tour of tuna and yellowfish farming pens in the bay and visit a mussel farm or visit the Seahorse Farm, the only one of its type in South Australia. Port Lincoln is the largest town on the peninsula and has plenty of good restaurants, cafes, galleries and shops.

Streaky Bay, Ceduna and the west coast

The main towns on the western side of the peninsula are Streaky Bay and Ceduna, both pretty seaside towns with great seafood to be had in the local pubs, cafes and direct from the oyster growers themselves. Highlights of this section include the Talia sea caves and the Point Labatt Australian sea lion colony. There is a viewing platform on the cliff top where you can watch mothers teaching their pups to swim, or you can get really up close and personal on a swimming with sea lions and dolphin tour run by Ocean Eco Tours out of Baird Bay. Take the scenic cliff-top drive five minutes from Elliston. The views are sensational with cliffs as stunning as those you'll see on the Great Australian Bight. From Streaky Bay you can continue north to Ceduna where you can head west across the Nullarbor or back east to Adelaide on Highway 1.

Gawler Ranges

Across the north of the peninsula, the Gawler Ranges are a line of volcanic rock hills more than 1500 million years old, a landscape of vast hills and gullies with rocky gorges and seasonal water flows and a barrier between the arable lands to the south and the dry outback deserts to the north. Most of the area is protected by national park.

Caravan and camping

In Lincoln National Park there is a variety of beachside camping. The most popular is Memory Cove, but you will need to book at Pt Lincoln Visitor Information Centre and it is 4WD access only. Other good campsites include Fishermans Point, Surfleet Cove, Taylor's Landing and September Beach (each with toilet facilities) and beach-side bush camping at Carcase Rock, MacLaren Point, Spalding Cove, and Woodcutters Beach.

In Coffin Bay the most popular campground is at Yangie Bay, a sheltered bay surrounded by dense shrub. All other campsites in the park are 4WD only and most have no facilities. Sensation Beach is quite exposed, while Big Yangie, Black Springs, Morgans Landing and The Pool near Point Sir Isaac all offer more sheltered beachside campsites.

In the Gawler Ranges there are several good reasonably shady campgrounds with views to red rocky outcrops although you will need a 4WD to access all of them and there are no facilities.

Fresh oysters. *(SATC)*

DON'T MISS

- **Cowell Jade Motel Showroom:** nephrite jade was discovered in 1965 in the nearby Minbrie Ranges and Cowell jade is recognised as the oldest and one of the largest deposits in the world, with a variety of colours and patterns not found elsewhere. Lincoln Highway, Cowell. Open daily.
- **Smoky Bay Oyster Farm:** tours Mon–Fri 3pm. Bookings essential. ☎ (08) 8625 7077.
- **Abalone Farm Tours:** tours Tue, Thu, Fri and Sun 10am. Bookings essential. ☎ (08) 8626 1377.
- **Elliston Crayfish Tours:** tours Mon, Wed and Fri 2pm. Bookings essential ☎ (08) 8687 9200.
- **Walking tours, Port Lincoln:** Mon, Wed, Fri and Sat 10.30am. ☎ 1800 629 911.
- **South Australian Seahorse Marine Services:** South Australia's only working Seahorse breeding facility. Tours available only with prior bookings through the Port Lincoln Visitor Information Centre. ☎ 1800 629 911. www.saseahorse.com
- **Boston Bay Wines:** wine tastings and sales. Lincoln Highway, Port Lincoln. Cellar door open weekends, public holidays and daily during December and January and school holidays, 11.30am–4.30pm. www.bostonbaywines.com.au
- **The Old School-house Museum:** pioneering relics of the Ceduna district, antiques and restored farm machinery. Also artefacts from the British atomic program at Maralinga and a medical room dedicated to the history of the Bush Church Aid Society. Park Terrace, Ceduna. Open Mon, Tue, Fri and Sat 10am–12 noon, Wed, 2–4pm and Thu, 10am–noon and 2–4pm, other times by arrangement.
- **Koppio Smithy Museum:** National Trust museum reflecting farming activities prior to the late 1940s. Other restored buildings include 'Glenleigh', a pine-log thatched-roof shepherd's hut, and the Koppio school house with its collections of photographs, early firearms and clerical machines. Open Tue–Sun and public holidays 10am–5pm, daily during school holidays 10am–5pm.
- **Axel Stenross Maritime Museum:** unique maritime museum in the original boat-building workshop and home of the late Axel Stenross, a Finnish boat-builder who set up his boat-building business in Port Lincoln in the late 1920s. The museum features relics and artefacts of the windjammer era including an extensive collection of early maritime photographs, a working slipway and blacksmith shop. 97 Lincoln Highway, Port Lincoln. Open Tue, Thu, Sun and public holidays 1–5pm, Sat during summer months 1–5pm. ☎ (08) 8682 2963.
- **Mt Dutton Bay Woolshed Museum:** shearing, farming, and fishing memorabilia in restored woolshed. Mt Dutton Bay. Open daily, 10am–5pm.
- **Murphy's Haystacks:** outcrop of pink granite boulders with walkways between the two outcrops and interpretive signage. 40km southeast of Streaky Bay.
- **Talia Sea Caves:** rocks have been hollowed by the sea to form limestone caves with a granite rock face and formations. 40km north of Elliston.
- **Point Labatt sea lion colony:** cliff-top viewing platform overlooking the colony 40km south of Streaky Bay. Take binoculars and a zoom lens for close-up views.
- **Ceduna OysterFest:** community festival held over the October long weekend each year on the foreshore lawns in Ceduna.

scenic highlights

Elliston Cliffs. (SATC)

The cold southern waters that wash this rugged coastline also produce some of the freshest and tastiest seafood in the country and the best way to taste it is to follow the seafood and aquaculture trail.

The self-drive trail hugs the peninsula's coastline, from Ceduna in the west to Port Lincoln at the southern tip and along the eastern coast to Wyhalla, and leads you to abalone and crayfish farms, oyster sheds, fish hatcheries and processors that open their doors for informative tours and even a seahorse farm. You could do the trip in two days, but if you want to really explore the area three or four days would be better.

There's a lot of competition on the peninsula about which oysters are the best, plumpest and juiciest, and you can begin your own taste testing in Ceduna at the Ceduna Oyster Bar, where you can snack on freshly-shucked oysters, sitting in the sun on the roof of the oyster shed overlooking the bay.

But according to Jeff Holmes, owner of the Smoky Bay Oyster Farm 38km down the road at Smoky Bay, the best way to eat them is cooked in the shell on the barbeque, with just a touch of freshly ground pepper. Jeff and his wife, Colleen, run tours of their oyster farm where you can learn all the hows and whys of oyster farming, see aquarium displays of local marine life, and of course, taste some of the fruits of their labour. Just like those at Ceduna, their oysters taste of the sea—just the way a good oyster should be.

These pristine waters also produce premium abalone, and at Streaky Bay (69km south) you can join an Abalone Farm Tour. This unique land-based abalone farm produces green and black lip abalone, supplying the insatiable Asian seafood market.

Although not officially part of the trail, it's worth stopping at Baird Bay, a tiny collection of houses clinging to the edge of Anxious Bay, home to a colony of rare Australian sea lions. Back on the trail, the road hugs the coast line, past sleepy Elliston, where you can take a short detour to follow the 5km cliff drive for some stunning views of limestone cliffs before taking a tour of the local crayfish farm. Here you'll learn how cray pots capture their prey, the life cycle of the crayfish, and hand pick your own crayfish to take home and cook.

It's 169km to Port Lincoln, the tip of the Peninsula and home to the largest commercial fishing fleet in the Southern Hemisphere. The one 'don't miss' attraction in Port Lincoln is the Seahorse Farm, the only one of its type in South Australia where you'll learn some of the finer points of seahorse life and lore on the guide tour: that there are 16 species native to Australian waters; that it is the male who gets pregnant and gives birth to live babies; that they eat sea monkeys, just like those you ordered in comic books as a child; and that, according to Asian herbal apothecaries, dried and ground seahorse is a great aphrodisiac.

Heading north, stop for a wine tasting with a view at Boston Bay wines, explore the seaside towns of Tumby Bay, try some more oysters at Cowell where you can buy them almost anywhere—direct from the oyster farmers along Oyster drive, from the bakery, the café, on the jetty... but the ones you really should try is an oyster kebab from the Cowell Commercial Hotel. These skewers of hot oysters wrapped in bacon and dipped in bbq sauce are a treat. If oysters aren't your favourite food (you may well be in the wrong place!) try the whiting, another Eyre Peninsula speciality.

Eyre Peninsula sunset. *(SATC)*

Bushwalks

The Investigator Trail is a 93km long-distance coastal loop trail in Lincoln National Park which takes its name from the *Investigator*, the ship commanded by Matthew Flinders while surveying the rugged coastline of Lower Eyre Peninsula in 1802. The trail is easy to walk and well marked through coastal heath, mallee corridors and along beaches and passes through magnificent coastal scenery including sheltered bays, views to offshore islands, mobile sand dunes and beautiful beaches. It can also be broken up into smaller sections.

Also in Lincoln National Park an energetic walk up Stamford Hill provides spectacular views of Boston Bay, Port Lincoln and Lincoln National Park. A monument commemorating Matthew Flinders voyage of discovery is located at the top.

The Parnkalla Walking Trail is a pleasant 14km walk that follows the shores of Boston Bay with breathtaking coastal views.

In Coffin Bay National Park there are a number of walking trails, mostly following old vehicle tracks. At Yangie Bay there is a short climb to Yangie Lookout with views overlooking Yangie Bay and Marble Range or you can extend it with the 40-minute Kallara Nature Walk, via Yangie Lookout or the 5km Yangie Island Trail that leads to a close up view of Yangie Island from the adjoining beach or walk between the vegetated dunes that come out on the expansive Long Beach, a 10km one-way walk from the Yangie Bay campground.

At Black Springs Well you can follow the coast around the headland overlooking sheltered Port Douglas. Black Rocks is a two-hour return walk to the rugged coastline of Avoid Bay with views overlooking Lake Damascus. In Whidbey Wilderness Area the Sudden Jerk Lookout Walk overlooks the rugged coastline out to Sudden Jerk Island. For a longer walk try the eight-hour, 23km return walk through coastal heath, samphire flats and mallee woodlands to Boarding House Bay, a rugged coastline of cliffs, beaches and offshore reefs.

In the township of Coffin Bay, the Oyster Walk is a 12km walk that meanders around the inner bays, past seaside shacks and boat moorings, with the lookout in Kellidie Bay Conservation Bay offering stunning views. Stop for lunch at one of the oyster sellers along the way.

adventure activities

Canoeing and kayaking

Take to the beautiful waters of Port Lincoln, Coffin Bay and their national parks on a guided sea kayaking adventure or enjoy a paddle with the dolphins at Dutton Bay with Out There Tours in Port Lincoln. Kayaking tours range from two-hour sunset marina tours paddling around the Lincoln Cove Marina, Lincoln Lakes and Porter Bay to watch the sun set over Australia's largest fishing fleet to full-day tours of Coffin Bay and Lincoln national parks. They also offer kayak hire on the Port Lincoln foreshore on hot days.

www.outtheretours.com.au

Diving

Each year between May and August, tens of thousands of Australian Giant Cuttlefish descend on the coastline of Fitzgerald Bay near Whyalla for their annual ritual of mating and spawning. This phenomenon is the greatest mass gathering of the animal anywhere and attracts thousands of divers from all over the world to see it.

You can snorkel among Australian giant cuttlefish in their annual spawning grounds just offshore from Whyalla, and watch as these 'chameleons of the sea' instantly change colour and texture to blend with any environment. Hire equipment from Whyalla Diving Services.

The waters off the Eyre Peninsula are also a renowned habitat for the great white shark, with mature sharks exceeding 4m in length and up to and over 7m. Film maker Rodney Fox, survivor of a great white shark attack in 1963, has been running Cage Diving expeditions in the waters off Port Lincoln since 1965. The four-day, three-night live aboard tours maximize your 'face to face' opportunities with great white sharks in the specially designed, submersible shark-proof cage. Adventures depart from Port Lincoln, and head out into the Southern Ocean to the Neptune Islands at the mouth of the Spencer Gulf, where the array of wildlife, including many bird species, dolphins, thousands of fur seals, and Australian sea lion, is the natural feeding ground of the great white shark. Sharks can be found in any month, and there are exceptions every season with both the weather and sharks reliability, however in general reliable sharks combined with the best weather is in January, the most reliable shark numbers are experienced from July through September and the largest sized sharks are often experienced in June–although the water is very cold at that time of the year. A dive ticket is not necessary, however, if you are certified you can go down 15-30m in the special submersible bottom cage. Non-certified divers can still have a full experience in the floating surface cages.

Caption. *(credit)*

www.rodneyfox.com.au

Fishing

With more than 2000km of coastline, and the largest commercial fishing fleet in the Southern Hemisphere, the Eyre Peninsula is one of the best fishing areas in Australia, and it is the most popular recreational activity with most visitors (and locals) with surf, jetty, rock and offshore fishing all excellent.

Spencer Gulf is one of the country's best snapper areas, especially around Whyalla and also Port Pirie, Port Augusta and Cowell. Arno Bay jetty is good for tommy ruff, squid, garfish, whiting and mullet; Redbanks rock platform for snapper and Tumby Bay jetty for whiting, tommy ruff, garfish, snook and squid. Tumby Bay is the gateway to the Sir Joseph Banks Group of islands, 12km to the southeast, which produces some of the best fishing in the state. With a reasonable boat (over 16ft) you can expect to catch a wide range of delicious eating fish such as whiting, snapper, sweep, trevally, snook, salmon, tommy ruff and garfish.

The foot of the Eyre Peninsula around Port Lincoln attracts more visiting anglers than any other part of the state. The local industry is celebrated each January during the three-day Tunarama festival, and trolling for bluefin tuna is popular with game anglers who also go offshore after shark. Head to Port Lincoln jetty for snapper, salmon, trevally, garfish and tommy ruff.

On the west coast big salmon are caught near Elliston and Streaky Bay and the beaches west of Fowlers Bay. Around Coffin Bay you'll get whiting, trevally, salmon, garfish, tommy ruff, flathead and snapper; Locks Well surf beach is famous for its salmon run; Elliston jetty is good for tommy ruff, garfish, snook and squid and Streaky Bay jetty for tommy ruff, salmon, trout and snook.

Fishing charters are available in Ceduna and Port Lincoln and larger towns along both the east and west coasts.

Off-road driving

Lincoln National Park has a number of 4WD-only scenic drives. The track in the rugged southern section of the park is largely along the cliff edges to the Sleaford sand dunes, an endless sea of towering white sand dunes leading to beaches pounded by enormous waves. The more

sheltered, northern section of the park has a string of pretty bays and calm beaches. Pick of the crop is Memory Cove, named by Flinders as a reminder of the tragic accident which took the lives of his eight crewmen, but you will need to get a gate key from the Visitors Centre in Port Lincoln before you go.

Coffin Bay National Park is on the western side of the Peninsula, about 40km from Port Lincoln and is great for 4WDs. You can drive the length of the peninsula to Point Sir Isaac, but be warned, the sand can trap even the most experienced four-wheel driver. Lower your tyre pressures and carry a compressor to re-inflate them–you will need to do this several times during the trip. It's only 55km from the ranger station but it will take around three hours each way. Much of the road is actually on the beach, so you need to check the tide chart before you set off. There are good camping spots along the way at Black Springs and Point Sir Isaac–both sites are practically on the beach and the fishing is good. You can also camp at Sensation Beach on the more exposed southern side.

The majority of tracks within The Gawler Ranges National Park are also 4WD only. All tracks and roads can become impassable in wet conditions.

Great Australian Bight Safaris, in Port Lincoln, offer a range of tag-along and guided 4WD tours of the Gawlers and various locations around the peninsula.

www.greatsafaris.com.au

Sailing

Yacht Away Cruising in Port Lincoln has a range of half-day and up to five-day cruises available, including visits to tuna farms, cruises around Boston Bay and overnight island cruises aboard the 10m Nantucket, *Free Spirit*.

www.portlincoln.net/yachtaway

Yacht-Away SA, based in Tumby Bay, also has a range of sailing cruises available aboard *Quasar*, a 55ft racing Van de Stadt sloop refitted for cruising that accommodates up to eight people (12 for sail training). With a separate aft crew-cabin for the skipper, it is also available for a kind of bare boat charter with the 'pilot' promising to keep a low profile and only called upon if required.

www.tumbybay.com/yachtawa.htm

Surfing

The stretch of coastline between Ceduna and Penong at the start of the Nullarbor Plain is known as the surf coast and is renowned for its string of surf beaches. Most famous of all, Cactus Beach, 21km south of Penong has three perfect surfing breaks, Castles and Cactus are both left handers and Caves is a powerful right-hand break, although these waves are not for novices. Although the surrounding land is private property, the owner permits camping in a natural environment. Toilets and bore water showers are provided, and firewood is supplied nightly.

Remember though, sharks are known to frequent these waters and there have been fatal attacks at this beach.

Sunset beach fishing. *(SATC)*

Swimming with sea lions

The cold southern waters off Baird Bay (just north of Port Kenny) are home to a large breeding colony of 70 or so Australian sea lions, one of the rarest of seal species. The entire population is only around 12,000, and about two thirds of the population live in South Australian waters. Ocean Eco Tours offer half-day trips swimming with sea lions, and depending on weather, swimming with the resident pod of bottlenose dolphins. But unlike some wildlife watching tours that spend hours chasing harassed marine animals around a bay, this one is all about conservation. The sea lions are never fed, and all interaction is initiated by the animals. They come to you. You must be able to swim and parents or guardians must accompany children under 12. The best season is from September through to May.

www.bairdbay.com ☎ (08) 8626 5017

Windsurfing and kitesurfing

Windsurfing is one of Port Lincoln's most popular aquatic pastimes. Popular spots include the inner area of Boston Bay and Sleaford Mere. Great wavesailing spots are spread all along the coast but beware of upsetting local surfers in towns like Cactus, where localism is strong.

www.oes-australia.com

MORE INFORMATION

- **Whyalla Information Centre:** Lincoln Highway. ☎ 1800 088 589.
- **Port Lincoln Information Centre:** 3 Adelaide Place. ☎ 1800 62 9911. www.visitportlincoln.net www.tep.com.au

weather watch

- January: 15–25°C
- July: 8–16°C
- Temperatures are moderate most of the year. Summer is usually much drier than the winter months.

riverlands

Beach fishing on the Limestone Coast. *(SATC)*

& limestone coast

▶ SOME OF AUSTRALIA'S most dramatic river scenery is found along the Murray River as it curves its way past a backdrop of vertical limestone cliffs, redgum forests, citrus orchards and vineyards.

In the north, the area called The Riverlands is the state's fruit bowl, producing more than 90 per cent of the state's citrus, stone fruits and nuts and half the state's wines.

To the south, the Murray empties into Lake Alexandrina on the coast, feeding the beautiful Coorong wetlands and the rugged eastern coastline, known as the Limestone Coast, a popular holiday destination with a string of pretty seaside towns. The area is also home to some of Australia's youngest (extinct) volcanoes, just 5000 years old, and fascinating cave systems.

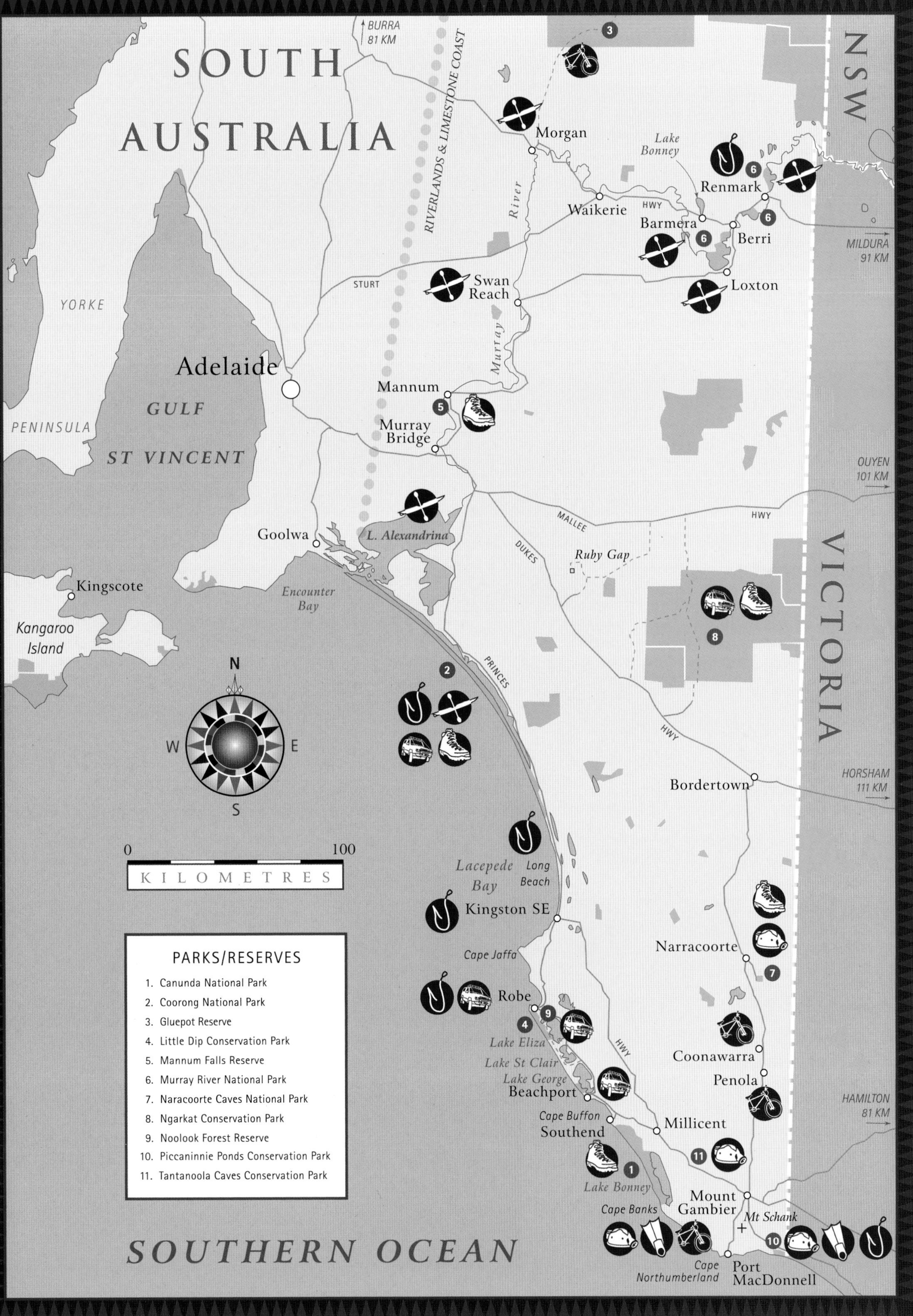

SOUTH AUSTRALIA
NSW
VICTORIA
BURRA 81 KM
RIVERLANDS & LIMESTONE COAST
Morgan
Lake Bonney
Renmark
Waikerie
HWY
Barmera
Berri
River
MILDURA 91 KM
STURT
Swan Reach
Loxton
YORKE
PENINSULA
Murray
Adelaide
GULF
ST VINCENT
Mannum
Murray Bridge
OUYEN 101 KM
MALLEE
HWY
Goolwa
L. Alexandrina
DUKES
Ruby Gap
Kingscote
Encounter Bay
Kangaroo Island
PRINCES
HWY
N
W
E
S
Bordertown
HORSHAM 111 KM
0
100
KILOMETRES
Lacepede Bay
Long Beach
Kingston SE
Narracoorte
Cape Jaffa
Robe
Lake Eliza
Lake St Clair
Lake George
HWY
Coonawarra
Penola
Beachport
HAMILTON 81 KM
Cape Buffon
Southend
Millicent
Lake Bonney
Mount Gambier
Cape Banks
Mt Schank
SOUTHERN OCEAN
Cape Northumberland
Port MacDonnell
PARKS/RESERVES
1. Canunda National Park
2. Coorong National Park
3. Gluepot Reserve
4. Little Dip Conservation Park
5. Mannum Falls Reserve
6. Murray River National Park
7. Naracoorte Caves National Park
8. Ngarkat Conservation Park
9. Noolook Forest Reserve
10. Piccaninnie Ponds Conservation Park
11. Tantanoola Caves Conservation Park

Coorong National Park. *(SATC)*

NATIONAL PARKS

Murray River National Park: this park, split into three sections, protects areas of floodplain and wetlands and is home to a large variety of water birds. The Katarapko, Kapunda Island, and Rilli Island section is opposite the town of Loxton and is 4km south of Berri. Lyrup Flats encompasses 2000 hectares along the floodplain on the northern side of the river, opposite the township of Lyrup. Bulyong Island is just out of Renmark.

Ngarkat Conservation Park: combined with the neighbouring Big Desert Park in Victoria this park forms a huge swathe of wilderness, a complex of sand dunes stabilised by a unique mosaic of heath and mallee. Early attempts to farm this country failed and you can explore farming ruins at Box Flat. Wildlife is plentiful and you'll often see the western grey kangaroos and emus, and if you are lucky, the rare mallee fowl.

Coorong National Park: a long, narrow stretch of windswept beach, coastal dunes, lagoons and wetlands extending 145km south-east from the mouth of the Murray River. This 50,000 hectare park is home to a great variety of birds, animals and fish including many species of migratory birds. The Coorong is also an archaeological site of national importance with middens and burial sites throughout the park giving evidence of Aboriginal occupation over many thousands of years. Highlights include the largest breeding colony of the Australian Pelican (*Pelicanus conspicillatus)* at Jack's Point Observatory.

Canunda National Park: stretching from Cape Buffon outside the town of Southend, to Cape Banks near the southern end of Lake Bonney, Canunda National Park features limestone cliffs, sea stacks, offshore reefs and low dense scrub in the north and mobile sand dunes and stretches of beaches in the south.

Naracoorte Caves National Park: South Australia's only World Heritage site, these 26 caves have acted as pitfall traps, collecting animals for at least 500,000 years, preserving the most complete fossil record we have for this period of time including the bones of megafauna such as *Thylacoleo carnifex* (marsupial lion), *thylacine, zygomaturus* and *sthenurine* kangaroos.

Renmark and Barmera

The river port towns of Renmark, Waikerie and Morgan boomed in the late 19th century when river trading was brisk and paddle steamers plied the waterways. They have maintained much of the charm and heritage with gracefully preserved buildings, historic wharves, wide streets and parklands. Houseboating is a popular holiday option and several restored paddle steamers cruise the river on day trips and overnight cruises. First settled by returned WWI soldiers, Barmera, on the shores of Lake Bonney is the centre of a rich citrus and grape growing area, thanks to an irrigation system established in the early 1920s.

Coonawarra

Just 12km long and 2km wide, the Coonawarra, with its fabled limestone-rich terra rossa soil, is some of Australia's most valuable wine real estate, producing high quality wines, particularly cabernet sauvignon.

Robe and seaside towns

One of the most attractive historic towns in South Australia, Robe is also one of the oldest. The historic walk in the town centre lists 45 historic buildings. Surrounded by spectacular rocky coastline Robe is a popular seaside holiday resort that feels like a small fishing village. Neighbouring seaside towns of Kingston, Cape Jaffa and Beachport are renowned for their fresh lobster.

Mount Gambier

Half-way between Melbourne and Adelaide near the state border, Mount Gambier is most famous for its Blue Lake, a 75m-deep lake filling an extinct volcanic crater with intensely blue water. It is at its bluest between November and March.

Caravan and camping

In Murray River National Park you can camp beside the river at Eckerts Creek, Lock 4, Main Katarapko, Black Box, Colligans and Lyrup Flats. There are nine campsites in Ngarkat Conservation Park, those at Pertendi Hut, Mt Shaugh and Mt Rescue

Robe Harbour. *(SATC)*

scenic highlights

Murray mouth. (SATC)

The Southern Ports Coastal Route, from Mount Gambier to Kingston SE is a lovely coastal drive that meanders through farmlands, past extinct volcanoes and rugged cliff tops, deserted beaches and charming seaside fishing villages.

Mount Gambier is Australia's youngest volcano, only 5000 years old, which in geological terms is practically new. There are three craters in the extinct volcano, including the famous Blue Lake, which turns a brilliant blue in summer. No definitive explanation for this has been found. Head up John Watson Drive, which circles the crater rim, for the best views. There is a memorial to poet Adam Lindsay Gordon, who, for a bet, made a spectacular leap on his horse over a fence close to the rim of the Blue Lake to land on a narrow ledge 70m above the water.

Head south to Piccaninnie Ponds, a top cave diving spot, and on to Port MacDonnell and Cape Northumberland on the coast road, which runs beside the beach. Once the second busiest port in South Australia, Port MacDonnell is home to the largest cray fleet in the state. At Cape Northumberland you can watch fairy penguins returning to their nests on the eastern side of the cliff top at dusk or take in the views from the historic lighthouse.

Drop into Dingley Dell, home of the daredevil horse riding poet and take a detour to Mount Schank, another very young dormant volcano and then on to Tantanoola Caves. The road now spears through radiata pine plantations and dolomite cliffs honeycombed with a network of decorated caves that rise sharply on one side of the highway. The museum at Millicent has one of the best collections of horse-drawn vehicles in the country as well as all sorts of salvaged items from the many shipwrecks that have occurred on this section of the coast.

Spear off towards the coast to Canunda National Park. If you can tear yourself away from the beaches and beautiful fresh water of Lake Bonney, continue west along the Southern Ports Coastal Route across drained wetlands to Beachport where the jetty is a great spot for fishing, past Lake George, Lake St Clair and Lake Eliza, all separated from the sea by sand dunes to Robe and through Noolook Forest to Kinston SE and the Coorong.

have toilets. In the Coorong there are campsites at 28 Mile Crossing, 32 Mile Crossing, 42 Mile Crossing, Barker Knoll, Godfreys Landing, overlooking the Coorong lagoon at Long Point, Loop Road, Mark Point, Old Coorong Road, Parnka Point (excellent views of the lagoon) and Tea Tree Crossing. In Canunda National Park you can camp at Boozy Gully, Cape Banks Lighthouse, Geltwood Beach, and Number Two Rocks and there are 10 powered sites and a large area for tents at Naracoorte Caves.

Bushwalks

In the Murraylands area there are nice boardwalks in the Rocky Gully, Swanport and Riverglade wetlands and a short walk in Mannum Falls Reserve. The 79km Federation Trail traverses the south-eastern flanks of the Mt Lofty Ranges from Murray Bridge, winding its way to the township of Tungkillo past historic rail yards, river wetlands, rugged gorges, forests, vast farming lands and the Monarto Zoological Park.

In Ngarkat Conservation Park the Mt Shaugh 3km walk is fairly tough, but gives panoramic views over the park, Western Victoria and Big Desert Wilderness Area. The hard, seven-hour, 17km Scorpion Springs Trek traverses stringybark mallee and native pines and joins with Nanam Well and Fishponds–only attempt it in cool weather.

The best walk in the Coorong is the Nakun Kungun Trek from Salt Creek to 42 Mile Crossing via Chinaman's Well. The 27km trail winds through different types of vegetation, passing ephemeral lakes and areas rich in wildlife. Allow around 48 hours. You can camp along Loop Road and at 42 Mile Crossing. Shorter walks in the Coorong include the 90-minute Godfrey's Landing Walk from Coorong Lagoon through the sand dunes and swales of the Younghusband Peninsula to the Southern Ocean beach but can only be accessed by boat. The 45-minute Journey to Gold Walk is an interpretive trail with signs recreating the story of Chinese fortune seekers on their way to the Victorian Goldfields.

In Canunda the one-hour Cape Buffon loop is a magnificent coastal cliff-top walk with intriguing cliffs, sea stacks and reef platforms. A variety of colourful wildflowers can be seen throughout the year. The 90-minute (one way) Seaview Walk is another great cliff-top walk featuring spectacular rock formations, sandy beaches, seabirds, coastal plants and scenic views. The 8.5km Coola Outstation Historical Trail winds through coastal habitats and lakeside vegetation to Coola Lookout for views of Lake Bonney, dunes and farmland. Interpretive signs tell the history of Coola Outstation.

Naracoorte Caves National Park has several good short trails, many with interpretative signage. In Mount Gambier, the Blue Lake Circuit around the circumference of the Blue Lake is very popular and the 5km Forest Dry Creek walking trail follows a creek bed past many active wombat holes and along a river trail which passes dense native vegetation and includes a lookout along the Glenelg River.

Blue Lake, Mount Gambier. *(SATC)*

DON'T MISS

- **Birds Australia Gluepot Reserve:** birdwatcher's paradise with 14 marked walking trails and five elevated bird hides. 64km north of Waikerie. Entry key available from Shell Service Station in the centre of Waikerie.
- **Loxton Historical Village:** large display of farm equipment, machinery, household goods and buildings depict a village from the 1890-1930s with 30 fully furnished buildings. On the riverfront, Loxton. Open Mon–Fri, 10am–4pm; weekends, 10am–5pm. www.loxtonhistoricalvillage.com.au
- **Monash Adventure Park:** family fun park with rope bridge, wave bridge, maze, mini basketball, flying fox and more. Madison Avenue, Monash. Open daily, 10am–5pm.
- **Olivewood:** historic home of Charles Chaffey, founder of the Renmark Irrigation Colony. Twenty-First Street, Renmark. Open Thu-Mon, 10am–4pm; Tue 2pm–4pm.
- **Brayfield Park Lavender Farm:** lavender, herb and display gardens and café. Placid Estates Road, East Wellington. Open daily, 9am–5pm. www.brayfieldpark.com.au
- **Mallee Heritage Centre:** collection of restored tractors, farm and household memorabilia, Printing Museum and other exhibits. Railway Terrace, South Pinnaroo. Open Mon–Sat, 10am–1pm.
- **Mannum Dock Museum of River History:** museum incorporating the paddle steamer *Marion* and the historic Randell Dry Dock. 6 Randell Street, Mannum. Open Mon–Fri 9am–5pm; weekends 10am–4pm.
- **Murray Bridge Regional Gallery:** contemporary and traditional art and craft exhibitions. 27 Sixth Street, Murray Bridge. Open Mon–Thu 10am–4pm; Sun 1pm–4pm.
- **Avenue Emus:** emu farm with emu products for sale, including emu oil, emu mettwurst and emu skin. Thomas Road, Avenue Range. Open Thu–Mon, 10am–4pm.
- **Big Lobster:** 17m high and weighing four tonnes with displays and lobster for sale. 17 Princes Highway, Kingston SE. Open daily, 9am–6pm.
- **Cave Gardens:** in the centre of Mount Gambier this sinkhole was the original source of water for the early settlers. Famous for its roses, there are also cave viewing platforms. Watson Terrace, Mount Gambier.
- **Mount Gambier Crater Lakes:** volcanic area made up of three main craters containing several lakes; amongst them are Brownes Lake, Valley Lake, Leg of Mutton Lake and the famous Blue Lake. Bay Road, Mount Gambier.
- **Aquifer Tours:** fascinating 45-minute tour at Blue Lake which takes visitors in a glass panelled lift down the original dolomite well shaft, from which water was originally extracted. Walk through a tunnel to see the Blue Lake at close range. Corner of Bay Road and John Watson Drive. Mount Gambier. Open daily, tours on the hour. www.aquifertours.com
- **Courthouse Gallery and Old Courthouse Museum:** historic courthouse and museum. 42A Bay Road, Mount Gambier. Open Mon–Fri, 11am–3pm.
- **Limestone Coast Cheese Company:** hand crafted gourmet cheeses. Roach Road, Lucindale. Open Wed–Sun, 11am–4pm.
- **Mary MacKillop Penola Centre:** commemorates the lives of Blessed Mary MacKillop and Father Julian Tenison Woods with displays, photographs, artefacts and history. Portland Street, Penola. Open daily, 10am–4pm.
- **Pool of Siloam:** a salt lake, reputedly seven times more salty than the sea alleged to possess therapeutic assets. Beachport.
- **Monarto Zoological Park:** 1000 ha open-range zoo where giraffes, lions, rhinoceros, zebra, antelope and cheetahs roam freely in a bushland setting. Princes Highway, Monarto. Open daily, 10am–5pm. www.monartozp.com.au

adventure activities

Murray River. *(SATC)*

Camel safari

Bush Safari Company, in Waikerie, offers camel rides fom November to April and half-day or full-day treks with beautiful cliff-top scenery. Two- and three-day treks along the Murray or into the semi-desert, are also available, as are camel/boat combinations and longer treks.

www.safarico.com.au

Canoeing and kayaking

There are some great canoeing trails along the Murray River, including Katarapko Creek near the Loxton irrigation area where the waterways vary from long open lagoons to narrow, densely vegetated creeks ideal for overnight trips. The 70km section of the Murray between Morgan and Swan Reach has several creeks that lead into wide lagoons, wildlife is plentiful and majestic river redgums line the river banks.

The Chambers Creek area near Barmera has good facilities for canoe access and camping and the Murray backwaters are great for birdwatching. At Chowilla Creek near Renmark, you can paddle through three states in a day (SA, Vic and NSW). The Chowilla Creek system has some of the most pristine country along the Murray, with plenty of wildlife, native vegetation and a rich aboriginal heritage. Paddlers are likely to have sections of the creeks to themselves. Further south, the Coorong and Lake Alexandrina also have some good paddling spots.

Caving

The south-east of South Australia is honeycombed with caves; the most famous is the Naracoorte Cave World Heritage Fossil Site. There are 26 caves in the park but not all are accessible as some are set aside for scientific research or for the protection of the cave and its contents.

General access cave tours include the Victoria Fossil Cave Tour which showcases the World Heritage values of Naracoorte Caves; a 30-minute tour of the richly decorated Alexandra Cave; a self-guided tour of Wet Cave with robust columns and stalactites and a Bat Tour of the Bat Observation Centre and the Blanche Cave, an important wintering site for the Southern Bentwing Bat.

There is also a range of adventure caving tours available. Blackberry Cave is low with lots of good crawls and squeezes and Stick-Tomato Cave is the section beyond what you'll see on the Wet Cave self-guided tour. The Starburst Chamber adventure tour visits Starburst Chamber as well as several other spectacular chambers in Victoria Fossil Cave. A prerequisite to this tour is either Stick-Tomato Cave or Blackberry Cave. The crawl is reasonably long, but is less strenuous than Fox Cave or Cathedral Cave.

Fox Cave is a worthwhile three-hour trip with lots of great scenes and extensive speleothem development. An important bat wintering site, it has a rare invertebrate colony and areas of fossils.

From the huge daylight entrance chamber, the Cathedral Cave tour progresses to a long small tunnel that emerges into a decorated chamber. Several fossil excavations have taken place here and the tour shows you where the work has been completed. Tantanoola Cave is one of only two dolomite caves in Australia. An ancient sea cave in a cliff face, it is stunningly beautiful, filled with giant stalactites, stalagmites and helictite formations developed over thousands of years.

Mount Gambier's city streets sit above a labyrinth of limestone caves, and you can also explore majestic gardens created in sinkholes and watch possums feeding at night in Umpherston Sinkhole.

Engelbrecht Cave, formed 30-40 million years ago, extends under seven city streets. It was once used as a dump by one of the city's local whisky distilleries but is now open for tours where you can see water which is making its way under the city towards the Blue Lake. The main viewing platform is 27m below the surface.

Further south near Port MacDonnell are the Piccaninnie and Ewens Ponds. You can snorkel across the top of 'The Chasm' at Piccaninnie Ponds and peer into depths of more than 40m or see crayfish and pygmy perch in the crystal clear waters of Ewens Ponds. Permits can be obtained from the local office of the Department for Environment and Heritage (DEH).

Ewens Ponds. (SATC)

Cycling and mountain biking

One of the most popular bike trails in this area is the Mount Gambier Crater Lakes Mountain Bike Trail beside Mount Gambier's extinct volcanic crater lakes. The route begins along a narrow track between the Valley Lake and Leg of Mutton Lake craters, with great views down steep cliffs to the bottom. Maps are available at Mount Gambier's Lady Nelson Visitor and Discovery Centre. There are a range of rides, from eight to 100km, throughout Penola and the Coonawarra region and trail maps are available at Penola Coonawarra Visitor Information Centre. In the Riverland area the Gluepot Reserve has a well maintained cycling track around the 55,000 hectare reserve.

Diving

Piccaninnie Ponds is one of the most famous freshwater sinkholes in the world, and attracts thousands of qualified divers to its clear water and interesting cave system. Cave diving qualifications are required and you'll need to purchase a permit–for diving or snorkelling–from DEH in Mt Gambier.

Ewens Ponds consists of three ponds, each about 40m in diameter and 6-10m in depth. Eels, fresh water crays and yabbies inhabit the ponds. The ponds can also be snorkelled. DEH permit required.

Engelbrecht Cave in Mount Gambier is also very popular with cave divers with dives in both the east and west sections of the cave. Get a key from Lady Nelson Visitor Information Centre. The Shaft, one of the world's most stunning cave dives, also in Mount Gambier, is a sinkhole dive with a tiny tube entrance that drops down into small lake chamber with a huge underwater chasm. Visibility is excellent and there is often an impressive shaft of sunlight visible in late spring, summer and early autumn. Depths of up to 120m have been explored, although for safety reasons (there have been several fatalities in this cave) the Cave Divers Association of Australia (CDAA) imposes a depth limit of 40m at all its sites. The longest submerged cave system in Australia, Tank Cave, also lies in this area. Much of Tank Cave is less than 15m deep, allowing divers long bottom times and some lengthy penetrations. More than six miles of crystal-clear tunnels have been charted to date.

www.cavedivers.com.au

Fishing

The Murray River was once one of the best inland fishing rivers in the country until the introduction of European carp reduced native fish stocks. That said, while you are more likely to catch carp than anything else you may be lucky enough to catch a Murray cod, which can grow up to 100kg or 1.8m in length. Your best bet is to try in deeper water near fallen logs. Callop (yellowbelly or golden perch) is one of the most sought-after fish in the River Murray and is excellent eating–try beneath overhanging willows, among fallen timbers and along clay banks. During the warmer months and when high river levels are falling is the best time to go after yabbies–try river backwaters and deep water areas.

Silver perch, catfish and Murray River crayfish are now totally protected and must be returned to the water immediately after being caught. On the other hand, European carp, mosquito fish and redfin are non-native fish–it is illegal to return them to the river or transport them live.

The Coorong is good for fishing most of the year. Long Beach, north of Kingston SE is approximately 100km long and is one of the best surf fishing destinations in Australia with an annual surf fishing competition each January long weekend. The Murray mouth is legendary for monster mulloway and the surf beach at Goolwa produces mullet and the Goolwa cockle.

The stretch of coastline between Port MacDonnell and Kingston SE is the state's best lobster fishing area but it's also good for mulloway and salmon from the beaches and shark and bluefin offshore.

Off-road driving

The Border Track is a 50km route through the Ngarkat group of parks along the border with Victoria. From Pinnaroo, travel along the Rosey Pine road to Pine Hut Soak just inside the park boundary, where you'll find picnic tables, camping areas and toilets.Head south on the Centre Track (the original Border Track is in very poor condition) across extensive native pine covered sand dunes. In the swales between the dunes the pines give way to square fruited mallee. The Centre Track is well signposted and brings to the Border Track further south where you'll travel beside the old dingo fence. From the Dogger's Hut

camping area you can return to the bitumen via Shaugh Track or continue south to Red Bluff and the Murrayville Track in Victoria. The best time to tackle the Border Track is April to November. In spring wildflowers carpet the desert-like landscape. Allow two days.

On the coast, some challenging off-road tracks are between the pretty seaside towns of Robe and Beachport. Big white dunes coupled with long sweeps of beach sand rate from hard-packed and easy to impossibly deep and extreme. Start at Cape Lannes behind Robe in the middle of the steep and vegetated dunes of Little Dip Conservation Park. Between Stony Rise and The Boundary there is around 15km of beautiful coastline. You could do it in three hours, but take your time and explore the park. To access the Beachport leg there's a short transit hop from The Boundary Track, picking up the gravel road that runs along lakes Eliza and St Clair, turning into the dunes at the Lake George Holiday Resort. Stick to the marked trail. Head into the Beachport Conservation Park where the going initially is deceptively easy. The track criss-crosses calcrete swales before being swallowed by the dunes again, the biggest and most mobile of which is Five Mile Drift. Deflate your tyres, carry a recovery kit and compressor and stick to the orange marker post tracks. The sea has claimed plenty of vehicles along these beaches, so watch the tides. The best time to visit is between October and May.

In the Coorong you can drive along the stunning narrow ribbon of sand called the Younghusband Peninsula for 150km from the Granites near Kingston SE to the mouth of the Murray River. Separated from the mainland by a chain of salt-water lagoons, huge flocks of waterbirds, gorgeous beaches and tough dunes make this a great drive, but should not be attempted in winter. (Keep an eye out for escape routes to safer terrain, dotted along the track.) The first section of the trip to 28 Mile Crossing is a wide and firm beach with some shellgrit 'speed-humps'. Between 28 and 42 Mile Crossings, shattered remains of four-wheel-drive chassis and motors pop out of the surf, a reminder of the dangers of beach driving. The beach track sits up in the foredune, with many turnouts and campsites, designated by green-topped posts. The best camp is Tea Tree, a flat grassy expanse between the claypipe lagoon and the coastal dunes.

Watersports

There are many safe beaches along the coast and in the Murray mouth. The Iceberg Team swim every day of the year from Robe's town beach with only a bathing cap and Speedos. The Southern Ocean is quite cool, even in summer, so a wetsuit is recommended for surfing and windsurfing. Robe has many reefs and beaches for snorkelling, a great bay for sailing and windsurfing and the town looks simply stunning from the water. The Robe Yacht Club runs races from Karratta Beach over summer. There are windsurfing spots to suit beginners and wave sailors, but there is no equipment hire in Robe. Beachport, between the Southern Ocean and inland Lake George, is a fabulous spot for windsurfing. Lake George is a renowned speed sailing venue with camping available at Fosters Point, where you can always find a peaceful spot under large tea-trees. As you enter Beachport the beach, known as Surfbeach, has the best surf in the area.

Renmark. *(SATC)*

MORE INFORMATION

- **Barmera Visitor Information Centre:** Barwell Avenue, Barmera. ☎ (08) 8588 2289.
- **Renmark Paringa Visitor Information Centre:** 84 Murray Avenue, Renmark. ☎ (08) 8586 6704. www.riverland.info
- **Murray Bridge Visitor Information Centre:** 3 South Terrace, Murray Bridge. ☎ (08) 8539 1142.
- **Mannum Visitor Information Centre:** 6 Randell Street, Mannum. ☎ (08) 8569 1303. www.murraylands.info
- **Lady Nelson Visitor Information and Discovery Centre:** Jubilee Highway East, Mount Gambier. ☎ 1800 087 187. www.thelimestonecoast.com
- **Penola Coonawarra Visitor Information Centre:** 27 Arthur Street, Penola. ☎ (08) 8737 2855. www.wattlerange.sa.gov.au
- **Department of Environment and Heritage:** ☎ (08) 8204 1910. www.dehaa.sa.gov.au

weather watch

- January: 12–24°C
- July: 5–16°C
- Summer temperatures are much higher away from the coast. Winter is generally wetter than summer.

the flinders ranges

Brachina Gorge. *(SATC)*

▶ THE FLINDERS RANGES in central South Australia is an ancient landscape, full of weathered crags in primeval colours, mountains of rich purples and deep blues, cut through with red rock gorges and surrounded by acres of white, yellow and purple wildflowers in spring. The countryside is one of the oldest on earth: the mountains, once higher than the Himalaya, are more than 600 million years old and are one of the richest geological areas in the country. The Aboriginal Dreamtime stories that are woven around the creation of these ancient landforms and gorges have been passed on for more than 40,000 years.

While the Flinders is remote and rugged, main roads are accessible to conventional sedans, but many side tracks are 4WD only. The best time to visit is in spring, when the ragged hills and valley floors are carpeted in wildflowers.

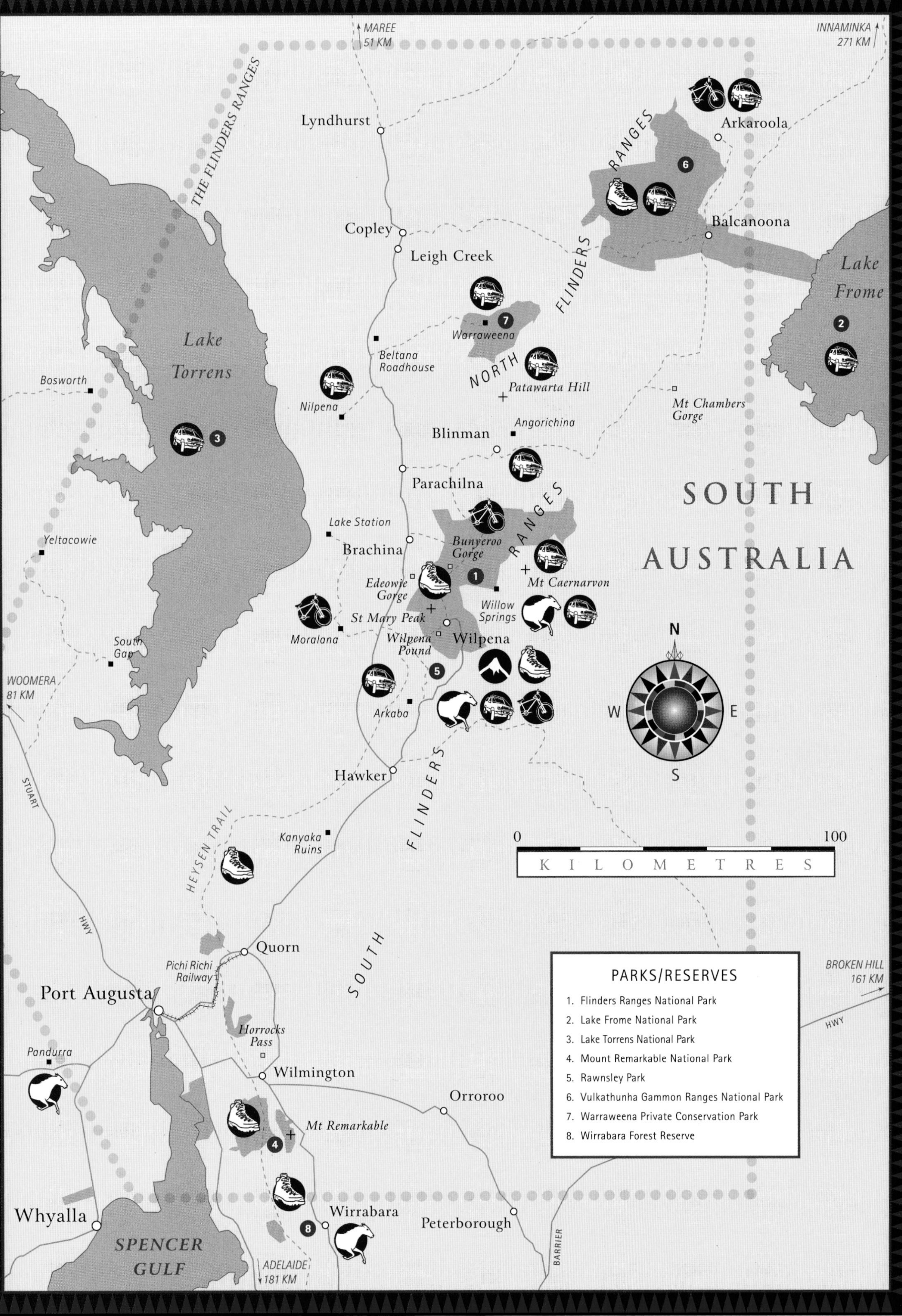
MAREE 51 KM
INNAMINKA 271 KM
THE FLINDERS RANGES
Lyndhurst
Arkaroola
RANGES
6
Copley
Leigh Creek
Balcanoona
FLINDERS
Lake Frome
2
Lake Torrens
7
Warraweena
Beltana Roadhouse
NORTH
Patawarta Hill
Bosworth
Nilpena
Mt Chambers Gorge
3
Blinman
Angorichina
Parachilna
SOUTH AUSTRALIA
RANGES
Lake Station
Yeltacowie
Brachina
Bunyeroo Gorge
1
Mt Caernarvon
Edeowie Gorge
Willow Springs
St Mary Peak
Moralana
Wilpena Pound
Wilpena
South Gap
N
WOOMERA 81 KM
5
W
E
Arkaba
S
STUART
Hawker
FLINDERS
Kanyaka Ruins
0
100
KILOMETRES
HEYSEN TRAIL
HWY
SOUTH
Quorn
Pichi Richi Railway
PARKS/RESERVES
1. Flinders Ranges National Park
2. Lake Frome National Park
3. Lake Torrens National Park
4. Mount Remarkable National Park
5. Rawnsley Park
6. Vulkathunha Gammon Ranges National Park
7. Warraweena Private Conservation Park
8. Wirrabara Forest Reserve
BROKEN HILL 161 KM
Port Augusta
HWY
Horrocks Pass
Pandurra
Wilmington
Orroroo
Mt Remarkable
4
Whyalla
Wirrabara
Peterborough
8
SPENCER GULF
ADELAIDE 181 KM
BARRIER

Flinders Ranges National Park. *(LA)*

NATIONAL PARKS

Flinders Ranges National Park: one of the most popular of all South Australian national parks, Flinders Ranges has rugged mountain ranges, spectacular gorges and dry creek beds lined with river red gums. Highlights include Wilpena Pound and Aboriginal rock art sites, fossil sites and rich geological history dating back some 500–600 million years.

Vulkathunha Gammon Ranges National Park: remote arid wilderness area in the northern Flinders Ranges with deep gorges and freshwater springs. A haven for wildlife, including the elusive yellow-footed rock-wallaby and the rare Balcoona Wattle. There are many good walking tracks and 4WD tracks within the park that lead to Aboriginal sites, waterholes and gorges.

Lake Torrens National Park: a stark wilderness to the west of Flinders, this ephemeral salt lake is 250km long and has filled with water only once in the past 150 years. Thunderstorms occasionally provide a small amount of water in the lake, when this happens the area is home to a variety of birds which seem to materialise from nowhere. Access to the lake is by either of two tracks, both of which are on private pastoral properties and you must get permission from the pastoralists to use the road or to camp alongside it. The two tracks are the Leigh Creek to Lyndhurst to Farina Ruins to Andamooka via Mulgaria Station track (permit required)—you must get permission to use this track from Mulgaria Station ☎ (08) 8675 8313; and Roxby Downs to Andamooka to Lake Torrens—you must get permission to use this track from Andamooka Station ☎ (08) 8671 0754.

Lake Frome National Park: another ephemeral salt lake 100km long and 40km wide that lies to the east of the ranges. Access to the lake is via Vulkathunha Gammon Ranges National Park.

Mount Remarkable National Park: The 16,000 ha park stretches from the coastal plain on the western side of the Flinders Ranges to the foothills above Wilmington. It is an interesting location, where South Australia's arid north and wetter southern regions overlap, and features pretty valleys and dramatic mountain scenery. Highlights include Mount Remarkable summit (960m), rugged ridges, sheer rock faces and Alligator Gorge.

Wilpena Pound. *(SATC)*

The Southern Flinders

Port Augusta at the top of the Spencer Gulf is considered the gateway to both the Flinders and the Outback, although it's not until you reach the historic railway town of Quorn 40km to the north-west that you really begin see the characteristic purple hills of the Flinders, which becomes increasingly more rugged and ragged the further north you travel, forming an imposing backdrop to the last real township of any size, Hawker.

Wilpena Pound

The centrepiece of the Flinders, Wilpena Pound is a crater-like pile of rock covering 83km^2 that rises sharply from the surrounding flat plains–the rim is actually the stumps of massive mountains, eroded down from a height that once approximated the Himalayas. The wooded interior–accessible through just one gorge–is 11km long and 8km across. The first settlers in the area were farmers who established sheep runs inside the Pound in the 1850s. The word 'Pound' was added because the farmers were struck by its resemblance to the enclosures for keeping sheep, which at that time were called pounds. The best way to really see the distinctive shape is on a scenic flight from the resort inside the Pound.

Northern Flinders

North of Wilpena, the road is gravel and much less trafficked, with the tiny blink-and-you'll-miss-it towns of Parachilna and Blinman not much more than a pub and a house or two, yet both manage to have truly good cafes and accommodation in the restored pubs, partly in thanks to the demand caused by visiting celebrities and filmmakers who often use the Flinders a backdrop for their films, particularly the Prairie Hotel at Parachilna. The restaurant is most well-known for its feral food–camel, kangaroo, emu and bush herbs and native spices–keep an eye out for the distinctive road signs advertising the menu on the way into the town.

Arkaroola is a privately-owned and operated 610km^2 wilderness sanctuary at the far northern tip of the Flinders. One of the most visually stunning places in the Flinders, it features rugged mountains, soaring granite peaks, deep gorges and waterholes. It is also home to more than 160 species of birds and the rare yellow-footed rock-wallaby. The four-hour ridge-top tour that travels along the spine of the mountains to a stunning lookout is a must, but you can

also follow one of the many self-drive 4WD tracks. With no light pollution it is also one of the best places to view the night sky and there are two observatories on the property.

Leigh Creek

Leigh Creek, at the northern tip of the Flinders on the edge of the desert where the dirt road rejoins the main road, is a modern coal mining company town founded in the early 1980s whose main claim to fame seems to be its neatness, a several-time winner of the tidy towns award. It is however, a handy place to restock supplies.

Caravan and camping

Wilpena Pound Resort has 30 powered sites and plenty of out-of-the-way bush sites throughout the Flinders Ranges National Park and also at Arkaba Station site off the Moralana Scenic Drive.

www.wilpenapound.com.au ☎ (08) 8648 0048

Arkaroola also has powered and unpowered sites and there are several caravan and camping areas within Gammon Ranges National Park with shower access available at Balcanoona Shearers Quarters for a small fee.

In Mount Remarkable National Park there are 53 unpowered sites at Mambray Creek campground, with flushing toilets, solar-heated showers, water supply, firewood supply (in season), rubbish disposal and communal fire-places. Facilities provided are suitable for disabled access. Advance bookings for individual campsites are essential for Easter, April and September school holidays and long weekends during the visitor season from March to November, and for group sites throughout the year. There are also 11 walk-in bush camp sites throughout the park.

A number of station owners in the Flinders allow camping, for a fee, but make sure you call into the homestead before you pitch your tent. Some stations provide keys which allow access to beautiful camping spots such as along a creek or river bank or by the edge of lakes which are filled after heavy rains. Ask at the visitors information centre in Port Augusta for details or visit:

www.flindersoutback.com

scenic highlights

You can explore the Flinders via a loop or along one of the many roads that cuts through the centre of the ranges. Start at Quorn, home to the Pichi Richi Railway, one of Australia's best-known steam train journeys. Originally the Port Augusta–Quorn Railway, it opened in 1879 and closed 77 years later in 1956. It was restored in 1974 by the Pichi Richi Preservation Society. The historic station buildings make for great photographs. There are also several galleries in town and a 45-minute historic building walk.

From Quorn, head for Hawker, the last town before the ranges, which are a picturesque backdrop to the town, but stop at Kanyaka ruins. In 1856 the Kanyaka Station covered 365 square miles (945km^2 or 94,500 hectares) and housed 70 workers and their families. Visit the grave of Hugh Proby, the third son of the Earl of Carysfort and owner of the station, who was swept away by flood waters while mustering sheep. His family shipped the 1.5 ton granite tablet from Scotland to mark the place of his burial.

The road is sealed to Wilpena, in the heart of Flinders Ranges National Park. Several good look-outs give great views of the Elder Range and the outer ramparts of Wilpena Pound.

The road turns to gravel just past Wilpena and it is around three hours drive to Arkaroola. Try and avoid driving at dawn or dusk as collisions with wildlife, particularly kangaroos, are common. There are several tracks cutting across the national park, and while all roads in this area are scenic, the Brachina and Bunyeroo Roads, and the Blinman–Parachilna road are even more so as they follow dry creek beds and ancient gorge lines deep into the heart of the ranges.

Stop at the former copper mining town of Blinman for a coffee and a slice of quandong pie at Wild Lime Café or a cold drink a the historic hotel, before continuing north to Arkaroola. Chambers Gorge, off a 10km rough and rocky side track, has an extensive Aboriginal rock engraving gallery. The best time to visit is late in the afternoon, when the setting sun turns the walls of the gorge to a deep, fiery red.

Spend some time exploring Arkaroola on one of the 4WD tours then head south and join the Copley Road heading to the tiny modern mining community of Leigh Creek. At Leigh Creek it's back on the bitumen for a quick run down to Parachilna and back down the highway to Hawker, the purple walls of the Flinders a constant companion to the left, before finally finishing the loop at Quorn.

Parachilna. (Sam Tinson)

Bushwalks

The Heysen Trail (1200km from Cape Jervis in the south to Parachilna) passes through both Mount Remarkable and Flinders Ranges national parks.

Popular shorter walks in Mount Remarkable National Park include the 90-minute loop walk through 'the narrows' in spectacular Alligator Gorge that returns to the main car park via Blue Gum Flat picnic area and the longer four-hour, 9km Alligator Gorge Ring Route which follows Alligator Creek upstream beyond the Terraces. The Hidden Gorge Walk is a beautiful seven-hour (18km) medium walk from the park headquarters at Mambray Creek that takes you into the gorge to sheer rock faces of red quartzite and beyond to the Battery Range for good views of the Spencer Gulf. The Mambray Creek to Alligator Gorge Walk follows the course of Alligator and Mambray Creeks for 13km and can be started from either Alligator Gorge or Mambray Creek. The climb to the summit of Mt Remarkable will take around five hours and the six-hour Mount Cavern Trek is a challenging trail crossing the high ridges of Black Range to the summit of Mt Cavern before descending steeply into Mambray Creek.

There are dozens of good bushwalks in the Flinders and Gammon Ranges parks, but many are quite challenging. The sun can be harsh, so always carry more water than you think you will need and register at Wilpena Pound or park headquarters before setting out and on your return.

In Flinders Ranges one of the most popular walks is the two-hour Hills Homestead Walk, an easy walk along Wilpena Creek to a restored 1914 homestead. You can also walk to Wangara Lookout from Hills Homestead, with information signs along the trail telling the story of Jessie Hill, the daughter of the first pioneering family to live in the homestead. There are breathtaking views of Wilpena Pound at the lookout. A shuttle bus service is provided to shorten the walk.

The Blinman Pools Walk is a pretty five-hour walk through a rocky creek bed to the Blinman Pools where there are cascading waterfalls, majestic river red gums and wedge-tailed eagles. The Mt Ohlssen Bagge Hike is a hard four-hour walk (6.4km) with some steep, rocky inclines but rewarding views of Wilpena Pound. St Mary Peak Trek is

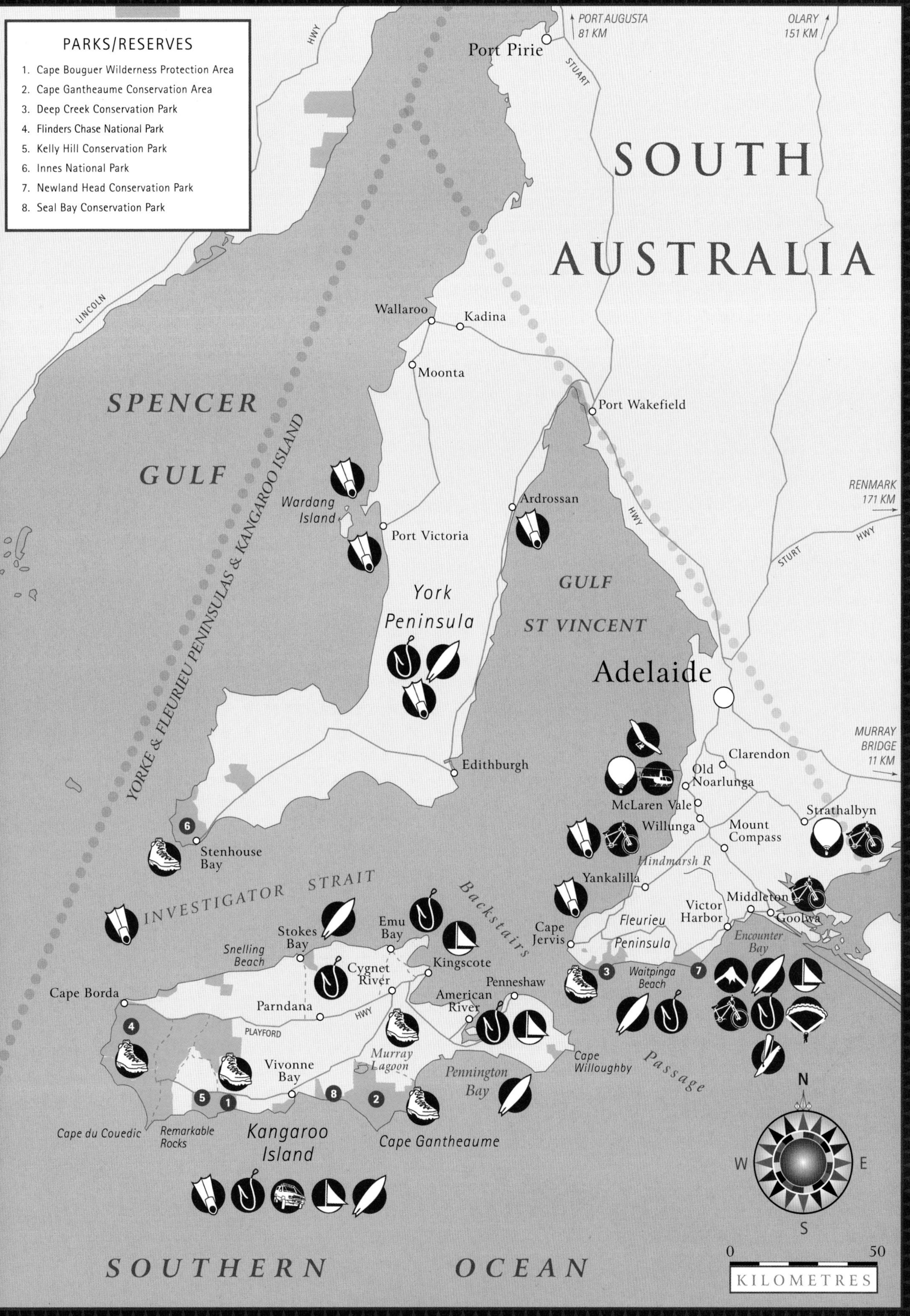

PARKS/RESERVES
1. Cape Bouguer Wilderness Protection Area
2. Cape Gantheaume Conservation Area
3. Deep Creek Conservation Park
4. Flinders Chase National Park
5. Kelly Hill Conservation Park
6. Innes National Park
7. Newland Head Conservation Park
8. Seal Bay Conservation Park
SOUTH AUSTRALIA
PORT AUGUSTA 81 KM
OLARY 151 KM
Port Pirie
STUART
HWY
LINCOLN
Wallaroo
Kadina
Moonta
Port Wakefield
SPENCER GULF
YORKE & FLEURIEU PENINSULAS & KANGAROO ISLAND
Wardang Island
Port Victoria
Ardrossan
RENMARK 171 KM
STURT HWY
York Peninsula
GULF ST VINCENT
Adelaide
MURRAY BRIDGE 11 KM
Clarendon
Edithburgh
Old Noarlunga
McLaren Vale
Willunga
Strathalbyn
Mount Compass
Stenhouse Bay
Hindmarsh R
Yankalilla
INVESTIGATOR STRAIT
Backstairs Passage
Middleton
Victor Harbor
Goolwa
Fleurieu Peninsula
Encounter Bay
Cape Jervis
Stokes Bay
Emu Bay
Snelling Beach
Cygnet River
Kingscote
Waitpinga Beach
Penneshaw
Cape Borda
American River
Parndana
PLAYFORD HWY
Murray Lagoon
Cape Willoughby
Vivonne Bay
Pennington Bay
Cape du Couedic
Remarkable Rocks
Kangaroo Island
Cape Gantheaume
N
W
E
S
SOUTHERN OCEAN
0
50
KILOMETRES

Innes National Park. *(SATC)*

NATIONAL PARKS

Innes National Park: on the southern tip of the Yorke Peninsula, Innes National Park offers great coastal scenery, from the rugged cliffs of Ethel Beach to the wide, sweeping expanse of West Cape and the beautiful protected sandy bays of Dolphin and Shell Beaches. Whale watch from the cliff tops for southern right whales during the winter at Stenhouse Bay and Cape Spencer and explore the historic ruins of Inneston mining village. Other highlights include 3000-year-old living stromatolites around the edges of the salt lakes and The Gap, an impressive wind and rain-eroded cutting in a 60m vertical cliff face.

Deep Creek Conservation Park: the largest remaining block of wildlife habitat on the Fleurieu Peninsula. Follow the extensive network of coastal trails for views out to Backstairs Passage and Kangaroo Island or the rugged Deep Creek Valley.

Newland Head Conservation Park: Seven kilometres west of Victor Harbor, Newland Head Conservation Park protects two long beaches and is popular with skilled surfers, fishers and beachcombers. Rolling hills and rugged cliffs provide panoramic views of the Waitpinga Creek, Encounter Bay, The Pages in Backstairs Passage and Kangaroo Island.

Flinders Chase National Park: one of Australia's largest reserve areas and containing many of KI's most popular attractions. Highlights include Cape du Couedic lighthouse, Admirals Arch and its colony of New Zealand fur seals, Remarkable Rocks, Cape Borda Lighthouse, Scott Cove and West Bay. At Rocky River you can see koalas and walk the Platypus Waterholes Walkway.

Seal Bay Conservation Park: Seal Bay's breeding colony of sea lions is a must for every visitor to KI. Guided tours allow you to walk amongst the sea lions on the beach, or take a self-guided tour along a boardwalk to a headland viewing platform.

Kelly Hill Conservation Park: bordering Cape Bouguer Wilderness Protection Area, this park is a vast undulating limestone ridge. Underneath the dense covering of mallee and stunted coastal heath is an extensive cave system. Adventure and show cave tours operate regularly. ☎ (08) 8559 7231 for bookings and details.

Cape Gantheaume Conservation Park: home to Murray Lagoon, KI's largest freshwater lagoon as well as spectacular coastal scenery.

York Peninsula

Flanked by the calm waters of the Gulf St Vincent to the east and the Spencer Gulf to the west, the Yorke Peninsula is today a peaceful, but popular, seaside holiday destination offering spectacular coastal scenery, great beaches, surfing and diving. But back in the mid 19th century, the discovery of copper at Moonta created a mining boom and the 'Copper Coast' (Moonta, Kadina and Wallaroo) is steeped in mining history and a strong Cornish heritage. Maritime heritage is also strong; the peninsula's ports, like Edithburgh and Port Victoria, were once amongst the busiest in the country when great windjammers and ketches loaded up with cargo bound for England and the northern hemisphere jostled for space at the wharves. These days, while some of the ports still export grain and dolomite around the world, most of the historical jetties are lined with anglers.

Fleurieu Peninsula

Practically on the outskirts of Adelaide, the Fleurieu Peninsula is the state's most popular and accessible holiday destination, famous for its wine, scenic coastline and gourmet produce. The heart of the wine-growing area is McLaren Vale, where olives and almond groves are scattered amongst the 50-plus vineyards. Pretty Strathalbyn was settled by Scottish immigrants in the 1830s, a heritage town with 30 or so historic buildings and popular place to shop for antiques and crafts. Victor Harbor on the Southern Ocean side is the most popular seaside resort with lots of family attractions.

Kangaroo Island (KI)

Kangaroo Island's gentle rolling hills, covered in rich pasture and studded with grazing sheep and cattle, belie a wilder heart. Close to half of the island is either natural bushland or national park, and it is home to some of the most diverse wildlife you'll find concentrated in one area anywhere in Australia. Four thousand penguins, 6000 fur seals, 600 rare Australian sea lions, 5000 koalas, 15,000 kangaroos, 254 species of birdlife and somewhere in between 500,000 and one million tammar wallabies. If you can't spot wildlife here then you simply aren't trying.

Caravan and camping

There are a number of good camping spots at Innes National Park on the Yorke Peninsula: four sites with no facilities at Jolly's Beach; 25 caravan and camping sites close to the beach, visitor centre and jetty at Stenhouse Bay; eight at Cable Bay with great views of the offshore islands, and 75 at Pondalowie with showers, flushing toilets and barbecues with easy access to the Fisherman's Village boat ramp and Pondalowie Bay–caravans and generators are permitted in the western end of the campground. The eight sites at Casuarina need to be booked at the Visitor Centre as a key is required to enter the campground. At Surfers Camp a boardwalk through the sand dunes runs to the popular surf break and viewing platform of Pondalowie Bay and there are eight shady sites at Shell Beach Campground, which is close to Shell Beach. Browns Beach has 10 sites alongside a steep sand dune

scenic highlights

Remarkable Rocks, Kangaroo Island. *(SATC)*

Spend a couple of days exploring the rugged wilderness of Kangaroo Island in three day-trips to three corners of the island: Cape Willoughby, Cape du Couedic and Cape Borda.

Kingscote is the biggest town on KI, so it is a good place to use as a base. It is also where flights arrive and depart for Adelaide. If you've travelled from Adelaide on the ferry, you'll arrive and depart from the sleepier town of Penneshaw, which is about 45 minutes from Kingscote.

Head east from Kingscote along Hog Bay Road through the pastoral heart of the island to Penneshaw. On the way, stop at Pennington Beach, a long expanse of white sand edged up against rugged limestone cliffs at the narrowest point on the island. Continue east through Penneshaw and onto the unsealed road that leads 30km out to Cape Willoughby on the far-eastern tip of the island. The lighthouse here is one of four on the island: it was also the first built in South Australia. Both Kingscote and Penneshaw have penguin colonies, but the best place to see them is on the guided boardwalk tour in Penneshaw, which is home to 1200 of KI's 4000 little penguins. The penguins spend most of the day feeding out at sea, returning to land just after dark, when you can see the parents come waddling out of the sea to clamber up the rocky beach to their burrow-like nests in the sand dunes to feed their stridently hungry chicks.

Day two, head south to Flinders Chase National Park and Cape du Couedic along the South Coast Road. At Seal Bay you can join a tour and stroll along the beach amongst dozens of huge, sleepy sea lions resting after spending three days at sea hunting for food. Seal Bay is the only place in Australia where you can get this close to the sea lions; all other colonies are perched amongst inaccessible rocky headlands. If you don't want to join a tour, there is a self-guided boardwalk, but it does not allow you to get onto the sand or as close to the sea lions.

From Seal Bay, drive on to the far-western reaches of the island to Flinders Chase National Park. Wander among Remarkable Rocks, a cluster of huge weather-sculptured granite boulders perched on a granite dome that swoops 75m to the sea, and then spear north to Cape du Couedic. The rocks below the lighthouse are home to a colony of New Zealand fur seals, wallowing in the sun or frolicking in the surf under the dramatic rock arch of Admirals Arch.

On they way home to Kingscote, watch for koalas in the tree tops beside the road, dawdling echidnas crossing in front of your car, and of course, the dozens of wallabies and kangaroos that are ubiquitous on the island.

The third main driving route on KI is to the far north-western tip at Cape Borda with side trips to the north coast. From Kingscote, head west on the Playford Highway. At Cygnet River, visit the Island Pure Sheep Dairy to watch the sheep being milked and taste some of their delicious haloumi cheese. Continue west through Parndana, where in late winter and spring, the roadside is carpeted in wildflowers, to Cape Borda; the last 38km or so cutting through the wilderness of Flinders Chase National Park. The unusually-shaped lighthouse here is 155m above sea level. Four kilometres to the east is Scotts Cove lookout, where you can see the spectacular cliffs of Cape Torrens and Cape Forbin.

Good side trips on the way back to Kingscote include Western River Cove, ideal for swimming, rock and surf fishing; Snellings Beach at the mouth of Middle River; Stokes Bay, where a walk through a headland of boulders brings you to a fine, white sandy beach surrounded by cliffs; and finally, Emu Bay, a lovely 3km-long beach with vehicle access on to the hard sand.

DON'T MISS

- **Ardrossan and District Historical Museum:** local historical exhibits. 16 Fifth Street, Ardrossan. Open Sun, 2.30–4.30pm.
- **Moonta Mines Museum:** museum is located in the former Moonta Mines Model School. Erected in 1878, this building now houses thematic displays on the Cornish miners' lifestyles. Verran Terrace, Moonta. Open Wed, Fri–Sun, 1.30pm–4pm.
- **Moonta Mines State Heritage Area:** covers most of the former Moonta Mining Company lease with tourist drive and walks exploring the ruins and historic buildings.
- **Moonta Mines Tourist Railway:** 50-minute round trip by narrow gauge rail. Departs from the station adjacent to the Moonta Mines Museum during school holidays.
- **Wallaroo Heritage and Nautical Museum:** extensive displays of the copper smelting era and other local history. Jetty Road and Emu Street, Wallaroo. Open Tue, Thu–Sun 2–4pm, Wed 10.30am–4pm.
- **Willunga Slate Museum and Courthouse Museum:** 61 High Street, Willunga. Open Tue 11am–4pm, weekends 1–5pm.
- **Archery Park:** all forms of archery for all levels. Piggott Range Road, Clarendon. Open weekends, 10am–5pm.
- **Encounter Coast Discovery Centre and the Old Customs and Station Masters House:** learn about the meeting between English and French naval captains Matthew Flinders and Nicolas Baudin in Encounter Bay in 1802. 2 Flinders Parade, Victor Harbor. Open daily, 1pm–4pm.
- **Granite Island Nature Park:** guided evening penguin tours at Victor Harbor. The Causeway, Granite Island, Victor Harbor. **www.graniteisland.com.au**
- **The Old Bank Artel:** co-operative of local craft workers. 141 Main Road, McLaren Vale. Open daily, 10am–5pm.
- **South Australian Whale Centre:** extensive collection of displays, murals, videos, hands-on opportunities and fun activities. 2 Railway Terrace, Victor Harbor. Open daily, 11am–4pm. **www.sawhalecentre.com**
- **Victor Harbor Horse Drawn Tramway:** Clydesdale horses continue their historic old-style passenger service across the Causeway at Victor Harbor. Open daily, 10am–4pm.
- **Penneshaw Penguin Centre:** the penguins are in residence at the colony all year except for the month of February, when they go out to sea. Tours daily 7.30pm and 8.30pm in winter, 8.30pm and 9.30pm in summer. ☎ (08) 8553 1103.
- **Emu Ridge Eucalyptus Distillery:** the only commercial eucalyptus distillery in operation in SA. Willsons Road, MacGillivray. Open daily, 9am–2pm.
- **Jumbuck Australiana:** watch shearers at work, learn about working sheep dogs, wool classing, spinning and knitting. Cnr Hog Bay Rd and American River Road. Open daily, 9.30am–1.30pm.
- **Penneshaw Maritime & Folk Museum:** local history exhibits including a special nautical section highlighting the shipping history of the island. Howard Drive, Penneshaw. Open Wed–Sun, 3–5pm from Sep–May.
- **Clifford's Honey Farm:** free tastings and sales of honey made from pure Ligurian bees—the only pure strain in the world. Elsegood Road, MacGillivray. Open daily, 9am–5pm.
- **Island Pure Sheep Dairy:** watch the sheep being milked and taste their delicious cheeses. Gum Creek Road, Cygnet River. Open daily 1–5pm. Milking 3–5pm.
- **Kangaroo Island Gallery:** jewellery, pottery, photography, woodcraft, paintings and sculpture from KI artists. Murray Street, Kingscote. Open daily, 10am–5pm.
- **Stokes Bay Bush Garden:** collection of KI and Australian native plants in beautiful bush garden setting. Stokes Bay Road, Stokes Bay. Open daily from 10am. Closed Sat and during Feb and Mar.

Moonta Mines *(SATC)*

Flinders Chase National Park. *(SATC)*

near the fishing beach, and secluded Gym Beach can be accessed from the Corny Point Road at the northern-most boundary of the park.

In Deep Creek National Park on the Fleurieu the Stringybark camping area is in a sheltered forest setting with 16 sites, hot showers, toilets and rain water, with unpowered caravan sites. Central to the main walking trails, Trig has open grassy areas with 25 well-sheltered and shady sites suitable for caravans and camp trailers. There are 18 sites at Tapanappa with spectacular coastal views and 10 at Cobbler Hill, close to Blowhole Creek Beach. Eagle Waterhole is a remote walk-in site on the Heysen Trail.

There is also camping at Waitpinga in Newland Head Conservation Park.

On Kangaroo Island the following beaches have caravan sites: Nepean Bay (Kingscote), Penneshaw, Antechamber Bay, Brown's Beach, Stokes Bay Emu Bay, Vivonne Bay and Western River and Rocky River in Flinders Chase National Park. Best camping in Flinders Chase is at Rocky River, Snake Lagoon, Harveys Return and West Bay. In Cape Gantheaume National Park camp at Murray's Lagoon or D'Estrees Bay.

Bushwalks

Innes National Park has an extensive network of coastal trails. One of the best is the three-hour, Thomson-Pfitzner Plaster interpretative trail that follows an old wooden horse-drawn rail line. It starts at and returns to Inneston Village. Other good short walks include the 5km Barkers Rock Walking Trail for coastal views, the three-hour Browns Beach to Gym Beach Walk and the two-hour return Royston Head hike with panoramic coastal views of offshore reefs and islands.

The Deep Creek Cove Walk from Tapanappa Lookout is a hard two-and-a-half-hour return walk that has stunning coastal views of the south coast, Backstairs Passage, Kangaroo Island and Deep Creek Cove. The Heysen Trail also passes through Deep Creek, with this 19.5km section between Blowhole Beach and Boat Harbour Beach featuring rugged coastal scenery and dense native scrub. Other shorter walks include the four-hour Boat Harbour Circuit, a rather hard walk through dense, closed forest and low coastal heath but with great views; the 11km, six-hour Aaron Creek Walk and the 3km Blowhole Beach Walk. A nice easy stroll, the 5km Spring Wildflower Walk is a loop from Stringy Bark campground along fire access tracks with beautiful wildflower displays in spring.

On Kangaroo Island the Cape Gantheaume Coastal Trek is a challenging 36km trail through the rugged south coast of the Cape Gantheaume Wilderness Protection Area. Also at Cape Gantheaume, the 11km Curley Creek walking trail follows an old fire track along northern boundary of Murray Lagoon to Bald Hill. In Flinders Chase National Park the 6km Breakneck River Trail follows the river valley to a small beach and coastal lagoon surrounded by cliffs while the Cape du Couedic Walk is a 40-minute loop taking in the east and west sides of the cape with views from the cliff-top lookout of Remarkable Rocks and the southern coastline. The walk joins the Admirals Arch Walk. The Platypus Waterholes Walk has part-disabled access to waterholes of the Rocky River with boardwalks, lookouts and viewing platforms where, if you are lucky, you may see platypus. Snake Lagoon Walk follows a ridgeline through mallee woodland, before reaching Rocky River crossing to the river mouth (two hours) and the 3km Weirs Cove Trail links the Cape du Couedic Lighthouse to the landing site at Weirs Cove, taking in spectacular coastal views. For a longer walk try the Hanson Bay Trail in Kelly Conservation Park, an 18km, six-hour return walk from caves to coast past lagoons, woodlands, rivers and dunes.

adventure activities

Goolwa. *(SATC)*

Abseiling and rock climbing

Abseiling down a cliff face first combines the thrill of bungy, with the control of abseiling, and for anyone who finds normal abseiling a bit tame, Forward Abseiling is the adrenalin roping sport! Live Adrenalin run three-hour sessions at the spectacular cliffs around Victor Harbor where you will get to run down a 35m cliff face at Rosetta Head, commonly known as The Bluff.

www.adrenalin.com.au

Aerobatic joy flights

Adelaide Biplanes, based in Aldinga on the Fleurieu Peninsula, offers Super Decathlon aerobatic and scenic flights over McLaren Vale and along the coast as well as more gentle scenic flights in the open-cockpit 1935 WACO biplane.

www.adelaidebiplanes.com.au

Ballooning

Adelaide Ballooning operates hot air balloon flights over the vineyards at McLaren Vale and Langhorne Creek, around Strathalbyn and over the Monarto open-range zoo, 70km east of Adelaide.

www.adelaideballooning.com.au

Camel safari

Camel Tours & Treks SA offer a range of camel rides on the Fleurieu Peninsula. The most popular trek is the two-hour camel riding beach tour of the Sir Richard Peninsula, but there are also short rides in Encounter Bay (Victor Harbor) and two-hour bush treks through tall pine forest and native scrub. Longer four-day treks on the Limestone Coast and Coorong National Park are also available.

www.cameltourssa.com.au

Cycling and mountain biking

The gentle rolling hills and beautiful coastal scenery makes the Fleurieu Peninsula a favourite for cyclists. The Coast to Vines Rail Trail is a 34km cycling trail from Marino to Willunga. The vineyards of McLaren Vale are nearby, the landscape has sea views, it is adjacent to the significant geological site of Hallett Cove Conservation Park, and there are plenty of good places to stay and eat.

The 30km Encounter Bikeway is a dedicated bike path between the Bluff and Signal Point at Goolwa Wharf. The sealed path is suitable for escorted toddlers on trikes through to those wanting a gentle, seaside cycle. Between May and October you may be able to spot southern right whales as you ride.

From Strathalbyn, a four-hour, 38km ride takes you into the hills–take the Ashbourne Road, climbing over several kilometres to the lookout on Gemmill Hill for views across the plains to Lake Alexandrina and to the sand dunes of the Coorong National Park. Continue along the gum-lined road to Ashbourne then turn toward Meadows, following the Bull Creek as it winds its way steadily uphill through the valley. Near the crest, turn sharply right towards Paris Creek. A string of beautiful dams, farms, ruins, dry stone walls and views of distant plains and lakes present as the road descends, almost continuously over the last 15km into Strathalbyn. There are also some good rides on Hindmarsh Island. Detailed maps covering some of the Fleurieu Peninsula rides are available at visitor's information centres.

Diving

The Yorke Peninsula is one of the country's key dive spots. The Adelaide Underwater Heritage Trail extends from Port Willunga to Ardrossan on the Yorke Peninsula. The Investigator Strait, between Yorke Peninsula and Kangaroo Island, is home to 26 shipwrecks, dating from 1849 to 1982, which are a habitat for a diverse range of marina flora and fauna, attracting divers from all over the world.

Wardang Island is a natural breakwater against south-westerly winds that buffet the western coast of Yorke Peninsula. Until 1909 there was no light on the island and wreckings were common. The Wardang Island Maritime Heritage Trail has eight shipwrecks within 16km to explore in clear shallow waters–ideal for novice shipwreck divers. Travel to them from Port Victoria. There are underwater plaques adjacent to each wreck. Edithburgh Jetty has some great diving for all levels of experience, with lots of marine life including big-bellied seahorses, Port Jackson sharks, leafy sea dragons, cuttlefish, a variety of other fish and colourful corals.

Lying 10 nautical miles southeast of Ardrossan, the *Zanoni* wreck is the most intact 19th century merchant sailing vessel located in SA. Divers need a permit from the Maritime Heritage Branch of the Department for Environment and Heritage.

The former Navy ship HMAS *Hobart* was scuttled off the Fleurieu coast near Yankalilla in November 2002–creating one of the best dive sites in Australia. As part of the preparation, many holes and hatches were cut to allow easy access to scuba divers and navigation throughout the wreck and much of the original equipment, instrumentation and many fittings–including filing cabinets, sinks, toilets and tools–are still in place. There are also some more challenging penetrations for more experienced scuba divers. There are several local dive operators that run trips out to the wreck.

Port Noarlunga Reef is a very popular spot, with easy access from the steps of Port Noarlunga jetty with fascinating rock formations, schools of small fish and extensive weed beds. The waters off Kangaroo Island also provide some fantastic temperate-water diving with walls of Gorgonia corals, red, orange and white sponges, magnificent fish (blue devil, harlequin, truncate coralfish and boarfish) and the leafy sea-dragon. More than 50 recorded shipwrecks have occurred around the Island's coastline, and the Kangaroo Island Maritime Heritage Trail is a dive trail that takes in 25 of those wrecks, which lie in varying conditions, from rugged coastlines to calm bays and from depths of 3-20m. Several tour operators run diving tours to the wrecks.

HMAS *Hobart*. *(SATC)*

Second Valley. *(SATC)*

Pondalowie Bay. *(SATC)*

Fishing

The Yorke Peninsula, a jetty anglers paradise, is dotted with historic jetties and surf beaches that are good for snaring snapper, garfish, salmon, tommy ruffs, mullet, crabs, squid and King George whiting. Dive for scallops just off the beach and rake the shallows for blue swimmer crabs. Browns Beach in Innes National Park is famous for its winter salmon run.

On the Fleurieu Peninsula, Victor Harbor is a good year round fishing destination. Jetties offer mullet, squid, garfish, tommy ruff, snook and salmon trout, and you'll catch squid, garfish and tommy ruff on The Causeway. The Hindmarsh River is productive for both bream and mullet. The fishing for Australian salmon is legendary at Waitpinga and Parsons Beach and other species include mulloway (jewfish), mullet, tommy ruff, salmon trout and shark. The river mouth at Waitpinga is also worth a try for bream. Boat fishing is good for snapper, shark, whiting, trevally, snook and mackerel. Garfish can also be taken in shallower waters around Granite Island. Tooperang Rainbow Trout Farm at Mount Compass is open to the public for bait fishing and private secluded fly-fishing on Saturday, Sunday and all public holidays.

The fishing is just as good on Kangaroo Island, with good jetty fishing at Kingscote, Penneshaw and American River wharves. High tide in the evening is the best time. Garfish, tommy ruffs and snook bite best on a fairly fast running tide. Jetties at Emu Bay and Vivonne Bay bring good results. For surf fishing head to the north coast around Emu Bay, Stokes Bay, Snellings Beach for bull salmon, mullet and large flathead. On the south coast D'Estrees Bay and Vivonne Bay are best for salmon and mullet where strong surf is running. Antechamber Bay is also good. Sweep provide the most popular rock fishing on the island and can be found most places where the water is deep off the rocks. Swallow tail can usually be caught in the same area. A popular sport is catching crayfish with a line, lump of red meat and a dab net. Middle River, Western River Mouth, Chapman River and Cygnet River all provide excellent bream fishing. At the mouth of the Cygnet, salmon trout, mullet and tommy ruffs may be caught. If you have a boat, snapper abound along the length of the north coast where the water is usually less turbulent than off the south coast. Whiting up to 1.5 kg are common. Trolling for snook is also popular around the entire coast.

Hang gliding

Airborne Action offers cable hang gliding at their property just off the Victor Harbor Road at Old Noarlunga. With all the trills and adrenalin spikes of hang gliding but without the risks, cable hang gliding is great for first timers and kids. Strapped into a harness and glider attached to main steel cable suspended between two steel support poles that are approximately 300m apart, the summit or launching platform is at the high end of the cable system and has a vertical height difference of 50m from the pole at the lower end. You are launched from the summit platform, and gravity takes over. It takes approximately 26 seconds to travel the 300m and can generate speeds of around 50km/h. You descend into the valley and once at the bottom you are winched back up to experience the thrill a second time. The whole experience takes around five minutes.

They also offer cable sky diving, operating with all the same safety procedures and equipment of the cable hang gliding–the trapeze of the glider is folded away and you are suspended below the apparatus. This time you launch yourself from the summit platform and experience the sensation of flying with the ability to steer yourself similar to a skydiver in high speed through the air. Once at the bottom you will be winched back to the launching platform for your second flight, but this time you will be launched backwards.

www.airborneaction.com.au

Parasailing

Go parasailing off the Granite Island Causeway near Victor Harbor on weekends and public and school holidays from November through to April, weather permitting, with Odyssey Adventures Parasailing. Choose from a single parasail (seven minutes) to a 10-minute tandem flight.

☎ 0418 891 998

Sailing

Clear water, sandy beaches, isolated coves and impressive scenery make for good sailing off Kangaroo Island. Nepean Bay offers all year round sheltered cruising for day sailing, and the north coast provides numerous spectacular anchorages on longer voyages. Skippered charter yachts operate from Kingscote and American River, offering day and overnight fully catered cruises.

http://homepages.picknowl.com.au/kisail/

Australis Charters departs twice daily from Screwpile Jetty on Granite Island near Victor Harbor (subject to minimum numbers and weather conditions). Bookings essential.

☎ (08) 8552 4191

Sky diving

Get the adrenalin pumping with a 25-minute tandem skydive over the southern coast of the Fleurieu Peninsula with Skydive Adelaide, where you'll get a bird's eye view of Victor Harbor, Goolwa and Port Elliot's Horseshoe Bay–you might even spot a whale or two in winter.

www.skydiveadelaide.com.au

Learn to surf on Goolwa Beach. *(SATC)*

Surfing

The tip of Yorke Peninsula and the beaches around Victor Harbor both have some of the best surfing in South Australia. Chinaman's, in Innes National Park, is a very powerful left-hand reef break for experienced riders only. Other good spots include Ethel Wreck, West Cape, Pondalowie Bay and Richards. Trespassers is outside the national park near Point Margaret, another powerful break for experienced riders only. Also worth surfing are Baby Lizards, just north of Point Margaret in Formby Bay; the Rock Pool south of Daly Head; Salmon Hole; Daly Head and Spits, just north of Daly Head. The Cutloose Ripcurl Yorke's Surfing Classic, held on the October long weekend in Innes National Park, is South Australia's most prestigious surfing event.

Victor Harbor has a range of waves to suit all levels from beginner to experienced surfers. Waitpinga is suitable for intermediate to experienced surfers but strong currents and powerful swells make this a no go zone for beginners as is Parsons Beach. Petrel Cove is a mix of beach breaks with some reefy bottom suitable for intermediate surfers; Chiton Rocks and the Dump suits beginner to intermediate. Bullies is a big wave spot only for experienced surfers while Middleton Point and Surfers offers right and left hand point breaks that are excellent for beginners when it is smaller. There are a number of surf schools in the area who offer fun, exciting and, most importantly, safe learn-to-surf experiences.

www.surfnsun.com.au www.surfcultureaustralia.com

On Kangaroo Island, Stokes Bay, Vivonne Bay and Pennington Bay are suitable for beginners, however the beach breaks can often produce good quality waves for more advanced surfers. There are numerous surfing spots around the island for experienced surfers and most are accessible by car.

MORE INFORMATION

- **The Farm Shed Museum and Tourism Centre:** 50 Moonta Road, Kadina.
  ☎ 1800 654 991. www.yorkepeninsula.com.au
- **Victor Harbor Visitor Information Centre:** The Causeway Building, Esplanade, Victor Harbor.
  ☎ (08) 8552 5738. www.tourismvictorharbor.com.au
- **Gateway Visitor Information Centre:** Howard Drive, Penneshaw, Kangaroo Island.
  ☎ (08) 8553 1185. www.tourkangarooisland.com.au

weather watch

- January: 14–24°C
- July: 9–15°C
- Relatively mild during both summer and winter. At times, cool ocean breezes make windproof clothing necessary, while inland areas occasionally experience temperatures of 35-40°C in mid-summer.

the outback

Cooper Creek. *(SATC)*

Outback wreck. *(SATC)*

► MORE THAN 70 PER CENT of South Australia is a harsh, often unforgiving, but beautiful ancient landscape. The transition from arable lands to outback sands is sudden and marked by a distinct change in vegetation between the scrub bushes known as mallee to the south and the arid salt bush to the north that is easily discernable from the air. This change forms a line across the state known as Goyder's Line, named after the Surveyor-General of the same name in the latter half of the 19th century. It almost exactly represents the demarcation of a long-term average of 254mm (10 inches) of rain per year, indicating the edge of the area suitable for agriculture. North of Goyder's Line, the land is only suitable for long-term grazing. The line starts on the west coast near Ceduna and goes south-east across the top of the Eyre Peninsula to the Spencer Gulf, continues north of Crystal Brook, south-east past Peterborough and the northern Clare Valley to the Victorian border near Pinaroo.

PARKS/RESERVES

1. Breakaways Reserve
2. Coongie Lakes
3. Elliot Price Conservation Park
4. Innamincka Regional Reserve
5. Lake Eyre National Park
6. Nullarbor National Park & Regional Reserve
7. Simpson Desert National Park & Regional Reserve
8. Strezlecki Regional Reserve
9. Tallaringa Conservation Park
10. Wabme Kadarba Mound Springs Conservation Park
11. Witjira National Park

NATIONAL PARKS

Lake Eyre National Park: about as remote as it gets! It's a stark, largely inaccessible and inhospitable wilderness where a vehicle breakdown can, and does, quickly develop into a life threatening situation, sometimes with tragic results. That said, it is an incredibly beautiful place that will linger in your imagination for many years.

Most of the time, the 'lake' is a vast, shimmering plain of bright, white salt. The lake fills with water, on average, around once every eight years, when it becomes a breeding ground for masses of waterbirds that have flown thousands of kilometres to the newly arrived body of water. Lake Eyre has filled to capacity only three times in the past 150 years.

There are two access tracks to Lake Eyre National Park. One turns off the Oodnadatta Track approximately 7km south-east of William Creek and runs to Halligan Bay (64 km). The second runs 94km north from Marree to Level Post Bay via Muloorina Station. Both tracks cross pastoral properties and are 4WD only. Reserves of fuel, water and food must be carried. There are no public access tracks into Elliot Price Conservation Park.

Nullarbor National Park and Regional Reserve: at the head of the Great Australian Bight, this park contains the world's largest semi-arid karst (cave) landscape and is rich in Aboriginal culture and the largest populations of the southern hairy-nosed wombat. The Nullarbor cliffs command spectacular views of the Southern Ocean coastline where southern right whales gather with their calves during winter.

Witjira National Park: 7,770km^2 of gibber, sand dunes, stony tablelands and floodplain country on the western edge of the Simpson Desert, the park is the former Mount Dare pastoral lease and includes Dalhousie mound springs, 70 or so thermal springs. The springs are home to unique species of fish such as the Lake Eyre hardy-head and other rare aquatic life. They are also a haven for birdlife.

Simpson Desert Conservation Park and Regional Reserve: the Simpson Desert is a sea of parallel red sand ridges some 300–500km across, covering a total area of 170,000km^2 and one of the world's best examples of dunal desert. It lies across the corners of South Australia, Queensland and the Northern Territory. Although it is called a desert, the dunes are home to a wide variety of desert flora and fauna, including spinifex grasslands and acacia woodlands. There are no facilities and you will need to be totally self sufficient with fuel, food and water and should carry long range communications equipment such as a satellite telephone or Royal Flying Doctor Service High Frequency radio. Summer temperatures can exceed 50°C.

Innamincka Regional Reserve—Coongie Lakes National Park: an oasis surrounded by vast expanses of sandy desert and arid plains, this park includes the gum-lined Cooper Creek, Innamincka township, and several beautiful waterholes. Part of the Reserve, Coongie Lakes National Park is listed as a Ramsar Wetland of International Importance, comprising of channels, waterholes, lakes, shallow floodplains and swamps which attract an enormous amount of waterbirds. The area is an important spiritual site for the Aboriginal people who inhabited the area as well as significant for the European history relating to early exploration and pastoralism. Four-wheel-drive access only to Coongie Lakes.

Strzelecki Regional Reserve: includes the vast pale sand dune country of the Strzelecki and Cobbler Deserts, and the mostly dry bed of the Strzelecki Creek. Access is via the 4WD Strzelecki Track.

Lake Eyre. *(SATC)*

The Nullarbor

West of the Eyre Peninsula lies the vast expanse of the Nullarbor–a 'treeless' plain stretching over a thousand kilometres from Ceduna to Norseman in Western Australia. The road across the plain hugs the coast of the Great Australian Bight and side tracks lead to lookouts over the Bunda cliffs, where the immense 250,000km2 plain abruptly falls into the Southern Ocean in a 200km unbroken line of cliffs.

Coober Pedy

Famous for both opals–70 per cent of the world's opals are found here–and its underground homes, Coober Pedy is the only town of any real size in the South Australian outback and the largest opal mining town in the world. The intense heat–and the inhabitants skill in digging underground–has created the biggest subterranean town in Australia. Outside temperatures can reach a sizzling 50°C, but the underground homes (dugouts) remain a constant 22–26°C. The main street is lined with opal showrooms and mines you can tour. You can even stay underground at the four-star Desert Cave Hotel. There is a public noodling reserve in the centre of town. Noodling or fossicking for opal among discarded rock heaps is free and some visitors do find good-sized opals.

Marree and William Creek

At the junction of the country's most popular outback tracks–the Birdsville and Oodnadatta–the tiny settlement of Marree began life as a major railhead. You can explore old train carriages still waiting at the end of the line and the crumbling ruins of a mail truck in the park in the centre of town. The trip to William Creek (one of the smallest towns in South Australia with a population hovering around seven) only takes a few hours, but there are several places to stop on the way, such as Lake Eyre North, (follow the Muloorina Homestead track on the edge of town) where tracks lead to lookouts with magnificent views over the bright, white salt vastness of Lake Eyre. Although the lakebed looks firm and safe to drive on, it is only a thin crust and many vehicles have come to grief sinking in the dark sticky ooze that lies just beneath the surface. Periodically, the lake fills with water and the dry salt pans are transformed into wetlands supporting large flocks of pelicans, gulls and terns.

Oodnadatta

Like Marree, Oodnadatta was also a busy railway town where the Great Northern Railway stopped and camels took over. When camels were replaced by trucks and road trains and the railway was moved 200km to the west the town's fortunes dwindled. There is a museum in the disused railway station and the landmark Pink Roadhouse is the place for supplies and information.

Innamincka

Surrounded by desert and gibber plains, 1065km north of Adelaide, Innamincka is a tiny outback settlement–just a general store, petrol station and pub on the banks of Cooper Creek. It's where ill-fated explorers Burke and Wills died. Wills' grave is 25km west of the town, a memorial to Burke lies along the creek to the east and the famous 'Dig' tree where supplies were left for the explorers is 55km from town.

scenic highlights

Coober Pedy golf course. *(Sam Tinson)*

Cooper Creek

When ill-fated explorers Burke and Wills died on the banks of Cooper Creek in the far north-east of South Australia they unjustly gave this beautiful watercourse a bad reputation. Sure it's remote, but far from being bleak and inhospitable, the Cooper is an oasis in the midst of harsh and stony desert country.

The Cooper, one of Australia's last unspoiled inland waterways, is a wide clean river that attracts a wealth of birdlife to its almost constant water supply. At sunrise and sunset the reflections of the river gums shimmer while hundreds of cockies screech and pelicans drift by feeding on fish. Among the must-see sites are the graves of Burke and Wills, Coongie Lakes, Cullyamurra Waterhole, King's Site and the Dig Tree.

Around Coober Pedy

Although Coober Pedy is in the middle of nowhere, there is lots to do outside the town limits. 32km north along the sealed Stuart Highway are the Breakaways, a series of flat-topped hills or 'jump ups' that seemed to have broken away from the Stuart Range. At sunset the sandstone pillars, pinnacles and gully edges glow pink, red, brown, purple, yellow and white—it's a great place to set yourself up with a picnic table, some nibblies and a nice bottle wine to watch the sundown show.

A 70km round trip from Coober Pedy will take you through the Breakaways, to the famous dog fence and the Moon Plains—the local nickname for the moon-like desert landscape along the fence. The 2m-high dog fence stretches across three states for more than 5300km in an effort to keep northern dingoes away from southern sheep and is the longest fence in the world.

Bush camp. *(SATC)*

Caravan and camping

No camping is permitted in Nullarbor National Park. There are camping areas at roadhouses or bush camping at rest areas. Note that limited water supplies are available between Norseman and Ceduna so be sure to stock up before crossing the Nullarbor.

For most other parks in the South Australian Outback you will need to purchase a Desert Parks Pass for access and camping (where permitted) for a period of 12 months. Parks covered include Simpson Desert Conservation Park, Simpson Desert Regional Reserve, Innamincka Regional Reserve, Coongie Lakes National Park, Lake Eyre National Park, Witjira National Park, Tallaringa Conservation Park, Wabma Kadarbu Mound Springs Conservation Park (camping not permitted) and Strzelecki Regional Reserve.

Desert Parks Passes cost $95, which includes a useful information pack and detailed maps.

www.parks.sa.gov.au ☎ 1800 816 078

Cooper Creek is a beautiful place to camp and there are good camping sites on the south side of Cooper Creek in the Innamincka Town Common, at other specified sites west of the township and at Cullyamurra Waterhole. Other good camp sites include those at Scrubby Camp Waterhole and Coongie Lake. In the Simpson you can camp within 100m of the public access tracks, but there are no facilities. The best places to camp are mostly located towards the salt lakes in the central region where gidgee woodlands provide shade, shelter and soft ground for camping. At Dalhousie Springs the area in front of the springs is a very pleasant camping spot and showers and toilets are provided. Camping is also available at Mount Dare Homestead, 3 O'Clock Creek and Purni Bore. Mount Dare has a full range of facilities. The bush camping area at 3 O'Clock Creek has drinking water, shady spots and firewood, but you will need to take your own water supplies and pick up firewood on your way to Purni Bore.

Along the Oodnadatta Track the best campsites are at Halligan Bay on the shores of south Lake Eyre, Coward Springs, Neales Crossing and beside the creeks running from the Alberga River, near Todmorden Station. These are bush camping, so you must be self sufficient with water and supplies.

Bushwalks

The extreme conditions of outback deserts are not conducive to bush-walking and there are few marked trails to follow. If you are stepping out, walking along a creek or between two dunes is the best way to go and will have the more wildlife and flora-spotting opportunities. Make sure you take lots of water and ensure you do not loose your bearings.

DON'T MISS

- **Bunda Cliffs:** six lookouts, the first is signposted shortly after Border Village.
- **Yalata Roadhouse Aboriginal Arts and Crafts:** good value art gallery. Open daily.
- **Umoona Opal Mine and Museum:** underground museum with Aboriginal Interpretive Centre, an underground home, and an on-site mine and opal showroom. Lot 14, Hutchison Street, Coober Pedy. Open daily with tours at 10am, 12noon, 2pm and 4pm. www.umoonaopalmine.com.au
- **Underground Potteries:** underground workshop and display area. Opposite golf course off Seventeen Mile Road, Coober Pedy. Open daily, 8.30am–6pm.
- **The Catacomb Church:** originally built in 1977 this unique church is cut out of the sandstone in the shape of a cross and with furniture fashioned from local mulga wood and an old miner's winch. Catacomb Road, Coober Pedy.
- **Serbian Orthodox Church:** underground church featuring rock carvings in the walls, high roof 'ballroom' style design, and stained glass windows. Flinders Street, Coober Pedy.
- **The Big Winch:** a lookout gives a good view of the town and surrounding opal fields. Opal shop next door contains fully fossilised shells of opal still embedded in the wall. Off Umoona Road, Coober Pedy. Open Mon–Sat.
- **Old Timers Mine & Museum:** original opal mine dating back to 1916. Crowders Gully Rd, Coober Pedy. Open daily. www.oldtimersmine.com
- **The Underground Art Gallery:** arts, crafts, opals and jewellery. Hutchison Street, Coober Pedy. Open daily.
- **Coober Pedy Opal Fields Golf Club:** 18-hole course has 'mod grass' (green plastic woven 'grass'), crushed rock fairways and no water hazards—although the dry creek beds make great sand traps. A special club rule is 'rock relief' if your ball lands on a rock. In summer, night golf is the way to go—using luminous balls and flag sticks. 3.5km north of town centre.
- **Moon Plain:** vast expanse of rocky plains with lunar-like landscape. Approximately 15km north-east of Coober Pedy.
- **Breakaways:** striking and unique example of arid scenery with flat-topped mesas and stony gibber desert plains. Approximately 33km north of Coober Pedy. Best colours are at sunset.
- **The Dog Fence:** longest continual construction in the world. Stretching some 5300km, it begins west of Surfers Paradise in Queensland and ends up north of Ceduna in the Great Australian Bite. Originally built to protect the sheep country in the south from the dingoes in the north. Approximately 15km north-east of Coober Pedy.
- **Museum Park, Marree:** beside the old railway line in the centre of town is the old mail truck which Tom Kruse used to transport mail from Marree to Birdsville along the Birdsville Track. Nearby, you'll see the abandoned rolling stock of the once busy rail line.
- **Mound Springs:** between Marree and William Creek there are several mound springs where waters from the Great Artesian Basin bubble to the surface, creating a small oasis in the midst of red sand hills. The largest and most accessible are Bubbler and Blanche Cup.
- **Old Peake Telegraph Station and Homestead:** now largely in ruin it was once an important centre for the Old Telegraph Line and until the early 1900s there was a small copper mining community here. There is also a memorial to explorer Ernest Giles, who made his base here on his western surveys.
- **Wrightsair scenic flights over Lake Eyre:** a great way to see the best of the vast salt plain. If there is water in the lake you'll see a prolific amount of birdlife—great flocks of pelicans, terns, ducks and black swans who feed on the thousands of fish in the normally dry lake. (Tip: the glare from the bright white salt is blinding so take good sunglasses as well as some bottled water as it gets hot in the small plane.) Flights depart from William Creek. ☎ (08) 8670 7962. www.wrightsair.com.au

Outback flying. *(SATC)*

adventure activities

Outback cattle drive. (SATC)

Camel safari

Coward Springs–previously known as Coward Springs Siding–is a private campground on the Oodnadatta Track beside the old Ghan railway line. A bore sunk in 1886 to service the railway has created an extensive wetland that attracts more than 100 species of birds. The campground runs semi-regular seven-day camel safaris along the eucalypt-lined Stuart Creek into the Turret Ranges, meandering through a changing landscape of gibber plains, sand dunes and mesas, travelling 12 to 20km each day.

www.cowardsprings.com.au

Canoeing and kayaking

Cooper Creek and Coongie Lakes are perfect for paddling and you can hire canoes and kayaks at the Innamincka Hotel. Ecotrek run nine-day camping and canoeing trips that include 4WD touring and paddling on both Cooper Creek and Coongie Lakes as well as general sight-seeing. Tours depart from and return to Adelaide.

www.ecotrek.com.au

Caving

The Nullarbor Plain is the largest single karst formation on the planet. The area was originally an ancient seabed, uplifted from the sea and subsequently weathered by wind and rain to form the extremely flat conditions that are seen today, along with many caves. Some are extremely large with several kilometres of passages. Murrawijinie Caves north of the Nullarbor roadhouse is open to the public. Koonalda Cave and Bunabie Blowhole may be viewed from the top, but other caves can only be entered in the company of National Parks and Wildlife Officers or as part of an organised accredited caving group. Strict regulations in the use of all caves apply and should be obtained from the Department of Environment and Natural Resources. Ask at Balladonia Hotel for more information on access to the safer and easier-to-get-to caves under the Nullarbor Plain.

Cycling and mountain biking

Cycling across the Nullarbor is increasing in popularity, but is not without its hazards. Avoid cycling at night and beware of road trains. Be ready to get right off the road if faced with oncoming traffic; a lack of seals shoulders means there is room on the road for a truck and a car to pass, but not for a truck, a car and a cyclist.

ROC Tours Australia run guided rides through Coober Pedy, down the Oodnadatta Track to the Flinders Ranges. Cycle the Mawson Trail, enjoy wine tasting in the Clare Valley and stand on the edge of the Great Australian Bight. The support vehicle is never far away.

www.cycletours.com.au

Fishing

Fishing is prohibited in the lakes of the Coongie Conservation Zone but is permitted in other areas of Innamincka Regional Reserve, including Cooper Creek, one of the few carp free rivers in Australia. Expect to get good bream, catfish and yellowbelly. The legal catch length for yellow-belly is 33cm with a bag limit of five per person per day. Up to 10 catfish per person per day may be taken. No more than two of these fish over 33 cm in length are permitted. There is no size limit on Barcoo Grunter with up to five fish per person per day able to be taken.

Off-road driving

The Birdsville Track: established as a 520km stock route in the 1880s from Marree SA to Birdsville Qld, is one of Australia's legendary outback tracks. Then, it took about a month to complete; the route was long and harsh and cattle often didn't survive the trip. Now the track is passable to conventional vehicles most of the year but is a favourite with 4WD. Highlights include white salt lakes, homestead ruins, crossing the dog fence and visiting the gushing hot water bores beside the track, the Natterannie sand hills where the Tirari and Strzelecki deserts meet and, of course, the famous Birdsville Hotel.

Oodnadatta Track: linking Marree in the south to Marla in the north, this 620km track traverses South Australia's remote outback, in the footsteps of explorer John McDouall Stuart, who crossed the continent from Adelaide to Darwin in 1862. The Overland Telegraph Line was built along his route just 10 years later, followed by the first Ghan railway line, opened in 1929. It can be a bumpy, dusty trip, but nothing like the horror stretch it once was. Today, with care, a conventional sedan can travel the main track, but after even a little bit of rain you'll need a 4WD. Explore old train carriages in Marree, have a beer at William Creek (population seven), visit the salty vastness of Lake Eyre, bubbling mound springs, old Telegraph Station and homestead ruins and the outback outpost of Oodnadatta.

Strzelecki Track: a 462km track from Innamincka to Lyndhurst, north of Leigh Creek. The original 'track' was blazed by Harry Redford and 1000 stolen cattle over untracked country from central Queensland to Adelaide. When Redford was caught, the jury was so impressed with his heroic effort that they declined to convict him.

The Simpson Crossing: the 650km crossing is one of the last frontiers of the outback, the last Australian desert to be explored by Europeans. Ted Colson first crossed the Simpson's expanse of red dunes by camel, in 1936, the first vehicle in 1962. Now, while thousands of people cross each year, you must be self sufficient: carry good maps and basic spares, make sure your vehicle is prepared and take water for several days. Crossing east to west is the easiest, from Birdsville to Dalhousie hot springs, and allow three days. Be alert for oncoming vehicles on dune crests. Use a UHF CB radio to scan frequencies and fly a bright flag high on whip aerials or a pole to alert others of your approach.

The Outback mail run: a full-day 4WD tour, delivering mail from Coober Pedy to Oodnadatta, William Creek, Anna Creek Station, several remote cattle stations and Lake Cadibarrawirracanna. It's a long 12-hour day–more than 600km. The outback mail run is a great way to meet some locals and see what its like to live on these isolated stations. The mail is usually met with excitement–especially if there are kids on the station. They will often take your hand and drag you to their schoolroom where they do their school of the air lessons and other favourite places. Their parents are often keen for a cup of tea and a chat. Stickers and postcards from your home town are a great hit with the kids. Tours depart from Coober Pedy on Mondays and Thursdays.

www.mailruntour.com.au ☎ (08) 8672 5558

Simpson Desert dunes. *(SATC)*

Horse riding

The Great Australian Outback Cattle Drive is a biannual event where some of Australia's most experienced drovers unite to drove 600 head of cattle by horseback down one of the legendary outback stock routes, such as the Birdsville or Oodnadatta Track. Cattle drives take five to six weeks between late April and June and are broken into five-day sections so you can join the cattle drive at various locations. Camp in a village of luxury tents with showers, bar and plenty of campfire cooking. Scenic flights and camel rides are available along the way.

www.cattledrive.southaustralia.com

Whale watching

At Head of Bight, on the coast 20km east of Nullarbor Roadhouse, there is a whale-viewing platform where, between June and October, you can see up to 100 southern right whales and their calves lolling in the water at the foot of the cliffs beneath. The whales come here each year during winter from the freezing Antarctic waters to give birth and it's one of the best whale watching places in the world. Whale watching permits available from the White Well Ranger Station on the Head of Bight Road and the Yalata Roadhouse. You can also take a scenic flight over the whale breeding grounds and along the cliff line, which can also be organised at the Nullarbor Roadhouse.

MORE INFORMATION

- **Coober Pedy Visitors Information Centre:** Hutchison Street, Coober Pedy. ☎ 1800 637 076. www.opalcapitaloftheworld.com.au
- **For information on Lake Eyre visit:** www.environment.sa.gov.au/parks/lakeeyre/visit.html, www.southaustralia.com, www.nullarbornet.com.au
- **For up-to-date road conditions:** call the Transport SA Hotline on ☎ 1300 361 033 or the Pink Roadhouse in Oodnadatta on ☎ 1800 802 074.

weather watch

- January: 21–45°C
- July: 4–19°C
- Summer can be extremely hot. Best time to travel is during the winter months when days are dry and warm but nights can be freezing.

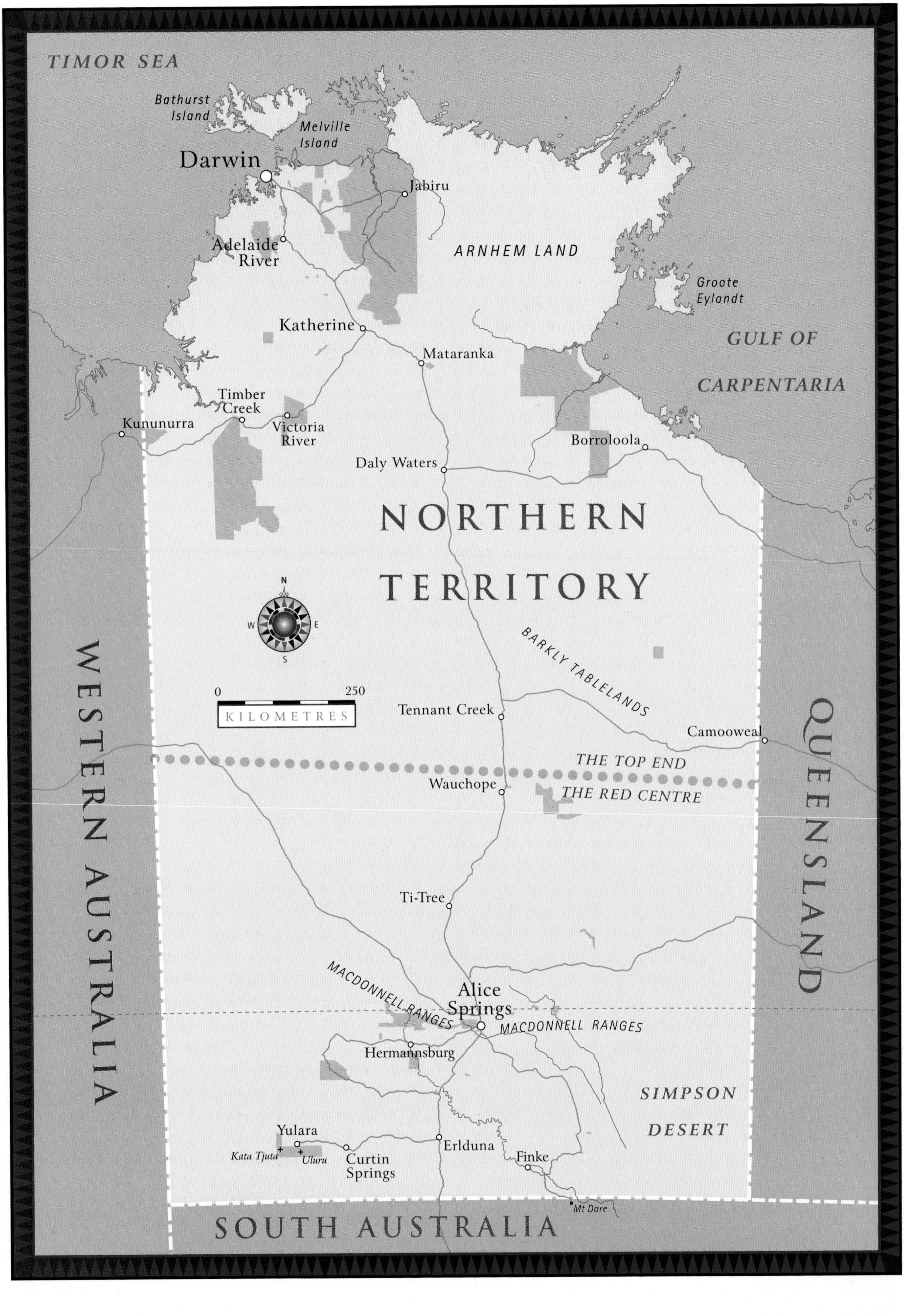

TIMOR SEA

Bathurst Island

Melville Island

Darwin

Jabiru

ARNHEM LAND

Adelaide River

Groote Eylandt

Katherine

GULF OF CARPENTARIA

Mataranka

Timber Creek

Kununurra

Victoria River

Borroloola

Daly Waters

NORTHERN TERRITORY

N

W

E

S

0 250

KILOMETRES

BARKLY TABLELANDS

Tennant Creek

Camooweal

THE TOP END

Wauchope

THE RED CENTRE

WESTERN AUSTRALIA

QUEENSLAND

Ti-Tree

MACDONNELL RANGES

Alice Springs

MACDONNELL RANGES

Hermannsburg

SIMPSON DESERT

Yulara

Kata Tjuta

Uluru

Curtin Springs

Erlduna

Finke

Mt Dare

SOUTH AUSTRALIA

northern territory

The Northern Territory is Australia's last wild frontier, the most barren and least populated area of Australia. It is a place of extremes, from the harsh red centre with its outback icons of Uluru, Kata Tjuta, Kings Canyon and West MacDonnell Ranges, to the steamy tropical forests of the Top End and the World Heritage Kakadu National Park. Home to less than one per cent of Australians, the Territory is administered by the Federal Government. There are vast tracts of Aboriginal land, including remote and wild Arnhem Land in the north-east. Its capital, Darwin, closer to Asia than the rest of Australia, is the country's most cosmopolitan city.

the top end

The Devils Marbles. *(Tourism NT)*

►AUSTRALIAN CAPITAL cities don't come much more tropical, or exotic, than Darwin. Perched on the edge of the Timor Sea at the very top of Australia, closer to Singapore than Perth or Sydney, Darwin is a heady mix of the tropics and the outback, of frontier hardiness and urbane sophistication, extreme weather and genuine friendliness blended in a crucible of cultural influences.

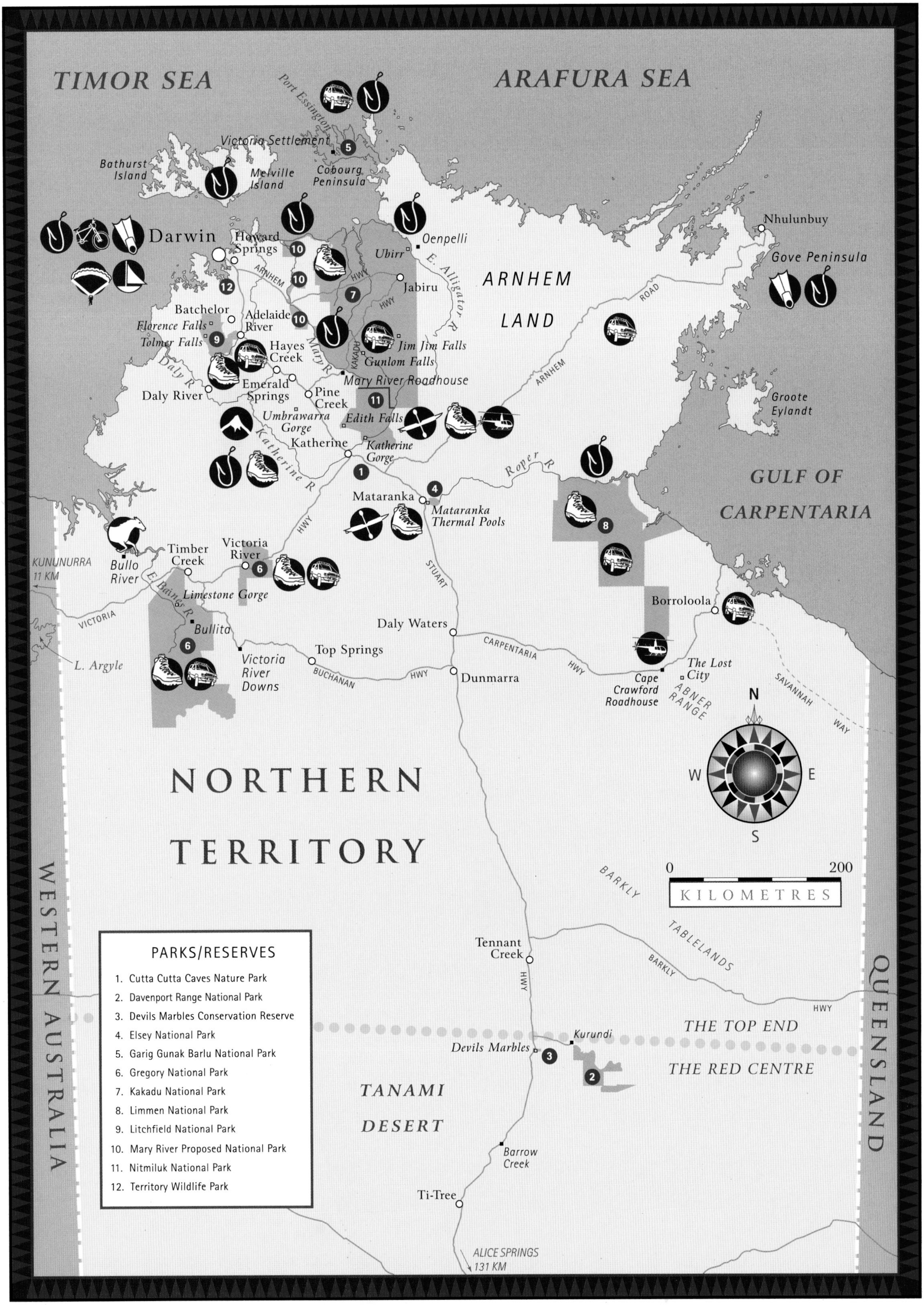

NORTHERN TERRITORY

TIMOR SEA

ARAFURA SEA

Port Essington

Victoria Settlement

Bathurst Island

Melville Island

Cobourg Peninsula

Darwin

Howard Springs

Oenpelli

Ubirr

E. Alligator R.

ARNHEM LAND

Jabiru

Nhulunbuy

Gove Peninsula

Batchelor

Florence Falls

Tolmer Falls

Adelaide River

Hayes Creek

Mary R.

KAKADU

Jim Jim Falls

Gunlom Falls

Mary River Roadhouse

Daly R.

Daly River

Emerald Springs

Pine Creek

Umbrawarra Gorge

Edith Falls

Katherine

Katherine Gorge

Katherine R.

ARNHEM HWY

ARNHEM ROAD

Groote Eylandt

Roper R.

GULF OF CARPENTARIA

Mataranka

Mataranka Thermal Pools

KUNUNURRA 11 KM

Bullo River

Timber Creek

Victoria River

E. Baines R.

Limestone Gorge

VICTORIA

Bullita

L. Argyle

Victoria River Downs

Top Springs

BUCHANAN HWY

STUART HWY

Daly Waters

Dunmarra

CARPENTARIA HWY

Borroloola

Cape Crawford Roadhouse

The Lost City

ABNER RANGE

SAVANNAH WAY

N

W

E

S

0 200 KILOMETRES

BARKLY TABLELANDS

BARKLY HWY

Tennant Creek

WESTERN AUSTRALIA

QUEENSLAND

THE TOP END

THE RED CENTRE

Kurundi

Devils Marbles

TANAMI DESERT

Barrow Creek

Ti-Tree

ALICE SPRINGS 131 KM

PARKS/RESERVES

1. Cutta Cutta Caves Nature Park
2. Davenport Range National Park
3. Devils Marbles Conservation Reserve
4. Elsey National Park
5. Garig Gunak Barlu National Park
6. Gregory National Park
7. Kakadu National Park
8. Limmen National Park
9. Litchfield National Park
10. Mary River Proposed National Park
11. Nitmiluk National Park
12. Territory Wildlife Park

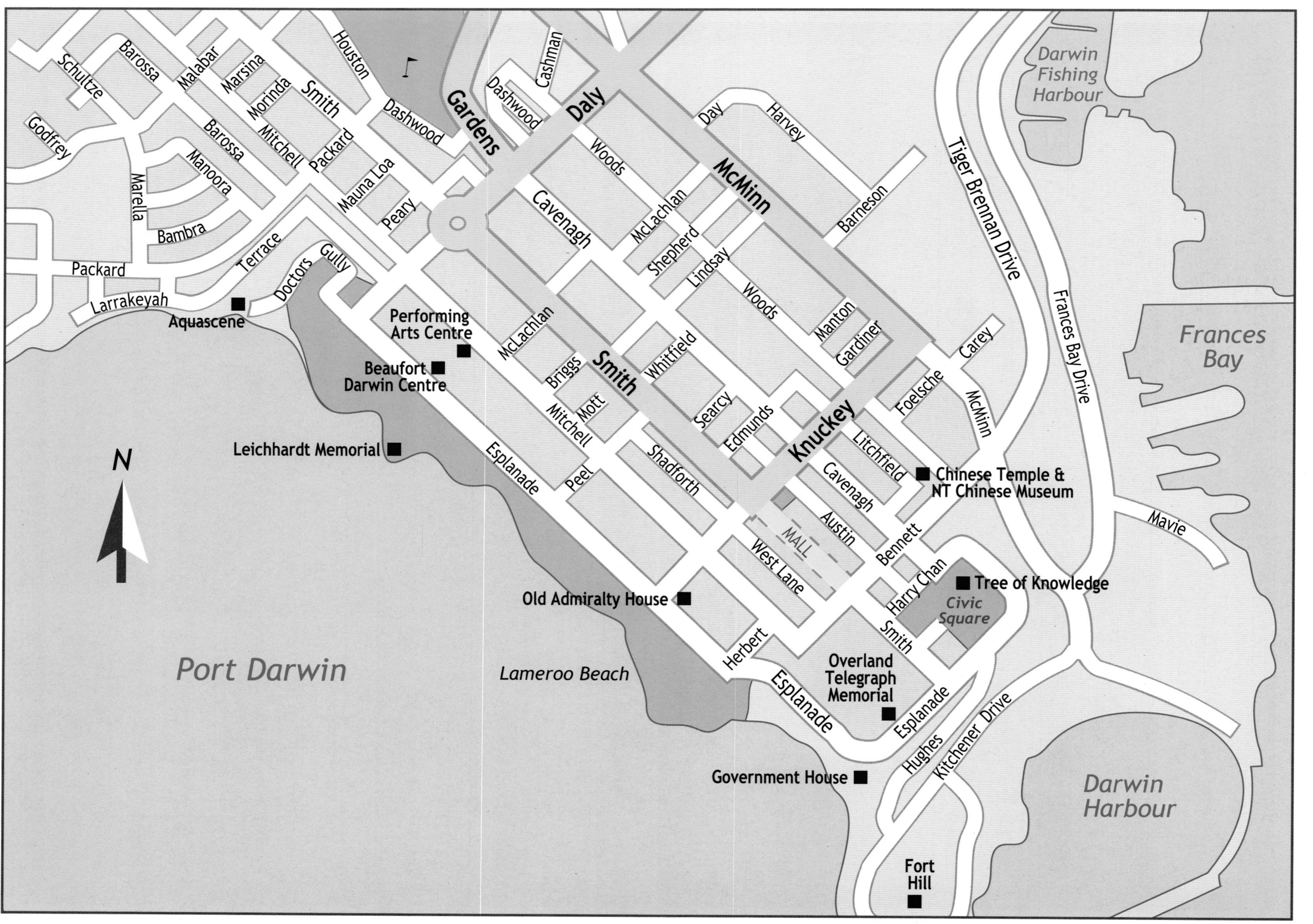

Darwin Fishing Harbour
Frances Bay
Darwin Harbour
Port Darwin
Lameroo Beach
N
Tiger Brennan Drive
Frances Bay Drive
Mavie
Kitchener Drive
Hughes
Esplanade
Herbert
Peel
Smith
Knuckey
McMinn
Daly
Gardens
Cavenagh
Woods
McLachlan
Shepherd
Lindsay
Manton
Gardiner
Carey
Foelsche
Litchfield
Austin
Bennett
Harry Chan
MALL
West Lane
Shadforth
Edmunds
Searcy
Whitfield
Briggs
Mott
Mitchell
Barneson
Harvey
Day
Cashman
Dashwood
Houston
Peary
Mauna Loa
Packard
Morinda
Marsina
Malabar
Barossa
Schultze
Godfrey
Marella
Manoora
Bambra
Terrace
Larrakeyah
Doctors
Gully
Aquascene
Performing Arts Centre
Beaufort Darwin Centre
Leichhardt Memorial
Old Admiralty House
Chinese Temple &
NT Chinese Museum
Tree of Knowledge
Civic Square
Overland Telegraph Memorial
Government House
Fort Hill

Cobourg Peninsula, Garig Gunak Barlu National Park. *(Tourism NT)*

NATIONAL PARKS

Kakadu National Park: one of the most popular, and magnificent, national parks in Australia, Kakadu covers more than 20,000km^2 and the entire catchment of the South Alligator River. The World Heritage area encompasses five main habitats: savannah woodlands; floodplains and billabongs; monsoon forest; rocky escarpments and tidal flats and coast. Birdlife is prolific and saltwater crocodiles inhabit most waterways. Spectacular waterfalls during the wet season. See Scenic Highlights section (over page) for more details.

Litchfield National Park: 100km south of Darwin via Batchelor. This is the place to see waterfalls, the four most spectacular in the park are all accessible in 2WD, and several of them are open for swimming—one of the few places, apart from resort swimming pools, in the Top End where it's safe to swim. Highlights include the magnetic termite mounds, a large group of two-metre high termite mounds, all aligned north-south—to keep the inside of the mound from overheating under the fierce sun; Buley Rockhole, a chain of spa-like pools linked by small waterfalls; Florence Falls; the Lost City, an area of bizarre sandstone block and pillar formations, formed by thousands of years of wind and rain erosion; Tolmer Falls and Wangi Falls, the largest in the park.

Nitmiluk National Park: the Katherine River carves 13 deep gorges through towering red sandstone cliffs, navigable in the dry season by canoe or commercial cruise. There is a nice swimming platform, and the river is supposedly free of saltwater crocodiles: the only ones they say you'll see here are the relatively harmless freshwater variety. Katherine is 90km south of Pine Creek.

Elsey National Park: numerous springs within the park feed the Roper River which, during April to September, flow gently through large waterholes and then tumbles over rocks and 'tufa' dams. Highlights include the Mataranka Thermal Pools where spring water rises from underground at a temperature of 34°C contained in a swimming pool surrounded by a paperbark and palm forest. The area around the pool is a natural breeding ground for the Little Red Flying Fox. The breeding season is traditionally in the wet season but often extends into the dry.

Cutta Cutta Caves Nature Park: 29km south of Katherine, the limestone Cutta Cutta Caves are about 15m below the earth's surface—the main cave system goes for 700m until it enters the water table. Back in the 1970s a caver lived for more than 60 days in this cave to get into the *Guinness Book of Records*. There are still remnants of his occupation further back in the cave. The caves are home to a variety of wildlife including the brown tree snake and rare orange horseshoe bat. Guided tours of the cave system are conducted throughout the day.

Garig Gunak Barlu National Park: on Arnhem Land's Cobourg Peninsula is the only area in the NT which contains adjoining land and marine park areas; it's a place of pristine beaches carpeted in sea shells where turtles come up to lay their eggs and the world's largest remaining wild herd of banteng roam in the monsoon forests behind the high tide mark. Even better, only 20 permits to enter the park are issued at any one time, so you know you've got the place pretty much to yourselves. Plan to spend at least three or four days here.

Gregory National Park: covers an area of around 13,000km^2 in the transition zone between tropical and semi-arid regions of the Northern Territory on the edge of the Kimberley region. The park features spectacular range and gorge scenery, extensive stands of boab trees and significant traces of Aboriginal culture, European exploration and pastoral history.

Limmen National Park: tucked away in a seldom-visited corner of the Gulf of Carpentaria west of Borroloola, this park is a remote and rugged place steeped in culture and history, with spectacular sandstone formations, numerous rivers and wetlands.

Devils Marbles Conservation Reserve: 100km south of Tennant Creek, the Devils Marbles are a collection of gigantic (some are four metres high and 13–33m wide) rounded granite boulders that are often precariously balanced on top of one another. Scattered heaps of these 'marbles' occur across a wide, shallow valley. The area is an important meeting place and rich in 'dreaming' sites for local Aboriginal people.

Davenport Range National Park: the park is 90km from Tennant Creek and features many large waterholes. Access is via Kurundi Station to the north of the Devils Marbles or via the Taylor's Creek Road to the north of Barrow Creek.

scenic highlights

Ubirr, Kakadu. *(Lee Atkinson)*

Despite its fearsome reputation as the last frontier, the Top End, and Kakadu, is surprisingly easy to get around, even without a 4WD, and none of the main sites involve long walks to access them. The main route through Kakadu, known as the Nature's Way, is fully sealed and links up with the Stuart Highway at both ends. It begins at the turn off to the Arnhem Highway, 34km south of Darwin and roughly forms two sides of a triangle, with the mining town of Jabiru at the apex, joining up with the Kakadu Highway running south to the Stuart Highway near historic Pine Creek.

First stop for most folks is at the Adelaide River Bridge, where you can join a 90-minute Jumping Crocodile Cruise. The Arnhem Highway then passes through the proposed Mary River National Park, a favourite with anglers and birdwatchers, although facilities at this stage are scant. The Kakadu park entrance is around 55km on. How much time you spend in Kakadu, and what you see and do is limited only by the amount of time you have. You really need a minimum of two days, and even then, you will only be seeing the highlights.

Spend a couple of hours watching magpie geese, egrets and countless other birds in the cool and breezy over-water shelter at Mamukala wetlands. Call in to the Bowali Visitor Centre near Jabiru to learn about the landscape and habitats in the park and time your trip to Ubirr for great sunset views over the Arnhem Land escarpment after viewing the ancient Aboriginal rock art galleries.

Take an early morning scenic flight from Jabiru, then do the one-hour walk around more rock art galleries at Nourlangie Rock. During the dry you can walk around the edge of Anbangbang Billabong at its base. Climb Mirrai Lookout for woodland views, before driving on to Cooinda, home of the Warradjan Aboriginal Cultural Centre, an excellent free interactive museum telling the stories of the traditional owners. The turn-off to Jim Jim Falls and Twin Falls is just before you reach Cooinda, but it is 4WD only and doesn't reopen after the wet season until early June.

At Cooinda make sure you do the Yellow Water billabong cruise, a two-hour cruise on a breathtakingly beautiful landlocked billabong fringed by pandanus, paperbark swamps and monsoon rainforest. Take the sunset or sunrise cruise and you'll see thousands of birds and more than likely a few big crocodiles as well.

It's about 82km from Cooinda to the boundary of the park. Along the way, take a detour to Gunlom Falls, one of the few you can see in the park without a 4WD.

Nature's Way officially ends at the Stuart Highway junction, 58km from the park boundary, a few kilometres south of Pine Creek, but continue south for 90km to Katherine and Nitmiluk National Park.

Darwin

The modern city of Darwin, which began life as Palmerston in 1869, was the fifth attempt at establishing a settlement on the northern coast of Australia. The previous four, which included Fort Dundas, Raffles Bay, Escape Cliffs and Port Essington on the Cobourg Peninsula, had all been failures and it wasn't until the construction of the Overland Telegraph 1870 that the fledgling town really had a sustainable reason for being.

Darwin has always had to have a strong will to survive. During World War II it was bombed more than 60 times, the harbour full of warships a prime target for the Japanese. Then, on the night of Christmas Eve 1974, the city was destroyed by Cyclone Tracy, Australia's greatest natural disaster.

But you'd never know it if you visit Darwin today. The harbourside city of more than 110,000 people is a bustling city with a relaxed personality, a great restaurant and bar scene, and as the locals like to tell you, 'the best shopping for 1000 miles'.

Tiwi islands

Melville and Bathurst Islands, known collectively as the Tiwi Islands, are just a short but beautiful 20-minute flight across the Timor Sea from Darwin. Together the two islands, which are separated by the 700m wide Aspley Strait, are 8000km^2 of monsoonal rainforest ringed by pristine beaches, scattered with tiny Aboriginal communities maintaining elements of a traditional existence mixed with modern-day influences.

One of the most important expressions of the traditional Tiwi culture, the burial poles, or *Pukumani*, are part of a religious ceremony that includes singing, dancing and the making of special carved poles called *tutini* as well as *tungas* and arm bands. These large poles are made from the trunk of the ironwood tree and are carved and decorated to celebrate the dead person's life and spiritual journey. The ceremony occurs approximately six months after the deceased has been buried and the Tiwi believe that the dead person's existence in the living world is not finished until the completion of the ceremony.

Arnhem Land

East of Kakadu National Park, the area known as Arnhem Land encompasses 91,000km^2 and is home to many Aboriginal people, most of whom continue to practice their traditional way of life. Split by the 500km-long Arnhem Land escarpment it is a place of wild coastlines, deserted islands, rivers teeming with fish, lush rainforests and savannah woodland, and one of Australia's most remote and least travelled regions. Cobourg Peninsula and the Aboriginal township of Oenpelli lies to the north-east of the Alligator River; on the western coast is Nhulunbuy on the Gove Peninsula where each August Australia's most significant indigenous festival, The Garma Festival, celebrates the practice, preservation and maintenance of traditional dance (*bunggul*), song (*manikay*), art and ceremonies of the Yolngu People. To visit Arnhem Land you must apply for a permit from the Northern Land Council.

www.nlc.org.au/html/permits.html

Mataranka Thermal Pool. *(Tourism NT)*

Katherine

Katherine, 316km south of Darwin, is at the junction of the Stuart Highway, which cuts a straight line down the middle of the Northern Territory linking Darwin and Alice Springs, and the transcontinental Savannah Way, which links Cairns in Queensland to Broome in Western Australia. The third largest town in the Northern Territory with a population of almost 11,000, it is accessible all year by sealed roads. The star attraction is Nitmiluk National Park, just 29km from the town centre, where the Katherine River carves a deep gorge through towering red sandstone cliffs to form 13 spectacular gorges each separated by a tumble of boulders and a string of rapids.

Caravan and camping

Litchfield National Park has some beautiful camping spots close to swimming holes at Wangi Falls, Buley Rockhole and Florence Falls. 4WD camping, during the dry season only, at Tjaynera Falls (Sandy Creek), Surprise Creek Falls and downstream of Florence Falls. There is caravan camping (unpowered sites only) at Wangi Falls.

DON'T MISS

- **Mindil Beach Sunset Markets:** more than 60 food stalls from more than 30 countries and 200 art and craft stalls. Shop for local souvenirs, have a massage, your palm read, a Tarot reading, watch the buskers, listen to the live bands or just sip a glass of wine on the beach and watch the sunset. April until October on Thursday and Sunday nights at Mindil Beach, Darwin.
- **Museum and Art Gallery of the Northern Territory:** includes an excellent exhibition of Aboriginal bark paintings, a collection of stone axes estimated to be up to 22,000 years old, and the Melville Island Pukamani Burial Poles. The Cyclone Tracy display includes a recording of the cyclone's screeching winds. Conacher Street, Fannie Bay, Darwin. Open Mon–Fri, 9am–5pm; weekends and public holidays, 10am–5pm.
- **East Point Military Museum:** the original bunker where the Australian army planned the Top End defence strategy. The oil storage tunnels, which were built as part of the war effort, are equally fascinating and wind beneath the city. East Point Reserve, Darwin. Open daily, 9.30am–5pm.
- **George Brown Botanical Gardens:** 42-hectare garden just two kilometres from the Darwin city centre includes a rainforest gully with hundreds of palms, a wetland, a coastal zone and a mangrove boardwalk. Open daily, 7am–7pm.
- **Aquascene:** hand-feed the hundreds of fish that come to shore in high tide at Doctors Gully, Darwin.
- **Aviation Heritage Centre:** exhibits include a B52 bomber that crashed 100km west of Tennant Creek in 1945 and was recovered in 1974, a Spitfire, a Wessex helicopter, a Sabre jet and more Australian aviation history. 557 Stuart Highway, Darwin. Open daily, 9am–5pm. Guided tours at 10am and 2pm.
- **Fannie Bay Gaol:** opened in 1883, the notorious gaol was home to criminals and their like for almost 100 years until 1979. East Point Road, Fannie Bay, Darwin. Open daily, 10am–4.30pm.
- **Crocodylus Park:** wildlife park with crocodiles, cassowaries, dingos and wallabies. 815 McMillans Road, Berrimah, Darwin. Open daily, 9am–5pm. Feeding/tour 10am, 12pm and 2pm.
- **Tiwi Islands:** Tiwi Tours (with Aussie Adventure Tours) run several different day trips to Bathurst and Melville Island and will organise the permits on your behalf. Tours include morning tea, lunch and return flights from Darwin. www.aussieadventure.com.au
- **Territory Wildlife Park:** operated by the Parks and Wildlife Commission of the Northern Territory, this 1000-acre park showcases the native plants and animals of the region. Cox Peninsula Road, Berry Springs. Free-flying birds of prey demonstrations twice daily (10am and 3pm). Open daily 8.30am–6pm. www.territorywildlifepark.com.au
- **Adelaide River Jumping Crocodile Cruise:** watch saltwater crocodiles leap out of the muddy river and see a huge variety of birdlife from the boat. 90-minute river cruises depart Adelaide River Bridge, Arnhem Highway, via Humpty Doo, several times daily, year round. www.jumpingcrocodilecruises.com.au
- **Window on the Wetlands:** this visitor centre at Beatrice Hill provides an overview of the wetlands, with information and displays on the wildlife, seasonal changes and the problems of feral animals and weeds. The centre commands superb views across the floodplains, especially during the early morning or late afternoon. Open daily, 7.30am–7.30pm.
- **Scenic flights:** half-hour and one-hour flights over the park depart Jabiru and Cooinda. ☎ 1800 089 113 for bookings.
- **Bowali Visitor Centre:** interpretative centre illustrating two ways at looking at Kakadu National Park; the *Gukburlerri* (Aboriginal) and *Guhbele* (non-Aboriginal) views though a series of interactive displays on Kakadu's habitats. Open daily, 8am–5pm.

Nhulunbuy locals. *(Tourism NT)*

- **Ubirr:** a major Aboriginal art site of Kakadu with galleries featuring an array of Aboriginal painting styles. The rocky outcrop is the location of a shelter used as a home for thousands of years. Beautiful sunset views over the floodplains and escarpment.
- **Nourlangie Rock:** allow at least an hour to walk around this site which is an ancient Aboriginal shelter with outstanding rock art galleries surrounded by a variety of natural features: creeks, sandy alluvial plains, woodland and sandstone escarpment.
- **Warradjan Aboriginal Cultural Centre:** developed by the traditional Aboriginal owners of Kakadu to display the stories they want to share with visitors, providing an insight into both traditional and contemporary Aboriginal culture. Open daily, 9am–5pm.
- **Yellow River Cruise:** two-hour billabong cruises. Home to crocodiles and an extraordinary array of birdlife and wildlife. Cruises depart several times daily, year round. Bookings essential, call ☎ (08) 8979 0145. www.yellowwatercruises.com
- **Injalak Art and Craft Centre:** indigenous artists and craftspeople gather at Gunbalanya (Oenpelli) most mornings to create traditional bark paintings, didgeridoos, pandanus weavings and screen printed fabrics. Visitors can obtain a permit to visit Oenpelli through the centre. www.injalak.com
- **Nitmiluk Gorge Cruise:** cruises through gorges carved out of sandstone rock by torrential summer rain over millions of years. See abundant bird, fish and animal life, including the fresh water crocodile. Wear comfortable walking shoes. Nitmiluk Tours, 6 Katherine Terrace, Katherine. ☎ 1800 089 103.
- **Katherine Museum:** originally built in 1944–5 as an air terminal, today houses an eclectic collection of artefacts, photographs, maps and farming displays, including the Gypsy Moth plane that belonged to Katherine's famous 'Flying Doctor', Clyde Fenton. Gorge Road, Katherine. Open Mon–Sat, 10am–1pm during wet season; weekdays 10am–4pm and 10am–1pm weekends during dry season.
- **Springvale Homestead:** managed by the National Trust on the Katherine River, is the oldest standing homestead in the Northern Territory and provides an insight into early pioneer days. Shadforth Road, Katherine. Open May and September; free tours at 3pm.
- **Katherine Hot Springs:** natural thermal springs on the bank of the Katherine River, signposted from the centre of town. It's a popular place to swim—the water is warm rather than hot and there are picnic grounds and walking tracks.
- **Adelaide River War Cemetery:** Australia's largest war cemetery, resting place for 54 civilians and 434 service men and women killed in the 1942 air raids on Darwin. Also remembered are 287 service personnel lost in Timor and other northern regions, but who have no known grave.

You can camp at more than 20 camping areas in Kakadu; seven of which have caravan sites. You can also camp beside the billabong at Shady Camp in Mary River Proposed National Park and at Couzen's Lookout camping beside the Mary River.

In Nitmiluk there are tent and caravan sites at the Gorge and Edith Falls (powered sites at the Gorge only); walkers and canoeists can bush camp elsewhere in the park.

There are two camp grounds in Garig Gunak Barlu: campground No. 1 (generators are not permitted), and camp ground No. 2 where generators are permitted. No. 2 is open and airy, while No. 1 is in a swamp that is prone to mosquitoes and where crocodiles have been known to come a little too close for comfort.

Gregory National Park has several campgrounds; Big Horse Creek has a boat ramp and is popular with anglers; Bulita is on the banks of the East Baines River near the historic Bulita homestead and Limestone Gorge has a beautiful swimming hole.

In Limmen National Park there are boat ramps and basic campgrounds at Towns River and Tomato Island. You can also camp at Butterfly Springs, a beautiful swimming hole surrounded by paperbacks and exquisite fern-leaved grevillea ablaze with dainty orange flowers during the dry season that attract hundreds of birds to the oasis. It's also home to thousands of common crow butterflies that cover the sandstone wall to the right of the pool and arise en masse when you approach.

Another good camping area, but without any facilities, is beside the Lomarieum Lagoon beside St Vidgeon ruins, not far from the Roper River, the large water-lily covered lagoon is a haven for birdlife.

Bushwalks

There are some lovely short walks in Litchfield National Park: at Wangi Falls, the most popular swimming area in the park, an interpretive nature trail leads from the camping and barbecue area to the top of the falls and back down to the car park. There is also a shady circuit walk (one-hour return) that winds through the monsoon forest beside the creek at Florence Falls. The Tabletop Track is a 39km loop that can be accessed at Florence Falls, Greenant Creek, Wangi Falls and Walker Creek.

In Kakadu there are good short walks at most of the major sites. Good longer walks include the Sandstone and River bushwalk, an easy 6.5km loop near Ubirr that takes you past Catfish Creek, floodplains, billabongs, sandstone outliers and the East Alligator River. The Barkk bushwalk is a difficult 12km walk (allow six to eight hours) through the sandstone country of Nourlangie and the Barrk Marlam walk is a challenging dry season only trail that branches off the Jim Jim Falls plunge pool track (6km return).

There are a range of walks available in Nitmuluk, all of which start near the visitors centre and climb the rocky escarpment of Katherine Gorge. They range from two hours to three days and all are rated medium or difficult but all offer fantastic gorge views and many lead to good swimming holes. All overnight walkers must register at the Nitmuluk Centre on departure and return. The Jatbula Trail is a challenging four- to six-day, 66km bushwalk from Katherine Gorge to Edith Falls that takes in diverse scenery, plunging waterfalls and Aboriginal rock art.

Lost City, Cape Crawford. *(Tourism NT)*

In Limmen National Park you can wander amongst towering rock pillars at the Southern Lost City. At 1.4 billion years in the making, these rocks are some of the oldest in the world. They consist of 95 per cent silica and are held together by an outer crust made mainly of iron, giving them their unique red colour, especially at sunset. It's a 3km track in from the main road with a 2km easy walking trail among the rock formations. The track winds its way through clumps of prickly spinifex and it is prime snake habitat, so wear long pants.

adventure activities

Canoeing in Katherine Gorge. *(Lee Atkinson)*

Abseiling and rock climbing

Umbrawarra Gorge, 22km south-west of Pine Creek, features a creek running through the middle of steep red cliffs and swimming pools with sandy beaches and is one of the territory's best climbing spots with around 30 moderate routes in good quality rock rising above a series of waterholes in a beautiful setting. Permits to climb or abseil must be obtained from the Batchelor or Palmerston Parks and Wildlife Services offices before you arrive at Umbrawarra.

Canoeing and kayaking

Canoeing the tranquil waters of the Katherine River is a highlight of many people's visit to the Top End. Take an extended trip with an experienced guide or launch your own canoe from the Katherine Low Level Bridge, five minutes from town. The upper gorges are accessible to canoes but portage can be quite strenuous, especially when the river is low. You will need to carry canoes and gear over the crossovers between various gorges. You can hire canoes at the Nitmiluk Centre in the national park. There a number of guided canoeing trips available–ask at the visitors information centre for details or visit the site below. You can also canoe at Mataranka thermal pools.

www.travelnorth.com.au

Cycling and mountain biking

In Darwin there is a nice cycle path at East Point Reserve and Lake Alexander at Fannie Bay. The 22km Darwin Rail Trail follows the route of the former North Australian Railway from the outer edge of Darwin to Palmerston.

Remote Outback Cycling Tours (ROC) combine mountain biking and 4WDs to provide fully-supported tours to a number of outback destinations, including a six-day cycling tour of Katherine and Kakadu, cycling up the Stuart Highway visiting the Devils Marbles, an old bush pub, Mataranka thermal pool, Katherine Gorge and two days in Kakadu National Park as well as a four-day trip in and around Kakadu and Litchfield National Parks.

www.cycletours.com.au

Diving

Darwin Harbour is twice the size of Sydney Harbour with sunken ships from World War II, Cyclone Tracy and confiscated Indonesian fishing vessels. Darwin Dive Centre runs dive trips in Darwin Harbour, and the wrecks are easy to dive, allow good dive times and have a diverse range of fish life and corals. However, as Darwin tides can vary up to 7m diving is only possible, on average–for four consecutive days per fortnight and compared to most other dive sites in the world–visibility is very low with an average of 2-5m during diving tides (neap tides).

www.divedarwin.com

The Gove Peninsula in Arnhem Land offers a multitude of dive sites on the reefs surrounding the many islands of the peninsula with a variety of hard and soft corals, an abundance of fish life including many clownfish and their anemones and bat fish. These reefs are home to manta rays, blue spotted rays, reef sharks and a few resident moray eels. During September to April water temperatures are 28-32°C and the visibility is around 15-25 metres. During May to August water temperatures are 24-28°C and the visibility is around 8-15 metres. Gove Sports Fishing & Diving Charters hires gear and runs snorkelling and diving trips.

www.govefish.com.au

Fishing

The inland billabongs, tidal rivers, mangrove-line estuaries and pristine coastal waters make the Top End one of the country's best sport fishing destinations. The prized barramundi is the most highly sought after fish and it's not uncommon to catch a 10kg fish with plenty weighing even more. Best time for barramundi is September to December and they can be caught in all coastal areas of the Territory -in the open sea, harbours, estuaries, creeks, rivers and billabongs. There are countless fishing charters available in Darwin and other major centres and many private fishing camps.

www.fishingtheterritory.com

The Barramundi Fishing Park at Howard Springs has a billabong stocked with more than 3000 barramundi–catching a fish is guaranteed.

☎ (08) 8983 1232

As well as barramundi the tropical waters yield huge queenfish, trevally, saratoga, Spanish mackerel, longtail tuna, threadfin salmon, mangrove jack, marlin and sailfish and reef dwellers such as black jewfish, coral trout, red emperor, golden snapper.

While the fishing is pretty much good everywhere, the standout areas include the Adelaide River, Borroloola and the Gulf Country, Cobourg Peninsula, Daly River, Darwin Harbour and coast, the Tiwi Islands, Gove, Mary River, Kakadu and Katherine.

Off-road driving

While you don't need a four-wheel drive to explore most of Kakadu and Litchfield National Parks, some sections are 4WD only. In Kakadu the Jim Jim and Twin Falls area is 4WD and dry season only, but are two of the most spectacular features of the park. Note that the falls stop flowing in the dry season and the very enticing plunge pools are occasionally home to saltwater crocodiles. A snorkel is recommended to get to Twin Falls Gorge as the 70km track includes a deep-water crossing of Jim Jim Creek. There are plenty of 4WD tours available.

In Litchfield there is a 4WD-only track to the Lost City, a group of fantastically-shaped eroded sandstone towers. The 10km track is mostly narrow and one-way; watch for oncoming vehicles and be prepared to pull off the track to let them pass. Another good 4WD route is the 44km track from the Litchfield Park Road to the Daly River Road via Tjaynera Falls (Sandy Creek Falls), a deep waterhole every bit as gorgeous as Wangi Falls, but without the crowds, and Surprise Falls, another of Litchfield's hidden gems that most visitors to the park don't know about. After a sweaty 10-minute trek and some rock hopping you'll end up at a superb gorge, two plunge pools falling into each other over sheer rock walls.

The road into to the Cobourg Peninsula and Garig Gunak Barlu National Park is pleasantly easy, although a couple of creek crossings could get tricky after rain.

In the Gulf country the 700km section of the trans-continental Savannah Way from Normanton in Queensland to Borroloola, is a well-made but unsealed road that's not strictly 4WD, but there are a few river crossings, easy enough in the middle of the dry season.

Sandy Creek Falls, Litchfield National Park. *(Tourism NT)*

Sunset sail on Darwin Harbour. (Tourism NT)

Access to the Western Lost City formations in Limmen National Park is 4WD only. You will need a key from the Ranger Station to unlock the gate at the start of the 28km track. It begins just north-west of the Nathan River Ranger Station and ends at a 300m walk and short climb to views over the O'Keefe Valley. Organise the key prior to your visit, as the Ranger Station is not always attended.

Also part of the Savannah Way, the Buchanan Highway from Dunmarra just south of Daly Waters to Timber Creek, is best tackled in a 4WD, is a 574km route through wide-open cattle country along a rough dirt road that can be a killer on tyres. Stop at Top Springs Pub to wash away the grime and camp underneath the boab trees, beside a swimming hole at Limestone Gorge in Gregory National Park.

The Davenport Range National Park in the Tennant Creek area also offers 4WD tracks. The Old Police Station Waterhole has an alternative access road via the 'Frew River Loop,' a demanding 17km track that should only be attempted by experienced four-wheel-drivers. Check road conditions with the Alekerenge (Ali Curung) police station on:

☎ (08) 8964 1959

Helicopter flights

Take a helicopter or fixed wing flight over Nitmiluk National Park for a bird's-eye view of the natural gorges carved through sandstone by the Katherine River. A 12-minute flight will take you as far as the sixth gorge and 25-minute flights include the whole gorge system. Sightings of the local wildlife are common and breathtaking views of the Arnhem Land plateau are also superb.

At Cape Crawford take a helicopter sightseeing tour over the Lost City, a large expanse of tall sandstone columns only accessible by air. It's a worthwhile joyflight that takes you over the Abner Escarpment onto a plateau on McArthur River Station. The area was once an inland sea, the water seeped into the rock and eroded it, breaking it into columns up to 25m tall, and from the air you get a good idea of how these natural sky scrapers were formed. You can also do a two-hour ground tour that includes a 1.5km walk around the base of a small section after being dropped off by the chopper, which returns to pick you up and fly you back later.

www.capecrawfordtourism.com.au

Horse riding

The iconic outback property, Bullo River Station, located 800km south-west of Darwin near the Western Australian border, is the 500,000 acre home of Marlee Ranacher, daughter of pioneering parents Charles and Sara Henderson, who established the property in the 1950s. Apart from the station stock horses that are the backbone of Bullo's cattle operations, there are horses available for guests to ride subject to your riding ability–only experienced horse riders are catered for and guided rides can be arranged with prior notice.

www.bulloriver.com

Sailing

Watching the sun fall into a blood-red sea from the deck of a restored schooner, 1950s pearling lugger, sailing ketch, catamaran or cruiser while sipping champagne is a Darwin moment not to be missed. There are several cruises available on the harbour, with sunset cruises the most spectacular.

www.topendsaltwateradventures.com.au www.sant.net.au

Sky diving

Skydive the Top End with Top End Tandems for scenic views of Darwin and surrounding islands and coastline whilst climbing to jump height–your choice of 8000, 10,000 or 12,000 feet. Trips depart from Darwin Airport, and your parachute ride is over Darwin's beaches with the chance to fly your own canopy before a beach landing at Lee Point Beach.

www.topendtandems.com.au

MORE INFORMATION

- **Tourism Top End:** corner Knuckey & Mitchell Streets, Darwin. ☎ 13 67 68. www.travelnt.com
- **Katherine Region Tourist Association:** corner Lindsay St & Katherine Tce, Katherine. ☎ 1800 653 142. www.krta.com.au

weather watch

- January: 24–33°C
- July: 18–32°C
- The dry season is early May to late October. Many roads are closed and impassable during the wet season.

Port Essington, Cobourg Peninsula. *(Tourism NT)*

the red centre

Kata Tjuṯa. *(Tourism NT)*

► AUSTRALIA'S RED CENTRE is a place of endless surprises. The bush stories and legends of Australia's harsh outback fail to prepare most people for its stark beauty. Just as the tales of starving pioneers and dying explorers mean many are surprised at the feast of bush tucker available.

The red centre is the spiritual and mythological heartland of the continent. The desert plains have been home to many groups of Aboriginal people—including the Anangu and Arrernte—for thousands of years, and the landforms, hills and riverbeds all have deep spiritual meaning and are associated with significant Dreamtime (creation) stories. In the past few decades, ownership of most of the land, including the national parks, has reverted to the traditional owners and you will need a permit to travel beyond the main tourist sites.

Europeans first settled in the region in the 1870s with the building of the Overland Telegraph Line and the first intrepid tourists made the journey to Ayers Rock, now Uluru, in the 1940s with tourism steadily booming since the 1970s. These days, staying in the desert can be as luxurious, or as rough, as you want to make it.

NORTHERN TERRITORY
WESTERN AUSTRALIA
QUEENSLAND
SOUTH AUSTRALIA
THE TOP END
THE RED CENTRE
SIMPSON DESERT
N
S
E
W
0
200
KILOMETRES
Tropic of Capricorn
PARKS/RESERVES
1. Alice Springs Desert Park
2. Alice Springs Telegraph Historical Reserve
3. Arltunga Historical Reserve
4. Chambers Pillar Historical Reserve
5. Finke Gorge National Park
6. Rainbow Valley Conservation Reserve
7. Ruby Gap National Park
8. Tnorala Conservation Reserve
9. Uluru-Kata Tjuta National Park
10. Wattarrka National Park
11. West Macdonnell National Park
HALLS CREEK 211 KM
Rabbit Flat Roadhouse
TANAMI
TENNANT CREEK 21 KM
Wauchope
HWY
STUART
Ti-Tree
Camooweal
BARKLY
HWY
MT ISA 111 KM
PLENTY
HWY
BOULIA 121 KM
ROAD
Papunya
MACDONNELL
RANGES
Gemtree
HARTS RANGE
Simpsons Gap
Alice Springs
Ruby Gap
MACDONNELL RANGES
Glen Helen Resort
Hermannsburg
DRIVE
LARAPINTA
HWY
Jesse Gap
Todd River
Hale River
Kings Canyon Resort
GEORGE GILL RANGE
Kings Creek
ERNEST
GILES
ROAD
Illamurta Springs
OLD
ANDADO
TRACK
Finke River
Chambers Pillar
Mt Ebenezer
Yulara
Curtin Springs
HWY
Erlduna
Kata Tjuta
Uluru
LASSETER
Mt Connor
Finke
Old Andando
WARBURTON 211 KM
STUART
COOBER PEDY 161 KM
Mt Dare
Dalhousie Springs

NATIONAL PARKS

Uluṟu and Kata Tjuṯa National Park: World Heritage-listed park, home to Uluṟu and Kata Tjuṯa. Your first trip to Uluṟu should begin at the cultural centre, where a series of exhibits, paintings, videos and interpretation boards explain the relationship that the Anangu have with the land, Uluṟu and Kata Tjuṯa. You can practise the language with audio recordings; learn about the way of life, their foods, traditional weapons and utensils, and how they manage the land today. Be aware that Anangu do not like to be photographed and ask that all visitors respect this wish. It is also an offence to Anangu culture to photograph or film areas of spiritual significance. These areas are clearly signposted. Do not take photographs of the cultural centre.

Watarrka National Park: the western end of the George Gill Range, with rugged ranges, rockholes and gorges. Highlight is Kings Canyon, with its ancient sandstone walls rising up 100m to a plateau of rocky domes.

West MacDonnell National Park: cool scenic gorges great for walking and swimming in swimming holes. Features of the landscape are significant in the stories of Western Arrernte Aboriginal culture. Highlights include the Ochre Pits, Ormiston Gorge and Simpsons Gap.

Finke Gorge National Park: includes Palm Valley, home to a diverse range of plant species many of which are rare and unique to the area, including the Red Cabbage Palm for which the park is well known. This species of palm is restricted to this area, with a population of around 3000 adult plants. You'll need a 4WD to travel the last 16km along the sandy bed of the Finke River.

Tnorala Conservation Reserve: 175km west of Alice Springs, Gosse Bluff is a huge crater some 20km across formed by a comet more than 140 million years ago, although, according to Aboriginal belief, Tnorala was formed in the creation time, when a group of women danced across the sky as the Milky Way. During this dance, a mother put her baby aside, resting in its wooden baby-carrier (a turna). The carrier toppled over the edge of the dancing area and crashed to earth where it was transformed into the circular rock walls of Tnorala. Access is via Larapinta or Namatjira Drive. A 4WD is recommended for the last 10km drive to the Reserve and a Mereenie Tour Pass is required to travel this road.

Ruby Gap National Park: a remote park 150km east of Alice Springs with beautiful gorges and rich mining heritage—in March 1886, explorer David Lindsay found what he thought were rubies in the bed of the Hale River. Access to Ruby Gap is via the Arltunga Historical Reserve. A high clearance 4WD is essential. Heavy rains may cause the roads to become temporarily impassable. From the park entrance there is a 5km drive along the river bed and then a 2km walk to reach Glen Annie Gorge.

Palm Valley *(Tourism NT)*

Rainbow Valley Conservation Reserve: scenic sandstone bluffs and freestanding cliffs that form part of the James Range, 75km south from Alice Springs along the Stuart Highway. Best time to visit is early morning and late afternoon when the rainbow-like rock bands are highlighted by the sun.

Chambers Pillar Historical Reserve: a sandstone obelisk towering 50m above the plain, formed by the erosion of sandstone deposits laid down in the area 350 million years ago. At sunrise and sunset, the Pillar glows red hot as the sun strikes its face. 160km south of Alice Springs, along the Old South Road on a turnoff to the west of Maryvale Station. The road is unsealed and may be closed after rain. After the Maryvale turnoff, a 4WD is required to negotiate the deep sand drifts and steep jump ups.

DON'T MISS

- **Sounds of Silence:** this dinner atop a sand dune in the desert near Ayers Rock Resort is not your average bush barbecue. After tucking into fine wines, fresh barramundi, lamb, kangaroo and emu steaks, bush vegetables and luscious desserts, the lanterns are dimmed, the port poured and the legends of the southern sky are explained by a local astronomer. Not recommended for children under 10.
- **Hermannsburg:** a mission station originally established by Lutherans and now a thriving Aboriginal community. Birthplace and former home of artist Albert Namatjira. Aboriginal art and artefacts are available at the tea rooms and painted nearby in the Old Colonists' House—visitors are welcome to observe the artists at work. National Trust buildings include a school, mess house, manse and quarters for the missionaries, as well as the church, which is now a museum.
- **Alice Springs Desert Park:** a zoo, botanic garden and museum all wrapped up in one superb arid landscape park with three major habitats—Desert Rivers, Sand Country and Woodland, featuring more than120 species of animals and 350 species of plants. Free-flying birds of prey display and rare and endangered animals in the largest desert nocturnal house in the world. Guides present aspects of life in the desert, including Aboriginal use of resources, bush foods and medicines. Open daily, 7.30am–6pm. **www.alicespringsdesertpark.com.au**
- **National Pioneer Women's Hall of Fame:** museum preserving the place of women in history and their special contribution to Australia's heritage. Old Courthouse, 27 Hartley Street, Alice Springs. Open daily, 10am–5pm, (closed mid-December until 1 February). **www.pioneerwomen.com.au**
- **The Alice Springs Cultural Precinct:** eight attractions in the one location—The Araluen Centre (performing arts), Aviation Museum, Grand Circle Yeperenye Sculpture, Memorial Cemetery, Museum of Central Australia, Namatjira Gallery, Strehlow Research Centre and Territory Craft. Cnr Larapinta Dr and Memorial Ave. Open daily, 10am–5pm.
- **Alice Springs Telegraph Station Historical Reserve:** marking the site of the first European settlement in Alice Springs, the Telegraph Station was established in 1872 to relay messages between Darwin and Adelaide. It is the best preserved of the 12 stations along the Overland Telegraph Line. 4km north of Alice Springs along the Stuart Highway.

Hermannsburg Church. (Tourism NT)

Alice Springs

One of Australia's best known country towns, Alice Springs was named after a telegraph official's wife. It is a sprawling town of 25,000 beside the perennially dry Todd River, home of the famous Henley-on-Todd Regatta held every August, a dry-river race where teams race through the deep coarse sand in a motley collection of bottomless yachts, bathtubs and other weird and wonderful 'floats'. Today 'The Alice' is the centre of a booming tourism industry based on the strength that it is close to Uluru. It is, in fact, a five-hour drive. But as far as five-hour drives go, it's a fairly quick and easy run due south along the Stuart Highway and west along the Lasseter Highway, both all-sealed, speed-limit-free highways.

To the west rise the breathtakingly beautiful West MacDonnell Ranges (west macs), where you find some of the country's best gorge scenery.

Alice Springs has some fabulous art galleries specialising in Indigenous art. While some tend to focus on cheap and tacky souvenir canvases, serious buyers and investors should head to either the Gallery Gondwana or Papunya Tula Artists, both located in Todd Mall.

Established in 1990, Gallery Gondwana in Alice Springs represents artists from the Western and Central Deserts, many of whom produce their work in the gallery's Alice Springs studio. The Gallery also extends its exhibitions program to encompass the diversity of other regions, including new works by leading and emerging Aboriginal artists from remote communities around the country.

The Papunya Tula Art Movement began in 1971 when a school teacher, Geoffrey Bardon, encouraged some of the men to paint a blank school wall. The murals sparked off tremendous interest in the community and soon many men started painting and in 1972 the artists successfully established their own company, which they named after Papunya, a settlement 240km north-west of Alice Springs, and one of the hills in the immediate locality, called Tula, a Honey Ant Dreaming site. The gallery represents around 120 artists, many of whom have work hung in major galleries and museums both in Australia and overseas.

scenic highlights

The 330km Mereenie Loop Road is a three-day drive that will take you to all the icons of the Australian outback: Alice Springs, Kings Canyon and Uluru. However, as there is so much to see and do in the red centre, you should plan to spend at least two or three days in each place.

From the Alice, head west on Larapinta Drive, driving across the desert plains beside the ancient West MacDonnell Ranges. The landscape here is all about colour: rich, vibrant and primary—red rocks and sand, blue sky, yellow spinifex and purple hills. Just minutes from Alice Springs is Simpson's Gap, a spectacular cleft in the red rocky range and a few kilometres further on is Standley Chasm, less than nine metres wide and towering to a height of 80m. The best time to see it is at midday, when the sun is directly overhead and lights up the walls and floor of the rocky chasm.

Travelling this road it feels as if you have stepped inside the frame of one of Australia's famous landscape paintings. You'll pass by the once Lutheran mission, Hermannsburg, birthplace and home of aboriginal artist Albert Namatjira. His paintings of red rock and dunes, hazy purple mountains and tall desert oaks are some of the most familiar images of outback Australia and you can see some of his work at the small gallery there.

Standley Chasm. *(Tourism NT)*

An alternative route is to take Namatjira Drive via Ormiston Gorge, Glen Helen Gorge and Tnorala (Gosse Bluff) Conservation Reserve to link up with the Mereenie Loop Road near Hermannsburg. Stop for an icy dip at Ellery Creek Big Hole, an intoxicatingly beautiful swimming hole that most tourists zoom past on their way to Serpentine Gorge and the Ochre Pits. Drop into Glen Helen Gorge for a cold drink at the caravan park-cum-resort with views of the rust red gorge walls. Just opposite the resort is the turn-off to Ormiston Gorge, where there is a short walk to a beautiful sandy swimming hole.

Just west of the Hermannsburg mission is Finke Gorge National Park. You'll need a 4WD to travel the last 16km along the sandy bed of the Finke River. The highlight of this park is Palm Valley, an oasis of ancient palms that is the remnant of the tropical rainforest that once covered the interior of Australia.

From Finke Gorge, continue west towards Watarrka National Park, home to Kings Canyon, where breathtaking 300m sheer cliffs cut deep into the ground. From Kings Canyon it's bitumen all the way to Uluru. If you are returning to Alice Springs, it's a run of around 445km on an all-sealed road.

Most of the land along the Meerenie Loop Road is Aboriginal, so you need a permit to travel ($2.20). These are available from Kings Canyon Resort, CATIA office in Alice Springs and the Central Land Office in Alice Springs and must be carried with you at all times whilst travelling through Aboriginal land. No alcohol is permitted in Aboriginal communities.

The road is unsealed from Kings Canyon east to Hermannsburg and Glen Helen Gorge and not generally suitable for caravans and 4WD is recommended, although there are plans to seal the Mereenie Loop Road by 2007. If travelling before the work is finished, carry at least one spare tyre, in addition to the space saver.

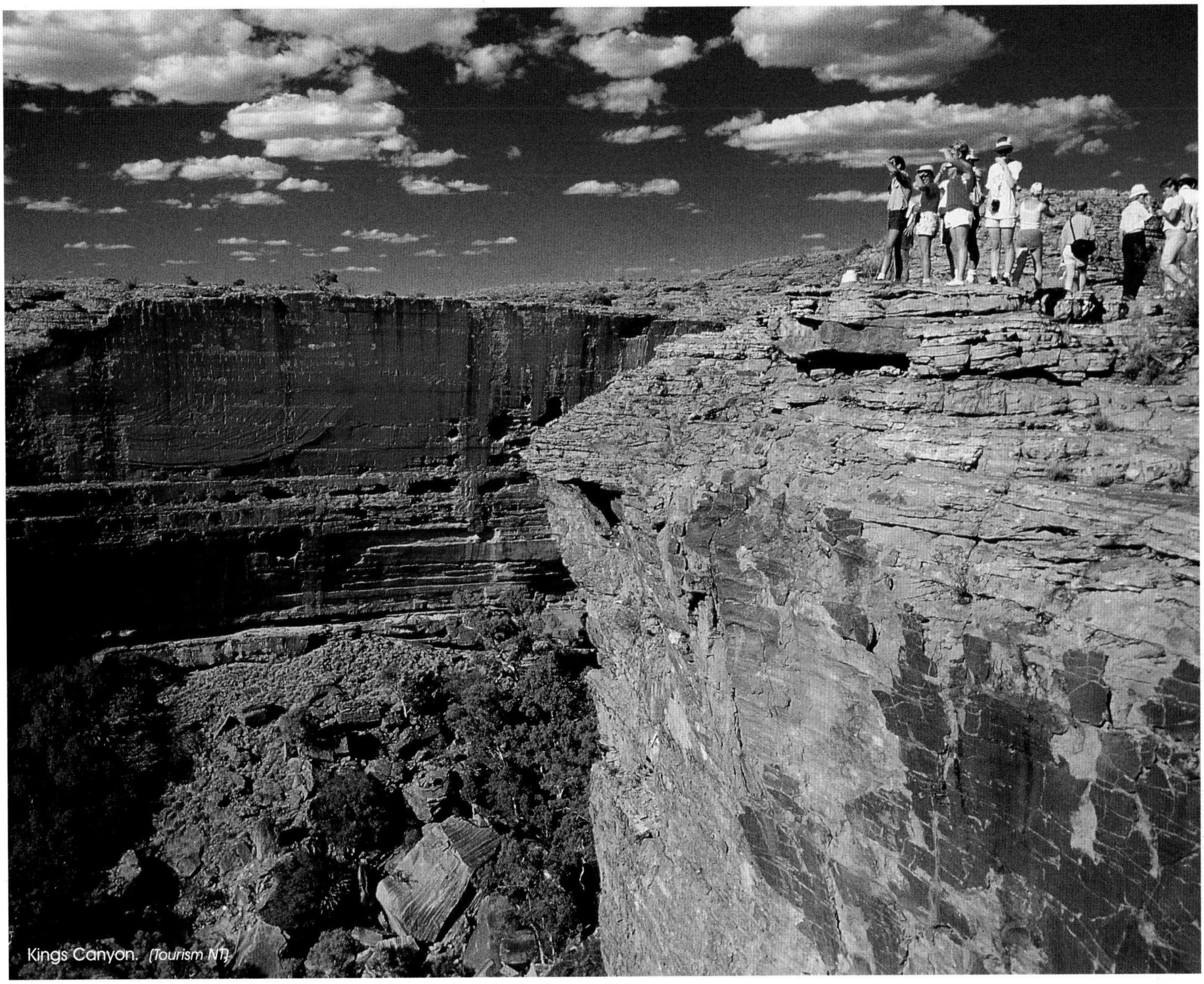

Kings Canyon. *(Tourism NT)*

Yulara

Yulara is the name for the 'village' 20km from Uluru (Ayers Rock), a collection of local services for the staff that work at Ayers Rock Resort and the visitors that stay there.

Australia's most identifiable icon, Uluru is a massive red rounded monolith rising 348m above the surrounding plains that reaches 6km below the earth's surface. The circumference measures more than 9km. The first European to see Uluru was explorer William Gosse in 1873. Its sister rock formation, Kata Tjuta, (The Olgas) which means 'many heads', is made up of 36 huge, weathered domes spread over 35km^2 and is just as impressive.

For many Uluru is a place of pilgrimage, an elemental landscape that strips away city-bred grime and attitude. Hyperbole aside, it really is that special: nobody is ever disappointed with their first glimpse of Uluru. Others come here just to madly scramble 350m up the sheer red face of the rock like small ants and then leave, just as quickly as they came. For the traditional owners, the Anangu people, Uluru, and nearby Kata Tjuta, are fundamental to their spiritual beliefs and relationship with the land. They do not climb Uluru and would prefer it if you didn't. Sunset and sunrise are the most spectacular times to visit Uluru, when the red rock takes on different colours with the changing light.

The third of the great red centre rock formations, Mt Connor (which countless first-time visitors to Uluru have mistaken for the Rock on the drive in from Alice Springs) is 100km east of Yulara, a huge flat-topped mesa rising from the desert plains. There is a good lookout just off the highway, or you can take a day tour from Yulara.

Kings Canyon

The western end of the George Gill Ranges rises sharply from the surrounding flat desert plains, producing a rugged landscape of ranges, rockholes and gorges–the best known of all being Kings Canyon in Watarrka National Park. Sculptured by the elements and rising up 100m to a plateau of rocky domes, Kings Canyon is home to one of the most dramatic short walks in the outback–the Rim Walk.

Trephina Gorge. (Tourism NT)

Caravan and camping

There are commercial camping and caravan facilities at Glen Helen Resort, Kings Canyon Resort and Ayers Rock Resort. In the west macs there are basic camping facilities at Ellery Creek Big-Hole and Redbank Gorge. Serpentine Chalet and 2-Mile (4WD only) also have camping sites with no facilities. Ormiston Gorge has camping facilities with showers and toilets.

There are also camping areas provided between Chambers Pillar and Castle Rock, at Palm Valley in Finke Gorge, Rainbow Valley and, at Ruby Gap bush camping (no facilities) along the river between the park entrance and Ruby Gap.

Bushwalks

There are a number of self-guided and ranger-guided walks available at Uluru-Kata Tjuta National Park. Two excellent Anangu-led walks are the Liru Walk and Kuniya walks. The Liru walk takes around two and a half hours but is only 2km of easy walking. It is even wheelchair accessible. It begins sitting in a *wiltja* (traditional shade structure) as an Aboriginal elder shows how to make *kiti*, a glue-like resin made from spinifex that was used to make spears and other tools, and how to ground 'flour' from grass seeds to make a traditional bread. On the rest of the walk you will learn how to make spears, spear throwers, bowls and other tools along with traditional bush skills and medicines. You will also learn about the ancient creation law and legends of Uluṟu.

The Kuniya tour, at sunset, visits Mutitjulu waterhole at the base of Uluṟu and caves with ochre and charcoal paintings. Here you will also learn about local bush foods and the Law of *Kuniya*, the sand python.

Other good self-guided shorter walks include the 1km (45 minutes return) Mutitjulu walk on the southern side of Uluṟu which takes you to a beautiful waterhole past rock art sites and the 2km (one hour) Mala walk on the north-west side of Uluṟu to the inspiring Kantju Gorge past several caves used by Anangu not so long ago. A full circuit around the base of Uluṟu is 9.8km (three to four hours) and is an excellent alternative to climbing the rock. The walk is quiet and you are unlikely to encounter large groups of people in most areas. Walk in a clockwise direction. It takes in the Mala and Mutitjulu walks along the way.

The 30-minute Dune Walk from the bus sunset car park takes you along a sand dune with views of both Uluṟu and Kata Tjuṯa. Keep an eye out for animal tracks.

The 8km 'Valley of the Winds' walk at Kata Tjuṯa winds along a rocky trail past sheer rock faces and unusual rock formations to a magnificent lookout. It can be steep, rocky and difficult in places and the walk is closed from Karu Lookout at 11am if the forecast temperature is 36°C or greater. The shorter (one hour return) Walpa Gorge trail takes you to the end of the Gorge where Spearwood vines flourish. The track gently rises as you go giving a good view of the surrounding country to the west.

The Kings Canyon Rim walk is one of the regions best half-day walks. The best time to tackle the 6km walk is either early in the morning, before the heat and flies begin to fray tempers, or late in the afternoon, when the setting sun lights up the sheer sandstone walls of the canyon to their best advantage. The first half-hour or so is a lung-busting, muscle-destroying climb up the side of the canyon, but if you can make it that far, the remainder of the two to three-hour walk is an easy stroll around the rim of the canyon where breathtaking 300m sheer cliffs cut deep into the rock. Highlights include the weathered, buttressed domes of the 'Lost City', and the 'Garden of Eden', a sheltered valley with permanent waterholes and lush vegetation.

The Larapinta Trail is an exciting long distance walking track that runs for 223km along the backbone of the West MacDonnell Ranges from Alice Springs west to Mt Sonder. It is divided into 12 sections.

There are a number of good walks in Finke Gorge. Kalaranga Lookout is an easy 20-minute climb (1.5km, 45 minute return) with spectacular views of the rock amphitheatre encircled by rugged cliffs. The Mpaara Walk, (5km, two hours return) introduces the mythology of the Western Arrernte Aboriginal culture. In Palm Valley, the Arankaia Walk (2km, one hour) and the longer Mpulungkinya Walk (5km, two hours return) meanders among lush oasis of slender palms and returns to the car park across the plateau.

Be aware that every year a number of visitors to the red centre suffer from heat stroke and heat exhaustion, so always wear a hat, strong shoes and sunscreen, walk in the cooler parts of the day and carry and drink at least one litre of water per hour.

adventure activities

Abseiling and rock climbing

Set in the desert above a dry riverbed, Ormiston Gorge is one of the NT's best climbing spots with about 30 moderate-grade routes on steep and deep red rock. The easy access, variety of great easy to moderate routes, and the swimming hole close by, have made this area a local favourite. Climbing is banned at all cliffs in the park except for Ormiston Bluff. Before climbing at Ormiston Bluff, call ahead on ☎ (08) 8956 7799 and let the rangers know you're coming, or at least book into the Rangers Station when you arrive.

Ballooning

Ballooning in the red centre is one of the country's most unforgettable experiences. Floating through the crisp dawn air, the flat, red, spinifex-studded landscape is shrouded in thin white mist. Sunlight beams behind the trees, creating crazy elongated shadows. The desert is still and quiet, and the views spectacular as you glide above the dusty plains and dry river beds that surround Alice Springs when suddenly the silence is broken by the screeching and coarse caterwauling of a flock of cockatoos and majestic red kangaroos bound across the plains beneath the floating balloon. There are a number of hot air ballooning companies based in Alice Springs that offer 30- and 60-minute dawn flights followed by champagne breakfasts in the desert.

www.outbackballooning.com.au www.balloonflights.com.au
www.ballooningdownunder.com.au

Camel safaris

Camels, ideally suited to the hot, dry climate of Australia's interior, were imported in the 19th century and remained the principal means of outback transport until railways and roads were established. Today there are an estimated 700,000 one-humped, dromedary-type camels in the wild. Ayers Rock Resort offers a range of camel safaris around Uluru including one-hour sunrise and sunset rides that include billy tea, freshly baked beer-bread (on sunrise tours) or champagne or beer and snacks (on sunset tours) as well as commentary. In addition to the sunrise and sunset tours, there's a special 'wagon' tour for those who may not be inclined to climb atop a camel but still want to experience their oddly graceful manner and unique character.

www.ayersrockresort.com.au/camel-tours

In Alice Springs, Frontier Camel Tours offer sunrise and sunset tours along the Todd River that include either a barbecue breakfast or dinner and daytime rides.

www.cameltours.com.au

The Outback Camel Company has a range of extended 10- and 14-day camel treks and even longer expeditions during the cooler winter months (April to September) through the parallel sand dunes of the Simpson Desert.

www.cameltreks.com.au

Todd River, Alice Springs. (Tourism NT)

Cycling and mountain biking

The Simpsons Gap Bicycle Path is a sealed 17km cycle path meanders between Flynns Grave on the outskirts of Alice Springs to Simpsons Gap. The path weaves cross-country with generally easy grades. The cooler months from April to October are the more pleasant for cycling. Don't use the path in hot weather as heat stress can be dangerous, even fatal. The path is open during daylight hours only as Simpsons Gap closes at 8pm. Camping is not permitted in the park.

ROC Tours (Remote Outback Cycling) combine mountain biking with four-wheel driving in a number of outback destinations, including a five-day/four-night cycling tour of the MacDonnell Ranges from Uluru to Alice Springs via Kings Canyon, Palm Valley and the West MacDonnells, cycling around half a day or around 40km at a stretch, the remainder of distance covered in 4WDs.

www.cycletours.com.au

Off-road driving

While the Lasseter Highway to Uluru and the road between Yulara and Kings Canyon, are sealed, to really explore much of the red centre you will need a 4WD. There are a vast number of local 4WD tours available from both Ayres Rock Resort and Alice Springs, most of which have access to otherwise prohibited Aboriginal lands and offer good commentary and bush tucker tours. Worth doing is the full-day 4WD safari to Cave Hill, an Aboriginal community across the state border in South Australia. The rock art found here dates back 20,000 years, and portrays the Yankunytjatjara version of the story of the Pleiades, or Seven Sisters.

www.ayersrockresort.com.au/cave-hill

If you have your own vehicle, good tracks include the Meerenie Loop Road (see scenic highlights page 378) and the track down the Finke River to Illamurta Springs and Watarrka National Park that begins at Finke Gorge. This trip requires careful planning and preparation. Talk to rangers to obtain guidance and directions before heading down the Finke River. An additional Finke 4WD information sheet is available from the Parks and Wildlife Services office in Alice Springs.

The Old Andado Track between Alice Springs and Mount Dare in the Simpson Desert is a challenging track through mountain ranges, rocky gibber plains, desert sand dunes and floodplains. You can extend this trip to include Dalhousie Springs or Finke. While the track is just less than 440km, you will need to allow at least two days to do this trip, and you will need to be prepared for anything to occur. It is very remote country so vehicles must be well equipped for emergency situations. Take sufficient fuel, food and water, as there is nowhere to stop and get supplies. You will also need recovery gear as well as some form of long distance communication such as HF Radio, or satellite phone. Camping is permitted at Old Andado and Mt Dare.

The Tanami Track is a great shortcut linking the Red Centre to the Kimberley in north-western Australia across one of Australia's great deserts–The Tanami. Although once a notorious 4WD track, it is now a graded dirt highway that offers a relatively easy, although very remote dry weather 4WD trip.

In the East MacDonnell Ranges, much of Ruby Gap National Park is extremely rugged and is only suitable for 4WD. Do not enter the Hale River if the sand is soft and wet after recent heavy rain. In the event of a mishap, stay with your vehicle. Do not attempt to walk back to Arltunga. The Hale River is susceptible to flash flooding following heavy rain. If it begins to rain heavily leave the park immediately. Do not attempt to cross flooded creeks. Wait on high grounds for creeks to recede. The Parks and Wildlife Service provides a 4WD Registration Scheme–you can register with credit card details by telephoning 1300 650 730 for the cost of a local call.

The Plenty Highway is an 830km sandy track from Alice Springs east to Boulia in western Queensland. On the Northern Territory side it is fairly well maintained, but is impassable when wet when the red sand soil turns to tyre-sucking mud. The flat red plains burst into bloom after rain when wildflowers such as billy buttons, bush daisies, poached egg daisies, yellow tops and native violets carpet the sides of the road where water collects in the gutters. Highlights include Trephina Gorge and John Huges Rockholes, Corroboree Rock and Emily and Jessie Gaps in the East McDonnell Ranges, the Hartz Range, Mt Palmer, gemstone fossicking areas and vast outback cattle stations.

Motor cycle tours

Explore the desert around Uluru on the back of a late model Heritage Softail Harley Davidson on a 90-minute Uluru Motorcycles Tour. Tours operate on demand and depart from Ayres Rock Resort 45 minutes before sunrise or sunset and include tea or coffee and hot croissants whilst viewing the sunrise or sunset.

www.ayersrockresort.com.au/Uluru-motorcycles

Central Oz Motorcycle Adventures, based in Alice Springs, also offer a range of escorted self-ride and passenger Harley tours to Uluru, through the west macs and even as far afield as Darwin. Tours range from one hour to seven days.

www.centraloz.biz

Alice Springs Motorcycle Tours also offer sightseeing tours of Alice Springs and surrounds from the back of a Harley.

www.aliceharley.com.au

Simpsons Gap. *(Tourism NT)*

Quad bikes

Blaze your own trail through the desert on a quad bike with Desert Quads, based in Alice Springs. They offer two tours: a two-hour guided Trail Blazer tour along a maze of sandy desert tracks, and the three-and-a-half-hour Outback Explorer tour across beautiful sand hills to an outback waterhole.

www.desertquads.com.au

Outback Quad Adventures, also in Alice Springs run quad bike tours at Undoolya Station, the oldest working station in the NT, 17km east of the town centre and overnight quad bike camping safaris between Undoolya and the neighbouring station, The Gardens.

www.outbackquadadventures.com.au

You can also ride quad bikes at Kings Creek Station near Kings Canyon, (motor cycle and camel safaris also available).

www.kingscreekstation.com.au

Scenic flights

The best way to really see the majesty of Uluru is from the air, and most commercial flights will point out the monolith if cloud cover permits, so try and get a seat on the right-hand side of the aircraft. For a more close-up aerial view, you can take a helicopter flight over Uluru from Ayers Rock Resort with Ayers Rock Helicopters. The 15-minute Rock Blasting flight takes off from a launch near Uluru and give good views of the Ayers Rock Resort, the waterhole Mutitjulu and the surrounding desert. The longer 30-minute flight offers the same views of the first but also include a bird's eye view of Uluru all the way to the rock formations of Kata Tjuta.

Murray Cosson's Australian Outback Flights in Alice Springs has a range of scenic flights available, including a full-day flight tour along the spectacular MacDonnell Ranges, past Gosse Bluff meteorite crater and on to Kings Canyon before flying over the great salt lake to Uluru and Kata Tjuta. Price includes a rental car at Uluru with lunch at the Ayers Rock Resort, before a leisurely flight back to Alice Springs, arriving before dark. The eight-hour Kings Canyon scenic flight flies along the West MacDonnell Ranges, over the crater and on past Kings Canyon to Kings Creek station, before heading by bus to Kings Canyon for climbing and sightseeing, lunch and the flight home.

www.australianoutbackflights.com.au

Helicopter tours are also available at Kings Canyon and Kings Creek Station. The 15-minute aerial tour flies over the canyon, the domes of the Lost City and the Garden of Eden, then along Kings Creek and over to Carmichael Crag. A longer 30-minute trip includes the spectacular cliffs of the George Gill Range to Carmichael Crag before returning via the Hidden Valley.

www.kingscanyonresort.com.au/helicopter-tours
www.kingscreekstation.com.au

Kings Canyon scenic flight. *(Tourism NT)*

MORE INFORMATION

- **CATIA Visitor Information Centre:** Gregory Terrace, Alice Springs. www.centralaustraliantourism.com
- **Northern Territory Tourism:** www.ntexplore.com.au ☎ (08) 8952 5800
- **Northern Territory Parks and Wildlife Service:** www.nt.gov.au/nreta/parks/ ☎ (08) 8951 8250

weather watch

- January: 22–37°C
- July: 4–19°C
- The temperature range is extreme. Winter days may be warm but nights can get very cold so take a warm jacket.

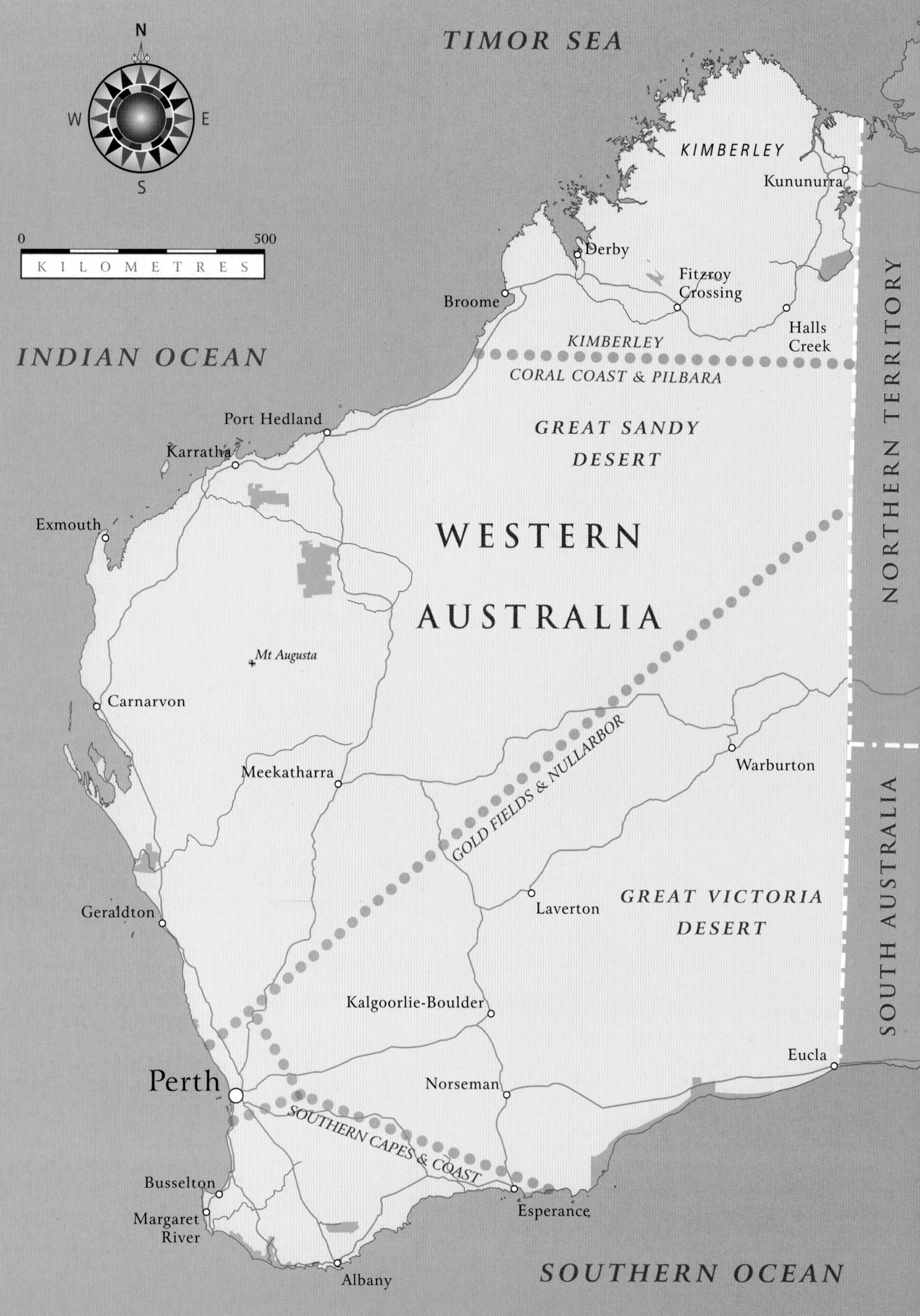

N
W
E
S
0
500
KILOMETRES
TIMOR SEA
INDIAN OCEAN
SOUTHERN OCEAN
WESTERN AUSTRALIA
NORTHERN TERRITORY
SOUTH AUSTRALIA
KIMBERLEY
Kununurra
Derby
Fitzroy Crossing
Broome
Halls Creek
KIMBERLEY
CORAL COAST & PILBARA
GREAT SANDY DESERT
Port Hedland
Karratha
Exmouth
Mt Augusta
Carnarvon
Meekatharra
GOLD FIELDS & NULLARBOR
Warburton
Laverton
GREAT VICTORIA DESERT
Geraldton
Kalgoorlie-Boulder
Eucla
Perth
Norseman
SOUTHERN CAPES & COAST
Busselton
Margaret River
Esperance
Albany

Australia's largest state is isolated from the eastern states by the inhospitable central deserts. Perth is the world's most isolated capital city. Most of the population live in the reasonably fertile south-west corner of the state, beyond that there are long empty spaces of sandy arid wilderness dotted with small mining communities and ghost towns, reminders of mineral booms and gold rushes past. Indeed, the state survives on the wealth of minerals beneath the surface. The coast is just as lonely as the interior, a long coastal highway links fishing and mining communities heading north to the spectacular wild gorges of the Kimberley, a place so remote that some of it still remains unexplored.

perth & surrounds

Perth's Swan River. *(WATC)*

Fremantle's West End. *(WA Tourism Commission)*

► WESTERN AUSTRALIA'S CAPITAL is a city that, no matter where you are, you're never far from water. The city centre straddles the Swan River at one of its widest points, and beachside suburbs stretch out in either direction along the cerulean blue Indian Ocean. With an average of eight hours of sunshine per day, Perth enjoys more hours of sunshine than any other capital city in Australia, so it's easy to see why most of the action happens in the great outdoors.

Founded by Captain James Stirling in 1829 as a free settlement when it was feared that the French would colonise the western coast of the continent, the Swan River settlement struggled until 1850 when the first shipment of convicts arrived. The discovery of gold in and around Kalgoorlie in the 1880s gave the fledging city a boost, as did the more recent diamond finds in the Kimberley.

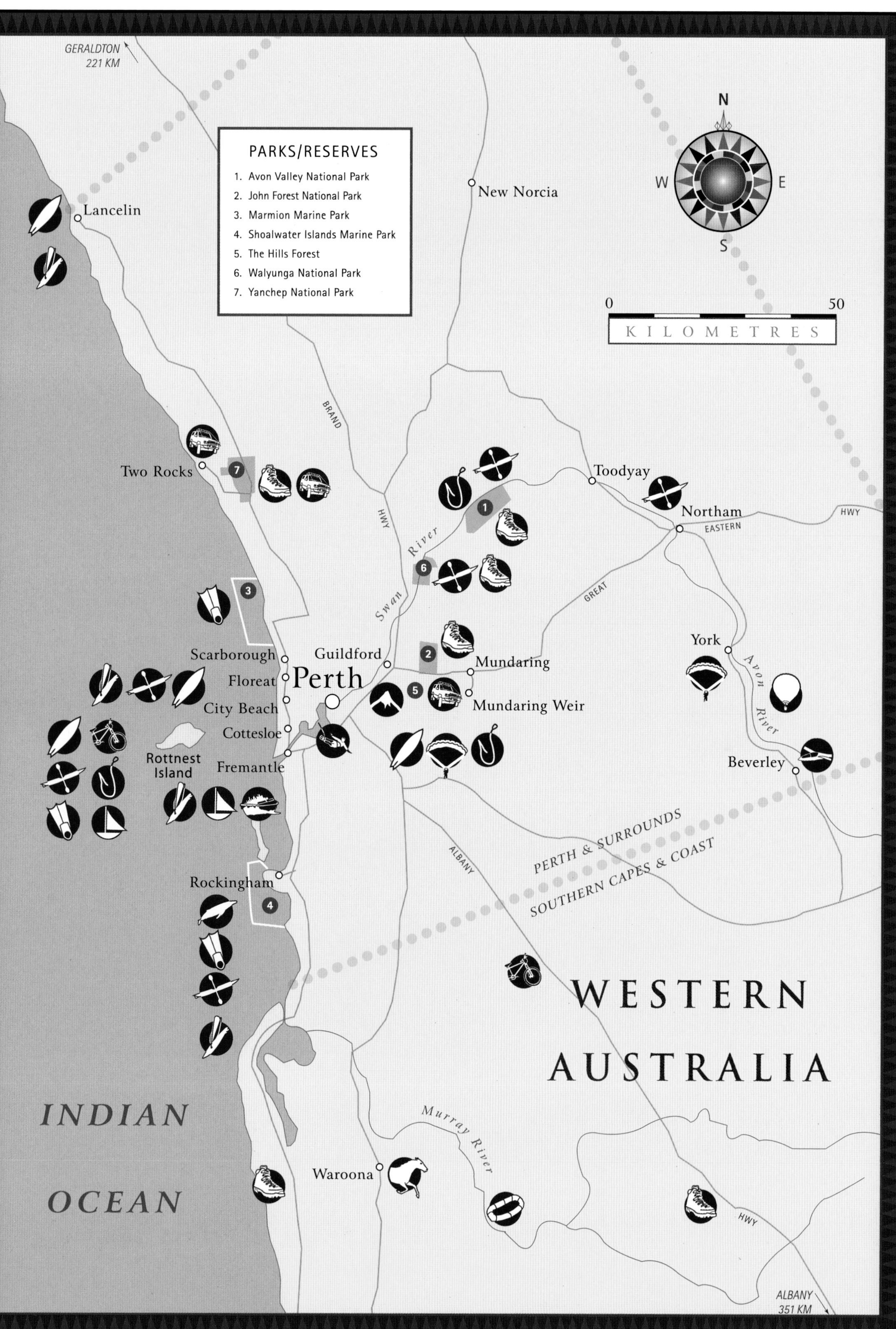

GERALDTON
221 KM
PARKS/RESERVES
1. Avon Valley National Park
2. John Forest National Park
3. Marmion Marine Park
4. Shoalwater Islands Marine Park
5. The Hills Forest
6. Walyunga National Park
7. Yanchep National Park
N
W
E
S
0
50
KILOMETRES
Lancelin
New Norcia
Two Rocks
BRAND
HWY
Toodyay
Northam
EASTERN
HWY
GREAT
Swan River
Scarborough
Guildford
Perth
Floreat
City Beach
Cottesloe
Mundaring
Mundaring Weir
York
Avon River
Rottnest Island
Fremantle
Beverley
ALBANY
PERTH & SURROUNDS
SOUTHERN CAPES & COAST
Rockingham
WESTERN
AUSTRALIA
INDIAN
OCEAN
Murray River
Waroona
HWY
ALBANY
351 KM

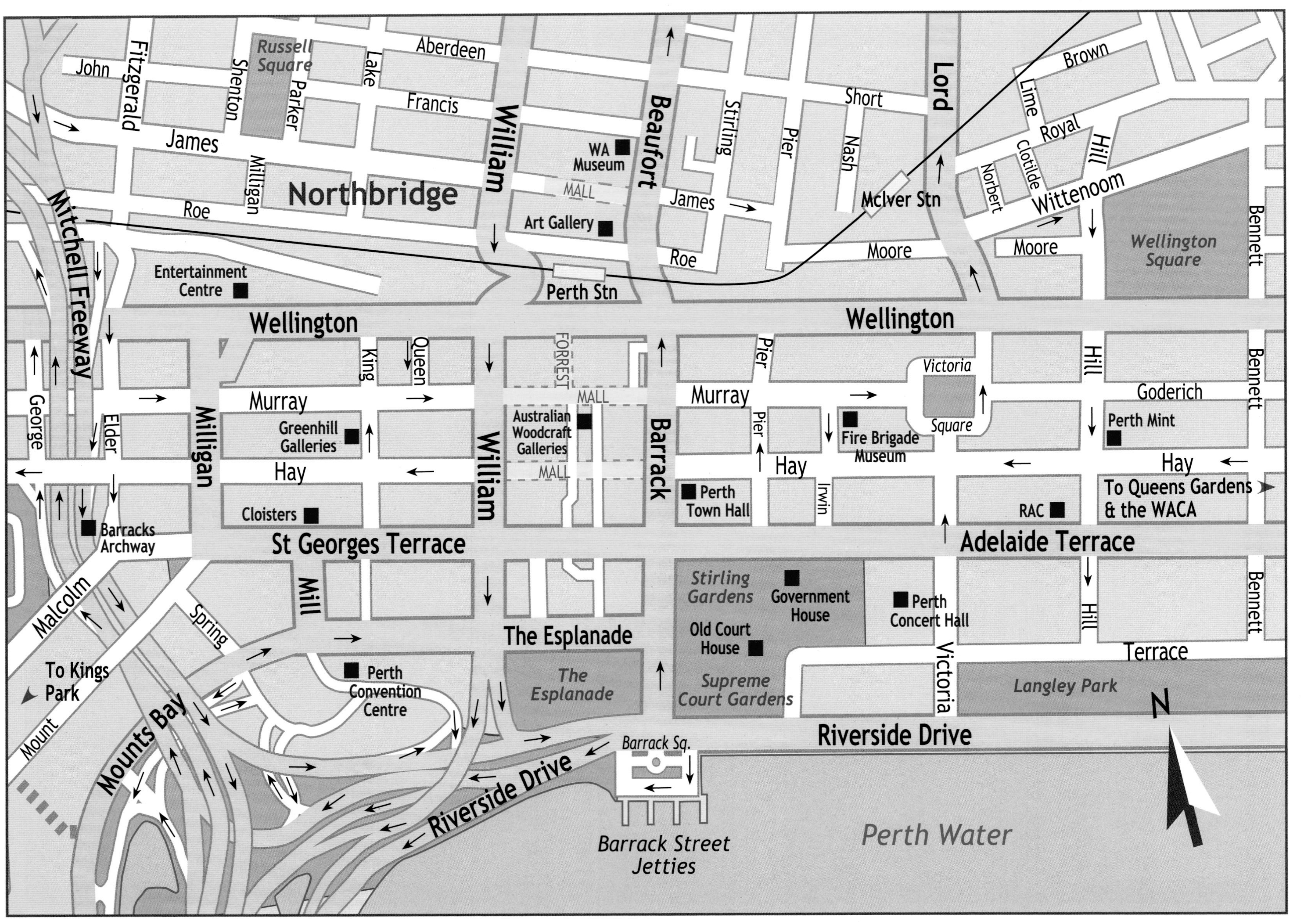

John
Fitzgerald
Russell Square
Shenton
Parker
Lake
Aberdeen
Francis
James
Milligan
Northbridge
William
WA Museum
MALL
Art Gallery
Beaufort
Stirling
Pier
Nash
Short
Lord
Brown
Lime
Royal
Clotilde
Norbert
Hill
Wittenoom
James
McIver Stn
Roe
Roe
Moore
Moore
Wellington Square
Bennett
Mitchell Freeway
Entertainment Centre
Perth Stn
Wellington
Wellington
King
Queen
FORREST
Pier
Victoria
Square
Hill
Bennett
Murray
Murray
MALL
Goderich
Perth Mint
George
Elder
Milligan
Greenhill Galleries
Australian Woodcraft Galleries
Barrack
Pier
Fire Brigade Museum
Hay
Hay
MALL
Hay
Cloisters
William
Perth Town Hall
Irwin
RAC
To Queens Gardens & the WACA
Barracks Archway
St Georges Terrace
Adelaide Terrace
Malcolm
Spring
Mill
The Esplanade
Stirling Gardens
Government House
Perth Concert Hall
Hill
Bennett
Old Court House
Terrace
To Kings Park
Perth Convention Centre
The Esplanade
Supreme Court Gardens
Victoria
Langley Park
N
Mount
Mounts Bay
Barrack Sq.
Riverside Drive
Riverside Drive
Perth Water
Barrack Street Jetties

City centre

The city centre is a mix of elegant colonial architecture and modern steel and glass towers. The CBD is compact and easily explored on foot, bounded by the loops of the Swan River and the city's crowning glory, its many parks and gardens which run along the banks of the river. Ask any local what's the first thing you should do in Perth and they'll straight away say 'Kings Park'. Set beside the Swan River in the heart of the city, the 406 hectare (roughly 1000 acres) park is the heart, lungs and soul of the city. A mix of bushland, botanic gardens, walkways and grassy lawns it's the place to go for lunch-time strolls and weekend picnics or barbecues. In spring, the park is home to some of the most impressive wildflower displays in the state and in summer, an outdoor cinema. Don't miss the Federation Walkway, which extends 620m through the Botanic Garden along a combination of on-ground pathways and a spectacular elevated 52m glass and steel arched bridge suspended amongst a canopy of tall eucalypts. Getting around is easy with an extensive network of shared, off-road cycle and pedestrian paths linking the city to surrounding suburbs.

City beaches

When not kicking a ball or taking a stroll in the park, you'll find the locals at one of the 19 city beaches. Cottesloe, just 15 minutes from the city centre, is a favourite, with its bustling cafes and children's playgrounds drawing young crowds and families for body boarding, surfing and snorkelling. City Beach and Floreat Beach are also excellent for body boarding and sunset beach fishing. You can find calm river beaches on the Swan at Peppermint Grove and Crawley, but surfers head further north to Scarborough Beach and Trigg Island, 15 minutes north-west of the city. The best time to go is in the morning, before the afternoon breezes kick in, unless of course you are a windsurfer, sailor or kitesurfer. The regular south-east sea breeze, the 'Fremantle Doctor' is a sailor's best friend and welcomed by land lubbers when it blows away the stifling summer heat.

Fremantle

The historic port of Fremantle is less than half an hour from the city centre. One of the best-preserved examples of a 19th-century port streetscape in the world, Fremantle has WA's largest collection of Heritage-listed buildings. It a popular place to go on weekends for markets, dozens of bookshops, boutiques and homeware stores, a brewery, countless cafes, restaurants and pubs, or to feast on fish and chips while wandering around the Fishing Boat Harbour.

Kings Park. *(WATC)*

John Forrest National Park. *(WATC)*

NATIONAL PARKS

Walyunga National Park: in the heart of the Darling Range, covers both sides of a deep valley. The river forms a string of placid pools along the valley floor in summer and a raging torrent with series of rapids in winter. In winter and spring this is one of the best places to see wildflowers. Walyunga contains one of the largest known Aboriginal campsites around Perth and used by the Nyoongar people until the 20th century. Archaeological evidence suggests that local tribes used the area for more than 6000 years.

Avon Valley National Park: the northern limit of the jarrah forests is an hour's drive north of Perth. The Avon River churns over spectacular rapids in winter and spring, home to the famous Avon Descent canoe race each August. During summer and autumn the river shrinks to a series of pools in a bed of granite boulders and tea-tree thickets.

The Hills Forest: 80,000 hectares of rolling hills in the Darling Ranges between the Great Eastern Highway and Brookton Highway, it includes state forest, five national parks, the Mt Dale Conservation Park and the picturesque Mundaring Weir area. The Hills Forest Discovery Centre is a focal point for activities.

John Forrest National Park: north of The Hills Forest, east of Perth, this is Western Australia's first national park, established in 1898 to conserve its many natural and cultural features. Highlights include magnificent views of the Swan coastal plain, walking trails through rugged wilderness along an old railway line or quiet pools and spectacular waterfalls.

Penguin Island: 42km from Perth, this small island in the Shoalwater Islands Marine Park, off shore from Rockingham boasts the largest colony of little penguins on the west coast. Since 1998 it has become one of the few breeding colonies of Australian pelican (*Pelicanus conspicillatus*). Ferry tours operate hourly from Mersey Point, mid-September to early June, or cruise Shoalwater Bay to view sea lions lazing on Seal Island. Penguin Island is limited to walk trails and demarcated beaches only. The rest of the island is a bird sanctuary and access is prohibited.

Yanchep National Park: includes pristine wetlands, a pretty freshwater lake, one of WA's largest koala colonies, limestone caves and a stunning array of wildflowers. Alongside the popular koala exhibits is the new Wangi Mia (talking place) offering a range of Nyoongar Aboriginal cultural experiences.

scenic highlights

New Norcia. (LA)

New Norcia, about 90 minutes drive north of Perth, is Australia's only privately-owned monastic town. It was founded in 1846 by Spanish Benedictine monks as a mission for the local Aboriginal people with the aim to create a largely self-sufficient village based on agriculture. More than 150 years later, it is still a working monastery, with 15 Benedictine monks in residence who adhere strictly to the abbey rules: no women allowed; prayer seven times a day; work or study in between; silence after 8pm. Although these days, the mission and four schools that catered for the local indigenous and settlers' children have long closed, and the main business of the town is tourism and the renowned New Norcia bakery.

New Norcia attracts thousands of visitors each year, most of whom come to marvel at the traditional mission architecture that rises from the surrounding parched grazing lands like a shimmering Spanish mirage, tour the abbey, museum and art gallery, and buy some of the delicious New Norcia bread, rich nut cakes and slightly sinful *pan chocolatti* that are cooked in a traditional wood-fired oven in the abbey bakery.

There are 27 heritage buildings in the town, in a variety of architectural styles and scale, including Spanish Mission, Gothic, Byzantine and Georgian.

Guided tours take around two hours, and include a history of the mission and tours of the historic college buildings, abbey church and monk's private chapel covered in beautiful frescos with ornately carved altar pieces. The museum and art gallery are also popular attractions, full of paintings by Spanish and Italian masters, including a tapestry cartoon by Raphael; gifts from the Queen of Spain; a collection of modern religious art and a fascinating array of artefacts and memorabilia.

Although most visitors come to New Norcia for the day, you can stay overnight and join the monks at any of the scheduled prayer services, which start at 5.15am. Most people, however, join the monks for mass at 7.30am in the Abbey Church, a classic example of what happens when Mediterranean architecture meets the Aussie bush—all lovely stonework, mud plaster, rough hewn trees and wooden shingles. Inside, you'll find the painting of Our Lady of Good Counsel, New Norcia's own miracle. In 1847 a bushfire threatened New Norcia and the founding abbott, Dom Salvado, grabbed the painting and pointed at the flames while praying. To the amazement of all, particularly the local Aborigines, the wind promptly changed direction and the bushfire burnt itself out. You can buy copies of the miraculous painting in the gift shop, where the image of Our Lady graces posters, T-shirts, post-cards and fridge magnets.

Swan Valley

Just a cork's pop from Perth, less than 30 minutes drive, the Swan Valley, Western Australia's oldest wine growing region, is often overlooked in favour of its big brother in the wine stakes, the Margaret River. But the 30 or so wineries in this pretty valley cut through by the lazy Swan River produce some very good chardonnay, shiraz, chenin blanc, verdelho and fortified wines, without much of the wine snobbery that you find in the glitzy cellar doors in the south of the state.

The best way to explore the Swan Valley is on the signposted, 32km Swan Valley Drive. It begins and ends in Guildford, which is 15km from the city via the Great Eastern Highway. Browse the antique shops that line the stately main street and visit Guildford Village Potters, a co-op of 21 potters.

Perth Hills

Take a half hour drive out to the region known as the Perth Hills, the western slopes of the Darling Range, and you'll feel as if you've left the city far behind. Mundaring is most well known for its weir, built in the 1890s to provide water for the Goldfields Water Scheme that still pumps water 400km to Kalgoorlie. Today the weir is a popular picnic spot and you can visit the museum in the No.1 Pump Station on Sunday afternoons.

Stop for a drink in the historic Mundaring Weir Hotel, or browse the very good selection of local art in the Mundaring Arts Centre, before heading off on the Bickely Valley Wine Trail, a picturesque sign-posted trail that winds through the valley visiting 11 wineries. The annual Bickley and Carmel Valleys Harvest Festival is held each May and includes performances, lunches and events at many of the wineries along the trail.

Maritime Museum. (WATC)

DON'T MISS

- **Aquarium of Western Australia (AQWA):** wander down the 98m tunnel aquarium and check out the thousands of colourful fish, sharks and stingrays as they glide around you. For an even closer look, head to the Discovery Pool, where you can touch the sharks and stingrays. Qualified divers can pay extra for a guaranteed face-to-face shark experience. 91 Southside Drive, Hillarys Boat Harbour, Perth. Open daily, 10am–5pm. www.aqwa.com.au
- **Berndt Museum of Anthropology:** one of Australia's best collections of traditional and contemporary Australian Aboriginal art and artefacts. University of Western Australia. 35 Stirling Highway, Crawley. Open Mon and Wed 2pm–4.30pm; Fri 10am–2pm. www.berndt.uwa.edu.au
- **Museum of Western Australia:** gallery of Aboriginal culture; a marine gallery with the skeleton of a 25m (82ft) blue whale; a gallery of dinosaurs and a good collection of meteorites, including Australia's largest. The museum complex also includes Perth's original prison, built in 1856 and used until 1888. Perth Cultural Centre, James Street, Perth. Open daily, 9.30am–5pm. www.museum.wa.gov.au
- **Swan Bells Tower:** one of the largest musical instruments on earth, housing the 12 bells of Saint Martin in the Fields church. Displays on the history of the bells and bell ringing, as well as stunning views. Barrack Street, Perth. Open daily, 10am–4pm. www.swanbells.com.au
- **Perth Observatory:** Australia's oldest continuously operating professional observatory. 337 Walnut Road, Bickley. Star viewing nights, daytime guided tours—bookings essential. www.wa.gov.au/perthobs ☎ (08) 9293 8255.
- **Western Australian Maritime Museum:** highlights include the 1983 America's Cup winner, *Australia II*, with its famous winged keel. Discover treasure at the Shipwreck Galleries, explore inside a submarine, and check out the sights of Fremantle's historic 'West End' maritime precinct. Victoria Quay, Fremantle. Open daily, 9.30am–5pm. www.museum.wa.gov.au
- **Fremantle Motor Museum:** featuring cars and motorcycles from the dawn of motoring to the present and includes pieces ranging from an 1898 De Dion to the Williams driven by 1980 Formula 1 World Champion Alan Jones. B Shed, Victoria Quay, Fremantle. Open daily, 9.30am–5pm. www.fremantlemotormuseum.net
- **Fremantle Prison:** built by convicts in the 1850s and closed in 1991 after 136 years of use, it now offers several tours including a spooky night-time candlelight tour and adventure tours through the labyrinth of tunnels 20m underneath the prison. The Terrace, Fremantle. Open daily, 10am–5pm. www.fremantleprison.com.au
- **Guildford Village Potters:** located next door to the Guildford Visitors Information Centre. Open Mon–Fri 9.30am–3pm; weekends and public holidays 9.30am–4pm.
- **Maali Mia Aboriginal Cultural Centre and Art Gallery:** paintings, artefacts, hand-made gifts. West Swan Road, Henley Brook. Open daily, 10am–5pm.
- **Swan Valley Cheese Company:** a boutique cheese factory producing a range of gourmet cheeses. Watch the cheese being made while you taste. Great Northern Highway, Herne Hill. Open daily, 10am–5pm.
- **Woodbridge Historic Home:** National Trust property built in 1883 by prominent farmer, newspaper proprietor and parliamentarian, Charles Harper. Ford Street, West Midland. Open daily 1pm–4pm (except Wed, Christmas Day and Good Friday). Closed in July.
- **Whiteman Park:** 2400-hectare reserve including a conservation area with walking trails. Also inside the park are a vintage electric tramway, a bushland railway and motor, bus and tractor museums. Picnic areas and village, including craft shops and a cafe. Open Wed–Sat, 10am–4pm and Sunday and public holidays, 10am–5pm.
- **Caversham Wildlife Park:** wide range of native and exotic fauna, and shady picnic and barbecue areas. Kiosk for light refreshments. Cnr Arthur and Cranleigh Street, West Swan. Open daily, 9am–5pm.
- **New Norcia Museum and Art Gallery:** community of Benedictine monks with 27 buildings classified by the National Trust. The buildings house richly decorated interiors, furnishings and post Renaissance art. www.newnorcia.wa.edu.au

Fremantle Prison. (WATC)

Avon Valley. *(WATC)*

Rottnest Island

When Perth locals want to escape the city for a night or two, they head for Rottnest Island. 'Rotto', 18km off the coast of Perth, is renowned for snorkelling, diving, surfing, fishing, boating and swimming in crystal bays, as well as its resident quokkas. They are almost unique to the island and resemble small kangaroos. Vehicles are not permitted on the island, but visitors can hire bicycles and pedal from bay to bay or catch the bus. Day tours and cruises are available, and if you're planning to stay overnight you'll need to book well in advance. Indeed, in a great example of Aussie egalitarianism, during peak holiday times, the accommodation is allocated by ballot.

Caravan and camping

You can camp in Walyunga National Park but you'll need to arrange it with the Ranger first. Contact the Swan Office of Conservation and Land Management (CALM).

☎ (08) 9368 4399

In Avon Valley National Park there are basic camping sites with wood barbecues, picnic tables and pit toilets. Water is available in the Bald Hill and Homestead camping areas. The steep and rough roads are not suitable for caravans and trailers. Bush camping is also available in most other national parks in the region. In New Norcia, there are tent and caravan stopover (with power) sites located behind the roadhouse.

☎ (08) 9654 8020

Bushwalks

Learn about Aboriginal myths and legends and see Walyunga's plants and animals through the eyes of the original inhabitants on the 45-minute Aboriginal Heritage Trail that meanders along the riverbank, between Walyunga Pool and Boogarup Pool. Other good walks in the park include a medium 5.2km, 2.5-hour return walk to Syd's Rapids along the grassy floodplain of the Swan River. The Kangaroo Trail is a medium 4km, two-hour loop that traverses granite outcrops and the 8.5km (four-hour loop) Kingfisher Trail is a medium walk with diverse plant life. The more challenging 10.6km (five hours) Echidna Trail gives breathtaking panoramas across the Swan and Avon Valleys.

Follow the old railway track, in John Forrest National Park, from the main picnic area to Hovea Falls or wander north-west to National Park Falls. Just past the falls is WA's only 'true' railway tunnel, the Swan View Tunnel built in 1893 is a major feature on the 10km John Forrest Heritage Trail through the park. A trail continues along the northern side of Jane Brook to Rocky Pool, where you can cross the creek and return along the John Forrest Heritage Trail. The falls and creek usually flow from the beginning of winter to about the end of October.

In the Avon Valley there is a nice riverside walk that begins at the picnic area at the end of 41 Mile Road.

The award-winning Bibbulmun Track is one of the world's longest walking trails stretching 1000km from Kalamunda in the Perth Hills to the south coast of WA. The track takes walkers through towering karri and tingle forests, down misty valleys, over giant granite boulders and along stunning coastal heathlands.

www.perthtrails.com.au

adventure activities

Hills Forest, Mundaring. (WATC)

Abseiling and rock climbing

Within a 100km radius of the city there are some 700 rock climbing routes offering a great variety of climbing from delicate slabs to cracks and steep walls. There are more than a dozen crags and quarries and about half a dozen boulder areas scattered throughout the Perth Hills. One of the most popular sites is Boya Quarry. Adventure Out and Live Adrenalin both offer one-day introductory abseiling and rock climbing days at Boya (Mountain Quarry) or Gooseberry Hill (Statham's Quarry).

www.adventureout.com.au www.adrenalin.com.au

Ballooning

The hot and windy summer weather in Western Australia between December and March is unsuitable for ballooning, but conditions are perfect in the cooler months. Windward Balloon Adventures conduct champagne balloon flights daily over the picturesque Avon Valley, Western Australia from April to late November.

www.windwardballooning.com

Bungy jumping

Leap from a 40m-high tower attached to a bungy cord at Bungee West, over looking Bibra Lake near Perth. Bungee West also offers abseiling from the top of the tower as a slightly more sedate alternative to the bungy jump.

www.bungeewest.com ☎ (08) 9417 2500

Camel safaris

Take a camel trek through native Australian bush of the Darling Scarp at the Calamunnda Camel Farm, set on 10 acres in the state forest east of Perth. Enjoy either a short camel ride or an extended camel trek. In season, you'll see magnificent displays of wildflowers, also native banksias, eucalypts, casuarinas, grass trees and age-old cycads. The forest echoes to the calls of native birds you'll often encounter kangaroos and wallabies as the camels carry you quietly through the forest.

www.camelfarm.com

Canoeing and kayaking

One of the world's greatest river races, the Avon Descent is a time trial for paddle craft and power dinghy craft covering 134km of the Avon and Swan Rivers, held annually in August. The event begins in the town of Northam, passes through Toodyay and the Avon Valley and Walyunga NatioÓal Parks and finishes at Riverside Gardens Reserve, Bayswater in Perth. First held in 1973 with just 49 competitors, no rules, no officials, no checkpoints and very few spectators, in the years since more than 25,000 people have competed in the Avon Descent, from novices and families to World and Olympic Champions.

www.avondescent.com.au

Race aside, the Avon offers experienced canoeists a great run through national parks facing grade 2 and 3 rapids. Ride the famous Bells Falls and experience some of the best white water in the world.

Snorkelling with sharks. *(AQWA)*

There are plenty of other locations for paddlers around Perth. Paddle the Swan River, along the limestone cliffs of Blackwall Reach–a popular 10m cliff jump into the river–or cruise the shoreline of Fremantle.

Hire a sea kayak and head out to the islands off Rockingham in the Shoalwater Islands Marine Park where you can view sea lions, penguins and dolphins. The more experienced paddler can head out to Rottnest Island, where coral reefs and isolated bays are waiting to be explored. Closer to shore, you can ride the waves at popular Trigg and Scarborough Beaches or explore the coastline's coves in a surf ski.

Between November and March, Western Blue Sea kayak run paddling trips to Penguin Island, home to Western Australia's largest colony of Little Penguins. See prolific birdlife, sea lions and dolphins as you discover places only accessible by kayak and take a guided snorkel in Shoalwater Islands Marine Park. Small groups with personalised service, friendly, experienced and knowledgeable guides promise a most memorable experience.

www.westernblue.com.au

Capricorn Kayak Tours also run paddling trips to Penguin and Seal Islands as well as Rottnest Island from November to April.

www.capricornkayak.com.au

Cycling and mountain biking

Nyoongar for 'path through the forest', the Munda Biddi Trail is a long-distance mountain bike (and walking) trail that will eventually reach from Mundaring near Perth to Albany. About one third of the distance will be on old railway formations making it one of the longest rail trails in the world. The first 332km section from Mundaring to Collie was finished in July 2004 and winds through ancient jarrah forests.

Pedal Oz has a number for cycling tours around Perth including packages for the Munda Biddi Trail, providing transport to and from the track, mountain bikes, camping equipment, panniers, repair and first aid kits, maps and satellite phones.

www.pedaloz.com.au

Dwellingup Adventures offer day or overnight, self-guided, supported tours to explore both the Munda Biddi Trail and local surrounds. Hire by the day to explore the forests and river valleys that make Dwellingup an ideal mountain biking destination.

www.dwellingupadventures.com.au

Cycling is the best way to get around Rottnest Island as no private vehicles are allowed on the island. Take you own or hire before arriving on the island.

www.rottnestexpress.com.au

Kitesurfing on Rottnest Island. (John Carter)

Diving

Marmion Marine Park lies offshore from Perth's northern suburbs, between Trigg Island and Burns Beach, and is a favourite diving and snorkelling spot. The reefs have ledges, caves and swim-throughs and are inhabited by an array of fish species and colourful invertebrates. Highlights include Boyinaboat Reef, just 75m from the sea wall of Hillarys Boat Harbour. Caverns in the reef provide homes for many fish. Offshore from Little Island, sponges, gorgonians, hydroids, sea urchins and sea squirts crowd beneath ledges and into caves, and sea lions laze on the island's beach, sometimes joining divers in the water. The seagrass meadows that grow in sandy areas around the island support a huge range of animals such as bailer shells. Little Island, North Lump, Wreck Rock, Cow Rocks and many other submerged reefs within the marine park are also favourite diving destinations. The *Centaur* was wrecked on the southernmost section of Marmion Reef in 1874.

Other good spots include Mettams Pool, a calm snorkelling spot 30 minutes from the city, ideal for families and beginners and Rottnest Island where there's a range of good diving and snorkelling locations. The Rottnest Shipwreck Trail tells stories of the 14 shipwrecks found along its coast–there are information plaques on the ocean bed.

Cavernous reefs, seagrass meadows and even more shipwrecks surround the islands of Shoalwater Marine Park, just an hour south of Perth. You'll find more sea lions here, and penguins. The cavernous reefs around the Penguin Islands provide good snorkelling and diving. The reef areas support a variety of temperate and subtropical marine life including sea stars, urchins and molluscs as well as a number of fish species.

Dolphin and whale watching

Between September and May, Rockingham Dolphins conduct trips in the shallows of nearby bays to go swimming with some of the 180 wild bottlenose dolphins that inhabit the local area. Once the dolphins have been located, it's on with mask and snorkel and you jump in the water with the wild animals. It's a wild encounter, so there are no guarantees, but the wildlife are consistent in their habits and successful encounters are reliable. Only one swim tour per day is conducted to ensure the dolphins remain wild. Tours includes wetsuits, snorkelling gear, a light lunch, refreshments and return transport to Perth.

www.dolphins.com.au

Fishing

Perth's surf beaches offer some great fishing for tommy ruff, tailor and mullet, especially when the tailor run, in summer. Fish the sand holes between the inshore reefs for tarwhine and yellow-finned whiting in summer. The Swan River estuary is good for tailor and black bream and there is great fishing around Rottnest Island, which is best known for tommy ruff and Australian salmon in autumn.

Kings Park. (WATC)

Off-road driving

A popular 4WD track close to Perth is the challenging 12.5km section of the Powerline Track near Mundaring, which follows the powerline service track through a series of steep valleys. In summer, when the track is dry it can be deeply rutted; in winter it's wet, slippery, muddy and very boggy. A challenging day trip is the back route from Mundaring to York, along the Powerline Track and the Wandoo Woodlands conservation area. For good sand driving head to the dunes of Wilbinga just north of Perth past Yanchep and Two Rocks. A popular spot with local 4WD clubs you can have some fun on all kinds of sand including sandy tracks, soft ruts, uneven sand hills, sand dunes, seasonal beach driving, steep ascents and descents.

Gliding

Beverley Soaring Society offer trial instructional glider flights and pilot training through to cross-country flying and racing most weekends, 130km east of Perth. Part of the Gliding Federation of Australia, they also provide a structured program of solo flying training where you can learn to fly at your own pace or attend one of their regular 'Learn to Fly' courses: five days of concentrated instruction running over two consecutive weekends, including one Friday and covers pre-solo training, post-solo development and cross-country coaching.

www.beverleysoaring.org

Horse riding

Lake Navarino Forest Resort at Waroona (90 minutes south of Perth) offer a range of guided horse riding trails around the fresh water lake and through State Jarrah Forest for all levels of riding experience. Moonlight rides with dinner stopovers are also available.

www.navarino.com.au

Jet boating

According to Westcoast Jet in Fremantle, 'wetta iz betta' and that's exactly what you'll get on their 20-minute open-ocean jet-boat ride. Reaching around 40 knots the *Okiedokie* is put through her paces with bucket stops, fancy fishtails, hilarious high-speed turns and, if the conditions are right, even a surf!

www.extremetourswa.com.au

Sailing

One of the country's most popular sailing locations, Fremantle was venue for the 1987 America's Cup yacht races and the Fremantle Sailing Club prides itself on a100-year-plus history and heritage. There are a number of sailing cruises and charters available, including bareboat charters.

South West Yacht Charters offers learn to sail holidays through their sailing school, Chardonnay Coast Sailing, sailing luxury Jeanneau yachts.

www.swyachtcharters.com.au

Starsand Luxury Yacht Charters in Fremantle offer overnight, day and twilight trips (or exclusive charter) aboard the 20m ketch rigged luxury yacht, *Starsand*, visiting Rottnest Island, Garden Island and Carnac Island, Cockburn Sound to Mindarie Keys and extended trips south to Naturaliste. You can either take an active part in the sailing of the yacht or simply relax and let the crew do all the work.

www.starsand.com.au

Leeuwin II is a three-masted barquentine with more than 810m^2 of sail and an overall length of 55m. Operated by the Leeuwin Ocean Adventure Foundation, a private non-profit organisation based in Fremantle, the tall ship is available for day sails and extended voyages. Climb the mast, take the helm, set the sails or settle back and enjoy the view on Australia's largest ocean-going tall ship.

www.leeuwin.com

Surfing

Perth has 19 city beaches, and almost all offer good surfing, with Scarborough one of the most popular. Rottnest Island is also popular with the Perth locals with swells often 2–3ft larger than Perth's beaches.

Learn to surf in Perth at Scarborough Beach Surf School and Lancelin Beach Surf School, which also offers great value surfing tours–from learn to surf day trips to extended surfing camps. On a surf camp you can progress from complete beginner to advanced surfing in just days. Both surf schools are fully accredited by Surfing Australia Surf Schools.

www.learntosurf.net.au

Avon River. *(WATC)*

Sky diving

Skydiving over Perth offers spectacular aerial coastal views out to Rottnest Island and as far south as Bunbury. The WA Skydiving Academy offers a wide range of tailor-made beginners first jumps, skydiving courses and freefall tandem jumps.

www.waskydiving.com.au

Skydive Express offer a similar range from their new Skydiving Centre at York and have won several awards for their facilities, which include a café, licensed bar and resort-style pool.

www.skydive.com.au

White water rafting

The Murray River, 80km south of Perth in the beautiful Dwellingup region, offers great winter white water rafting. Hang on tight and experience the thrill of rapids such as 'tricky dicky', 'columbines', 'fast eddies' and 'gobbly guts', with the day culminating in the 1km long 'terminations', dropping 90m over 8km.

Combine abseiling the Wellington Dam quarry then white water rafting on the Collie River. The one-day trip begins with an abseil at the Wellington Dam quarry followed by whitewater rafting on the magnificent Collie River in two-man inflatable rafts (aka inflatable crocs). The Collie River's pristine waters are great for floating along and relaxing and the thrill of rapids with names like '3 drops' and 'waterfalls'. The Collie River is a grade 2 river.

www.adrenalin.com.au

MORE INFORMATION

- **Western Australian Visitor Centre:** corner Forrest Place and Wellington Streets, Perth. ☎ 1300 361 351.www.westernaustralia.com
- **Fremantle Visitor Centre:** Town Hall, Kings Square, Fremantle. ☎ (08) 9431 7878. www.fremantlewesternaustralia.com
- **Swan Valley and Eastern Region Visitor Centre:** corner Meadow and Swan Streets, Midland. ☎ (08) 9379 9400. www.swanvalley.com.au

weather watch

- January: 16–32°C
- July: 7–18°C
- Summer is normally dry and warm. Almost all the region's rain falls during the winter months.

southern & capes coast

Two Peoples Bay, Albany. *(New Holland Image Library)*

Munda Biddi bike trail. *(WATC)*

► THE SOUTH-WEST CORNER of Western Australia incorporates the Margaret River wine region, a stretch of rugged coastline where the Indian and Southern oceans meet and towering old-growth jarrah and karri forests dominate. To the east, the area known as The Great Southern includes the beautiful Stirling Ranges, more wineries and the town of Albany, the oldest white settlement in Western Australia. Even further east, the beautiful turquoise coastline continues to Esperance, before giving way to the inhospitable sheer cliffs of the Nullarbor and Great Australian Bight across the centre of the continent towards South Australia.

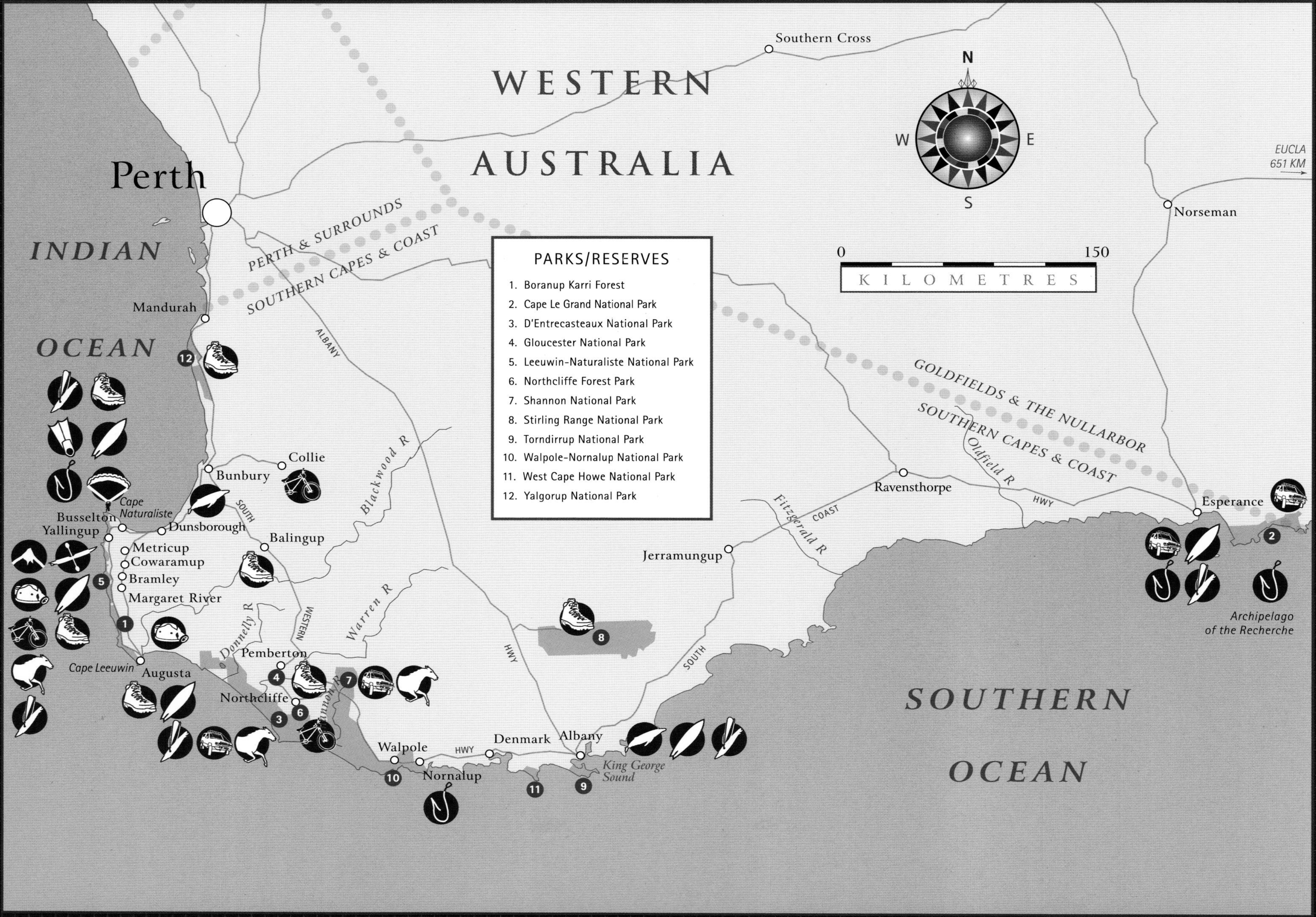
WESTERN AUSTRALIA
Perth
INDIAN OCEAN
SOUTHERN OCEAN
Southern Cross
Norseman
EUCLA 651 KM
N
S
E
W
0
150
KILOMETRES
PERTH & SURROUNDS
SOUTHERN CAPES & COAST
GOLDFIELDS & THE NULLARBOR
SOUTHERN CAPES & COAST
PARKS/RESERVES
1. Boranup Karri Forest
2. Cape Le Grand National Park
3. D'Entrecasteaux National Park
4. Gloucester National Park
5. Leeuwin-Naturaliste National Park
6. Northcliffe Forest Park
7. Shannon National Park
8. Stirling Range National Park
9. Torndirrup National Park
10. Walpole-Nornalup National Park
11. West Cape Howe National Park
12. Yalgorup National Park
Mandurah
Bunbury
Collie
Busselton
Cape Naturaliste
Dunsborough
Yallingup
Metricup
Cowaramup
Bramley
Margaret River
Balingup
Cape Leeuwin
Augusta
Pemberton
Northcliffe
Walpole
Nornalup
Denmark
Albany
King George Sound
Jerramungup
Ravensthorpe
Esperance
Archipelago of the Recherche
Blackwood R
Warren R
Donnelly R
Fitzgerald R
Oldfield R
ALBANY
SOUTH
WESTERN
HWY
COAST

Stirling Ranges National Park. *(WATC)*

NATIONAL PARKS

Leeuwin-Naturaliste National Park: rugged sea cliffs, windswept granite headlands, and formations such as Canal Rocks and Sugarloaf Rock dominate the coastline of Leeuwin-Naturaliste National Park, which stretches 120km from Bunker Bay in the north to Augusta in the south. Highlights include the Boranup Karri Forest, the historic homestead at Ellensbrook, bushwalking, snorkelling, surfing, salmon fishing during the annual spawning run in May and June and self-guided tours of Calgardup and Giants Caves.

Walpole-Nornalup National Park: best known for the huge buttressed red tingle trees, unique to the Walpole area, this 20,000 hectare park also protects towering karri forests, coastal heath and wetlands. One of the most popular attractions in the park is the Valley of the Giants Tree Top Walk, a walkway 38m above the canopy of a magnificent tingle forest. Other highlights include the Frankland River Circular Pool and Falls, Coalmine Beach with a high lookout above cliffs, The Knoll, a peninsula dividing Nornalup and Walpole Inlets and accessible by the one-way sealed Knoll Scenic Drive, and Conspicuous Cliff, one of only three places around Walpole that offer car access to the coast. (The others are Peaceful Bay townsite and Mandalay Beach.)

Yalgorup National Park: protects a chain of 10 lakes on the western edge of the Swan Coastal Plain just south of the Dawesville Channel near Mandurah. Lake Clifton is one of only a few places in Western Australia where living thrombolites (rock-like structures built by micro-organisms too small for the human eye to see) survive. These peculiar structures live on the eastern edge of the lake and are most easily seen in March and April.

D'Entrecasteaux National Park: along with its inland neighbour the Shannon National Park, this park surrounds one of Western Australia's largest inlets. Spectacular coastal cliffs, beaches, mobile sand dunes, vast coastal wildflower heaths and pockets of karri are all highlights of this wilderness park. Major streams and rivers, including the Warren, Donnelly and Shannon, drain through D'Entrecasteaux and empty into its coastal waters. High sand dunes and limestone cliffs on the sea coast give way to coastal heathlands and a series of lakes and swamps further inland. These include Lake Yeagarup and Lake Jasper, which is the largest freshwater lake in the southern half of Western Australia. Vast areas of wetlands behind the coastal dunes are known as The Blackwater. Another feature is the Yeagarup Dune, an impressive mobile dune 10km long and the basalt columns west of Black Point: a close-packed series of volcanic hexagonal columns slowly being eroded by the sea.

Gloucester National Park: home of the Gloucester Tree, Western Australia's most famous karri tree. This 60m-high giant towers above the forest surrounding Pemberton. In the past, foresters maintained a regular fire lookout from its lofty crown. Today, you can climb to the cabin in its upper branches for sensational views of the surrounding karri forest.

Stirling Range National Park: the jagged peaks of the Stirling Range stretch for 65km from east to west and include Bluff Knoll, the highest peak in the south-west of Western Australia. The main face of the bluff forms one of the most impressive cliffs in the Australian mainland. It takes three to four hours to complete the 6km return climb.

West Cape Howe National Park: south-east of Denmark, West Cape Howe National Park protects an area of the rugged southern coastline. The park is popular for hang gliding over spectacular Shelley Beach and is also popular with scuba divers.

Torndirrup National Park: the Southern Ocean has moulded the rugged coastline into some spectacular rock formations, including the granite Natural Bridge and the Gap, where the waves rush in and out with tremendous ferocity. Nearby are a series of Blowholes where a crack in the granite, 'blows' air and occasionally spray as waves hit the rocky shore.

Cape Le Grand National Park: wild coastal scenery, rugged granite peaks, and sweeping heathlands are the attractions of this national park near Esperance, which includes attractive bays with wide sandy beaches set between rocky headlands. In the south-west corner of the park, massive rock outcrops of granite and gneiss form an impressive chain of peaks including Mt Le Grand, Frenchman Peak and Mississippi Hill.

DON'T MISS

- **Eco-caveworks:** learn about the local geology and how the network of some 350 caves was formed. Open daily. ☎ (08) 9757 7411
- **Cape Leeuwin Lighthouse:** 10 minutes drive south of Augusta. Precinct open daily 8.45am–5pm. Visit www.margaretriverwa.com/lighthouse.asp
- **Cape Naturaliste Lighthouse:** open every day 9.30am–4pm (last tour 3.30pm), except: summer school holidays 9am–5pm (last tour 4.30pm) and other school holidays and long weekends 9.30am–4.30pm (last tour 4pm). ☎ (08) 9755 3955.
- **Busselton Jetty:** walk or ride the train along the southern hemisphere's longest pier and check out the underwater life in the Underwater Observatory. Jetty open 24 hours, observatory open daily except Christmas Day, 8am–5pm in summer (Dec–Apr) and 9am–4pm during winter (May–Nov). Bookings are essential, particularly during peak periods. ☎ (08) 9754 3689.
- **Boranup Galleries and Yallingup Galleries:** For a wide selection of good quality hand-made furniture, sculpture, paintings, jewellery and design pieces try Boranup Galleries and Yallingup Galleries, both of which have several rooms packed with innovative and beautiful locally-made pieces. Boranup at Caves Road, via Margaret River. Open daily, 9.30am–5pm. Yallingup, also on Caves Road, open daily, 10am–5pm.
- **Ollio Bello:** guided olive oil tastings, and sales of olive-based products and homewares. Cowaramup Bay Road, via Cowaramup. Open Thu–Mon, 10am–4.30pm.
- **Margaret River Chocolate Factory:** watch chocolate being made before you buy. There's also a cheap and cheerful deli with sandwiches to go to eat in the gardens out the back. Harmans Mill Road, Metricup. Open daily, 10am–5pm.
- **Margaret River Dairy Company:** boutique cheese and yoghurt maker. Free tastings of cheese and yoghurt—the cheddar is excellent—old-fashioned milkshakes and ice cream. Bussell Highway, Metricup. Open daily, 9.30am–5pm.
- **Whale world:** whale displays and whaling museum on the site of the Cheynes Beach Whaling Station, which ceased whaling operations in 1978. Frenchman Bay Road, Albany. Open daily, 9am–5pm. www.whaleworld.org
- **Replica of the Brig *Amity*:** replica of the ship that brought the first settlers to Albany in 1826. Parade Sreet, Albany. Open daily.

Cape Naturaliste Lighthouse. *(WATC)*

Cape le Grand National Park. *(WATC)*

scenic highlights

Boranup karri forest. *(WATC)*

The town of Margaret River is more or less in the middle of Caves Road, a 110km scenic drive that stretches cape to cape, and even though the entire drive could be done in an hour or so, if you really want to explore the area you should split the drive into two days, one day for the south, the other for the north.

From Margaret River to Cape Leeuwin is around 45km, and forms the southern half of Caves Road. Call in to Boranup Galleries and wander through several rooms of hand-made furniture, sculpture and paintings. At Eco-Caveworks you can learn about the local geology and how the network of some 350 caves were formed before touring some of the caves. Take a detour off Caves Road to wind your way through the Boranup Karri Forest and stroll amongst the 90m-high trees; meander past barely-there beach-side communities; stop for a fabulous fish burger at the bakery in Augusta; and finally reach Cape Leeuwin, the most south-westerly tip of Australia. The lighthouse here has watched over the point where the Indian and Southern oceans meet since 1895.

The Caves Road Loop north of Margaret River hits the sea in Geographe Bay at Cape Naturaliste, cutting through the heart of the main wine-producing area and is a food and wine lover's dream drive. There are around 50 wineries clumped together in a stretch of around 15km.

The mouth of Margaret River. *(New Holland Image Library)*

Margaret River

Think Margaret River and most people automatically think 'great wine'. The Margaret River region, a wild knob of land jutting into the sea off the bottom corner of WA, crowned in the north by Cape Naturaliste and Cape Leeuwin in the south, is home to some of the finest white wines (and plenty of terrific reds) produced in Australia. It is also home to some of the best surfing breaks in the country, an extensive network of caves and vast forests of karri, one of the world's tallest hardwood trees. In the south the town of Augusta overlooks the country's most south-westerly point, while in the north, Busselton is a popular diving and snorkelling spot and a great place to see whales during spring.

Albany

The very pretty town of Albany, set on a beautiful harbour in King George Sound, was officially founded in 1827 by a party of 21 soldiers and 23 convicts who arrived on the *Amity*. Situated on the main whale migration route it soon became a busy whaling station and later, a bustling port for shipping travelling between Europe and Asia and eastern Australia. Lovely churches, public buildings and historic harbourside stores and wharves, combined with stretches of dramatic coastline make this a popular tourist destination.

Esperance

Esperance is a water sports paradise with fishing, diving and snorkelling, surfing and windsurfing all popular on the beautiful beaches around the town. The short 30km Ocean Road Loop that twists and turns along the stunning coastline lined with white sand beaches lapped by calm turquoise water is one of the country's most beautiful short drives.

Caravan and camping

There are plenty of commercial caravan parks in various coastal communities along the coast. Best campsites in Leeuwin-Naturaliste National Park are the campgrounds at Conto, Point Road (4WD) and Boranup. In D'Entrecasteaux National Park there is a campground at Lake Jasper with a shaded camping area, barbecues, picnic tables, water and toilets as well as at Black Point, Moore's Hut, and Crystal Springs. In the Stirling Ranges you can camp at Moingup Springs and there are good campgrounds in Yalgorup National Park. There are two camping grounds at Cape Le Grand National Park, one at Lucky Bay, and the other at Le Grand Beach. Facilities include flush toilets and showers.

Cape Naturaliste. (WATC)

Bushwalks

One of the most famous walks in the region is the Bibbulmun Track which stretches for nearly 1000km between Kalamunda in Perth and Albany. The track runs through or near the towns of Collie, Balingup, Pemberton, Northcliffe, Walpole, and Denmark before finishing in Albany. Along its path are areas of old growth forest, pretty farmland, rugged coastal cliffs and remote beaches. It even passes near some of the regions most popular attractions like the Gloucester Tree in Pemberton and the Tree Top Walk near Walpole.

In the Margaret River wine region the Cape to Cape Walk is a 140km walk between Cape Naturaliste and Cape Leeuwin and with breathtaking coastal scenery and wildflowers from August to November. Between June and December, you can also spot migrating whales. You can join the track at popular spots such as Sugarloaf Rock, Canal Rocks near Yallingup, Injidup Point and Hamelin Bay.

The Possum Spotlighting Trail in the Tuart Forest near Busselton is an easy 1.5km walk designed to be completed at night with a spotlight or large torch, so the nocturnal inhabitants of the forest can be spotted. You are highly likely to see the rare western ringtail possum and the more common brushtail possum. Red reflectors on the trail markers and information plaques guide the way. The Cosy Corner to Skippy Rock Walk near Augusta is a challenging 20km full-day hike through magnificent but rugged country and involves long stretches of sand and scrambles along narrow rock platforms. Vehicle pick-up is essential.

There are a number of forest walks available, the most popular being the Valley of the Giants Tree Top Walk and the 3km Gloucester Tree Walk at Pemberton. The 12km walk from the Gloucester Tree to the Cascades passes through karri forest and by Eastbrook Valley. The Great Forest Trees Walk in Shannon National Park is a medium 8km, three-hour return walk that follows an old forestry track. The trail is steep in places, particularly where it crosses the Shannon River. In D'Entrecasteaux National Park the steep 30-minute walk to the top of Mt Chudalup offers great views but is dangerous in windy weather and not recommended for children or frail people.

adventure activities

Jewel Cave, Augusta. (New Holland Image Library)

Abseiling and rock climbing

Margaret River's spectacular sea cliffs (Willyabrup) and steep limestone crags of Wallcliffe and Bob's Hollow are popular rock climbing spots. Within a 40km radius of Margaret River there are more than 200 routes. Peak Charles near Esperance is a popular climbing spot–a large granite dome with many smaller faces and gullies offers a range of climbing styles and grades.

Live Adrenalin run regular abseiling, rock climbing and caving adventure weekends with sea cliff abseils and climbs at Willyabrup Sea Cliffs and adventure caving in the underground tunnels of the Leeuwin-Naturaliste Ridge, accessed by rope over a 35m overhang.

www.adrenalin.com.au

Adventure IN, based in Margaret River, run full-day abseiling and rock climbing days in the Boranup Forest or the sea cliffs at Willyabrup.

http://users.highway1.com.au/~abseil

Canoeing and kayaking

Bushtucker River and Winery Tours offer a half-day canoe paddling trip up the Margaret River through wilderness forest, past huge cliffs, caves, ancient trees and wildflowers, with bush tucker tastings and a canoe race home to the surf beach.

www.bushtuckertours.com

Caving

The limestone ridge of the Leeuwin-Naturaliste National Park hides a series of caves, many of which are open to the public. Calgardup and Giants Cave are both unlit self-guided caves. The floor of the two main caverns in Calgardup Cave is covered in water, which throws up beautiful reflections–there are elevated viewing platforms. Giants Cave is a unique 'walk through' cave that you can enter on one side and reappear out of another opening. Elevated platforms and marked paths are provided along its 800m length. Jewel Cave just north of Augusta is home to one of the longest straw stalactites to be found in any tourist cave. Inside Lake Cave near Margaret River is a stunning pristine chamber with a tranquil lake reflecting the delicate formations. Mammoth Cave houses the ancient fossil remains of numerous extinct animals. Ngilgi Cave, just north of Yallingup, offers stunning display of stalactite, stalagmite, helicitite and shawl formations plus an interpretative area detailing the caves rich history.

Adventure IN runs adventure caving courses in the 60m-deep Bride Cave that involves lowering yourself across a rocky overhang and then abseiling 33m into the sink hole. It is a free-fall abseil where feet do not touch the wall. The main features of the cave are gigantic flow stone and stalactites and stalagmites. The exit is via a rope haulage system or aluminium and wire flexible ladder and safety belay system.

http://users.highway1.com.au/~abseil/caving.htm

Beneath Busselton Jetty. *(WATC)*

Cycling and mountain biking

Nyoongar for 'path through the forest', the Munda Biddi trail is a long-distance mountain bike (and walking) trail that will eventually reach from Mundaring near Perth to Albany. About one third of the distance will be on old railway formations making it one of the longest rail trails in the world. The first 332km section from Mundaring to Collie through ancient jarrah forests is now open.

Other good mountain bike trails in the south-west include the Sika Circuit near Collie, a looped trail that comes off the Munda Biddi near the Wellington Dam. One of the state's most challenging trails, it is a mixture of single and dual use tracks with hill climbs and descents running alongside the picturesque Collie River.

The 600m-long Federation Track for mountain biking and a 7.7km time trial track are both situated in the Northcliffe Forest Park. The Linkage Trail starts at the Visitor Centre and connects with the 6km State Championship Track at the Boorara Conservation Park, which follows firebreaks and single tracks through dense karri forest. There are a couple of creek crossings and sections that are downhill. This is a difficult track that will challenge experienced mountain bikers. The Northcliffe Linkage Trail provides a link to the Boorara State Championship Trail. It is an easy 36km return trail with some moderate slopes and river crossings in season.

There are also several rail trails in the region. The 20km section between Cowaramup and Margaret River, known as the Busselton-Flinders Bay Rail Trail is now complete and ready to ride and links with the Ten Mile Brook Trail to Rusden Picnic Site and also to the 10km sealed pathway between Margaret River and Prevelly. The 33km Denmark to Nornalup Heritage Rail Trail near Albany features forests and ocean views and links with the Wilson Inlet Heritage Trail (7.5km) from the Denmark River mouth to Crusoe Beach. The 39km Hopetoun-Ravensthorpe Railway Heritage Walk, which can also be cycled, follows an isolated former private railway built to connect mines to a port that operated from 1909 to 1935.

Pedal Oz run tours around WA including the 'Margaret River Meander', a two-day wander through the vineyards, Boranup Karri Forest and includes an exploration of Mammoth Caves.

www.pedaloz.com.au

Diving and snorkelling

With an extensive coastline and crystal-clear turquoise water, the Capes region is a paradise for divers and snorkellers with abundant marine life and numerous shipwrecks. The Busselton Jetty, Eagle Bay, Meelup and Castle Rock are calm and ideal for snorkellers. The Busselton Jetty has formed one of the greatest artificial reefs in the southern hemisphere, where an abundance of marine growth encrusts the pylons of the jetty, which offers safe diving in the pristine and sheltered waters of Geographe Bay.

Surfing Margaret River. *(WATC)*

Located near Dunsborough, the HMAS *Swan*, a 120m-long naval destroyer–scuttled off Meelup in 1997, is one of Western Australia's most spectacular artificial reefs and is a mecca for scuba divers. The largest wreck in the state is HMAS *Perth* which is sunk to 36m at Albany. Off Bunbury is the *Lena*, previously an illegal fishing vessel.

There are a number of local dive operators who run trips out to various wrecks and other dive sites.

Dolphin and whale watching

Geographe Bay provides a rest stop for whales and their calves on their southern migration to Antarctica, the sheltered waters a nursery for the young as they prepare for the long journey ahead. You can also sometimes see the rare and endangered blue whales, the world's largest animal, in these waters. Sea Eco Yacht Cruises run whale watching sailing trips in a 11m yacht out of Dunsborough between October and December.

www.seaeco.com

Naturaliste Charters Ecotours also run whale watching tours in Geographe Bay out of Dunsborough from September to December (June to September in Flinders Bay out of Augusta). The cruises are three hours, and include a light lunch of sandwiches.

www.whales-australia.com

In Albany you can go whale watching with Silver Star cruises between June and November in the waters of King George Sound, who promise that if you don't see a whale, you can cruise again for free.

www.whales.com.au

Fishing

The clarity of the waters of the south-west means you can often see the fish you want to catch. Most common catches are tommy ruff (known locally as herring) from both beach and jetty, Australian salmon and silver trevally on the beaches and flathead, garfish and whiting just off shore. The Busselton Jetty is a great place to catch fish, squid or crabs. Esperance is home to some of the largest silver trevally (skipjack); huge samson fish and snapper can be caught in the Recherché Archipelago; King George whiting in Nornalup Inlet and the prized Westralian jewfish is found offshore from Cape Naturaliste.

Off-road driving

There are plenty of opportunities for off-road exploring in the south-west. Just east of Esperance on the Southern Ocean are some excellent remote coastal areas where you can drive on the beaches near Cape Le Grand and Cape Arid. There are some good but challenging 4WD tracks in Shannon, Brockman, D'Entrecasteaux and Warren National Parks that provide spectacular scenery ranging from towering karri forests to endless sand dunes. Callcup hill, a 240m high sand dune, gives extensive views of Warren Beach. The most challenging sections are in D'Entrecasteaux National Park, which is largely wilderness with few facilities, so expect isolated beach campsites, wild coastal views and excellent fishing. Some tracks are closed between June and November.

Horse riding

Tour the wineries on horse back with Margaret River Horseback Tours, who offer scenic ride through the Bramley hinterland, overnight camping treks as well as winery tours.

www.margaretriverhorse-backtours.com

Shannon Horseback Adventures specialised in extended three-, four- and seven-day rides through the D'Entrecasteaux and Shannon national parks riding over sand dunes, along remote beaches, through karri forests and overnight camps in mustering and fishing huts with campfire tucker.

http://members.iinet.net.au/~shanadvs/

There are several other horse riding schools that offer trail rides through the bushland and along the coast and beaches as well as natural horsemanship (horse whispering). Check with visitor information centres for details.

Motor cycle tours

Albany Down Under Motorcycle Tours run personalised tours of the Albany area on Harley-Davidson motorcycles or trike, promising to take you anywhere you want to go, and back again!

www.harleytours.ws

Sky surfing

Southern Skydivers operate out of the Busselton Regional Airport and offer tandem jumps as well as accelerated free fall (AFF) and solo jump courses. If you have done 100 or more jumps and have an Australian

Windsurfing Margaret River. *(John Carter/Starboard)*

Parachute Federation 'C' License or overseas equivalent you can sign up for a sky surfing course, a cross between skateboarding and sky-diving in which you jump out of an aircraft with a board strapped to your feet. You use the board during free fall to execute acrobatics by working against the slipstream, so you really are surfing, but on air rather than water.

www.southernskydivers.com.au

Surfing

The Margaret River region is one of the country's top surfing destinations with more than 75 top class surf breaks spread over 130km of pristine coastline from Cape Naturaliste to Cape Leeuwin. Powerful ground swells generated in the notorious Roaring Forties 1000km to the south of Cape Leeuwin march north-east and meet with the reefs and beaches of the region. The result is consistent, spectacular, high-quality surf. The ocean temperature varies little throughout the year, the water is as clean as you can get and there are no crowds. The biggest and most spectacular surf hits the coast in winter and spring, but summer and autumn also offer consistent swells. It is very rare to find the ocean flat for more than a few days, even in summer. A wide variety of breaks offer varying difficulty, and a number of small beach breaks that are perfect for inexperienced surfers and novices. Several surf schools exist in the area, check with visitor information centres for more details.

The Esperance area is full of hundreds of islands and reefs that also offer excellent waves. Between Esperance and Albany there are miles of uncrowded waves although access can be difficult along rough tracks through kilometres of unmarked dunes.

Windsurfing and Kitesurfing

If Margaret River is a top destination for Australian surfers, it is also a mecca for the world's best windsurfers. International champions and pro sailors come here in their off season to live, train and just soak up the laid back local atmosphere. In recent years kitesurfers too have improved their skill level and earned enough respect from the fiercely protective surfing community to shred Margaret's demanding and dangerous breaks. Definitely a 'bring your own gear' destination.

MORE INFORMATION

- **Margaret River Visitor Centre:** 100 Bussell Highway, Margaret River. www.margaretriver.com ☎ (08) 9757 2911. www.downsouth.com.au
- **Albany Visitor Centre:** Old Railway Station, Albany. ☎ 1800 644 088. www.albanytourist.com.au
- **Busselton Visitor Centre:** 38 Peel Terrace, Busselton. ☎ (08) 9752 1288. www.geographebay.com
- **Esperance Tourist Bureau:** Museum Village, Dempster Street, Esperance. www.visitesperance.com ☎ (08) 9071 2330. www.australiassouthwest.com

weather watch

- January: 14–25°C
- July: 7–16°C
- Summer is normally dry and warm, although tempered by sea breezes. Almost all the region's rain falls during the winter months.

coral coast & pilbara

Ningaloo Reef. *(WATC)*

Sandboarding the Geraldton dunes. *(accent)*

► THE STRETCH OF COAST from Perth north to Port Headland, where the red deserts meet the astonishingly blue waters of the Indian Ocean, is an ancient landscape of reefs, gorges, cliffs and startling rock formations. World Heritage-listed Shark Bay is a marine-life wonderland with dugongs, dolphins, whales and billion-year-old stromatolites. Mount Augustus is an ancient piece of granite twice the size of Uluru and Ningaloo Reef is Australia's largest and most accessible fringing reef system.

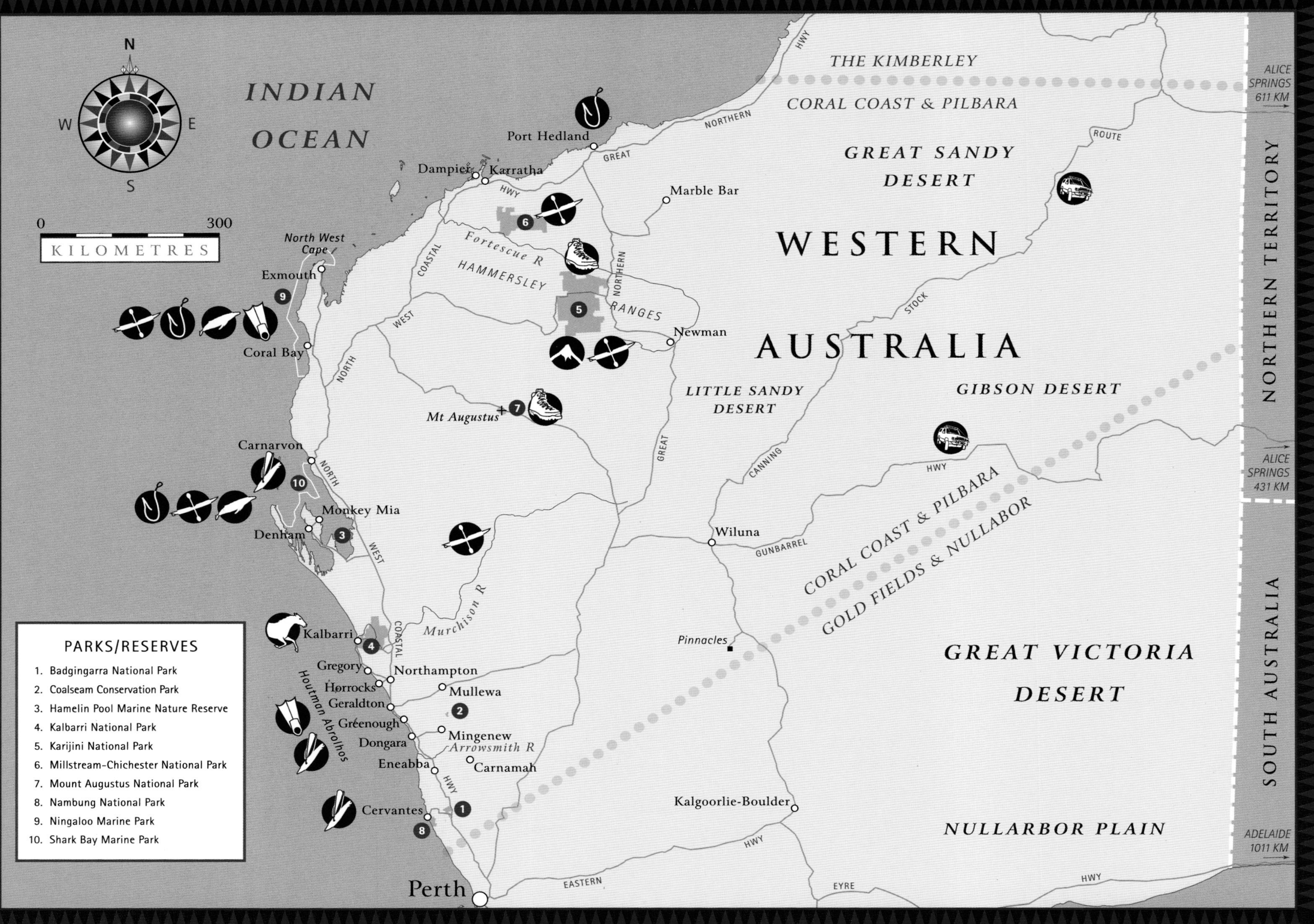

N
W
E
S
INDIAN OCEAN
0
300
KILOMETRES
THE KIMBERLEY
CORAL COAST & PILBARA
GREAT SANDY DESERT
WESTERN AUSTRALIA
LITTLE SANDY DESERT
GIBSON DESERT
CORAL COAST & PILBARA
GOLD FIELDS & NULLABOR
GREAT VICTORIA DESERT
NULLARBOR PLAIN
NORTHERN TERRITORY
SOUTH AUSTRALIA
ALICE SPRINGS 611 KM
ALICE SPRINGS 431 KM
ADELAIDE 1011 KM
Port Hedland
Dampier
Karratha
Marble Bar
North West Cape
Exmouth
Coral Bay
Fortescue R
HAMMERSLEY
RANGES
Newman
Mt Augustus
Carnarvon
Monkey Mia
Denham
Murchison R
Wiluna
Pinnacles
Kalbarri
Gregory
Horrocks
Northampton
Mullewa
Geraldton
Greenough
Houtman Abrolhos
Dongara
Mingenew
Arrowsmith R
Eneabba
Carnamah
Cervantes
Kalgoorlie-Boulder
Perth
NORTHERN
GREAT
HWY
ROUTE
STOCK
CANNING
GUNBARREL
COASTAL
WEST
NORTH
EASTERN
EYRE
PARKS/RESERVES
1. Badgingarra National Park
2. Coalseam Conservation Park
3. Hamelin Pool Marine Nature Reserve
4. Kalbarri National Park
5. Karijini National Park
6. Millstream-Chichester National Park
7. Mount Augustus National Park
8. Nambung National Park
9. Ningaloo Marine Park
10. Shark Bay Marine Park

NATIONAL PARKS

Mount Augustus. *(WATC)*

Mount Augustus National Park: one of the most spectacular solitary peaks in the world Mount Augustus, or Burringurrah as it is known by the local Wadjari Aboriginal people rises 717m above a stony, red sand plain of arid shrubland and is clearly visible from the air for more than 160km. The rock itself is about 8km long—about twice the size of Uluru, which makes it the biggest 'rock' in the world.

Kalbarri National Park: magnificent red and white banded gorges formed by the Murchison River, sea cliffs and vast, rolling sand plains are just some of the spectacular scenery in this national park. Along the coast, wind and wave erosion has exposed the layers of the coastal cliffs that rise more than 100m above the ocean. From Red Bluff, extensive views south overlook colourful coastal limestone and sandstone ledges. There are scenic sites at Mushroom Rock, Rainbow Valley, Pot Alley and Eagle Gorge. Kalbarri is also famous for its wildflowers, most of which bloom from late July through spring and into early summer.

Nambung National Park: thousands of huge limestone pillars rise out of a stark landscape of yellow sand in the area known as the Pinnacles Desert. In places they reach up to 3.5m tall. Some are jagged, sharp-edged columns, rising to a point; others resemble tombstones. Other highlights in the park include the white sandy beach at Hangover Bay with good snorkeling, windsurfing, surfing and beachcombing and frequent sightings of bottlenose dolphins and sea lions, and the coloured desert.

Hamelin Pool Marine Nature Reserve: one of only two places in the world with living marine stromatolites, or 'living fossils', they are able to survive here because Hamelin Pool's water is twice as saline as normal sea water. They look like rocky lumps strewn around the beach but are actually built by microscopic living organisms, up to 3000 million individuals per square metre, that use sediment and other organic material to build stromatolites up to 1.5m high—up to 10 million times their size. Because they grow very slowly, a metre-high stromatolite could be about 2000 years old.

Shark Bay Marine Park: World Heritage area home to turtles, whales, prawns, scallops, sea snakes, fish and sharks, communities of corals, sponges and other invertebrates, together with a unique mix of tropical and temperate fish species and the largest area of seagrass with the most number of species ever recorded in one place in the world. Dugongs and marine turtles are frequently seen in the bay. The waters of Monkey Mia, where several bottlenose dolphins regularly visit the beach, are also within the marine park.

Karijini National Park: formerly Hamersley Range National Park this is the second largest national park in WA. Huge termite mounds rise from the surrounding spinifex and in the north, small creeks hidden in the rolling hillsides—dry for most of the year—plunge into sheer-sided chasms up to 100m deep. They are spectacular but can be extremely dangerous. Further downstream, the gorges widen and their sides change from sheer cliffs to steep slopes of loose rock. In Dales Gorge, a stream with pools, waterfalls, and ferns contrast with the red, terraced cliffs. At Oxer Lookout, the junction of Weano, Red, Hancock and Joffre Gorges, tiers of banded rock tower over a pool at the bottom of the gorge. To explore these gorges you must be fit and prepared to submerge in near-freezing water, follow narrow paths and cling to rock ledges.

Millstream–Chichester National Park: the Chichester Range rises sharply from the coastal plain and includes rocky peaks, tranquil gorges, and hidden rock pools. A highlight is the Millstream oasis, where fresh water springs from an aquifer to create the lushly tropical Chinderwarriner Pool on the Fortescue River, ringed by paperbark and palm trees.

Ningaloo Marine Park: stretching some 300km from Bundegi Reef in Exmouth Gulf around North-West Cape to Amherst Point, south to Red Bluff, the park extends about three nautical miles out to sea and protects the 300km-long Ningaloo Reef. Whales, dolphins, dugongs, manta rays, huge cod and massive whale sharks can be seen in their natural habitat and the reef offers world class diving alongside safe family snorkelling in sheltered lagoons crammed with coral gardens. The largest fringing coral reef in Australia, it is the only large reef in the world found so close to a continental land mass; about 100m offshore at its nearest point and less than 7km at the furthest.

From mid-March to mid-May each year visitors from all around the world converge on Ningaloo to dive with whale sharks, the world's biggest species of fish. Ningaloo Reef is the only easily accessible place in the world where these giants appear in large numbers at predictable times of the year. They swim close to the surface, so even snorkellers can get close.

Exmouth and Coral Bay are also perfect places to view the mass coral spawning, a three-day event that begins a week or so after the full moon, during March and April. Each night, many species of coral simultaneously release millions of bright pink egg and sperm bundles, which float to the surface of the water, creating a huge floating slick of coral spawn.

Geraldton

Home to the largest lobster fleet in the world, Geraldton is one of the state's most popular winter-time resort towns, boasting an average of eight hours of winter sunshine each day. An important regional centre for the surrounding wheat belt and dry hinterland, it is also one of Australia's top windsurfing locations, with thousands of keen windsurfers and kitesurfers arriving from around the country and overseas each year.

Monkey Mia

Around 400 bottlenose dolphins live in the waters of Shark Bay near Monkey Mia, and most mornings, several of the wild dolphins drift into the shallows to be hand fed by scores of eager tourists. It's also home to the world's largest population of dugongs, the stromatolites at Hamelin Pool, and the remarkable Shell Beach made up of millions of tiny coquina shells.

Monkey Mia. *(WATC)*

Exmouth

First discovered by Dutch sailors in the early 17th century, the most famous being Dirk Hartog and Abel Tasman, Exmouth began life as a pearling outport before finally being settled in 1899, although it was not until the establishment of a naval base in 1963 that the town really began to develop. Stretching along 260km of coastline near Exmouth, and sometimes less than 100m from shore, Ningaloo Reef is home to huge whale sharks, humpback whales, green turtles, dolphins and dugongs as well as an array of corals and other sea life.

The Pilbara

Western Australia survives on the wealth of its mining industry, and nowhere is this more apparent than in the Pilbara. The rugged, ochre-coloured Hamersley Range sits above the world's richest deposits of iron ore and the port towns of Dampier and Port Headland are busy iron-ore shipping ports. Offshore from Karratha is the huge North West Shelf Gas project, Mt Whaleback at Newman is the largest open cut iron ore mine in the world and 185km south-west of Port Headland is Australia's hottest town–Marble Bar–where for 161 consecutive days in 1924 the temperature never dropped below 100°F (37.8°C), a record that still stands.

Shell Beach, Denham. *(WATC)*

DON'T MISS

- **The Blowholes:** a powerful jet of water is forced with terrific pressure through a hole in the rocks, sometimes to a height of 20m, 70km north of Carnarvon.
- **Shell Beach:** stunning beach formed from billions of tiny shells and is one of only two in the world. It stretches for approximately 110km and is between 7–10m deep. 45km from Denham.
- **Yarra Yarra Lake:** spectacular salt lake system which changes colour dramatically from salty pink to blood red in summer, to milky green to azure blue in winter. Off Carnamah/Eneabba Road, Three Springs.
- **Vlaming Head Lighthouse:** restored lighthouse built in 1912 from local stone and Australia's only kerosene burning lighthouse. Cape Range, Exmouth. Open for tours. ☎ (08) 9949 1176.
- **Westoby Banana Plantation:** guided tours of the banana plantation. 500 Robinson Street, Carnarvon. www.westobyplantation.com
- **Rainbow Jungle Australian Parrot Breeding Centre:** world leader in the breeding of endangered species of parrots, cockatoos and exotic birds, with the largest parrots in free-flight walk-in area in Australia. Red Bluff Road, Kalbarri.
- **Oakabella Homestead & Tearooms:** 1860s Heritage-listed homestead fully furnished in the period style, together with its original unique barn and restored shearing shed. Starling Road, Oakabella, Northampton.
- **HMAS *Sydney* Memorial:** situated on Mount Scott overlooking Geraldton, impressive memorial commemorates the deaths of the entire crew of the HMAS *Sydney* (645 men) on November 11, 1941, in an exchange with the German raider *Kormoran* in the Indian Ocean.
- **Carnarvon Heritage Precinct:** includes Carnarvon One Mile Jetty, the Carnarvon Tramway and the Lighthouse Keepers Cottage Museum plus many other attractions. Annear Place, Babbage Island, Carnarvon.
- **BHP Billiton Iron Ore Mt Whaleback Mine:** world's largest open cut iron ore mine. 90-minute mining tours depart from the Newman Visitor Centre corner of Fortescue Avenue and Newman Drive, Newman. ☎ (08) 9175 2888. www.newman-wa.org
- **Turtle nesting:** between September and April hundreds of marine turtles come ashore on the islands and mainland beaches of the Pilbara to lay their eggs on the warm quiet beaches, hatching after 8–10 weeks. After laying up to 160 eggs, they take to the ocean again.

scenic highlights

Grass trees, Kalbarri. (WATC)

Western Australia is renowned for its stunning wildflower displays, when inland areas explode into a riot of colour between June and November and roadsides are lined with flowers of all descriptions. There are several wildflower trails/drives you can follow including the Everlastings Trail, North West Trail or the Cape Range Trail.

The area from Cervantes to North Eneabba and Arrowsmith River region is the richest wildflower belt along the coast with more than 2000 species of flowering plants including smokebush, black kangaroo paw, cats paw, scarlet feather flower, scholtzia, thryptomine, cowslip orchids, woody pear and banksia.

The towns of Badgingarra, Carnamah, Eneabba, Mingenew and Mullewa (part of the Everlastings Trail) are most famous for the wreath flower; see black and yellow varieties of kangaroo paw along the 2km nature trail through the Badgingarra National Park and carpets of everlastings in Coalseam Conservation Park.

Dongara-Denison, Greenough, Geraldton, Northampton, Horrocks, Port Gregory, Chapman Valley and Kalbarri are also home to dense populations of flowers, and while less prolific the further north you travel, you will still see roadside flowers as you head up towards Shark Bay, which is home to 700 species of flowering plants including the State emblem: the red and green kangaroo paw.

The Pilbara area produces yellow native hibiscus, bluebells, sticky cassia, mulla mulla, native fuschias and many more.
www.westernaustralia.com

Weano Gorge, Karijini National Park. *(New Holland Image Library)*

Caravan and camping

Not all the national parks allow camping, so commercial campsites and caravan parks in town centres are probably the best way to go. That said, one of the most delightful places to camp is in the shady bush-style camping areas at Crossing Pool and Snake Creek in Millstream–Chichester National Park where pit toilets are provided and there are good swimming areas in Deep Reach and Crossing Pool, which also has gas barbecues. You can also camp in Karijini National Park at the new Savannah Campground, 10km south of Weano.

Bushwalks

There are a number of good short walks in Mt Augustus National Park. Goordgeela is a small recreation spot at the base of the rock and there's a short, steep trail that runs to a cave from which there are good views of the Lyons River and the Godfrey Ranges to the north. The Saddle Trail is a 2km walk with views into The Pound, a natural basin used last century for holding cattle before droving them to Meekatharra. The six-hour, 12km return walk to the top of the mountain is only for fit and experienced bushwalkers. From the summit there are extensive views over the surrounding plain to the distant ranges. Edney's Trail is a 6km return walk to Edney's Lookout.

In Kalbarri, the Mushroom Rock Nature Trail is a leisurely two-hour return walk. The longer Coastal Trail (8km one-way) takes in the views from many of the sea cliffs. Arrange to be dropped off at Eagle Gorge and picked up at Natural Bridge. The six-hour Around the Loop walk begins and ends at Nature's Window.

There are also some lovely walks in the Hamersley Ranges. The short 800m walk at Circular Pool is quite arduous, so allow two hours. It's a loose, steep

Nature's Window, Kalbarri. *(WATC)*

descent, then an easy ramble to the hidden gardens of Circular Pool. The Dales Gorge Walk is a 4km return trail that runs along the bottom of the gorge and there is also a 1.2km return trail that runs along the rim of the gorge. At Fortescue Falls you can walk down through the changing vegetation of the iron-rich gorge walls to the park's only permanent waterfall (800m, two-hour return) or take the three-hour track down this steep, narrow Hancock Gorge to Kermit's Pool. At Joffre Gorge a short track runs from the car park to the lookout overlooking the falls, which are usually dry, and the plunge pool at their base. Follow the marked route into the bottom of the gorge to the first pool downstream of the waterfall (three hours return). There are three walks of varying lengths and difficulty to the top of the second tallest peak in WA, Mt Bruce, called Bunurrunha by the Aboriginal people: Marandoo View is 500m and takes 30 minutes return; Honey Hakea Track is 4.6km–allow three hours and the walk to Mt Bruce Summit is 9km–allow five hours for the return trip. This walk is recommended only for fit and experienced walkers.

The Chichester Range Camel Trail is an 8 km, three-hour one-way Heritage Trail that crosses the rugged sandstone Chichester Range, following part of the old camel road linking Mt Herbert and Python Pool.

Monkey Mia dolphin. *(WATC)*

adventure activities

Abseiling and rock climbing

The spectacular sandstone gorges of Kalbarri National Park are one of the most popular places to go abseiling and rock climbing on the WA coast. Kalbarri Abseil runs full-day tours, for all levels of experience, in the Murchison River Gorges, where the sheer rocks walls are famous for their many different colours. Explore the gorges on a rope, climbing a wall, walking down a rock face, hiking through the river bed and swimming in the river pools.

☎ (08) 9937 1618

Canoeing and kayaking

Kalbarri is also a popular spot for rafting and canoeing when, after heavy rains, the Murchison River becomes deep enough to navigate. It is however, a trip for experienced and well equipped paddlers only as it can be quite hazardous. Contact park rangers before making the trip.

For a more tranquil paddle head to Millstream-Chichester National Park where row boats, canoes, rafts and windsurfers are welcome at both Deep Reach and Crossing Pool.

Rivergods Paddle Adventures run five-day sea kayaking trips to Monkey Mia and Ningaloo Reef as well as rafting trips on the Murchison River after cyclonic floods (at short notice).

www.rivergods.com.au

Diving

Shark Bay and Ningaloo Reef are, along with Queensland's Great Barrier Reef, the country's premier diving and snorkelling locations. Best places are Jurien Bay Marine Park, Ningaloo Marine Park, Abrolhos Islands, Navy Pier, Murion Islands and Lighthouse Bay. Snorkelling and diving equipment is available for hire at a number of towns throughout the region and there are a variety of tours available. Highlights include:

Broadhurst corals: a large coral patch around 5m in diameter swarming with colourful sea life and both soft and hard corals. Keep an eye out for the bright purple sponges the area is famous for.
Sandy Point: on the eastern side of Dirk Hartog Island, where blue, purple, green and brown staghorn corals, as well as brain and plate corals, form a beautiful underwater garden.
Coral Bay foreshore: great for novices, this dive or snorkel begins directly from the foreshore of Coral Bay with the coral beginning only metres from the shore.
Turquoise Bay: 65km south of Exmouth with a rich diversity of coral, fish and other marine life close to shore including several large coral bombies as well as numerous smaller coral colonies, particularly brain coral and the slow-growing massive coral.
Pilgramunna Ledges: beautiful coral formations, multitudes of colourful reef fish and occasional oceanic fish species, as well as rays, sharks and diverse invertebrates, all within 10m of the shore.

There are also a number of good wreck dives along the coast. The *South Tomi* is a confiscated fishing vessel scuttled three nautical miles from Geraldton. The hulls and holds now host newly growing corals, seaweeds and a profusion of fish life. The Abrolhos's Wallabi Group was scene of the infamous *Batavia* mutiny in 1629. The Dutch East Indies Trading Ship, *Batavia*, was wrecked on Morning Reef in the Abrolhos Islands in 1629, and its survivors made it to land, only to face a bloody mutiny resulting in the murder of 125 men, women and children. You can dive on the *Batavia*'s wreckage and view the outline of the hull, fully equipped with cannons and anchors. The wreck of the Dutch ship *Zuytdorp* lies on the seabed against the cliff face at the southern extremity of the Shark Bay World Heritage area. The ship was wrecked in winter 1712 whilst on a voyage from Holland to Batavia in the East Indies. The *Zuytdorp* was carrying more than 250 passengers and crew and a cargo of trade goods and silver including 248,000 guilders in newly minted coins. The *Gudrun* is rated by the Western Australian Maritime Museum as one of the state's best wreck dives. From the Lighthouse Bay beaches in Exmouth, you can also see the wreck of the SS *Mildura*, a cattle ship that was lost en-route from the Kimberley during a cyclone in 1907.

Rattler, the Pit, Kalbarri. *(onsight.com.au)*

Windsports thrive all along the WA coast. (WATC)

Dolphin and whale watching

Dolphins and whale sharks are two of the main reasons many people visit this area of Western Australia.

For face-to-face encounters with dolphins go to Monkey Mia, where bottlenose dolphins are hand fed at the beach each day. The dolphins are wild, come and go as they please, and CALM (Conservation and Land Management) insists they are not reliant upon humans for their complete diet. At the beach they are fed up to three times per day under the guidance of CALM officers. The dolphins receive a maximum of 2kg of fish per day, their average daily intake is between 8-15kg, so they remain self sufficient. The dolphins are not fed after 1pm. There are also a number of dolphin-watching cruises available.

Also in Monkey Mia, take an afternoon Dugong Cruise to see nature's only vegetarian sea mammal. It feeds only on sea-grass, and Shark Bay's massive meadows of sea grass mean it is home to about 10 per cent of the world's dugong population around 10,000 or so.

www.monkeymiawildsights.com.au

The Ningaloo Reef is the only place in the world where the massive, but harmless whale sharks, measuring up to 18m in length, are known to visit on an annual basis, in large numbers, so close to the coast. They are filter feeders and are believed to visit the waters of Ningaloo Reef for the coral spawning and rich plankton that is in the water and they swim just beneath the surface. The best time to swim with whale sharks is between April and early July. Coral Bay Adventures run swimming with whale shark trips during the season, as well as year-round trips swimming with huge manta rays at Ningaloo Reef.

www.coralbayadventures.com.au

The north-western coast is also a great place to see humpback whales on their annual winter time migration to and from warmer waters.

Fishing

The region's coastal waters are home to some of the ocean's most prized eating fish with tailor, mulloway and herring (tommy ruff) the main catches. Off shore there is good sport fishing for marlin, mackerel, coral trout or snapper. Temperate and tropical water fish congregate in Shark Bay providing a veritable feast of fish. There is good rock fishing from the base of Cape Cuvier cliffs and Ningaloo Reef has good fishing inside the reef with big game fish such as sailfish and marlin in the deep water outside. The coastal waters around Port Headland are also renowned for an abundance of sailfish. But the area is most renowned for its lobster season, November to June, when hundreds of boats fish the Coral Coast waters.

Off-road driving

Two famous tracks cut through this region: the Gunbarrel Highway and The Canning Stock Route. The Gunbarrel was the first desert road built by legendary surveyor Len Beadell in the 1960s as part of the Woomera missile range and weapons testing facility. This isolated and remote track is for experienced desert travellers only. The 1400km long, dead-straight desert track runs from Wiluna to Yulara (via Jackie Junction and Docker River), is heavily corrugated in sections with washaways and some sandy sections. You will need permits before you travel from the Central Land Council and Ngaanyatjarraku Council:

☎ (08) 8951 6320 ☎ (08) 8950 1711

The Canning Stock Route is a 2013km track following an old stock route through the Gibson and Great Sandy Deserts from Wiluna to Halls Creek and is one of the most remote and isolated 4WD tracks in the world, and a long way from help if anything goes wrong. You must be extremely well prepared before undertaking this trek, with all supplies, water, emergency medications and communication equipment as well as enough fuel to last 1185km. There are more than 900 steep sand dunes to cross (be aware of head-on collisions) as well as extreme conditions and some boggy sections around wells. Your vehicle must be in excellent condition. Do not do this trek on your own and do not travel in summer.

Horse riding

Big River Ranch in Kalbarri has 500,000 acres of magnificent country and more than 50 horses on the edge of the national park and runs daily two-hour trail rides down to the Murchison River.

www.bigriverranch.net

Sandboarding

Massive sand dunes south of Geraldton provide a fantastic sandboarding playground, just off the main road. Kalbarri Sandboarding run full-day 4WD and sandboarding adventures on the local 45-degree razorback dunes progressing to the adrenalin-pumping Superbowl, a 85m-high sand crater before cooling off swim and snorkel in Lucky Bay Lagoon.

www.sandboardingaustralia.com

Sandboarding, Geraldton. *(accent)*

Surfing, windsurfing and kitesurfing

Geraldton's consistent summer winds have made it the country's windsurfing and kitesurfing capital. Although officially known as Sun City, most of the locals refer to Geraldton as the Windy City. The windy season is from October through to March with the predominantly southerly sea breezes, the Fremantle Doctor, blasting in from 20 knots and occasionally up to 40 knots. Some of the world's best sailors travel to WA for the summer windsurfing circuit that includes the 'Screaming Leeman' downwind marathon, held each January in Leeman.

Favourite spots include Point Moore, renowned for its variety of breaks, with a protected bay, 'Kiddies Korner' and the more ferocious outer reef known as 'Hells Gates'. Experienced windsurfers head for Sunset Beach while St Georges Beach is great for beginners. Coronation Beach is a popular spot for wave jumping and Jacques Point is renowned among surfers for its superb reef break. Flat Rocks, 30km south of Geraldton hosts a round of the State Surfing Championships in June each year. Further south the crayfishing town of Cervantes is a stunning windsurfing location with wind-blasted chop on the south of the long, sandy point and a smooth speedway on the protected northern side. The clear, green water has to be seen to be believed. Denham on beautiful Shark Bay also offers an unforgettable sailing experience.

Sailwest, located at Point Moore in Geraldton, sell and hire windsurfing and kitesurfing equipment as well as organising complete windsurfing holiday packages, including rental cars that are ready to roll with roofracks fitted.

www.sailwest.com.au ☎ 08 9964 1722

MORE INFORMATION

- **Pinnacles Visitor Centre:** Cadiz Street, Cervantes. ☎ 1800 610 660.
- **Geraldton Visitor Centre:** 90 Chapman Road, Geraldton. ☎ 1800 818 881.
- **Kalbarri Visitor Centre:** 70 Grey St, Kalbarri. ☎ 1800 639 468.
- **Denham & Monkey Mia Visitor Centre:** 29 Knight Terrace, Denham. ☎ (08) 9948 1010 or 1300 135 887.
- **Carnarvon Visitor Centre:** 11 Robinson Street, Carnarvon. ☎ (08) 9941 1146.
- **Exmouth Visitor Centre:** Murat Road, Exmouth. ☎ 1800 287 328. **www.australiascoralcoast.com**
- **Karratha Visitor Centre:** Karratha Rd, Karratha. **thecentralpilbaracoast.com** ☎ (08) 9144 4600
- **Port Headland Visitor Centre:** 13 Wedge Street, Port Headland. ☎ (08) 9173 1711.

weather watch

- January: 22–39°C
- July: 11–27°C
- Summer is normally dry and warm. Almost all the region's scarce rain falls during the winter months.

the kimberley

Hiking in the Bungles. *(WATC)*

▶ LESS THAN 25,000 people live in the remote north-western corner of Australia known as the Kimberley, an area bigger than Germany. It is a rough and rugged, but breathtakingly beautiful place, with jagged mountain ranges, spectacular gorges, beautiful waterfalls, serene billabongs, ancient rock art galleries and wild uninhabited wilderness. The oldest rocks in the Kimberley were formed approximately 2000 million years ago. There has been so little geological activity in the area since that the landscape has remained relatively unchanged, making it some of most ancient land on earth.

One of the last areas in the country to be settled by Europeans, the Kimberley was first explored in 1879 by Alexander Forrest, brother of John Forrest, WA's first premier. Forrest was soon followed by some of the most colourful characters in Australia's pastoral and farming history such as Durack, Buchanan and MacDonald, who drove huge mobs of cattle from as far away as Goulburn in New South Wales and Thylungra in south-western Queensland across largely uncharted territory to take up large tracts of land, many more than a million acres in size, in the newly opened north-west.

It is one of Australia's true last frontiers, where everyday is an adventure. Crocodiles, both the saltwater and freshwater varieties, inhabit the creeks and rivers, which flood during the wet season making this remote area even more isolated. One of the regions most spectacular landforms, Purnululu or the Bungle Bungles, was unknown (apart from a few pastoralists and the local Aboriginal community) until 1982. To explore beyond the main sealed highway you'll need a 4WD, even then some places are accessible only by air or by boat. Wherever you go, you'll need to be pretty much self-sufficient, carry spares and tools and be willing to camp most nights.

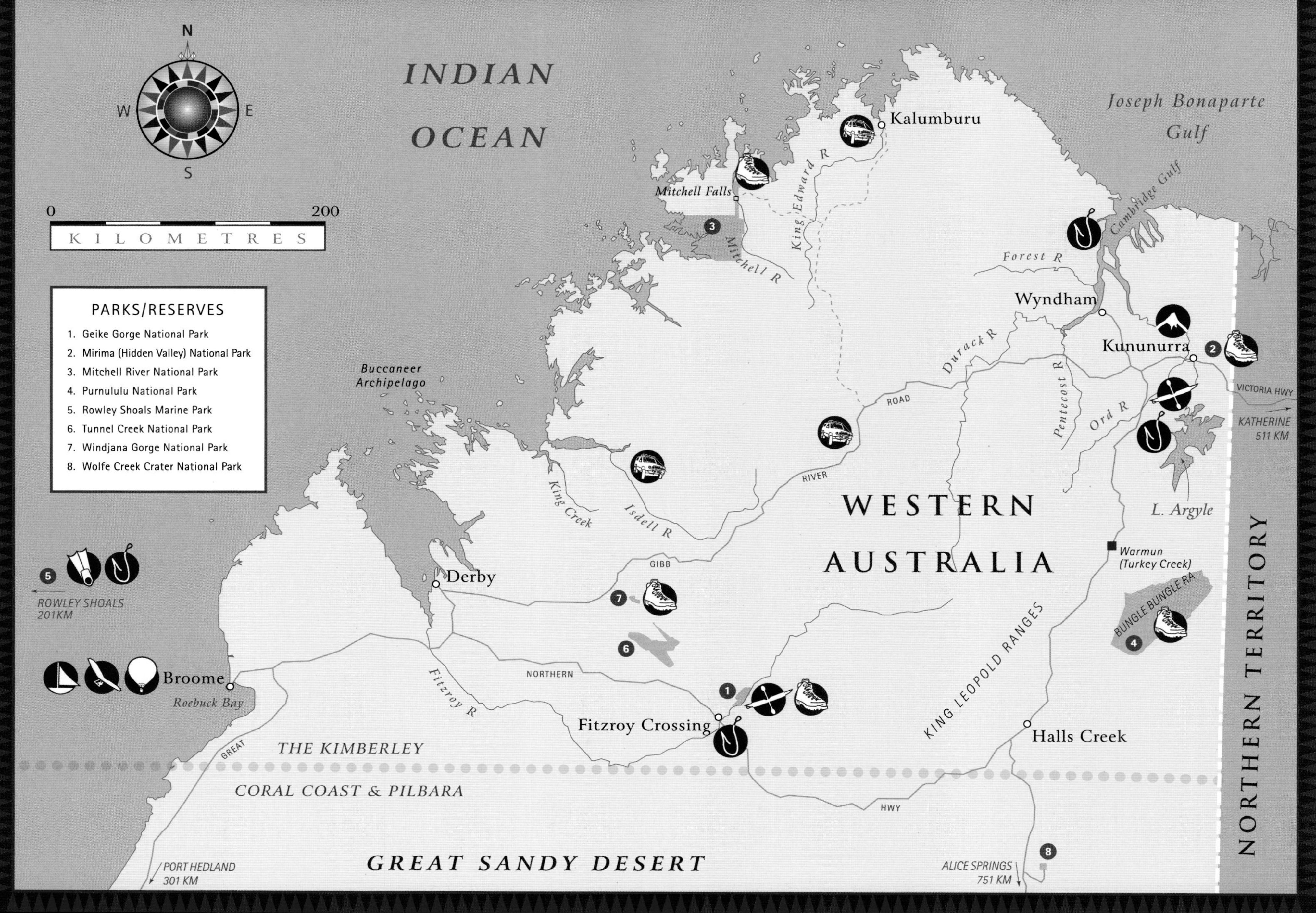

N
W
E
S
INDIAN OCEAN
0
200
KILOMETRES
PARKS/RESERVES
1. Geike Gorge National Park
2. Mirima (Hidden Valley) National Park
3. Mitchell River National Park
4. Purnululu National Park
5. Rowley Shoals Marine Park
6. Tunnel Creek National Park
7. Windjana Gorge National Park
8. Wolfe Creek Crater National Park
Joseph Bonaparte Gulf
Kalumburu
Mitchell Falls
King Edward R
Mitchell R
Cambridge Gulf
Forest R
Wyndham
Kununurra
Durack R
Pentecost R
Ord R
VICTORIA HWY
KATHERINE 511 KM
L. Argyle
Buccaneer Archipelago
ROAD
RIVER
GIBB
King Creek
Isdell R
WESTERN AUSTRALIA
Warmun (Turkey Creek)
BUNGLE BUNGLE RA
NORTHERN TERRITORY
ROWLEY SHOALS 201KM
Derby
KING LEOPOLD RANGES
Broome
Roebuck Bay
Fitzroy R
NORTHERN
Fitzroy Crossing
Halls Creek
GREAT
THE KIMBERLEY
CORAL COAST & PILBARA
HWY
GREAT SANDY DESERT
PORT HEDLAND 301 KM
ALICE SPRINGS 751 KM

Tunnel Creek. *(WATC)*

NATIONAL PARKS

Windjana Gorge National Park: an ancient coral reef, eroded by the Lennard River to create a wide, 100m-high gorge that cuts through the limestone of the Napier Range exposing countless fossils. You can take a self-guided 7km return walk along the length of the gorge beside the river.

Tunnel Creek National Park: Western Australia's oldest cave system famous as a hideout used in the 19th century by an Aboriginal leader known as Jandamarra. Tunnel Creek flows through a tunnel beneath the Napier Range. You can walk 750m through the tunnel. Take a torch.

Mitchell River National Park: one of the most remote national parks in the Kimberley, access is by 4WD only and is two days of rugged and very rough driving from Kununurra. The Mitchell River, flowing northwards, drains into the Admiralty Gulf, carving gorges and waterfalls though the Mitchell Plateau. Highlights are the three-tiered Mitchell Falls and crystal clear Surveyors Pool as well as the extensive stands of *Livistonia* fan palms.

Purnululu National Park: countless orange and black striped beehive-shaped mounds rising steeply from the surrounding flat plains and hiding a world of gorges and pools, with fan palms clinging precariously to walls and crevices in the rocks. The park is open only between April and September. Access is 4WD only. Scenic flights are available.

Geike Gorge National Park: flood waters of the Fitzroy River have carved a 30m-deep gorge through the limestone at the junction of the Oscar and Geike Ranges. During the wet season, the Fitzroy River rises about 16.5m, staining the walls of the gorge and flooding the national park with 7m of water.

In the dry, between April and November, the river is a quiet stream strung out beneath the towering cliffs of the Devonian Reef. Unlike modern reefs—which are built by corals—algae and a group of now extinct lime-secreting organisms built the bulk of this reef.

Mirima (Hidden Valley) National Park: a kind of mini-Bungle Bungles just 2km from Kununurra. The area abounds in wildlife with lots of lizards, birds and rock wallabies as well as very photogenic boab trees that grow on the rock faces.

Wolfe Creek Crater National Park: although it has long been known to Aboriginal people, who called it *Kandimalal*, the Wolfe Creek meteorite crater 145km from Halls Creek was only discovered by Europeans in 1947, during an aerial survey. It is the second largest crater in the world—880m across and almost circular, the floor 60m below the rim. Dating of the crater rocks and the meteorite have shown that it crashed to Earth around 300,000 years ago—relatively recently in geological terms. It would have weighed more than 50,000 tonnes and is thought to have been travelling at 15km a second, a speed which would have taken it across Australia in five minutes. Aboriginal Dreaming, however, tells of two rainbow snakes who formed the nearby Sturt and Wolfe Creeks as they crossed the desert. The crater is believed to be the place where one snake emerged from the ground.

Rowley Shoals Marine Park: a chain of coral atolls 260km offshore from Broome with shallow lagoons inhabited by corals and abundant marine life. Each atoll covers an area of around 80–90km^2. The Shoals rise with nearly vertical sides from very deep water. Mermaid Reef, the most northerly, rises from about 440m, Clerke from 390m and Imperieuse from about 230m. The boat trip to the Rowley Shoals takes approximately 12 hours from Broome. Charter operators usually depart from Broome at sunset and arrive at the Shoals at around sunrise.

scenic highlights

Wandjina Aboriginal rock art, West Kimberley. *(WATC)*

While in Kununurra, take a scenic flight over Lake Argyle, which also takes in the diamond mine and the Bungle Bungles. Argyle Diamonds is the world's largest diamond mine, the true size of the massive open-cut mine is best seen from air. The diamonds mined here are found in a stunning range of colours—pink, blue, yellow, orange, champagne and brilliant white—and include the world's only intense pink diamonds. A number of local outlets in town display the pink diamonds from the mine along with other local precious gems, but if you want to see the gems in the rough you will need to join a mine tour.

Most flights also fly over Purnululu National Park or the Bungle Bungles. The distinctive beehive-shaped towers of the Bungle Bungle massif are made up of sandstones and conglomerates, their alternating orange and black or grey banding are caused by a skin of silica and algae and are inaccessible unless you have a 4WD.

Closer to Broome, Derby is a good base for scenic flights and cruises to the magnificent Buccaneer Archipelago, a beautiful area consisting of some 800 to 1000 rocky islands surrounded by turquoise water. It is part of a drowned coastline with rugged and sparsely vegetated islands of ancient massive sandstone. The area has huge tidal ranges up to 12m, creating such natural phenomena as the horizontal waterfall in Talbot Bay. The falls are caused by the differential created when the tide flows between narrow island gaps. Saltwater crocodiles are common in the waters and mangrove fringes. Sea snakes, sharks, swordfish and a great variety of tropical fish are found in the pristine waters and coral lagoons. The area is remote and accessible only by boat or plane.

Broome's spectacular 'Staircase to the Moon' is a natural phenomena caused by the rising of a full moon reflecting off the tidal mud flats of Roebuck Bay. It's visible only for three nights each month between March and October, but well worth planning a trip around. As the huge blood-red sun slowly drops into the ocean crowds of locals and tourists make their way to Town Beach, laying out picnic blankets on the grassy parklands or tucking into steaming bowls of spicy noodles cooked fresh at one of the many food stalls at the full-moon night-markets held specially to coincide with the event. Buskers, fire dancers and local bands provide free entertainment, stalls offer weird and wonderful clothes, crafts, souvenirs and delicious snacks and the beach begins to resemble a raucous but cheerful street party until suddenly, as the sky darkens and the moon begins to creep above the horizon, the crowd moves as one to the point for the best vantage spot and silence descends. As the moon rises, its tangerine reflection builds a slow but steady staircase to heaven as the crowd cheers. The show only lasts a few minutes, but it's one of those unforgettable, uniquely Australian celebrations that lingers in the imagination much longer.

Kununurra

The Kimberley's youngest town, Kununurra, was built in the early 1960s to serve the Ord River Irrigation Project. Kununurra means 'big water' in the local Aboriginal language, and Lake Argyle, the body of water created by the Ord River Scheme, is world's largest man-made body of water. It's a great place to watch the sun go down with a glass of wine on a sunset cruise or to spot wildlife (the waters are home to an estimated 25,000 fresh water crocodiles) and birdlife on a morning cruise.

Broome

For sheer spectacle, there is no better place to watch the sun set than at Broome. By day, Cable Beach, where an impossibly turquoise Indian Ocean laps up against 23km of dazzling white sands, is breathtaking, but come sunset it's the place to be, whether driving your 4WD on to the sand for a picnic dinner and a spot of fishing, sipping a cocktail at a beachside bar in one of the string of resorts beside the beach or swinging precariously from the back of a camel.

Originally settled in the 1880s as a port with facilities for the pearling industry, the frontier outport boomed as the price of mother of pearl shell escalated. The lustre of the pearl shell lured thousands of immigrants to the town, and the population became a cosmopolitan mix of Malays, Chinese, Japanese, Filipinos, Europeans and Aborigines.

Take a wander through the town centre and you'll see plenty of evidence of the town's history. There's some unique corrugated iron architecture; a bustling Chinatown that was once full of gaming houses, pubs, eating houses and brothels; the largest Japanese cemetery in Australia; the restored pearl luggers and the remains of flying boats bombed during a Japanese air raid in 1942 that can be seen in Roebuck Bay during low tide all testify to the town's tumultuous past.

Wyndham

Western Australia's most northerly town sits on the edge of the crocodile-infested Cambridge Gulf, surrounded by desert plains, salt lakes and a sea of mud. The best view of all this is from Five Rivers Lookout, which provides panoramic views over five rivers (the Durack, King, and Pentecost to the south, Forrest to the west and Ord to the north) and the vast mud flats which sprawl in every direction.

Just before you hit town, head out to the Grotto (signposted at the west of the road). Staircases carved out of the rock lead to a quiet waterhole oasis in a kind of cool amphitheatre. Other attractions include the Prison Tree (23km along the King River Road) one of several hollowed out old boab trees across the Kimberley which were once used as a temporary lockup by the local police and, slightly harder to miss, the giant 20m-long concrete crocodile in the main street.

Caravan and camping

Camp along the banks of Bell Creek under the shade of majestic boab trees or at Silent Grove, where 10 sites are strung out along the riverside and each one has its own fireplace and flushing toilet. These sites are on a ticket system with first come, first choice so try and get in early.

Mitchell Falls and King Edward River have basic bush camps, although a few have fire places and toilets. In Purnululu, there are two camp sites at Walardi or Kurrajong Camp, and both sites have toilets and water. You can also camp at Wolfe Creek Crater where there are toilets but no water available, and at Windjana Gorge. There is a shady camping area with toilets at the start of the Punamii-Unpuu (Mitchell Falls Track) in Mitchell River National Park.

Geike Gorge is a day use area only so camping is not allowed, although there is a very good commercial campground with a large, shady grass camping area at nearby Fitzroy Crossing as well as plenty of caravan sites. There are also caravan parks at Broome, Halls Creek and Kununurra and several stations along the Gibb River Road offer camping for a small fee.

Bushwalks

Get a bird's eye view of Kununurra on one of two good, short walks in Mirima National Park. The Wuttuwutubin Trail is a short and narrow trail within a gorge to a lookout point over Kununurra, while the harder Didbagirring Trail climbs up steep slopes, with some loose rock, for an expansive view over the township and the park's many intricate rock formations.

The Windjana Gorge walk is a 7km return walk along the length of the gorge beside the river, getting a close up look at the gorge's resident fruit bats, corellas and freshwater crocodiles.

Geike Gorge Reef Walk is a pleasant 3km walk along the base of one of the gorge walls. It's best in the early morning and late afternoon. The 20-minute river walk is along the banks of the Fitzroy River to the Sandbar, a popular fishing and swimming place.

In Purnululu the most popular walk is the short walk into Cathedral Gorge or the challenging two-day hike into Picaninny Creek and Gorge. The deeper you go, the more spectacular it gets, but for your safety you must tell a ranger before setting out.

The regions best walk, however, is the 4-6-hour walk to Mitchells Falls. It's a moderate to difficult trek from the camping area across rough and rocky country, skirting several dangerous cliffs and passing by Little Mertens Falls (500m from the camping area and great for swimming) and Big Mertens Falls (2.5km from the camping area) along the way. Beware of snakes. The Aunuayu Walk is a moderate, 8km walk to Surveyors Pool from the Surveyors Pool car park.

Historic boab tree. (LA)

Lake Argyle. (LA)

DON'T MISS

- **Lake Argyle and Argyle Homestead museum:** reconstructed homestead of the pioneering Durack family originally on Argyle Downs Station but moved to its present site when the lake was proposed. Open daily, May–Oct 8.30am–4.30pm.
- **Argyle Diamonds:** the world's largest diamond mine is situated south of Kununurra. A number of local outlets display the pink diamonds from the mine along with other local precious gems.
- **Lake Argyle Cruises:** morning and sunset cruises on Lake Argyle near Kununurra, including a swimming stop and wildlife watching, ☎ (08) 9168 7687. **www.lakeargyle.com**
- **Alligator Airways:** scenic flights over Lake Argyle, the diamond mine and the Bungle Bungles in specifically designed aircraft with large windows for good photography opportunities. Hangar 5, Kununurra Airport. ☎ 1800 632 533. **www.alligatorairways.com.au**
- **Pearl Luggers:** museum of Broome pearling industry, including two restored 1957 pearling luggers. 31 Dampier Terrace, Broome. Tours presented by pearl divers daily, April to November: 9am, 11am, 2pm (4pm tour also available): Nov–Mar: daily 11am and 2pm, weekends 11am only.
- **Willie Creek Pearl Farm:** tours aboard the *Willie Wanderer* to learn about modern pearling techniques and see the pearl panels suspended in the creek. You'll also see how the pearls are produced as your guide demonstrates the intricate process of culturing pearls, including the seeding of a live oyster shell. 38km north of Broome. Bookings essential. **www.williecreekpearls.com.au**
- **Gantheaume Point:** home of 130-million-year-old dinosaur footprints which can be seen at very low tides. While there, take in the vibrant colours of the red sandstone cliffs that spill into the water and see Anastasia's Pool—built by a former lighthouse keeper for his arthritic wife. Just north of Broome.
- **Japanese Cemetery:** graveyard for more than 900 Japanese pearl divers, the most fearless of the Broome divers.
- **Malcolm Douglas Crocodile Farm:** see some big crocodiles up close. Cable Beach Road, Cable Beach. Open April to November, Mon–Fri 10am–5pm, Sat–Sun 2pm–5pm; feeding tours Wed–Sun 3pm.
- **Boab Prison Tree:** huge, hollow boab tree once used as a gaol for Aboriginal prisoners. Nearby Myall Bore which feeds a huge 120m-long cattle trough, reputed to be the longest in the southern hemisphere. 7km south of Derby.
- **Yariyil Art Centre:** co-operative art gallery showcasing the best of local Aboriginal art. Duncan Road, Halls Creek. Open Mon–Fri 9am–noon and 1–4pm or by arrangement, ☎ (08) 9168 6466. **www.yarliyilarts.com**
- **Warmun Art Centre:** studio and sales/exhibition space for artists of the Warmun (Turkey Creek) community, led by Rover Thomas and Queenie McKenzie. Warmun Community, halfway between Halls Creek and Kununurra, along the Great Northern Highway. Open Mon–Fri, 9am–4pm; weekends by prior arrangement. **www.warmunart.com**
- **Geike Gorge boat tours:** take a one-hour cruise with national park rangers or a five-hour cruise with local Aboriginal guides, to learn about the ecology, geology and history of the gorge. Geike Gorge National Park, near Fitzroy Crossing.

adventure activities

Cable Beach, Broome. (LA)

Abseiling and rock climbing

There are a number of good abseiling and rock climbing spots in the Kimberley, although you usually must have a guide as many are in national parks or on private or Aboriginal lands. Go Wild Adventure Tours in Kununurra have a range of tours including the Grotto, a sandstone gorge with a 40m abseil onto land or water; Andy's Chasm which features a swim through a sandstone chasm, ranging from 1-6m wide, with water slides, waterfalls and an underwater tunnel with a 10m abseil into the chasm and 40m in the chasm centre. Other adventures include a beginner's cliff at Elephant Rock, a 75m vertical drop at Black Rock Falls, hard core climbing at Mt Nyulasey, figured to be the Kimberley's best, adventure caving at Jeremiah Hills and abseiling and flying fox at Carlton Gorge on the scenic upper Ord River.

www.gowild.com.au

Ballooning

Walk the skies over Roebuck Plains Station near Broome in a hot air balloon with Outback Ballooning between June 1 and September 30. Both dawn and sunset flights are available–with red dirt, endless flat plains and 22,000 head of cattle on one side, the bay and ocean on the other–it is always a special flight. Afternoon flights are subject to weather conditions; check at time of booking.

www.outbackballooning.com.au/broome.php

Camel safaris

Almost every visitor to Broome takes a sunset camel ride along Cable Beach and there are a number of camel safaris on offer. Just head down to the beach in the late afternoon and you'll find yourself a willing ride, or ask at the visitors centre in Broome.

Canoeing and kayaking

During the dry season, April to November, boats, kayaks and canoes are allowed access to Geike Gorge after 4.30pm, just in time to see the creamy walls of the gorge glow in the late afternoon light. You must notify rangers before launching your boat.

There's also plenty of paddling opportunities in Lake Argyle and Go Wild Adventure Tours run one-, two- and three-day self-guided paddling trips on the Ord River near Kununurra with boat pick up and camping equipment supplied.

www.gowild.com.au

Cycling

Ride the World Heritage Bungle Bungle National Park in a truly exceptional way with ROC Tours departing from Darwin. This is an 11-day, fully supported mountain bike tour through the Bungle Bungles and the Kimberley. Cycle the famous Gibb River Road, swim in majestic gorges, camp under the stars and finish at Cable Beach in Broome.

www.cycletours.com.au

Diving

The Rawley Shoals is one of the country's best diving spots, but due to its remoteness, it's explored by less than 400 divers each year. With a clear water visibility up to 60m, and an average water temp of 27°C, you can dive amongst underwater gardens displaying more than 200 vivid species of coral and swim with a menagerie of more than 700 species of vividly coloured tropical fish including giant potato cod and curious maori wrasse. The Rowley Shoals dive season is limited, extending from September through to December when conditions are usually calm, clear and warm. It's a 12-hour boat trip from Broome, so most diving trips are several days long. The Great Escape Charter Company specialises in live aboard dive trips to the Shoals.

www.kimberleyescape.com

Kimberley sunset. *(WATC)*

Fishing

Like most of northern Australia, the Kimberley offers fantastic fishing, with barramundi and large sport fish the most sought-after catches. The more remote, the better the fishing and there are numerous private fishing camps scattered throughout the region.

Rowley Shoals offers unsurpassed fishing although fishing is not permitted at Mermaid Reef. You can fish at Clerke and Imperieuse Reefs, although potato cod, maori wrasse, coral trout, Queensland groper and all shellfish within 1.6km of the reefs are fully protected. You should throw these species back immediately. Bag limits also apply for most other species.

More accessible rivers include the Fitzroy and the Ord–the former is one of the state's best barramundi waterways. Lake Kununurra is good for sooty grunter and catfish, as is Lake Argyle, which is home to a commercial fishery. Near Kununurra, Ivanhoe Crossing, the old concrete causeway over the Ord River, is a favourite fishing spot for locals who go there to catch wild barramundi. Be careful though, it's also a favourite spot with saltwater crocodiles.

Off-road driving

The Gibb River Road is one of the country's most famous outback tracks. It starts 45km west of Kununurra, and cuts through the heart of the Kimberley to meet the sea at Derby, though the heart of Durack country, the pioneering cattle droving family who were among the first Europeans to explore and settle in this remote area. Their history is immortalised in the Australian classic, *Kings in Grass Castles* by Mary Durack.

The Gibb River Road crosses the Pentecost River, rolls through undulating country and past stands of boab trees to the turn off to Kalumburu. There is a rough 240km track to Mitchell Falls, through thick red bulldust with several creek crossing and corrugations, but the trip through the changing landscape of *Livistonia* Palms up to the Mitchell Plateau with its gorge walks, clear swimming holes and magnificent waterfalls is a highlight.

Permits are necessary to visit Kalumburu because you are entering Aboriginal land. Arrange your permit in advance or obtain one on arrival.

Back on the Gibb, the track cuts through several gorges. One of the most spectacular, Bell Gorge, is a breathtaking series of cascading waterfalls where the Isdell River slashes its way through the mountains forming several excellent swimming holes. 95km further east, Windjana Gorge is an ancient coral reef, eroded by the Lennard River to create a wide, 100m high gorge that cuts through the limestone of the Napier Range exposing countless fossils. Windjana Gorge is 145km from Derby, and the Gibb turns to bitumen about halfway along the way.

For those without their own vehicle, or who prefer to travel in a group, there are a wide variety of 4WD tours and tag-alongs available in Kununurra and Broome.

Mitchell Falls. *(WATC)*

Microlight flights

Broome Trike Flights is the only microlight aircraft school in the world permitted to operate at an international airport alongside passenger jet planes. Introductory flights include a Student Pilots Licence which allows you to try the controls (if you wish). Take off and touch down with a 737 waiting to taxi out onto the same runway! Sunrise and sunset flights are available, and often include a beach landing.

☎ (08) 9193 5697

Sailing

Take a sunset sail around the turquoise waters of Gantheaume Point and Roebuck Bay in Broome in a traditional schooner or pearling lugger. Longer Kimberley coast and Buccaneer Archipelago cruises are also available.

www.pindansailing.com www.redsky.com.au
www.williecruises.com.au

MORE INFORMATION

- **Broome Visitor Centre:** cnr Broome Highway and Bagot St. ☎ 1800 883 777. www.broomevisitorcentre.com.au www.derbytourism.com.au www.westernaustralia.net

weather watch

- January: 24–37°C
- July: 11–33°C
- Roads are impassable November to April. The dry 'winter' season, May to October is the best time for travelling.

goldfields & nullarbor

Lake Ballard. [WATC]

► THE SOUTH-EASTERN PLAINS OF WESTERN AUSTRALIA, 600km east of Perth where the wheat belt gives way to a vast landscape of alluvial flats and salt pans, hide a wealth of gold underneath the rocky surface. Gold was first discovered in this region in 1892 and in a few months the rush was in full swing with thousands of men swarming to the outback to try their luck. The towns along this stretch—Southern Cross, Coolgardie and Kalgoorlie-Boulder—are full of grand gold rush-era buildings that testify to the riches that were found here. WA still supplies 75 per cent of Australia's total gold production and about eight per cent world-wide. A lot of it is dug from the ground along Kalgoorlie's Golden Mile, which has more than 3000km of old underground workings and has yielded more than 49,000,000 ounces of gold so far.

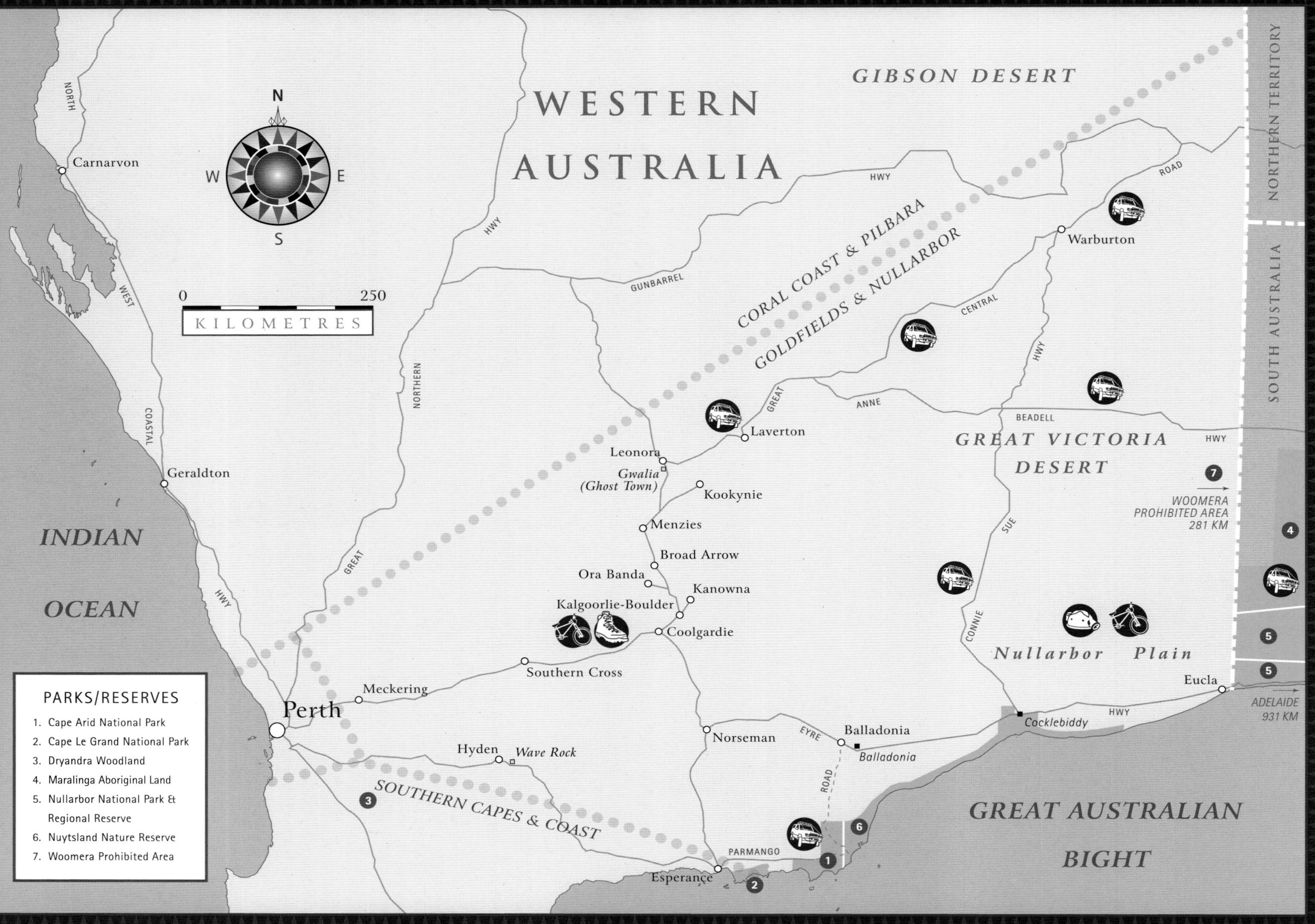

WESTERN AUSTRALIA
GIBSON DESERT
NORTHERN TERRITORY
SOUTH AUSTRALIA
N
E
S
W
0
250
KILOMETRES
Carnarvon
NORTH
WEST
COASTAL
Geraldton
HWY
INDIAN OCEAN
GREAT
NORTHERN
HWY
GUNBARREL
HWY
CORAL COAST & PILBARA
GOLDFIELDS & NULLARBOR
Warburton
ROAD
CENTRAL
HWY
GREAT
ANNE
BEADELL
HWY
Laverton
Leonora
Gwalia (Ghost Town)
Kookynie
Menzies
Broad Arrow
Ora Banda
Kanowna
Kalgoorlie-Boulder
Coolgardie
Southern Cross
Meckering
Perth
Hyden
Wave Rock
SOUTHERN CAPES & COAST
Norseman
EYRE
ROAD
Balladonia
Balladonia
PARMANGO
Esperance
GREAT VICTORIA DESERT
WOOMERA PROHIBITED AREA 281 KM
SUE
CONNIE
Nullarbor Plain
Eucla
Cocklebiddy
HWY
ADELAIDE 931 KM
GREAT AUSTRALIAN BIGHT
1
2
3
4
5
5
6
7
PARKS/RESERVES
1. Cape Arid National Park
2. Cape Le Grand National Park
3. Dryandra Woodland
4. Maralinga Aboriginal Land
5. Nullarbor National Park & Regional Reserve
6. Nuytsland Nature Reserve
7. Woomera Prohibited Area

Wheatfields. *(WATC)*

NATIONAL PARKS

Nullarbor National Park and Regional Reserve: at the head of the Great Australian Bight, this park contains the world's largest semi-arid karst (cave) landscape. It is rich in Aboriginal culture and has the largest populations of the southern hairy-nosed wombat. The Nullarbor cliffs command spectacular views of the Southern Ocean coastline where southern right whales gather with their calves during winter.

Dryandra Woodland: numbats, woylies, tammar wallabies, brushtail possums, tawny frogmouths, kangaroos and wallabies are regularly seen by visitors to Dryandra, which includes a predator-proof compound containing core populations of western barred bandicoots, banded hare-wallabies, boodies, bilbies and rufus hare-wallabies, built to provide a safe environment for breeding. More than 100 species of birds live in the area, including the mound-building malleefowl. It is a very scenic area with magnificent woodlands and spectacular wildflowers in spring. The open eucalypt woodlands of white-barked wandoo and powderbark once covered much of the wheatbelt before it was cleared for farming. A highlight is the Barna Mia animal sanctuary.

The wheat belt

The wheat belt extends several hundred kilometres in a rough semi-circle from Perth and is known as the golden heartlands of the state. It is a gently undulating landscape of dusty golden paddocks studded with windmills and clusters of brilliant wildflowers in spring. Attractions include Kellerton Hill, the third biggest monolith in Australia, Wave Rock and the 1968 earthquake fault line at Meckering.

Kalgoorlie

Kalgoorlie is one of Australia's greatest gold mining towns. Unlike many other towns born of the 19th century rush for gold, Kalgoorlie is still a gold town, sitting atop the richest goldfield in the world. You can see the workings of the modern day mining industry at the lookout over the Super Pit on the outskirts of town. It is simply an enormous hole in the ground 3km long, 1.4km wide and 330m deep that makes the huge caterpillar trucks carrying the ore–more than 6m high and 7m wide–look like tiny toys.

Ghost towns

With boom comes bust and there are a number of deserted towns littered throughout the goldfields. Kanowna is 20km north-east of Kalgoorlie. In 1905 the population was 12,000 with 16 hotels, two breweries, many churches and an hourly train service to Kalgoorlie, however today nothing remains. A Heritage walk booklet is available from the tourist centre. Broad Arrow is 38km north of Kalgoorlie. In 1900 the population was 2400 with eight hotels and two breweries, today the population is about 20 and all that is left is a hotel. At Ora Banda, 66km north of Kalgoorlie there is little else than a recently restored historic tavern, while Menzies, 132km north of Kalgoorlie, which had a population of 10,000 in 1905, has many stately buildings remaining, including the town hall, railway station and the Menzies clock, although population has dwindled to around 400.

Little remains of Kununalling, 40km north of Coolgardie, except for chimneys and the ruins of the Premier Hotel. In 1905 Kookynie, 200km north of Kalgoorlie, was home to 1500 people and boasted six hotels, electric streetlights, public baths, a brewery and many brick buildings. Today the population is about 12 and there is hotel accommodation, fuel, museum and a caravan area. Within 1km are many old workings and tailings dumps ideal for fossicking.

Leonora-Gwalia is 237km north of Kalgoorlie. Leonora has a population of 2600 but Gwalia is a ghost town with miners' cottages, woodline loco, excellent museum, heritage trails, State Hotel, picnic spots and lookout over the open cut mine.

Gwalia ghost town. *(WATC)*

scenic highlights

Bunda Cliffs. (LA)

The drive from Perth to Ceduna across the Nullarbor is a long trip—it will take you at least four days just to get to Ceduna, which is still a long way from Adelaide. And there's also no denying it's flat with long sections of empty straight road between tiny settlements where shopping, nightlife and good coffee is non-existent. But once you've done the trip you could never argue that it's boring, nor could you say there's nothing to see. And as for the driving, well quite simply, it's Australia's greatest road trip.

The journey across the Nullarbor really begins at Norseman where the road gets straighter and longer between stops, with the first real stop of any note being Balladonia, a couple of hours east. From Balladonia you are now on the Nullarbor Plain, where the road runs due east with hardly a turn or hill along the way, and the only stops along the way are roadhouses. After crossing the WA/SA border you'll reach the section of highway closest to the sea. Side tracks spear off to the right, each leading to a lookout over the Bunda cliffs where the immense, treeless Nullarbor Plain abruptly meets the Southern Ocean and the Great Australian Bight in a 200km line of cliffs.

At Head of Bight, the dip in the coastline 20km east of Nullarbor Roadhouse, there is a whale viewing platform where, during the whale season between June and October, you can see up to 100 southern right whales and their calves lolling in the water at the foot of the cliffs beneath. The whales come here each year during winter from the freezing Antarctic waters to give birth and it's one of the best whale watching places in the world.

The lands surrounding the highway east of Nullarbor Roadhouse until almost as far as Nundroo, 145km to the east, are owned by the Anangu people. The Yalata Roadhouse, the best on the Nullarbor, also has an Aboriginal art gallery where paintings, carvings and other work by local artists is sold at a fraction of the price you'd find in city galleries.

From Yalata, the scenery begins to subtly change, with more trees and homesteads along the way as you head towards the Eyre Peninsula. Take a short detour off the highway to tranquil Fowlers Bay, a tiny fishing village by the sea with a general store, a few holiday shacks and not much else. Perfect however, for dozing in the sun and a lazy walk along the long jetty that juts into the ocean where, before roads trains took over, the grain ships would load the wheat that is the main farming activity on the Peninsula. From the Fowlers Bay turn-off it's 140km to Ceduna and the beginning of the Eyre Peninsula. You are now travelling through a much lusher landscape, as the saltbush gives way to vast undulating fields of wheat. Townships appear on the horizon at regular intervals until finally, you reach Ceduna. The name Ceduna comes from the Aboriginal word *Chedoona*, which means 'resting place'. After almost 2000km of driving, it's a welcome one indeed.

Eucla sand dunes. *(WATC)*

The Nullarbor Plain

Norseman, named after a horse who pawed the ground in 1894 and uncovered a gold nugget, is the gateway to the Nullarbor Plain, a 250,000km² treeless limestone slab that was once part of the seabed, and the last 'town' as such until you reach Penong, 720km away on the edge of South Australia's Eyre Peninsula. In between there's a scattering of roadhouses and tiny settlements such as Balladonia, (population 9) the site of the dramatic crash landing of the American Sky Lab Space Station in 1979. According to the locals, the Dundas Shire Council presented NASA with a littering fine, and President Jimmy Carter even rang the Balladonia Roadhouse to make his apologies, and caused a (rather good natured) diplomatic event with Canberra's American Ambassador visiting the region to inspect any damage that may have been done.

Caravan and camping

You camp at Congelin Campground in Dryandra, where basic facilities are provided, but you'll need to bring your own water. Bromus Dam, 32km south of Norseman, is a popular local swimming, camping and picnic spot. No camping is permitted in Nullarbor National Park. There are designated camping areas at Roadhouses or bush camping at rest areas. Note that limited water supplies are available between Norseman and Ceduna so be sure to stock up before crossing the Nullarbor.

Bushwalks

There are a series of working trails in Dryandra Woodland. However, be aware that there is no water available on any of the walks or trails. Make sure you carry sufficient water when attempting any of the longer walks, especially in summer (at least two litres per person in summer or one litre per person in cooler months).

The Ochre Trail is a 5km return walk with interpretive signs along the way that explain the special relationship between the Nyoongar people and the natural environment. The 5.5km Woylie walking trail takes you through a number of different vegetation types, including woodlands of powderbark and jarrah, kwongan heathlands and mallet plantations. One of the highlights is a thick stand of rock sheoak, featuring a lush fern understorey in winter. Keep an eye out for the diggings and scratchings of woylies in this area. The Wandoo Walk is a short half-hour walk through wandoo woodland and good for bird watching, and the 8km Kawanda Road Walk is one of the best places in Dryandra to see kangaroos and brush wallabies. If you are lucky, you might even see a malleefowl. Longer walks include the 12.5km Lol Gray Trail to the picnic area and back and the steep Lol Gray Loop which follows the old telegraph line down the hill from the picnic area.

Kalgoorlie Arboretum is a semi-arid zone woodland park in the centre of the city with a number of interpretive walking trails. Features include a wide variety of indigenous flora, with more than 60 species of planted trees, a remanent woodland area, 65 bird species, recreation facilities on a grassed area under the shade of river gums, and a small dam that attracts waterbirds.

DON'T MISS

- **Sounds of Dryandra Drive Trail:** 25km radio drive trail through Dryandra Woodlands. Short-range, solar-powered transmitters, hidden from view in nearby treetops, broadcast commentaries as you move from site to site along the trail with tales of the local Nyoongar Aborigines, early forestry days, bush railways and some of Dryandra's unique wildlife. 164km south-east of Perth and 22km north-west of Narrogin. Signposts to Dryandra are located on the Albany Highway at North Bannister, on the Great Southern Highway at Cuballing and at Narrogin.
- **Wave Rock:** rising 15m above the ground and more than 100m long, Wave Rock looks a giant surf wave of multicoloured granite about to crash onto the bush below. 4km east of Hyden.

Wave Rock. *(WATC)*

- **Goldfields Pipeline:** an incredible feat of engineering, the pipeline was the vision of Charles Yelverton O'Connor, Chief Engineer of Western Australia from 1891–1902, who managed what many people considered was impossible: to pump 22,700 cubic metres of water from Mundaring Weir near Perth, lift it 355m with only eight pumping stations and deliver it to the thirsty goldfield towns 600km away. Sadly, parliament and the media subjected both the pipeline and his work to prolonged criticism and scepticism. He took his own life in March 1902, just before the water was turned on. **www.goldenpipeline.com.au**
- **Australian Prospectors and Miners Hall of Fame:** gold pouring demonstrations, tours of the underground mine, surface displays, gold panning and the new $21 million Prospectors & Miners Hall of Fame. 5km north of Kalgoorlie along the Goldfields Highway. Open daily, 9am–4.30pm. ☎ (08) 9026 2700.
- **Langtrees 181 Brothel Tours:** $3 million entertainment complex retells the colourful and all too often sad tales of Kalgoorlie-Boulder's working girls. Hay Street, Kalgoorlie. Tours last an hour and include a guided walk through 12 fantasy-themed rooms. Tours Tue–Sun at 1pm, 3pm and 6pm.
- **Super Pit Lookout:** overlooks the open cut mine that is part of the original Golden Mile. Signposted off the Goldfields Highway, Boulder. Open daily, 6am–7pm. Check with the visitors centre to confirm blast time.
- **Goldrush Tours:** tours include the History and Heritage Tour, the Coolgardie (the Old Camp) Tour, and the Golden Mile to Golden Feather Tour. ☎ 1800 620 440. **www.goldrushtours.com.au**
- **Goldfields and Coolgardie Museum:** introduction to the early colourful social history of the Coolgardie goldfields with photographic displays, period rooms, historical memorabilia and aboriginal cultural artefacts. Includes the Waghorn Bottle Collection, one of the largest and most comprehensive antique bottle displays in Australia with bottles and glassware dating from 300BC through to the present day. Bayley Street, Coolgardie. Open Mon–Fri, 9am–4pm; weekends 10am–3pm.
- **Old Coolgardie Gaol:** see how prisoners were kept during the gold rush era. The gaol is part of the main Government Building complex which includes the Post Office and the early Telegraph Office built in 1895. Bayley Street, Coolgardie. Open daily.
- **Coolgardie Pharmacy Museum:** extensive collection of 18th and 19th century medicines and antique tools of the chemists' trade on display. Located in the Old Gaol Complex.
- **Gwalia Historical Museum:** cultural and historical displays of the former gold mining town, now largely a ghost town. Tower Street, Gwalia. Open daily, 10am–noon and 2–4pm.
- **Mulka's Cave:** well preserved examples of Aboriginal art in the form of hand outlines. 18km north of Wave Rock off Lovering Road, Hyden.
- **Balladonia Interpretive Centre:** displays within the museum cover everything from Balladonia's early pioneering days to the dramatic crash landing of the Skylab space station in 1979. Open daily.
- **Eyre Bird Observatory:** surrounded by the Nuytsland Nature Reserve, this area is home to more than 240 species of birds, many rare and endangered. Access the observatory by a turn-off 17km east of Cocklebiddy. To drive all the way to Eyre Bird Observatory you'll need a 4WD. Conventional vehicles can travel along the access road as far as the microwave tower, where there is a car park, and a pick up and drop off point for visitors, by prior arrangement. ☎ (08) 9039 3450.
- **Eucla Telegraph Station Ruins:** large sand drifts have repeatedly covered and uncovered the telegraph station, which was established in 1887. Today the telegraph station remains in ruin and the area is reportedly haunted by a ghost.
- **Bunda Cliffs:** six lookouts, the first is signposted shortly after Border Village.
- **Yalata Roadhouse Aboriginal Arts and Crafts:** good value art gallery. Open daily.

adventure activities

Cave diving

Beneath the Nullarbor Plain lies an extensive network of limestone caves, including Australia's (and one of the world's) longest underwater caves, Cocklebiddy Cave. The object of numerous cave diving expeditions over the years and several world record attempts, the entrance chamber is more than 300m long and leads to a 180m-long lake. The cave then consists of a single, straight tunnel more than 6km long, of which more than 90 per cent is underwater. The Nullarbor is unique as it is the only desert region with extensive caves that contain large quantities of water. This water varies in salinity with some of it being used for stock watering. The water in the caves is remarkably lifeless with only a few of the wet caves having any form of (microscopic) life in the water. Most of the Nullarbor caves are difficult or dangerous to locate and enter, and the cave environment and inhabitants are extremely fragile and can easily be damaged or destroyed; these caves are considered the sole preserve of expert cavers and can be explored only through organised caving expeditions.

www.cavedivers.com.au

Cycling and mountain biking

Cycling across the Nullarbor is increasing in popularity, but is not without its hazards. Avoid cycling at night and beware of roadtrains, be ready to get right off the road if faced with oncoming traffic; there is room on the road for a truck and a car to pass, but not for a truck, a car and a cyclist.

A less arduous ride is Gribble Creek Cycle Way that winds along the creek and through the Kalgoorlie Arboretum.

ROC tours run a fully supported cycle and 4WD tour across the Nullarbor to Margaret River (11 days Adelaide to Perth). This adventure lets travellers cycle along some of the Nullarbor Plain before detouring south to beautiful Esperance then up to Perth via the majestic karri forests and vineyards of the Margaret River region.

www.cycletours.com.au

Off-road driving

This sparse area of Western Australia is criss-crossed with rough dirt tracks that need a 4WD drive, although many are accessible to two-wheel drives in the dry.

The Parmango Road between Balladonia and Esperance on the coast (known locally as 'The Track') is a fairly rough gravel road and a good short cut to Cape Le Grande and Cape Arid. Check road conditions with Balladonia Roadhouse staff before venturing off the Eyre Highway.

Most of the other major 4WD tracks in this area were built by Len Beadell, a famous Australian surveyor, explorer and author instrumental in the surveying and building of 6000km of desert roads through the Great Victoria, Gibson and Great Sandy deserts of Australia in the early 1960s.

The Nullabor Plain. *(New Holland Image Library)*

The Anne Beadell track, named after Len's wife, is an inland-alternative to travelling the Nullarbor that traverses more than 1342km of remote outback country between Coober Pedy in South Australia and Laverton in the gold fields. The trip will take around six or seven days, allowing for sightseeing along the way. It is a very remote desert track and you will need to be totally self sufficient. There are no fuel supplies en route and you will need to arrange four different permits (Desert Parks Pass (or at least a camping permit for Tallaringa Reserve), Unnamed Conservation Park, Woomera Prohibited Area and Maralinga Aboriginal Land) before you go. The track is sandy with some washed out sections, corrugations and passes through a vast wilderness of vegetated dunes and gibber rises. Temperatures can rise to 50°C in summer and it has been known to get as high as 60°C.

The Connie Sue Highway, named after Len and Anne's daughter Connie Sue who actually spent five months of her infant life living 'on the road' with her parents, is a 1022km track (don't let the word 'highway' mislead you) from Kalgoorlie to Warburton. It provides an almost straight line shortcut to Warburton providing quick access to the many other desert tracks in the area and runs mostly north-south through the heart of extremely remote desert country, intersecting both the Anne Beadell Highway and also the Great Central Road. It crosses the Aboriginal land reserve known as Yapuparra near the Hann Breakaways just before reaching the junction of the Great Central Road and for this section you must have a permit. There are no supplies or water along the length of this trip so carry all fuel, water and food.

Gold prospecting

Western Australia's goldfields are popular haunts for gold fossickers armed with high-tech metal detectors searching for gold lying near the surface. A miner's right, which permits the holder to prospect on vacant crown land, is essential for all prospecting in Western Australia. It is also possible to prospect on pastoral leases and mining claims with the permission of the leaseholder or tenement holder. Always request permission however, and be prepared to accept no for an answer, otherwise you might find yourself in trouble. Prospecting can not be carried out in national parks, nature reserves, Aboriginal and Heritage sites or within town sites or other classified areas such as cemeteries.

www.mpr.wa.gov.au

Finders Keepers Gold Prospecting Adventures offers a range of tours that include lesson on how to use a metal detector along with safety and communication equipment (GPS and handheld radios) and transport to and from gold prospecting sites, relic hunting and ghost towns. Tours depart from Kalgoorlie Goldfields Visitor Centre.

Horse riding

The Contine Bridle Trail in Dryandra Woodlands is a five-hour 27km bridle trail designated specifically for horse riding. It takes in some of the other blocks of Dryandra, surrounding farmland, wandoo woodland and mallet plantations.

Cooling off. *(WATC)*

MORE INFORMATION

- **Kalgoorlie Goldfields Visitor Centre:** 250 Hannan Street, Kalgoorlie. ☎ (08) 9021 1966. www.kalgoorlie.com
- **Nullarbor:** www.nullarbornet.com.au

weather watch

- January: 10–40°C
- July: 4–25°C
- Summer can be extremely hot. Best time to travel is during the winter months when days are dry and warm but nights can be freezing.

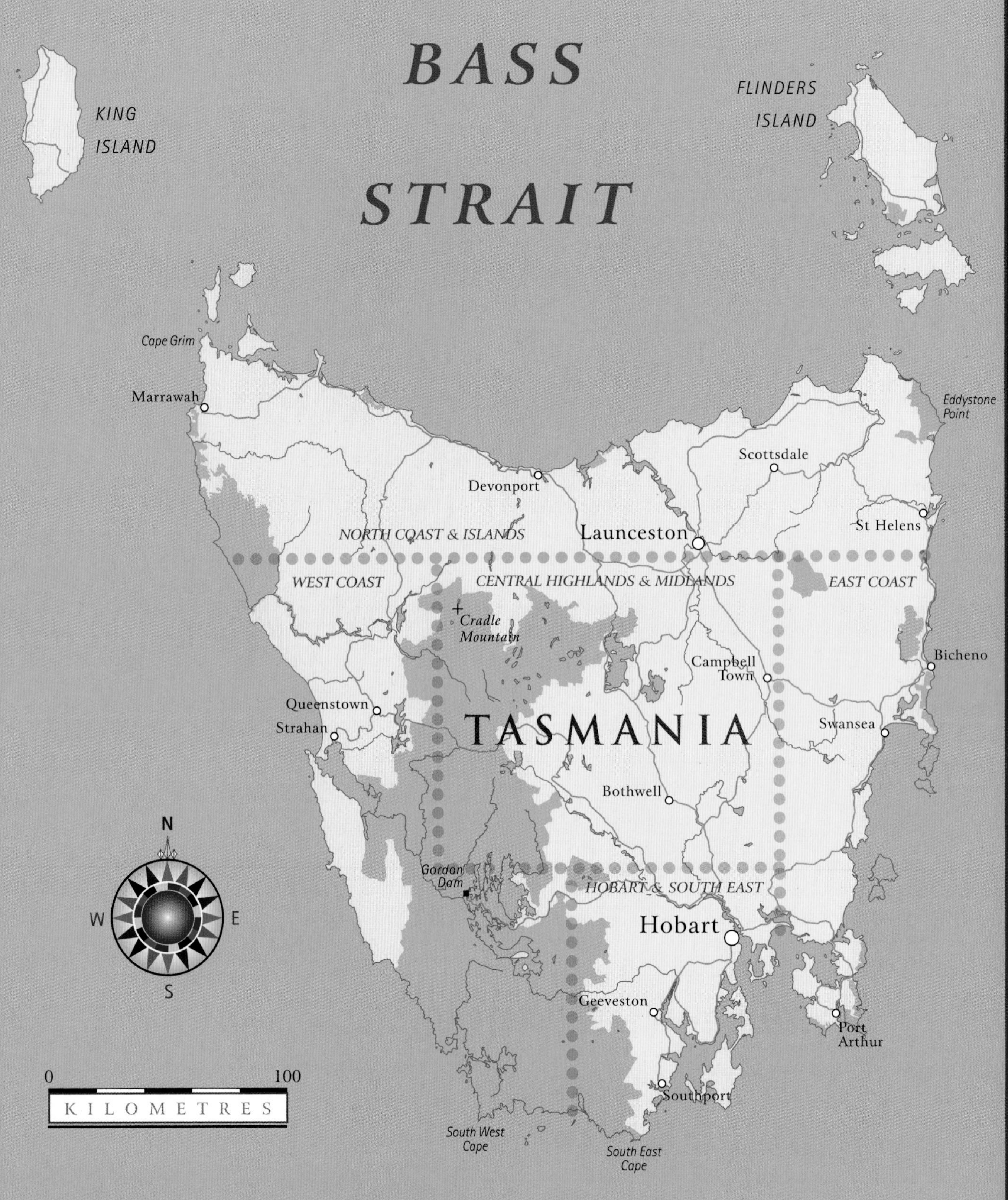
BASS
STRAIT
KING
ISLAND
FLINDERS
ISLAND
Cape Grim
Marrawah
Eddystone
Point
Scottsdale
Devonport
St Helens
Launceston
NORTH COAST & ISLANDS
WEST COAST
CENTRAL HIGHLANDS & MIDLANDS
EAST COAST
Cradle
Mountain
Campbell
Town
Bicheno
Queenstown
Strahan
TASMANIA
Swansea
Bothwell
N
W
E
S
Gordon
Dam
HOBART & SOUTH EAST
Hobart
Geeveston
Port
Arthur
0
100
KILOMETRES
Southport
South West
Cape
South East
Cape
SOUTHERN OCEAN

Australia's only island state was first settled as a penal outpost and has more historic ruins and remains than any other state. This small island is packed with varying landscape, microclimates and huge tracts of untouched wilderness, despite the heavy industries of mining and forestry, thanks to a strong state-wide conservation movement. With everything from snow-covered mountains to dense rainforest, raging rivers and gentle valleys, Tasmania is an incredibly diverse state with a fascinating, if sometimes brutal history.

tasmania

hobart & south east

Hobart's waterfront. *(Lee Atkinson)*

► CLINGING TO THE EDGE of a small island on the edge of the world, Hobart, Australia's smallest capital city, is a maritime city. Squashed into a narrow wedge of land between towering Mount Wellington, the Derwent River and a deep harbour port, there's no escaping Hobart's seafaring heritage.

The thriving waterfront, with its beautiful honey-coloured Georgian and Victorian architecture, still caters primarily for shipping trade, which really sets Hobart apart from its mainland cousins. You don't need to spend your time in museums, although there are good ones in the city, to soak up all that history: it's all around you. Wander down to the busy dock, stop for some fresh fish and chips and watch the world sail by.

Stroll a little further and you'll find Salamanca Place with its terrace of warehouses dating back to the whaling days of the 1830s, now mostly boutiques and galleries. It comes alive on Saturdays with a huge outdoor market selling everything from crafts to organic vegetables. Nearby Battery Point and Macquarie and Davey Streets boast over 60 National Trust classified buildings.

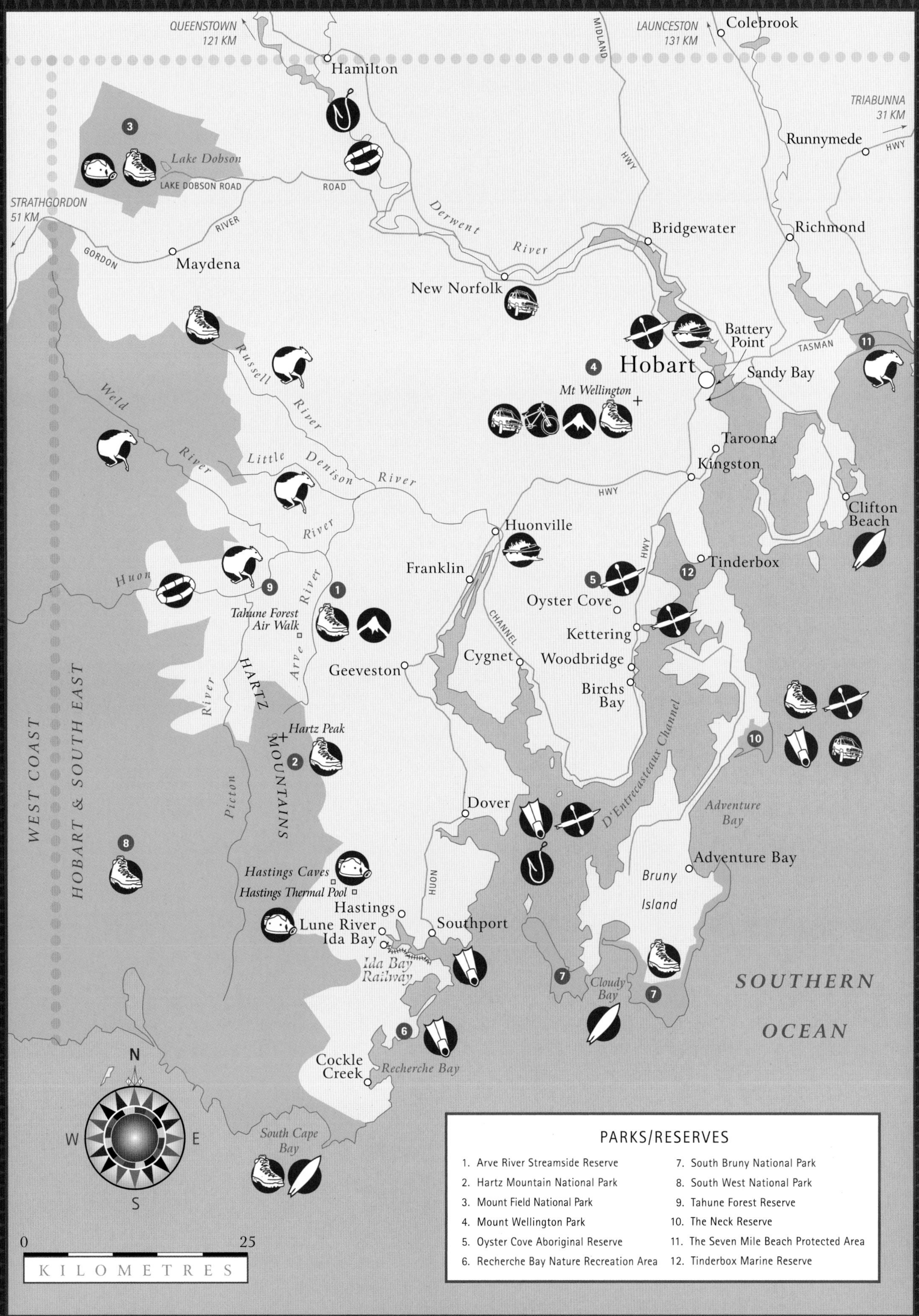

QUEENSTOWN 121 KM
LAUNCESTON 131 KM
Colebrook
Hamilton
MIDLAND HWY
TRIABUNNA 31 KM
Runnymede
HWY
Lake Dobson
LAKE DOBSON ROAD
ROAD
STRATHGORDON 51 KM
GORDON RIVER
Maydena
Derwent River
Bridgewater
Richmond
New Norfolk
Battery Point
TASMAN
Hobart
Sandy Bay
Mt Wellington
Russell River
Weld River
Little Denison River
Taroona
Kingston
HWY
Clifton Beach
Huonville
River
Huon
Franklin
Tinderbox
Tahune Forest Air Walk
Arve River
Oyster Cove
Kettering
CHANNEL
Cygnet
Woodbridge
Geeveston
Birchs Bay
HARTZ MOUNTAINS
Hartz Peak
River
WEST COAST
HOBART & SOUTH EAST
Picton
D'Entrecasteaux Channel
Adventure Bay
Dover
HUON
Adventure Bay
Bruny Island
Hastings Caves
Hastings Thermal Pool
Hastings
Lune River
Ida Bay
Southport
Ida Bay Railway
Cloudy Bay
SOUTHERN OCEAN
Cockle Creek
Recherche Bay
South Cape Bay
N
W
E
S
0
25
KILOMETRES
PARKS/RESERVES
1. Arve River Streamside Reserve
2. Hartz Mountain National Park
3. Mount Field National Park
4. Mount Wellington Park
5. Oyster Cove Aboriginal Reserve
6. Recherche Bay Nature Recreation Area
7. South Bruny National Park
8. South West National Park
9. Tahune Forest Reserve
10. The Neck Reserve
11. The Seven Mile Beach Protected Area
12. Tinderbox Marine Reserve

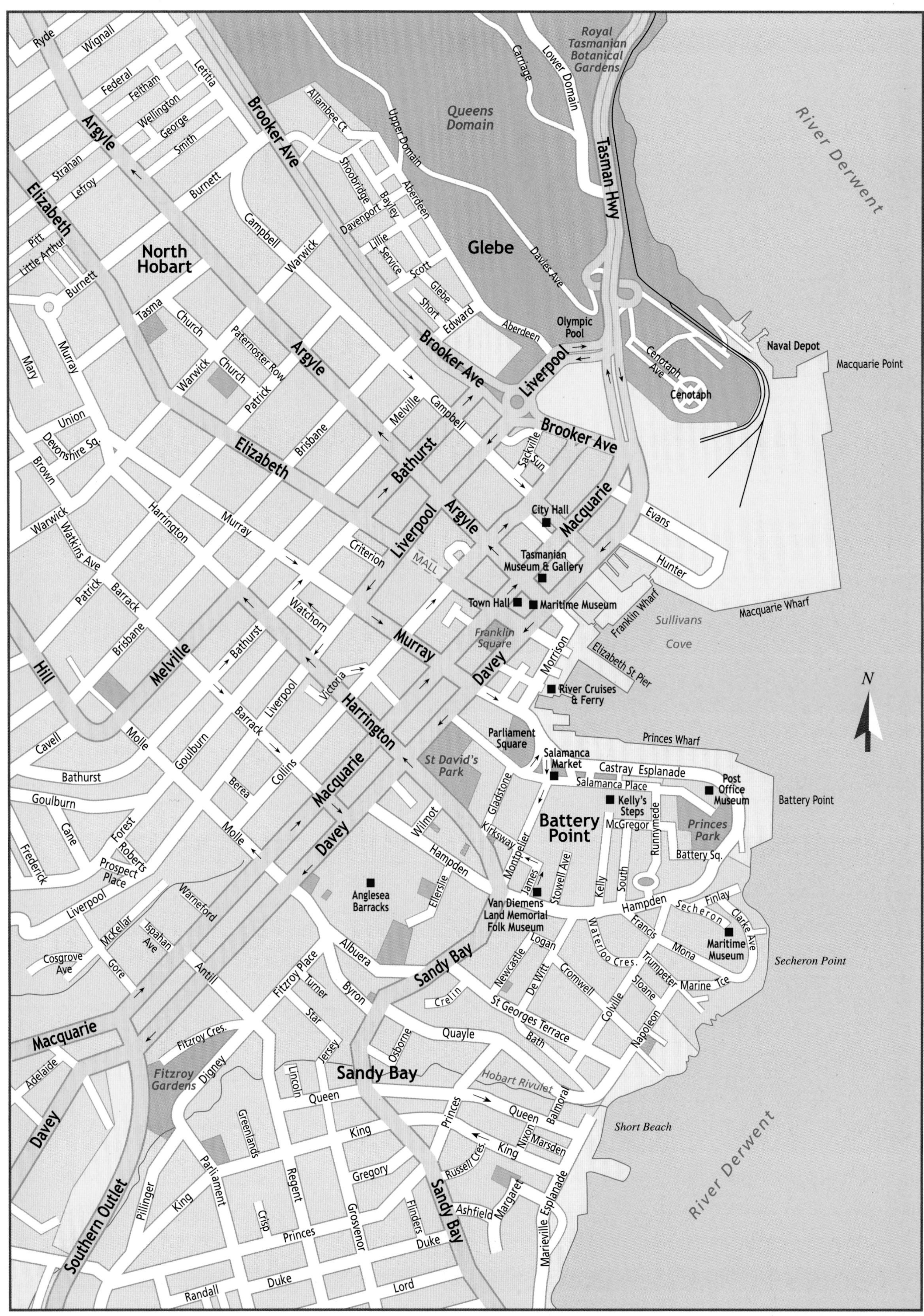

Royal Tasmanian Botanical Gardens
Queens Domain
River Derwent
Tasman Hwy
Glebe
North Hobart
Olympic Pool
Naval Depot
Macquarie Point
Cenotaph
City Hall
Tasmanian Museum & Gallery
Town Hall
Maritime Museum
Franklin Square
Sullivans Cove
Macquarie Wharf
Franklin Wharf
Elizabeth St Pier
River Cruises & Ferry
Parliament Square
Princes Wharf
Salamanca Market
Castray Esplanade
Salamanca Place
St David's Park
Kelly's Steps
Post Office Museum
Battery Point
Princes Park
Battery Sq.
Anglesea Barracks
Van Diemens Land Memorial Folk Museum
Maritime Museum
Secheron Point
Sandy Bay
Hobart Rivulet
Fitzroy Gardens
Short Beach
River Derwent
Southern Outlet
N

Derwent Valley

Less than an hour to the north-west of the city are the green rolling hills of the very pretty Derwent Valley, all farmlands, hop fields, forests and remnants of rainforest. Historic towns, such as New Norfolk and Bridgewater are full of convict era buildings and Mount Field National Park is the oldest park in the state.

Huon Valley

South of Hobart the Huon Valley, between the Hartz Mountains to the west and the D'Entrecasteaux Channel, is a fertile farming district most famous for its apples, although these days you'll also find vineyards, berry farms, salmon fisheries and boutique cheese makers. Further south still are the tall southern forests and the wild Hastings Caves and South Cape Bay, closer to the Antarctic winter ice shelf than it is to Cairns.

Bruny Island

Formerly home to Tasmania's most well-known Aboriginal, Truganini, tragically famous for being the last of the island's full-blood Aboriginals, the island is a sleepy place with gentle countryside and wild coastlines, great walks, spectacular beaches, fishing, wildlife and a rich heritage of sealers, whalers and explorers.

Caravan and camping

Camping is permitted in some areas of Mount Wellington Park, however there are no formal camping sites or facilities. Free camping and unpowered caravan sites are available near the Visitor Centre at Tahune Forest Reserve as well as good tent sites upstream beside the Huon River. There are a number of campsites at Cockle Creek in the south-east section of Southwest National Park (see West Coast chapter, page 458) with pit toilets (no water or firewood) at Recherche Bay Nature Recreation Area and at Boltons Green. The road to Cockle Creek is often rough in places, although the Tasmanian Parks & Wildlife Service advises that caravan access is possible with care. There is a private campground at Mount Field, offering powered and unpowered sites and facilities include amenities block, toilets, showers, hot water and basins, coin-operated washing machine and dryer. On Bruny Island there are two camping grounds at Cloudy Bay. The Pines is small with a pit toilet, the second, Cloudy Bay Corner Beach campground, is 4WD-only with access via the beach. At Jetty Beach on Cape Bruny there is a larger campground with pit toilets, tank water (seasonal only), picnic shelters, and sheltered swimming for children with caravan access. The Neck Reserve, outside the national park, has free camping and caravan (unpowered) sites with a pit toilet, day use shelter, open fireplace (no wood supplied) and tank water (seasonal only).

Bushwalks

No trip to Hobart is complete without a pilgrimage to the top of Mount Wellington. Standing sentinel 1271 metres over Hobart and its harbour, the summit is just a 20-minute drive from the centre of the city. On a fine day you can see the city spread below, the D'Entrecasteaux Channel, the east coast, the Derwent Valley, the south west and the Tasman Peninsula. There are a number of walking tracks criss-crossing the mountain, but be warned, the wind is often cold so coats and warm weather gear are always needed. In fact, it's not uncommon to see the top of Mount Wellington dusted in snow, even in mid summer. One of the best walks on the mountain is the four-hour Organ Pipes Walk that leaves from the Springs and takes walkers beneath the fluted columns known as the Organ Pipes, a section of towering, columnar, dolerite cliffs. A shorter alternative is Sphinx Rock 45-minute return walk.

Russell Falls. *(Tourism Tasmania)*

NATIONAL PARKS

Mount Field National Park: Tasmania's oldest national park, and one of its most popular, with a rich variety of vegetation from tall swamp gum forests and massive tree ferns at the base of the mountain, through rainforest along the Lake Dobson Road, to alpine vegetation at the higher elevations. Highlights include Russell Falls, stunning walks through enormous fern forests and some of the tallest trees in the world, Lake Dobson and winter skiing.

Hartz Mountain National Park: just west of Geeveston and part of the World Heritage Wilderness Area, the Hartz Mountains National Park features a range of walking tracks through subalpine woodlands to ice-carved crags, lakes and alpine moorlands. On a clear day Hartz Peak (1255m), provides panoramic views into the heart of the southwest.

Tahune Forest Reserve: part of the State Forest rather than a national park, this forest reserve is home to the Tahune Forest AirWalk and Visitor Centre. Apart from the elevated walkway there are several lookouts and short walks leading off the Arve Forest Drive. The 10-minute riverside loop at the Arve River Streamside Reserve is a terrific walk, as is the 20-minute Huon Pine boardwalk underneath the AirWalk.

South Bruny National Park: at the southern tip of Bruny Island this national park features wonderful coastal scenery with towering cliffs, muttonbird rookeries, gardens of kelp seaweed and long sandy beaches. Adventure Bay and Jetty Beach provide sheltered areas for swimming, while Cloudy Bay is a popular spot for experienced surfers.

scenic highlights

Huon River. *(Tourism Tasmania)*

The best way to explore the Huon Valley south of Hobart is via the Huon Trail, a sign-posted route that travels south of Hobart along the banks of the Huon River and out into the forests, before returning to trace the coastline and loop back to Hobart. It's an easy one-day drive with plenty to see and do along the way.

From Hobart take the Southern Expressway and follow the signs to Huonville, through apple orchards that in early spring blanket the slopes in white and pink blossoms. Here the road begins to meander its way south beside the Huon River: follow it to Franklin, home of the Wooden Boat Centre, a showcase for traditional boat building skills, and on to Geeveston, a sleepy timber-getting town on the edge of the Southern Forests. It's a lovely 29km winding drive though the Arve Forest on a sealed road (watch for logging trucks) to Tahune Forest Reserve, where you can wander above the treetops on the Tahune AirWalk, see some rare Huon Pine on a 20-minute boardwalk or picnic beside the river.

From Tahune, backtrack to Huonville and head south on the right bank of the Huon to Cygnet. Stop at a roadside stall to buy some fresh fruit, browse through one of the many small art and craft studios along the way or snap a photo at one of the lookouts as you wind your way south along the coast through Verona Sands and Gordon to Peppermint Bay, the place to linger over a long lunch as you gaze out over the D'Entrecasteaux Channel towards Bruny Island. If time is short, you can cut across from Cygnet via Gardners Bay—the views of the Channel and Woodbridge as you crest the hill are spectacular.

Hobart is about an hour away, via a succession of sleepy farming and fishing communities and beautiful coastal stretches with plenty of perfect picnic sites. Stop on the way at the historic shot tower at Taroona and take the coast road back to the city via Sandy Bay and the waterfront suburbs of Hobart.

The 20-minute, wheelchair accessible circuit of Russell Falls takes you through a mixed forest of towering swamp gums (the tallest flowering plant on Earth), and species typical of wet forests and cool temperate rainforests, such as dogwood, musk and myrtle. Towards the falls, the track is framed by stunning tall tree ferns. The one-hour-and-45-minute Lady Barron Falls Circuit features the best of the Mt Field National Park's lower altitude tracks and includes Russell Falls, Lady Barron Falls and the Tall Trees Walk. The Pandani Grove walk (40 minutes) circles Lake Dobson and, as the name suggests, features many of the unique pandani. Keep an eye out for platypuses in the lake, especially at dusk and dawn.

There are a number of good short walks in South Bruny National Park, with two of the most popular being the 90-minute Grass Point walk and the longer Fluted Cape walk which continues on from Grass Point with impressive cliff and ocean views.

Hartz Peak is a three-hour to five-hour moderate climb but gives great views of the south west wilderness including Federation Peak, but be aware that blizzard weather conditions can occur with little warning, in any month.

The four-hour South Cape Bay walk starts from the end of Australia's most southerly road and is the eastern end of the popular seven-day South Coast Track to Port Davey.

Tahune Forest Walk. *(Tourism Tasmania)*

DON'T MISS

- **Tasmanian Museum and Art Gallery:** highlight is the display on the Thylacine, or hyena-like Tasmanian Tiger, thought to be extinct, although weird and outrageous sightings are occasionally reported. 40 Macquarie Street, Hobart. Open daily, 10am–5pm. **www.tmag.tas.gov.au**
- **Maritime Museum of Tasmania:** collection of historic items, paintings and ships models and stories on the exploits of early explorers, the whaling industry, and the central role of sailing ships and steam ships in the colony. Cnr Davey and Argyle Streets, Hobart. Open daily, 9am–5pm. **www.maritimetas.org**
- **Royal Tasmanian Botanical Gardens:** set amidst sprawling lawns with great views of the Derwent River and best known for its magnificent spring displays. Queens Domain, Hobart.
- **Narryna Heritage Museum:** housed in one of Hobart's earliest Colonial homes (1836) with one of the most comprehensive collections of 19th century items. Open Tue–Fri 10.30am–5pm, weekends 2.30–5pm. Closed all July. 103 Hampden Road, Battery Point.
- **Wooden Boat Centre:** watch students and master craftsmen at work. Main Road, Franklin. Open daily, 9.30am–5pm. **www.woodenboatcentre.com** ☎ (03) 6266 3586
- **AirWalk:** part of Tahune Forest Reserve, the 600m elevated treetop walk leads out over the canopy of the wet eucalypt forest to a cantilever 50m above the ground for stunning views of the Huon and Picton Rivers. Open daily. ☎ (03) 6297 0068.
- **Forest and Heritage Centre:** forestry museum and interpretive centre with displays on woodworking, forest management and timber. Church Street, Geeveston. Open daily, 9am–5pm.
- **Grandvewe Cheesery:** Australia's only organic sheep dairy, specialising in hand-made sheep and cows-milk cheeses. Watch the sheep being milked daily at 4pm (Oct–Mar). 59 Devlyns Road, Birchs Bay. Open daily, 10am–5pm (closed Tue in Jul and Aug). **www.grandview.au.com** ☎ (03) 6267 4099.
- **Dorans Jam Factory:** Australia's oldest surviving jam factory established in 1834. View the factory in operation, browse the museum of antique machinery and sample the products. Pages Road, Huon Valley. Open daily, 10am–4pm. **www.doransjams.com**
- **Shot tower:** the only remaining circular sandstone shot tower left in the world, erected in 1870. Climb the 58m tower to see how the lead was dropped to form shot as well as great views of the Derwent River Estuary. Channel Highway, Taroona. Open daily from 9am.
- **Peppermint Bay:** two-hour journey from Hobart down the Derwent River to the spectacular cliffs and coastline of the channel district. You've a good chance of seeing dolphins, seabirds, seals, penguins and the occasional whale. Underwater 'spy ball' cameras provide you with a close up view of sea life, colourful kelp and coral gardens where parrot fish and leafy sea dragons are often seen. Cruises depart Hobart at noon. **www.hobartcruises.com** ☎ 1300 137 919.
- **Ida Bay Railway:** a narrow gauge bush railway with 7km of track extending from the main road to a disused jetty near Southport passing scenic and historic sites. Located at Lune River. **www.idabayrailway.com.au**

adventure activities

Organ Pipes, Mount Wellington. *(Tourism Tasmania)*

Abseiling and rock climbing

Hobart's most popular rock climbing spot is the Organ Pipes on the side of Mount Wellington, a series of dolerite columns ranging up to 125m tall. The climbing ranges from single pitch to multi pitch. There are a few short, completely bolt protected, face routes now at Lost World, New World and Teardrop Wall.

Aardvark Adventures run a range of abseiling tours in and around Hobart, including a 25-metre abseil off the famous Tahune AirWalk where you'll descend from the forest canopy into to the lush under story of ferns and tea trees–group bookings only.

www.aardvarkadventures.com.au

Canoeing and kayaking

Hobart has some of the world's best sea kayaking at its doorstep. Roaring 40's Ocean Kayaking, based in Kettering, offer a range of overnight and day trips exploring the scenic coves of the nearby D'Entrecasteaux Channel visiting Oyster Cove Aboriginal Reserve, an Atlantic salmon farm, an old whaling station or the Iron Pot Lighthouse, Egg Islands, Fortescue Bay and Variety Bay on Bruny Island. They also offer a range of longer, multi-day wilderness trips to points further north and south to Recherché Bay and beyond.

www.roaring40skayaking.com.au

Blackaby's sea kayaking tours range from paddling on the Hobart waterfront with fish and chips or pizza to paddling around the historic ruins of Port Arthur, B&B sea kayaking tours on the Tasman Peninsula, and seven-day Gordon River Wilderness Expeditions.

www.blackabyseakayaks.com

Caving

Tasmania's limestone and dolomite caves feature lots of squeezy passages, underground rivers, constellations of glow worms and richly decorated chambers.

Hastings Caves and Thermal Springs are 90-minutes drive south of Hobart. Newdegate Cave is the largest tourist cave in Australia and occurs in dolomite rather than limestone. Parks and Wildlife Service conduct daily 45-minute tours through the large highly-decorated cavern which features large and spectacular formations including flowstone, stalactites, columns, shawls, straws, stalagmites and unusual helictites. The Thermal Pool is fed from a spring that supplies water at around 28°C all year round and is surrounded by forest and ferns.

Southern Wilderness Eco Adventure Tours (S.W.E.A.T.) specialises in small group adventures and offer glow-worm and adventure caving tours in the Southwest World Heritage Area. Day and night tours are available and depart from Dover.

www.tasglow-wormadventure.com.au

Mountain biking trails and opportunities abound. *(Getty Images)*

In and around Mount Field National Park there are more than 500 known cave entrances, including many deep and long caves. Niggly Cave (375m), which is located inside the park, is probably the current deepest explored cave in Australia. Other important caves are Junee Cave (at Junee Cave State Reserve), Beginners Luck, Welcome Stranger, Frankcombes Cave, Cashions Creek Cave and Growling Swallet. The majority of caves in the area are accessible only to very experienced cavers, only Junee Cave is suitable for visits by the general public.

Cycling and mountain biking

Mount Wellington is the undisputed king of mountain biking in Hobart: boasting an adrenalin pumping 21km downhill ride. Bike riding is permitted on formed roads, fire trails and nominated walking tracks on the mountain. Glenorchy Mountain Bike Park was designed by world-renowned course designer Glen Jacobs (Sydney Olympics, World Cup, World Championships) and caters for all levels and types of mountain bike riding.

www.tasbikepark.com

Other good bike trails include the 26km track from Ferntree along Pipeline Track to Mt Wellington Falls; the 32km Margate to Pelverata Falls track; 27km Margate-Snug Tiers-Kaoota-Margate loop; the 55km Margate to Cygnet via Snug Tiers and the 100km ride starting and ending at Salamanca Place and going through the townships of Richmond, Pontville, Campania and Bridgewater. The 91km Hobart-Tahune AirWalk route is another good ride.

www.biketas.org.au

You can also cycle the Tasmanian Trail, a 480km long distance trail for walkers, mountain bikers and horse riders, extending from Devonport on the northern coast of Tasmania to Dover in the south. The trail links up existing forestry roads and fire trails, country roads and occasionally crosses private land. Up to 90 per cent of the Trail is on some form of made road or track.

www.parks.tas.gov.au/recreation/tastrail.html

Island Cycle Tours offer a range of cycling tours, including paddle and pedal trips and the Mt Wellington descent.

www.islandcycletours.com

Diving

The D'Entrecasteaux Channel and waters off Bruny Island offer some excellent diving with popular spots including Acteon Island, Recherche Bay and South East Cape.

Gateway to the D'Entrecasteaux Channel is the Tinderbox Marine Reserve. The mid-channel area is popular with divers, particularly Huon Island, Arch Island, Simpson's Point and Nine Pin Point. The area is used by a lot of diving courses and there is a snorkelling trail to the south with underwater information plaques and permanently erected dive flags. The best diving in the reserve is north towards Piersons Pt. The climb down the cliff at Fishermans Haul is worth the effort.

There are extensive kelp forests in the area from Dover on Port Esperance down to Southport. Some of the most popular Tasmanian wrecks are also not far from Dover, including the 440 tonne barque *Katherine Shearer*, which blew up on a voyage out from England in 1855.

Aquatic playground ... in the Roaring 40s. *(Boards and More GesmbH)*

Fishing

Fishing is practically the state sport in Tasmania, and although most fishing in centred on the great wild fisheries of the highland lakes and country streams, the pristine southern waters offer some great opportunities for fishing. There is good fishing right in the heart of Hobart in the Derwent estuary and up river with mackerel, cod, flathead, Australian salmon and bream the most sought after catches. It is at its best at the end of winter though, when sea-run trout and bream are prevalent. In the D'Entrecasteaux Channel the wharves and jetties, coves and bays offer great fishing and you'll often land an escapee from one of the Atlantic salmon farms. There are dozens of fishing guides and charters available.

www.discovertasmania.com.au

Off-road driving

Tasmania is rugged and thickly forested and many sections of the spectacular coastline are inaccessible to conventional vehicles, which makes for some great four-wheel-driving, although most of the tracks are short day trips.

The Jefferys Track is a medium track through beautiful bush scenery that runs across the Wellington Range from Lachlan (near New Norfolk) to Crabtree and provides a through route from the Derwent Valley to the Huon Valley. The track joins the Crabtree Road northwest of Crabtree, 8km from the Huon Highway at Grove. It is 14km long, and there may be some snow cover during winter. Look out for other users on this track, including cyclists and walkers.

Closer to Hobart there are some challenging fire trails on Mount Wellington with steep, rocky and sometimes difficult terrain. The most popular routes are the East West trail via Montrose Road and either out via Collins Cap trail or Jefferys Track and the East West Trail via Jefferys Track and out via the Collins Cap trail. Access points are gated–call for details of track conditions, possible closures due to weather and where to obtain an authority and key.

☎ (03) 6233 6560

Most of the roads on Bruny Island are fine for 2WD with care, but there are large unsealed sections and some campsites are accessible only by 4WD via the beach. Driving on the beach is best at low tide and is only permitted for access to the camping area and for boat launching and retrieval. A 40km speed limit applies. You must stay below the high tide mark so as not to disturb shorebird nesting sites or destroy other wildlife and vegetation.

Horse riding

The Seven Mile Beach Protected Area consists of 27km^2 of pine forest and long stretches of beach near Hobart, perfect for a brisk canter or more leisurely trail ride though the forests. Seven Mile Beach Equestrian Centre offer one-hour throught to three-hour scenic trail rides along Seven Mile Beach, Five Mile Beach or through a pine forest laced with trails for all levels of riding ability.

☎ (03) 6248 5420

In the Huon Valley you can explore the beautiful valleys and mountains around the Huon, Weld, Russell and Little Denison Rivers on horseback with Huon Valley Horsetrekking. Rides are tailored to your experience, from slow and relaxed to fast, daring and adventurous. Saddlery and helmets included and overnight camps are available.

☎ (03) 6266 0343

Jet boating

Take a thrill ride tour of Hobart Harbour and the lower Derwent River with Hobart Harbour Jet. Tours include photography opportunity stops and the high-speed thrills of jetboat manoeuvrability. Look for the jetboat at Watermans Dock, Murray Street Pier in Sullivans Cove, near the Salamanca Market area. The jetboat can seat up to nine passengers.

www.hobartharbourjet.com.au

Huon River Jet Boats, based in Huonville, will give you 35 minutes of stunning scenery and exhilaration as you alternate between zooming along the river and stopping to see Huon Pine and reflections on the water, remnants of the early days of river trade, old houses and open farmland.

www.huonjet.com

Surfing

Despite the often chilly weather, surfing is popular in Tasmania all year, with plenty of uncrowded breaks with clean, powerful waves. Close to Hobart, Park and Clifton Beaches are the favourite spots. Further south, Bruny Island's Cloudy Bay faces the wide Southern Ocean so the surf there can be huge. So does South Cape Bay–but you'll need to carry your board on a 7km bushwalk through the World Heritage Area to reach this South Coast beach.

The South Coast Surf School, which proudly calls itself Australia's 'coolest' surf school, runs daily surf lessons at Clifton Beach. Bring your wetsuit–you'll need it.

www.tassiesurf.com/Surf_School.htm

White water rafting

Tasmania is the white-water capital of Australia. And while the big rapids are in the rivers of the south-west, you can bounce gently down the lower Picton into the Huon River, which flows through lush rainforest, studded with huon pines, blackwoods, myrtles and interspersed with giant eucalypts; or float down the Derwent as it flows through open farmland, past hop fields and grazing cattle with grade 1-2 rapids.

Both trips are great for first-time rafters or families.

www.aardvarkadventures.com.au www.raftingtasmania.com

Derwent River. *(Tourism Tasmania)*

MORE INFORMATION

- **Tasmanian Travel Centre:** cnr Davey and Elizabeth Streets, Hobart. www.discovertasmania.com.au
  ☎ 1300 655 145

weather watch

- January: 9–22°C
- July: 1–12°C
- Rain is frequent in this area of Tasmania. Roads can be icy during winter.

east coast

Bay of Fires. *(Tourism Tasmania)*

▶ TASMANIA'S EASTERN SEABOARD is a spectacularly scenic coastline; a long, ragged strip of peninsulas, islands, channels and windswept beaches, flanked by rugged mountains with gorges, waterfalls and forests. One minute you are driving through open paddocks and farmlands, through quaint historic villages full of convict-built stone houses, following the course of a twisting, shallow river when suddenly you find yourself in dense, lush rainforest. A few hours down the road you are winding through pristine sub-alpine wilderness with snow-dusted mountain ranges looming above you.

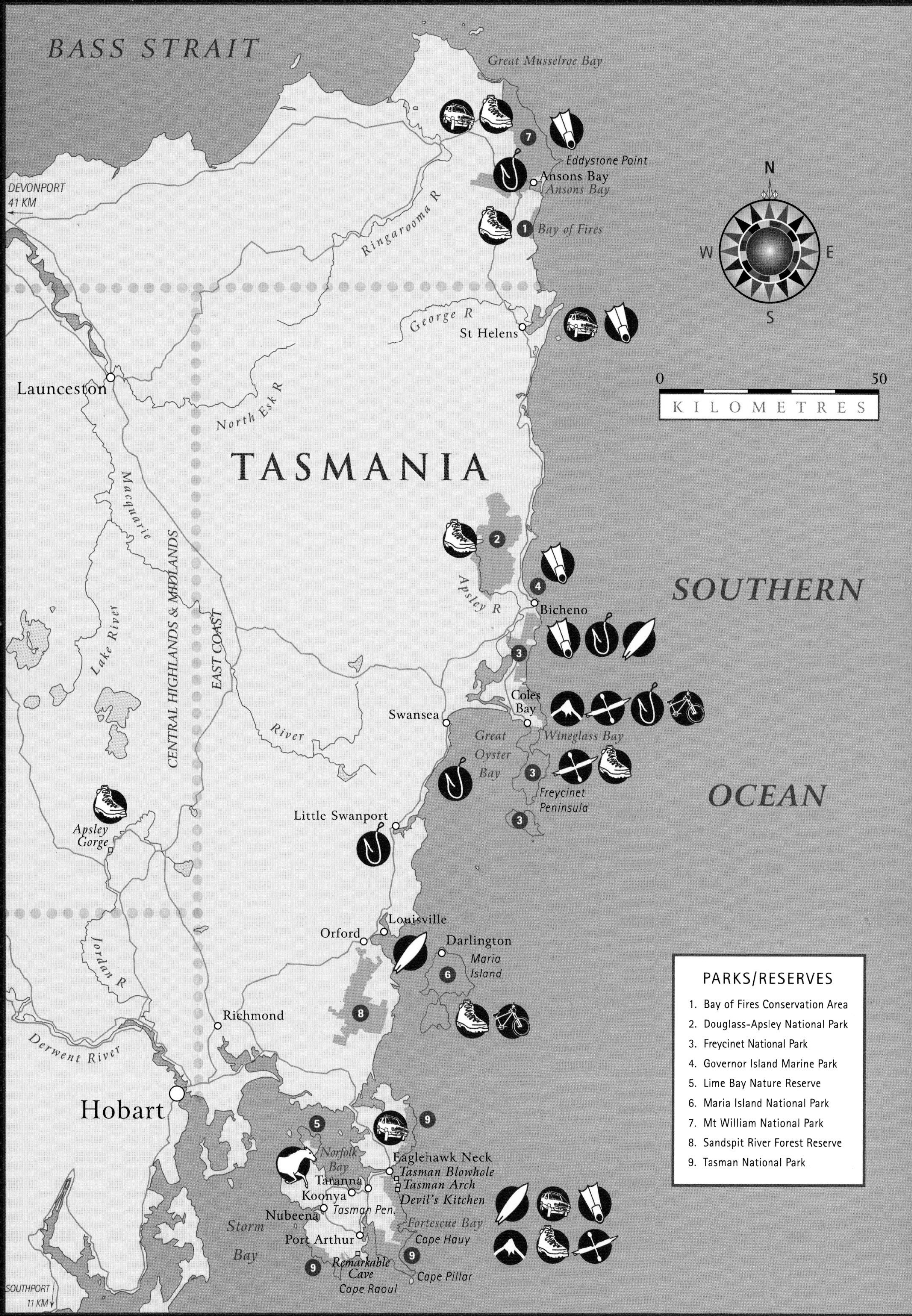
BASS STRAIT
Great Musselroe Bay
Eddystone Point
Ansons Bay
Ansons Bay
Bay of Fires
DEVONPORT
41 KM
Ringarooma R
George R
St Helens
Launceston
North Esk R
TASMANIA
Macquarie
CENTRAL HIGHLANDS & MIDLANDS
EAST COAST
Lake River
Apsley R
Bicheno
Coles Bay
Swansea
River
Great Oyster Bay
Wineglass Bay
Freycinet Peninsula
Apsley Gorge
Little Swanport
Louisville
Orford
Darlington
Maria Island
Jordan R
Richmond
Derwent River
Hobart
Norfolk Bay
Eaglehawk Neck
Tasman Blowhole
Tasman Arch
Devil's Kitchen
Taranna
Koonya
Nubeena
Tasman Pen.
Storm Bay
Fortescue Bay
Port Arthur
Cape Hauy
Remarkable Cave
Cape Raoul
Cape Pillar
SOUTHPORT
11 KM
N
W
E
S
0
50
KILOMETRES
SOUTHERN
OCEAN
PARKS/RESERVES
1. Bay of Fires Conservation Area
2. Douglass-Apsley National Park
3. Freycinet National Park
4. Governor Island Marine Park
5. Lime Bay Nature Reserve
6. Maria Island National Park
7. Mt William National Park
8. Sandspit River Forest Reserve
9. Tasman National Park

Maria Island. (Tourism Tasmania)

NATIONAL PARKS

Tasman National Park: scattered around various coastal sections of the Tasman Peninsula, Tasman National Park has wonderful sea views, rock formations, sea caves and hidden bays. Highlights include the dramatic formations of Tasman Arch and Blowhole, Devils Kitchen, the full-day coastal track that winds along the shoreline from Eaglehawk Neck to Fortescue Bay and Cape Raoul.

Freycinet National Park: jutting out from the sea the rugged and beautiful Freycinet Peninsula is largely national park and consists of bare granite mountains (known as the Hazards) surrounded by azure bays and white sand beaches. The one-hour climb up to the lookout over Wineglass Bay is one of the best short walks in Australia and the breathtaking view is worth the steep slog.

Maria Island National Park: originally settled by whalers and sealers, the island became a penal colony in 1825. The island was soon infamous for the number of escapes—one unlucky group drifted across the channel on a raft only to walk ashore into the arms of two lost police constables according to local legend—and was known among convicts as a place of ease. By 1832 the convict settlement was abandoned in favour of Port Arthur. Explore the convict settlement site at Darlington, which is also the ferry landing from Louisville, just north of Orford. Other highlights include the Fossil Cliffs and the Painted Cliffs. No cars are permitted on the island.

Douglas-Apsley National Park: dry sclerophyll forest with riverside walking tracks, swimming holes, birdlife and Oyster Bay pines just north of Bicheno. Highlights are deep river gorges, waterfalls and a dolerite-capped plateau, colourful heath and pockets of rainforest.

Mt William National Park: empty beaches with large granite boulders, coastal wildflowers, fishing, diving and camping are the main attractions of this park in the far north-east corner of Tasmania. It is also a great place to see wallabies, wombats, kangaroos (including the Forester kangaroo, unique to Tasmania) and Tasmanian devils, at their most active at dawn and dusk, or in the case of the devils, at night.

Tasman Peninsula

Tasmania's Tasman Peninsula, an easy day drive from Hobart, is, all hyperbole aside, an area of intense natural beauty. Think pockets of lush rainforest, pristine beaches, rugged wind-swept headlands pock-marked with sea caves and fantastically-shaped rock formations and gentle rolling hills studded with contented black and white cows and you'll have the picture.

Beautiful it is, but the main reason people come here is the dramatic history–which is so pervasive that you can almost hear the clanking of the convict chains as you drive past convict-built houses and explore the ruins of convict settlements, the highlight of which is Port Arthur, one of the country's most significant historic sites.

Practically cut off from mainland Tasmania by a strip of land less than 100 metres wide called Eaglehawk Neck, surrounded by shark infested waters and wild beaches and towering cliffs, the Tasman Peninsula was a natural penitentiary, or so thought the colonial powers at the time.

Richmond

This historic town just north of Hobart has more than 50 buildings classified by the National Trust, with many built by convicts, and is home to Australia's oldest bridge, built in 1825. Today it is a popular tourist town with lots of galleries, craft shops and boutiques.

Freycinet Peninsula

Jutting into Great Oyster Bay the rocky peaks of the Freycinet Peninsula are among the most readily recognisable in the state–the distinctive pink granite peaks of the Hazards dominate the scenery as you drive along the edge of the bay to the tiny town of Coles Bay, a collection of holiday houses clinging to the shore line. There are many secluded beaches in the national park, with beautiful Wineglass Bay the most popular of them all. Take a drive up to the lighthouse at Cape Tourville for good sunset views and whale and dolphin watching in season.

Bicheno, St Helens and Maria Island

The east coast is home to many of Tasmania's commercial fishing fleet and the seaside towns of Bicheno and St Helens are low-key holiday-cum-fishing towns where you can watch the fishing boats unload their catch or tend their dockside chores. Both offer beautiful seemingly endless stretches of pristine white beaches close to town. Offshore, granite outcrops form underwater cliffs and the clear waters are home to a diverse range of marine life and offer some fantastic diving.

Tiny Maria Island, just 20km long and 13km wide and a 20-minute ferry ride from Orford is a restored penal settlement that operated from 1825-51. It is now a national park.

Caravan and camping

One of the best kept beach-side camping secrets in Australia, beautiful Lime Bay near the Coal Mines Historic Site on the Tasman Peninsula has shady campsites with million dollar water views. There are also basic camping facilities and unpowered caravan sites at Fortescue Bay in Tasman National Park. Freycinet National Park is a popular place to camp, with good reason: camping at Freycinet is by the beach and each camp site has fantastic views. There are plenty of shady sites to choose from, including powered sites for campervans and caravans up to 17ft. There is also good camping at the Friendly Beaches close to the border of the park. On Maria Island there is a large open camping area close to the creek at Darlington with a number of fireplaces, but a portable stove is recommended.

Port Arthur. *(Tourism Tasmania)*

DON'T MISS

- **Eaglehawk Neck:** the Officers Quarters, built in 1832 and reputed to be the oldest wooden military building remaining in Australia, has been restored as a museum interpreting the history and life at Eaglehawk Neck. Open daily, 9.30am–4pm.
- **Tessellated Pavement:** a short walk to an unusual geological formation near Eaglehawk Neck that looks as if the coastline has been tiled by a giant.
- **Port Arthur:** Tasmania's biggest tourist attraction, the site covers more than 40 hectares and 30 historic buildings, ruins and gardens, including fully restored and furnished houses. Highlights include the Interpretation Centre in the Visitors Centre, an interactive museum chronicling the life of many convicts and very popular with kids. Tickets are valid for two days and include guided walking tours and harbour cruises. Evening ghost tours, Isle of the Dead and Point Puer tours also available. Open daily, 8.30am–dusk. **www.portarthur.org.au** ☎ 1800 659 101.
- **Devils in the Dark:** night-time tour and feeding of Tasmanian devils and other nocturnal native animals at the Tasmanian Devil Park. 5990 Port Arthur Highway, Taranna. Park open daily. Devils in the Dark tours nightly from dusk—times vary. (Tue, Wed, Fri and Sat; Easter–September). **www.tasmaniandevilpark.com**
- **Coal Mines Historic Site:** wander freely among the evocative ruins of Saltwater River Convict Station, with its cramped and gloomy underground cells. The spectacular water views mitigate the harshness of the lives the convicts must have endured here. 20km off the highway at Taranna via Premaydena. Open daily.
- **Remarkable Cave:** sea cave 6km from Port Arthur. Views to Cape Raoul from the lookout above the beach, or climb down to the sand to explore the cave.
- **Wineglass Bay:** one of Tasmania's most photographed views over the white sands and perfectly shaped beach of Wineglass Bay. The fairly steep one-hour climb to the lookout is well worth the effort. It's another two hours return to walk from the saddle down to the beach. Freycinet National Park.
- **Kate's Berry Farm:** berries, jams, sauces and Devonshire tea, plus a small winery specialising in table wines made from berries, fruit and grapes. Addison Street, 2km south of Swansea. Open daily, 9am–6pm. ☎ (03) 6257 8428.
- **Swansea Bark Mill & East Coast Museum:** historic plant built in the 1880s to process the bark from Black Wattle for tanning leather. East Coast history museum, tearooms, and wine and wool centre retailing wines from more than 50 Tasmanian wineries and Tasmanian knitwear. 96 Tasman Highway, Swansea. Open daily. ☎ (03) 6257 8382.
- **Sea Life Centre:** exhibition of live Tasmanian fish, seahorses, Tasmanian crayfish, some of the world's lagest crabs, baby crayfish, trumpeter, octopus, cowfish and other intriguing creatures. 1 Tasman Hwy, Bicheno. Open daily, 9am–5pm.
- **East Coast Natureworld:** wildlife park set in natural parkland beside a lagoon. Tasman Hwy, 6km north of Bicheno. Open daily, 9am–5pm. **www.natureworld.com.au**

scenic highlights

Coal Mines Historic Site. *(Tourism Tasmania)*

In Tasmania the past is never very far away—particularly its convict beginnings and the grand bridges, colonial buildings and haunting ruins that were built by their labour. The best place to explore convict history and its legacy is on the Tasman Peninsula, home to Port Arthur penal settlement, a mixture of intact buildings and atmospheric ruins and one of Australia's most significant historical sites. This drive can be done in a day, but there is so much to see and do, as well as some very good evening tours, that it's worth spending the night.

From Hobart, head north out past the airport to Sorell, then cut across to Dunalley and wind down to Eaglehawk Neck. This narrow isthmus of land—only a few hundred metres wide—is the reason Port Arthur was chosen as the site for a maximum security prison in 1830—the tiny strip of land was easily patrolled, in those days very few people could swim, the surrounding bush was dense and inhospitable and, if all else failed, a line of snarling dogs roused the soldiers if any brave prisoners tried to sneak past.

The coastline of the Tasman Peninsula is riddled with dramatic rock formations, extraordinary rock pillars and sea stacks. The Tessellated Pavement, a stretch of coastline resembling giant tiles, is on the north side of Eaglehawk Neck and the Tasman Blowhole and the ruins of once huge sea caves at Tasman Arch and the Devils Kitchen are on the southern side.

Hugging the shores of Norfolk Bay the road winds its way to Taranna, where you can begin a small loop, visiting Port Arthur Historic Site (plan to spend at least half a day here, if not longer, exploring the 30 historic buildings and ruins, joining one of several walking tours and ferry cruises) and the thriving farming community of Nubeena before heading up along the western edge of the Norfolk Bay to the Coal Mines Historic Site. Tasmania's first operational mine, the site was developed both to limit the colony's dependence upon imported coal from New South Wales, as well as a place of punishment for the 'worst class' of convicts from Port Arthur and provides a very different, self-guided look at our convict past than the more popular Port Arthur site.

From the Coal Mines site, head back to Taranna, reconnecting with the highway back to Hobart, about two hours drive.

Water is provided from a centrally located tap. Campsites are also available at French's Farm and Encampment Cove some three or four hours' walk away.

Douglas-Apsley National Park is a fairly new park, so facilities are still basic, but there is a small bush camping area near the Apsley Waterhole, 10 minutes walk from the car park off Rosedale Road. For those walking the Leeaberra Track there are remote bush campsites near Heritage Falls and Tevelein Falls, both on the Douglas River. In Mt William National Park there are several sheltered camping areas at Stumpys Bay in the north of the park. There is also a camp site at the far northern end of the park, just before Musselroe Bay township and at the end of the beachside road from Eddystone Point to Deep Creek in the southern end of the park

Bushwalks

The one-hour climb up to the lookout over Wineglass Bay in Freycinet is one of the best short walks in Australia and the breathtaking view is worth the steep climb. What's more, while you'll see a few people on the trek, if you continue down to the beach (two hours return), you're just as likely to have it to yourself, as the walk unjustly deters most day trippers, who seem happy enough to snap a picture of this most photographed beach in the world, and continue on their way.

The 30km Freycinet Peninsula Circuit travels around the Hazard Mountains to Hazards Beach. The track continues south to Cooks and Bryans Beaches then crosses the peninsula over a heath-covered plateau next to Mount Freycinet (spectacular views) before descending to the white, quartz sands of Wineglass Bay.

On the Tasman Peninsula the three- to five-day Tasman Coastal

Tasman Island. *(Tourism Tasmania)*

Trail follows the coastal cliffs from Waterfall Bay through to Fortescue Beach, out to Cape Hauy and on to Cape Pillar. Highlights include some of the highest sea cliffs in Australia; Waterfall Bay with its spectacular view across the cliff-lined bay to a waterfall which, after rain, plummets straight into the sea; the squeaky white sands of Fortescue Bay; large kelp forests and spectacular dolerite columns and cliffs at Cape Hauy. Be aware that the Tasman Peninsula is exposed to the weather–especially Cape Pillar where places like Tornado Ridge and Hurricane Heath often live up to their descriptive names. You can break the walk into shorter sections if desired. A good stand-alone short walk is the five-hour return walk to Cape Raoul, although there are some rough uphill sections, but the views are worth it.

On Maria Island the 90-minute return walk from Darlington to the Painted Cliffs features beautifully patterned sandstone cliffs created by the movement of mineral-rich water though the rock, and by the eroding action of wind and waves. The peaceful beaches and shoreline also have a wealth of fascinating tidal-zone marine life.

Good walks in Douglas-Apsley National Park include the 20-minute return stroll to the Apsley Waterhole, the three-hour Apsley Gorge circuit and the three-day north-south bushwalk through the park.

In Mount William, walks range from easy strolls on the beach to coastal and heath walks of half a day or longer. The entrance to the Bay of Fires–Binalong Bay (10 minutes from St Helens) is one of Tasmania's most beautiful beaches and provides some great views and walks along the stunning coastline. The four-day Bay of Fires walk is a commercially-run guided walk, with accommodation in a luxury lodge.

www.bayoffires.com.au

adventure activities

Tasman Island. *(Tourism Tasmania)*

Abseiling and rock climbing

The coastal cliffs that rise dramatically from the sea near Coles Bay on the Freycinet Peninsula are probably one of the best known climbing areas in Tasmania, with climbs varying from the less accessible routes on the Hazards (an impressive 300m high, pink granite dome) to the more popular, shorter but steeper, well protected climbs found closer to Coles Bay. It's also a popular place with abseilers and there are several companies that offer full-day climbing and abseiling courses.

www.aardvarkadventures.com.au
www.freycinetadventures.com.au

The spectacular dolerite columns and cliffs along the coastline of the Tasman National Park are also popular areas for climbing and abseiling. The sea stacks north of Fortescue Bay, the 'Candlestick' and 'Totem pole' at Cape Hauy and the cliff lines around Mount Brown are the most commonly climbed areas.

Canoeing and kayaking

Paddling is one of the most popular ways to explore the clear blue waters, sandy white beaches and dramatic coastline of the Freycinet Peninsula and there are many places you can hire a kayak or canoe in and around Coles Bay. There are also a number of excellent guided paddling tours available. Freycinet Adventures is probably the biggest with daily tours, both morning and twilight, departing from Muir's Beach in Coles Bay as well as range of three- to five-day adventures, or you can hire your own kayak from them and go it alone.

www.freycinetadventures.com.au

Blackaby's Sea Kayaks and Tours also do guided kayaking trips on the Tasman Peninsula to the amazing sea cliffs of Fortescue Bay, the sea caves and sandstone formations near the Coal Mines Historic Site and Norfolk Bay and Port Arthur, where you'll paddle past the sandstone prison buildings, out to the Isle of the Dead and past Point Puer where young boys were imprisoned, gliding over vast kelp forests and past sea caves and perhaps an Australian fur seal or two, to get a completely different perspective on the notorious, but very picturesque, prison.

www.blackabyseakayaks.com.au

Cycling

With no cars allowed on Maria Island cycling is a great way to explore the length of the island and there are a number of tracks where bike riding is permitted. You can download a map from

www.parks.tas.gov.au/natparks/maria/bike.html

You can also hire mountain bikes from Freycinet Adventures in Coles Bay, which includes a map of tracks in the area, and guided tours are available by arrangement.

www.freycinetadventures.com.au

Preparing for a day's kayaking. *(Tourism Tasmania)*

Tasman National Park. *(Tasmania Tourism)*

Diving

Both the Tasman and Freycinet peninsulas boast some of the best temperate water diving in the world with the famous Waterfall Bay caves, the historic wreck of the *SS Nord* with huge schools of fish, giant kelp forests and bizarre seadragons just some of the highlights.

Cathedral Cave at Waterfall Bay is the most popular dive site in south-east Tasmania, a maze of caverns, passageways and narrow swimthroughs. The entrances of the system have walls that are adorned with jewel anenomes, yellow zoanthids, sponges, asidians, bryzoans and other species that are often only found in deeper water. Visibility is often 30 to 40 metres in the winter months and ideal for photography.

The Eaglehawk Dive Centre runs boat dives to Cathedral Cave, through the giant kelp forests of Fortescue Bay, the wreck of the SS *Nord* (one of Australia's best wreck dives for deep divers with experience to 40m) and other locations including seal dives to Hippolyte Rock and Cape Pillar where sharks often visit the colonies looking for an easy meal. The water surrounding Hippolyte Rock drops down to 90m and offers spectacular wall diving but is not for novices as good all-round skills, particularly buoyancy control, are necessary.

www.eaglehawkdive.com.au

There is also good diving around Bicheno in Governor Island Marine Reserve where the coarse-grained granite bedrock has created spectacular underwater scenery with sheer vertical walls and overhanging rock faces covered with invertebrate life and deep fissures and caves are full of fish. At depths below 30m, the granite reef slopes into sandy-bottomed trenches scattered with boulders. The Castle, Hairy Wall and Mr Whippy are some of the names given by divers to underwater features. However, the waters around Governor Island are deep and subject to strong currents and swells so diving is recommended for experienced divers only.

Further north, there is also good diving at Georges Rocks and Eddystone Point off the coast from Mt William National Park and in the clear waters off St Helens.

Fishing

The sheltered bays around the Tasman Peninsula and Great Oyster Bay offer superb fishing, abounding with a variety of table fish including flathead, Australian salmon, trevally, trumpeter and squid. Coles Bay is an excellent base for big game fishing, especially during the autumn when the giant bluefin tuna run. The Swan River and Little Swanport have some of the state's best bream fishing. The warm East Australian Current washes the east coast north of Bicheno, bringing with it large numbers of fish, making the area a favourite with saltwater anglers who fish from the sheltered bays, beaches and rocks for salmon, flathead, bream, trumpeter and tuna. Lots of boat launching ramps also add to the coast's fishing attractiveness. Ansons Bay has long been recognised as a good spot for bream fishing. It is also one of the few places in Tasmania where you can catch Australian bass.

Off-road driving

Good four-wheel-drive opportunities along the coast include the scenic 12km drive through one of the state's oldest working forest areas to Fortescue Bay in Tasman National Park and the Taranna Forest Drive near Port Arthur. Although accessible to 2WD the dirt road through the Wielangta Forest from Rheban to Kellevie is very pretty. The Sandspit Forest Reserve has picnic facilities, forest interpretation boards and scenic forest walks. The road also provides access to the Thumbs picnic area and lookout near Orford and the network of East Coast Forest Roads. Highlights of this 118km trip are the coastal and forest scenery together with access to Lost Falls, Meetus Falls and Hardings Falls. Access is from the Tasman Highway just north of the Little Swanport Bridge via Bresnehans Road and then McKays Road. The route extends to the Tasman Highway about 4km south of St Marys, crossing Lake Leake Road and Old Coach Road along the way.

The Peron Dunes track (St Helens Point Road) near St Helens offers more of a challenge–access can be difficult for 4WD vehicles because of steep loose sand at the entry point and you'll need to deflate your tyres on the dunes due to the soft sand. The area is used by all types of recreational vehicles, including dune buggies and all terrain vehicles, so care is needed. To get there, travel south-east from St Helens on the A3 for about 2km and turn left onto St Helens Point Road C851. The dunes are a further 6km on. Coastal camping is available at Humbug Point and Dianas Basin.

In Mt William National Park there is a nice loop road providing access to Stumpys Bay for camping, fishing and boating. The loop rejoins Musselroe Road, which also provides access to the Musselroe Bay Conservation Area. The access road to the coast provides excellent coastal views and free campsites on Crown Land where dogs are permitted.

Horse riding

Seaview Riding Ranch at Koonya on the Tasman Peninsula offers a variety of trail rides for beginners and experienced riders. Choose from rainforest or light bush riding trails. The one-hour rides meander through the bush and into paddocks while the two-hour ride is up through a fern gully, which is quite spectacular. Horses are suitable for all ages as well as beginners. 90-minute rides are also available.

☎ (03) 6250 3110

Surfing

Eaglehawk Neck on the Tasman Peninsula usually has a wave, and all up the east coast from Orford to Bicheno there'll be somewhere breaking. The famous monster waves of Shipstern Bluff are off the coast of Port Arthur. 42 South Surfschool in Scamander has soft board and wetsuit hire as well as a mobile surf school with locations at Falmouth in Scamander, Redbill Beach at Bicheno, Eaglehawk Neck on the Tasman Peninsula and others.

www.surfingaustralia.com

Giant Kelp Forests *(Tourism Tasmania)*

MORE INFORMATION

- **Tasmanian Travel Centre:** cnr Davey and Elizabeth Streets, Hobart. www.discovertasmania.com.au ☎ 1300 655 145

weather watch

- January: 11–19°C
- July: 6–11°C
- Most rain falls during the winter months. Roads can be icy during winter.

west coast

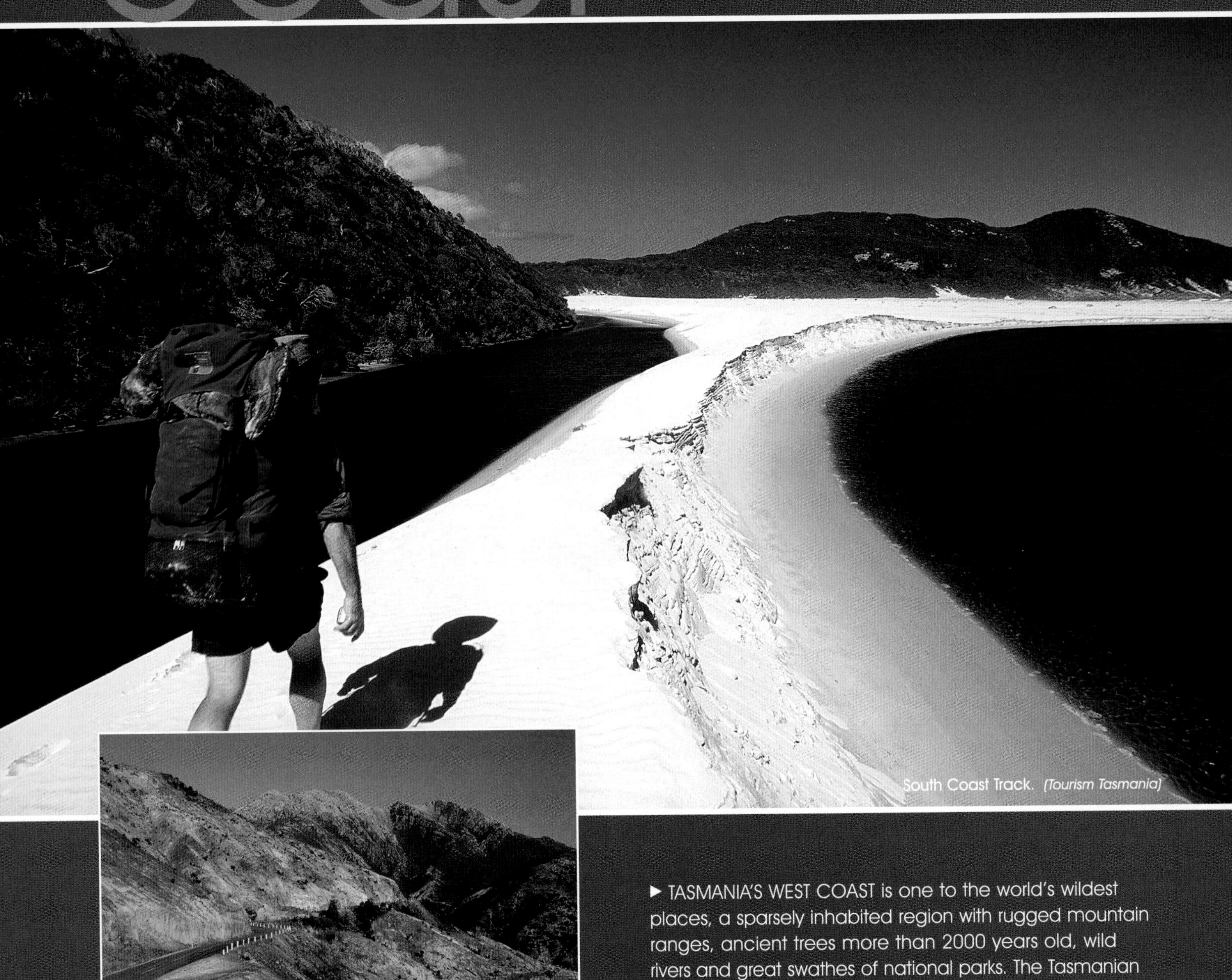

South Coast Track. *(Tourism Tasmania)*

Road to Queenstown. *(Tourism Tasmania)*

▶ TASMANIA'S WEST COAST is one to the world's wildest places, a sparsely inhabited region with rugged mountain ranges, ancient trees more than 2000 years old, wild rivers and great swathes of national parks. The Tasmanian Wilderness World Heritage Area protects one of the last true wilderness regions on earth and encompasses a greater range of natural and cultural values than any other region on the planet.

The southern corner of the state is largely untouched and inaccessible except by air, on foot or by the river and all of it challenging, preserved thanks to the efforts of conservationists in the 1980s who fought vigorously against proposed hydro-electric dams, making headlines around the world and kick-starting the green movement in Australia.

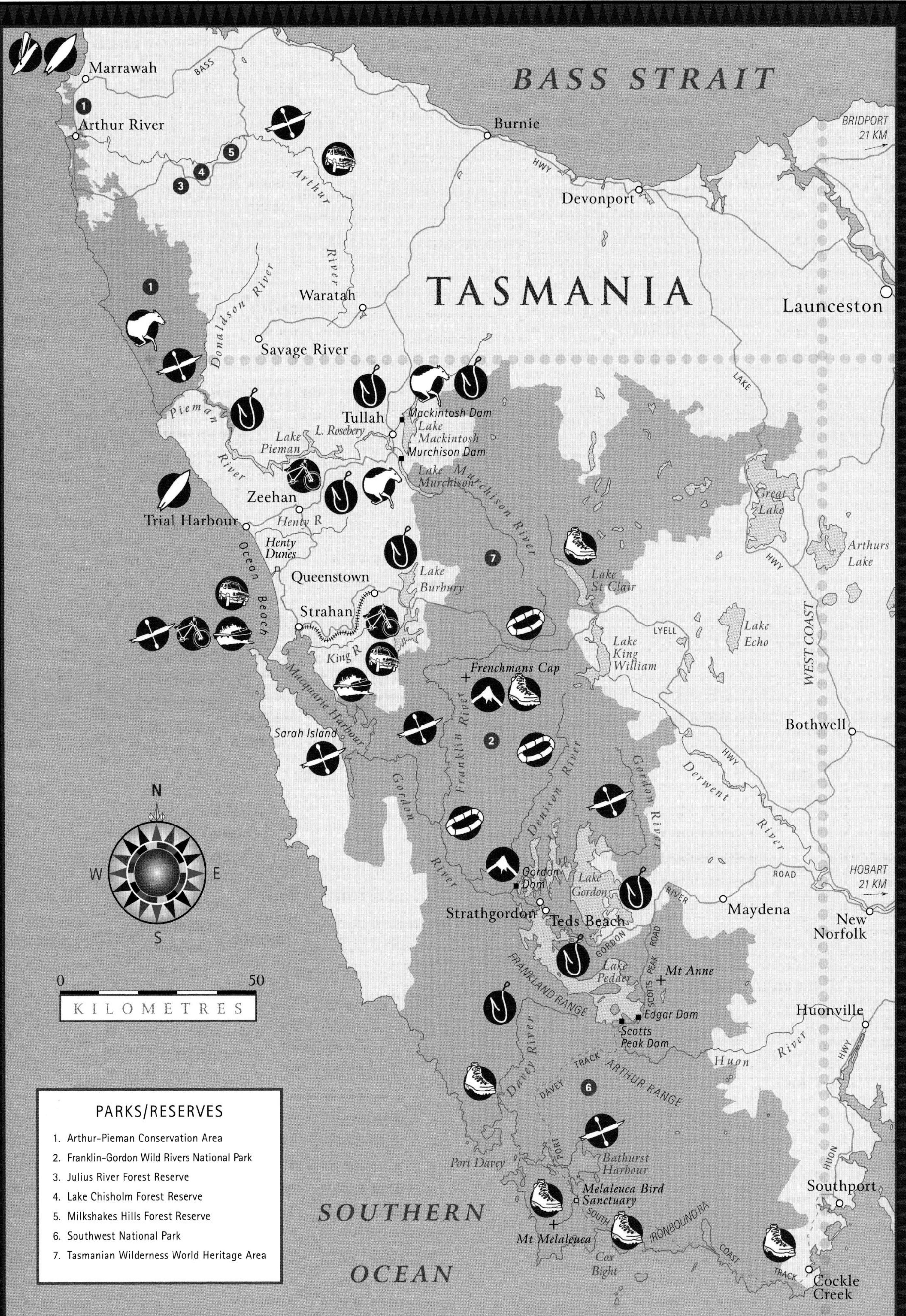

BASS STRAIT
TASMANIA
Marrawah
Arthur River
Burnie
Devonport
Launceston
BRIDPORT 21 KM
Waratah
Savage River
Donaldson River
Arthur River
Tullah
Mackintosh Dam
Lake Mackintosh
Murchison Dam
Lake Murchison
L. Rosebery
Lake Pieman
Pieman River
Zeehan
Henty R
Trial Harbour
Henty Dunes
Ocean Beach
Queenstown
Strahan
King R
Lake Burbury
Murchison River
Lake St Clair
Great Lake
Arthurs Lake
Lake Echo
Lake King William
LYELL
WEST COAST
HWY
LAKE
Frenchmans Cap
Sarah Island
Macquarie Harbour
Franklin River
Gordon River
Denison River
Derwent River
Bothwell
Gordon Dam
Lake Gordon
Strathgordon
Teds Beach
Maydena
ROAD
HOBART 21 KM
New Norfolk
Lake Pedder
Mt Anne
SCOTTS PEAK ROAD
FRANKLAND RANGE
Edgar Dam
Scotts Peak Dam
Huonville
Huon River
Davey River
DAVEY TRACK
ARTHUR RANGE
PORT DAVEY
Port Davey
Bathurst Harbour
Melaleuca Bird Sanctuary
Mt Melaleuca
SOUTH COAST TRACK
IRONBOUND RA
Cox Bight
Southport
Cockle Creek
SOUTHERN OCEAN
N
W
E
S
0
50
KILOMETRES
PARKS/RESERVES
1. Arthur-Pieman Conservation Area
2. Franklin-Gordon Wild Rivers National Park
3. Julius River Forest Reserve
4. Lake Chisholm Forest Reserve
5. Milkshakes Hills Forest Reserve
6. Southwest National Park
7. Tasmanian Wilderness World Heritage Area

Arthur Pieman Conservation Area. *(Tourism Tasmania)*

NATIONAL PARKS

Southwest National Park: part of the Tasmanian Wilderness World Heritage area this 600,000 hectare park is the largest in the state. A region of wild rivers and jagged mountain ranges, rolling buttongrass plains and silent and green rainforests, it encompasses some of the finest wilderness country in Australia. The Gordon River and Scotts Peak roads wind through sections of the park, sometimes opening out onto breathtaking views of rugged mountains like the Saw Back, Anne, Western Arthur and Frankland ranges. In the southeast, the park is accessible from Cockle Creek—the most southerly point in Australia that you can reach by road –you can walk to the coast from there. Bathurst Harbour and Port Davey are drowned river valleys, joined by the deep and narrow Bathurst Channel.

Franklin-Gordon Wild Rivers National Park: joining Southwest National Park this park is also part of the Tasmanian Wilderness World Heritage Area and also features dramatic mountain peaks, beautiful rainforest, deep river valleys and spectacular gorges. The park is famous for the wild and pristine rivers that twist their way through the wilderness. The Franklin River itself has become synonymous with Australia's largest conservation battle—the battle to save the Franklin from a proposed hydro-electric power scheme which would have flooded the river—and is of one of the world's great white water rafting destinations. The Lyell Highway winds for 56km through the heart of the national park and there are several short walks and picnic stops along the way. The park is also visited by cruise boats which operate out of Strahan.

Arthur-Pieman Conservation Area: 100,000-hectare reserve that stretches along the wild and beautiful north-west coast between the Arthur River in the north, the Pieman River in the south and the Frankland and Donaldson Rivers to the east. The Roaring Forties generate enormous swells and sand dunes and lichen-painted rocks fringe the beaches. The area has a rich Aboriginal heritage with middens, hut depressions, artefacts and rock art.

Queenstown

The surreal landscape surrounding the copper, gold and silver mining town of Queenstown provides a stark and shocking contrast to the surrounding national parks and bushland; the alpine wilderness has been transformed into a moonscape of treeless, eroded hills where the vegetation has been killed by almost 100 years of tree felling, bushfires and sulphurous pollution from smelters. Although bizarre, the landscape does have a certain kind of strange and unique beauty. The steep drive down the mountain's hairpin turns to the town centre is quite exciting.

Strahan and Zeehan

The hub of the west coast, Strahan, is a pretty little village beside the sea at the mouth of Macquarie Harbour, the second biggest natural harbour in Australia. This is the jumping off place for the Gordon River Cruises. Most cruises leave in the morning, although during summer there are some afternoon cruises. Thrill seekers can try the 50-minute jet boat ride to King River, another surreal legacy of copper mining pollution. Alternatively, if the weather is nasty, you can always while away the afternoon sitting by the fire in Hamers Hotel with a bowl of soup and watch the fishing boats laden up with cray pots dock at the wharf.

A short drive north is the small mining township of Zeehan, where it is worthwhile stopping into the West Coast Pioneers Memorial Museum–14 galleries chronicle the life and history of the west coast, with a major emphasis on mining and minerals.

Caravan and camping

There are several campsites along both the Gordon River Road and Scotts Peak Road in the Southwest National Park. These vary from very basic sites with no facilities to sites with toilets and tank water. Teds Beach has toilets and electric barbeques (open fires are not allowed). Edgar Campground has toilets and fireplaces and firewood is provided. The Huon Campground has a shelter, composting toilets, fireplaces and firewood. In Franklin-Gordon Wild Rivers National Park there is a basic campsite with a pit toilet at the Collingwood River, the starting point for rafting and canoeing trips down Franklin River. At Arthur River there are three campgrounds with water and toilet facilities. There are no powered caravan sites available within the conservation area, although there is a caravan park, Arthur River Cabin Park, 2km north of Arthur River.

Bushwalks

Two of the country's most challenging wilderness walks are in the rugged southwest. The 70km Port Davey Track links Scotts Peak Road and Melaleuca, while the 85km South Coast Track traces the magnificent coastline between Cockle Creek and Melaleuca. There are no roads to Melaleuca, so you must fly, sail or walk in and out. About 200 people walk the Port Davey track each year, taking four to five days, but be warned, there are some steep and muddy sections. You can either fly out at Melaleuca or continue along the South Coast Track–about 1000 people tackle the South Coast Track each year and most take about six to eight days to complete it. The Ironbound Range rises to 900m where the weather can change rapidly; a warm sunny day can quickly turn to a day of high winds, hail, sleet and snow, even in summer. At times of heavy seas and high tides, some rocky sections of the track can be unexpectedly inundated by ocean waves. Particular care needs to be taken at Granite Beach and the bluff on the eastern beach at Cox Bight. The track surface is rough and muddy over extended sections and is only for experienced and self-sufficient walkers.

For those after something a little less demanding there is the 20-minute boardwalk known as the Creepy Crawly Nature Trail through a lovely section of

Gordon River Cruise. *(Tourism Tasmania)*

DON'T MISS

- **Queenstown Mine Tours:** underground and surface tours of copper mines. Douggies Underground Mine Tours, 2 Orr Street, Queenstown. ☎ (03) 6471 1472.
- **West Coast Wilderness Railway:** historic 35km railway of tight curves and spectacular bridges through the rugged wilderness, dense rainforest and steep gorges between Strahan and Queenstown. Trains run daily. **www.puretasmania.com.au**
- **Galley Museum:** displays and information on Queenstown and surrounding areas housed in the original Imperial Hotel, built in 1897. Corner Driffield and Sticht Streets, Queenstown.
- **Gordon River Cruises:** several cruises depart every day, twice daily during summer, from the wharf area at Strahan. **www.worldheritagecruises.com.au www.puretasmania.com.au**
- **Seaplane Tours:** scenic flights over World Heritage Area, including a river landing. Wilderness Air ☎ (03) 6471 7280.
- **West Coast Pioneers Museum:** excellent museum of local and mining history. Main St, Zeehan. Open daily, 8.30am–5pm.
- **Sarah Island:** remote penal settlement established in Macquarie Harbour in 1821, making it Tasmania's oldest convict settlement. Pining and shipbuilding were among the trades carried out by the convicts and it was once the largest shipbuilding yard in Australia. Full day cruises to the Gordon River include a visit to Sarah Island.
- **Ocean Beach:** stretching for more than 30km from Macquarie Heads in the south to Trial Harbour in the north, Ocean Beach is the longest beach in Tasmania. Giant windswept sand dunes, roaring surf and ocean sunsets. Thousands of shearwaters (muttonbirds) breed here during summer and provide an amazing wildlife spectacle each night at dusk as they return from their feeding forays over the ocean. There is a walkway over the dunes to a viewing platform. To get to Ocean Beach, drive out of Strahan towards Zeehan and turn left at the first intersection past the caravan park. Follow this road for 4km and park behind the dunes.

cool temperate rainforest near Frodshams Pass along the Scotts Peak Road. The Eliza Plateau walk is a five- to six-hour return walk with spectacular views over nearby ranges and lakes. Its starts from Condominium Creek car-park about 21km south along the Scotts Peak Road and is a long steep climb up an exposed ridge following a sometimes very muddy track and a steep scramble over large boulders to get to the summit. The challenging eight-hour Lake Judd trail, also off Scotts Peak Road, takes you to a deep, ice-carved lake surrounded by precipitous mountains.

The Franklin River Nature Trail is a one kilometre, easy nature trail that winds through stunning cool temperate rainforest to two wild rivers: the Franklin and the Surprise, and is suitable for wheelchairs. For experienced bushwalkers the return trip to the summit of Frenchmans Cap takes four to five days but the Donaghys Hill Wilderness Lookout Walk is a 30-40 minute return walk on a well-graded track that gives a spectacular wilderness panorama, taking in the Franklin River valley and Frenchmans Cap, which at 1443m dominates its surroundings and often retains some of its snow well into summer. Even when the snow has melted it remains white and shiny due to the quartzite rock which makes up the half-dome peak. This unusual formation was said to resemble a cap worn by French men–hence the name.

The Nelson Falls Nature Trail, about 4km west of Victoria Pass, is a pleasant 20-minute return walk along a well-graded track takes you through cool temperate rainforest to the spectacular Nelson Falls.

scenic highlights

Lake Rosebery. *(Tourism Tasmania)*

The Gordon River and Scotts Peak roads, in Southwest National Park, were built in the late 1960s and early 1970s as part of the controversial Middle Gordon hydro-electric power scheme which flooded the original Lake Pedder. The routes are lined with rainforest trees such as myrtle, sassafras and celery top pine. In season you will also see wildflowers and berries including silver wattle, leatherwood, Tasmanian waratah and snow berries. Bird life is prolific and there are numerous lookouts along both roads.

The 70km Gordon River Road, from Maydena to Strathgordon, the main construction village for the development of the power scheme, is fully sealed. However it is often steep and winding, is subject to ice and snow, and in places passes quite close to deep water and has a speed limit of 60km/hour.

To reach the Scotts Peak Road turn off the Gordon River Road at Frodshams Pass, 28km from the Maydena gate. On a clear day the views from this road are superb and include the dark dolerite mass of Mt Anne—the highest peak in the southwest—contrasting with the grey quartzite of the surrounding ranges and the green of the forested slopes. The road winds about 36km to the Huon Campground, is unsealed and will take around 90 minutes. There are some steep, rough and corrugated sections, and can be subject to snow and ice, so drive with care.

The drive from Lake St Clair to Strahan is also spectacular. The first 80km section winds through the Franklin-Gordon Wild Rivers National Park, where it seems as if a new jagged-edged mountain rises up around every curve of the road. The bizarre contrast when you reach Queenstown is quite shocking.

The best way to really come to grips with the immensity of the south west wilderness area is to take a 80-minute scenic flight from Strahan in a sea plane that circles above the harbour and Ocean Beach before following the Gordon and Franklin Rivers way beyond the reach of the cruise boats to land on a steep-sided section of the Gordon River at Warners Landing, site of the Franklin River blockade in the 1980s. After a five-minute board walk into the rainforest to view the very pretty Sir John Falls and some ancient huon pines, the tiny seaplane taxis upriver to take off again, following the Gordon River back to Strahan.

adventure activities

Off-road descent near Queenstown. (Tourism Tasmania)

Abseiling and rock climbing

The world's highest commercial abseil, 140 metres in one continuous drop down the Gordon Dam wall, is run by Aardvark Adventures. If you're not quite up for the big one you can also try the optional 30 or 70 metre abseils. It's a full-day tour departing Hobart.

www.aardvarkadventures.com.au

Frenchman's Cap, a magnificent white quartzite dome 1446m high and the most prominent mountain peak in the Franklin-Gordon Wild Rivers National Park, is popular with rock climbers who aren't daunted by the 25km walk in.

Canoeing and kayaking

The Lower Franklin and Gordon Rivers are popular with sea kayakers. Strahan Adventures run four-day combined Steam, Sail and Kayak Tours from Hobart which includes a trip aboard the West Coast Wilderness Railway from Queenstown to Strahan, sailing the vast Macquarie Harbour at sunset on the yacht *Stormbreaker*, and exploring the lower Franklin and Gordon Rivers by kayak and a cruise boat back to Strahan with a guided tour of the former convict settlement on Sarah Island. Camp each night under a canopy of trees.

www.freycinetadventures.com.au

Roaring 40s Ocean Kayaking run three and seven-day sea kayaking trips to Port Davey and Bathurst Harbour. Both expeditions begin with a spectacular light aircraft flight, the only access to the area other than by way of a five-day hike, and use a combination of double and single 'Feathercraft' collapsible kayaks. Some previous kayaking experience is recommended for these wilderness trips.

www.roaring40skayaking.com.au

For a do-it-yourself paddling adventure hire a canoe at Arthur River and explore the rivers in Arthur-Pieman Conservation Area.

Cycling

The west coast has a number of good rail trails for walkers and mountain bikers–the dense bush land is riddled with historic railways and smaller mining tramways built to connect the mines and the ports. It was not until the construction of the Murchison Highway in the 1960s that the railways finally gave way to road transport. The Montezuma Falls Rail Trail is a 19.5km trail in the Zeehan Area from Williamsford to Melba Flats and features the 105m high Montezuma Falls. Following the route of the former North East Dundas Tramway, which ran from Zeehan to Williamsford, the trail travels through lush rainforest with leatherwood, myrtle and sassafras. You can also continue

Rafting on the Franklin River. *(Tourism Tasmania)*

along the Melba Flats to Zeehan trail parallel line between Zeehan and Melba Flats through open grasslands. The 6km Spray Tunnel and Comstock Tramways loop from Zeehan follows four connected disused mining tramways, one with a tunnel. The Strahan to Regatta Point Rail Trail is a lovely 3km trail around the foreshore of Strahan following the former railway that connected the Abt rack railway (now the West Coast Wilderness Railway) from Queenstown with the main line north to Zeehan and Burnie.

The 16km Magnet Mine Trail is a run through lush rainforest to the site of the Magnet Mine. The mine site has good places to camp and relics to explore. The trail begins 1.75km west of Waratah at the local tip and follows the route of the former Magnet Tramway, built in 1901 to carry silver-lead ore from the Magnet Mine.

South of Queenstown, the 12km North Mount Lyell Rail Trail follows an old railway route through lovely rainforest inside the World Heritage Area to Kelly Basin and Pillinger, historic town sites on the shores of Macquarie Harbour. A 5km section from the Bird River turnoff to Bird River is suitable for 4WD and bicycles. From Bird River the trail is for walking only. Allow a full day for the walk to Pillinger.

Fishing

With much of the west coast being inaccessible, fishing destinations are limited compared to other areas of Tasmania. That said, there is some great fishing to be found within the Southwest National Park. Trout fishing, using artificial lures only, is permitted in Lakes Gordon and Pedder all year but is not permitted in any river or stream leading into the lakes. Teds Beach, which has a boat launching area, about 4km before Strathgordon, is popular as is the Edgar Dam area, 30km along the Scotts Peak Road, just before Scotts Peak. The lower reaches of the Gordon River are good for brown trout during spring. Lake Burbury near Queenstown also offers some great fishing opportunities and is most well known for its large numbers of medium-sized brown and rainbow trout. Lakes Rosebery and Mackintosh and the Pieman and Henty rivers are also good for trout.

Off road driving

Much of the south-west is true wilderness with few long-distance tracks, but there are still opportunities to go off road. The Bird River Track is an easy drive through spectacular rainforest in the Wilderness World Heritage Area. It's 42km from Queenstown via Mt Jukes Road then Kelly Basin Road to the Bird River Bridge and car park.

Follow the Montezuma Falls via Melba Flats rail trail or the Ring River alternate route that comes out near Renison Bell. This second track is graded hard and should not be attempted after rain.

There is a 15km beach run on Ocean Beach near Strahan, but beware of quicksand around the mouth of the Henty River. The Mt Huxley Track is more challenging but provides views of Queenstown, Lake Burbury and surrounding mountains. The return trip from Queenstown skirts the northern and eastern slopes of Mt Huxley and has some very steep, rocky terrain at the summit. The 22km Mt McCall Track from Queenstown has superb scenery and ends at the top of an old haulage way, 300m above the Franklin River.

The South Arthur Forest Drive from Kunnannah Bridge to Roger River is an easy forest drive with picnic facilities and forest walks at

Julius and Milkshakes Forest Reserves. Other places include the Sumac Lookout and a pretty walk through Lake Chisholm Forest Reserve to a beautiful sinkhole lake.

Arthur River, 16km south of Marrawah, to Sandy Cape is a challenging 62km drive with fantastic coastal scenery and beautiful camping spots. The first section to Temma is quite easy, but from Temma to Greenes Creek (12km) is tricky after rain with deep-water sections. The beach drive from Greenes Creek to Sandy Cape (12km) is rated hard and vehicle groups are recommended because of the frequent occurrence of quicksand. Alternatively stop at Greenes Creek and return to the Balfour/Greenes Creek Road junction and take the 16km Balfour Track. It has a 70-metre-long canal-like stretch of water, but is otherwise a medium-difficult trail. Interesting features at Balfour include the unique settlement, historic cemetery and old mine sites. You'll need a permit from Parks and Wildlife Service's Arthur River office before starting the trip.

Horse riding

Tullah Horseback and Boat Tours run fully escorted horseback tours of Tullah and the shores of Lake Rosebery. Horseback and boating tours range from one hour through to full day and include a tour of Mackintosh Dam and river by boat and a ride out to the Murchison Dam to view the cliffs on one side and the river on the other. The one-hour tour is a bush tour around the lake area and good for riders with limited experience. A two-day Pioneer Adventure Trail Ride is a pack horse trail ride to the old mine workings around Tullah, spending the night in a hut on the banks of Lake Rosebery with traditional bush cooking around a campfire.

www.tullahhorseback.com.au

If you have your own horse there are some great trails in the radiata pine plantations on the west coast. Riders are also permitted to ride on the designated off-road tracks and beaches within the Arthur-Pieman Conservation Area. Contact the Ranger for details and advice. Holding yards for horses are available at Marrawah, Arthur River and Rebecca Creek.

Jet boating

A 50-minute jet boat ride follows the rain-forested gorges of the King River. From Strahan you will cross Macquarie Harbour to the King River, where 100 years of mining waste has created a vast 400-hectare delta–the river banks devastated to the high water mark. The life in the river has been destroyed by mining pollution, but the scenery is nonetheless bizarre and haunting. Upstream you'll see stands of ancient huon pine and learn about the area's fascinating past when copper-laden trains rattled through the once bustling river port of Teepookana, now a ghost town.

You can take a 4WD trip from the valley floor to the Teepookana Plateau where you can walk on an elevated walkway that meanders through a stand of mature huon pines, some of which are 2000 years old, to a viewing tower with stunning 360-degree views of surrounding forests and mountain ranges with Macquarie Harbour and the Southern Ocean visible on clear days. Jet boats leave daily from Strahan Wharf.

www.wildriversjet.com.au

Sandboarding

The Henty Dunes are a series of giant, 30m-high dunes about 14km from Strahan on the Zeehan Road and a great place for sandboarding or tobogganing. Boards are available for hire from the Strahan Activities Centre on the Esplanade in Strahan.

Surfing and Windsurfing

The wild west coast is for experienced surfers only, with roaring surf rolling in generated by the legendary Roaring Forties winds, wild weather and rips and currents that come and go without warning. Top spots include Trial Harbour in the south and around Marrawah in the north. The powerful winds make Marrawah, in particular, a world class wavesailing location which hosts the annual SmackFest competition. The wind blows from both tacks, with an average strength around 25 knots but regularly reaches 35 knots or more, so small sails are a must. With water temperatures around 15–17 degrees a short-arm or full-length steamer is recommended and bring as many spares as possible. The Great Southern Ocean can be unforgiving and there is no windsurf shop for miles.

www.smackfest.net/loc.html

White water rafting

The Franklin River, one of the world's last major wild rivers, is Australia's premier white water rafting destination. Rafting this river is challenging with rapidly fluctuating water levels, unpredictable weather and demanding portages, but it is a magnificent wilderness adventure through deep gorges, superb rapids and awesome scenery. Not a river for first timers or the unfit, it has claimed several lives. If you are planning to raft the river privately check out the national parks rafting notes at:

www.parks.tas.gov.au/recreation/boating/frankl.html

Most trips take between five and 10 days and there are numerous rafting companies that specialise in Franklin River expeditions.

www.raftingtasmania.com www.tas-ex.com

MORE INFORMATION

- **West Coast Visitor Information and Booking Centre:** The Esplanade, Strahan. ☎ (03) 6471 7622 or visit www.discovertasmania.com.au

weather watch

- January: 12–22°C
- July: 2–12°C
- Most of the coast is exposed to cold, wet, southerly winds. Rain falls on average every second day during summer and more often in other seasons.

central highlands

Dove Lake from Cradle Mountain. *(Tourism Tasma*

& midlands

▶ TASMANIA'S FERTILE MIDLANDS and rugged central highlands are rich in colonial history and magnificent scenery. The undulating midland plains that stretch along the island's spine between Hobart and Launceston are home to many of the country's most significant colonial houses and farming properties, elegant mansions and convict built bridges.

In the centre of the island is the rugged wilderness of Cradle Mountain—Lake St Clair, a mecca for bushwalkers; the central lakes are a fisher's paradise and towards the east the Ben Lomond Range is the state's centre for downhill skiing.

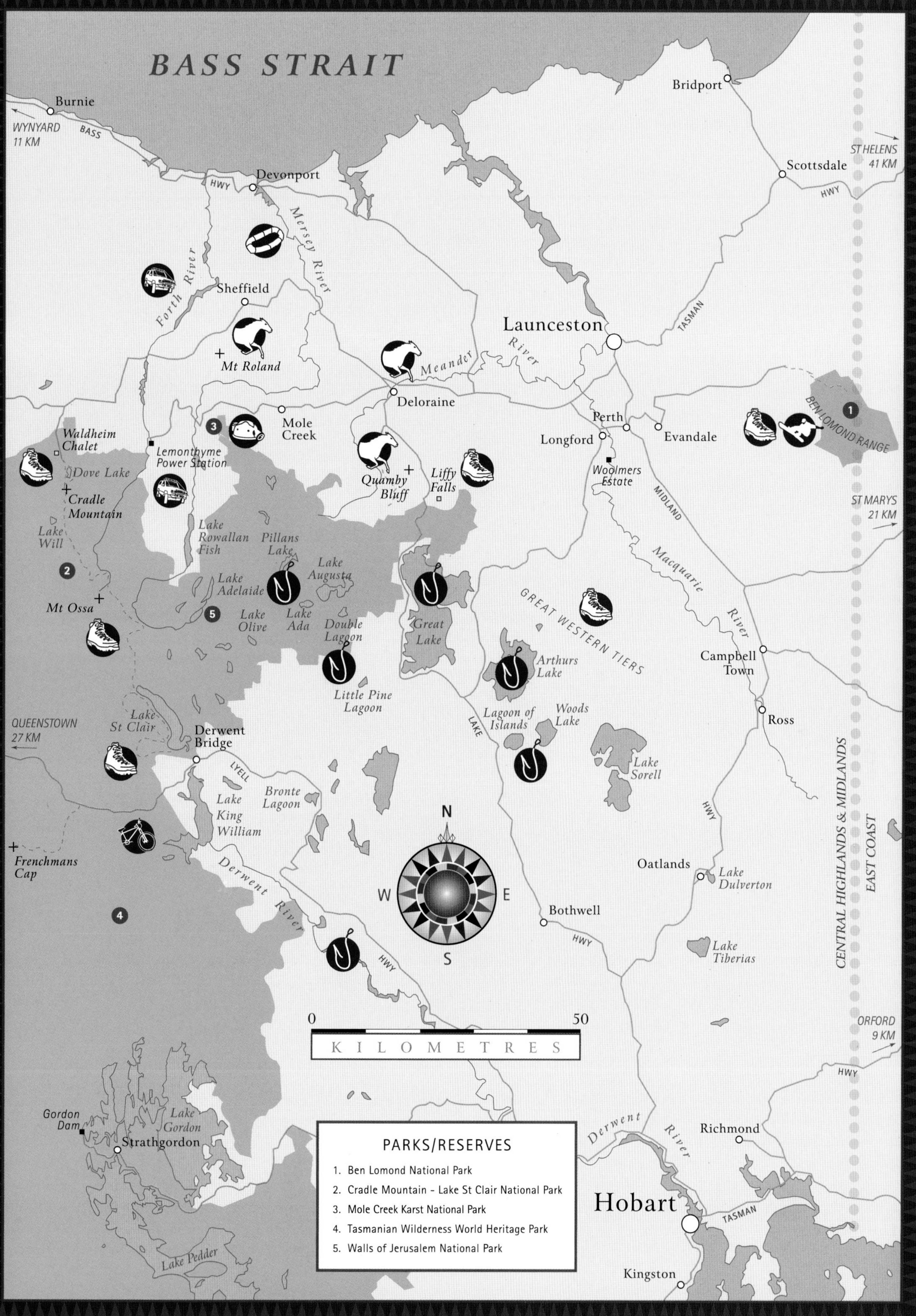

BASS STRAIT
Burnie
WYNYARD 11 KM
BASS HWY
Devonport
Mersey River
Forth River
Sheffield
Mt Roland
Meander River
Launceston
Bridport
Scottsdale
ST HELENS 41 KM
HWY
TASMAN
Deloraine
Mole Creek
Perth
Longford
Evandale
BEN LOMOND RANGE
Waldheim Chalet
Lemonthyme Power Station
Dove Lake
Cradle Mountain
Quamby Bluff
Liffy Falls
Woolmers Estate
MIDLAND
ST MARYS 21 KM
Lake Will
Lake Rowallan
Fish
Pillans Lake
Lake Augusta
Lake Adelaide
Mt Ossa
Lake Olive
Lake Ada
Double Lagoon
Great Lake
GREAT WESTERN TIERS
Macquarie River
Arthurs Lake
Campbell Town
Little Pine Lagoon
Lagoon of Islands
Woods Lake
Ross
QUEENSTOWN 27 KM
Lake St Clair
Derwent Bridge
LAKE
LYELL
Lake Sorell
Lake King William
Bronte Lagoon
HWY
N
W
E
S
Frenchmans Cap
Derwent River
HWY
Oatlands
Lake Dulverton
Bothwell
HWY
Lake Tiberias
CENTRAL HIGHLANDS & MIDLANDS
EAST COAST
0
50
KILOMETRES
ORFORD 9 KM
HWY
Gordon Dam
Lake Gordon
Strathgordon
Lake Pedder
Derwent River
Richmond
Hobart
TASMAN
Kingston
PARKS/RESERVES
1. Ben Lomond National Park
2. Cradle Mountain - Lake St Clair National Park
3. Mole Creek Karst National Park
4. Tasmanian Wilderness World Heritage Park
5. Walls of Jerusalem National Park

NATIONAL PARKS

Cradle Mountain-Lake St Clair National Park: part of the Tasmanian Wilderness World Heritage Area this park is one of the most spectacular in the state. In the north, the jagged peaks of Cradle Mountain are among the most well-photographed in the country and the starting point for the famous six-day walk that takes you through the heart of some of the finest mountain terrain. Ancient rainforests, alpine heathlands, buttongrass plains, stands of colourful deciduous beech, icy streams, rugged mountains including Mt Ossa, the state's highest peak (1617m), glacial lakes and a wealth of wildlife are just some of the highlights. At the southern end of the park, carved out by glaciers over the last two million years, Lake St Clair is the deepest lake in Australia and the headwaters of the Derwent River.

Walls of Jerusalem National Park: adjoining Cradle Mountain-Lake St Clair National Park and also part of the Tasmanian Wilderness World Heritage Area this park is remote and not accessible via road—an area of true wilderness whose dolerite peaks and alpine vegetation are exposed to the extremes of Tasmania's changeable weather. Bushwalkers who do venture into the park must be well equipped and self sufficient—tracks are practically non-existent and ironstone deposits within the region may affect compass readings. There are no visitor facilities.

Ben Lomond National Park: the main focus of downhill skiing in Tasmania with the state's only skiing facilities—there are six ski lifts on the downhill slopes and they operate only in the snow season. Visible over much of the northern midlands of Tasmania, the magnificent mountain of Ben Lomond features imposing and precipitous cliffs. The plateau is roughly 14km in length, 6km wide and more than 1300m high—the summit is the second highest point in Tasmania (1572m).

Mole Creek Karst National Park: Marakoopa and King Solomons Caves are two show caves in an area that has more than 300 known caves and sinkholes. Other typical karst features in this area include gorges and large underground streams and springs. The glow-worm display in Marakoopa Cave is the largest in any public access cave in Australia.

Mount Ossa. *(Tourism Tasmania)*

Ross

Most famous for its decoratively carved bridge, the historic village of Ross, founded in 1812, has many fine examples of convict-built stone buildings and colonial architecture, and is one of Australia's best preserved 19th century towns. The celebrated bridge over the Macquarie River was built by convicts in 1836–making it the third oldest bridge still standing in Australia–and features 186 ornate carvings of birds, fish, animals, insects, plants and ghoulish faces on its sides. There are more than 40 historic stone buildings in and around the township.

Deloraine

Lying in the shadow of the Great Western Tiers, this pretty town on the banks of the Meander River is also full of graceful historic buildings, many of which now house art galleries and boutiques. Nearby Mole Creek is home to a very good wildlife park and the ground is riddled with limestone caves.

Sheffield

This enterprising town south of Devonport managed to put itself on the tourist map by wearing it history on its sleeve–or on its walls in this case. Taking inspiration from the Canadian town of Chemainus, which revitalised the town's dwindling fortunes by covering its buildings with murals depicting the history of the town and region, Sheffield has covered every blank wall in the village with bright and colourful murals and the new tourism attraction is said to entice more than 120,000 visitors to the town each year.

Caravan and camping

Due to the delicate nature of the environment and the large number of visitors to Cradle Mountain, camping is not permitted inside the day visitor area. There is a commercial campground 3km outside the park and rustic cabin accommodation available at Waldheim inside the National Park (book at the Cradle Mountain Visitor Centre).

☎ (03) 6492 1110

Overland Track walkers cannot camp until they reach either Waterfall Valley Hut or the Scott-Kilvert Hut. There are basic, unattended huts at various stages along the track, which provide bunks (without mattresses), tables and either coal-burning or gas heaters. These huts are used on a first-come, first-served basis and may be full when you arrive, so you will also need to carry a tent. Walkers are encouraged to use huts or the tent platforms provided to minimise campsite impacts–if they are fully occupied you can camp in the areas adjacent to the huts. At Lake St Clair you can camp at Cynthia Bay where there are showers and laundry facilities.

There is a small camping area one kilometre inside the boundary of Ben Lomond National Park and another several kilometres below the summit. There are six unpowered sites that are suitable for tents or campervans, flush toilet, drinking water and a lookout. Otherwise, there are no other camping facilities in the national park, although bush camping is permitted anywhere in the park but not within 500 metres of any road. You must use a fuel stove.

It's also bush camping only at Walls of Jerusalem National Park and no camping is permitted at Mole Creek.

Cradle Mountain. *(Tourism Tasmania)*

Bushwalks

Undoubtedly the most famous walk in Tasmania is the six-day, 65km Overland Track between Cradle Mountain and Lake St Clair (see Top 100 page 32). It travels through spectacular dolerite mountains, beside beautiful waterfalls, through a variety of landscapes including alpine pastures, swamps and beech forests, includes a side trip to climb Tasmania's tallest mountain, Mt Ossa, and finishes at Australia's deepest lake, Lake St Clair. Although much of the walk is on boardwalk in order to protect the fragile alpine environment there are some steep and challenging sections. Bookings are required for each walking season (1 November to 30 April).

www.overlandtrack.com.au

If you don't fancy, or don't have the time, for the six-day walk there are a number of excellent short walks that leave from the visitors centre at Cradle Mountain. The two-hour Dove Lake Loop Track is a great introductory walk to the park, and takes you under the shadow of Cradle Mountain, through the tranquil Ballroom Forest and back along the western shore of the lake. There is a short 10-minute rainforest walk behind the visitor centre that has great views of the beautiful Pencil Pine Falls and the 20-minute Weindorfers Forest Walk from Waldheim chalet is an easy stroll through a forest of King Billy pines, celery-top pines and myrtles. The half-hour Enchanted Walk passes by waterfalls, pools, moorland and rainforest before returning to the Cradle Mountain Lodge.

At the Lake St Clair end you can take a gentle stroll around the lakeshore at Cynthia Bay or follow the easy one-hour Watersmeet trail along the crest of a glacial moraine for beautiful wildflowers in spring. You can continue on to Platypus Bay on the Larmairremener tabelti–Aboriginal cultural walk which will take you back to Cynthia Bay via fern glades, moorlands, rainforest and towering eucalypt stags and provides interpretation of the Aboriginal heritage of the area. Allow 90 minutes for the return trip.

On Ben Lomond there are two cross country ski routes which are also used as walking routes. They are not formed trails but are marked by snow poles. The Carr Villa to Alpine Village walk is a 90-minute walk with some steep sections–it takes you up onto the plateau and then along the plateau to the highest point. You can continue on to Little Hell (90 minutes return) for good views across the southern part of the plateau to Stacks Bluff.

The Tasmanian Trail is a 480km trail designed for mountain cyclists, walkers and horse riders that traverses the centre of the island from Devonport in the north to Dover in the south through farmlands, highlands, forests and towns. See the cycling section (page 94) for more information.

scenic highlights

Although you can drive the 200-odd kilometres between the state's two main cities, Hobart and Launceston, in just a couple of hours, you would miss out on some of the island's most beautiful scenery and rich history. Known as the Heritage Highway, the road travels through some of the first lands settled by farmers in the early days of the convict colony. The sleepy villages with their quaint Georgian coaching inns and gracious colonial houses, convict-built bridges and 19th century sandstone road markers are reminiscent of the English countryside, if you can discount the screeching cockies and tall stands of -eucalypt wilderness beyond the cultivated farmlands.

Highlights along the way include Oatlands with its collection of Georgian houses including the National Trust Callington Mill, one of the oldest windmills in the country, the second oldest Supreme Courthouse and the convict-built gaol; the historic township of Ross with its famous bridge and the Tasmanian Wool Centre; historic Longford settled in 1813 and full of National Trust buildings, large farming estates and beautiful churches and Evandale, a National Trust village of well-preserved 19th century buildings, many dating back to the early 1800s. One of Australia's most unusual carnivals, the National Penny Farthing Championships are held here on the last weekend of February every year. Just a few kilometres from town is one of the Trust's finest properties, Clarendon. Built in 1838 for James Cox, wealthy woolgrower and merchant and son of William Cox, who pioneered the first road over the Blue Mountains in NSW, the elegant Georgian mansion has been restored and is fully furnished with extensive gardens.

Oast House. *(Tourism Tasmania)*

Callington Mill (Tourism Tasmania)

DON'T MISS

- **Callington Mill:** built in 1837 is the third oldest windmill in Australia and the only working, authentic 19th Century flour windmill in the country. The complex consists of the mill, a miller's cottage, stables, the proprietor's house and outbuildings. Oatlands.
- **Tasmanian Wool Centre:** heritage museum and wool exhibition and an extensive range of Tasmanian woollen products. Church Street, Ross. Open daily. **www.taswoolcentre.com.au**
- **Trowunna Wildlife Park:** specialises in Tasmanian Devils, wombats and koalas. Mole Creek Rd, Mole Creek. Open daily, 9am–5pm (8pm in summer). Tasmanian devils tours and talks are held at 11am, 1pm and 3pm. Nocturnal tours also available. **www.trowunna.com.au**
- **Deloraine Museum:** local exhibits housed in a collection of historic buildings including cottage, pub, Jimmy Possum snug and the exhibition gallery, garden, dairy, blacksmith's shop, and a vehicle shed. Also includes the Yarns Artwork in Silk exhibition—a four-panel tapestry telling the story of the Great Western Tiers Kooparoona Niara region. More than 300 people from the region helped create the artwork that took more than 10,000 hours to complete. Each panel is 3.4m x 4m and depicts a different season. 98 Emu Bay Rd, Deloraine. Open daily.
- **Liffey Falls:** beautiful waterfall in a forest of tree ferns, old growth myrtles and eucalypts. Golden Valley near Deloraine.
- **Brickendon Historic Farming Village and Gardens:** National Estate listed gardens surrounded by 170-year-old trees and more than 180 varieties of old fashioned roses. The Historic Farm Village depicts the lives of Tasmania's convicts and free settlers on a working farm with displays, old-time games, farm animals, seasonal farming activities and trout fishing. Longford. Open Tue–Sun, 9.30am–5pm. **www.brickendon.com.au**
- **Woolmers Estate:** one of the most outstanding examples of 19th century rural settlements in Australia, Woolmers Estate was established in 1816 and is also home of the National Rose Garden. Conducted tours of the main house, self-guided tours of the out buildings, gardens and National Rose Garden of Australia. 7km from Longford. Open daily, 10am–4.30pm. **www.woolmers.com.au**
- **Clarendon House:** one of the great Georgian houses of Australia, Clarendon was built on the banks of the South Esk River in 1838. Tour the National Trust House, wander the formal gardens and enjoy a coffee in the sunny conservatory café. New Evandale, close by Launceston airport. Open daily, 10am–5pm.

adventure activities

Mole Creek Karst National Park. *(Tourism Tasmania)*

Caving

The Mole Creek Karst National Park contains more than 200 caves, which began to form about 30 million years ago. Marakoopa Cave features two underground streams, a large display of glow-worms, large caverns, rim pools, reflections and shawl and flowstone features. Two tours, one to the lower chamber and one to the large cavern known as the Great Cathedral, are available several times daily. King Solomon Cave is also lavishly decorated with shawls, stalactites and stalagmites. Tours are approximately 45 minutes in duration and cater for all age groups and levels of fitness.

Wild Cave Tours run regular tours of the undeveloped wild caves of Mole Creek. No previous caving experience required as there is no vertical ropework, however the caves have no paths, steps or fixed lighting. Caving gear, helmets and overalls are supplied. Minimum age is 14. Second tours are available for repeat clients in a more remote, sensitive and/or difficult cave and those tours can include abseiling.

www.wildcavetours.com

Cycling

Tasmania is a great place for cycling as traffic is relatively light and towns are close together, allowing for comfortable distances to be covered each day. The 480km Tasmanian Trail stretches from Devonport in the north to Dover in the south, linking existing forestry roads and fire trails, country roads and occasionally crossing private land. From its conception it was intended for use by walkers, mountain bikers and horse riders, so it differs from other trails that usually started as walking tracks and are therefore restricted in use.

Up to 90 per cent of the trail is on some form of made road or track. It passes through a wide range of environments including some of the most beautiful and fascinating areas of Tasmania, through forests and farmlands, across highland plateaus and past the buildings and bridges of some of Australia's oldest towns. For more information go to:

www.parks.tas.gov.au/recreation/tastrail.html

There are a number of tour companies that specialise in Tasmanian cycling holidays. For details see the Tourism Tasmania website:

www.discovertasmania.com

Fishing

Tasmania is the wild trout capital of Australia and the remote lakes of the central highlands and sparkling rivers and streams of the midlands offer some of the country's best fly fishing. There are countless fishing guides and fishing lodges scattered throughout the area but the best, and most popular places to go are Arthur's Lake, Great Lake (the largest lake in the Central Highlands), Little Pine Lagoon, the Western Lakes around the Nineteen Lagoons area surrounding Lake Augusta, Lake Burbury, Bronte Lagoon and Lagoon of Islands. Best time to fish is January and February.

Off-road driving

The Patons road is a medium-rated 4WD track partly in the Tasmanian Wilderness World Heritage Area that runs from Lemonthyme Power Station along the Forth River valley to an old wolfram mine around 20km upstream and features great forest and

Lake Saint Clair. *(Tourism Tasmania)*

High country rides. *(Tourism Tasmania)*

river views. The road is closed at Oakleigh Creek, 1km from the former mine site and is subject to flooding and blockage by fallen trees and is not maintained.

Horse riding

Silver Ridge Retreat, on the slopes of Mount Roland in the heart of the Cradle Mountain and Lakes district offers accompanied trail rides of varying difficulty and length, ranging from one to four hours along bush and logging tracks around Mt Roland.

www.silverridgeretreat.com.au

Central Highlands Trail Rides in Deloraine offer three-hour rides around Quamby Bluff or day, overnight and extended rides around the Central Plateau.

☎ (03) 6369 5298

Cradle Country Adventures are a Tasmanian company with extensive local knowledge who offer a range of half day, full day or multi day rides around their 6000-hectare property Armitstead, near Deloraine. Half-day rides take you through undulating areas of old growth forest, grazing land and bluegum plantation with morning or afternoon tea served on the bank of the beautiful Mersey River, home to lots of platypus. Full-day rides cater for the more experienced rider as do the two and three-day rides.

www.cradleadventures.com.au

River rafting, a great day out. *(Tourism Tasmania)*

If you have your own horse you can ride all, or sections of the 480km Tasmanian Trail, which passes through some of the most beautiful and fascinating areas of Tasmania: forests and farmlands, highland plateaus and past some of Australia's oldest towns.

www.parks.tas.gov.au/recreation/tastrail.html

White water rafting

Aardvark Adventures run regular one-day rafting trips down the Mersey River White Water Race Course, 40km west of Mole Creek. The section of the river rafted is graded 2/3, with some challenging rapids, and is suitable for the whole family. The course takes around 90 minutes to navigate, and is followed by a smorgasbord lunch beside the river. The trip is then repeated, with the opportunity to try your hand at steering the raft through the rapids.

MORE INFORMATION

- **Great Western Tiers Visitor Centre:** 98 Emu Bay Road, Deloraine. www.discovertasmania.com.au
- **Cradle Mountain Visitor Centre:** located just inside the national park entrance. ☎ (03) 6492 1110

weather watch

- January: 9–22°C
- July: 1–12°C
- Most rain falls in winter, when snow falls are not uncommon and roads can be icy.

north coast

The Nut, Stanley. *(Tourism Tasma*

& islands

► TASMANIA'S NORTHERN COASTLINE is one of its best-kept secrets. It is a place of rugged beauty, where fertile farmlands spill into the wild waters of Bass Strait. The spectacular Bass Highway follows the coast from Ulverstone in the east to Stanley in the west, Tasmania's own version of the Great Ocean Road. Cape Grim on the far-western tip has the world's cleanest air, the village of Penguin is home to a large colony of, you guessed it, penguins, the Tamar Valley north of Launceston is home to some of the state's best wineries and the windswept islands of the Bass Strait produce world famous cheeses and other highly-sought after gourmet produce.

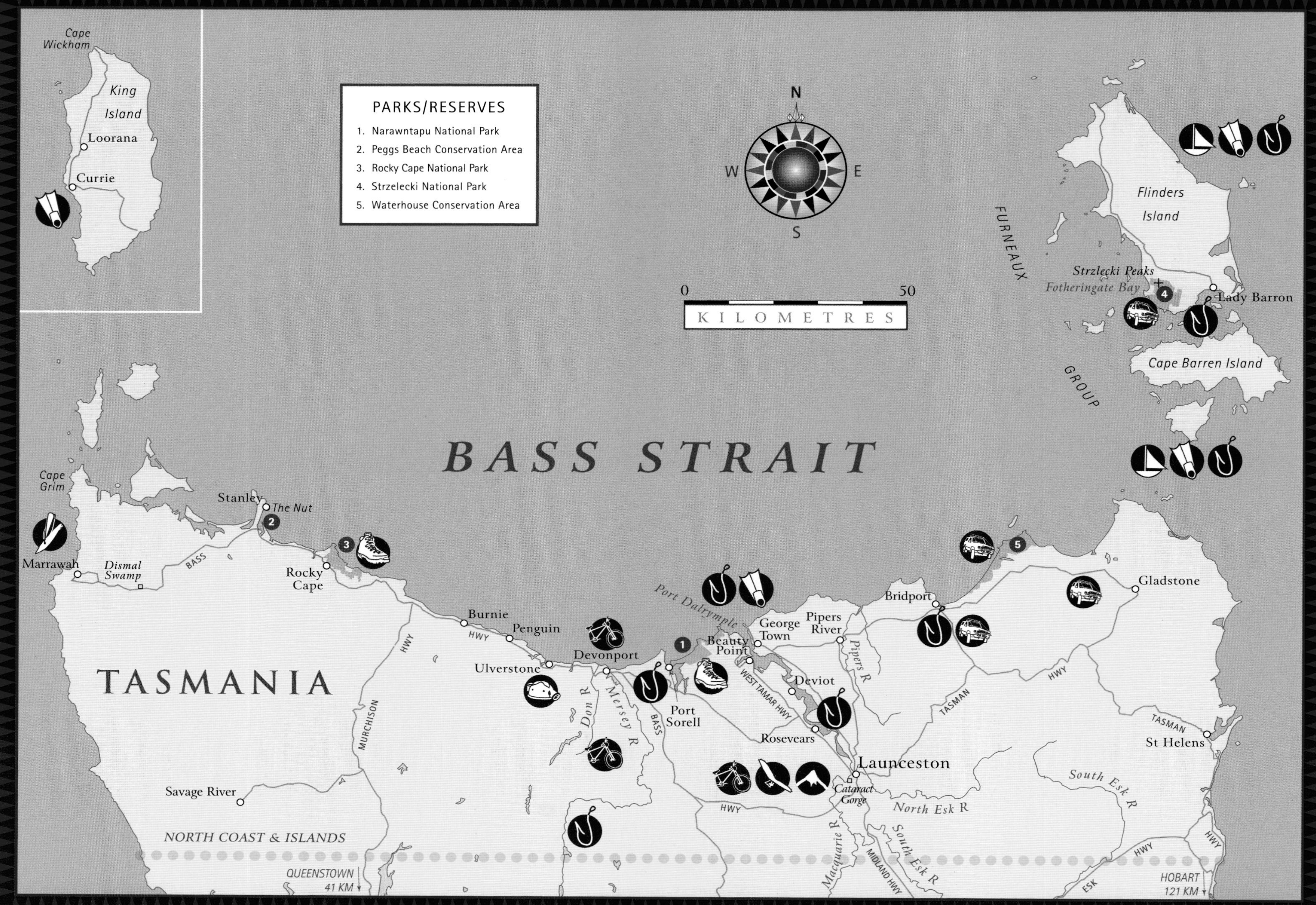

PARKS/RESERVES
1. Narawntapu National Park
2. Peggs Beach Conservation Area
3. Rocky Cape National Park
4. Strzelecki National Park
5. Waterhouse Conservation Area
BASS STRAIT
TASMANIA
NORTH COAST & ISLANDS
KILOMETRES
0
50
N
S
E
W
Cape Wickham
King Island
Loorana
Currie
Cape Grim
Marrawah
Dismal Swamp
Stanley
The Nut
Rocky Cape
Burnie
Penguin
Ulverstone
Devonport
Port Sorell
Port Dalrymple
Beauty Point
George Town
Pipers River
Pipers R
Deviot
Rosevears
Launceston
Cataract Gorge
Bridport
Gladstone
St Helens
Flinders Island
Strzlecki Peaks
Fotheringate Bay
Lady Barron
Cape Barren Island
FURNEAUX
GROUP
Savage River
Don R
Mersey R
North Esk R
South Esk R
Macquarie R
BASS
HWY
MURCHISON
WEST TAMAR HWY
TASMAN
MIDLAND HWY
ESK
QUEENSTOWN 41 KM
HOBART 121 KM

Rocky Cape National Park. (Tourism Tasmania)

NATIONAL PARKS

Narawntapu National Park: formerly known as Asbestos Range National Park, and dubbed the 'Serengeti of Tasmania', the park boasts a rich array of easily observed animals that come out in the evening to graze on the grasslands that stretch from the low coastal ranges to the long Bass Strait beaches. Highlights include an historic farm, a complex of inlets, small islands, headlands, wetlands, dunes and lagoons. Asbestos and other minerals were once mined around the edges of the Asbestos Range, hence the earlier name of the park—and the name change.

Rocky Cape National Park: a small coastal park about two hours drive west of Launceston with sweeping views, Aboriginal heritage, ship wrecks, fabulous rock formations and an incredible variety of flowering plants.

Strzelecki National Park: in the south-western corner of Flinders Island, this national park, named after the Polish scientist and explorer Count Paul Edmund Strzelecki who climbed a number of the mountain peaks on Flinders Island in 1842, features spectacular coastal and granite mountain landscapes. Rocky headlands and beaches at Trousers Point and Fotheringate Bay offer camping, picnicking, swimming, fishing, snorkelling and diving.

Launceston

Wherever you are in Launceston, you're never far from the river. Situated 50km from the north coast at the junction of the North Esk, South Esk, and Tamar Rivers, Launceston is Tasmania's second largest city, and the third oldest city in Australia (after Sydney and Hobart). Its mix of Victorian and Georgian architecture and abundance of parks and gardens make it one of the country's prettiest cities.

Cataract Gorge, a 10-minute walk from the city centre, is a piece of wilderness in the heart of the city. The spectacular gorge extends from the mouth of the South Esk River at King's Bridge and winds its way up the river to the Trevallyn hydro electric dam 5km upstream. The reserve is popular with walkers, river rafters, rock climbers and abseilers. The chairlift crossing the gorge is the longest single span one in the world and there is a restaurant and a kiosk in the grounds. On the southern side of the basin is a 50-metre swimming pool which includes a full length wading pool for young children.

Devonport

This large town and port at the mouth of the Mersey River is the terminal for the Bass Strait ferry service–the *Spirit of Tasmania*, which arrives from Melbourne. Attractions include the Tiagarra Aboriginal Culture and Art Centre, the Maritime Museum, the Don River Railway and Museum and Home Hill, the home of Australia's only Tasmanian prime minister, Joseph Lyons.

scenic highlights

The Tamar Valley Wine Route is a triangular loop drive from Launceston along the banks of the wide Tamar River and across to George Town and back via Pipers River. There are 21 wineries along the way, producing some of the state's best cool climate wines, with pinot noir, sauvignon blanc and chardonnay the main varietals you'll find, although aromatic gewurztraminers, reislings and pinot gris are making an appearance on more cellar door release lists.

There's enough on the trail to fill two full days, although you can easily break the trip into two day trips, one following the western bank of the river 60km north towards Beauty Point on the Bass Strait coastline; the other heading slightly inland to follow the eastern apex of the triangle on the other side of the river, through the hills of the Pipers Brook area to George Town at the mouth of the river.

From Launceston, head north across the Kings Bridge over the river on the West Tamar Highway (A7), through the northern outskirts of the city, past rambling, sometimes crumbling, hillside manor houses and across the river flats to the Tamar Island Wetlands Centre, where you can stroll the boardwalk watching for birdlife.

The blink-and-you'll-miss-it riverside village of Rosevears is just a few minutes up the road, and home to Strathlynn, with its cellar door for Pipers Brook and Ninth Island wines, neighbouring Moorilla Estate's church-like cellar door at St Matthias vineyard and Rosevears Estate, where if all the imbibing and lunching has become too much, you can stay in one of eight luxury cabins overlooking the vineyard and river below.

Continue north, taking the meandering waterfront road to Deviot and Beaconsfield, once a thriving gold rush town where you can visit the Grubb Shaft Gold and Heritage Museum, a collection of buildings from the gold mining era between 1877 and 1914 and the original Tasmania Gold Mine. Although the mine only operated for 37 years it produced 26 tonnes of gold.

Beauty Point is just 7km down the road, where you can learn about seahorses at Seahorse World, and right next door, platypuses at the Platypus House. But if you're really here for the wine, then cross the river via the Batman Bridge and head up to George Town (where you really should visit the historic lighthouse at Low Head—even just to admire the views and try to spot one of the fairy penguins who burrow in the coastal scrub, although they mostly sleep during the day) and spear east to Pipers Brook Vineyard and Jansz Wine Room to taste some of the best sparkling wines produced in Australia.

There are several more wineries along the way back to Launceston, as well as apple orchards, a strawberry farm and cheese factory. At Providence Vineyards you can taste from a selection of their own wines, or up to 60 of the smaller lesser-known Tasmanian vineyards that are not so easy to get to.

Back in Launceston, finish off your day with a cleansing ale or a brewery tour at J Boag & Son.

Cataract Gorge on the Tamar River. *(Tourism Tasmania)*

Bass Strait islands

The remains of a land bridge that once connected mainland Australia and Tasmania, the windswept, storm-lashed islands of the Bass Strait are home to thousands of seabirds and animals and a few small communities of hardy islanders, descendents of the sealers and whalers who first settled these remote and mountainous islands in the middle of the sea.

Flinders Island, the largest of the 53 islands that make up the Furneaux group, features dramatic pink and grey granite cliffs and rolling, green farmland. Surrounding islands host huge colonies of shearwaters, who return to the same burrow each year after their annual migration to the Artic.

Around 1700 people live on King Island, farming dairy and beef cattle on the lush grasses that are the secret to the succulent local beef, rich cream and wonderful hand-made cheeses the island is famous for; gathering bull kelp washed ashore by the turbulent seas of harvesting cray fish and abalone. Cape Wickham lighthouse is the tallest lighthouse in the southern hemisphere and the surrounding seas are full of shipwrecks, making the island a favourite with divers. Reid Rocks, 12km offshore, is home to a major breeding colony of Australian fur seals.

Strzelecki Peaks Flinders Island. *(Tourism Tasmania)*

Stanley

Most well known for the distinctive 152-metre-high flat-topped circular headland called The Nut that looms above the town, Stanley is a pretty fishing community at the western end of the north coast. The Nut is actually the stump of a volcano, and it's a steep climb to the top (or take the chair lift) where there's a 40-minute circular track with great coastal and ocean views.

Caravan and camping

In Narawntapu National Park you can camp at Springlawn, the horse yards, Bakers Point and Griffiths Point and except for large groups, bookings are not necessary. Most campsites have fire-places, tables and pit toilets although at Springlawn there are septic toilets, a shower block, powered sites and electric barbecues. Rocky Cape is mainly a day use park, so no camping areas are provided, although there is camping with facilities at Rocky Cape township and Crayfish Creek, and bush camping at Peggs Beach Conservation Area. On Flinders Island you can camp at the southern end of Trousers Point, Allports Beach, Lillies Beach and North East River, where there are toilets and fireplaces. Camping is also permitted on crown reserves and this covers most of the Flinders Island foreshore as well as sections of the foreshore on Cape Barren Island.

Bushwalks

There are a number of good short walks in Narawntapu National Park including the easy (one hour) Springlawn nature walk through a coastal thicket to the lagoon bird hide and back via the thickly vegetated dunes; and the two-hour walk to Archers Knob for good views over Bakers Beach, Badger Head and beyond. Longer walks include the six- to eight-hour Copper Cove/Badger Head walk from Springlawn, a sea-side walk that zig zags up to Little Badger Head from the eastern end of Bakers Beach before descending to Copper Cove where there is a good picnic spot. From the cove the track continues around the headland to the tiny settlement of Badger Head. The seven- to nine-hour Coastal Traverse is a magnificent walk between Bakers Beach and Greens Beach. The Point Vision Track (allow six to eight hours return) takes you to the highest parts of the range. It is mostly open and fairly easy walking in fine weather. Views from the top are spectacular.

At Rocky Cape there are a number of 10–20 minute walks to caves filled with shells, bones and other remains from thousands of years of Aboriginal occupation. Please do not enter the caves as it is disrespectful to the Aboriginal community. The one-hour Banksia Grove/Caves Circuit leaves from near the Sisters Beach boat ramp at the eastern end of the park and climbs in to the heath-covered hills to an extensive stand of saw banksias with spectacularly large cylindrical flowers. This tree-sized variety of banksia is common in parts of mainland Australia, but is found only around Sisters Beach in Tasmania. From Banksia Grove take the link track towards the coast to the Aboriginal shelter, Lee Archer Cave, set dramatically above the rocky shore. A platform allows viewing of the cave while protecting midden material.

DON'T MISS

- **Seahorse World:** take a tour of the seahorse farm; see exotic seahorses, sea dragons and other endangered fresh water species. Interpretive centre and touch pool for kids. Beauty Point, Tamar Valley. Open daily from 9.30am. Tours on the half hour, last tour 3.30pm. **www.seahorseworld.com.au** ☎ (03) 6383 4111.
- **Queen Victoria Museum and Art Gallery:** once derelict railway workshops have been transformed into an innovative industrial museum with art galleries housing Australian colonial art, contemporary craft and design, blacksmith's shop, railways and migration exhibitions and more. Inveresk, Launceston, open daily, 10am–5pm. Sister site (linked by riverside walkway) at Royal Park open daily, 10am–5pm. **www.qvmag.tas.gov.au**
- **Design Centre:** showcasing the best of Tasmanian timber design and craftsmanship. Changing exhibitions of everything from furniture to sculpture in the specially-designed gallery space, plus well-stocked shop selling Tasmanian-made art and furniture. City Park, corner Brisbane and Tamar Streets, Launceston. Open daily, 9.30am–5.30pm. **www.twdc.org.au**
- **City Park:** the largest and most impressive of Launceston's many beautiful parks and gardens. Developed in the 1820s by Australia's first horticultural society, the park's 13 hectares feature fine Victorian gardens, a troop of Japanese macaques at Monkey Island, a giant chess board, a bandstand, and a beautiful conservatory full of exotic hot house plants.
- **National Automobile Museum of Tasmania:** $8 million collection of cars and motorbikes from across the motoring era. 86 Cimitiere Street, Launceston. Open daily, 9am–5pm; 10am–4pm during winter. **www.namt.com.au**
- **Boag's Centre for Beer Lovers:** take a guided tour of the Boag's Brewery, which has been brewing on the banks of the Esk River since 1883. The tour includes a free tasting at the end of the visit. 39 William Street, Launceston. Open Mon–Fri, 8.45am–4.30pm. **www.boags.com.au**
- **Tamar Island Wetlands Centre:** unique urban wetlands reserve just a 10-minutes drive from the centre of the city and a haven for variety of wild birdlife such as pelicans, cormorants, swans and flightless native hens as well as frogs, dragonflies and lizards. Boardwalk, bird hide and wetlands interpretation centre. West Tamar Highway, just north of Riverside. Open daily.
- **Low Head Penguin Tours:** night time penguin watching tours at Low Head on the eastern side of the Tamar River, near the river mouth. Tours run each night just after sunset. Return transport available from Launceston if required. **www.penguintours.lowhead.com**
- **Devonport Maritime Museum:** Tasmanian and local maritime history housed in old harbour master's residence near mouth of Mersey River. 6 Gloucester, Ave, Devonport. Open Tue–Sun 10am–4pm winter; Tue–Sun 10am–4.30pm in summer.
- **Imaginarium Science Centre:** more than 50 interactive, colourful and exciting exhibits together with stimulating science shows and demonstrations. 19–23 MacFie Street, Devonport. Open Mon–Thu, 10am–4pm; weekends noon–5pm.
- **Home Hill:** home of a former Prime Minister, Joseph Lyons. 66 Middle Rd, Devonport. Open daily except Mon and Fri, 2–4pm.
- **Tiagarra Aboriginal Culture and Art Centre:** award-winning interpretation centre with several buildings designed to resemble Tasmanian Aboriginal huts housing more than 2000 artefacts in 18 different displays, among them two large murals by Tasmanian artist Max Angus. Bluff Rd, Devonport. Open daily 9am–4.30pm.
- **Don River Railway:** one of the largest Steam Preservation Railways in Australia. Forth Rd, Devonport. Open daily, 9am–5pm. **www.donriverrailway.com.au**
- **Pioneer Village Museum:** outdoor museum recreating Main Street Burnie as it was in 1900 at the height of the town's first economic boom. Burnie. Open Mon–Fri, 9am–5pm; weekends, 1.30–4.30pm.
- **Dismal Swamp:** a giant sinkhole, filled with ancient blackwood trees and other forest trees. Follow the walkway, take the buggy or slip down the 110-metre slide to the swamp floor 40 metres below. At the bottom, four boardwalks on the swamp floor make it easy to get to know life in a swamp without getting your feet wet. Local artists display artwork throughout the site and there is a cantilever suspended off the sinkhole rim at the edge of the visitor centre deck. On the Bass Highway, 30 minutes drive south-west of Smithton. Open daily, 9am–5pm Nov–Mar; 9am–4pm other months. **www.tasforestrytourism.com.au/pages/site_nw_dismal.html**
- **King Island Historical Society Museum:** housed in a former lighthouse keeper's cottage with displays on the island's history and shipwreck relics. Lighthouse Street, Currie. Open daily, 2pm–4pm; closed Jul and Aug.
- **King Island Dairy Fromagerie:** taste the cheese that has made the island famous. On the hill next to factory at Loorana. Open Mon–Fri, 9am–4.30pm and Sun 12.30–4pm.

The walk then heads down to Wet Cave and to the coast with a rock-hop of 100m or so back to the Sisters Beach boat ramp. The Postmans Track, named after the route used for horseback postal deliveries early last century, circles the easternmost section of the park, near Sisters Beach, around a two-hour loop. The Rocky Cape Circuit Walk (two and a half hours return) offers extensive coastal views and spectacular displays of Christmas bells in summer. The 15km Inland Track follows the Rocky Cape circuit track to Postmans Pass, then continues inland over the Sisters Hills (almost 300m high) before descending to Sisters Beach. There are magnificent views down to the coast and back inland.

The Coastal Route (four hours one way) is a rugged coastal alternative to the Inland Track. You can combine the coastal and inland routes to make a full-day 25km circuit walk of the park.

In Strzelecki National Park there is a well-marked 3km walking track to the summit of the Strzelecki Peaks. It's not an easy walk–the climb, through wooded slopes and damp fern gullies, takes about four to five hours return. Be aware that the weather may close in while at the summit, which can be disorientating.

adventure activities

Abseiling and rock climbing

Launceston's Cataract Gorge is a popular spot for abseiling and rock-climbing. According to Tasmanian Expeditions there are more than 200 short climbs within five minutes of the centre of the city, ranging in difficulty to suit first timers through to seasoned climbers. They run half- and full-day guided climbs, and abseiling courses, in the gorge for all level of experience.

www.tas-ex.com

Caving

Gunns Plains Cave, around 20km south of Ulverstone, was formed by an underground river that still flows and contains giant freshwater lobster, fish and eel. Platypus sleep and nest in the sandy banks along the river. The cave consists of a series of short passages and lofty caverns containing varied formations including magnificent calcite shawls. The caves are open for tours daily and involves a couple of ladders but otherwise easy, albeit damp, walking.

Cycling

The Don to Devonport Cycleway is a 7.5km rail trail and is a great way to explore Devonport. Parts of the trail follow the route of a former tramway. You can follow the trail from the Don Railway Station to central Devonport, with the option of a loop trail along the opposite bank of the Don River.

There are also a number of cycling trails in and around Launceston: the North Esk River Trail runs alongside the North Esk river between Henry St and Hoblers Bridge Road; the Rocherlea Old Rail Trail runs along an old railway track behind the Mowbray Golf Course; the River Edge Trail connects the Seaport Boardwalk, Kings Park Trail and the Royal Park Trail and makes a great loop beside the river and back through Royal Park. There are also a number of trails in the Heritage Forest–the most popular one is the loop trail around the exterior of the forest.

Tasmanian Expeditions run cycling tours of the Tamar Valley and include bike hire, accommodation and all the necessary gear, as well as a support vehicle for those that taste too much wine along the way.

www.tas-ex.com

Diving

The rough seas and fierce westerlies that howl across the waters of Bass Strait have resulted in hundreds of shipwrecks. Australia's worst maritime disaster occurred off the coast of King Island in 1845, when the *Cataraqui,* bound from Liverpool to Melbourne with more than 400 passengers and crew, was wrecked 100 metres from the shore in heavy rain and seas. Of the 400 people on board only nine reached the beach alive. Today the wreck lies in 10 metres of water and makes an unforgettable dive.

King Island Dive Charters specialise in the eerie and exciting experience of diving these wrecks, however the island also offers amazing underwater scenery unique to the area with marine life growing around the island not normally found in such shallow depths. Southern rock lobsters up to six kilos can be found on most dives with dolphins and whales often encountered throughout the season.

Adventure Caving. *(Tourism Tasmania)*

www.kingislanddivecharter.com.au

Flinders Island Dive provides full-day and half-day diving trips around the islands on the west coast of Flinders Island. Extended trips to the Cape Barren and Clarke Island areas can also be arranged. Dive courses are also available.

☎ (03) 6359 8429

Seal and Sea Adventures will take you to one of Tasmania's most accessible seal colonies on Tenth Island in Bass Strait–a colony of around 600 Australian fur seals, and about 60 breeding pairs of New Zealand fur seals about 3km off the coast. You can snorkel or scuba dive with the seals (a Shark Shield device is available). Tours depart from the Pilot Station at George Town, on the eastern side of the Tamar River.

www.sealandsea.com

Fishing

The coastal waters of northern Tasmania can often be rough, but there is good fishing in the sheltered bays and estuaries. On the north-western coast, the islands of the north-western tip around Hunter Island and the shallow waters of the Mersey River are good for Australian salmon, flat-head, barracouta and whiting. Port Sorrel and Port Dalrymple offer good safe fishing, as do the pontoons along the Tamar River, which make ideal fishing platforms. Towards the east, Bridport offers good jetty, beach and boat fishing. The Bass Strait Islands also offer superb coastal fishing, from the beaches, rocks and jetties as well as charter boats. Flinders Island is renowned for its fishing–it is the main industry at Lady Barron on the southern tip: shark, trevally, yellowtail kingfish, tuna and Barracouta are the main catches.

Off-road driving

The St Albans Bay track is a challenging but scenic coastal drive. From Bridport, take the Sandy Points Road to Lades Beach. The 22km track travels though the sand dunes and long the beaches to Bellingham. There are several reasonably sheltered campsites along the track near the dune area and the there is plenty of opportunity for bird watching and surf fishing. Do not drive around either headlands as they are bird breeding areas. An easier track is the 60km Waterhouse Road between Bridport and Gladstone. It provides access to the beautiful Waterhouse Conservation Area via Homestead Road and Blackmans Lagoon Road.

All off-road use of vehicles in the reserve must have written authority from the Parks and Wildlife Service

www.parks.tas.gov.au ☎ (03) 6336 5312

Once you have the permit you can drive on West Tomahawk Beach (sometimes called East Ransons Beach) east of the boat-launching site at the end of Homestead Road. At Blackmans Lagoon (good trout fishing) there is a track through to Waterhouse Beach and beach driving is permitted to the southern limit of the reserve. You can bush camp at various sites within Waterhouse Conservation Area along the Homestead Road.

Sailing

Cruise the waters and wilderness of Bass Strait in style and comfort aboard a 50-foot sailing catamaran with Resolution Adventures, based on Flinders Island. Day trips exploring the sheltered waters amongst the many islands of the Furneaux Group as well as extended three- and five-day charters to uninhabited islands–set the sails, beach comb, kayak, snorkel, catch your lunch–or simply relax and unwind from the comfort of the boat.

www.resolution.org.au

Hang-gliding

Experience all the thrills of hang-gliding without any of the spills with cable hang-gliding at Trevallyn Dam near Launceston. A support frame on the glider is attached to a main cable to ensure you remain safe during your flight. Soar over an 18-metre cliff, landing 200m from your take-off point to enjoy a short flight that gives you the experience of normal hang-gliding under controlled conditions. This is a ride that thrill-seekers of almost any age can take.

www.cablehanggliding.com.au

Cable hang-gliding, Launceston. *(Tourism Tasmania)*

MORE INFORMATION

- **Launceston:** Cornwall Square, 12–16 St John Street. ☎ (03) 6336 3133. www.discoverlaunceston.com www.tamarvalley.com.au
- **Devonport:** 92 Formby Road. www.discovertasmania.com.au ☎ (03) 6424 4466
- **Stanley:** 45 Main Road. www.kingisland.org.au ☎ (03) 6458 1330 www.focusonflinders.com.au

weather watch

- January: 10–23°C
- July: 2–11°C
- Summer is mild, winter tends to be the wetter season.

About the author

Lee Atkinson is one of Australia's leading experts on travelling in Australia.

Author of *On the Road: 40 great driving holidays in Australia* and former editor of the country's highest circulating motoring and travel magazine, *The Open Road,* Lee has been writing about her adventures on and off the road since 1991.

Past president of the Australian Society of Travel Writers, Lee was also co-editor of an anthology of Australian travel writing, *Best Foot Forward* and commissioning editor of the series of international and domestic drive travel guides, including the bestselling, *2000 Things to See and Do in Sydney, Great Drives of NSW, Short Holidays in NSW, Great Drives of Australia* and *Great Driving Adventures.*

Lee's work also appears regularly in *Royal Auto, The Road Ahead* and *SA Motor, The Australian, The Sun Herald, The Age* and the *Sunday Herald Sun* newspapers as well as glossy travel magazines such as *Out There, Unwind, Friday, Audi* and various international inflight magazines.

When not travelling on assignment, Lee divides her time between Sydney and the NSW mid-north coast.

Contributors

Andrew Bain—cycling

Melbourne writer Andrew Bain has cycled in Indonesia, the United States and Canada and once spent 14 months pedalling 20,000km around Australia, a journey that became the book *Headwinds.* He is the author of Lonely Planet's *A Year of Adventures* and lead author of the Lonely Planet *Walking in Australia* guidebook. He has two children but three bikes, which may say something about his priorities.

Melanie Ball—bushwalking

Melanie Ball likes nothing better than to lace up a pair of hiking boots and go bush. Nothing, perhaps, except sleeping in a swag under the stars in the Australian outback after a day on her feet.

A member of the Australian Society of Travel Writers, she has written about independent and guided walks in every Australian state and territory, as well as other adventures, for *The Age, The Herald Sun* and the *Sunday Telegraph* newspapers. She also contributes travel articles and photographs to Australian magazines including *Royal Auto, On The Road, House & Garden* and *Australian Doctor.*

Melanie has worked as an updating editor on Fodor's *Australia* guide for the last four years.

John Borthwick—surfing

Based in Sydney, John, a lifelong surfer, has chased (and caught) waves in most Australian states, as well as in Samoa, Indonesia, the Maldives, New Zealand and Hawaii. He is the author of countless travel articles, plus collections of his travel stories, such as *Chasing Gauguin's Ghost* and *The Circumference of the Knowable World.* His professional recognitions include multiple awards from the Australian Society of Travel Writers for Travel Writer of the Year and Photograph of the Year. In 2004 the Thai government presented him with a prestigious 'Friend of Thailand' award.

Jim Darby—skiing

Jim Darby is the editor of *theSKImag* and *Alpine Style* magazines and co-author of *The Snow Guide to Australia and New Zealand.* He has worked in the mountains as a ski lift operator, ski instructor, ski patroller, summer maintenance worker and resort planner. A ski-writer for 25 years, Jim has been the snow columnist for the *Sydney Morning Herald* and *Melbourne Herald Sun* and has contributed to magazines and newspapers around the world, including the Melbourne *Age,* the Sydney *Sun Herald,* the London *Times,* the *Denver Post, Action Asia, UK Ski and Board* and international inflight magazines. Jim is a three-time winner of Skiing Australia's print media award.

Cathy Finch—diving and snorkelling

Cathy Finch is a travel writer and photographer based in Central Queensland. She writes for leading metropolitan newspapers and magazines throughout Australia and overseas.

Cathy gained her diving certification in the Red Sea, Egypt, and continued to travel and dive various locations around the world. On her return to Australia her love of diving was fuelled by the beauty of our Australian reefs and the unique opportunity to work onboard a vessel used as a filming platform for a series of underwater documentaries, visiting important dive locations around the country.

Cathy considers spending a day in the water with whale sharks as one of her most memorable diving moments.

Louise Goldsbury—rock climbing

Louise Goldsbury is a travel writer with a passion for all outdoor adventure. Louise has bungy jumped, parasailed, abseiled, sea kayaked, jet-skied, whitewater rafted, skied, biked and hiked around the world. She recently discovered the joys of rock climbing with her boyfriend, a rock climbing instructor who has climbed extensively throughout mainland Australia and Tasmania for the past 13 years.

A former resident of Darwin, Taiwan and London, Louise is now based in Sydney. Her articles appear in *The Australian, Sunday Telegraph, Daily Telegraph,* various travel and inflight magazines and *The Independent, The Guardian, The Times* and *Sunday Observer* newspapers in Britain.

Briar Jensen—sailing

Briar Jensen is a Sydney-based writer specialising in travel and boating. Briar learnt to sail at 16 during a 10-day trip aboard the sail-training ship *Spirit of Adventure* (New Zealand). She now lives in Sydney with her husband and two children. They own a NZ designed and built Noelex 30 yacht, which they keep on Cowan Creek, Ku-ring-gai Chase National Park, NSW. Briar's articles have appeared in all the leading boating magazines in Australia as well as sailing magazines in America, Britain and South Africa. Her travel articles have appeared internationally in newspapers and magazines.

Kerry Lorimer—responsible travel and safety

Kerry Lorimer has been operating and promoting responsible travel for 15 years. Over two decades she has worked and travelled in more than 100 countries on all seven continents and sailed most of the oceans in between. She has guided low-impact treks and tours in South America, Africa, the Himalaya, Antarctica and Australia. Kerry was the co-ordinating author of Lonely Planet's *Code Green: Trips of a Lifetime that Won't Cost the Earth.* She is a writer and photographer who heads up Splash Communications, a Sydney-based marketing communications consultancy specialising in nature-based travel.

Kris Madden—whale watching

Journalist and ecotourism consultant, Kris Madden, has a special interest in wildlife conservation and the development of responsible tourism. She is also an avid whale watcher. Her travels take her around the world to view whales in their natural habitat. She has observed whales and dolphins in several Australian states, New Zealand, the South Pacific, Antarctica and the northern hemisphere. She is an active member of ORRCA (Organisation for the Rescue and Research of Cetaceans in Australia) a not-for-profit voluntary organisation dedicated to the rescue and research of marine mammals in Australia.

Alistair McGlashan—fishing

Alistair McGlashan is one of Australia's leading fishing photojournalists. An accomplished author with a number of books to his name Alistair also contributes to dozens of magazines in Australia and overseas.

Spending more than 250 days a year on the water, Alistair also happens to be an accomplished angler who has passion for catching everything from giant black marlin through to Australian bass and everything in between. In his words all he wants to do is 'be on the water fishing'.

An adventurer at heart Alistair has tramped all over Australia and abroad always searching for somewhere new and unexploited to fish. He hopes that his writing and images will encourage others to get out and enjoy the great outdoors.

Isabelle Quartly—birds

Sydney-based Isabelle Quartly has always been interested in 'furry' animals, but her love for birds did not really develop until she became a wildlife photographer, as she explains: 'In the beginning my business was not making enough money for travel, so I photographed what I could find in driving distance from my house. In Sydney this was mainly birds and, in spending that time with them, I really discovered how interesting birds are. These days I can't get enough of them!' she says. Isabelle has been a professional photographer for five years, is published in both magazines and books and says she wouldn't want any other job.

Rob Woodburn—Australian wildlife

English-born freelance writer and photographer, Rob Woodburn grew up in Africa. The legacy of those formative years is a deep and abiding sense of wonder concerning all wild animals, great and small. Now a resident of Sydney, he relishes any opportunity to spend time observing and learning about Australian fauna in its natural state. 'It never ceases to amaze me', he says, 'how nature adapts to different living conditions. In the harsh, desiccated and forbidding environment that is much of central Australia, I have witnessed the most miraculous strategies of survival. Although Australia lacks the big game of Africa, it certainly can boast some of the world's most remarkable creatures.'

D

E

F

G

H

N

Y

Z

APPROXIMATE DISTANCES IN KILOMETRES	ADELAIDE	ALICE SPRINGS	BRISBANE	BROKEN HILL	BROOME	CAIRNS	CANBERRA	COOBER PEDY	DARWIN	MELBOURNE	MOUNT GAMBIER	MOUNT ISA	PERTH	PORT AUGUSTA	SYDNEY
ADELAIDE		1540	2068	510	4290	3145	1209	855	3050	730	458	2749	2730	315	1427
ALBANY	2696	3587	4350	2799	2801	5427	3951	2903	4859	3411	3141	4793	407	2371	4102
ALICE SPRINGS	1540		3009	1649	2741	2322	2815	687	1513	2268	1993	1204	3628	1226	2645
BORROLOOLA	2758	2742	2735	3334	1715	2188	4486	1886	965	3488	3214	931	3736	2443	3307
BRISBANE	2068	3009		1550	4648	1720	1259	2516	3412	1675	2173	1815	4382	1981	1000
BROKEN HILL	510	1649	1550		4401	2633	1152	964	3165	855	869	2403	2840	433	1169
BROOME	4290	2741	4648	4401		3962	5218	3711	1863	5020	4739	2841	2252	3974	5234
CAIRNS	3145	2322	1720	2633	3962		2610	3011	2730	3052	3201	1124	5955	2686	2544
CANBERRA	1209	2815	1259	1152	5218	2610		2424	4259	651	801	2379	3993	1588	286
CARNARVON	3635	2821	6599	3745	1485	4979	4839	3861	3294	4543	4091	3722	905	3320	5129
CHARLEVILLE	1769	2349	748	1256	3990	1382	1174	3035	2751	1673	2128	1151	4090	1680	1245
COOBER PEDY	855	687	2516	964	3711	3011	2424		2201	1583	1310	1882	2947	541	1973
DARWIN	3050	1513	3412	3165	1863	2730	4259	2201		3781	3509	1607	4043	2734	3997
DUBBO	1207	2410	867	749	4821	2209	400	1719	3582	840	1204	1978	3589	1178	419
ECHUCA	750	2177	1530	670	5870	3250	586	1605	3690	208	660	2509	3480	1065	756
EUCLA	1271	2170	2931	1380	3880	4011	2469	1490	3685	1999	1726	3379	1452	950	2386
INNAMINCKA	1074	1716	1827	733	4457	2363	1885	1031	3229	1588	1602	1106	3804	756	1902
KALGOORLIE	2197	3107	3865	2314	2991	4908	3411	2385	4622	2931	2657	4310	602	1843	3482
KATHERINE	2735	1199	3101	2851	1553	2410	3944	1877	316	3463	3195	1293	3726	2421	3688
KULGERA	1266	274	3334	1776	3015	2596	2475	411	1787	1996	1724	1478	3502	952	2693
MEEKATHARRA	3310	4217	4969	3421	1464	5359	4515	3495	3263	3501	3769	4231	766	2961	4386
MELBOURNE	730	2268	1675	855	5020	3052	651	1583	3781		419	2825	3456	1042	870
MILDURA	397	1941	1663	302	4682	2934	872	1254	3445	552	579	2705	3126	711	1022
MOUNT GAMBIER	458	1993	2173	869	4739	3201	801	1310	3509	419		3280	3177	772	3096
MOUNT ISA	2749	1204	1815	2403	2841	1124	2379	1882	1607	2825	3280		4830	2426	2392
PERTH	2730	3628	4382	2840	2252	5955	3993	2947	4043	3456	3177	4830		2407	4148
PORT AUGUSTA	315	1226	1981	433	3974	2686	1588	541	2734	1042	772	2426	2407		1599
PORT HEDLAND	4182	3291	5194	4301	612	4500	5392	4368	2405	4381	4640	3375	1639	3831	5260
PORT LINCOLN	659	1570	2325	777	4318	3030	1932	885	3078	1386	1116	2770	2336	344	1943
PORT MACQUARIE	1876	3416	879	2247	5527	2599	685	2731	4291	1455	1907	2694	4606	2680	413
ROCKHAMPTON	2381	2509	637	1879	4145	1079	1597	2849	2912	2037	2488	1311	4715	2305	1638
SYDNEY	1427	2645	1000	1169	5234	2544	286	1973	3997	870	3096	2392	4148	1600	
TENNANT CREEK	2073	531	2486	2182	2221	1799	3058	1211	986	2801	2523	677	4152	1753	3065
TOWNSVILLE	3127	2090	1373	2607	3723	345	2322	3580	2491	2763	3221	883	5444	3034	2339